BAPTISM IN THE NEW TESTAMENT

THIS BOOK treats Christian baptism, not as an optional extra in Christian life, as a sort of "post-graduate" field of study for the specialist, but as basic to the whole New Testament teaching concerning the Church of God.

Dr. BEASLEY-MURRAY goes at once to the heart of the subject by taking the New Testament documents and expounding their witness to Christian baptism and assessing the implications of that evidence. He scrutinizes and assesses the traditions and practice of different schools of interpretation, and calls upon the churches to re-think their attitudes to this apostolic ordinance in view of its significance in personal witness as well as in movements for closer unity in the Body of Christ.

By the same Author:

JESUS AND THE FUTURE

A COMMENTARY ON MARK THIRTEEN

Titles in this Series

BAPTISM IN
THE NEW TESTAMENT

BY

G. R. BEASLEY-MURRAY
M.A., M.Th., Ph.D.

EXETER:
THE PATERNOSTER PRESS

ISBN: 0 85364 134 x

This Paperback Edition published 1972 by
The Paternoster Press by arrangement with
Macmillan & Company Ltd

TO MY WIFE

AUSTRALIA:
Emu Book Agencies Pty., Ltd.,
1, Lee Street, Sydney, N.S.W.

SOUTH AFRICA:
Oxford Univeristy Press
P.O. Box 1141, Oxford House, 11, Buitencingle St.,
Cape Town

Made and printed in Great Britain for
The Paternoster Press, Paternoster House,
3 Mount Radford Crescent, Exeter, Devon
by Redwood Press Limited,
Trowbridge, Wiltshire

PREFACE

THIS work is the outcome of an invitation to deliver annual lectures under the auspices of the Dr. W. T. Whitley Lectureship during the academic year 1959–60. They were delivered in November 1959 in Regent's Park College, Oxford, and in February 1960 for the Bangor Baptist College at the University College, Bangor, North Wales, by courtesy of the University Authorities. I thank most warmly Dr. G. Henton Davies, Principal of Regent's Park College, and Rev. T. Ellis Jones, Principal of Bangor Baptist College, for the kindness they showed me on these occasions.

Opportunity has been provided for me to test the major theses of the book among more varied audiences and in more distant places than these. Dr. K. Duke McCall, President of the Southern Baptist Theological Seminary, Louisville, Kentucky, invited me to give the Norton Lectures in connection with the Centennial Celebrations of the Seminary in March 1959; some of the chief themes of the book formed the subject of those lectures. In the same period arrangements were made for me to deliver lectures on various aspects of this subject by the Presidents of the Southeastern Baptist Seminary, Wake Forest, North Carolina, the New Orleans Baptist Theological Seminary, and the Southwestern Baptist Seminary, Fort Worth, Texas. These visits were memorable, not alone by reason of the lavish Southern hospitality showered upon my wife and myself, but also for the interest and sympathy displayed with respect to viewpoints by no means characteristic of the Churches in those areas. The Baptist ministers of Italy, meeting for their annual conference in 1959 at the seminary in Rivoli, Torino, were a responsive audience for lectures and discussions on this theme. The conference of Baptist ministers in Holland, meeting at De Vinkenhoff, Utrecht, in the summer of 1960 similarly accorded a sympathetic hearing to lectures on the subject. Perhaps the liveliest interest was manifested by the students of the Betelseminariet, Stockholm, and the ministers who joined them, when six lectures were given under the Broady Foundation in November 1960 and keen discussion took place on a variety of topics connected with baptism, particularly in relation to the ecumenical issues which they raise.

The book is intended to offer a Baptist contribution to the discussions on baptism that are taking place throughout the Christian world. But the indefinite article should be observed; the impression must not be given that my interpretations are characteristic of Baptist thought generally. At most it can be claimed that they represent a trend gaining momentum among Baptists in Europe. I have striven to interpret the evidence of the New Testament as a Christian scholar, rather than as a member of a particular Christian Confession. The bulk of the work could conceivably have been written by a scholar in any Christian Communion, for Biblical exposition has increasingly refused to be fettered by confessional limitations in recent years. For this reason the controversy concerning infant baptism has been rigorously kept from the body of the work and has been reserved for the last chapter. That section inevitably reflects a frankly confessional standpoint and I cannot but expect dissent from many who may conceivably sympathize with much of the exposition contained in the earlier part. If I offend any, I ask for pardon. I have endeavoured to state a viewpoint in candour and, I trust, with courtesy. At least I hope that I shall enable members of other Christian Churches to understand better the difficulties felt by Baptists on the issue that separates them from their fellow believers.

There is no body from whom I have learned so much on the subject as the European section of the Faith and Order Commission on Christ and the Church, led by Bishop Nygren. I am indebted to them alike for their patience and forbearance, their incisive criticism and their profound theological insight. For their sakes alone I could have wished it had been possible for me to write differently in the closing chapter. They at least will understand that it has not been written with a light heart. The pain of ecumenical discussion has to be experienced to be understood. I hope that readers who dissent from my views will appreciate the controlling motive in my mode of statement, namely the necessity for ruthless honesty and truthfulness, for the sake of the Truth after which we all strive and which we but partially see.

It remains for me to acknowledge a debt of gratitude to Rev. J. J. Brown, B.D., of Dagenham, who willingly undertook the labour of providing indices for this book; to Miss Iris Copping, whose eagle eye in proof-reading has spared the book from many errors; and to my secretary, Mrs. M. Moody, who painstakingly typed the MS. for me.

CONTENTS

ABBREVIATIONS

CHAPTER I

THE ANTECEDENTS OF
CHRISTIAN BAPTISM

(i) *Lustrations in the Old Testament*

As with other institutions in the religion of Israel, a long history lies behind the legal enactments of the Old Testament concerning ritual ablutions. The regulations as to their use are far from primitive; on the contrary they are comparatively advanced and presuppose an age-long development of thought and practice in the matter of purification of persons and things connected with the service of God. This is by no means a unique phenomenon. In the Old Testament lustrations are linked with sacrificial worship; but no one is under the illusion that sacrifices to Deity were first observed among the Jews, nor are people generally surprised to learn that the ordinances as to their performance and significance are not unrelated to sacrificial thought and practice that go back to remote times among many peoples. So also ritual cleansings in water were practised from immemorial antiquity and if their history has been largely forgotten, their associations have shown an extraordinary tenacity of life.

At the outset a warning may not be amiss. It may be thought, on the one hand, that to consider the beliefs of ancient Semites about the supernatural properties of water is superfluous and should be left to those who have an inclination to pursue antiquarian interests. The hard fact must nevertheless be faced that those early beliefs have never died; they did not die in Israel, they did not die in the Church and they persist (in fashions both less and more refined) to this day. On the other hand there are some who tend to be over-impressed with the lowly origins of religious lustrations and to draw exaggerated negative inferences as to their value in the light of these origins. Heitmüller, for example, who spent a great deal of time in research in other religions concerning ideas associated in the early Church with baptism, and did it to excellent effect, came to the conclusion that sacramental theology can logically exist only where primitive views of sin and demonism are held, and that its continuance alongside developed religious concepts represents a survival that has no real justification.[1] That however is a non sequitur. It is a universally recognized canon of interpretation that one must not confuse the origins of institutions and ideas with their developments or with phenomena that are related but transfigured to bear new conceptions. It would be possible to draw a direct line of development from the witch doctor and his practices to the modern medical practitioner and his methods, but we do not normally confound the latter with the former. More pertinently, one could draw a line revealing basic connections between primitive sacrificial practices, the covenant sacrifices of the Old Testament, the New Testament teaching on the new covenant in Christ's blood and the present day celebrations of the Communion of the Lord's Supper, but it would be monstrous to confound the Christian eucharist with, say, the sacrificial rites of Canaanite religion or with those of certain primitive African tribes today. So too the recognition that baptism has essential precedents in animistic views of the supernatural nature of water and the destructive power of holiness must not blind us to the differences between an early Semite washing in a sacred spring, the High Priest of Israel bathing himself in the Temple on the Day of Atonement, publicans and sinners responding in Jordan to the call for repentance from John the Baptist, and the Christian believer confessing in baptism his identification with Christ in his redemptive action and thereby anticipating the renewal of the universe.

Recognizing therefore the nature and the limits of this introductory study, we may give ungrudging acknowledgement to certain fundamental ideas that lie behind early ritual lustrations and that conditioned both their existence and development. Chief of these are the following: (i) the belief that certain waters, notably of sacred springs and streams, can be impregnated with the power of deity so as to become, as one has expressed it, 'the living organism of a demoniac life',[2] capable of communicating its power to persons and objects plunged in them; (ii) the danger entailed in contact with deity, in view of the power of the divine holiness to destroy unworthy man; (iii) the complementary danger of contact with demonic powers, particularly at times when man is peculiarly exposed to their operation, above all

---

[1] Consider the following typical utterance: 'Whenever and wherever sin is apprehended in a moral-religious sense as disobedience against God, as a moment of willing and doing, and the materialistic estimate of sin is overcome, then it follows that a bathing in water, a "baptism", which can set aside sin, is basically a survival from a stage of development that has been left behind', *Taufe und Abendmahl im Urchristentum*, Tübingen 1911, p. 9. Heitmüller apparently did not consider the possibility of baptism itself being 'moral-religious'.

[2] Robertson Smith, *Lectures on the Religion of the Semites, First Series*, 1889, p. 128.

in circumstances connected with birth, sickness and death; (iv) the unitary view of nature, of body and soul, flesh and spirit, embracing an inclusive view of disease, sin and uncleanness even in higher reaches of religion, so that an application of a remedy without can affect the whole person. It requires little reflection to realize that all these conceptions are capable of interpretation on different levels, ranging from the extreme of materialistic crudity to a lofty height of sublimated religion. The Old Testament provides glimpses of considerable variety between the extremes. We shall consider briefly each of these issues in turn.

(i) There is good ground for believing that the efficacy of water to cleanse religiously was originally conceived of in a highly realistic manner and was connected with the veneration of deities resident in the water. As all movement connotes for the primitive man life on analogy with his own, so the bubbling energy of a stream and the refreshing, not to say life-sustaining, property of a spring are interpreted as indicating mysterious powers of the spirits therein active.[1] The relation sustained by the deities to the waters was variously conceived and expressed. Sometimes the spring or stream was thought to be the dwelling of beings which could come forth in human or animal form. Various myths point to the idea that the waters contain the blood of the deity, since blood was generally considered to be the principle of life.[2] By an easy transition the life force of the god who had died in the water could be thought to have passed into the fish of the stream, the eating of which was believed to be able to kill a man, or into a serpent or a dragon or the like. The differences are unimportant. In some way expression is given to the idea that the waters were imbued with the vital energy of the deities to which they were regarded as consecrated. It is easy to understand the progression of thought which passed from a veneration of the waters to the idea that to bathe in them was to do homage to the divine spirits resident in

[1] 'Of all inanimate things, that which has the best marked supernatural associations among the Semites is flowing, or as the Hebrews say, "living" water. . . . Sacred wells are among the oldest and most ineradicable objects of reverence among all the Semites, and are credited with oracular powers and a sort of volition by which they receive or reject offerings,' Robertson Smith, op. cit., pp. 127 f. He pointed out that as healing springs and sacred springs are everywhere identified, the Arabs still regard medicinal waters as inhabited by *Jinn*, usually of serpent form; and that Hannibal, in his covenant with Philip of Macedon, when he swears before all the deities of Carthage and of Hellas, includes among the divine powers to which his oath appeals, 'the sun, the moon and the earth, rivers, meadows and waters'.

[2] To this Milton alluded in his *Paradise Lost*, i. 450, in dependence on Lucian:

> Smooth Adonis from his native rock
> Ran purple to the sea, supposed with blood
> Of Thammuz yearly wounded.

them, and then to the belief that such waters bestowed 'blessing' — divine energy which effected release from the infection of demonic powers, hence healing of sickness and the protection of the god.

Naturally, these ideas are characteristic of animistic religion and have no place in the religion of the Law and Prophets of the Old Testament. More correctly, they *ought* to have had no place in such a faith; in fact, they are of the kind of ideas that dies hard and they find expression in multifarious ways and places, not alone in the Old Testament but in the Christian Church. Conceptions of cleansing through lustration did, of course, undergo a drastic purgation and sublimation in the Old Testament legislation, so that in due course their original associations and significance became buried in a long forgotten past.[1] What is surprising is their fresh emergence in new guises at times when the strictest monotheism prevailed. The angel of the pool of Bethesda in the interpolated passage at Jn. 5.4 is a case in point.[2] Tertullian unwittingly links the saving efficacy of baptismal waters with downright animism.[3] As late as the time of Epiphanius it could be said of a heretical baptizing sect, that among them 'the water is reverenced and is esteemed as divine'.[4] Clearly these primitive notions lived on and continued to exert a powerful influence in the time of the Christian Church; they require to be taken into account when examining the development of thought on baptism in the Christian Church.

(ii) Primitive ideas of holiness represent it in terms of a power with dread effects, like electricity which can consume a man who comes into contact with too much at once. The conviction that things and persons in touch with deity can become charged with this dangerous

[1] See below, pp. 6–10.

[2] Pagans would have ascribed the healing power of the water to a god, who signified his presence in the stirring of the waters; the Jews, who could recognize no deity but the Lord, preserved essentially the same idea but modified the status of the spirit who gave the water its healing virtue to that of an angel. Bultmann agrees, see *Das Evangelium des Johannes*, Göttingen 1956, p. 180, n. 4.

[3] After recalling heathen belief in the cleansing power of water, he observes: 'Do not unclean spirits in other ways also, and without any religious rite, brood over the waters, pretending to imitate the up-bearing of the Divine Spirit at the beginning? Witness all shady fountains, and all unfrequented streams, and the pools at the baths, and all the conduits and cisterns in houses, and the wells which are said to carry men off, to wit, by the power of the noxious spirit. . . . To what purpose have we related these things? *that none should think it too hard a thing that the holy angel of God should be present to prepare the waters for the salvation of man, when the bad angel hath oft-times unholy dealings with the same element for the destruction of man*'. From his further comments on the angel of the waters, there can be little doubt that Tertullian thought of a real angel-spirit present to make the baptismal waters effective, as the angel-spirit was held to give healing power to the pool in Bethesda. See *De Baptismo*, V–VI.

[4] τετίμηται δὲ τὸ ὕδωρ, καὶ τοῦτο ὡς θεὸν ἡγοῦνται, *Epiphanius*, 53.1, cited by Bousset, *Hauptprobleme der Gnosis*, Göttingen 1907, p. 280.

power is at the root of the idea of 'taboo', a term applying to something which must not be touched because of its association with the god. Such a concept is related to the awe and fear with which man views the supernatural, and it can become the basis of that reverence for God which is indispensable for true worship. Perhaps the clearest example in the Old Testament of the awful power of the holiness of God is seen in the account of the theophany at the giving of the Law on Sinai, Ex. 19. Moses is bidden, 'Go down and warn the people lest they break through to the Lord to gaze and many of them perish. And also let the priests who come near consecrate themselves, lest the Lord break out upon them' (vv. 21 f). Despite their 'consecration' and washing of garments in preparation for the epiphany (vv. 10 f), the people are not permitted to draw nigh, and the priests themselves are warned that they would perish if they come too near the appearance of the glory.

The Book of Leviticus reflects the calmer atmosphere of the legislator, yet the description of the rites of the Day of Atonement presumes a like basic conviction. Aaron must not come at any time into the Most Holy Sanctuary, lest he die (Lev. 16.2). When he does enter on the appointed day he has to bathe his body in water, put on 'holy garments' (v. 4), offer a sacrifice to make atonement for himself and his house (v. 6), and in the Most Holy Sanctuary burn incense, 'that the cloud of the incense may cover the mercy seat which is upon the testimony, *lest he die*' (v. 13). It would seem, accordingly, that the necessity for the High Priest to bathe himself before appearing 'before the Lord' is part of the conditions under which he may approach the divine holiness and still live. Significantly, after concluding the atoning for 'the holy place and the tent of meeting and the altar' and sending off the scapegoat into the wilderness, Aaron has to 'bathe his body in water in a holy place' and put on his ordinary garments before proceeding into the (less holy) court where the people are assembled (v. 24): there is no question of his having contracted defilement in the Holy of Holies or through confessing Israel's sins over the head of the scapegoat; it would seem that a reminiscence is here preserved of the necessity of removing the effects of contact with the divine Presence before returning to ordinary relationships of life.[1]

[1] The parallel description of the changes of clothing to be worn by the Levitical priests in Ezk. 44.15 ff seems to make this indubitable. On entering the gates of the inner court the priests are to wear linen garments and have nothing of wool on them: 'And when they go out into the outer court to the people, they shall put off the garments in which they have been ministering, and lay them in the holy chambers; and they shall put on other garments, *lest they communicate holiness to the people with their garments*' (v.19.). See further W. Brandt, *Die jüdischen Baptismen*, Giessen 1910, p. 23.

(iii) If man must take steps to approach aright the deity, he requires to be protected from the evil powers that are ready to exercise malevolence at any time propitious to them. Such occasions especially centre in the processes of birth, sickness and death.[1] Examination of the regulations concerning the purifications of ordinary people (i.e. as distinct from the priests and all objects connected with the cultus) will show that they are concerned with precisely these three conditions in the main. The prescriptions concerning everything to do with birth, and therefore including the sexual organs and sexual acts, are meticulous: from Lev. 15.8 it would seem that a husband and wife should bathe themselves after every occasion of intercourse; any kind of discharge from the genitals requires cleansing (Lev. 15.1 ff); the mother after birth, as all women after menstruation, suffers a period of uncleanness and must undergo a lustration at the end of it (Lev. 12). A leper is unclean (Lev. 13) and therefore any contact with a leprous person entails a defilement which requires a cleansing (Lev. 13.4 f). Any contact with death causes a condition of defilement from which one must be cleansed (Num. 5.1 ff, 19.1 ff, 31.19 ff). The origin of these rites of lustration lies in the dim past when protection against demonic assault was sought. Nevertheless two observations should be made. First, it is reasonably certain that such ideas were far from the minds of those responsible for drawing up the Priestly Code. Secondly, it is very possible that the consciousness of Israel's exclusive relationship to Yahweh lent to these rites a polemical aspect; Israel's neighbours resorted to all kinds of magical rites to secure the aid of the gods in these critical aspects of life, but the answer of the priests to these, as to all worship of foreign gods and contact with animals sacred to idolatrous cults, was to be *clean* from them all and to be exclusively devoted to the Lord.[2]

(iv) The unitary view of nature and of man in early thought requires effort on our part to be grasped. We naturally think of ourselves as persons, with a relative independence of our physical frame

---

[1] Lods represents the judgment of many scholars that the 'uncleanness' of the dead, as of everything that came into contact with them, was originally due to the terror inspired by the spirit of the dead; that sexual uncleanness was the result of the dread inspired by the supernatural powers presiding over generation; that the uncleanness of the leper was due to the fear of the demon which possessed him, and the uncleanness of certain kinds of animals was attributable to the belief in the supernatural capacities they possessed. See *Prophets and the Rise of Judaism*, E.T. 1937, pp. 291 f.

[2] Compare W. Eichrodt: 'The close connection especially of the Canaanite divinities with procreation and birth and of the Egyptian divinities with the cult of the dead may have contributed to the emphasis on these prescriptions', *Theologie des Alten Testaments*, I. 5th ed. 1957, p. 79.

standing over against an impersonal nature; the primitive man pictured himself rather as an animated body existing in an animate nature, every part of which was very much alive. Not only was the soul conceived of in a materialistic fashion (as a kind of breath) and the body a psychical entity, every part of which had both physiological and psychical functions; it would seem that the distinctions connoted by those two terms, physiological and psychical, did not exist for the primitive.[1] When one adds to this the conviction that man is open to all the spirit-influences of the spirit-controlled environment in which he lived, there is no questioning the ability of such elements as sacred water or blood powerfully affecting a man in his totality of being.

When we consider the lustrations of the Old Testament we again have to make considerable adjustments of thought. By the time these lustrations came to be regulated we have entered an environment of exclusive monotheism, in which the dominating influence to which man is open is that of the *Spirit of the Lord*. But man is still a unitary being whose characteristic element of personality is body. F. Gavin pointed out that the classic definition of a sacrament as 'an outward and visible sign of an inward and spiritual grace' could scarcely have originated in Judaism, for it assumes a dualistic view foreign to its genius.[2] In my judgment Gavin has exaggerated the Jewish inability to distinguish between 'outward and visible' and 'inward and spiritual', for the Psalmists, taught by the Prophets, have given us indubitable evidence that some of Israel's finest minds were concerned to make the 'inward and spiritual' conform to the 'outward and visible' in life and worship. Nevertheless it is true that the Jew maintained a sense of the unity of being which is not native to us, and which made the sacramental idea so natural to him as to be accepted without question. The remarkable feature of this is not that the Jew or later Judaism *could* not distinguish between outer and inner but that he *would* not separate them when he did understand the distinction. A hint of this may be perceived even in the book of Leviticus. This writing, that lays so much stress on lustrations, is notable for two other features: its presentation of the laws of sacrifice and its preservation of the so-called Law of Holiness, chs. 17–26. The former emphasized the gravity of sin;[3] the latter, with its reiterated refrain, 'You shall be holy for I the

---

[1] Wheeler Robinson, *The Christian Doctrine of Man*, 3rd ed. 1926, p. 6.

[2] *The Jewish Antecedents of the Christian Sacraments*, London 1928, p. 7.

[3] 'What is new in the post-exilic Law is no fresh conception of the existence of the nature of sin, but a greater emphasis on the exceeding sinfulness of sin', H. H. Rowley, *The Rediscovery of the Old Testament*, 1945, p. 154.

B

Lord your God am holy', entailed a concept of holiness no longer exclusively divine but a characteristic to be shared by the people of God. If therefore from one point of view, Leviticus represents a strong tendency to legality, it hints of something more: the giving of spiritual depth to the idea of cleansing, which is related to both atonement and moral renewal. The intention of the book was not to secure ritual purity alone, nor obedience as a bare religious principle, still less ethical purity divorced from the other two, but to secure all three together. Such an outlook was possible only where men viewed creation as inseparable from the Creator, where body and soul were viewed together, and where the individual had a truly self-conscious existence, though vitally linked to the community. The worship of Israel is built on the acceptance of such an attitude as axiomatic, for without it the Temple cultus is impossible to conceive. We may agree, therefore, with Gavin when he affirms: 'As partners, not enemies, the Jew thought of flesh and spirit; as two parts of a whole he thought of "ceremonial" or "ritual" or "legal" and "spiritual". The antonym of spiritual is neither "material" nor "legal" but un- or non-spiritual'.[1]

We have been concerned to set the lustrations of Israel in the light of their origins in primitive religion, but it has already become plain that in the Old Testament they have become integrated into a God-relationship of a different order. Admittedly we cannot at this distance be sure how these lustrations were interpreted by those who handed on the prescriptions for their use and by those who submitted to them. We are fairly safe in assuming that they were viewed in different ways by different individuals, even by contemporaries as well as by those separated by the centuries.[2] It should never be forgotten that the period of the Law was the great period for the Psalms, but that many of the Psalms were composed for use in connection with the Temple cultus. In this connection Ps. 24 is noteworthy:

[1] Op. cit., p. 13. Compare also Eichrodt: 'Because the physical and spiritual life of man is not yet torn asunder, but man is taken seriously in his totality as a spirit-body creature, man participates as a creature of sense in his relationship to God. In the outward cultic action the divine blessing is bestowed on man in his concrete form of existence; the sacred action thus becomes a sacrament', op. cit., p. 54.

[2] Lods, it is true, speaks scathingly of the 'ritualist movement' in Israel as representing a reversion to primitive religion in face of the contrary witness of the prophets, op. cit., pp. 251 ff. The view of G. F. Moore is surely more in keeping with the facts: 'It would be a mistake to imagine that this increased importance of the law in principle, or the elaboration of ritual and rule, choked ethical and spiritual religion. The literature of these centuries — the Psalms, Job, Proverbs — prove, on the contrary, that the influence of the prophetic teaching had never before been so widespread or so deep as in this period', *History of Religions*, Vol. II, 1920, p. 45.

> Who shall ascend the hill of the Lord?
> And who shall stand in his Holy Place?
> He who has clean hands and a pure heart,
> Who does not lift up his soul to what is false
> And does not swear deceitfully.

The pilgrim at the Feast who comes to worship requires not alone external ablutions but inward purity; the prophetic corrective of priestly religion has borne fruit.[1]

More precious still is the fruit observable in Ps. 51.6 ff, surely the climax of Old Testament yearning for true cleansing:

> Behold thou desirest truth in the inward being . . .
> Purge me with hyssop, and I shall be clean;
> Wash me, and I shall be whiter than snow . . .
> Hide thy face from my sins,
> And blot out all my iniquities.
> Create in me a clean heart, O God,
> And put a new and right spirit within me.

As a leper is cleansed by blood sprinkled from a sprig of hyssop and by the washing of water, so the man who prayed this prayer, a self-confessed sinner, desires spiritual cleansing. Whether he made it the accompaniment of ablutions and worship in the Temple we cannot say; certainly those who preserved the prayer and the many who subsequently repeated it would have so used it. Wheeler Robinson rightly observed that this psalm illustrates how 'the Temple worship, like all ritual, was really a framework of different spiritual values experienced by the differing worshippers'.[2] It should not go unnoticed that the important anticipation of divine cleansing in the last day, 'I will sprinkle clean water upon you, and you shall be clean from all your uncleannesses, and from all your idols will I cleanse you', (Ezk. 36.25) comes from a prophet-priest and conjoins spiritual cleansing with ceremonial purity. It is a further hint of the manner in which the ablutions used in connection with the worship and service of God had become spiritualized in the minds of many in Israel.

---

[1] See especially Is. 1.10 ff. N. A. Dahl has suggested that since the Levitical system of purifications was so complicated, to live according to it could at best be an ideal; consequently the purifications gained the character of rites of consecration, or even initiation, for worship at the Temple and so applied above all to the pilgrims at the festivals, hence the sentiment of Ps. 24.3 ff. If this were true it would add force to the conviction that the Old Testament lustrations are vitally important precedents for New Testament baptism. See Dahl's article, 'The Origin of Baptism', in *Interpretationes ad Vetus Testamentum pertinentes S. Mowinckel*, Oslo 1955, p. 39.

[2] 'The Inner Life of the Psalmists', in *The Psalmists*, ed. D. C. Simpson, 1926, p. 62.

It is not to be gainsaid that the emphasis on the Law as a summary of the divine demands on man led to a tendency to view the carrying out of rites of worship as the due part of obedience in respect to the Law, with an inevitable diminution of their intrinsic worth. This happened in later Judaism, with unequal results. In the case of the nobler minded it underscored the recognition that only God could cleanse from sin.[1] That for others it led to an emphasis on outward manifestations of piety and worship, to the neglect of the appropriate inward attitude of faith, is seen in the controversy of Jesus with the Pharisees. The blessing pronounced upon the 'pure *in heart*' (Mt. 5.8) contains a silent rebuke against a purity consisting in external observances alone. More explicitly, Jesus condemns those who 'cleanse the outside of the cup and of the plate but inside are full of extortion and rapacity', and He bids them 'first cleanse the inside of the cup and of the plate, that the outside also may be clean' (Mt. 23.25 f). Yet Jesus did not abolish ritual lustrations, despite his strong condemnation of their misuse.[2] On the contrary, his submission to the baptism of John and rebuke of the Pharisees for not doing likewise[3] indirectly taught the desirability of a radical cleansing, expressed in a single effective lustration. Such a complete cleansing in a once-for-all lustration is known to the Old Testament only in eschatological hope, but the hope is significant: the prophets look for the Day when a fountain will be opened to cleanse the house of David from sin and uncleanness (Zech. 13.1), when the Lord will 'sprinkle clean water' upon his people and put within them a new heart and a new spirit (Ezk. 36.25), and when He will refine his people as with fire and with fuller's soap (Mal. 3.1 ff). Till that time the Israelite, according to the Old Testament, should continue in the offering of worship, cleansed through the lustrations commanded by the Law, and await the purgation that the new age alone can give.

---

[1] D. Daube cites in this connection the well known statement of R. Akiba: 'Blessed are ye, O Israel. Before whom are ye made clean, and who makes you clean? Your Father in heaven. As it is written, And I will sprinkle clean water upon you and ye shall be clean. And again it says, O Lord, the hope, *miqwe* (which may also signify "immersion-pool") of Israel: as the *miqwe* cleanses the unclean, so does the Holy One cleanse Israel', *The New Testament and Rabbinic Judaism*, London 1956, p. 107.

[2] For the significance of Mk. 7.15, which in the first instance relates to the inability of eating with unwashed hands to defile a man, see Rawlinson, *St. Mark*, 1925, pp. 92 ff.

[3] If Lk. 7.20 is a comment of the Evangelist's and not a word of Jesus, the parable of Mt. 11.16 f implies rebuke for refusing John's message; and the purport of the question concerning the authority of John's baptism was correctly understood by the Jewish leaders: 'If we say, "From heaven", he will say, "Why then did you not believe him?" ' (Mk. 11:31 f).

(ii) *Jewish Baptizers and the Qumran Community*

It was mentioned above that complete conformity to the Levitical demands for purity through the prescribed lustrations was an ideal that few Jews could maintain. The rites of purification tended to assume the character of rites of consecration or initiation to Temple worship, especially pertinent for pilgrims at the feasts.[1] A quite opposite movement was set in motion about the middle of the second century B.C., which not alone inculcated the ritual lustrations commanded in the Law but added to their number and made of them hall marks of godliness. How it began and whence its inspiration came are uncertain. There is reason to believe that it coincided with the rise in influence of the Chasidim, who sought to live in strict accord with the Law's demands and from whom the Pharisees later developed; it is possible that the Jewish baptizers came into being as a result of the same enthusiasm for the Law.[2] This supposition is strengthened by the fact that the most notable of these groups, namely that which had its headquarters at Qumran, originated from within the priesthood. Their origin among priests would have led them to emphasize the adherence to the ritual law, yet their abandonment of the sacrificial worship of the Temple cut them off from some of the most outstanding elements of that law; it was not unnatural that they laid stress upon the ritual observances that were left to them, viz. those which related to rules for the maintenance of ritual cleanness, and developed them according to their own characteristic theology.[3] This coincided with their earnest desire for purity of body and soul. Moreover their eschatological views were taken from the Old Testament. It is likely that this group, who, presuming they either were or subsequently developed into the Essenes, had affiliated groups throughout the cities

[1] The belief that the prescriptions concerning ritual ablutions were given mainly in connection with the worship in the temple led eventually to their abandonment by male Jews; they insisted on their continued observance by their women folk in the appropriate circumstances (a demand which continues in force among orthodox Jews to this day, Brandt, op. cit., p. 55), but according to I. W. Slotki, the Jewish women themselves made them increasingly onerous, see the Soncino Talmud, Niddah, p. xxvii.

[2] Cf. Bousset, *Die Religion des Judentums*, 3rd ed. 1926, p. 457; H. H. Rowley, *The Zadokite Fragments and the Dead Sea Scrolls*, Oxford 1952, p. 80.

[3] A. Büchler suggested that the Essenes' idea of taking a *daily* ablution may have been an adaptation of the daily guilt-offerings sacrificed in the Temple in their day. 'If it is remembered that the pious men of the beginning of the first century in Jerusalem brought every day a guilt-offering for doubtful sins to cleanse themselves from every error possibly committed, Kerith 6.3, Tos. 4.4, the substitution of the daily immersion by the Essenes for such daily atonement will be better understood', *Studies in Sin and Atonement in the Rabbinic Literature of the First Century*, 1928, p. 369, n. 1.

of Israel, started a fashion that became popular in Jewry. It continued for centuries in the sects of the Jordan valley, *all* of whom were Jewish.[1] In the fourth century Epiphanius wrote about seven allegedly pre-Christian heresies among the Jews and examined their effects on Christianity; all had in common the custom of frequent baptizing and all were situated in Transjordan. It was in this area that John the Baptist exercised his ministry and where the Elchasaites developed, absorbing many of the other baptizing sects and communities. The Mandaean writings appeal continually to the virtue of the river Jordan and of bathing in it and the primitive Mandaean sect also lived in this territory. It is reasonable to suppose that this whole diverse movement sprang directly from a spontaneous application of the Levitical rites by priestly enthusiasts to a wider area of life than was envisaged in the Law.[2]

Thanks to the discovery of the Dead Sea Scrolls, we now possess first hand testimony from one of the most influential of the Jewish baptizing groups. There would seem to be more reason in favour than against the supposition that the Qumran Community was closely related to the Essenes; they should be viewed as either an early example of Essene order, possessing their own characteristic viewpoints not necessarily shared by the other related orders, or, more probably, as the forerunners of those Essenes known to history through Josephus, Philo, Pliny etc.[3] If such a connection between the Community and the Essenes were denied, we would be compelled to the admission that the custom of frequent lustrations must have been widely in vogue among the Jews about the beginning of the Christian era, seeing that such considerable and unrelated groups practised them.

The selection of the desolate area at the northern end of the Dead

---

[1] 'We have not found in the country of Syria any evident trace of pagan "baptists"; the Jewish world had the monopoly of this new kind of religious formation', Thomas, *Le Mouvement Baptiste en Palestine et Syrie*, 1935, p. 270.

[2] Fundamentally I think this is sound. But the possibility must be recognized that the whole movement was either sparked off by an outside influence or was early affected by such. See Bousset, *Hauptprobleme der Gnosis*, pp. 158, 285, *Die Religion des Judentums*, p. 461; Reitzenstein, *Das mandäisch Buch des Herrn der Grösse*, 1919, pp. 41 ff; von Gall, *ΒΑΣΙΛΕΙΑ ΤΟΥ ΘΕΟΥ*, Heidelberg 1926, pp. 430 ff. Granting that an early Mesopotamian influence might here have been effective in this realm, the evidence nevertheless is more satisfactorily accounted for on the assumption that the existing Jewish rites of cleansing received an extension of application among a group of priestly separatists, and that the development of their use and meaning may at certain times have been subjected to extraneous influences.

[3] See especially H. H. Rowley, *The Zadokite Fragments and the Dead Sea Scrolls*, Oxford 1952, pp. 78 ff. The identification of the Qumran Community with the Essenes is now generally accepted, though dissentient voices continue to be raised against it.

Sea for the Community's chief habitation may not be unconnected with its comparative proximity to the Jordan; certainly the later baptizing groups chose the Jordan valley for the sake of the water supply and also probably because of the sacred character of the waters of Jordan.[1] But Qumran is not situated on the Jordan; to judge from the map it must be quite seven miles from the river. Brownlee points out that the writers of the Sect have themselves given us the clue to the reason for their choice. In the Manual of Discipline, it is said of the initiates who have completed their period of preparation: 'They will separate themselves from the midst of the habitation of perverse men and go to *the wilderness* to *clear the way of the Lord*, as it is written:

> "*In the wilderness clear the way of the Lord;*
> *Level in the desert a highway for our God.*"

This means studying the Law which He commanded through Moses, so as to do according to all that was revealed time after time and according to that which the prophets revealed through his Holy Spirit' (viii.13 ff). The 'arabah' in which the 'highway for our God' was to be prepared fitly designated the depression in which the Jordan and Dead Sea lie. 'It was here the glory of the Lord would be revealed in the person of the Messiah(s). The study and practice of the law and the prophets would bring in this glad day'.[2] Here we see the creative force of the eschatological motif, which has been added to the traditional use of lustrations. Their conjunction has brought forth a new thing in Israel. These 'covenanters' have gone out into the desert, as ancient Israel did in the Exodus, with the intention of entering into the new covenant of the last days and of preparing for the advent of the Kingdom of God. They are thus, as F. M. Cross expressed it, 'priestly apocalyptists', followers of an 'eschatological asceticism'.[3]

Here we must remind ourselves of the fact, frequently pointed out, that the members of this sect had a clear understanding of the limitations of lustrations. They aspired to something more than ceremonial purity[4] and they knew that lustrations of themselves could not bestow

---

[1] Thomas, op. cit., p. 271.
[2] Brownlee, *John the Baptist, in the Scrolls and the New Testament*, ed. K. Stendahl, London 1958, pp. 34 f.
[3] *The Ancient Library of Qumran*, London 1958, pp. 56, 180.
[4] An example of the lofty ethical ideal of the Community may be seen in the Manual of Discipline, IV, the Book of Hymns, ch. v and the Covenant entered into by the initiates, Zadokite Document, vi.11 ff.

the moral purity they sought. In the Manual of Discipline it is stated, 'No one is to go into the water in order to attain the purity of holy men. For men cannot be purified except they repent their evil' (v). The well known statement of this conviction in chapters 2 and 3 of the Manual declares that the man who persists in walking in the stubbornness of his heart is not to be admitted to the community of God's truth; for 'he cannot be cleared by mere ceremonies of atonement, nor cleansed by any waters of ablution, nor sanctified by immersion in lakes or rivers, nor purified by any bath. Unclean, unclean he remains so long as he rejects the government of God and refuses the discipline of communion with Him. For it is only through the spiritual apprehension of God's truth that man's ways can be properly directed. Only thus can all his iniquities be shriven so that he can gaze upon the true light of life. Only through the holy spirit can he achieve union with God's truth and be purged of all his iniquities.[1] Only by a spirit of uprightness and humility can his sin be atoned. Only by the submission of his soul to all the ordinances of God can his flesh be made clean. Only thus can it really be sprinkled with waters of ablution. Only thus can it really be sanctified by waters of purification'. Clearly, the 'waters of purification' were of themselves powerless to cleanse the impenitent; the purging of iniquities is 'through the holy spirit' and obedience to the commands of God. Here is a striking example of the Jewish ability to distinguish between 'outward and visible' and 'inward and spiritual', the ritual and the moral, flesh and spirit, yet a refusal to separate them. Water cannot cleanse the rebellious spirit, but submission to the ordinances of God can cleanse the flesh. The desire of the Covenanters evidently is to have an outward cleansing accompanied by an obedient spirit, for in the conjunction of both the desired purity of body and soul is gained.

It is remarkable to what extent the sectaries succeeded in maintaining this conjoint emphasis on ritual cleansing and moral endeavour. The lustrations were so marked a feature of their life, it would have been easy for ethical effort to have been dissipated in the concern for negative ritual purity through avoidance of contact with the unclean. Yet the stress on moral demand was tremendous. The

[1] Does this signify the necessity of cleansing by the Spirit of God, as in Mk. 1.8, Mt. 3.11? or does it refer to the holy spirit of a man, as in the Zadokite Document, Ch. vii, 'No man shall make abominable his holy spirit'? The latter alternative is the more likely. In the passage here cited 'the holy spirit' appears to be synonymous with 'a spirit of uprightness and humility' in the following sentence, and is replaced by 'his soul' in that which succeeds it.

community was one of volunteers who committed themselves with
binding oath to return with all the heart and soul to the commandments of the Law of Moses (Manual of Discipline, v. 7 f) and the
covenant had to be renewed, not merely annually in the Community,
but daily by the individual member.[1]

There has been no little dispute as to whether the lustrations can
legitimately be viewed as 'baptisms', in the technical sense which that
word has acquired. H. H. Rowley has protested at the too ready assumption that the ablutions of the Covenanters had a similar significance as the baptism of John. He maintains that there is no clear
statement that a first ablution had the character of an initiatory rite.
From the description in Josephus of the stages whereby an initiate
into the company of the Essenes reached full status, it would appear
that at the conclusion of his first probationary year he was permitted
to use the waters of purity, and after a second year he was allowed to
use the purer kind of water reserved for the full members of the sect.
Rowley concedes that the first admission of the novice to the ablutions
of the sect in the water reserved for the members will have had a
special character, but in his view it was nevertheless not comparable
with an unrepeatable baptism. Nor is there any evidence that this
first ablution differed in form from those that followed: 'It is not an
administered rite, but a bath'. Accordingly, it must be said, 'There is
not a single feature of John's baptism for which there is the slightest
reason to go to Qumran to look for the source'.[2] It is salutary to
receive this check on too ready an identification of the Qumran lustrations with the practice of baptism in the strict sense of the term. The
frequency of the lustration should have warned us against that. Indeed, Josephus conveys the impression that the baths of the Essenes
were taken not simply once daily, as is commonly assumed, but
at least three times per day: after the passage of a stool, before
the midday meal and before the evening meal.[3] Such frequency of
ablution stands in strong contrast to the once-for-all rite of baptism.

On the other hand, it is essential that we do not under-estimate the
genuinely sacramental nature of these lustrations. And the view that

[1]   'With the coming of day and night
                     I shall come ever anew
                     Into God's covenant'.
Hymn of Initiates, col. 10 of the Manual of Discipline.
   [2] 'The Baptism of John and the Qumran Sect', in the *New Testament Essays,
Studies in Memory of T. W. Manson*, ed. by A. J. B. Higgins, Manchester 1959,
pp. 219-23.
   [3] *Wars of the Jews*, II, viii.5, 9.

the first lustration of a novice partook of the character of a formal initiation has much to commend it. Unfortunately our documents are vague at the point where we could have wished for clarity. Regulations concerning the admission of novices are given in the Manual of Discipline in chs. 5 and 6. In the latter passage it is laid down that an applicant for admission to the community is to be examined by the superintendent of the general membership, and if the man is willing to enter on a course of training he is to 'enter into a covenant to return to the truth and turn away from all perversity'. Later he appears for examination before the whole company and is voted into the membership if found satisfactory; but he is not admitted to the 'purity' until the completion of a full year's probation, at the end of which he is once more examined and voted on for acceptance into full status and the communal sharing of goods. In ch. 5 a parallel statement is made, but with less precision. Anyone admitted to the formal organization of the community is to 'enter into a covenant in the presence of all fellow-volunteers in the cause and to commit himself by a binding oath to return with all his heart and soul to the commandments of the Law of Moses'. He must keep himself separate from all 'forward men that walk in the path of wickedness'. The writer then declares, 'No one is to go into the water in order to attain the purity of holy men. For men cannot be purified except they repent their evil.' Such is the rendering of Gaster, and he interprets it as a protest against the idea that the act of immersion can by itself absolve sins. F. M. Cross, however, considers this to be closely related to the context; he interprets the subject as the impenitent of whom the preceding paragraph speaks: '(Such a candidate) shall not enter into the water (and as a result) come into contact with the Purity of the holy men; for they are not purified (thereby) except they repent from their wickedness'.[1] If this be an acceptable translation, it not alone signifies a prohibition for the unworthy to enter the 'purity' of the holy men, but has a positive implication for the action of the penitent: his entry into the purity of the holy men in a spirit of repentance will effect his purification and so number him among the 'holy'. There is no sense of crisis, such as attaches to the baptism of John and Christian baptism, but there is also no question but that *a man who enters for the first time the purity of the holy men thereby is purified and becomes one of their number*. The same impression is conveyed by the passage 2.25–3.12, which speaks of the impotence of waters to purify the stubborn man:

[1] Op. cit., p. 70, n. 96.

THE ANTECEDENTS OF CHRISTIAN BAPTISM

'Only by the submission of his soul to all the ordinances of God can his flesh be made clean. Only thus can it really be sprinkled with waters of ablution. Only thus can it really be sanctified by waters of purification'. 'Only thus' — but when the spirit of obedience is present, the waters of ablution cleanse from sin, the waters of purification sanctify! Of a man so cleansed and sanctified it is written: 'Then indeed will he be acceptable before God like an atonement offering which meets with his pleasure, and *then indeed will he be admitted to the covenant of the community for ever*'. Taking these passages together it looks as though the first ablution of a novice was more than simply a first bath: it signified an entrance on to the state of purity and consequently an entrance into the company of the purified.[1]

It should further be borne in mind that the lustrations of the Qumran Community and of the later Essenes had a more than ceremonial significance. On our understanding of the passages just cited from chs. 5–6 of the Manual of Discipline, the lustrations were effective for the cleansing of moral impurity where they were accompanied by a spirit of penitence and submission to the will of God. It is evident from Josephus that by his day certain lustrations were practised among the Essenes with a special sacramental import. In one passage he makes reference to a practice of divining the future 'by reading the holy books and using several sorts of purifications and being perpetually conversant in the discourses of the prophets'; the effectiveness of such method receives honourable mention; 'it is but seldom that they miss in their predictions!'[2] If that was an application of the lustrations confined to a few, there was another far more widespread, which also was undergone with the intention of procuring a precise and powerful effect; it would seem that the married members of the sect subjected their brides to special lustrations with a view

---

[1] The belief that the first bath of a novice virtually had the character of an initiation is maintained by Brownlee, op. cit., pp. 38 f; Cullmann, 'The Significance of the Qumran Texts for Research into the Beginnings of Christianity', in *The Scrolls and the New Testament*, ed. Stendahl, p. 21; F. M. Cross, op. cit., p. 70, n. 96; Gaster, op. cit., p. 44. Both Bousset, *Hauptprobleme der Gnosis*, p. 283, and Brandt, op. cit., pp. 66 f, had affirmed the same concerning the ritual lustrations of the Essenes on the basis of the information available in Josephus and Philo. It may be worth noting that the later Ebionites had *both* a baptism for the forgiveness of sins and inheritance of the Kingdom *and* a daily baptism; see Brandt, op. cit., pp. 21 f, 96. This, however, was probably due to a combination of Christian baptism with the practice of daily lustrations and is not proof of similar views among the Qumran Community; at best it indicates that among a people who had much in common with the Qumran Covenanters it was possible to conceive of an initiatory baptism and daily ablutions.

[2] *Wars*, II, viii.12.

to their early conception and child-birth.[1] There is no smoke without a fire; applications of the lustrations in ways such as these — and there may well have been others of which we are ignorant — could never have arisen unless some sacramental efficacy attached to the ordinary ablutions. In this I read a significant lesson: if the more innocent daily lustrations could be developed in special ways by certain members of the community, it would not be remarkable if a prophetic individual who knew of them adapted them in a far more radical manner, more in harmony with their spiritual intent. There *is* a bridge from Qumran to John the Baptist and it has more than one track: for the Covenanters and for John, the End is near; it requires drastic moral preparation; and lustration apart from the Temple worship, albeit necessarily conjoined with repentance, is effective for that purpose. In each case John is more radical in his teaching and more genuinely prophetic; but the Covenanters prepared the Way of the Lord better than they knew — by preparing the way of the Forerunner.

(iii) *Jewish Proselyte Baptism*

Our paramount interest in this chapter is to examine Jewish *antecedents* to Christian baptism. The question whether Jewish proselyte baptism was historically antecedent to the ministries of John the Baptist and Jesus, and if so the extent to which it influenced the Christian rite, are extraordinarily difficult to answer with any degree of confidence. The issues are more complex than is generally admitted. Whereas the pre-Christian origin of proselyte baptism is regarded by the majority of investigators as axiomatic,[2] it remains that the authors

---

[1] Such seems to be the meaning of the statement in Wars II, viii.13: δοκιμάζοντες μέντοι τριετίᾳ τὰς γαμετάς, ἐπειδὰν τρὶς καθαρθῶσιν εἰς πεῖραν τοῦ δύνασθαι τίκτειν, οὕτως ἄγονται. Whiston translates: 'They try their spouses for three years; and if they find that they have their natural purgations thrice, as trials that they are likely to be fruitful, they then actually marry them'. But a woman's experience of menstruation three times in three years is an extraordinary test for her fitness for marriage! Nor can the language imply menstruation in three successive months at some point in the three years. Whiston is surely missing the meaning of the passage. The 'being cleansed' three times with a view to proving whether the woman can bear child must relate to a lustration received on three different occasions within the three years *in order to aid her in conceiving*; if, in spite of such powerful aid, no conception is forthcoming, it is interpreted that the woman is incapable of bearing child and that she is therefore unfit for marriage. The raison d'être for such a test is manifest: among the Essenes marriage was entered upon for the sole purpose of procreation and to secure the continuance of the race; on such a basis marriage to a woman incapable of childbearing was without point. I observe that this interpretation is in harmony with Brandt's understanding of the passage, op. cit., p. 67.

[2] Such is the opinion of Schürer, *The Jewish People in the time of Jesus Christ*, II, vol. 2, p. 322; Plummer, *Hasting's Dictionary of the Bible*, vol. I, pp. 238 f; Oesterley & Box, *The Religion and Worship of the Synagogue*, London 1911, p. 281;

of the two best known works devoted to the examination of baptism among Jews and Jewish sects show a marked caution in this respect and incline to minimize the extent to which proselyte baptism was practised in the first half of the first century A.D.[1] In my judgment a fresh investigation requires to be made of all the issues in the light of our fresh knowledge of Jewish sources, including those from Qumran, and of Christian origins. In this discussion I can but point to some of the controverted issues and put forward a few tentative suggestions. Of their soundness I am far from certain.

Before considering the evidence I would raise a preliminary question: If proselyte baptism was a universally accepted institution in Judaism before the Christian era, how are we to explain the fact that there is not one clear testimony to it in pre-Christian writings and its complete absence of mention from the writings of Philo, Josephus and the Bible, particularly the New Testament? The silence of these authorities is the more unexpected when it is recalled how interested they all were in the relations of Jews to Gentiles. Many scholars, it is true, deny any significance to this phenomenon. Schürer, for example, speaking of Philo and Josephus, stated 'No one has ever been able to point out a single passage in which those writers were necessarily called upon to mention the matter'.[2] Strictly speaking he is right in his assertion and always will be, for it is quite impossible to prove that at any one point a writer *must* have mentioned the practice. Nevertheless, Zeitlin is not unreasonable in holding that the account in Josephus of

Gavin, op. cit., pp. 55 f; Abrahams, *Studies in Pharisaism and the Gospels, First Series*, 1917, p. 37; Strack Billerbeck, vol. I, pp. 102 ff; Starr, 'The Unjewish Character of the Markan Account of John the Baptist', *Journal of Biblical Literature*, New Haven 1932, p. 231; H. H. Rowley, 'Jewish Proselyte Baptism', *Hebrew Union College Annual*, Cincinnati 1940, p. 316; Marsh, *The Origin and Significance of the New Testament Baptism*, Manchester 1941, p. 9; Oepke, article 'Βάπτω' in Kittel's *T.W.N.T.*, p. 533; Flemington, *The New Testament Doctrine of Baptism*, London 1948, p. 4; Jeremias, 'Der Ursprung der Johannestaufe', *Z.N.W.* 1929, pp. 341 ff, *Hat die Urkirche die Kindertaufe geübt?* Göttingen, 2nd ed. 1949 ff, p. 16, *Die Kindertaufe, in den ersten 4 Jahrhunderten*, Göttingen 1958, pp. 37 f, *Jerusalem zur Zeit Jesu*, Göttingen, 2nd ed. 1958, p. 192; T. W. Manson, 'Baptism in the Church', *S.J.T.*, vol. 2, 1949, p. 392, n. 7; Levison, 'The Proselyte in Biblical and early Post Biblical Times', *S.J.T.*, vol. 10, 1957, pp. 49 ff; Crehan, *Early Christian Baptism and the Creed*, London 1950, p. 4. Torrance, 'Proselyte Baptism', *New Testament Studies*, vol. 1, 1954, p. 154, 'The Origins of Baptism', *S.J.T.*, vol. II, 1958, p. 161 ff; *The Biblical Doctrine of Baptism* (Church of Scotland Study Document), 1958, p. 13; J. Heron, 'The Theology of Baptism', *S.J.T.*, vol. 8, 1955, p. 45; Gilmore, 'Jewish Antecedents', in *Christian Baptism*, London 1959, pp. 67 ff. J. Schneider believes that proselyte baptism is probably pre-Christian in origin but it played no part in the development of Christian baptism, *Die Taufe im Neuen Testament*, Stuttgart 1952, pp. 20 ff. Lampe seems to hold a similar view, *The Seal of the Spirit*, London 1951, p. 86.

[1] Brandt, *Die jüdischen Baptismen*, 1910; Thomas, *Le Mouvement Baptiste en Palestine et Syrie*, (150 av. J.C.–300 ap. J.C.) 1935.

[2] Op. cit., p. 323.

the conversion of Izates, King of Adiabene, comes near to fulfilling the condition, for the narrative is very detailed; much is said of circumcision, but not a word about the proselyte's bath.[1] It is similarly very surprising that the Gospels, despite their interest in the baptism of John, the ritual lustrations of Jews and Christian baptism, yet pass over proselyte baptism in silence, as also do Acts and Paul, although debate concerning the relation of Gentile Christians to circumcision continued over a prolonged period. Perhaps even more striking is the lack of reference to proselyte baptism in the Jewish work Joseph and Aseneth. This book, described as a piece of Hellenistic Jewish propaganda from Egypt, records the conversion of the Gentile Aseneth to the Jewish faith.[2] In Kilpatrick's view, 'the tract seems to represent conversion to Judaism under the guise of initiation into a mystery'.[3] No mention is made of baptism. This confirms Kilpatrick in his belief that the book is early, possibly 100–30 B.C. Kühn, however, though prepared to date the work in the first century A.D., doubts that it should be placed earlier than this.[4] It follows that in an area in which proselyte baptism might be expected to flourish, it was not practised by at least one group bent on proselytizing about the beginning of the Christian era. On the other hand, the group admittedly may have isolated itself from the main body of Jews in Egypt. And the silence of the major writers earlier mentioned *could* represent a curious accident of history.

Turning to the positive evidence for the early institution of proselyte baptism, in Schürer's judgment one simple observation was sufficient to scatter all objections: A Gentile, who did not observe the Levitical regulations concerning purity, was unclean as a matter of course, and so could not be admitted into Jewish communions without a tebilah, a ritual bath of purification. 'This general consideration is of itself so conclusive that there is no need to lay any very great

---

[1] See his article, 'The Halaka in the Gospels and its relation to the Jewish Law at the Time of Jesus', *Hebrew Union College Annual*, I, 1924, p. 359. Izates embraced the Jewish faith and wished to become circumcised, but entreaty was made to him to desist from taking the step for the sake of his crown and of his personal safety. He was finally stung into action by one Eleazar, who told him that he was guilty of impiety in neglecting to obey the command to be circumcised. In the circumstantial narrative of Josephus, it is curious that he neither made Eleazar to mention baptism with circumcision, nor narrated the king's submission to it along with the operation; nor did Ananias refer at all to it when attempting to dissuade the king from taking the dangerous step of circumcision. See *Antiquities of the Jews*, XX.2, 4.

[2] Kilpatrick, 'The Last Supper', *E.T.*, vol. LXIV, 1952, p. 5.

[3] Op. cit., p. 6.

[4] 'The Meal', in *The Scrolls and the New Testament*, ed. Stendahl, p. 261, n. 33.

stress upon individual testimonies.'[1] Most writers on the subject express themselves similarly. Yet it appears to me to oversimplify the issue. For if Gentiles were unclean 'as a matter of course', by virtue of their not observing Levitical ordinances, they must have been so viewed from the time that the Jews adopted those regulations; then, since Israel had always known the 'stranger within the gates', proselyte baptism is as old as the Levitical code!

In reality, there are two separate questions here, namely the nature of Gentile uncleanness and the manner of its removal. The evidence as to the former is tantalisingly uncertain;[2] even where it was taken

[1] Op. cit., p. 322.

[2] In Zeitlin's view the Gentiles were not regarded as unclean until the year A.D. 65, when Jews were forbidden to associate with them, as a measure intended to promote Jewish nationalism in face of the threat from the Romans, and it was after this declaration that the necessity for proselyte baptism arose ('The Halaka in the Gospels', *H.U.C.A.*, 1924, p. 360). Finkelstein replied to Zeitlin by urging that too much importance should not be attached to the date A.D. 65, since the conclave of that year re-enacted many laws and gave sanction to many customs which had been prevalent before it, and that concerning Gentiles and proselyte baptism may have been among those so confirmed (*J.B.L.*, 1933, pp. 207 f). In fact, it must be admitted that the uncleanness of Gentiles is assumed in various passages of the Gospels and Acts, e.g. Jn. 18.28, Acts 10.28, 11.12, and possibly Mt. 8.7 (viewed as a question). Jeremias interprets this as implying the Levitical uncleanness of the Gentiles. Indeed, he lays it down with precision: 'In the time of Herod the uncleanness of the Niddah (a menstrual woman) was ascribed to the Gentiles; in the first decades of our era the uncleanness of a corpse; in the last time before the destruction of the temple the uncleanness of the Zab (=a man with a seminal issue)' (*Z.N.W.*, 1929, p. 313). He finds a fixed point in the fact that Simon, Son of Kamithos, High Priest A.D. 17–18, was not able to officiate in the Day of Atonement ceremonies through accidentally being spat on by an Arab (*Kindertaufe* . . ., p. 30). We can find an example possibly even earlier than this: Josephus says that when one of the lower order of the Essenes touched a member of the highest grade, the latter washed himself 'as though he had associated himself with a foreigner' (*Wars*, II, viii, 10). Yet, over against these testimonies, one must set the rabbinical discussion in Pes. 91b, wherein the Hillelites laid down a particular ruling about a proselyte on the ground that, 'he (the proselyte) will not understand that the previous year he was a *heathen and not susceptible to uncleanness*, whereas he is now *an Israelite and susceptible to uncleanness*'. The Shammaites took issue with the Hillelite ruling, but not with their view of the heathen's lack of susceptibility to uncleanness. On the strength of this, Daube is convinced that proselyte baptism was outside the levitical sphere: 'Pagans were not susceptible of levitical uncleanness, so in principle there was simply no room for purification' (op. cit., p. 107). I can see no solution to this problem other than postulating a distinction between the uncleanness to which the Jew is susceptible and the uncleanness of the Gentile. A. Büchler has a long discussion on the distinction between levitical uncleanness and what he terms 'religious' uncleanness in the Old Testament and in Rabbinical literature; the distinction is undoubted, though it is covered up frequently by the habit of Jewish writers of using levitical terminology for defilement of every kind, and it could well apply in this sphere (see Büchler's *Studies in Sin and Atonement in the Rabbinic Literature of the First Century*, 1928, pp. 212 ff). On this basis it would be possible to maintain that, in the case mentioned by Jeremias, the Arab was unclean under one category (as a Gentile) and that through him the High Priest was rendered unclean under another (as a Jew, susceptible to levitical laws). Something like this was evidently in the minds of Strack-Billerbeck when they wrote, 'Even if a Gentile, because he did not stand under the law, could not be levitically unclean in the sense of the law, yet he was considered unclean simply as a Gentile' (op. cit., I, p. 102). But if this distinction were to be

for granted, it can by no means be assumed that baptism was the needful means of taking it away. In the Joseph and Aseneth story, Joseph refuses to kiss Aseneth because she was unclean, but on conversion she was cleansed without baptism — by her penitence and perhaps by participating in a sacral meal. We must return to this point later.

Jeremias has revived a view that proselyte baptism is to be found in Test. Levi 14.6: 'Out of covetousness you will teach the commandments of the Lord; wedded women you will pollute, and the virgins of Jerusalem you will defile; and with harlots and adulteresses you will be joined, and the daughters of the Gentiles you will take to wife, *purifying them with an unlawful purification*'. Jeremias interprets the last clause of proselyte baptism, which the writer of the Testaments regards as 'unlawful' and combats on the ground that it encourages immorality; he dates the book in the closing years of the first century B.C.; in that case it becomes the earliest reference to proselyte baptism yet known.[1] Unfortunately the matter is far from clear. No two scholars seem to agree on the interpretation of the relevant clause. Charles thinks it may refer to lay observance of customary purifications, or it may be a declaration that any purification is unlawful.[2] Zeitlin relates it to purification after the menses.[3] Finkelstein first suggested that it relates to proselyte baptism,[4] then withdrew the suggestion, partly because he thought that opposition to such a practice would have to be more explicit and partly because in any case marriage between priests and proselytes would not have been sanctioned by the writer of the Testaments with *any* form of purification; he therefore gave up the present form of the text and proposed to amend it so as to read, 'betrothing them against the law'.[5] In a context of immoral dealings of priests, Charles' first suggestion is plausible; but on this basis, why do we not read of 'unlawful purifications', in

granted, would the uncleanness suffered by a man 'simply as a Gentile' be subject to a law directed to removing levitical uncleanness, viz. by a bath? In my judgment the difficulty of answering in the affirmative is twofold: (*a*) the lateness of the emergence of proselyte baptism in face of such a statement as Amos 7.17, 'Thou shalt die in an unclean land', implying all lands beyond Israel as unclean; (*b*) the role of circumcision as the traditional mode of entrance into Judaism, to which the bath was attached with uncertain significance and relation. It should be noted that G. F. Moore, like Daube, also divorced proselyte baptism from levitical cleansing, though from a different viewpoint, (*Judaism*, vol. I, pp. 332 ff) and Büchler could not find proof of the idea of purification of sin by immersion in first century Jewish writers: 'There is no evidence for the assumption that the immersion prescribed for the proselyte was instituted to wash off symbolically his numerous sins', op. cit., p. 373. This united testimony of Rabbinic experts deserves more consideration than it has thus far received.

[1] *Die Kindertaufe*, p. 30.   [2] *Apocrypha and Pseudepigrapha*, vol. II, p. 313.
[3] *J.B.L.*, 1933, p. 78.
[4] Quoted by Starr from a verbal communication to him, *J.B.L.*, 1932, p. 231.1.16.
[5] Reading ותקדשׁו instead of ותטהרו; *J.B.L.*, 1933, p. 204 f.

the plural? Moreover the date of the passage raises a complication. Jeremias favours the end of the first century B.C. for the composition of the book. That suits his view of the time when belief in Gentile uncleanness arose. But most scholars place the book in the second century B.C.[1] Such a date would make very difficult the possibility of reference to proselyte baptism, and on Jeremias' view it would rule it out altogether, for there was no call for such an institution, the Gentiles not being regarded as unclean. On the other hand Torrey sets the Testaments in the first century A.D.,[2] as also Schnapp;[3] that would alter the potential application of the saying, but the possibility that proselyte baptism was regarded by some Jews in the first century A.D. as 'unlawful' is an interesting one to contemplate![4] At least it should be admitted that a saying whose significance and origin are so dubious as this has no claim to confidence as a means of determining so complex an issue as that under review.

The first indubitable references to proselyte baptism belong to the first century A.D. They are generally set in the closing decades of the century, though some authorities would date one or two of them earlier. Epictetus at the end of the century makes mention of baptism as a distinguishing feature of the real convert to Judaism.[5] A passage in the fourth Sibylline Oracle, dated about A.D. 80, is believed by most to relate to proselyte baptism.[6] More important is the Rabbinic

[1] E. G. Charles, op. cit., pp. 289 f; Pfeiffer, *History of New Testament Times*, 1949, p. 64; Moore, op. cit., p. 193; Rowley, *Relevance of Apocalyptic*, 2nd ed. 1947, pp. 63 ff; Oesterley and Robinson, *A History of Israel*, vol. II, 1932, pp. 306 ff; Herford, *Talmud and Apocrypha*, 1933, p. 233; Albright, *From the Stone Age to Christianity*, 1940, p. 279.

[2] *The Apocryphal Literature*, 1945, p. 131.

[3] Kautzsch's *Apokryphen und Pseudepigraphen des Alten Testaments*, vol. II, 1900, pp. 459 f. Schnapp does not rule out the second century A.D. as impossible for the composition of the Testaments.

[4] I forbear to consider de Jonge's belief that the Testaments originated about A.D. 200, a hypothesis which has many difficulties in the way of its acceptance. See M. de Jonge's, *The Testaments of the Twelve Patriarchs*, 1953.

[5] 'When we see a man playing a double game we are accustomed to say, "He is not a Jew but pretends to be one". But when he accepts the experience of the baptized and chosen, then he is in name and reality a Jew', *Dissert*, II.9.9–21. Thomas follows Polster in interpreting the term 'experience', τὸ πάθος, as a euphemism for circumcision: in which case the passage attests both circumcision and baptism as the real test of whether a man is a genuine proselyte, op. cit., p. 361.

[6]   Ah; miserable mortals, change these things,
       Nor lead the mighty God to wrath extreme.
       But giving up your swords and pointed knives,
       And homicides and wanton violence,
       Wash your whole body in perennial streams,
       And lifting up your hands to heaven seek pardon
       For former deeds and expiate with praise
       Bitter impiety.
The date is uncontested. See e.g. Lanchester in Charles' *Apocrypha and Pseudepigrapha*, II, p. 373.

evidence. In the Mishnah a discussion is recorded as having taken place between R. Eliezer, a Shammaite, and R. Jehoshua, a Hillelite, as to the relative importance of circumcision and baptism;[1] the controversy is placed about A.D. 90. A further difference between representatives of the two schools concerned the right of the newly circumcised to participate in the passover: 'The School of Shammai maintain, If a man became a proselyte on the day before the Passover he may immerse himself and consume his Passover offering in the evening. And the School of Hillel say: He that separates himself from his uncircumcision is as one that separates himself from the grave'.[2] On this basis the Hillelites made a man wait for seven days after circumcision before taking the bath. How far back the difference of viewpoint extended we do not know; the passage in the Pesachim is generally admitted to be earlier than the controversy between R. Eliezer and R. Jehoshua, and some would set it even prior to the destruction of Jerusalem.[3] While uncertainty attaches to this, more confidence may be placed in the brief notice in the same tractate, Pes. viii: 'R. Eleazar b. Jacob says: Soldiers were guards of the gates in Jerusalem; they were baptized and ate their Paschal lambs in the evening'. Abrahams is inclined to view this piece of evidence as more weighty than that earlier cited, for Eleazar ben Jacob the Elder was one of the most trustworthy reporters of Temple events and rites, which he knew from personal experience. It would seem that Roman soldiers were converted and baptized on the day before the Passover, while the Temple still stood. The precise date cannot be fixed, but the opinion of Graetz, that it took place in A.D. 67, is commonly accepted.[4] Abrahams observes that this still leaves us without evidence that proselytes were baptized half a century earlier but considers that this last datum greatly increases the probability.[5] On reflection, I am inclined to agree with him. It would be unreasonable to suggest that these men were the first proselytes to receive baptism; an established

---

[1] R. Eliezer said that a circumcised man even without the bath is a proselyte, for our fathers were circumcised but did not take the bath. R. Jehoshua maintained that a man who has taken the bath but has not been circumcised is a proselyte, for our mothers took the bath but were not circumcised. See Yeb. 46a.

[2] Pes. 91b–2, taken from Danby's translation.

[3] So H. H. Rowley, op. cit., p. 316. Jeremias considers that the difference must be set before A.D. 30, on the assumption that the Shammaites must have taken a stricter view of the uncleanness of the heathen in the time of Jesus (Jn. 18.28); *Jerusalem zur Zeit Jesu*, II, p. 192. Such an inference seems to me unjustifiable from the Johannine text. See the extended note on Gentile uncleanness, p. 21, n. 2.

[4] Abrahams, op. cit., p. 37. Jeremias, as in the previously cited passage from Pesachim, again places the incident before A.D. 30 for the same reason, ibid.

[5] Ibid.

custom is being observed.[1] What cannot be answered with any confidence is how much earlier than the ministries of John and Jesus this custom is to be dated, and, more pertinently, how widespread it was. For, barring a decree such as Zeitlin suggested, it is not obvious that proselyte baptism should suddenly have sprung into being and secured instant recognition in all Israel and the Dispersion. Ideas sometimes have to win their way gradually; the evidence suggests that it may have been so with this one.[2]

Granting the possibility, if not the probability, that Jewish proselyte baptism was practised when the Christian Church first began to make known its message and to administer its own baptism, the question arises whether the Jewish rite exercised a dominant influence on the Christian. Here certain scholars speak with emphasis and with confidence: both the form and theology of Christian baptism depend on those of Jewish proselyte baptism. The following points are currently made, notably by Jeremias in his most recent work:[3]

(i) The *baptismal terminology* of the New Testament is held to be derived from that used of proselyte baptism. For example, since the basic terms βαπτίζειν and its derivatives are not used in a sacral-technical sense in non-Jewish Hellenism, they come from Jewish-Greek usage. The formula εἰς τὸ ὄνομα, 'in the name', also reproduces the Hebrew term לְשֵׁם, used to signify the intention of the rite.

(ii) The *baptismal catechetical instruction* of the New Testament

---

[1] Professor Daube further observed to me that it is difficult to think of two Rabbinical scholars discussing the relative importance of circumcision and proselyte baptism if the latter were an innovation in their own lifetime.

[2] Daube, in his lecture 'A Baptismal Catechism' (*The New Testament and Rabbinic Judaism*, pp. 106 ff), points out that whereas circumcision is required of a man, in the case of a woman 'even Judaism regarded baptism as the only indispensable rite of reception — a point not always given its due weight by those interested in the origins of the Christian ceremony' (p. 106). In his view proselyte baptism must have been introduced long before the Christian era, possibly several centuries earlier, since female proselytes were always more numerous than men and without the rite they would have entered Judaism with no outward sign of initiation at all. I stand in perplexity before the suggestion, in part to comprehend how our sources, including the Old Testament, could have so completely hidden the matter from us had it been so, but also admittedly puzzled by the problem presented. All the evidence suggests that proselyte baptism was secondary to the circumcision of the proselyte; it is difficult to believe that it was instituted with women mainly in view. And a beginning of the practice had to be made some time, prior to which the women must have been accepted without it. The phenomenon of Ruth the Moabitess, which deeply influenced the thought of proselyte reception, must have suggested the possibility of a woman entering Judaism without baptism. But it is equally comprehensible that a time had to come when the position was regularized, so as to conform in measure with the reception of the males, and that the baptism of female proselytes speedily became more numerous than the reception of males.

[3] *Die Kindertaufe in den ersten vier Jahrhunderten*, pp. 34 ff.

reproduces that given in connection with proselyte baptism. This is most plainly seen in 1 Peter and the Didache (chs. 1-6), which latter document incorporates the scheme of the Jewish teaching on the Two Ways.

(iii) The *baptismal rites* of the early Church follow the pattern of those used in proselyte baptism. The regulations in the Didache concerning the kind of water to be used in baptism are clearly taken from Judaism.[1] The same is true of the necessity, mentioned in the Hippolytan manual of Church Order (16.6), that women let down their hair and remove their ornaments before baptism; it reflects the Jewish ordinance, designed to ensure that the baptized was completely immersed and came into contact with the water in every part of the body.[2]

(iv) The *baptismal theology* of the New Testament is believed to have had its origin in the Jewish understanding of proselyte baptism. The concept of dying and rising in baptism appears to be reflected in the rabbinical saying, already quoted, 'One who separates himself from circumcision is like one who separates himself from the grave'.[3] In the view of D. Daube this dictum implies that, spiritually, heathenism equalled existence in a tomb, hence conversion meant a passage from death to life;[4] it is presumed to be the source of the Pauline doctrine of baptism in Rom. 6.1 ff. Moreover in a rabbinical discussion on lawful marriages the judgment is given, 'One who has become a proselyte is like a child newly born';[5] it is considered to be the source of the New Testament teaching on regeneration.[6] The allusion in 1 Cor. 10.1 f to the Fathers being baptized in the cloud and in the sea at the Exodus is thought by Jeremias to reflect an early form of the Rabbinical mode of justifying proselyte baptism from the

---

[1] 'Having first recited all these things, baptize in the name of the Father and of the Son and of the Holy Spirit in living water. But if thou hast not living water, then baptize in other water; and if thou art not able in cold, then in warm'. Did. 7.1 ff. Compare the 'six degrees of gatherings of water' in the tractate Mikwaoth, ch. 1, given in an ascending order of value: (*a*) water of pits; (*b*) water of rain drippings; (*c*) a gathering of water ('mikweh') containing forty seahs; (*d*) a fountain; (*e*) 'smitten' water, i.e. salty water or hot water from a spring; (*f*) living waters.

[2] In the same tractate, Mikwaoth ch. 9, a list of causes that prevent complete contact between the water and the body is given, commencing with 'threads of wool and threads of flax and the ribbons on the heads of girls'. Rowley, in discussing these regulations, considers that the custom in the early centuries of baptism taking place in nudity, attested by Chrisostom and Cyril of Jerusalem, is also due to the influence of proselyte baptism; op. cit., pp. 323 ff.

[3] Pes. 91b.

[4] *The New Testament and Rabbinic Judaism*, 1956, pp. 109 f.

[5] Yeb. 22a.

[6] Daube points out that in the majority of conversions to Judaism, which were those of women, this new birth was effected by baptism alone, op. cit., p. 114.

Scriptures.[1] On reviewing these agreements between the teaching on the significance of Christian baptism and of proselyte baptism Jeremias concludes: 'In this matter the possibility of an accidental agreement or an independent analogy is absolutely excluded; we can only be dealing with a genetic connection'.[2]

This demonstration of the 'genetic connection' between the two rites is at first sight striking, but I am persuaded that it is fallacious. There is no doubt that we are dealing with closely connected forms and thought, but the fallacy is committed through postulating that the middle term on every occasion is proselyte baptism. An examination of the points that have been made will make this clear.

(i) The terminology used of baptism in the New Testament has general, not particular antecedents. The verb $\beta a \pi \tau i \zeta \epsilon \iota \nu$ and the noun $\beta a \pi \tau \iota \sigma \mu o i$ occur in Mk. 7.4 of ordinary Jewish washings; in Heb. 6.2 the plural noun $\beta a \pi \tau \iota \sigma \mu o i$ includes Christian baptism and lustrations used by other religious groups, both Jewish and pagan, with an implicit contrast between the Christian and other usages; in neither passage can proselyte baptism be considered in any way determinative of the language. Nor is there any likelihood that $\beta a \pi \tau \iota \sigma \mu a$, as distinct from $\beta a \pi \tau \iota \sigma \mu o s$, reflects the special use of *tebilah* for proselyte baptism; apart from the figurative use of the term in Mk. 10.38 f, Lk. 12.50, its occurrence in the Gospels and Acts is exclusively reserved for *John's* baptism. The group of words connected with $\beta a \pi \tau i \zeta \epsilon \iota \nu$ reflect contemporary terminology used of lustrations of all kinds practised among the Jews. It is true that the term לשם is likely to have been determinative for the primitive use of the phrase $\epsilon i s \ \tau o \ \check{o} \nu o \mu a$, however that phrase may have been interpreted among Gentile Christians; but its background was so general and its application, even in a religious sense, so wide, it is superfluous to suggest that a restricted application in relation to proselyte baptism is the cause of its employment in relation to Christian baptism.[3]

---

[1] The Hillelites deduced from the statement in Num. 15.4 that the proselyte was taken up into the Sinaitic covenant in the same manner as the people were at Sinai. No mention is made in Exodus that the Fathers were baptized. Nevertheless a baptism was deduced from Ex. 24.8, 'Moses took blood and sprinkled the people therewith', on the ground that, 'It is valid tradition that there is no sprinkling without a (previous) ablution', Yeb. 46b. Paul's statement of baptism in the cloud and in the sea is considered to be a different, and probably earlier, mode of presenting this belief; that it has not been preserved in a rabbinical source known to us is purely accidental. This argument of Jeremias is presented in detail in the article, 'Der Ursprung der Johannestaufe', in the *Z.N.W.*, 1929, pp. 314 ff, and more briefly in *Hat die Urkirche die Kindertaufe geübt?*, p. 16, and *Die Kindertaufe in den ersten 4 Jahrhunderten*, pp. 37 f. [2] *Die Kindertaufe*, p. 43.

[3] See pp. 90–92, and observe especially the flexible use of לשם in the quotation given concerning the purpose of an offering: it is presented 'in the name' of the offering, the offerer, God, the altar fires, the sweet savour, and the good pleasure (of God).

(ii) Parallels between the mode of administering Christian baptism in the early Church and the enactments concerning proselyte baptism are indubitable, but two observations must be made in respect to them. First, the regulations framed for proselyte baptism themselves reflect basic procedure in Jewish lustrations generally; e.g. those pertaining to the *amount* of water required for ablutions and the *kind* of water to be used ('living' if possible, cold rather than warm etc.) were of universal application, as also was the demand for nakedness in ablutions.[1] Secondly, the authorities in which the Jewish pattern is so strikingly taken up and developed belong to the second century A.D., and in the case of Hippolytus to its closing decades. To assume, as is so frequently done without question, that the rite of baptism in Hippolytus is identical in all its particulars with the administration of baptism in the earliest Church is to overlook a great deal of very significant evidence.

(iii) The view that conversion from heathenism to Judaism implies a new life, whether a dying and rising again,[2] or a new birth,[3] is firmly attested in the Talmud. If the question were asked, however, 'By what means was this new life conceived to begin?' there can originally have been but one answer: 'By submission to circumcision'. This is attested by the saying already quoted from Pesachim 91b: whereas the Shammaites permitted a man to become proselyte on the day before the Passover, to immerse himself at once and eat the Passover sacrifice in the evening, the Hillelites said, 'He that separates himself from his uncircumcision is as one that separates himself from a grave'. The enactment in Num. 19.16 ff is in view: 'Whoever in the open field touches one who is slain with a sword, or a dead body, or a bone of a man, or *a grave*, shall be unclean seven days. For the unclean they shall take some ashes of the burnt sin offering, and running water shall be added in a vessel; then a clean person shall take hyssop and dip it in the water and sprinkle it upon . . . him who touched the bone, or the slain, or the dead, or the grave; and the clean person shall sprinkle upon the unclean on the third day and on the seventh day; thus on the seventh day he shall cleanse him, and he shall wash his clothes and bathe himself in water, and at evening he shall be clean'. The inference from the Rabbinical saying is clear: the newly circumcised has come from a grave and must endure the customary seven days period

---

[1] The necessity for no 'separation' between the water and the body was especially strict in the case of a woman after menstruation.

[2] 'One who separates himself from his uncircumcision is like one who separates himself from the grave', Pes. 91b.

[3] 'One who has become a proselyte is like a child newly born', Yeb. 229.

of uncleanness and then bathe himself: *the decisive turn from 'death' therefore was the circumcision already undergone, not the bath taken seven days later.*[1] The proselyte's bath enabled the freshly made Jew to enter upon his privileges of worship; it did not make the heathen a Jew. Hence it is a mistake to read back the New Testament theology of Christian baptism into the Jewish understanding of proselyte baptism.

It is possible, through this very saying, to trace a part of the development through which proselyte baptism passed. The Hillelites applied the saying to women.[2] Now manifestly this was a secondary application, however understandable. The 'uncircumcision' meant, in the first instance, the state of uncircumcision of the male.[3] Yet it was an easy transition to employ the term to represent 'the uncircumcised' generally, and so the heathen world or heathenism. In this sense the saying could be applied to a woman. Through the bath of the proselyte she 'separates herself' from her old 'uncircumcised' life and the world of paganism. On the analogy of the male, whose circumcision marked his departure from the old life, the female proselyte celebrated her prior renunciation of the old life at her baptism. But inasmuch as the commandments already learned were repeated while the proselyte was actually in the water, there must have been an inevitable tendency to attach the theology of transition, fashioned with respect to circumcision, to the bath itself. There is, indeed, evidence to show that while the Shammaites continued to lay emphasis on the importance of circumcision, the Hillelites laid increasing stress on proselyte baptism as the crucial point of transition, with the prime intention of assimilating the entry of the male proselyte to that of the female and because the latter was far more common than the former.[4]

[1] I observe that Strack-Billerbeck drew a similar deduction from this difference between the Shammaites and Hillelites. 'When the School of Shammai, which was the unyielding representative of the received tradition, allowed the bath of the proselyte to take place immediately on circumcision, then it may be assumed that the older view considered that the conversion of the proselyte was completed in his circumcision; that which followed after, the bath and the sacrifice, was an accident, the chief thing remained the circumcision', vol. I, p. 104.

[2] Tos. Pes. 7.13. See Strack-Billerbeck, I, p. 105 and Daube, op. cit., p. 110.

[3] So clearly in the translation of the Talmud by Louis Goldschmidt, *Der Babylonisch Talmud*, Berlin 1930, Pesachim, p. 603; Danby's translation of the Mishnah, p. 148; The Soncino edition of the Talmud, Pesachim, p. 491.

[4] See Strack-Billerbeck, vol. I, pp. 104 f, and compare their observation on p. 102: 'It is not to be denied that in the course of the first Christian century a certain change in the estimation of proselyte baptism took place. Whereas at the beginning circumcision was the decisive act, through which the conversion was perfect, the first bath of the proselyte gradually gained more and more an independent character alongside circumcision, so that in the end it was commonly regarded as the decisive mark of conversion'. In spite of this Daube is strongly

This consideration illuminates the significance of the close relations between the catechetical instruction given to the Jewish proselyte and the baptismal catechesis in the New Testament. There is no doubt that the latter has been greatly influenced by the former. But this instruction is basically concerned with the new privileges and obligations entered upon by the convert and is not affected by the fact that he undergoes baptism. The teaching would have been the same prior to the introduction of proselyte baptism as after its establishment. This issue, accordingly, has no bearing on the relationship between Jewish proselyte *baptism* and Christian baptism.

It is noteworthy that the Jewish theology of conversion as life from the dead and regeneration appears in the writing earlier alluded to, Joseph and Aseneth, in which proselyte baptism has no place. Joseph prays for the penitent Aseneth: 'Lord God of my father Israel . . . who didst quicken all things and summon them from darkness to light and from error to truth and from death to life, do thou bless this maiden also and quicken and renew her with thy spirit'. The angel declares to Aseneth at the end of her period of penitence: 'Be of good courage Aseneth . . . from this day thou shalt be *renewed* and *refashioned* and *quickened*'.

Whether the New Testament writers took over the concept of dying and rising and of regeneration from Jewish thought about the proselyte it is difficult to say. Presumption would indicate that those who shaped the thought of the primitive Church could hardly have been ignorant of this teaching. On the other hand the New Testament theology of baptism revolves about two poles of thought not associated with proselyte baptism: unity with the Messiah who is Son of Man and Second Adam and who rose for the race; and, closely connected therewith, the belief that the age of resurrection and the life of the Kingdom of God has dawned in the rising of the Messiah. It would seem plausible that the familiar concepts of Jewish conversion

---

inclined to attach the idea of rising to new life to the proselyte's baptism. He finds confirmation of this in the Tannaitic statement, 'When he has undergone baptism *and come up, tabhal we'ala*, he is like an Israelite in all respects'; the 'coming up' was the decisive moment of emerging into the new existence. Daube finds this echoed in the Markan description of the baptism of Jesus, 'Jesus . . . was baptized by John in the Jordan. And immediately *coming up* out of the water he saw the heavens opened . . .' (the phrase is also in Mt. 3.16 but not in Lk. 3.21; it is assumed that Luke did not understand its significance). If this is a true interpretation of the Tannaitic statement, it is a development from the earlier views represented by the School of Shammai, but I find it difficult to receive. If the 'coming up' was so critical for the meaning of resurrection in baptism, how is it that Paul does not allude to it, although it would so admirably have suited his theology of baptism? The interpretation above given of the language used of circumcision seems to me to be incontrovertible.

theology were given a fresh orientation and greater depth and power by the Christian understanding of the redemptive action of the Messiah. That it came to be more closely associated with baptism was natural in that Christian baptism is baptism to the crucified and risen Lord.[1]

Our discussion of the relationships between Jewish proselyte baptism and Christian baptism has not been wholly negative, for it has yielded some important data. If we have been compelled to stress the uncertainty attaching to the date of the emergence of proselyte baptism we have yet recognized the probability of its priority in time over Christian baptism. That it exercised a decisive influence on Christian baptism we have not found, but the theology of conversion in Judaism we have seen to be an important factor in the shaping of Christian thought on initiation. Jewish practice and thought was itself apparently undergoing modification and consolidation in the period when the Christian Church took its rise, hence the controversy that arose concerning the place and significance of proselyte baptism among Jewish thinkers in the latter part of the first century A.D.

In reaching this conclusion we have paid scant attention to the earliest and most important witness to baptism, John the Baptist. Is he to be regarded as an exception to the rule? Did he perhaps find his inspiration in the practice of Jewish proselyte baptism? If not, what was the origin of his baptism and its significance? To this problem we now turn.

(iv) *The Baptism of John the Baptist*

It would seem to be expedient, before considering the sources and

[1] It has sometimes been urged that a special employment of Jewish conceptions of proselyte baptism has been made in 1 Cor. 10.1 ff. Doubtless, Paul's allusions to the Fathers being baptized in the cloud and in the sea at the Exodus makes use of Rabbinic traditions, as the ensuing reference to the 'Rock that followed them' in the desert. Jewish exegesis conceived of the Israelites marching through tunnels in the water and of their being surrounded on all sides by the cloud. It would have been easy to advance from such a picture to the idea of the Israelites being baptized in the cloud and sea, but no record of the Rabbis so characterizing the event is preserved. They thought of the 'baptism' of the Fathers taking place at Sinai, in conjunction with the sacrifice that accompanied the making of the Covenant. Jeremias thinks that this omission is accidental and that Paul has reproduced an early tradition, whose original formulation was due to the desire to demonstrate that the Fathers were baptized and hence that proselytes should be baptized also. The guess is ingenious, but it remains — a guess. Inasmuch as Paul's use of the tradition concerning the manna and the rock as a foreshadowing of the Christian eucharist was a free and independent adaptation of Rabbinic materials, it is a priori likely that his use of the sea and cloud tradition as a foreshadowing of Christian baptism was due to an equally free and independent adaptation of the traditions. In 1 Cor. 10.1 ff the same spontaneous employment of Jewish traditions immediately ensues in the adducing of the experiences of the Israelites in the desert as 'types' for the instruction of the Christian readers. At no point in 1 Cor. 10.1–13 does Paul's exposition require a special Jewish theology of initiation and sacraments for its explanation; the insistence that such a theology of proselyte baptism was present to his mind goes beyond the evidence.

relations of John's baptism, to attempt to elucidate its significance and so ensure that our comparisons are rightly drawn.

Despite the brevity of the record of John's labours in Mark, the Evangelist has indicated with sufficient clarity two primary factors in John's baptism, namely its eschatological orientation and its integration with repentance. The former is hinted at in the opening citation from 'Isaiah the prophet': John is the Preparer of the way of the Lord, sent to perform a task that shall issue in the revelation of the glory of the Lord, that 'all flesh' may 'see it together' (Is. 40.3–4). He is himself an eschatological figure, whose activity sets in motion the process that shall culminate in the judgment and the redemption of the Messiah. As his own activity is embodied in the rite he administers, so the action of the Messiah is characterized as a powerful baptism — in the might of the Spirit who is the power of God (Mk. 1, 7–8). The baptism of John is thus eschatological in import, by virtue of the character of the administrator and the Person to whom it points. One baptism initiates the eschatological event, the other forms its heart and conclusion.[1]

Contrary to what is generally asserted, Mark's account of John's teaching is not wholly negative. John is not presented as a prophet of doom, with a message in tongues of fire against a background of storm clouds. 'Repent and be baptized, for the Almighty Messiah is at hand!' certainly includes warning, for the Jews were prone to overlook that the judgment must meet them; but He that is mighty to judge is mighty to deliver, and so Mark probably intends us to infer by his reference to the coming baptism by the Spirit. Mark's vagueness of statement, both as to the negative and positive aspects of the Messiah's ministry, is replaced by emphatic declarations in Matthew. On the one hand the evangelist sums up the message of John in words identical with those he later uses to summarize the message of Jesus: 'Repent, for the kingdom of heaven has drawn near' (Mt. 3.2); on the other he reproduces John's stern warnings concerning the inescapable judgment that faces the Jewish nation. Curiously both elements of Matthew's report have been misunderstood: the demand to the Jews not to appeal to Abraham (i.e. the promises made to him and merits attributed to him) on the ground that God can raise sons to Abraham from stones, has been interpreted as indicating a rejection of the Jew and advocacy of universalism on John's part; and it has been denied that the Baptist can have heralded the coming of the Messianic *King-*

[1] See Lohmeyer, *Das Urchristentum*, I, 'Johannes der Täufer', Göttingen 1932, p. 81.

dom. But John's protest was not directed against the belief that God would fulfil the promises made to the covenant people. He rejected the notion that the Jew had a right to the Kingdom, *simply as a Jew*;[1] on the contrary, none but the repentant members of the covenant people would find acceptance with the Messiah. What John thought about the relation of the Gentiles to the Kingdom we have no means of knowing; he ministered solely to the Jews and gave no word about the fate of the Gentiles.

Again, whatever form of words John employed, it is inharmonious with the literature of this period to postulate that he would have dissociated the judgment from the Kingdom, as though the issue of the messianic judgment could be in doubt. The Messiah is to use a winnowing fan, not however with the chief intent of gathering chaff for burning, any more than the farmer with whom the comparison is made is primarily concerned with dust; winnowing is for grain and grain is for the barn. The Messiah comes to gather the People of God and establish the Kingdom of God, and neither John nor his hearers could have thought otherwise.

The importance of this contention for the understanding of John's baptism is obvious. The forward look in baptism related to both judgment and redemption, since the Messiah was to come to judge the wicked and deliver the righteous. In baptism a transition was sought from the condition and destiny of the unrighteous to that of the righteous. It sealed the repentant as members of the covenant people fitted for the appearing of the Messiah, and therefore with hope of inheriting the Kingdom of the Messiah.[2]

What, then, was repentance to John and what was its relation to the baptism he administered? Brandt, noting the frequent conjunction of fasting, sack-cloth and ashes and repentance in Judaism (cf. Jonah 3.5 ff), toyed with the idea that John's baptism of repentance (μετανοίας) (Mk. 1.4) was an act of *penance*.[3] Recognizing the hardihood of that solution, he then suggested that μετανοίας was an

---

[1] See Strack-Billerbeck, I, pp. 116 ff for illustrations of this popularly held belief. It is well summarized in two oft quoted maxims: 'All Israelites are sons of kings' (=the patriarchs), Bar. Shab. 128a, and, 'The Circumcised do not go down to Gehinnom', Ex.R.19 (81c); it comes to crude expression in Justin's statement to Trypho, 'Your teachers think that the eternal kingdom will be given to those who are Abraham's seed according to the flesh, even if they are sinners and unbelieving and disobedient towards God'. Dial. 140.

[2] So Shailer Mathews, *The Messianic Hope in the New Testament*, 1905, pp. 64 f; Thomas, op. cit., p. 72; Evander, *Det kristna dopet*, 1938, p. 40.

[3] In the Vita Adea et Evae, Adam bids Eve, 'Let us repent with a great penitence. Perchance the Lord will be gracious to us and will pity us'. When Eve asks, 'What sort of penitence am I to do?' Adam bids her stand in the river Tigris with water to her neck for 37 days, while he stands in the Jordan for 40 days fasting, chs. 4–7.

epexegetic genitive: repentance, manifest in righteous living, is the fruit of baptism; hence baptism of repentance (Mk. 1.4) is a baptism demanding a repentant life, as Matthew saw when he paraphrased Mark's expression by a baptism *for* repentance (εἰς μετάνοιαν, Mt. 3.11).[1] Interpretations of this kind suffer from a basic defect: it is now generally agreed that μετάνοια and μετανοεῖν in the New Testament can be rightly represented only by terms that connote *turning* or *conversion*.[2] This 'conversion' does not primarily refer to a moral change from evil to righteous conduct but to a change in a man's relationship to God. The baptism to which John called the Jewish people was therefore a 'baptism of conversion';[3] it marked the individual's turning from sin to God that he might henceforth live in obedience to Him. Thus, though 'religious' in its basic meaning, conversion had radical consequences in the moral life.

But we must pause. What was the relationship between 'conversion' and baptism in John's preaching? Did the baptism symbolize the conversion, marking its actuality in the life of the baptized, or did it effect it? Lohmeyer strongly contended for the latter over against the former view. He insisted that John preached not a baptismal *repentance* but a repentance *baptism*. Only Matthew reports John as proclaiming the demand, 'Repent!' The other Evangelists know nothing of such a preaching; Luke does not even use the term repentance in connection with John. Repentance or conversion did not lead a man to baptism; he came to baptism to receive it. *John called on men to be baptized in order that they might become converted.*[4] It is unfortunate that an exegete should so strongly contend for what is

---

This certainly is a curious parallel, but fasting and silence for 40 days in deep water is hardly to be called a baptism; it is a lustration transformed into an act of self inflicted punishment to make a prayer more acceptable to God.

[1] Op. cit., pp. 78, 84. A. Büchler has a not dissimilar view. *Studies in Sin and Atonement*, pp. 367 ff.

[2] 'In the New Testament, as in the Hellenistic-Jewish writings, μετανοέω and μετάνοια represent what the religious language of the Old Testament expressed through שׁוּב and the theological terminology of the Rabbis expressed through תְּשׁוּבָה, תְּשׁוּבָה or עָבַד תְּתוּבְתָא, תְּתוּבְתָא', Behm, article μετανοέω and μετάνοια, Kittel's *T.W.N.T.*, IV, p. 994.

[3] The phrase is used by Schniewind, 'Das Evangelium nach Markus' (*N.T.D.*, vol. I), 5th ex. 1949, p. 44; Lohmeyer, *Das Evangelium des Markus (Meyerkommentar)*, 11th ed. 1951, p. 9; Behm, op. cit., pp. 995 f. Because of this relation of the term μετάνοια to God, Schlatter preferred to render it by Bekehrung rather than by Umkehr, since the former more distinctly connotes a conversion to God than does the latter, *Die Geschichte des Christus*, pp. 59 f.

[4] 'It is not the man who decides for conversion but God converts the thought and being of the man through conversion. . . . For John repentance is a divine act on a man; the means through which this miracle is given and is experienced is baptism', *Johannes der Täufer*, pp. 68 f. See also his commentaries *Das Evangelium des Markus*, p. 14, *Das Evangelium des Matthäus*, ed. Schmauch, Göttingen 1958, p. 44.

manifestly a one-sided emphasis; it demands decision on an 'either-or' which the New Testament writers would not have recognized. While Lohmeyer understandably calls Matthew to witness in support of his interpretation (since Matthew has replaced Mark's baptism of repentance by baptism for repentance, 3.11), he has already admitted that Matthew represents John as a preacher of repentance (3.2). This coincidence of language used in respect of the preaching of John and the preaching of Jesus is very significant; the demand made both by the Forerunner and the Messiah on the nation is summed up in the term, 'Repent — *Turn to God!*' It is not feasible that either Jesus or John meant by that word, 'Come to baptism that God may turn you!' That Matthew did not so interpret John is plain from his report of the Baptist's insistence that only the truly repentant should come to his baptism; John rebuked the Pharisees and Sadducees, lest their repentance, expressed in their desire for baptism, be without due seriousness.[1] On the other hand it is Matthew who delivered to us the phrase 'baptism for repentance'; he evidently saw in baptism a divine work, the fruit of which was conversion. But are not both aspects inextricably intertwined? Conversion is of man and of God. If the command Μετανοεῖτε be rightly rendered, 'Turn to God!' the human element in the appeal cannot be eliminated with justice, and baptism from the point of view of the candidate will be 'the expression and pledge of repentance'.[2] Yet in so far as baptism *issues in* conversion it presumes the activity of God, who therein accepts the baptized man turning to Him and makes of the act the pledge of his forgiveness and seal of the baptized into the Kingdom. Both the conversion and the baptism involve human and divine actions.

Granting that John's baptism represented a conversion to God and sealing unto the Kingdom, what kind of a baptism did he anticipate that the Messiah would perform? 'He will baptize you with Holy Spirit', is the record of Mark (1.8); 'He will baptize you with Holy Spirit and fire', write Matthew (3.11) and Luke (3.16). Chrysostom's interpretation that fire is a symbol of the Spirit, as shown by the Pentecost narrative (Acts 3.3), is still represented by Lagrange,[3] but few are prepared to adhere to it. The employment of fire in the next sentence to denote judgment would surely involve too harsh a change for it to symbolize the Spirit in v.11. Most scholars question whether a reference to the Spirit is in place in the logion. Margoliouth, follow-

---

[1] See Schlatter, *Der Evangelist Matthäus*, 3rd ed. Stuttgart 1948, p. 72.
[2] Swete, *The Gospel according to St. Mark*, London, 3rd ed. 1913, p. 4.
[3] *Évangile selon Saint Matthieu*, Paris, 7th ed. 1948, p. 53.

ing the Syriac scholar Merx, called attention to the reverse order of
Matthew's saying in the Sinaitic Syriac: instead of reading 'He shall
baptize you with Holy Spirit and fire', it runs 'He shall baptize you
with fire and Holy Spirit'. Change of word order is often a pointer to
interpolation; the antithesis between baptism with water and baptism
with fire is a striking one; Margoliouth, therefore suggested that John
had Mal. 3.1 in mind ('He is like a refiner's fire') and spoke of the
Messiah baptizing with fire only; this was interpreted by Christian
writers in the light of Pentecost, and the explanatory phrase 'and Holy
Spirit' was added; the order was then reversed to place the more important element first; finally the fire was omitted from the saying, as
in Mark.[1] This interpretation has now become generally accepted
among critical scholars.[2]

Yet the issue is not so clear cut as this unanimity would suggest. It
is doubtful that the Old Syriac has preserved the right reading of Mt.
3.11 against the otherwise universal manuscript tradition of Matthew
and of Luke; for Luke's order in 3.16 is the same as Matthew's, and
the difference in the word order is too small to call for such textual
accommodation as this. Moreover the tendency to 'christianize' John
must not be exaggerated; the tradition continued to preserve his
teaching on the Messiah's coming to Judgment, and there remains
much in the four gospels and Acts to indicate that many saw John and
his baptism as forming the water-shed of the new order but not included within it.[3] We have earlier reminded ourselves that John anticipated the Kingdom as well as the judgment of the Messiah; the
prophetic writings have frequent mention of the activity of the Spirit
in the last times, and some passages mention the Messiah's equipment
with the Spirit; there is therefore no a priori reason why John should
not have linked the ministry of the Messiah with that of the Spirit.[4]

---

[1] See 'Baptizing with fire', *The Expositor*, 8th Series, vol. XIII, pp. 446 ff.
[2] So J. Weiss, *Die Schriften des Neuen Testaments*, 2nd ed. 1907, I, p. 70; Creed,
The Gospel according to St. Luke, 1930, p. 54; T. W. Manson, *Message and Mission
of Jesus*, 1938, p. 333; J. Klausner, *Jesus of Nazareth*, 1925, p. 247; C. J. Cadoux,
The Historic Mission of Jesus, p. 56, n. 3; W. F. Flemington, *The New Testament
Doctrine of Baptism*, 1948, p. 19; R. Bultmann, *Die Geschichte der synoptischen
Tradition*, 3rd ed. 1957, p. 116, n. 1; V. Taylor, *The Gospel according to St. Mark*,
p. 157; E. Percy, *Die Botschaft Jesu*, 1953, p. 6.
[3] Mt. 11.11, Jn. 1.6 ff, 3.22–30, Acts 18.24–19.7.
[4] For the sending of the Spirit, see Is. 32.15, Ezk. 39.29, Joel 2.28 f, and for the
Spirit of the Messiah, Is. 11.1, 61.1. Israel Abrahams points out that the symbolism
of water and the use of such terms as 'pour out' in connection with the Spirit, both
in the Old Testament and Rabbinic writings, would have made such a sentiment as
baptizing with the Holy Spirit quite natural to Jewish ears; *Studies in Pharisaism
and the Gospels*, I, p. 43. See further Schechter, *Studies in Judaism*, 2nd series,
2nd ed. 1945, pp. 109 f; Lampe, 'Baptism in the New Testament', *Scottish Journal
of Theology*, vol. 5, 1952, pp. 163 ff; Marsh, op. cit., pp. 29 f.

It would be possible therefore to accept the statement of Mt. 3.11, Lk. 3.16 as it stands and interpret it of the dual task of the Messiah to redeem and to judge mankind.

It is worth considering, however, whether the concepts 'redemption and judgment' are adequate to convey what John may be presumed to have had in mind in his utterance. Is it feasible that John might have contrasted his baptism with water as one mode of cleansing and renewal with the Messiah's baptism with Spirit and fire as more powerful means of cleansing and renewal? Here it is necessary to observe the strict parallelism of language used by the evangelists in contrasting the two baptisms: in Mark, 'I baptized you with water ($\H{v}\delta a\tau\iota$), but he will baptize you with Holy Spirit ($\pi\nu\epsilon\acute{v}\mu a\tau\iota$ $\acute{a}\gamma\acute{\iota}\omega$)'; in Matthew and Luke, 'I baptize you with water ($\acute{\epsilon}\nu$ $\H{v}\delta a\tau\iota$) . . . he will baptize with ($\acute{\epsilon}\nu$) Holy Spirit and fire'. This ought not to be interpreted as meaning, 'He will baptize by the *agency* of water, by the *gift* of the Spirit and by the *agency* of fire'; the $\acute{\epsilon}\nu$ as well as the simple dative signify in each case the instrument or means employed in the baptism.[1] The Spirit is an agency comparable with water and fire. It happens that in Is. 4.2 ff we have an extraordinarily apt parallel to John's language:

> In that day the branch of the Lord shall be beautiful and glorious and the fruit of the land shall be the pride and glory of the survivors of Israel. And he who is left in Zion and remains in Jerusalem will be called holy, everyone who has been recorded for life in Jerusalem, when the Lord shall have washed away the filth of the daughters of Zion and cleansed the bloodstains of Jerusalem from its midst *by a spirit of judgment and by a spirit of burning*. (LXX $\acute{\epsilon}\nu$ $\pi\nu\epsilon\acute{v}\mu a\tau\iota$ $\kappa\rho\acute{\iota}\sigma\epsilon\omega s$ $\kappa a\iota$ $\pi\nu\epsilon\acute{v}\mu a\tau\iota$ $\kappa a\acute{v}\sigma\epsilon\omega s$). Then the Lord will create over the whole site of Mount Zion and over her assemblies a cloud by day and smoke and the shining of a flaming fire by night; for over all the glory there will be a canopy and a pavilion' (Is. 4.2–5).

Here the Spirit of the Lord, normally thought of in the Old Testament in terms of creative or life-giving power, is the agent of God's cleansing away the filth of the city in judgment. The passage is the more significant in that the 'branch of the Lord' will certainly have been interpreted messianically in later times: the issue of his glorious appearing and the cleansing work of the spirit of judgment will be the resting of the Shekinah glory over the city of God in the Kingdom of

---

[1] Schlatter recognizes this, though he has a different idea of the 'cleansing' from what is here proposed, see *Der Ev. Matthäus*, p. 80. To similar effect, Lohmeyer, *Ev. des Markus*, p. 19.

God. Such a passage would provide an excellent source for John's conception of the Messiah's appearing in might and majesty to baptize with Spirit and fire. And the passage is not alone in the Old Testament. The prediction of the outpouring of the Spirit in the last days, Joel 2.28 f, is immediately followed by a description of the dawning of the day of the Lord in 'blood and fire and columns of smoke', the deliverance of all who call on the name of the Lord and the judgment of the nations in the valley of Jehoshaphat. In Malachi the prediction of the sending of the messenger to prepare the way of the Lord is given in answer to the sceptical cry, 'Where is the God of justice?' (2.17). The messenger is to come for judgment, but not, observe, for annihilation:

> 'Who can endure the day of his coming, and who can stand when he appears? For he is like a refiner's fire and like fuller's soap; he will sit as a refiner and purifier of silver, and he will purify the sons of Levi and refine them like gold and silver, till they present right offerings to the Lord. . . . Then I will draw near to you for judgment; I will be a swift witness against the sorcerers, against the adulterers . . . against those who do not fear me, says the Lord of hosts. For I the Lord do not change; therefore you, O sons of Jacob are not consumed' (3.1-6).

With this oracle Mal. 4.1 should be compared:

> 'For behold the day comes, burning like an oven, when all the arrogant and all evildoers will be stubble; the day that comes shall burn them up, says the Lord of hosts, so that it will leave them neither root nor branch.'

This twofold use of fire for refinement and consuming judgment suggests that John the Baptist also could have had both aspects in mind. The Messiah's baptism with Spirit and fire will be applied to all, since He is to judge the whole world: for the people of God it will be their refinement for the Kingdom, as in Mal. 3.1 ff; for the wicked it will be with consuming power, as in Mal. 4.1. On this view Mt. 3.12 is not a precise exegesis of 3.11 but an application of it in respect to the wicked.[1]

The conception of judgment by fire is not strange to Judaism,[2] nor is it unknown to the New Testament.[3] Whether John restricted the

---

[1] For this reason I do not adhere to the interpretation of C. K. Barrett, that the Spirit is to be viewed as the wind (πνεῦμα) that blows away the chaff from the threshing floor and the fire which consumes it when gathered; *The Holy Spirit and the Gospel Tradition*, London 1947, p. 126. The interpretation here offered is in harmony with that adopted by Gray, *Isaiah 1–27* (I.C.C.), 1912, p. 80 and Herntrich, *Jesajah 1–12* (A.T.D.), 2nd ed. 1954, p. 71 and suits the more personal view of the Spirit in the prophetic passages likely to have influenced John.

[2] Strack-Billerbeck, op. cit., pp. 121 f; Abrahams, op. cit., pp. 44 f.

[3] Compare especially 1 Cor. 3.13 ff with 2 Thess. 1.7 f.

Spirit's work to this aspect of the messianic action we are not in a position to say; in view of the teaching of the prophets it is likely that he would have extended the function of the Spirit beyond it, even as he would certainly have expected the Messiah to do more than refine the righteous and judge the wicked; but it is doubtful that we ought to read an extension of the Spirit's ministry into this tradition of John's sayings handed down to us. While we could have wished for more information, we have enough to enable us to see how well integrated is this element of his teaching into the record of his proclamation and how comprehensible was the enlargement of its scope in Christian circles.[1]

The baptism of John thus had two focal points: it inaugurated the new life of the converted, so assuring the baptized of forgiveness and cleansing from sin; it anticipated the messianic baptism with Spirit and fire, so giving assurance of a place in the Messiah's kingdom.[2] If the sources of this baptism be sought, the nearest place to look would be in the area wherein John conducted his ministry. Mt. 3.1 describes the location of John's work as 'the wilderness of Judea' and Luke extends it by the phrase 'the whole area about the Jordan' (Lk. 3.3); the territory defined thus embraced the area north west of the Dead Sea and the Jordan Valley; that is, the area of the Qumran sect and the Jordan baptizers! Leaving aside speculations as to John's earlier relations with the Qumran sectaries, it is nevertheless impossible that he could have been ignorant of their existence. They thought of their lustrations as a means of (moral and religious) cleansing, when combined with penitence, and they cherished ardent eschatological expectations, conceiving of their task as preparers of the way of the Lord. No other major group in Israel used or interpreted lustrations in this manner (though comparable practices and ideas were probably maintained by smaller groups and individuals); and we know of no other major group who conceived of their vocation after this manner. Such a striking coincidence in ideas shared by John and a neighbour-

---

[1] This interpretation is in harmony with that given by M'Neile, *The Gospel according to St. Matthew*, 1915, pp. 29 f; Abrahams, op. cit., pp. 44 f; H. von Baer, *Der Heilige Geist in den Lukasschriften*, 1926, pp. 159 ff; N. A. Dahl, op. cit., pp. 44 f.

[2] The debate whether John's baptism bestowed a *present* forgiveness or the *promise* of forgiveness at the Messiah's coming in judgment is not unlike the dispute as to whether conversion is human or divine. On the interpretation here offered it is both. A conversion to God, accompanied by confession of sins and expressed and completed in baptism, would have been considered by John in terms of cleansing — not levitical but moral and spiritual, hence as mediating the divine forgiveness. But the final cleansing and renewal was to be performed by the Messiah in his baptism of Spirit and fire, by a judgment which would also witness the ultimate vindication of his own.

D

ing group of Jews is not likely to be accidental; it points to a positive relation between the Baptist and the Covenanters. On the other hand, the differences between them ought not to be minimized. Everything in John's practice and preaching was more radical than that of the Covenanters: the eschatological expectation was more immediate; the call to repentance was more urgent; it was expressed in a once-for-all baptism; the message of warning and offer of the Kingdom hope was addressed to the whole nation and not to a privileged few — hence John could not be contained within a cloister. It is clear, therefore, that John did not take over the ideas of the sectaries of Qumran and the Jordan valley without modification; on the contrary he transformed whatever he adopted. Yet that he *did* receive a basis on which to work seems indubitable. John was indebted to the sectaries for raw material hard to come by elsewhere.

Was John also indebted to the practice of proselyte baptism and the theology attaching thereto? If the institution was widely known at this time, it would be natural to presume that he took the idea of a single baptism from it, since this is the most obvious difference between John's baptism and that of the sectaries. Our one method of testing is to see if any dependence of John on the theology of proselyte baptism can be traced. Jeremias believes that such a dependence can be shown. He considers that John's ministry was set in the wilderness with the belief in view that the first redemption is the type of the last: Moses is the type of the Messiah and the generation in the wilderness is the type of the messianic community; John goes into the desert to prepare this community and, doubtless taking the hint from Ezk. 36.25 ('I will sprinkle clean water upon you . . .'), he uses the same method to prepare the people as the Fathers in the desert employed when they received the salvation and the covenant — baptism.[1] Heron followed this with the further suggestion that the Old Testament associations of טבל with 'overwhelm' made it likely that John interpreted his baptism as an acted parable of drowning; the candidate went down into the water to end his old life and begin a new one, even as the proselytes in baptism died to their Gentile life and emerged new born as Israelites.[2] He that has followed through our discussions thus far will perceive the weakness of these deductions. The Qumran Community had gone into the desert long before John to fulfil the prophecy of Is. 40, and so to prepare the way of the Lord. They sought to be the people of the New Covenant and their lustrations were adapted to this end. But there is not the slightest likelihood that they were moved by the consideration that, as the Fathers were baptized in the desert to offer Covenant Sacrifice, they should receive ablutions thrice daily. Nor indeed was proselyte baptism itself produced by such a motive; the 'explanation' came after the practice, not vice versa. The motives that led to the application of the bath to the Gentiles were quite different from those that prompted the daily ablutions of the Qumran Covenanters. The O.T. Scriptures that John the Baptist appears to have had in mind in his adaptation of the lustrations are connected with the prophetic expectations of divine cleansing, and the refining and judging work of the Messiah, rather than with the typology of Sinai and the ritual of the covenant. Moreover there is no intimation that John interpreted his baptism in terms of death and resurrection; not a hint is given of his preaching that he had ever heard of such a view of baptism.[1] The differences between John's baptism and proselyte baptism are as striking as the coincidences between John's baptism and the lustrations of the Qumran sectaries. Of the two chief points that John and the Qumran group had in mind, namely 'religious' cleansing through ablution and the presence of strong eschatological hope, the former is of uncertain relation to proselyte baptism and the latter is absent from it. On the other hand, common to John and Qumran was their lack of relation to the temple worship (and to sacrifice in particular), whereas proselyte baptism was closely related to the offering of sacrifice. Above all, proselyte baptism was for the purpose of enabling the Gentile to become a Jew; we have no ground for believing that John regarded all Jews as virtually Gentiles (such a conclusion from Mt. 3.9 would be a misuse of the passage) or that he had abandoned hope for the nation and sought to create in its place a small remnant. John's message was

---

[1] The belief that John may have conceived of baptism as entailing a death and resurrection has become widespread, but the grounds are always general and evidence from John's own teaching is never forthcoming. Lundberg e.g. considered that John's baptism had the character of submission to death and an expiation for sins, for the river Jordan was identified with the sea of death, *La Typologie baptismale dans l'ancienne Église*, Leipzig and Uppsala 1942, pp. 224 f. Fridrichsen evidently shared the same notion, considering that John would have viewed Jordan as an outreach of the waters of death in the underworld, an earthly counterpart to the heavenly river of fire, *Johannes' vattendop och det messianska elddopet*, 1941, pp. 9 f (cited by Percy, op. cit., p. 8, n. 6). Precisely the same idea occurs in Badcock, 'The Significance of the Baptism of Christ', *The Interpreter*, vol. 13, 1916–17, p. 156. Less speculatively the view is espoused by Schniewind, *Ev. nach Markus*, p. 44; Dibelius, *Art. Johannes der Täufer*, R.G.G., 2nd ed., vol. III, Col. 318; G. W. H. Lampe, 'The One Baptism and the One Church', *Bulletin of the World Council of Churches, Division of Studies*, vol. III, 1957, pp. 10 f; Leenhardt, *Le Baptême Chrétien*, 1946, p. 15. The belief is opposed by Oepke, art. βάπτω in Kittel's *T.W.N.T.*, vol. I, p. 535; Lohmeyer, *Johannes der Täufer*, p. 80; Percy, op. cit., p. 8, n. 6.

addressed to the whole nation. He did not retire into a monastery like the Essenes, nor did he restrict his ministry to a few capable of receiving it, like the Rabbis. He addressed himself to all, since all needed to repent and the Kingdom was for all who manifested repentance. The saying concerning raising sons to Abraham from stones is directed against the pride of the Jew, who thought himself secure simply because he was a Jew and so turned the promise of grace into an immoral security. But God *could* raise up sons to Abraham if necessary! The covenant had not been abrogated.[1] The idea that the people of God were no longer the people of God finds no place in John's teaching; he was sent to them precisely because they were such.

In short, there is no point at which contact can be found between John's baptism and proselyte baptism; there seems to be no ground therefore for the repeated assertion that the former was derived from the latter. The basic ideas behind the two institutions had little or nothing in common.

In view of this discrepancy between John's baptism and Jewish proselyte baptism, and the scant attention hitherto paid to the Jewish baptizing sects, it is not surprising that a number of exegetes have declined to see any other inspiration for John's baptism than the Old Testament.[2] Certainly there is much in the Old Testament which could have provided John with precedent for his baptism. The levitical lustrations would have had abiding significance for him, since he came from a priestly family. Many well known prophetic sayings exhort to moral cleansing under the figure of cleansing with water, e.g. Is. 1.16 ff, Jer. 4.14, and others anticipate a cleansing by God in the last times, notably Ezk. 36.25 and Zech. 13.1. We also recall that Is. 44.3 conjoins with the future purification the gift of the Spirit. Dahl has attempted to combine these priestly and prophetic strains by suggesting that John may have conceived of the assembly of the saved at the end of the age in terms of a great eschatological festival; the Israelites required to be prepared for this by a baptism in the wilderness, just as the priests and pilgrims had to be cleansed by ablution before they entered the temple, and the Messiah himself would conduct the last great 'baptism' when the 'festival' was about to commence.[3] The idea is ingenious but somewhat far-fetched. It would

---

[1] See the excellent discussion in Schlatter, *Die Geschichte des Christus*, pp. 59 ff.

[2] So Cheyne, art. 'John the Baptist', *Encyclopaedia Biblica* vol. II, 1901, col. 2499; Evander, op. cit., p. 23; Schweitzer, *Mysticism of Paul the Apostle*, 1931, p. 232; Klostermann, *Das Markusevangelium* (H.N.T.), 4th ed. 1950, p. 6; Lampe, *Seal of the Spirit*, 1951, p. 25; N. A. Dahl, op. cit., p. 44.

[3] Op. cit., pp. 44 f.

seem more plausible that John recognized in the newer use of lustrations among Jewish groups like the Essenes a means whereby the Old Testament predictions of cleansing in the last day, prior to the great Messianic purgation, should be fulfilled.

It is not impossible that John was influenced in his understanding of baptism by the phenomenon of prophetic symbolism. Not that he is likely to have deliberately selected (still less created) a form of baptism as a parallel for his generation to the public actions of Isaiah, Jeremiah and Ezekiel etc. But the psychological and religious outlook that lay behind the symbolic acts of the prophets could have been present with him and found a natural instrument in the practice of ablution for religious cleansing.[1] The chief element in that outlook would be the belief that the word of the Lord can be *performed* as well as spoken, and that such prophetic action has sacramental character.[2] Of this action certain features stand out: first, it expresses the will of the Lord, hence it is an instrument of his action; secondly, it sets in motion the action it represents; thirdly, in the case of John's baptism it involved the co-operation of the one baptized, since there could be no baptism without his coming for it and only those could be baptized who made sincere profession of 'turning to the Lord'. Nothing could more clearly illustrate the position earlier laid down, that conversion and baptism are acts wherein the human and divine come together; the initiative and the power of both are with God, but neither is conceivable without the responsive human subject. Moreover, since the baptism 'with water' is performed in prospect of the Messiah's baptism 'with Spirit and fire', the eschatological action represented in John's baptism is joined by the power of God to the eschatological action of the Messiah's baptism: the will of God effectively expressed in the first and to be manifest in the second binds the two together.

[1] The theme has been dealt with by H. Wheeler Robinson in many of his publications, notably in the essay, 'Prophetic Symbolism', in *Old Testament Essays, Papers read before the Society for Old Testament Study*, 1927, pp. 1 ff, and 'Hebrew Sacrifice and Prophetic Symbolism', *J.T.S.*, vol. 43, 1942, pp. 132 ff. In his first article he drew attention to the significance of this phenomenon for the understanding of the Christian sacraments; he eventually came to believe that it held the key to their right understanding. It is worthy of note that so far back as 1919 Joh. Lindblom included acts of prophetic symbolism among conjunctions of word and action in the Old Testament significant for the understanding of Christian baptism; see his *Jesu Missions- och Dopbefallning*, pp. 196–201. The idea has been widely taken up in recent baptismal discussions, above all by W. F. Flemington, who has argued that John's baptism should be understood as an extension of the symbolic actions of the prophets, op. cit., pp. 20 ff. See further the excellent treatment of the theme by A. Gilmore in *Christian Baptism*, pp. 75 ff.

[2] 'The prophet might equally well have said "Thus doth Yahweh", of his own prophetic act, as he does say, of his own spoken word, "Thus saith Yahweh" ', Robinson, *J.T.S.*, 1942, p. 132.

That John would have analysed his baptism in this manner is hardly to be conceded. That he participated to this extent in the prophetic consciousness is altogether likely. The uniqueness of his baptism was bound up with the uniqueness of his vocation. In him the age-long traditions of ritual lustrations combined with prophetic anticipations of judgment and redemption and found a medium in the ablutions of men that looked for redemption in Israel. The success of the instrument was greater than he could have dreamed: to it the Messiah himself submitted, then invested it with power for the community of the Kingdom.

CHAPTER 2

THE FOUNDATION OF
CHRISTIAN BAPTISM

(i) *The Baptism of Jesus*

STUDENTS of the Gospels, whatever their primary interest, sooner or later find themselves confronted with the problem of the messianic consciousness of Jesus. The Baptism of our Lord provides a major piece of evidence in the quest for ascertaining whether He believed Himself to be the Messiah, how He arrived at the conviction and how He conceived of His function. In discussions of the event the chief point of interest has commonly been the nature of the experience itself — what happened to Jesus in the Baptism, and what effect it had upon Him. This is, of course, an aspect of vital importance, but for those concerned to understand the attitude of Jesus to baptism the focus of interest has to remove to an earlier point of time: Why did Jesus come to the baptism of John, and what significance did He attach to His submission to it? The question became a matter of concern to the Church at a comparatively early date, as the Gospel to the Hebrews attests, but it is curious how frequently modern commentators on the Gospel pass by it in silence,[1] while no little confusion has been aroused by the attempts made to answer it. It will clarify the issues if we pass in review the chief solutions advanced to explain the problem.

First it may be remarked that an element of perplexed embarrassment is to be discerned in not a little discussion of the subject, which has occasioned some unfortunate exegesis. We may illustrate from no less a writer than Oepke. In his article on baptism[2] he lists four reasons for the baptism of Jesus: (i) His sinlessness was not a ready made and fixed conviction at this early date; (ii) He could not withhold Himself from John's revival movement; (iii) His baptism was His consecration as Messiah; (iv) the Messianic conception in Deutero-Isaiah included the necessity of the Messiah ranging himself

---

[1] It is not mentioned e.g. by Swete and Lohmeyer in their commentaries on Mark and it is scarcely touched on by Lagrange in all his three commentaries on the Synoptic Gospels.
[2] Kittel, *T.W.N.T.*, i. 1933, p. 536.

along with sinners. If the first of these reasons holds good, why bring in the fourth? For there is no virtue in one who shares the normal consciousness of sin taking a stand with sinners; he is one of them. Yet the significant point in the Deutero-Isaiah passage is the willingness of the *innocent* to number himself with the guilty; the conception has relevance to the baptism only if Jesus views His action in this light; in that case the first contention needs modifying. The presumed desire of Jesus to identify Himself with John's movement by no means implies the necessity of His submission to John's baptism. Did anybody baptize John? Why is Jesus not found standing alongside him as a fellow-worker, baptizing with him the penitents of Israel, instead of standing with them to receive it at his hand? And how does Jesus view as an appropriate means for messianic consecration a rite generally viewed as a means of acquittal at the judgment of the Messiah? The question is answerable, but it involves modifying both the messianic idea and the conception of his consecration, changes that are too important to be taken for granted or passed over in silence.

The 'embarrassment', referred to above, is already apparent: it arises from the submission of Him whom Christians acknowledge as Son of God to a rite characterized by the earliest Evangelist as 'a conversion baptism for the forgiveness of sins' (Mk. 1.4), which fits a man for the last judgment and gives him hope to be numbered with the saints. How could Jesus, presuming Him to be what the Church holds Him to be, occupy such a position?

One resort is no longer open to us: we cannot ignore the difficulty, nor can we assent to anything that smacks of evasiveness. For this reason the common view, that Jesus in His baptism dedicated Himself to His messianic task, cannot be accepted on the common terms, for the Messiah was not usually thought of as a sinner. Alfred Plummer attempted to defend the position[1] by reducing the idea of the repentance involved in Jesus' baptism: 'He, like others, could bury His past beneath the waters of Jordan, and rise again to a life in accordance with God's will. The change with them was from a life of sin to a life of righteousness. . . . The change with Him was from the home-life of intellectual and spiritual development (Lk. 2.52) to the life of public ministry as the Messiah'.[2] This alien importation and adaptation of Pauline theology is unrealistic and fails to meet the difficulty to which it is directed. If the baptism of Jesus was a mes-

---

[1] 'The people were consecrated to receive salvation, and He was consecrated to bestow it', *H.D.B.*, i. 1898, p. 240.

[2] Comm. on Matthew ad. loc.

sianic consecration, other factors entered in to give it its peculiar character.

Since John's baptism was an expression of repentance and desire for forgiveness, why not boldly acknowledge that Jesus knew His need for forgiveness and was baptized to receive it? Frederick Strauss thought that no other view was possible.[1] To Johannes Weiss it was 'almost painful' to hear it asserted that Jesus did not really need his baptism: 'With especial earnestness He will have made the vow of a new life, renewed faithfulness and devotion to the will of God'.[2] Middleton Murry further urged: 'Whatever this man was, he was the incarnation of honesty. He would not have sought baptism for the remission of sins had he not been conscious of sin'.[3] Certainly the honesty of Jesus is not to be impugned, but other elements in His character require to be taken into account. Above all there is manifest in His words and deeds a unique relation to the divine sovereignty, by which He proclaimed its imminent coming and spoke and acted in its present power. In that consciousness He forgave sins (Mk. 2.10) and pronounced judgment on them (Mt. 11.20 ff), demanded repentance of all (Mk. 1.15) and proclaimed the higher righteousness (Mt. 5–7), befriended publicans and sinners, but ever as physician of the sick (Mk. 2.17) and shepherd who seeks to save the lost (Lk. 15.3 ff, 19.10). Jesus had a ministry to all, and we sense the distance He felt between Himself and those to whom He ministered; such a 'distance' is presumed in the way Jesus addresses His hearers as, 'You, who are evil' (Mt. 7.11), to which no counterpart exists in His teaching, 'We, who are evil'. Such features belonged, so far as we know, to the teaching and work of Jesus from the beginning of His ministry; they are seen in yet more impressive clarity as He advances to His death as a ransom for the many (Mk. 10.45) and speaks in terms of being Assessor and even Judge in the last day (Mt. 10.32 f, 25.31 ff). He who so taught, lived and died, with a moral consciousness that did not falter from the baptism to the cross, was assuredly not baptized as a sinner seeking mercy of the Judge; if it was for sins, it was sins not His own.

'If it was for sins. . . .' Is it possible that it was *not* 'for sins'? A not inconsiderable number of exegetes have urged that to raise the question of the relation of our Lord's baptism to a consciousness of sin on His part is pedantic, since one could have received baptism with more

---

[1] *Life of Jesus*, E.T., 1846, p. 352.

[2] *Die Schriften des Neuen Testaments*, 1907, vol. 1, p. 70.

[3] *Life of Jesus*, 1926, p. 31. See further Bethune-Baker, *The Faith of the Apostles' Creed*, p. 117, J. Mackinnon, *The Historic Jesus*, 1931, pp. 61–2.

than one motive in mind. Holtzmann, at the beginning of the century affirmed, 'He simply took His place in the movement called forth by the Baptist; there is no hint to the contrary concerning bearing sins of others, participation in the general sinfulness and the like'.[1] Loisy was more persuasive: 'The baptism of repentance did not render guilty those who received it without sin; a righteous man could submit to it in order to signify his intention to live purely, without confessing sins which he had not committed; he manifested his resolution to prepare himself, according to his ability, for the coming of the kingdom'.[2] In more recent times, when the eschatological aspect of John's message has been more fully appreciated, the forward look of John's baptism has been stressed, so that the significance of the rite is thought of as more 'aspiration for the future' than 'regret for the past'.[3] So, too, T. W. Manson stated, 'Jesus recognizes in John's efforts to create a new Israel the purpose of God and willingly enters into it'.[4]

Despite the eloquence of these writers, it is doubtful whether their contentions do justice to the baptism of John. For a baptism which is characterized as a conversion baptism for the forgiveness of sins becomes radically different if there is neither conversion nor request for forgiveness. In view of the picture in the Synoptic Gospels of the nature of John's baptism, we have no right to presume that Jesus weakened its meaning in His own case. Loisy's statement is purely theoretical. Who are these people who received John's baptism 'without sin'? John recognized none. At best there was one alone, and we are trying to discover why he received it! Moreover the difficulty is intensified by the invoking of eschatological categories, for it was precisely the forward look of John's baptism that gave it urgency; it enabled a man to face the righteous judgment of the Lord's Anointed with hope and so look for a place in the Kingdom. Such is the context of John's baptism in Mt. 3.11-12: his water-baptism witnesses to the powerful baptism in Spirit and fire which the Messiah is to exercise at His coming. The modern exegete may theorize, if he will, as to the possibility of Jesus, or any other, coming to his baptism without confession of sin; it is hard to think of the prophet, who denied any advantage of Abraham's sons in the judgment, permitting it.[5]

[1] Die Synoptiker, 1901, p. 198.
[2] Les Évangiles Synoptiques, 1907, p. 405.
[3] Streeter, cited approvingly by B. T. D. Smith, Matthew C.G.T., 1927, p. 85.
[4] Message and Mission of Jesus, 1937, p. 441. Similar view may be seen in Klostermann, Das Matthäusevangelium, p. 173; Lindblom, Handbok till Nya Testamentet, 2.1, Matteusevangeliet, 1917, p. 21; Montefiore, Synoptic Gospels, vol. 1, p. 45; Marsh, op. cit., p. 102; R. E. O. White, Christian Baptism, 1959, p. 93.
[5] Note Mk. 1.5, ἐξομολογούμενοι τὰς ἁμαρτίας αὐτῶν.

Not infrequently an answer to our quest has been seen in the words of Jesus to John in Mt. 3.15: 'Thus it is fitting (πρέπον) for us to fulfil all righteousness'. The πρέπον presumably indicates in an indirect manner the divine will. A. Fridrichsen suggested that it is simplest to view this saying as a declaration of our duty to accomplish all that God asks of us; only in the application before us it is evident that Jesus has received an intimation that God desires Him to be baptized. 'Here is an idea perfectly in accord with Jewish thinking: the divine will must be blindly obeyed, without asking the reason for it.'[1] Leenhardt agrees with this motif of obedience but pursues further the thought of the righteousness of God that leads Jesus to baptism: God wills to bring about a new covenant through Him, and in the baptism He sees his purpose accomplished; hence by adoption in Christ sinners are to be brought to the knowledge of God, and by the Holy Spirit, sent at the baptism, the reign of God will be manifested and the people of God constituted.[2] Such conceptions are not wrong, but they leave out some decisive elements and bear an uncertain relationship to the thought of Jesus. In particular, it is difficult to extract from the Gospel narratives the notion that the divine righteousness is established through sinners receiving the adoption of sons in Christ, and that such was the purpose of His baptism. The idea that Jesus viewed His baptism as a religious duty in no way explains how He related it to His vocation. Schlatter did not consider that this element of command absolves us from the necessity of asking questions, for the above citation prefaces his whole discussion. We, too, must go further.

In the conviction that the Gospels demand the recognition that Jesus was baptized, as all others, for sin, the view is becoming dominant that in His baptism He took his first step in bearing the sins of the world. If we feel sympathy with this view, we must yet exercise care in our statement of it, for some doubtful exposition on the basis of it is now current.

Oscar Cullmann argues the following thesis. (i) The voice at the baptism has no relation to Ps. 2.7, it cites Is. 42.1 alone. It is true that the texts say that Jesus is addressed as 'son', but the ease with which υἱός (son) and παῖς (boy) could be confused is well known, and the Semitic original presumably addressed Jesus as אֶבֶד, 'servant'. Since the Servant of Is. 42.1 is he who must fulfil the mission described in Is. 53, Jesus is made known as the Son who takes the guilt of his

[1] 'Accomplir toute justice', *Congrès d'Histoire du Christianisme*, Jubile Alfred Loisy, I, 1928, pp. 169–70. Schlatter had an essentially similar interpretation, *Der Evangelist Matthäus*, p. 85.
[2] Op. cit., p. 21 ff.

people upon Himself in suffering and death, and this sinbearing begins in His baptism. (ii) Jesus Himself said that by His baptism He would 'fulfil all righteousness', i.e. 'effect a general forgiveness'. This must mean that His baptism points forward to the cross, in which He will achieve a general baptism for the sins of the world. (iii) That for Jesus 'to be baptized' means 'to suffer death for the people' is shown by Mk. 10.38 and Lk. 12.50, in both which 'to be baptized' means 'to die'. (iv) This view is confirmed by Jn. 1.29–34, which is the first commentary on the Synoptic account of the baptism. Above all the Baptist proclaimed Jesus as the Lamb of God that takes away the sin of the world (Jn. 1.29); he thus deduced from the heavenly Voice that Jesus was called to fulfil the mission of the Servant of the Lord. Here therefore, in our Lord's experience of baptism, is the root of the baptismal doctrine of Rom. 6.1 ff, and it can be traced throughout the whole New Testament.[1]

These points adduced by Cullmann must be examined, since they are basic to the later discussion. (i) In my judgment it is a questionable procedure that stresses the Servant concept in the baptism of Jesus to the detriment of the Messianic. While the tradition of the Voice could admittedly have been corrupted from an original, 'Thou art my Servant', to 'Thou art my Son', it remains that the latter has come down to us without dissent in our textual authorities; it is most naturally taken as an echo of Ps. 2.7, interpreted as a divine acclamation of the King-Messiah.[2] It is equally natural to regard the phrase, 'In thee I am well pleased' (ἐν σοὶ εὐδόκησα), as an allusion to Is. 42.1, in spite of the difference between this rendering and that of the LXX (προσεδέξατο αὐτὸν ἡ ψυχή μου). The rendering in Mark is almost identical with that in Mt. 12.18, where the passage from Is. 42.1 ff is reproduced in extenso with reference to the ministry of

---

[1] *Baptism in the New Testament*, pp. 15 ff. This exposition has been immensely influential and has encouraged yet further developments in the same direction. See e.g. G. W. H. Lampe, *The Seal of the Spirit*, 1951, pp. 33 ff, *The Scottish Interim Report on Baptism*, May 1955, pp. 8 f., H. W. Bartsch, 'Die Taufe im Neuen Testament', *Evangelische Theologie* 1948–9, pp. 90 ff.

[2] The lack of evidence in Jewish literature for the use of 'Son of God' as a messianic title should not be pressed against this interpretation, since we are dealing with sources stamped by One whose re-creative powers of thought were especially directed to the messianic concept. But Mk. 14.61 ought not to be overlooked, where the equivalent term is placed in the mouth of the High Priest. Test. Levi 18.6 is particularly noteworthy, since it provides a striking parallel to the baptismal scene and yet depends on Ps. 2.7:

> The heavens shall be opened,
> And from the temple of glory shall come upon him sanctification,
> With the Father's voice as from Abraham to Isaac.

See R. H. Charles, *Apocrypha and Pseudepigrapha*, vol. II, 1913, p. 314.

Jesus.[1] It would seem that the widely accepted view, that the 'Voice' fuses the diverse concepts of King-Messiah and Servant of the Lord, is to be retained until more convincing evidence to the contrary is forthcoming. The immediately ensuing narrative of the Temptation confirms this understanding of the passage, since it tests the conviction that Jesus is *Son of God*, and the Temptations themselves are best understood as popular means of pursuing the *messianic* task; but the freshly acclaimed King-Messiah has a different path to tread. It is not said what that path is, nor where it will lead, but the Lord is evidently intent on keeping to the way that is 'well pleasing' to the Father.

(ii) The complex, rather than simple, conception of Messiah in Mk. 1.11 makes the testimony of John the Baptist in Jn. 1.29 ff more comprehensible. It is witness to Jesus as Messiah, and that of no ordinary kind. In my view it is likely that the saying in v. 29, 'Behold, the Lamb of God, who takes away the sin of the world', was truly uttered by John, and that for him it had an apocalyptic significance. The 'Lamb' is the Leader of God's flock, mighty to judge (Rev. 6.16) and to conquer the enemies of God (Rev. 17.14). Just as in the Testaments of the Twelve Patriarchs the Messiah is a Lamb who delivers the flock of God from attacking beasts (Test. Jos. 19.18), and in his days sin comes to an end, the lawless cease to do evil, Beliar is bound and the saints tread on the evil spirits (Test. Levi 18), so the Messiah in John's proclamation will judge and cleanse the earth by his power (Mt. 3.11): 'His winnowing fan is in His hand and He will thoroughly cleanse his threshing floor, and He will gather his wheat into the barn, but the chaff He will burn up with unquenchable fire' (Mt. 3.12). Here is a cleansing by Spirit and fire — a taking away of the sin of the world, with never a thought of the rejection of the Messiah or His death as a sacrifice.[2] That this conception of the Warrior Lamb was known and preserved in Johannine circles is apparent from the two citations given from the Book of Revelation.[3] The latter Book goes further: it indicates that in these circles the apocalyptic conception of

---

[1] Morna Hooker, who is unwilling to see in Mk. 1.11 an allusion to Ps. 2.7 and Is. 42.1, concedes the likelihood that Mt. 12.18 ff is dependent on a Greek translation unknown to us, and which perhaps is also to be presumed in Mk. 9.7. Why should not a like tradition lie behind Mk. 1.11 also? See *Jesus and the Servant*, 1959, pp. 69 ff.

[2] See the discussion of this passage by C. H. Dodd, *The Fourth Gospel*, 1953, pp. 230 ff.

[3] That there was a close link between the authors of the Fourth Gospel and the Book of Revelation must surely be posited, as R. H. Charles acknowledges: 'The Evangelist was apparently at one time a disciple of the Seer, or they were members of the same religious circle in Ephesus', *Commentary on the Revelation of St. John*, 1920, vol. i, p. xxxiii.

the Messiah as the Warrior Lamb had been fused with the Christian idea of the Lamb slain for the sins of the world (Rev. 5.6—12. 11). The synthesis achieved by the author of the Book of Revelation could have been accomplished by the Fourth Evangelist also; only in his case it is likely that his stress on Christ's dying as God's passover Lamb (Jn. 19.37) would have caused that type to predominate over the more general thought of the sacrificial lamb or the lamb of Is. 53.7. Thus, at least two strands of Messianic thought come together in Jn. 1.29. But Jn. 1.30 introduces yet a third idea, that of the pre-existent Messiah, which has no contact with the traditional views of the Davidic Messiah or apocalyptic Lamb, or the Servant of the Lord. This is a specifically Johannine element, reflecting the Son of Man — Son of God — Logos Christology of the Fourth Gospel. Significantly, the conclusion of the testimony of John, summing up the lesson of the Baptism of Jesus, is recorded as 'I have seen and borne witness that *this is the Son of God*' (Jn. 1.34). It is plain that varied messianic concepts have gone to the making of Jn. 1.29 ff; they do not permit the reduction of the testimony of the Voice at the Baptism to the simple idea of Jesus as the Servant of the Lord.

(iii) It is a reasonable conjecture that Jesus had reflected in some measure, even before His baptism, on the person of the Messiah, the nature of his task, his relation to the Kingdom of God, how the Kingdom would come, and like questions. His contemporaries in Judaism had well defined ideas on these matters and He must have considered them. It is, however, highly dubious to presume that our Lord, on the basis of His reading of the Old Testament, had a complete understanding of the way his ministry would develop, that He knew that it would end in rejection and death on the cross and that such was the will of God for Him. In particular, it is scarcely legitimate to argue that because a divine revelation *consequent* on his baptism alluded to Is. 42.1, Jesus must have consciously *advanced* to his baptism with the intention of thereby initiating the process of suffering and sin-bearing described in Is. 53. Is it seriously maintained that the four Servant Songs of Deutero-Isaiah had been separated out from their contexts and a programme of action formed on their basis? In the light of what we know of modes of exegesis in our Lord's time, that is hardly conceivable. It does not accord with the tenor of our Lord's preaching, nor to the use made of the Servant idea in the Gospels. We find various allusions to passages linked with the Servant motif in the Gospels, such as the preaching in Nazareth, Lk. 4.16 f, in which Jesus is reported to have applied Is. 61.1 to His own ministry; Mt. 11.5, combining the same testimony with one from the joyous description of Is. 35.5; Mt. 12.18 f cites Is. 42.1–4 as illustrating the gentleness of the messianic ministry exercised by Jesus; Mt. 8.16 f sees in the healing ministry of Jesus a fulfilment of Is. 53.4, and Jn. 12.38 quotes Is. 53.1 in connection with Israel's unbelief. The two dominical citations referred to above make no mention of the Servant Songs, though they presume a messianic task harmonious with that of the Servant of the Lord. And, curiously, none of the passages used by the Evangelists is made to illustrate the sufferings of Jesus, not even those from Is. 53. That may be a coincidence, but it shows how the passages could be used for motifs other than the chief one which impresses the modern student. We have no wish to ascribe to our Lord such an artificial mode of exposition of Is. 53 as we find in the near contemporary Rabbinical writings, which interpret the Servant as the Messiah but ascribe all the sufferings to others.[1] But neither are we at liberty to affirm that He included in his anticipation of the messianic task every element of the picture there delineated, any more than He would have included every item of the sufferings of the Righteous Sufferer in the Psalm in the list of adventures — or misadventures — that lay ahead of Him. His preparedness to accept anything from His Father's hand, to be 'well pleasing' to Him at all costs, would have included a willingness to leave the path ahead for the Father's direction. But its course was not immediately discernible.[2]

(iv) The belief that the baptism of Jesus anticipated his general baptism for the sins of the world is bound up with a dubious understanding of Mt. 3.15 and an equally uncertain inference from Mk. 10.38, Lk. 12.50. Cullmann interprets Mt. 3.15, 'Thus it is fitting for us to fulfil all righteousness', as meaning that Jesus had to be baptized, because his baptism prefigured the event in which He was to achieve a righteousness on behalf of all. Apparently the saying is intended to convey the notion: 'Let Me be baptized, for it is a right and proper thing that *thus*, in a manner comparable to baptism, namely by My suffering a vicarious death, I should perform an act in which the total demand of God laid on all men should be rendered'. But is it conceivable that the term οὕτω, *thus*, should bear such an

[1] See C. R. North, *The Suffering Servant in Deutero-Isaiah*, 1948, pp. 11 ff.

[2] For other expressions of the viewpoint here adopted see C. J. Cadoux, *The Historic Mission of Jesus*, 1941, pp. 196 f; R. Schnackenburg, *Das Heilsgeschehen bei der Taufe nach dem Apostel Paulus*, 1950, p. 209; W. G. Kümmel, *Theologische Rundschau*, 1950, p. 39; E. Schweizer, *Erniedrigung und Erhöhung*, p. 50, n. 207. M. D. Hooker has an interesting treatment of the Isaianic passages in the Gospels, op. cit., pp. 83 ff.

imponderable weight of meaning, indicating both the nature of the baptism of Jesus as a prefiguration of his death, and the significance of that event as a representative act of righteousness rendered on behalf of the human race? Would such an idea have been even remotely conceivable to John the Baptist? I doubt it. If the saying is a construction of the Evangelist, and he wished to convey such a meaning, he succeeded in obscuring it fairly completely. I shall refer to this saying again shortly; meanwhile it may suffice to remark that a more plausible interpretation views it as meaning that the baptism of Jesus is an *instance* of the way in which Jesus must fulfil all righteousness, and that this latter obligation perpetually rests upon Him. That later the Lord will render to God a sacrificial obedience in which righteousness, human and divine, is consummated, is a truth at the heart of the Christian faith, but it is not set forth in Mt. 3.15.

The use to which Mk. 10.38 and Lk. 12.50 are put suffers from a like failure to take into account the historical context in which the sayings of Jesus are set; but whereas Mt. 3.15 is read in the light of the end of the ministry, these two sayings are made to reflect back on the beginning. 'Can you . . . be baptized with the baptism with which I am baptized?' 'I have a baptism to be baptized with, and how I am constrained till it is accomplished!' In both these sayings the term *baptize* connotes suffering and possibly death. Cullmann deduces from these utterances that for Jesus 'to "be baptized" from now on (i.e. from his baptism) meant to suffer, to die, for his people'.[1] It is suggested that this is why Jesus did not Himself baptize; for the meaning of baptism, His own death for others, cannot be attributed to other baptisms. But this is difficult reasoning. Is it justifiable to conclude that because Jesus towards the end of His ministry used the term 'baptism' to connote suffering and death, He attributed this meaning to baptism invariably, and in particular to His own baptism at the beginning of His ministry? That becomes even harder if we accept the testimony of Jn. 4.1, that Jesus made and baptized more disciples than John; for though the Lord did not himself administer the baptism, it was nevertheless authorized by Him. If these many 'disciples' were baptized into His death, it may be confidently presumed that neither the Twelve who administered the baptisms nor the people who received them had any idea that this was so. Moreover, we cannot take it for granted that the term 'baptize' in the two dominical sayings specifically harks back to Jesus' baptism in Jordan; for in the Marcan saying the figure of baptism is paralleled by that of drinking a cup, a

[1] Op. cit., p. 19.

figure manifestly taken from the Old Testament, where it frequently refers to the cup of wrath meted out by God (see e.g. Ps. 75.8, Is. 51.17, 22 ff, Jer. 49.12 f, Lam. 4.21); it is antecedently likely that the metaphor of baptism was also taken from common usage, for which there exist both wider precedents and reasonably close parallels, in Scripture and profane writings.[1] There is therefore some reason for assuming that the verb 'baptize' was capable of yielding a literal and a figurative sense, without undue confusion. It is doubtful that the idea of judgment unto death attached to the baptism of John, but it is comprehensible that when the Lord was aware that suffering and death lay ahead of Him He should have been encouraged to apply the terms baptize and baptism to His destiny, in accordance with the precedent of which He was not improbably aware. Nor need we exclude the possibility that by this time He had come to see the grimmer implications of His own baptism in the Jordan; if so, He does not seem to have dwelt on it in His instruction of the disciples, for there is no trace of such a view in the apostolic preaching and Epistles. There is thus no encouragement to adopt the procedure of Cullmann and read back into the baptism of Jesus the conceptions inherent in Mk. 10.38, Lk. 12.50.

This discussion as to the meaning of the baptism of Jesus has so far been negative; it is time that I gave more positive indications as to its presumed significance. I would venture the following assertion: *Jesus came to the baptism of John, among the penitents of Israel responsive to John's proclamation, to begin the messianic task in its fullness as He interpreted it from the writings of the Old Testament.*

In developing this thesis I would take up some of the affirmations made by writers earlier considered, but it will be necessary to draw some distinctions not infrequently overlooked.

(i) Our Lord's submission to the baptism of John constituted a clear assent to John's authority, in respect both to his message and to his ministry. The work and proclamation of John will have served as a clarion call to Jesus to begin that work which it was His vocation to achieve. Hence the preaching of Jesus began with a similar appeal to John's: 'The time of judgment and redemption is at hand, repent!' That Jesus added, 'and believe the good news!' is indicative of the difference of emphasis between Him and John in their life and teaching, but that does not concern us here. The chief point I would make, which is admittedly incapable of proof but which seems to suit the

[1] See pp. 73-7.

evidence best, is that Jesus went to the baptism of John, not as a private individual, but as one convinced of His vocation to be the Messiah and therefore as *a representative person*.

I am aware that it is commonly believed that the baptism of Jesus was the occasion wherein it was revealed to Him that He was the Messiah, but it is doubtful if the implications of this view have been sufficiently taken into account. It would imply that Jesus went to baptism in the same spirit as the rest of His fellow Jews, viz. for the remission of sins and enrolment among the heirs of the kingdom; we have already seen how difficult of acceptance such an idea is. Moreover one must recall the greatness of the conception of Messiah which Jesus had; His contemporaries might be satisfied with the idea of a merely human messiah (ἄνθρωπος ἐξ ἀνθρώπων γενήσεται, Trypho in the Dialogue of Justin Martyr, 49), so that even the rabbi Akiba could consider the pretender Bar-Cochba to be the Messiah, but for Jesus the Messiah possessed, or was to possess, the quasi-transcendental features of the Son of Man, just as John the Baptist proclaimed the 'Coming One' to be the Mighty Judge. The conviction that He was such a Messiah must have had deep roots. And so it did. It was almost certainly grounded in His consciousness of a unique filial relationship to God; and it is intolerable to imagine that *that* began only at His baptism on hearing the divine Voice. There is not a hint in the Gospels of any development of messianic conviction in the teaching of Jesus or of any modification of views He held in this respect; it is the more doubtful that they sprang into existence, ready made, as it were, at the baptism. Indeed, it is hard to believe that the unique elements in our Lord's teaching did not go back prior to His baptism.[1] Hence even Loisy, though holding the popular view of the baptism as the occasion of revelation to Jesus of His messiahship, felt obliged to affirm, 'That this revelation was strictly the first revelation, that it had not been prepared by the entire previous life of Jesus and that it was not later completed, the tradition, in fact, has never held and criticism cannot admit it. The revelation of the baptism could have been addressed only to a soul disposed to receive it'.[2]

Herein is contained the puzzle that lies behind Mt. 3.15, viz. why the *Messiah* comes to the baptism of John. We shall perhaps never be

[1] For example, He will almost certainly have formed His attitude to the Law in the quiet years at Nazareth and even at that time rejected the Pharisaic interpretation and way of life modelled on the 'Traditions of the Fathers'; such a formulated attitude is embodied in the fact of His baptism, which was impossible for one who insisted on holding Himself separate from the common mass of people.

[2] *Les Évangiles Synoptiques*, I, 1907, p. 408. See also Creed, *The Gospel according to Luke*, 1942, p. 56.

able to give a verdict satisfactory to all on the question of the authenticity of the saying. The pungent observation of Schlatter is worth
pondering: 'The belief that Jesus went to His baptism without any
ideas and then, taken aback by the sign, returned home as the Messiah,
was as impossible for Matthew as the notion of a baptism performed
without any exchange of words'.[1] John would not have baptized Jesus
without questioning Him; Mt. 3.15 is our only hint in the Gospel
record as to the nature of the conversation. The narrative of John's
embassy from prison to Jesus, recorded in Mt. 11.2 ff, is best understood as reflecting an earlier belief now weakening, that Jesus was the
Messiah; and that belief must have arisen either at the baptism or not
long after. Whatever one's view on this question, it must be granted
that no hint is given in the narrative that John objects to baptizing
Jesus on the ground of the sinlessness of Jesus. The previous context
contrasts John's water baptism with that of the Messiah. The statement of John in Mt. 3.14, 'I need to be baptized by you, and are you
coming to me?' may therefore best be understood as, 'I need *your*
baptism and You are coming to receive *mine*?' When the Messiah submits Himself to the water baptism of the Forerunner, the situation is
topsy-turvy! The reply of Jesus is no mere concession: 'That may be
true, but never mind . . .'. Rather it is a command: 'Let it be so — *at
once*!'[2] The matter is of urgent importance! 'To do thus is fitting; for
it is fitting for us to fulfil all righteousness'. Baptism is not a prescription of the Law, yet Jesus views it as a divinely imposed duty (πρέπον).
Why? One answer at least could run: because every strand of messianic teaching in the Old Testament depicts the Messiah as inseparable from his people. He that is 'meek and lowly in heart', and who
calls 'them that labour and are heavy burdened' to Himself, begins
His ministry by identifying Himself with them in their need. He
companies with sinners according to the will of God.[3]

(ii) Here it is needful, in face of current exegesis, to distinguish
between the concepts of solidarity and substitution.[4] When the baptism of Jesus is included under the latter category, Jesus is thought of
as taking the place *of* the sinner; when the former category is em-

---

[1] *Der Evangelist Matthäus*, p. 86.
[2] So Fridrichsen, op. cit., pp. 168–9; Lindblom, op. cit., p. 20; M. Barth, op.
cit., p. 67.
[3] See, besides the article of Fridrichsen, G. Bornkamm, 'Die neutestamentliche
Lehre von der Taufe', *Theologische Blätter*, 1938, p. 44 and 'Enderwartung und
Kirche im Matthäusevangelium', in the Festschrift for C. H. Dodd, *The Background of the New Testament and its Eschatology*, 1956, p. 245.
[4] Marcus Barth calls attention to this distinction, but apparently it is not important to him, for he works chiefly with the idea of the baptism of Jesus as a
substitutionary act, op. cit., pp. 62 ff.

ployed, Jesus is viewed as taking a place *alongside* the sinner.
Admittedly there is a vicarious aspect even in the idea of Jesus
establishing a solidarity with the people, but this is inherent in the
very notion of a Messiah Who acts on behalf of His people.

We have already observed that the Messiah is a representative
person. This is fundamental to the messianic concept in the Old
Testament. The real concern of the Old Testament is the relation between God and His people. The Messiah appears comparatively little
in its pages, but the mediatorial function is present from first to last;
whether the Messiah is accorded a major or minor role, His significance lies in His representing God to the people and the people to
God. The dominant messianic figure of the King-Messiah of David's
line appears in Isaiah chiefly as the ruler appointed as Yahweh's
representative (e.g. Is. 9.11), but in Jeremiah (30.21) and Ezekiel
(chs. 45–46) he acts rather as the representative of the people towards
God; moreover in the latter two books the personal Messiah has been
replaced by a line of kings. The present inclination to find the origin
of this conception in an institution of sacral kingship in Israel is of
note here, for on such a theory the king is viewed as essentially a
mediatorial figure, with whose person and destiny the fortunes of
Israel are bound.[1] The *Servant of the Lord* could well be such an individual, viewed under one aspect of his representative functions. The
majority of scholars, however, dissociate the Servant from the traditional messianic figure, even where they incline to see him as an
individual rather than a group. From our point of view it is noteworthy that the Servant notion hovers between the plainly corporate
concept (as in Is. 44.1) and the apparently individual application (as
in Is. 52.13 ff). In both cases the function of the Servant is representative, first as the Servant of the *Lord*, and then as Servant of his
fellow men (see especially Is. 49.5 ff). Similar remarks may be made
about the *Son of Man* of Dan. 7. It is hard to deny that in the interpretation of the vision, afforded in the latter part of the chapter (vv.
15 ff), the Son of Man is replaced by the 'saints of the Most High';
i.e. he represents the saints. The Son of Man is a corporate figure.
But he may be so in a more than pictorial sense. It is possible that, just
as the beasts of the vision symbolise four *kings*, who in turn represent
their kingdoms (v. 17), so the Son of Man symbolises the *Messiah* who
represents the kingdom of God; i.e. He represents the interests both
of God the universal Sovereign and of the saints as the heirs of the

[1] See e.g. A. Bentzen, *King and Messiah*, 1955; A. R. Johnson, *Sacral Kingship in Ancient Israel*, 1955.

Kingdom. Of this there can be no certainty, but it would assist our understanding of some difficult sayings of our Lord if He did so interpret the passage.

It may be worth remarking that if any justification exists for linking the concept of King-Messiah with the sacral functions of the king of Israel, then each of the three chief strands of Old Testament messianic tradition combine suffering with sovereignty, though in varying measure. By viewing certain of the Psalms (such as Ps. 18, 89, 101, 118) as having particular application to the king in the cultus, A. R. Johnson can speak of the Davidic king as suffering Servant and humble Messiah, in whose deliverance the people see their deliverance from death and establishment of righteousness.[1] The destiny of the Suffering Servant, in experiencing both abasement and exaltation, is too well known to need comment. But it is easy to forget that the Son of Man who receives the kingdom stands for the people suffering at the hands of an 'anti-christ' for faithfulness to the Most High, His worship and His laws. In this last case not a hint is provided that the Messiah will suffer, either with the saints or for them: but this is bound up with the situation of the prophecy of Daniel, coming as it does out of the heart of the affliction, and in earnest expectation of deliverance. The omission is rectified in the teaching of Jesus, for whom it is precisely the *Son of Man* who treads the path of humility and suffering associated with the Servant of the Lord.

These considerations are seen in their true perspective when it is recalled that, far from diminishing the place of the Messiah in the achievement of the divine purpose, Jesus heightened it, as his followers in dependence on Him.[2] We are realizing with increasing clarity that the message of Jesus, in respect both to the presence and future of the Kingdom, took shape by reason of His conviction as to its relation to Himself, His action, His proclamation. His consciousness of being the bearer of the Kingdom of God expressed itself in His messianic actions, proclamation and claims, while that same consciousness was almost certainly at the root of His so-called 'near expectation' of the final triumph, since it was bound up with His decisive action and the generation that experienced it. The parable of the Strong Man Bound, Mk. 3.27, shows that this consciousness of the Kingdom at work in Him cannot be limited to the latter part of the ministry, but belongs to the earlier also. On the view that the declaration of the Voice at the

[1] Op. cit., pp. 104, 116.
[2] R. H. Charles urged that this constituted a major difference between the writings of Judaism and the New Testament. See *Eschatology*, 2nd ed. 1913, 362 f; *Religious Development between the Old and New Testaments*, 1914, pp. 93 ff.

baptism confirmed convictions already nurtured in His mind, rather than conveyed a fresh revelation to Him, this consciousness will have been with Jesus as He descended into the waters of Jordan. Called to be the Agent of the judgment and redemption proclaimed by John, He knew Himself appointed to the most awful destiny given to man, by which the divine promise and human need, implied in the messianic patterns of the Old Testament, were to meet in Him.

(a) As Messiah, representative of people needing deliverance, Jesus demonstrates and effects his solidarity with them in their need. As such it is a momentous action, fraught with consequences to be revealed in the Kingdom and the Judgment. In submitting to the baptism of John, the Lord condemns the self-righteous and the wicked for their lack of repentance and takes His stand with the publicans and sinners, as well as more respectable members of society, who look for the Day of the Lord. It is not for us immediately to turn to the conclusion of the Gospel to see whither this solidarity of the Messiah with sinners would lead Him; we should turn over one page at a time and see Him in the midst of the struggling humanity whom He would relieve — at the table of Levi the publican with others of his ilk, in the homes and by the lake side, hemmed in by the ceremonially unclean seeking cleansing — a Messiah of the common folk, cursed by the learned religious because they did not know the Law. Here is divine life in human form, identifying itself with the irreconciled. In declining to read our Gospels too quickly we wish to recognize what those same documents surely teach, that the Lord who pledged His unity with the poor and needy, did so in obedience to the call of God and *in dependence on Him for the revelation of the next step*. A Messiah who would fulfil the total messianic pattern of the Bible and go all the way in unity with the lost must be prepared for humiliation and suffering to the uttermost on their behalf. So much would be clear to Jesus and we need not doubt that He dedicated Himself to this end without reserve. But to all facile ideas that He trod a straight path from His baptism to His cross, with never a look to the right or left, the immediately ensuing narrative of the Temptation is a rebuke. For there Jesus faces, not the impossibility of His being a Messiah, but the possibilities of His way as Messiah; and the ways He declined were those which would have destroyed His solidarity with the people He had come to save.

(b) As Messiah, called to be representative of the divine sovereignty, Jesus consecrated Himself to His Father in Jordan, that that sovereignty might be perfectly manifested in judgment and redemption. Herein especially lies the significance of the divine response to the baptism. The heavens were 'torn apart' (Mk. 1.10); Bornkamm suggests that this signifies not so much a personal vision as an eschatological event, an apocalyptic sign, for the Lord of Hosts is to work through His Anointed.[1] The Spirit came down as a dove upon Him. One recalls that the Spirit of the Lord is to rest on the King-Messiah (Is. 11.2) and on the Servant (Is. 42.1, 61.1). In both cases the Spirit enables the messianic task to be achieved, the former within the Kingdom, the latter in the process of its establishment; but fine distinctions of stages within the eschatological process would not be currently drawn: both the Messiah and the Spirit belong to the age to come. The opened heaven, the sending of the Spirit and the Voice from the Father all indicate that the last times have dawned, redemption is about to appear. If this be related to the proclamation of John the Baptist, it would be natural to conclude that the Messiah in His baptism is not merely equipped by the Spirit for the work of the Kingdom, but He becomes the 'Bearer' of the Spirit, that He might baptize in Spirit and fire.[2]

The baptism of Jesus takes on a fuller significance from this viewpoint. Far from being a simple acceptance of the death sentence it indicates the initiation of the divine intervention, the downfall of the powers of darkness, the dawn of the new creation, the promise of life from the dead! And this, indeed, is the spirit in which Jesus departed from the Jordan. In His Temptation He defeated the Strong Man by the Spirit Who was with Him; in His proclamation He made known the good news of the coming of the Kingdom; in His ministry He exercised the powers of the coming age. By the finger of God He cast out demons (Lk. 11.20; Matthew's paraphrase, 'By the Spirit of God . . .', 12.28, is a correct exposition). By the same power He performed such signs of the Kingdom as making the lame to walk, the deaf to hear, the dumb to speak, in accordance with the expectation of Is. 35 (Mt. 11.5). By the same authority He forgave sins (Mk. 2.10 f), proclaimed the righteousness of the Kingdom, revealed the love of the divine sovereignty and made known the nature of the times. We do

[1] *Theol. Blätter*, 1938, p. 45.

[2] Lohmeyer considers that the coming of the Spirit to Jesus is not strictly an endowment of spiritual power but a personal theophany, as Yahweh once came to Abraham: the Spirit 'comes down' to Jesus as Jesus 'comes' to John. On such an interpretation Jesus receives not an impersonal powerful inspiration but a Helper for His messianic task. See *Das Evangelium des Markus*, 1951, p. 21 ff, *Das Evangelium des Matthäus*, 1958, p. 51. For the idea that the coming of the Spirit on Jesus signifies the dawn of the new creation, see Holtzmann, op. cit., p. 44; Loisy, op. cit., p. 410; Leenhardt, *Le Baptême chrétien*, 1944, pp. 24 f.

not wonder that this mode of eschatological fulfilment puzzled John the Baptist, but it is thoroughly of a piece with what we have conceived the messianic ideal of Jesus to have been; whereas John awaited a Messiah who should sweep away the sinners, Jesus acted as one concerned for them and therefore brought precisely to *them* the gracious blessings of the new order. This, too, was an implication of His baptism.

It is clear that the significance of the baptism of our Lord is more complex than is often recognized. In particular, to make it the first step of his Via Dolorosa is not only too simple but misleading. The baptism of the Messiah is unto the carrying out of the whole purpose of God in judgment and redemption. A deeper and higher signification for baptism could not be imagined. At what point in His life Jesus knew that in bringing the redemption He should endure the judgment it is impossible for us to say. Nor is it necessary, for His baptism embraced every eventuality.

(iii) The foregoing discussion may have prepared us to exercise caution in attempting to define the relation between the baptism of Jesus and Christian baptism. No little uncertainty attaches to the problem; it is rendered more difficult by differences in interpreting the significance of Jesus' baptism, and not least by the paucity of our sources.

We may perhaps be pardoned for briefly dismissing the critical opinion that regards the narratives of the baptism of Jesus as modelled on the precedent afforded by Christian baptism. Such is the position maintained by Bultmann. He admits that the baptism was an historical event, but he believes the account to be legendary, since it sets forth the baptism as a messianic consecration and the earliest traditions of the life of Jesus are unmessianic. After explaining how the legend arose, Bultmann suggests that the final stage in the development was the making of it as the prototype of the Christian rite.[1] For those who cannot admit the cogency of the basic objection, viz. that the earliest traditions of Jesus did not present Him as Messiah, the argument is without force.

What Bultmann saw as the final stage in the development of the 'legend', viz. the making of the baptism of Jesus the foundation of Christian baptism, is the dominant view in present-day baptismal theology. To question it may appear needless pedanticism, but the reasons adduced for the unanimity are hardly compelling and the whole matter needs restatement.

The chief ground for the view is the conviction that the baptism of

---

[1] *Die Geschichte der synoptischen Tradition*, 3rd ed. 1957, pp. 263 ff. The same view is adopted by E. Percy, *Die Botschaft Jesu*, 1953, p. 13.

Jesus prefigured His death and resurrection, which in turn are the determinative redemptive acts lying behind Christian baptism. In the light of the foregoing exposition of the significance of Jesus' baptism it will be understood why I cannot accept this argument. The baptism of Jesus was directed to the accomplishment of the total eschatological action assigned to the Messiah; there are insufficient grounds for supposing that Jesus marked out from that total action a death and resurrection, removed from the final judgment and deliverance by an indeterminate period of time, and that He anticipated by His baptism this dying and rising as a means of entering the Kingdom. If the baptism initiated a new creation, its goal must be its completion in the final kingdom. Nothing less than that was the aim of the messianic consecration at the Jordan.

A different line of approach, favoured by not a few British scholars, stresses the similarity of the results of Jesus' baptism with those of Christian baptism. W. F. Flemington points out that for Jesus His baptism expressed and effected His oneness with the new Israel, bestowed a new experience of the Holy Spirit and witnessed a deeper conviction of His being the Son of God. The parallel with the Apostolic doctrine of baptism, which associates it with entrance into the Church, the reception of the Spirit and the adoption of sons, is striking, and Flemington feels that it cannot be accidental: 'It may be that this event has exercised a more considerable influence than has hitherto been recognized upon the origin of the Christian rite'. He suggests that in the early Church baptism was 'the counterpart in the life of the believer of the baptism of Jesus Himself'.[1] This is a plausible and attractive interpretation. We know that the baptism of Jesus came to occupy a prominent place in the later Church.[2] It is natural to assume that in the first generations also it was seen as the archetypal baptism, the pattern for all subsequent Christian baptism, and that its place in the Gospel narratives was intended to serve such a purpose. That it might be expected that such should take place we freely admit; but there is a fatal objection to the belief that it did actually happen, viz., the all but complete silence of the New Testament writers concerning this supposed relationship between the two

[1] Op. cit., pp. 27 ff, 121. So, more confidently, D. M. Baillie, 'It seems *obvious* that when the early Christians baptized into the name of the Lord Jesus, their thoughts went back to that incident which in the general tradition stood immovably at the beginning of His public ministry. . . .', *The Theology of Sacraments*, 1957, p. 77.

[2] W. Robinson pointed out that in the Eastern Church the Feast of Epiphany represents, not the showing of Jesus to the wise men, but the baptism of Jesus, Sacraments and Eschatology, *Theology*, vol. 55, p. 54, n. 6.

baptisms. Despite attempts to prove the contrary it would seem that
*no writer of the New Testament brings the baptism of Jesus into relation
with Christian baptism.*[1]

An explanation of this phenomenon lies to hand: though Jesus was
baptized with others, it was recognized that no other baptism was
strictly comparable to His, for He was baptized as the Messiah.
Therein He commenced His messianic ministry with a view to the
bringing in of the new creation; therein He was acknowledged by the
Father as the Christ; therein the Spirit came to Him, to manifest
through Him the Kingdom in grace and power. In all this the note is
uniqueness rather than likeness with us in our experience. Moreover,
the New Testament writers never make the mistake[2] of viewing the
baptism as the accomplishment of redemption, not even when the
qualifying adjective 'sacramental' is added; they saw this as the
inauguration of the messianic ministry and viewed it as essentially of a
piece with what followed. True, the eschatological accompaniments of
the baptism gave promise of Kingdom, power and glory, but the
setting was ambiguous — a baptism into solidarity with sinners and
obedience of the Father could not be other than a stepping into the
unknown. It would of course, be anachronistic to attribute to the
Apostolic Church a scrupulous anxiety to achieve a historical reconstruction of the stages in our Lord's understanding of His Father's
will; but the Apostolic theologians had enough historical sense to
realize that the significance of Christian baptism is determined by the
whole course of our Lord's messianic action, with emphasis on the
death and resurrection in the past and the parousia in the future.
From every point of view, accordingly, it seems fitting to view the
foundation of Christian baptism as *the total redemptive action which
the baptism of Jesus set in motion.* As P. Ryndholm so well put it, 'The
institution of Christian baptism is not a momentary action but a
history'.[3] For which reason, we may add, it was commanded when
the 'history' was accomplished, at least in respect to the Reconciliation,
viz. in the Resurrection (Mt. 28.18 ff). It will find its true goal in the
event which the Resurrection anticipates — the Parousia.

[1] This was recognized by A. Schweitzer, *The Mystery of Paul the Apostle*,
E.T., 1931, p. 234; J. Schneider, *Die Taufe im Neuen Testament*, 1952, p. 80;
R. Schnackenburg, op. cit., p. 209; H. G. Marsh, *The Origin and Significance of
New Testament Baptism*, 1941, p. 107; K. V. Rasmussen, *Dopet, Dåben, Dåpen, Tre
nordiska teologiska uppsatser*, 1957, p. 321. I can think of one passage only in the
New Testament which could claim to be an exception to the above statement, viz.
1 Jn. 5.6 ff. In the exposition of this passage however I suggest reasons for caution
in the use to which we put it. See pp. 236–42.
[2] As H. W. Bartsch did, *Evangelische Theologie*, 1948–9, pp. 90 ff.
[3] *Det heliga Dopet*, 1921, p. 31, cited by H. Evander, *Det Kristna Dopet*, 1938, p. 48.

On the other hand, we recognize that because our Lord's baptism was messianic, it could not be unrelated to our baptism. The Messiah is representative of God *and man*. Yet even when He is baptized as man, He is still *representative man*. Herein may be seen the clue to both the likeness and difference between the baptism at Jordan and Christian baptism: as in all His messianic action, Jesus makes His baptism a medium for His mediatorial and creative activity, but the identical outward action in our case expresses our dependence on Him and receptivity of the fruits of His action. For example, it is true that Jesus joined the Remnant in His baptism and we join the Church in ours; but how different is the action in each case! He stooped to become one with penitent sinners, we rise to join the saints — through union with Him. He fashioned the Remnant anew through attaching its members to Himself, even as He was subsequently to make of them a new creation by their participating in His resurrection; we are incorporated into that Risen Body. It is thus misleading to speak of Jesus and ourselves 'joining' the Remnant by the common rite of baptism, even though it is undeniably true; for the Messiah comes to the people in baptism for creative action, while the people come, not to the people, but to *the Messiah* in their baptism, and only through Him do they become the people of God. While, therefore, baptism and church are conjoined in the baptism of Jesus and in ours, it is unfitting in this respect to speak of our Lord's baptism as the ideal Christian baptism, for the realities they represent are so different.

Jesus was acknowledged Son of God at Baptism (Mk. 1.11) and in Him we become sons of God in baptism by faith (Gal. 3.26 f). The former citation is a proclamation of the messianic office of Jesus, the latter indicates the creation of a filial relationship to God. There is therefore a vast difference between the two experiences, yet there is also a connection between them. It is because Jesus the Messiah went down to Jordan to identify Himself with the unredeemed, and continued the same process of identification unto the cross and resurrection, that we can share His sonship; that sonship is rooted in the prior filial relation of Jesus to the Father, and the goal of our appropriation of it lies yet in the future, when sonship will be perfected in us (Rom. 8.23, 1 Jn. 3.2). Here again, we see that the baptism of Jesus is critical in the process whereby this goal is achieved, but in a theology of the Incarnation it cannot be viewed as the pattern of Christian baptism. A messianic acknowledgement of the Son by the Father is not the same as the adoption of a sinner by the Father.

The most striking parallel between Jesus' baptism and ours is the descent of the Spirit on Him and our reception of the Spirit in like circumstances. Again, however, the nature of the gift is different; for He comes to aid Jesus in the messianic task, while the believer is made anew through Him (Tit. 3.5 f). For Jesus this is presage of the gift to be given to Him in the Resurrection for 'all flesh' (Acts 3.22); the believer is receiver only, never giver of this gift. Yet one must underscore the term 'presage'; for the time for bestowing the gift had not arrived with the baptism in the Jordan; something further must take place before the Spirit of the Messiah could be poured forth. The frequently uttered view, that by His baptism Jesus transformed John's baptism to become a baptism of Spirit, suffers from the same lack of historical realism to which we have often referred; for John continued to baptize in water, without any manifestation of the Spirit, and according to the Fourth Evangelist Jesus authorized baptisms (Jn. 4.1 ff) in which the Spirit was not given (Jn. 7.39). The conjunction of baptism in water with baptism in Spirit awaited the crucial event wherein the Son of Man should be lifted up and exalted to the right hand of the Father (Jn. 16, 7, 20, 22). Even after that event, it is noteworthy that in Apostolic teaching the descent of the Spirit at the Messiah's baptism is eloquent of who *He* is rather than what Christian *baptism* is (Acts 10.38, 1 Jn. 5.6 ff). We do well to observe this example of Apostolic reserve.

There is, however, one feature in the baptism of Jesus, the siginicance of which, for Christian baptism, is frequently overlooked. Our Lord recognized in the proclamation and activity of John the summons of his Father to fulfil His vocation, but in the nature of the case His submission to baptism among sinners was made *in freedom*. He dedicated Himself with a perfection of love and obedience that brought the approval of the Father and the presence of the Spirit — as later His perfect obedience in love on the cross received the response of the Father in resurrection and exaltation. Now it belongs to the essence of Christian baptism that the believer comes as receiver. He hears the summons of the Gospel, and in making the baptismal confession, 'Jesus is Lord' (Rom. 10.9), he casts himself on the saving grace of the Sovereign Redeemer. Yet that same baptismal confession could not be uttered without the baptismal candidate conjoining with humble trust a willing submission to the Saviour Sovereign. He receives the Lord, and gives — himself. There is no little irony in the fact that the zeal with which many theologians claim the baptism of Jesus as the archetypal baptism has the end result of ensuring that the generations to come shall not approach their baptism in the spirit of free dedication that Jesus approached His. Is not this a matter to ponder and, if possible, to redress?

(ii) *Did Jesus Baptize During His Ministry?* John 3.22 ff, 4.1 ff

Among the differences between the presentation of the ministry of Jesus in the Fourth Gospel and that of the Synoptics, those concerning the relations of Jesus and John and the attitude of Jesus to baptism are striking. While each of the Synoptists gives an account of the baptism of Jesus, the Fourth Evangelist merely presumes it without mentioning the event (Jn. 1.32 f). On the other hand, the Synoptists are silent about any administration or authorization of baptism by Jesus, but the Fourth Evangelist refers twice to such an activity on the part of our Lord (Jn. 3.22 ff, 4.1 ff). Nor can it be said that the Evangelist views this work as an insignificant aspect of the ministry of Jesus; the account is part of his exposition of the relations between Jesus and John. He implies that there was a period when the ministries of John and Jesus were exercised concurrently (3.22 ff) and, somewhat surprisingly, that the baptizing ministry of Jesus was more successful than that of his forerunner: John's disciples tell him that 'everybody' was going to Jesus for baptism (3.26), and Jesus learns that the Pharisees heard He was making and baptizing more disciples than John (4.1). Since the response to John's preaching was widespread ('There went out to Him *all* the country of Judea and *all* the people of Jerusalem'! Mk. 1.5), this represents a far-reaching claim for the success and importance of the baptizing work of Jesus. According to Jn. 4.1 ff, the departure of Jesus from Judea to Galilee, is occasioned by this success; it is inferred that the Pharisees had become incensed by the large numbers baptized by Jesus and that He had deemed it wise to remove Himself from a possible attack at this juncture — an interpretation the more plausible if, as is likely, we are to understand that by this time the Baptist had been thrown into prison.

What are we to say about this report? Doubtless our answer will be coloured by our prior view of the Fourth Evangelist's attitude to history. If we believe that the Evangelist is interested solely in the exalted Christ and the Church of his generation and not in the Jesus of Palestine, we shall regard this passage as another creation of the Evangelist; his motive — whether it be to contrast external purification by water with the spiritual power of Christian baptism[1] or to

---

[1] Loisy *Le Quatrième Évangile*, 1903, pp. 331 ff.

provide a reason for the Church's adoption of John's water baptism[1]
— is of secondary importance. Some critics, who are unwilling
radically to reject the Johannine history, are yet disturbed by the
apparent contradiction between Jn. 3.22, which says that Jesus baptized, and Jn. 4.2, which says that He did not; they see here an
instance of patchwork employment of conflicting sources, and therefore consider that the passage cannot be used as evidence for a baptismal activity of Jesus.[2] It may be viewed as a sign of the times that a
majority of scholars now reject both viewpoints and see in this passage
a further example of the Fourth Evangelist's preservation of a valuable tradition lost to the Synoptists. It can no longer be held that the
Evangelist had no concern in the Jesus of Palestine. Nor is it reasonable to exaggerate the 'contradiction' of Jn. 4.2; at most the latter
statement may be viewed as an editorial addition that leaves unaffected
the major issue of a baptism authorized by Jesus.[3] As it happens, most
critics are prepared to accept 4.2 as a parenthesis from the hand of the
Evangelist.[4]

It is, of course, impossible to prove the reliability of the Fourth
Evangelist at this point, but there are some weighty considerations in
favour of accepting his statement that Jesus authorized baptisms
during His ministry. Above all we must take into account that the
first messianic act of the Lord was to be baptized in company with the
penitents. This was no action on impulse; He had come to the conclusion that John's baptism was 'from heaven' (Mk. 11.30) and He
demonstrated that belief in the strongest manner by receiving that
baptism. We have stated it as our view that Jesus was baptized in
solidarity with the people, not in their stead. There is therefore no
reason to believe that He saw His own baptism as cancelling the
desirability of all further baptisms. In baptism He had begun his
messianic work, not completed it; if He had been baptized unto the
bringing in of the Kingdom, there was no reason why people should
not be baptized with a view to entering it, even while He was engaged
in His messianic task. Especially would this relate to the earliest stage
in the ministry. MacGregor voiced the opinion that the authentic

[1] A. Schweitzer, *Mysticism of Paul the Apostle*, pp. 234 ff.
[2] So E. K. Lee, *Theology*, vol. LVII, 1954, p. 413.
[3] So Bernard, who thought that the motive of the Redactor was the idea that it
would detract from the dignity of Jesus to administer baptism, *Gospel According to
St. John*, 1928, vol. I, p. 133. MacGregor suggested that the Evangelist originally
wrote, 'When therefore Jesus knew that he was making and baptizing more disciples
than John, He left Judea and went away again into Galilee'; it is presumed that the
Evangelist wished to show that Jesus avoided the appearance of rivalry with John,
The Gospel of John, 1928, p. 93.
[4] Bultmann raises no query on this matter in his commentary.

tradition is wholly against the idea that our Lord's ministry at any time overlapped that of John.[1] That is a doubtful pressing of the silence of the Synoptic gospels. What right have we to suppose that Jesus was baptized but a few days before John was thrown into prison? It would indicate a peculiar tardiness on His part to recognize the authority of John's mission. The Synoptic gospels themselves exclude the possibility that Jesus returned to Nazareth for a period of inactivity after His baptism. What kind of a ministry then, is it supposed that Jesus exercised while John continued to preach and baptize? He preached concerning repentance and the Kingdom. Matthew reports the earliest proclamation of John in Judea and of Jesus in Galilee in exactly the same words (Mt. 3.2, 4.17); some scholars have doubts as to the legitimacy of the precise identification, but the eschatological appeal for *repentance* on the basis of the nearness of God's great intervention was undoubtedly the same, except that it received a yet greater note of urgency in the preaching of Jesus, through His consciousness of being the Agent of the divine sovereignty. The people, then, must repent. John demanded its expression in baptism. Did Jesus decline to ask for baptism? Then He must have set His face against it, choosing to stop the practice in His own ministry. He could not have ignored the rite of baptism; He had to resolve not to use it and thereby dissociate Himself from John's practice. In that case we are confronted with the situation that Jesus and John at the same time were demanding repentance in view of the imminence of the divine intervention, that Jesus had acknowledged that the repentance-baptism of John was ordained by God, that He had submitted to it, and in the act had received the approval of the Father and the presence of the Spirit, but He now declined to permit anyone coming in the sphere of His influence to submit in like manner to God's call. This is the more difficult to accept if we bear in mind that the crowds that came to Jesus must have associated Him with John and believed that they both preached the same message; the people went to John to get baptized: did those who went to Jesus never ask for baptism? And did He refuse it? Marsh protested that such an idea is impossible: 'He ought not to be accused of prohibiting an experience which in His own case had brought a divine revelation'.[2]

[1] Op. cit., p. 90.
[2] Op. cit., p. 122. So also Kittel, 'Die Wirkungen der christlichen Wassertaufe nach dem Neuen Testament', *Theologische Studien und Kritiken*, 1914, p. 27; Schlatter, 'Das Evangelium nach Johannes', *Erläuterungen zum Neuen Testament*, vol. 3 (1947), p. 55, *Der Evangelist Johannes*, 2nd ed. 1948, p. 103; Barrett, *Gospel according to St. John*, 1955, p. 192.

It may be taken as probable, therefore, that Jesus authorized baptism for at least the earliest period of His ministry.[1] The simplest explanation for the lack of its mention in the Synoptic gospels is that it was confined to the beginnings of the ministry, before John's imprisonment, and in the area south of Galilee, since the Synoptics do not take account of activities of Jesus prior to the Galilean ministry.[2] Admittedly one cannot press this restriction, in view of the fragmentary nature of the gospel records. Even the two Johannine references to the early baptismal activity of the disciples of Jesus serve only to introduce other topics; the first provides the context for an argument about baptismal purification between John's disciples and a Jew and leads to the final testimony of John to Jesus (Jn. 3.25 ff), the second explains how Jesus came to leave Judea and traverse the usually avoided territory of the Samaritans (4.1 ff); in neither case is baptism the subject under discussion. It is not impossible that the lack of further mention of the matter in the Fourth Gospel, as its total omission from the Synoptics, is due to the focussing of interest on the more critical developments of the ministry.[3] If Jesus did refrain from letting His disciples baptize in the later ministry, we have to admit that the reason is shrouded in uncertainty. Johannes Schneider suggests that the Messiah's task is to bestow the messianic baptism of Spirit, not the pre-messianic water baptism;[4] but this would have applied to the beginning of the ministry equally as to its end. Schweitzer more plausibly considers that Jesus viewed His own presence as having sacramental significance; he who attaches himself to the Messiah is assured of the Messiah's kingdom.[5] Would this notion, however, have applied to a baptism administered by disciples on Mission, away from the presence of their Master? Possibly the reason for the cessation of baptism had a less theological basis. If it is difficult to conceive of Jesus preaching in the Jordan valley at the same time as John and denying the appropriateness of baptism as the expression of repentance towards God, it is equally hard to believe that He could have determined to pursue a similar course as John's and remain *a Messiah in the wilderness*, waiting for the populace to

[1] Leenhardt thinks that the baptisms referred to in John 4.1 ff must have belonged to an even earlier situation than the Evangelist has indicated, op. cit., p. 34, n. 2.

[2] See W. F. Flemington, op. cit., p. 31.

[3] Marsh contests the view that the baptism administered by the disciples of Jesus was limited to the early ministry only, believing that the teaching and the life of Jesus overshadowed the observance of ritual and custom in its significance for the Gospel, op. cit., p. 125.

[4] Op. cit., p. 27.

[5] Op. cit., pp. 235 ff.

come to baptism. The Jordan may have been an ideal place for preaching in Judea, and in John's time there was no lack of congregations. But Jesus must go to the villages and towns and preach the good news to people who did not and would not come to the Jordan. 'Let us go elsewhere and preach', said Jesus, when the Galileans would restrain Him from leaving them, 'for to this end I came forth' (Mk. 1.37 f). By tradition and convenience a baptizing mission was more suitable for the Jordan valley than the villages and towns of Galilee. Not that baptism was impossible in Galilee, for Gennesaret was there; but the mission of Jesus was conceived on different lines from that of John. He was no ascetic, settled by the water's edge, but the Messiah who thrust forth into the press of humanity with the message that must be faced *now*. Other factors there may have been that led Jesus to modify John's emphasis on baptism, but this is surely not irrelevant.[1]

Our sources do not put us in a more favourable position when we attempt to assign a significance to a baptism administered during the ministry of Jesus. The two obvious alternatives, that it was virtually identical in character with John's baptism or that it was substantially the same as Christian baptism, were represented in the Fathers[2] and are still advocated today.[3] The difficulty of equating Jesus' baptism with John's is the unavoidable implication that the Messiah's ministry is no better than the Forerunner's, an idea which would have astonished John even as it perplexes us; but to make a baptism before the cross, resurrection and sending of the Spirit identical with that which was administered after these redemptive events is to diminish their cruciality and contradict the self-confessed theology of the Evangelist (Jn. 7.39). Hoskyns tried to rise above the dilemma by reading a theological intention in the Evangelist's narrative: the Evangelist has in view the variety of baptisms current in his day — those of the Jews, of John the Baptist and of the Church; the Jews were satisfied with their baptisms, John was not, but the disciples baptized in the visible presence of the Messiah; since He is Son of God and dispenses

---

[1] Such a view would be consonant with the possibility that Jesus made less of the demand for baptism, rather than abolished it immediately. In the latter part of the ministry, the shadow from the impending event that would enable baptism to be bestowed in Spirit and power would tend to diminish further the accent on a preparatory baptism.

[2] Darwell Stone cites for the former view Tertullian, *De Baptismo*, 11, Chrysostom in Joan, Ev. Hom xxix.1, and for the latter Augustine, In Joan, Ev. Tract. xv.3, Ep. xliv.10, cclxv.5, Peter Lombard, Sent. IV. iii, 7; cf. Thomas Aquinas, S.T., III, lxvi, 2: see *Holy Baptism*, p. 222, n. 15.

[3] Among proponents for the former view are Westcott, *The Gospel according to St. John*, pp. 57–9; Wotherspoon, p. 157, n. 2; Schlatter, *Der Evangelist Johannes*, p. 103; Evander, op. cit., p. 50; for the latter see MacGregor, op. cit., p. 93; Lightfoot, *St. John's Gospel*, 1956, p. 119.

the Holy Spirit, the Evangelist would have us know that Jesus is the
answer to the inadequacy of all visible historical baptism by water.[1]
This characteristic utterance of Hoskyns has at least a seed of truth in
it: *any baptism authorized by Jesus the Messiah is differentiated by its
relation to Him*. A baptism in the name of the crucified and risen Lord
will not be the same as a baptism authorized by the Lord who preaches
in Judea and Galilee but it will still be a unique baptism. This the
Evangelist hints of in 4.1, where the statement, 'Jesus made and baptized more disciples than John did', implies that those baptized at the
bidding of Jesus stood in a relation of disciple to Him as those baptized by John did to John.[2] There is no doubt that those baptized
under the preaching of Jesus would feel themselves more closely
bound to Him than they would to John. Is it wrong to suggest that,
baptized at the bidding of the Messiah, they stood in more immediate
relation to the Kingdom that He was in process of introducing?

It would seem that we have here an example of the ambiguity of the
messianic ministry of Jesus. Through His proclamation, as His
action, the Kingdom was drawing near, and was being actualized;
hence He could authoritatively speak the word of forgiveness (Mk.
2.5) which strictly awaited the time of redemption, just as He brought
deliverance from the evil powers that belonged to the final deliverance
(Mt. 12.28). The Kingdom was being realized in the ministry of the
Messiah, but not as it was shortly to be; so the baptism that belonged
to the time of redemption was being adumbrated, but not with the
power that it should shortly have. The baptism of the ministry therefore was neither Jewish, nor Johannine, nor Christian; it was a baptism in obedience to the messianic proclamation, under the sign of the
messianic action and in anticipation of the messianic deliverance.
More than that we cannot say.[3] For our purpose it is significant as
indicating that Jesus did not despise baptism but valued it enough to
authorize it in His ministry.

(iii) *The Significance of Mark 10.38, Luke 12.50*

These two dominical sayings are unique in that they, and they
alone in the Gospels, refer to the coming passion of Jesus in terms of a
baptism: He is to be plunged, not into water but into calamity unto
death. In both statements the term βάπτισμα is used, which to this

---

[1] *The Fourth Gospel*, 2nd ed. 1947, p. 227.

[2] Bultmann, op. cit., p. 128, note 7, makes this point and observes that a similar
loose use of 'disciples' for a wider circle of adherents is presupposed in 6.60 ff.

[3] Two writers who have come close to this view are H. Cremer, *Taufe, Wiedergeburt und Kindertaufe in Kraft des Heiligen Geistes*, 3rd ed. 1917, p. 21, and H.
Strathmann, *Das Evangelium nach Johannes* (N.T.D.) 1955, pp. 77 f.

day has not been discovered in any non-Christian literature. The conviction is gaining ground therefore that since Jesus Himself employed the term, it reflects His understanding of the *rite* of baptism.

We have already noticed Cullmann's view, that these utterances confirm the belief that Jesus regarded His own baptism as a consecration to a death for the sin of the world.[1] It has been also suggested that since Mark and Luke consciously employed the technical term for Christian baptism, they intended to convey in these sayings what they understood the teaching of Jesus to be on the baptism practised in the Church, viz. that it was into the death of the Messiah.[2] From this point of view it is not unnatural to push on a stage further and see in the connection of baptism and death an illumination of the nature of the death that Jesus is to suffer: just as baptism is an immersion into and an emergence from the waters, signifying a dying to sin and a rising to righteousness, so the death of Jesus is to be followed by a new and greater life; it will bring for Him liberation from the limitations imposed by an earthly existence to enjoy the wider powers and ministry of a resurrection life.[3]

This attempt to read the two sayings in the light of the developed baptismal theology of the Church is questionable. Our primary object is to discover, not the secondary use to which the Evangelists might have put the sayings, but their meaning on the lips of Jesus. At once therefore it should be observed that in Mk. 10.38 the two clauses are parallel in meaning: a *cup* is to be drunk, a *baptism* is to be endured. The idea of drinking a cup of suffering is frequent in the Old Testament, but significantly it is most commonly used of the cup of wrath which God apportions to sinful peoples; see especially Is. 51.17, 21 ff, Jer. 25.27 ff, Ezk. 23.32 ff, Hab. 2.16. The metaphor is employed in the same sense in Rev. 14.10, 16.19 to represent the divine judgment which is to be meted out to the Beast and to the harlot city Babylon. It would seem that, in speaking of the passion lying ahead as a cup to be drunk, Jesus sees it as ordained by God and connected with His judgment on the sinful people. It is natural therefore to understand

---

[1] Op. cit., p. 19. See also the *Church of Scotland Interim Report 1955*, pp. 8 ff; Lampe, op. cit., p. 39.

[2] A. Richardson, *An Introduction to the Theology of the New Testament*, London 1958, p. 340. In similar vein H. W. Bartsch contests the idea that Mk. 10.38 has in view blood-baptism, i.e. martyrdom: 'It is said that the disciples *in their baptism* take on themselves the death of Christ', *Evangelische Theologie*, 1948–9, p. 86.

[3] This interpretation is by no means uncommon and is not recent. See Wellhausen, *Das Evangelium Marci*, 2nd ed. 1909, p. 84; Johannes Weiss, *Die Schriften des Neuen Testaments*, 2nd ed. 1907, p. 174; E. F. Scott, *Kingdom and Messiah*, 1911, pp. 229 f; W. E. Flemington, op. cit., p. 32; M. Barth, op. cit., p. 42; J. A. T. Robinson, *Jesus and His Coming*, 1957, p. 41.

the parallel figure of baptism in the light of the Old Testament language, wherein sinking beneath waters symbolises the experience of overwhelming calamity.[1]

The familiar objection to this view, viz. the non-appearance of the term $\beta \acute{a}\pi\tau\iota\sigma\mu a$ outside Christian writings, is inconclusive. Its absence from the LXX is hardly surprising in view of the fact that its Hebrew equivalent טְבִילָה does not appear in the Hebrew Old Testament; the verb $\beta a\pi\tau\acute{\iota}\zeta\epsilon\sigma\theta a\iota$, used in the two dominical sayings, is attested in a metaphorical sense; and the *idea* represented by the noun and verb is very common in the Old Testament.

This interpretation is strengthened by the similarity of terms and ideas in Lk. 12.49–50. The closeness of connection between vv. 49 and 50 indicates that the two sayings have been handed down together in the tradition and were originally spoken together.[2] In this case we have the image of a baptism to be undergone paralleled with that of a fire to be kindled. Once more the item paralleled with baptism is a figure common in the Old Testament to represent the infliction of divine judgment: see e.g. Deut. 32.22, Ps. 21.8 f, 89.46, Is. 66.15 f, with similar examples of the symbolism in the New Testament, I Cor. 3.13 ff, 2 Th. 1.8, Heb. 12.29, 2 Pet. 3.7. Interestingly enough, one passage (Ps. 11.6) actually conjoins the two figures of *fire* (as in Lk. 12.49) with the *cup* (as in Mk. 10.38) to express the thought of the divine judgment:

> On the wicked he will rain coals of fire and brimstone;
> a scorching wind shall be the portion of their cup.

In Is. 30.27–28 the two figures of *fire* and *flood* are placed in imme-

---

[1] Note the four parallel phrases in Ps. 18.4 f: the cords of death, the torrents of perdition, the cords of Sheol, the snares of death. Ps. 69.14 sets in parallelism the mire, enemies, deep waters; it proceeds: 'Let not the *flood* sweep over me, or the *deep* swallow me up, or the *pit* close its mouth over me'. The writer of Ps. 88 compares himself to the forsaken among the dead and the slain in the grave; 'Thou hast put me in the depths of the pit, in the regions dark and deep, Thy wrath lies heavy upon me, and thou dost overwhelm me with all thy waves' (vv. 6 f). Clearly, the figure of the overwhelming waters that symbolize danger and death was common. In none of these passages however, does the term $\beta a\pi\tau\acute{\iota}\zeta\epsilon\iota\nu$ appear. But the LXX contains the extraordinary rendering in Is. 21.4, $\acute{\eta}\ \acute{a}\nu o\mu\acute{\iota}a\ \mu\epsilon\ \beta a\pi\tau\acute{\iota}\zeta\epsilon\iota$, which comes fairly close to the desired meaning, 'Lawlessness overwhelms me'. Delling further points to the rendering of Ps. 69.3 by Symmachus, $\acute{\epsilon}\beta a\pi\tau\acute{\iota}\sigma\theta\eta\nu\ \epsilon\acute{\iota}\varsigma\ \acute{a}\pi\epsilon\rho\acute{a}\nu\tau o\upsilon\varsigma$ $\kappa a\tau a\delta\acute{\upsilon}\sigma\epsilon\omega\varsigma$ and that of Job 9.31, by Aquila, $\acute{\epsilon}\nu\ \delta\iota a\phi\theta o\rho\hat{q}\ \beta a\pi\tau\acute{\iota}\sigma\epsilon\iota\varsigma\ \mu\epsilon$. The citation from a papyrus of about 153 B.C. is well known: $\kappa\hat{a}\nu\ \acute{\iota}\delta\eta\varsigma\ \acute{o}\tau\iota\ \mu\acute{\epsilon}\lambda\lambda o\mu\epsilon\nu\ \sigma\omega\theta\hat{\eta}\nu a\iota$, $\tau\acute{o}\tau\epsilon\ \beta a\pi\tau\iota\zeta\acute{\omega}\mu\epsilon\theta a$, which seems to mean, 'And if you have seen (in a dream) that we will be rescued, precisely then shall we be submerged', i.e. engulfed by the calamity; see further Moulton and Milligan, *Vocabulary of the Greek Testament*, p. 102; G. Delling, *Novum Testamentum*, vol. 2, 1957, pp. 100 f.

[2] It is unlikely that the same applies to the ensuing verses, 51–3, since they come from Q (see Mt. 10.34 ff) but Lk. 12.49–50 belong to the Lucan source (L).

diate juxtaposition to express the idea of the action of God in judgment:

> Behold the name of the Lord comes from far,
> burning with his anger, and in thick rising smoke,
> His lips are full of indignation,
> and his tongue is like a devouring *fire*;
> His breath is like an overflowing *stream*
> that reaches up to the neck;
> to sift the nations with the sieve of destruction,
> and to place on the jaws of the peoples a bridle that leads astray.

In view of these parallels it can hardly be doubted that the 'baptism' anticipated by our Lord is seen as an enduring of the judgment of God. Yet the Lucan passage implies that Jesus not alone suffers judgment but is to exercise it. He came to *cast fire* on the earth; i.e. create a blaze that should purge the world and bring the Kingdom. Here is an extraordinary conjunction of ideas: the Messiah has come to judge the world and be judged for the world! Delling suggests that the figure and idea hark back to the preaching of John: the Coming One is to perform a baptism of fire (Mt. 3.11), but Jesus sees the necessity for enduring that baptism Himself; it will involve His disciples, but it will also have the more catastrophic consequence of setting off the general conflagration that ushers in the new age.[1] This savours of an over-simplification of the process envisaged, but the basic interpretation is reasonable: the Messiah has both to take the cup of wrath from the hand of God and be plunged beneath the waters of affliction. This He does on behalf of His own and the world. But 'He that is near me is near the fire', runs an apocryphal saying; to be of the company of the Messiah in the day of His enduring judgment is to know burning. In this respect a difference of aspect appears between the Lucan and the Marcan sayings; in Luke the baptism is of the One, just as the judgment is exercised by One, but in Mark the disciples are called to drink the cup of woe and be baptized with the baptism of Jesus — they are to suffer along with Him. This is not solitary in the teaching of the New Testament, for the Lord called on men to take a cross with Him to Jerusalem (Mk. 8.34) and Paul sought to enter into the sufferings of the Christ for the sake of the Body (Col. 1.24). Indeed, fellowship in the sufferings of the Messiah is needful if men would know the fellowship of the Messiah in His Kingdom. The above quoted apocryphal saying continues, 'But he that is far from me is far from

---

[1] βάπτισμα βαπτισθῆναι, *Novum Testamentum*, vol. 2, 1957, pp. 108 ff.

the Kingdom', implying something akin to the Pauline dictum, 'Through many tribulations we must enter the Kingdom' (Acts 14.22).[1] The baptism and judgment alike have to do with the Kingdom. The Messiah must be the chief Actor in both. By His baptism of death He will endure judgment that men may become heirs of the Kingdom; by His exercise of judgment of fire He will remove that which hinders and bring in the final perfection. Note that He will *bring* it; we must not interpret the Lucan saying to mean that by His submission to suffering Jesus will pull down the world on His head and engulf all in ruin. The two sentences in Lk. 12, 49–50 are complementary in their parallelism, not synonymous. The Lord is to go to a death for the life of the world and come for the judgment of the world. A fuller exposition of the same theme is given in another Lucan passage, the so-called Q-Apocalypse, Lk. 17.22 ff. The major topic is 'the days of the Son of Man', v. 22. The Son of Man is to appear as the lightning, v. 24. But a catastrophic event is to take place before that day: 'First He must suffer many things and be rejected by this generation', v. 25. Then the sequence must surely follow: the judgment, as suddenly as Noah's flood, vv. 26 ff, as unexpectedly and cataclysmically as the fire that fell on Sodom, vv. 28 ff. Learn the lesson, then: 'Whoever seeks to gain his life will lose it, but whoever loses his life will preserve it', v. 33. Here we have the same fundamental outlook as is presupposed in Lk. 12.49–50. In the Q-Apocalypse we must suppose that the disposition of the sayings owes not a little to Luke, but the baptism and fire passage is unitary. The evangelist in arranging his material has not misread the tradition.

What may we learn then concerning the attitude of our Lord to baptism in the passages under review? However disappointing it may be, it would seem that we can gain very little that illuminates His conception of *baptism*. We learn much as to His understanding of His *death* and its relation to the Kingdom. For His death is as a baptism of suffering, a drinking of the cup of wrath; He advances to it in a spirit of dedication and sees it as needful to the coming of the Kingdom as the Last Judgment will be. The use of these two sayings in the current baptismal debate has made us overlook that the subject of our Lord's words is His death, not His baptism, and that it is His death which is likened to a baptism, not His baptism which is likened to a death. It is unlikely that Jesus would have applied the comparison

---

[1] The apocryphon is cited by Delling, op. cit., p. 115. Origen knew the saying and was sceptical about it. The Alexandrine Didymus gives the Greek text:

ὁ ἐγγύς μου ἐγγὺς τοῦ πυρός·
ὁ δὲ μακρὰν ἀπ' ἐμοῦ μακρὰν ἀπὸ τῆς βασιλείας.

here made to the elucidation of the meaning of baptism generally, still less to the baptism of John; nor was this the time for the exposition of the significance of the baptism that His followers would receive between the cross and judgment. The manner in which the Marcan and Lucan sayings conjoin the baptismal figure with another drawn from the Old Testament suggests that the use of baptism to represent His sufferings was inspired by the Old Testament precedents, rather than by His own experience of baptism. Nevertheless, there is no need to exclude the possibility that at this juncture the baptism in Jordan had taken on a deeper significance for Him; neither are we at liberty to exaggerate that factor. In particular, there seems no ground for imagining that Paul developed his doctrine of baptism on the basis of these two sayings; for that there is not a shred of proof. It is altogether likely that he came to his interpretation of baptism through reflection on the primary elements of the kerygma (1 Cor. 15.3 f) as they related to the believer and were experienced by him.

(iv) The Missionary Commission of the Risen Lord and Baptism: Matthew 28.18–20

It has long been an element of critical orthodoxy to regard Mt. 28.18–20 as unauthentic, a product of second generation Christianity, reflecting a theology characteristic of the end of that generation rather than its beginning. Heitmüller, in his major work on baptism and the name of Jesus, judged it needless to discuss the matter.[1] N. P. Williams, anxious to hold on to the Dominical institution of baptism if possible, did not feel he could go farther than regard the passage as 'the feather which may decisively weigh down that scale of historical balance which represents "Dominical Institution", if sufficient indirect evidence can be gathered from the rest of the New Testament to invest this hypothesis with considerable likelihood'; should testimony to the contrary be forthcoming, he adjudged, the passage would have to be rejected, 'not being more than a feather'![2] With such a prevailing attitude, it is not to be wondered at that New Testament scholars have declined to use the Matthaean text as evidence of the instruction of our Lord on baptism, or even as shedding light on the origins of Christian baptism. Nevertheless, the basis for this unanimity is by no means as firm as is represented, and there are signs of withdrawals from the ranks of the critically orthodox. It may be

[1] 'It would be superfluous to show all over again that the direct institution of baptism through Jesus, as it is recounted in Mt. 28, is historically untenable', *Im Namen Jesu*, 1903, p. 270.

[2] *Essays Catholic and Critical*, edited by E. G. Selwyn, 1926, pp. 407 f.

timely to take a fresh look at the objections raised against the Commission and the second thoughts being entertained about them.[1]

The chief points made against the authenticity of the Commission in Matthew are as follows: (i) The tradition is found only in Matthew's Gospel. No authentic strand of Gospel teaching contains a command to baptize. (ii) The original text probably contained no mention of baptism. (iii) The use of the trinitarian formula is late; Paul and Acts uniformly represent baptism as administered 'in the name of the Lord Jesus'. (iv) The attitude of the earliest Church to the Gentile mission is irreconcilable with its possession of a commission from the Risen Lord to preach the Gospel to all nations. The Commission is accordingly viewed as a summary of the Church's experience of baptism; its attribution to the Risen Jesus is to be seen either as reflecting the Church's conviction that its practice of baptism is according to the will of God revealed in Jesus Christ,[2] or as due to taking a word uttered 'in' the Lord to be a word 'from' the Lord.[3] It need hardly be said that such a viewpoint is not necessarily inconsistent with respect for the authority of the Commission for the Church, since it could well be a true reflection of the will of God in Christ, even as a word 'in' the Lord could be divinely given. On such a basis the issue will be to determine how early the intimation of the Commission was given to the Church, whether by the Lord to the disciples in the time of the resurrection appearances or by the same Lord in later years. In that case the spiritual authority of baptism has to be distinguished from the question of its historical origin, and there can be little doubting that the former is of greater consequence. Yet the matter is of such intrinsic interest as to make it worth considering with care.

(i) It seemed to Heitmüller, in his later work on the sacraments, to be a grave count against the Matthaean text of the Commission, that neither Mark nor Q contains a commission to baptize; we are to presume that in the circles in which these two most important repositories of evangelic tradition arose, and at the time of their writing, the baptismal commission was unknown. The gravity of this consideration is increased by the likelihood that the Q source comes from

---

[1] I venture the view that if the discussion of the problems surrounding Matthew 28.18–20, contained in J. Lindblom's *Jesu Missions-och Dopbefallning, Tillika en Studie över det kristna Dopets Ursprung*, Uppsala, 1919, had been issued in English or German, the swing of the pendulum observable in Europe at the present time would have taken place long since. I gratefully acknowledge my indebtedness to Lindblom's work.

[2] Leenhardt, op. cit., p. 43.

[3] Lohmeyer, *Das Evangelium des Matthäus*, 2nd ed. 1958, p. 423.

Palestinian churches.[1] It is necessary, however, to query at once both the assertion and the inference. Admittedly Q has no baptismal commission: neither does it contain an account of the passion and resurrection of our Lord; how then can it be expected to convey a commission of the Risen Lord to evangelize and baptize the nations? In view of the severe limitations imposed upon the Q source, who can say what the Palestinian circles in which it arose did or did not know about resurrection traditions? Similarly, what critic will today venture to define the precise limits of Mark's knowledge of the resurrection of Jesus? If Mark ended his Gospel at 16.8, then he chose to omit all resurrection narratives and to conclude with the announcement of the empty tomb: if his gospel was originally longer, we can conjecture as to what it may have contained but say little as to what it did not, for the conclusion seems to have been lost by the time that Matthew and Luke were written and speculations about its influence on the resurrection narratives of John and the Gospel of Peter do not carry us far. This *argumentum e silentio* is, in respect to Mark and Q, invalid.

It would be more to the point to raise the question why Luke's version of the commission to evangelize the nations does not include the command to baptize (Luke 24.46 f). The omission was taken by Kirsopp Lake to prove that Luke could not have known of such a command.[2] Certainly the omission is strange, but it is surely due to the manner in which Luke has chosen to cast his version of the missionary commission, viz. as a fulfilment of Old Testament prophecy: 'Thus it stands written that the Messiah must suffer and rise from the dead on the third day and that repentance for the forgiveness of sins be proclaimed in his name to all the nations. . . .'. It is a consistent aim of Luke to underscore the proclamation of the gospel to the nations as part of the divine will announced beforehand by the prophets (see especially Acts 10.43, 'To him all the prophets bear witness that every one who believes in him receives forgiveness of sins through his name'). For this he had excellent grounds, but he was too discreet to claim that the prophets foretold Christian baptism! Instead he couched the prophetic announcement in terms reminiscent of baptism. The prophets had foretold 'that repentance for forgiveness of sins should be preached in his name' ($\kappa\eta\rho\nu\chi\theta\hat{\eta}\nu\alpha\iota$ $\dot{\epsilon}\pi\dot{\iota}$ $\tau\hat{\omega}$ $\dot{o}\nu\dot{o}\mu\alpha\tau\iota$ $\alpha\dot{\nu}\tau o\hat{\nu}$ $\mu\epsilon\tau\dot{\alpha}\nu o\iota\alpha\nu$ $\epsilon\dot{\iota}s$ $\ddot{\alpha}\phi\epsilon\sigma\iota\nu$ $\dot{\alpha}\mu\alpha\rho\tau\iota\hat{\omega}\nu$,[3] Lk. 24.47). With this should be compared the summary of John the Baptist's work as 'preaching the

---

[1] *Taufe und Abendmahl im Urchristentum*, 1911, p. 2.
[2] *Encyclopaedia of Religion and Ethics*, vol. 2, 1909, p. 381.
[3] Reading with most modern editors $\epsilon\dot{\iota}s$, instead of $\kappa\alpha\dot{\iota}$ as in the Koine text.

baptism of repentance for forgiveness of sins', (κηρύσσων βάπτισμα μετανοίας εἰς ἄφεσιν ἁμαρτιῶν, Lk. 3.3), and Peter's preaching on the day of Pentecost, 'Repent and be baptized every one of you in the name of Jesus Christ, for forgiveness of your sins', (Μετανοήσατε καὶ βαπτισθήτω ἕκαστος ὑμῶν ἐν τῷ ὀνόματι Ἰησοῦ Χριστοῦ εἰς ἄφεσιν τῶν ἁμαρτιῶν ὑμῶν, Acts 2.38). The reference to the name of Jesus is naturally absent from the preaching of the Baptist, even as the resurrection passage omits reference to baptism, but the coincidence of thought and language is striking. It is difficult to believe that Luke's lack of mention of baptism in 24.47 is due to his historical conscience in respect to a knowledge that Jesus did *not* command baptism; on the contrary, by the language employed he has indicated that the prophetic announcement should be fulfilled through the proclamation of the Gospel with baptism.

The account in Jn. 20.21 ff stands by itself among the resurrection narratives. It is so compressed and so characteristically Johannine in expression, it is difficult to compare it with the other traditions of the resurrection commission; moreover, as in the case of the eucharist, the sacramental teaching of the Fourth Gospel requires to be considered as a whole when one is thinking of the institution of the two sacraments in this Gospel. Nevertheless it may be significant that, as in Luke, the declaration of mission (v.21) is followed by an authorization to forgive sins (v. 23): it is possible that we should see in this enigmatic statement at least an allusion to the baptizing activity of the disciples.[1]

It should not be overlooked that the Longer Conclusion of Mark preserves in 16.17 a tradition of the commission to baptize, closely parallel with that in Matthew but probably independent of it; for the compiler of this Conclusion seems to have depended for his information chiefly on Luke and Acts;[2] in this matter he could have drawn on oral tradition.[3] Denny's observation therefore has force: 'In all its forms the commission has to do either with baptism (so in Matthew and Mark) or with the remission of sins (so in Luke and John). These are but two forms of the same thing, for in the world of New Testament ideas baptism and the remission of sins are inseparably associated'.[4] In view of the nature of their testimony, it is unlikely that the bearers of these ideas in the second, third and fourth gospels wished to imply that it was otherwise with Jesus.

---

[1] So Gardner-Smith, *Saint John and the Synoptic Gospels*, Cambridge 1928, p. 83; Barrett, *The Gospel according to St. John*, 1955, p. 475.
[2] Streeter, *The Four Gospels*, 1927, p. 350.
[3] So Swete emphatically, *The Gospel according to St. Mark*, 3rd ed. 1909, p. 404.
[4] *The Death of Christ*, 4th ed. 1903, p. 73.

(ii) It is well known that Eusebius cited the Commission of Mt. 28.18 ff in more than one form; besides that known to us in our texts, he reproduced v. 19 not infrequently as, 'Go and make disciples of all nations in my name' (πορευθέντες μαθητεύσατε πάντα τὰ ἔθνη ἐν τῷ ὀνόματί μου). F. C. Conybeare, in an oft cited article,[1] examined the citations of the text in Eusebius and concluded that Eusebius did not know the longer form of the text until the Council of Nicea, when the trinitarian doctrine became established. Since he thought he found support for a like ignorance in Justin and Hermas, the question naturally suggested itself: 'Is the Eusebian and Justin's reading of Mt. 28.19 original?' To E. Klostermann there could be but one answer to that: If the evidence from Eusebius and Justin shows the existence of a short text of this nature, it must undoubtedly be preferred as original.[2] In this conviction he was not alone, but the number of supporters for the Eusebian reading is, in fact, surprisingly few.[3] The real difficulty is to determine whether we have any right to speak of a 'Eusebian reading'. E. Riggenbach, in a lengthy reply to Conybeare's article,[4] showed that Eusebius exercised considerable freedom in quoting the Matthaean text, as is evidenced in the fact that the text appears in various forms, even in one and the same work; after Nicea Eusebius cites the commission in both longer and shorter forms; while (in Riggenbach's view) in the letter written by Eusebius in 325, during the Council at Nicea, the manner in which he cites the common form of the text suggests that he had been familiar with it for long. This exposition of the facts received widespread support,[5] but the suggestion that Eusebius' habit of citing the text in a reduced form was due to the influence of the *arcani disciplina* (teaching on

---

[1] 'The Eusebian Form of the Text Matt. 28.19', *Z.N.W.*, 1901. The article was recapitulated in the *Hibbert Journal*, 1902.

[2] 'Das Matthäusevangelium', in Lietzmann's *Handbuch zum Neuen Testament*, p. 357.

[3] I have discovered only W. C. Allen, *The Gospel according to S. Matthew* (I.C.C.), 3rd ed. 1912, pp. 307 f; Wellhausen, *Das Evangelium Matthaei*, 1904; K. Lake in his article, 'Early Christian Baptism', Hastings' *Encyclopaedia of Religion and Ethics*, vol. 2, 1909, p. 380, and in that shared with Foakes Jackson, *The Beginnings of Christianity*, part I, vol. I, 1942, p. 336. E. Loymeyer supports the Eusebian reading on the ground of the structure of the passage — four lines bound together by the occurrence in each of the word 'all'. The parallelism looks more impressive in German than in Greek and can hardly be regarded as objective support for the shorter reading; see *Das Evangelium des Matthäus*, pp. 421 f.

[4] 'Der trinitarische Taufbefehl Matth. 28.19 nach seiner ursprünglichen Textgestalt und seiner Authentie untersucht', in A. Schlatter's and H. Cremer's *Beiträge zur Förderung christlicher Theologie*, 1903.

[5] T. Zahn stated, 'For any reasonable critic the matter is settled', *Das Evangelium des Matthäus*, 1910, p. 720, n. 7. Riggenbach's views were substantially adopted by F. H. Chase in his article, 'The Lord's Command to Baptize', *Journal of Theological Studies*, 1905.

baptism and the Trinity was unsuitable for uncircumcised ears) was
less happy. Lake thought it an impossible idea, since the quotations in
Eusebius are not found in works intended for unbelievers or for catechumens.[1] Lindblom by other means supported his protest: he
pointed out that Eusebius, in his work Contra Marcellum, cites Mt.
28.19 to prove that the teaching on the triune God had been hidden
from Moses and the prophets but was revealed through the Son to be
made known to *all* men; clearly a man who believed the teaching on
the Trinity to be integral to the gospel could not at the same time have
regarded it as an *arcanum*. Lindblom therefore scrutinized afresh the
citations of Mt. 28.19 in Eusebius and examined the context in each
case. He came to two conclusions: first, that Eusebius draws on
various passages in the New Testament when citing the missionary
commission, combining with Mt. 28.19 items from Mt. 10.8, 24.14,
Jn. 20.22, and that his 'in my name' ($\dot{\epsilon}\nu$ $\tau\hat{\omega}$ $\dot{o}\nu\dot{o}\mu\alpha\tau\acute{\iota}$ $\mu o\nu$) is due to the
example of Lk. 24.47 along with Mk. 16.17; secondly, the form of the
citation is made to suit the purpose in view at the moment of writing;
the full text is employed when Eusebius is concerned about some
aspect of the teaching on baptism or the Trinity, the shorter is used
when the interest is centred on the mission to the nations.[2] A just
estimate of these contentions requires a following of Lindblom's
presentation of the evidence, but it appears to me more plausible than
the alternative suggestions that have been made. The great majority
of critics and commentators have felt themselves unable to forsake the
unbroken testimony of the texts and versions for the very uncertain
witness of Eusebius; indeed, Lagrange characterized adherence to
'Conybeare's whim', as he described it, as 'a real defiance of textual
criticism'.[3] The objection to the authenticity of Mt. 28.19 on the basis
of sound principles of textual criticism therefore can scarcely be said
to have maintained itself.

(iii) The contrast between baptism in the name of the Trinity, in
Matthew, and baptism in the name of the Lord Jesus, in Acts and
Paul, is often regarded as the weightiest objection adduced against the
Matthaean Commission; for, as H. Evander pointed out, there is not
one example in the whole New Testament literature of a baptism
taking place in the name of the Father, Son and Holy Spirit.[4] On the
other hand the importance of this observation and the extent of its
implication should not be exaggerated, for at most it concerns one
phrase of the Commission; it raises the issue whether a command to

[1] *E.R.E.*, vol. 2, p. 380.   [2] Op. cit., pp. 16–26
[3] *Évangile selon Saint Matthieu*, 7th ed. 1948, p. 544.   [4] Op. cit., p. 15.

baptize in the name of the Lord Jesus was later conformed to Church terminology, so as to become a baptism in the name of Father, Son and Holy Spirit, but the authenticity of the commission as a whole cannot be called in question from this point of view.

We must first make up our mind whether Mt. 28.19 reflects a baptismal formula in current use in the Church, or whether it is intended to describe the nature of Christian baptism. Several notable exegetes have supported the latter alternative. Schniewind considered that a baptismal formula is as little intended here as in the evangelic traditions of the Beatitudes, the Lord's Prayer and the Last Supper.[1] F. C. Grant more recently has expounded a similar view: the baptismal statement combines the disciples' inherited Jewish faith in God ('the name of the Father'), their new faith in the Son (i.e. Son of Man) and their experience of the Holy Spirit, the earnest of the New Age.[2] While one appreciates the common sense of these assertions, it is hard not to feel that Mt. 28.19 *in its present form* is a liturgical formula. Here we must distinguish between the presumed origin of the tradition embodied in the Commission and the use to which it was early put. It is possible that the Matthaean text represents a primitive tradition of the instruction of the Risen Lord to his disciples, the formulation of which has been stamped by the liturgical needs of the Church. Such is the view of Otto Michel, who suggests that vv. 18–20 represent three originally distinct sayings that were subsequently combined, as happened to many other passages of the Gospels.[3] Is it possible to suggest an earlier form of v. 19? Yes, it is. A whole group of exegetes and critics have recognized that the opening declaration of Mt. 28.18 demands a Christological statement to follow it: 'All authority in heaven and on earth has been given to Me' leads us to expect as a consequence, 'Go and make disciples *unto Me* among all the nations, baptizing them in *My* name, teaching them to observe all *I* commanded you'. In fact, the first and third clauses have that significance: it looks as though the second clause has been modified from a Christological to a trinitarian formula in the interests of the

---

[1] *Das Evangelium nach Matthäus*, 5th ed. 1950, p. 480.

[2] *The Gospels, Their Origin and their Growth*, 1959, p. 150. Paul Feine's position may be worth mentioning here. When writing his article on baptism in the *Realencyclopädie für Theologie und Kirche* (vol. xlx, 1907) he argued that this was a baptismal formula and unauthentic. In his later *Theologie des Neuen Testaments* he changed his mind; the words are to be understood as a brief description of the nature of baptism and they were understood so by the Apostles; not till later were they interpreted as a baptismal formula, op. cit., p. 141.

[3] 'Der Abschluss des Matthäusevangeliums', *Evangelische Theologie*, 1950, pp. 16 ff. Michel compares v. 18 with Mt. 11.27, v. 19 with Mk. 16.15, v. 20 with Mt. 18.20.

liturgical tradition existing in the Evangelist's day.[1] This supposition
would be increased to well nigh certainty if we agreed with Michel and
Jeremias[2] that Mt. 28.18 ff represents a fulfilment of the vision of the
exaltation of the Son of Man in Dan. 7.13 f, conceived on the lines of
the old oriental coronation of a king: v. 18 declares the assumption of
universal authority by the Risen Lord, v. 19–20a the proclamation of
that authority among all the nations, v. 20b announces the power of the
Lord in his guardianship of His Apostles. In such a scheme there
would be no ground for bringing in the triune name, for baptism is
the appropriation of the disciple-subject to the Son of Man.

Again we are brought to a position where a way forward seems
reasonably clear, but which we recognize to be no more than plausible.
At least, it should be conceded that another objection to Mt. 28.19
has proved highly questionable. Instead of eliminating the text, investigation strengthens the case for the authenticity of the baptismal
command, for the concept of discipleship in this passage is consonant
with the use of baptism, and some would even say that it demands
it.[3]

(iv) If the evangelic record of a commission of the Risen Christ to
take the gospel to all the nations be authentic, how is the slowness of
the Apostles to obey it to be explained? And how are we to account for
the resistance of the primitive Church to the efforts made by Paul to
evangelize the heathen? In some critics' estimate, the situation is un-
accountable to the point of being intolerable; they propose that the
history in Acts must be given precedence over the Matthaean tradition and that the latter be dismissed as incompatible with the history.[4]
It is considered that the universality of the Christian message was
learned through the spiritual experience of the Apostle to the Gentiles
and that, once accepted by the Church, it was assigned to the direct
command of the Lord.[5]

As with the trinitarian issue, it would be possible to view this as a

---

[1] This suggestion was made independently by Lindblom, op. cit., p. 175, and by
Bultmann in his *Geschichte der synoptischen Tradition*, 3rd ed. 1957, p. 163, n. 1.
Lindblom was followed by H. Evander, op. cit., p. 59, and Bultmann by Michel,
op. cit., p. 21 and J. Schneider, *Die Taufe im Neuen Testament*, 1952, p. 31.

[2] 'Jesus' Promise to the Nations', *E.T.*, 1958, p. 39.

[3] Lohmeyer was unique in maintaining the originality of the Eusebian shorter
form of v. 19 but affirming at the same time that the Commission involves the command to baptize, since the concept 'make disciples' includes within itself the necessity of baptism, *Matthäus*, p. 420.

[4] So Jackson and Lake: 'According to Acts it never entered into the mind of the
Twelve to leave Jerusalem and evangelize the Gentiles until circumstances forced
them to do so: to accept Matthew 28.19 is to discredit the obedience of the Twelve
beyond all reasonable limits', *Beginnings of Christianity*, vol. 1, p. 328, n. 2.

[5] M'Neile, *The Gospel according to St. Matthew*, p. 435.

matter of the terms in which the Commission has been handed down to us. It is conceivable that a command was given to take the good news to all, without any definition or prescription of area or peoples (such an indefinite commission is, in fact, contained in Jn. 20.21 ff); this could have been understood later as logically involving the whole world and the form of the Commission modified so as to express this more explicitly. By this means justice would be done to the unanimous tradition of the Evangelists, that the Apostles were commissioned by the Risen Lord, and at the same time recognition made that a period of time had to pass for the universal implications of the commission to be grasped. Such a solution of the problem is not to be dismissed out of hand, but the matter is more complicated than at first sight appears; for we have to do not alone with the Matthaean commission but with the persistent strain of universalism in *all* the resurrection traditions, to say nothing of that in the teaching of the Lord in the ministry. Moreover the basic theological setting of Mt. 28.18 ff is involved: this is not a simple case of adding the term ἔθνη to πάντα; the meaning of the resurrection is at stake.

First, it ought no longer to be regarded as matter for debate that the controversy between Paul and the conservative elements in Jerusalem centred on the *terms* of the admittance of Gentiles into the Church, not on the *legitimacy* of a mission to the Gentiles. The mission itself was never in question. The real difficulty concerned the relationship of Law and Gospel: should Gentiles become Jews before entry into the Church, with all that involved in fellowship at the table of the Lord and in daily association? If the narrative of Acts 15 gives the impression that only a hard shell of conservative Pharisaic Christians demanded that Gentiles submit to the Law on coming into the Church, it is also true that Acts 10-11, indicates that neither Peter nor the Church in Jerusalem had faced the possibility of Gentiles joining them without first becoming proselytes. The way of a Gentile was hard, but to the early Jewish Christians that was of the divine ordering, and they saw no way out of the difficulty. How to carry out a Gentile mission was doubtless a problem to them, even though their own Jewish heritage taught them that one day the Gentiles would be converted. This practical difficulty facing the Apostles in the earliest days of the Church should not be overlooked by us as we consider their attitude towards a general mission charge.

Secondly, it is wrong to attribute a complete lack of concern on the part of the Jerusalem Church for the Gentiles and to assume that no mission work among the latter was undertaken before Paul's missionary enterprise. Taking Acts as our guide, it should be noted that the mission to Samaria and the first preaching to Gentiles in Syria, leading to the foundation of the church in Antioch, were parallel movements consequent on Stephen's martyrdom and were begun prior to the conversion of Paul (see Acts 8.4 ff, 11.19 ff). It is likely that this work was carried on by members of the Hellenist wing of the Jerusalem Church, whose most notable representative was Stephen. From the account of Stephen's activities and preaching in Acts 6–7, it appears that he led in the van of a movement for a universalism that not alone included a preaching to Gentiles, but affected basically the whole Christian outlook. In sharing and developing these views, Paul must be seen as the champion of an existing concept of mission, rather than its creator. Luke leads us to believe that Stephen found trouble because he represented views dangerously akin to the offensive elements in his Master's teaching (Acts 6.13); the Twelve had heard this same teaching but had not reproduced it; that was due perhaps less to disobedience than to their inability to adapt inherited ideas to the new teaching given and the new situation created by the Lord after the cross and resurrection. Is it possible that the openness of the Hellenists to the universalism of Jesus enabled them to give a quicker response than the Twelve to the demands of the mission itself?

Whatever the attitude of the Apostles to the Gentiles, it is in every way likely that they would have felt their responsibility to Israel to be a prior charge. 'To the Jew first, and also to the Greek' was the watchword even of the Apostle Paul; how much more would it have been adopted by his predecessors? Moreover, it would have required more insight and organisation than the Twelve could be expected to possess for them to plan a simultaneous mission to the Jews and to the Gentiles, dividing forces for the purpose. Israel must hear the Word of the Gospel first, and then the nation as a whole would fulfil the prophetic expectation and undertake the evangelism of the nations! That hope must have been cherished from the beginning by the Apostles, but they would have thought less after the long term strategy of a modern missionary society than the speedy and even miraculous taking of the Word to the world and the conversion of the nations to God in the end of the times.[1]

Here we must make an effort to understand the eschatology of the

[1] See Jeremias, *Jesus' Promise to the Nations*, 1959, pp. 42 f.

primitive Church and how it would have affected its members. We have already pointed out the possible relation between Mt. 28.18 ff and Dan. 7.12. By the resurrection Jesus has been exalted to the lordship of the world. It is not to be objected that such is an 'advanced' Christology; on the contrary it is primitive. It is presumed in the simple confession, 'Jesus is Lord', confessed by the man who is baptized in belief that God has raised Him from the dead (Rom. 10.9). It is the doctrine implied in the snatch of confession in Rom. 1.3–4. It is the teaching embodied in the Christological hymn of Phil. 2.6–11. For the Redeemer-Messiah, resurrection includes exaltation and exaltation means sovereignty. The Risen Lord has entered on His reign. The parousia has not yet happened but it has been anticipated. If the intensity of this rule is limited by the decree of the sovereign God, the extensity could not be so conceived; the world, not simply the Holy Land, belongs to the King-Messiah, and His claim must be laid upon it in its totality. Hence a restricted proclamation of the Gospel is irreconcilable with the concept of an enthroned Messiah. The disciples must have been conscious of this, even as they knew they were living in a new age, the age of the Spirit's outpouring. They also knew that the world to come had not yet arrived, but in their consciousness of the achieved redemption of the Lord and his resurrection to the right hand of God, they were certain that the time before the end must be short. He Himself was leading them in their mission to Israel and He would lead them in the time of the end to accomplish the miracle of the world's conversion — 'Lo, I am with you always, even to the end of the age'.

If this be consonant with the facts of the situation, it would indicate that the chief difference between the Hellenists and the Judaistic Christians in Jerusalem was in their understanding of the significance of Easter. The former believed that with the Resurrection of the Messiah the new age had dawned and the time of the mission to the nations had arrived, hence they embarked on that work without delay. The majority in Jerusalem concentrated on the proclamation to their own nation and looked for the Last Day as the time when the Gentile mission would be accomplished. Both groups could claim eschatological traditions for their outlook.[1]

The conclusion to which we are led by the previous discussion is that the authenticity of the Commission to baptize, far from being

---

[1] With modifications, this exposition is in harmony with views expressed by Schniewind, op. cit., p. 279; Michel, op. cit., p. 22; Lohmeyer, op. cit., p. 416; and especially Jeremias, whose work, *Jesus' Promise to the Nations*, deals with this theme.

discredited by examination of the evidence, is reasonably well supported by it. That the earliest disciples demanded and administered baptism in the name of the Lord Jesus from the beginning of the Church's existence is comprehensible if they believed that they had a command from their Lord to do so; it is much more difficult to accept the idea that their practice was due to a spontaneous revival of Johannine baptism among them, still less that they adopted the baptism of proselytes to Judaism for converts to the Church. There would seem to be good reason for Stauffer's dictum: 'How this Christian practice of baptism originated is a puzzle that only begins to be solved if we come at last once more to conclude that the tradition of the Risen Lord giving a missionary charge is to be taken seriously'.[1]

Our discussion concerning critical questions surrounding the Great Commission has served in no small measure to illuminate its significance. We have especially considered its context in the exaltation of Jesus to universal sovereignty: as Messiah He is Lord of all, *therefore* (οὖν, v. 19) all should know it and acknowledge that sovereignty by becoming His disciples. The root idea is that of kingship;[2] but since the Messiah is Redeemer as well as Ruler, the term *disciple*, with its personal associations of companying with the earthly Jesus, is a more fitting term than the less personal subject.

'Make disciples of all nations', runs the command.[3] How is this brought about? It might be considered as self-evident that disciples are made by the preaching of the gospel; that such as have become disciples are then baptized, and the baptized proceed to instruction; the two participles baptizing ... teaching ... successively follow the action of the main verb. Objection has been taken to this interpretation, however, for since the New Testament Epistles do not appear to reckon with the phenomenon of an unbaptized disciple, how can one become a disciple and then be baptized? Accordingly it is proposed that the participles describe the manner in which a disciple is made: the Church is commissioned to make disciples *by* baptizing men and

---

[1] *New Testament Theology*, E.T., 1955, p. 160. See also F. M. Rendtorff, *Die Taufe im Urchristentum*, 1905, p. 37; Lindblom, op. cit., p. 60; A. Oepke, *T.W.N.T.*, vol. 1, 1933, p. 537; J. Crehan, op. cit., pp. 72 ff.

[2] Lindblom, op. cit., p. 95.

[3] It is generally agreed that the Latin rendering of μαθητεύσατε by *docete*, followed by Luther in his translation, 'Lehret alle Völker', is mistaken. Rengstorf writes, 'Unlike the Greek outside the New Testament, μαθητεύω in the New Testament is always used transitively for "make disciple" (Mt. 13.52, 28.19, Acts 14.21)', *T.W.N.T.*, vol. IV, 1942, p. 465. See further the lengthy discussion in Lindblom, op. cit., pp. 124–32; he concludes that in our passage μαθητεύσατε may be rendered as Χριστιανοὺς ποιήσατε.

putting them under instruction. An explanatory note to this effect has been inserted in the current edition of the Luther Bible, and it has actually governed the translation of the passage in the Danish version of the Bible.[1] Its influence has been felt even in England's shores.[2] Now whatever the merits of the baptism, which this exegesis is intended to support, the exegesis itself is dubious. From the linguistic point of view, Lindblom has pointed out that when participles in Greek are co-ordinated with the main verb they are linked by means of a καί, or τε. . . καί, or δέ: if they follow one another without any such binding conjunction or particle they must be viewed as depending on one another or depending in differing ways on the chief verb.[3] This accords with the situation envisaged in the Commission, that proclamation of the redemption of Christ should be made and those responding in repentance and faith should be baptized and come under instruction. Baptism and instruction do not stand in the same relation to the action of making disciples. The chief action in the main verb is preaching, the plain commonsense of which is doubtless the reason for its lack of mention; but the preaching must be received if a hearer is to become a disciple, so the reception of faith is also presupposed in the verb μαθητεύσατε, 'Make disciples'. It is when a hearer believes and is baptized that he becomes a full disciple; which is the same as saying that a disciple is made such *in baptism by faith*. The relationship denoted by the participle 'baptizing' to the verb 'Make disciples' (μαθητεύσατε), therefore, cannot baldly be stated as instrumental, even if it expresses more than manner or accompanying circumstances. The truth is that the mystery of God's redemptive dealings with man by the Spirit of Christ cannot be compressed into the ordinary rules of syntax, however true it be that the latter can shed light on them. Baptizing belongs to the means by which a disciple is made. The instruction comes after. Grammatically that is expressed by saying that the participle διδάσκοντες (teaching) is to be seen as subordinate to the whole expression μαθητεύσατε βαπτίζοντες (Make disciples, baptizing), theologically by observing that the kerygma precedes the didache, the offer of grace before the ethics of

[1] 'Gå derfor hen og gør alle folkeslagene til mine disciple, idet I døber dem i Faderens og Sønnens og Helligåndens navn, og idet I laerer dem at holde alt det, som jeg har befalet jer'. This is a remarkable example of translators forgetting to remove confessional spectacles when rendering the Scriptures into their own tongue, and fortunately a rare one.

[2] See the popular brochure on baptism issued by the Church of England, *Church Albums*, No. 1.

[3] See his lengthy discussion, op. cit., pp. 236–72, especially 251 f. The rule concerning participles is given also in Blass-Debrunner's *Grammatik des n.t.lichen Griechisch*, 10th ed. 1959, par. 421.

discipleship, and it is when the gospel of grace is received that the ethics of gratitude may be learned and applied.[1]

The convert is baptized 'in the name of the Father and of the Son and of the Holy Spirit'. What is the significance of the phrase 'in the name of'? In view of our knowledge that the terms it translates in both the Greek εἰς τὸ ὄνομα and the Hebrew-Aramaic לְשֵׁם (לְשׁוּם) were well known formulae, it is surely a mistake not to acknowledge the a priori likelihood that the common use is intended in our passage. The difficulty is to decide which formula is the controlling one, the Greek or the Hebrew. Heitmüller argued that anyone who admitted that Mt. 28.19 did not reproduce a 'word of the Lord', and thus did not go back to an Aramaic original, had no ground to deny the characteristic Greek meaning of the phrase εἰς τὸ ὄνομα; it signified in our passage 'appropriation to the Father, Son and Holy Spirit with the use of this name'.[2]

Undoubtedly this meaning would fit the drift of the passage well; the peoples are to become disciples of the sovereign Lord and baptism is a means to this end; the idea of appropriation, dedication, submission, belonging, that attaches to the Greek use of εἰς τὸ ὄνομα, perfectly accords with the major motif of making disciples.

But what if, contrary to Heitmüller, one believed that Mt. 28.19 had connection with a 'word of the Lord', and thus that the saying was dependent on an Aramaic original? What then is the significance of εἰς τὸ ὄνομα? Curiously, in the last resort, not much difference from the former, although the route by which the result is reached diverges considerably. The basic meaning of the Hebrew לְשֵׁם is 'with respect to'; it can denote both the basis and purpose of that which is named. For example, in Mt. 10.41, to receive a prophet 'in the name of a prophet' (εἰς ὄνομα προφήτου) is to welcome him *because* he is a prophet; while in the more famous Mt. 18.20, the two or three who meet 'in my name' (εἰς τὸ ἐμὸν ὄνομα) do so *in the interests of* the cause of Jesus. Strack-Billerbeck give three examples from Rabbinical literature to illustrate the meaning of εἰς τὸ ὄνομα in Mt. 28.19, and they are worth recounting. (i) Heathen slaves on their

---

[1] It is not to be thought that this interpretation is due to the writer's confessional relationships; it is the one most commonly found in the standard commentaries, including those on Matthew by the Roman Catholic Lagrange, the Anglicans A. Plummer, W. C. Allen, such varied Lutherans as Klostermann, Lindblom, Schlatter, Michel, the Presbyterian theologian John Murray (*Christian Baptism*, p. 45) etc. It should further be noted that this is the understanding of the Commission reproduced in the Longer Conclusion of Mark, where the Matthaean μαθητεύσατε πάντα τὰ ἔθνη, βαπτίζοντες αὐτούς is replaced by κηρύξατε τὸ εὐαγγέλιον πάσῃ τῇ κτίσει, ὁ πιστεύσας καὶ βαπτισθεὶς σωθήσεται, Mk. 16.15 f.

[2] *Im Namen Jesu*, p. 121.

entry into a Jewish house were compelled to receive a baptism לְשֵׁם שִׁפְחוּת, 'in the name of slavery', i.e. to become slaves; similarly on their being set free they were to be immersed לְשֵׁם שִׁחְרוּר, 'in the name of freedom'. Baptism thus sets a man in that relationship which one has in view in the performance of it. On this analogy baptism, in the name of the Father, etc., sets the baptized in a definite relation to God; the Father, Son and Holy Spirit become to the baptized what their name signifies. (ii) An offering is slaughtered in the name of six things, לְשֵׁם שִׁשָּׁה דְּבָרִים: in the name of the offering, in the name of the offerer, in the name of God, in the name of the altar fires, in the name of the sweet savour, and in the name of the good-pleasure (before God). Here again לְשֵׁם defines the purpose in view, which varies considerably in this context. The offering is made *with respect to its intention*, i.e. whether for burnt offering or peace offering or passover offering etc.; *for the benefit of* the offerer; *for the sake of* (the true) God; *with regard to* the altar fires (that they be properly kindled); *in view of* the sweet savour and the delight that it yields to God. From this point of view baptism in the name of the Father, etc. takes place for the sake of God, to make the baptized over to God. (iii) An Israelite can circumcise the Samaritan, but a Samaritan must not circumcise an Israelite because the Samaritans circumcise 'in the name of Mount Gerizim', i.e. *with the obligation of venerating the God of the Samaritans* who is worshipped there. Strack-Billerbeck conclude after their survey: 'Baptism grounds a relation between the triune God and the baptized, which the latter has to affirm and express through his confession to the God in whose name he is baptized.'[1]

The fundamental likeness between the Greek and Semitic traditions is striking, a fact which Lindblom, writing before the appearance of Strack-Billerbeck's commentary, recognized. He urged that a baptism with respect to, with thought for, for the sake of, the Father, Son and Holy Spirit, in a context of becoming a disciple, was virtually entering into a relationship of belonging to the triune God; hence it amounted to more or less the same thing as the Greek tradition would have expressed.[2] That is a remarkable conclusion and has implications for our understanding of the relationship between the Semitic and Greek views of baptism in the early Church. Nevertheless, it is well for us to bear in mind the distinction between the two approaches, for

---

[1] *Kommentar zum Neuen Testament aus Talmud und Midrasch*, vol. i, 1922, pp. 1054 f.
[2] Op. cit., p. 169.

the Semitic phrase is undoubtedly more elastic and it has enabled the richer development to take place in the conception of the nature of the relationship of the baptized to God such as we see in the writings of the Apostle Paul.

Finally we should observe that the authority of Christian Baptism is of the weightiest order. It rests on the command of the Risen Lord after His achieving redemption and receiving authority over the entire cosmos; it is integrated with the commission to preach the good news to the world, and it is enforced by His own example at the beginning of His messianic ministry. Such a charge is too imperious to be ignored or modified. It behoves us to adhere to it and conform to it as God gives grace.

CHAPTER 3

THE EMERGENCE OF CHRISTIAN
BAPTISM: THE ACTS OF THE APOSTLES

(i) *Baptism an Institution in the Earliest Church*

IN discussing the representation given by the author of Acts of the
practice and views of the primitive Church relating to baptism, it
is impossible to avoid the critical question as to the accuracy of his
portrayal. It is not merely, nor even chiefly, a matter of determining
the author's supposed distance from or nearness to the events he
records. The claim for the authenticity of his picture would certainly
be strengthened on the view that Acts was written in the year A.D. 63,[1]
but as all know, it is impossible to prove that Acts was composed so
early; on the majority view that the two volume work Luke-Acts was
written in the eighties of the first century,[2] it would not be surprising
if some of the features of the earliest days had become blurred in
memory and Luke had sharpened them in the light of contemporary
usage. The difficulty of reducing to orderliness the variety of phenomena connected in Acts with the administration of baptism has
strengthened the supposition that this has, in fact, taken place; it is
believed that Luke has endeavoured to present the evidence of his
sources so as to conform it to the ecclesiastical practice of his day,
instead of allowing us to see a natural process of development taking
place in the life of the churches; his failure to subject the material to
his purpose has caused a confused picture to emerge, from which it is
our duty to recover the authentic outline. It would be misleading to
give the impression that such was the usual estimate of Luke's account of baptism in his history, on the contrary it is held by a
minority of scholars; but minorities are not necessarily wrong and their
eminence in this case adds to the necessity of examining their views
seriously.

Johannes Weiss notes that the three thousand converts of the day
of Pentecost were said to have been baptized, but he asks: How about
the hundred and twenty, the Apostles and brethren of the Lord and

---

[1] So Adolf Harnack, *The Date of the Acts and of the Synoptic Gospels*, E.T.,
1911.
[2] See the discussion in B. H. Streeter, *The Four Gospels*, 1924, p. 540.

the women (1.14)? Were they the only Christians who remained unbaptized? For it is self-evident that they did not receive Christian
baptism. Moreover Apollos appears in Acts 18 as an outstanding and
ardent Christian, who knew accurately and preached 'the things concerning Jesus', i.e. His life and death, but he had not received
Christian baptism, and we have no record that he did subsequently.
The men of Ephesus, whose story is immediately recounted (Acts
19.1 ff), were called 'disciples', i.e. Christians, though they had received only the baptism of John. These narratives show that baptism
was not from the outset a necessary mark of the Christian profession;
therefore, concludes Weiss, we must infer that the author has ante-
dated the situation when he introduces baptism as early as the first
Pentecost.[1] Jackson and Lake adopted a similar position.[2] They
suggested that Acts 1.4–2.4 embodies a primitive source, in which it
is represented that John's baptism in water has been replaced by
Christian baptism in the Holy Spirit; that Peter's speech on the Day
of Pentecost, explaining the manifestation of the Spirit's presence in
the outburst of 'tongues', is unsuitably, even inconsistently, followed
by the appeal for baptism to receive the Spirit (2.38), and the demand
that Cornelius and his friends be baptized after they had experienced
a like outpouring of the Spirit is superfluous and almost certainly
secondary.[3] They observe that in the narratives concerning Philip in
ch. 8 baptism is not connected with the gift of the Spirit, for the latter
is given only through the laying on of hands; a hint is thereby provided that the application of baptism in the name of the Lord Jesus
was introduced by the Seven and not by the Twelve. This would
correspond with the probability that the Seven were Hellenist Jews,
who would have been more open to the influence of the Diaspora than
the majority of the Jerusalem Church.[4]

In this kind of study it must be admitted that certainty is difficult,
if not impossible, to obtain. But if probability be the guide of life, I
am of the opinion that the way forward is tolerably clear here.

First, it cannot be without influence on our discussion that the
tradition of an administration of baptism in the earliest days of the

[1] *The History of Primitive Christianity*, E.T., 1937 (from the German *Das.
Urchristentum*, 1917), pp. 50 f.

[2] This contrasts with the views expressed by Lake in his article in the *E.R.E.*, in
which he explicitly repudiated the necessity to postulate a variety of sources in Acts
with different views on baptism, op. cit., p. 383.

[3] *The Beginnings of Christianity*, vol. 1, 1920, pp. 338 ff. Silva New expressed
an essentially similar view in her essay, 'The Name, Baptism and Laying on of
hands', in vol. v of the same work, 1933, p. 135.

[4] Op. cit., p. 341.

Christian community is taken for granted by Paul. The Apostle himself had been baptized and the allusions to baptism in his letters assume that all other Christians have been baptized. Weiss recognized that this was a difficulty for his view, especially if the conversion of Paul be dated not long after the death of Jesus. He could only suggest that Paul may have been baptized later, perhaps in Antioch, or that baptism was practised in Damascus from the very beginning.[1] But the former alternative is most unlikely. Paul's language in Rom. 6.1 ff, 1 Cor. 12.13, Col. 2.12 (and 1 Cor. 6.11, if it be a baptismal passage) implies that baptism is an initiation into life in Christ and the Church. I do not think that Paul could have bracketed himself with other Christians in his use of the first person plural in Rom. 6.1 ff if baptism had not been for him, as for others, the critical turning point in life, marking his deliverance from sin and experience of the new life of the Spirit. We are asked to assume an intolerable position if it be suggested that baptism could have brought that experience to Paul several years after his conversion. So also, the speculation that the Church in Damascus practised baptism from the beginning, at a time when the mother Church of Jerusalem did not, is without foundation and has nothing to commend it. It becomes yet more difficult of acceptance if we believe, as Lake did, that Paul's conversion took place only two years after the death of Jesus.[2] Why should the infant Church at Damascus introduce so momentous an innovation into the structure of the new community and depart from the ways of the mother Church and its Apostles? This is a suggestion born of embarrassment. In truth, Paul's witness to the primitive observance of baptism is of more decisive importance than Luke's, even though it is less direct, for it comes from within the situation. Whether or not Luke's sources imply a development of *thought* on the nature of baptism, it is doubtful that they imply a development in the *practice* of baptism, from its disuse to its application in the churches.[3]

The idea that the narrative of Pentecost is inconsistent with Peter's preaching of baptism is by no means clear, as also the similar judgment on his request that Cornelius and his company be baptized. The group on whom the Spirit came at Pentecost were disciples of Jesus. The crowd listening to Peter's address was a mixed group of Jews, proselytes and Gentile 'God-fearers'.[4] Since the Spirit was given by

---

[1] Op. cit., p. 196, n. 2.   [2] *Introduction to the New Testament*, 1938, p. 250.
[3] Bultmann considers that the witness of Paul is decisive as evidence for the primitive observance of baptism in the earliest Church, *Theology of the New Testament*, vol. 1, E.T., 1952, p. 39.
[4] Acts 2.5, 10. See Haenchen, *Die Apostelgeschichte*, 1957, p. 135.

the exalted Christ (Acts 2.33) and baptism expressed repentance and attachment to Him, it is not incomprehensible that the people were exhorted to repent and be baptized if they would share the same gift as the disciples of the Christ. The case of Cornelius will be considered later, but at this point we may say that the gracious bestowal of the Spirit, marking his acceptance with God, would naturally lead an Apostle acquainted with baptism to view this as a sign that Cornelius should be sealed as the Lord's in baptism and that he, though a Gentile, was fit to receive it.

Johannes Weiss is no more successful in his appeal to Pauline texts to prove that, over against the Lucan account, the oldest Christian view was 'entirely enthusiastic and supernatural'. From Rom. 5.5, Gal. 4.6, he deduced that the Spirit fell on men to show that God had chosen them, and baptism carried out in an earthly manner what God had already determined, but in Acts 2.38 we see the reverse order — baptism performed in hope that the baptized will receive the Spirit![1] Is it just, however, to cite Rom. 5.5, Gal. 3.2 for the 'enthusiastic' view, when the former passage is followed by the very realistic baptismal exposition of Rom. 6.1 ff and the latter by equally clear baptismal theology in Gal. 3.26? In both baptismal texts the significance of baptism is not less than that implied in Acts 2.38. The latter passage, it is true, is only incipiently christological, whereas the Pauline texts are explicitly so; but since the repentance of Acts 2.38 has relation to the crucifixion of Christ, and it is the exalted Lord who has sent the Spirit, the difference is of theological maturity, not of substance. Both Paul and the author of Acts recognized the work of the Spirit before baptism, in baptism and after baptism, precisely as they saw the Spirit at work before conversion, in conversion and after conversion. We must beware of exaggerating distinctions in the various stages of what the New Testament writers probably saw as a unitary process. We shall return to this theme in dealing with the relation of baptism to the Spirit in Acts, but at this juncture it cannot be said that the position of Weiss and Lake is supported by the evidence we have considered.

Recognition must certainly be taken of the fact that the first company to receive the Spirit at Pentecost had not received Christian baptism. It is not immediately apparent however that Apollos and the Ephesian 'disciples' should be regarded as on the same footing as they, despite Luke's employment of the term 'disciples' ($\mu\alpha\theta\eta\tau\alpha\iota$) for the latter. The Ephesian disciples of John were on the fringe of the

[1] Op. cit., p. 624.

Church, and it is not right to determine the nature of Christian baptism by reference to them. In the period of transition, when the effects of the ministries of John and of Jesus overlapped with that of the Apostles and their contemporaries, borderline cases were sure to occur; but the position of most men was not on the border and it is with the appropriation of salvation by mankind that we are concerned. I do not think that the lack of baptism of the hundred and twenty at Pentecost should be regarded as an insoluble puzzle. They had lived as the associates and disciples of the Christ, and to them and in them first was manifest the intrusion of the new creation into this, signified by the sending of the Spirit from the exalted Christ. The old disciple-relationship was set in a new key, enriched with new grace, and for this the experiences of the resurrection had prepared them. Granted that this meant a new beginning (they would not have understood the terminology of 'the Body of Christ') it was most surely the climax of the whole dealings of the Christ of God with them. For which reason it is false to set the circumstances of the Apostles on the day of Pentecost on a level with those of Cornelius and his company. It is understandable that Peter should have asked for the baptism of *these* people: it would have been absurd for Peter to have asked John to be baptized after the Pentecostal outpouring, or for John to have asked for Peter's baptism. In the mission of the Church to the world no group can be compared with the company of witnesses of the Resurrection, gathered in the name of the Lord on the day of Pentecost in expectation of the fulfilment of the promise. It is a misguided logic that deduces from their experience a primitive theology of the needlessness of baptism or the insignificance of any baptism that may have been administered by them. Grant that the mother of Jesus may not have been baptized, that James and his brother and sisters may not have been baptized, that even some others of their company may not have been baptized: their relationship to Christ was unique and their experience of his Spirit was unique; we cannot leap from them to the motley assembly that witnessed their ecstasy at Pentecost and the world without that was to hear their gospel. These had to listen to the good news and respond to it in repentance and faith; and if the Apostolic proclamation included the demand that this repentance and faith be objectified in baptism, and gave promise that God would answer such expression of repentance and faith, neither Pentecost nor Easter morning makes the demand inconsequential and the promise ridiculous. Equally this does not of necessity confine the miracle of Pentecost to Apostolic administration nor imprison it within water;

both Acts and Paul make that clear, and who that seeks a doctrine of baptism would have it otherwise? It is Jesus, crucified and risen, Who is the secret of Pentecost and of baptism alike; neither is explicable without Him and neither is insignificant with Him.

That leads us to a further observation. On the whole, the representations of baptism in Acts are primitive. They are not inconsistent with the developed views of baptism in Paul, the Pastorals, and the Fourth Gospel, but neither are these views to be found in the book; we also recall the absence from Acts of any baptism in the name of the Trinity, as in Mt. 28.19. Baptism is administered in the name of the Lord Jesus and takes no little of its significance from that fact, as we shall show later. An indication of this primitive atmosphere has been found in Acts 4.10 ff, where reference is made to *healing* in the name of Jesus and *preaching* in the name of Jesus, with a hint of *baptism* in the name of Jesus; the Risen Christ is thus at the centre of all three activities.[1] With this primitiveness of theology the primitiveness of context may be noted. Schlatter pointed out that from the first, Christian baptism was associated with repentance, and in the Jerusalem of the earliest days of the Church that message had a sharp edge: the Jews had rejected and killed the Messiah of God. This was a crime against God and responsibility for it lay upon the whole people (cf Acts 2.23). One recourse alone was open to them: they must repent their wickedness, confess it and seek reconciliation with God. To this end baptism was a fitting conclusion to the gospel proclamation; for baptism in the Name of the Lord Jesus connoted not alone a cleansing from sin but an expression of dissociation from the rejectors of the Messiah and a means of association with the Messiah and His people. In that historical context a more appropriate expression and means of turning to God could hardly be devised.[2]

Finally, it may be permitted at this point to recall the strength of the testimony that Jesus authorized baptism during the early period of His ministry (Jn. 3.22 ff, 4.1 ff) and the evidence for the authenticity of the command of the Risen Lord to baptize (Mt. 28.18 ff). This cannot but affect our view of the reliability of the witness in Acts as to the primitive administration of baptism in the early Church;

---

[1] The hint of baptism is in the connection of salvation (σωτηρία) with the *name* of Jesus, just as the appeal that men believe on the name of Jesus and be saved (σωθῆναι) is conjoined with baptism, Acts 2.40, 16.31 ff. See Heitmüller, *Im Namen Jesu*, p. 298; Schlier, 'Zur Kirchlichen Lehre von der Taufe', *T.L.Z.*, 1947, p. 326; Bultmann, *Theology of the New Testament*, p. 133.

[2] See Schlatter, *Theologie des Neuen Testaments, zweiter Teil, Die Lehre der Apostel*, 1910, pp. 419 f, *The Church in the New Testament Period*, E.T., 1955, pp. 26 ff.

for while it is comprehensible that the leaders of the Church in Jerusalem should be slow in carrying out their task among the nations of the world, there is no reason to believe that they hesitated to fulfil it among their own people. Moreover, the fellowship of those who responded to their proclamation was fostered by and expressed in the 'breaking of bread' (Acts 2.42). This fact shows, as F. Büchsel observed, that the piety of the primitive community was not without its 'cultic acts', in which the fellowship of the Spirit was experienced. Büchsel added: 'A religious possession, that includes in itself the cultic, does not originate without a cult act. It follows logically that the fellowship with the exalted Lord, that includes within itself a cultic act like the Lord's Supper, is also founded through a cult act like baptism'.[1] In the light of the evidence provided in Acts, that is not an unreasonable observation. Taken in conjunction with the foregoing argument, it would seem that the testimony of Acts as to the early administration of baptism is sound.

(ii) *The Nature of Early Christian Baptism*

If then baptism was practised in the earliest church, what significance was assigned to it? In the judgment of Bultmann, the rite at this period must have been essentially similar in import to the baptism of John; it was 'a bath of purification for the coming Reign of God'.[2] Is it likely, however, that a community constituted by the conviction that its Master had been 'installed Son of God in power by the resurrection from the dead' (Rom. 1.4), and exulting in its present possession of the Spirit of the age to come, should consider itself to be in the same position as the people about the Forerunner? If the ecclesia of the Risen Lord waited for the Consummation, it yet had entered on the inheritance; hence it had a *gospel*, which its preachers proclaimed with joyous certainty. The response to that good news was called for in terms of repentance, faith and baptism. W. F. Flemington therefore characterized the baptism of the earliest Church as a 'sacrament of the Gospel'.[3] Schlatter had the same point in view when he described the typical Apostolic sermon as 'a baptismal sermon': 'Its purpose was not merely the acceptance of an idea; it demanded a definite act'.[4] This is said from the aspect of baptism as a response to the gospel and acceptance of its gifts. There are grounds for going further and suggesting that the fitness of baptism to be a means of

---

[1] *Der Geist Gottes im Neuen Testament*, 1926, p. 258.
[2] Op. cit., p. 39.   [3] Op. cit., p. 124.
[4] *The Church in the New Testament Period*, p. 26.

response to the offer of the gospel is grounded in its fitness to be an embodiment of the gospel.

(i) As has been mentioned, baptism in Acts is always administered 'in the name of Jesus Christ' or 'in the name of the Lord Jesus' (2.38, 8.16, 10.48, 19.5). In our discussion on the meaning of εἰς τὸ ὄνομα, it was pointed out that in the last resort there is not much difference between Heitmüller's view, that 'in the name of' signified 'dedication to . . . with the use of the name', and that of Strack-Billerbeck, that it meant, 'with respect to, for the benefit of, for the sake of', though the latter was preferred as being consonant with the Semitic background of the command to baptize and as having greater elasticity of application. The same applies to its use in Acts, especially as it generally appears in passages with a Semitic background. From Acts 22.16 it would seem that the name of Jesus was invoked by the baptismal candidate; it is also likely that the name was called over the candidate by the baptizer.[1] Leenhardt not unreasonably concluded from this that we have to do with a rite which draws its whole meaning from the person of Christ and the relationship established with Him.[2] The believer was baptized 'for the sake of' the Lord Jesus and made over to Him. But who was this 'Lord'? The crucified One, raised and exalted by the Power of God to be the Messianic King. However rudimentarily it may have been grasped and defined in the earliest days of the Church, the baptism it practised proclaimed that a Redemption had been accomplished, the new age was dawning (the idea of resurrection could not be dissociated from the Kingdom and new creation), the new covenant had been made whereby it might be entered, and the Spirit who was its first fruits and pledge could be received. There is no question as yet of the Pauline idea of baptism as participating in the death and resurrection of the crucified and Risen Lord, but the idea at the root of that conception was of necessity present, viz. that baptism related the believer to the Redeemer, who by His redeeming acts had won redemption. To compare this with the baptism of John is to see that in the baptism of the Community of the Risen Lord we have a different sacrament.

(ii) That the Name was on the lips of the candidate baptized as well as uttered by the baptizer is harmonious with the dual nature of baptism as an act of man and an act of God.

Taking the former aspect first, it is to be observed that the declaration of the Name was made before man and before (unto!) God. It was therefore uttered in *confession* and *prayer*. That baptism should

---

[1] Such is a possible implication of Jas. 2.7.   [2] Op. cit., p. 36.

be both an occasion of confession and itself a confession is wholly natural. Heitmüller thought that the ancient practice of tattooing was the closest parallel to the use of the Name in baptism; soldiers commonly scratched in the skin or branded themselves with the sign of their commander, and still more commonly a worshipper of a god bore on himself the name or emblem of the divinity he served.[1] The parallel is interesting, but there is hardly need to invoke it. Baptism is an overt, public act that expresses inward decision and intent; since it is performed in the open, and not in secret, it becomes by its nature a confession of a faith and allegiance embraced. If baptism 'in the name of Jesus' is a baptism 'with respect to Jesus', and so distinguished from all other kinds of baptism by its relation to Him, then to submit to it becomes a confession of trust in Him. It is but natural that what is involved in the event itself should be brought to explicit mention and that the confession, 'Jesus is Lord', be *uttered* by the one baptized. Surprisingly enough, we have no certain instance in Acts of this confession being made at baptism, but the well known Western text of Acts 8.36 ff provides one. The Ethiopian eunuch, on hearing the gospel, asks Philip what prevents his being baptized; according to this tradition Philip replies, 'If you believe with your whole heart, it is permissible', and the eunuch affirms, 'I believe that Jesus Christ is the Son of God'; upon this he is baptized. Despite the preparedness of Cullmann[2] and Crehan[3] to champion the authenticity of this reading, its absence from our most reliable textual authorities compels a *non liquet* to the claim. Nevertheless its simplicity suggests its early date of composition, and it is agreed that it exemplifies the primitive custom of confessing Jesus as Christ and Lord at baptism, of which Rom. 10.9, Eph. 5.26, 1 Pt. 3.18 ff provide further hints.

The name of the Lord Jesus is *confessed* by the baptismal candidate and is *invoked* by him. Just as baptism is an occasion of confessing faith in Christ and is itself a confession, so it is the occasion of prayer by the baptizand and is itself an act of prayer. This has been questioned by some exegetes, but perhaps through lack of imagination (not to speak of lack of experience of being baptized as a believer and of witnessing such baptisms). Baptism in the name of the Lord Jesus, whatever else it came to imply, was in the earliest time a baptism 'for the sake of' the Lord Jesus and therefore in submission to Him as Lord and King. He that in baptism 'calls on the name of the Lord'

[1] *Taufe und Abendmahl*, p. 12.
[2] *The Earliest Christian Confessions*, E.T., 1949, p. 19, n. 4; *Baptism in the New Testament*, p. 71.
[3] *Early Christian Baptism and the Creed*, 1950, p. 9.

(Acts 22.16) undergoes baptism in a prayerful spirit; it becomes the supreme occasion and even vehicle of his yielding to the Lord Christ. Here is an aspect of baptism to which justice has not been done in the Church since its early days: baptism as a means of prayer for acceptance with God and for full salvation from God, an 'instrument of surrender' of a man formerly at enmity with God but who has learned of the great Reconciliation, lays down his arms in total capitulation and enters into peace. Baptism is peculiarly appropriate to express such a meaning, especially when the Pauline depth of signification is added to it. No subsequent rite of the Church, such as confirmation, adequately replaces it. The loss of this element in baptism is grievous and it needs to be regained if baptism is to mean to the modern Church what it did to the earliest Church.

(iii) The name of the Lord Jesus is called over the baptized. He therefore *dedicates himself to* the Lord and *is appropriated for Him*; since this is done by the command of the Lord, an act performed on His behalf, we must view it as an appropriation *by* Him. This implies an effective action by which the Messiah enrols the baptized as one of His subjects and accords to him a place in the Kingdom of God. He that is so recognized by the Christ becomes an heir of the future glory and a recipient of its present redemptive powers.

We are presuming here, of course, that ideal conditions prevail; the New Testament writers never question that when they speak of baptism. They take it (as we must) that the candidate is neither a liar nor a hypocrite and that the action is performed, not for the automatic fulfilment of the predestined purpose, but as a meeting point for a penitent sinner and a merciful Redeemer. If baptism be an 'instrument of surrender' by one conquered by the love of Christ, it is equally the gracious welcome of the sinner by the Lord who has sought and found him. Consequently, baptism is regarded in Acts as the occasion and means of receiving the blessings conferred by the Lord of the Kingdom. Admittedly, this way of reading the evidence is not characteristic of our thinking, but the intention of the author is tolerably clear.

(*a*) In the passage already cited, Acts 22.16, the exhortation to Paul, 'Rise and be baptized, and wash away your sins, calling on His name', implies that his sins will be washed away in his baptism accompanied by prayer. The word of Peter in Acts 2.38 conveys a similar impression: 'Repent and be baptized in the name of Jesus Christ for the forgiveness of your sins' ($\epsilon \grave{\iota}_S$ $\check{\alpha} \phi \epsilon \sigma \iota \nu$ $\tau \hat{\omega} \nu$ $\dot{\alpha} \mu \alpha \rho \tau \iota \hat{\omega} \nu$ $\dot{\upsilon} \mu \hat{\omega} \nu$). Markus Barth has pleaded the view that this means that baptism is received *in hope of* forgiveness: as in John's baptism (Lk. 3.3), repentance is the point of departure for baptism and forgiveness is the point of arrival, but baptism stands between as the promise but not the occasion of receiving the blessing.[1] This is surely pressing language expressive of purpose in a manner never intended. In the baptismal passage of Rom. 10.10 it is said:

> For with the heart faith is exercised for righteousness ($\epsilon i s$ δικαιοσύνην),
>
> And with the mouth confession is made for salvation ($\epsilon i s$ σωτηρίαν).

Here it is evident that faith is directed to the Lord for the purpose or with the result of receiving righteousness, and confession is made in order to receive, or with the effect of receiving, salvation; the point of time of the bestowal of the gift is not mentioned, but it is not needful to do so; faith turning to the Lord receives the grace sought, just as the confession made in baptism receives the salvation of God. That the baptism administered by John awaits the Messiah's advent for its ratification in divine vindication, and the baptism administered in the name of Jesus receives immediate response, is due to the distinction between the time of the Forerunner and that of the Risen Lord. Cleansing is the primary meaning of baptism in all religious groups that have practised it; but when baptism is administered in the name of the Lord who died and rose for the 'blotting out' of sins (Acts 3.19), this aspect of its significance is immeasurably strengthened.

(*b*) The outward act of confession and dedication to Jesus as Lord has as its corollary identification with the people who acknowledge Him as Messiah. This desire of the baptized to number himself with the people who invoke the Name of Jesus is answered by his graciously being incorporated in baptism into the community of those who inherit the Kingdom. The outward and inward aspects of this transition would have been viewed in the primitive Church as unitary, even as the free decision of the convert and the gracious act of God are simultaneously expressed in baptism. It is worth noting that the consciousness of baptism as a passage from the unbelieving world (or unbelieving Israel!) to the believing people of the Messiah seems to have existed from the beginning of the Church. After the appeal of Peter on the day of Pentecost, 'Repent and be baptized in the name of Jesus Christ' (2.38), a final summary of his message is added, 'Save yourselves *from this crooked generation*' (2.40); whereupon, 'They that received his message were baptized, and on that day about three

[1] Op. cit., p. 140.

thousand souls were *added* (*to the Church*)' (2.41). Apart from an explicit statement, words could hardly have expressed more clearly the conviction that by baptism the convert forsakes the Israel that had rejected the Messiah, to join the community that owned His sovereignty.

It needed but a short period of time for this outward demarcation of the people of the Messiah Jesus provided by baptism to become clear; so soon as hostility towards the Church was manifested by the authorities, it would have become a notorious sign. This situation is reproduced in our own day in communities inimical to Christianity, when baptism involves a breach with the entire unbelieving population.[1] On the other hand baptism as incorporation into the people of the Kingdom is an element of baptismal teaching that was destined to be developed by Paul in his characteristic doctrine of baptism as incorporation into the Body of Christ.

(*c*) The third and perhaps most impressive gift of God in baptism is the Spirit, the possession of which was frequently accompanied in the earliest Church by spectacular charismatic gifts and signs. That the gift should be associated with baptism is to be expected. For baptism in the name of the Messiah Jesus related the believer to the Lord of the Kingdom, who had received the Spirit from the Father that He might pour Him forth upon His people and so fulfil the promise given through the prophets (Acts 2.33); if Pentecost saw the corporate fulfilment of that promise in the waiting Church, the baptism of faith, confession and prayer to the King-Messiah individualized it for the believer.[2]

At this point we must pause and ask whether this is not simplifying a complex and much debated issue: is the relation between baptism and the gift of the Spirit really represented in Acts as that of the occasion and/or means of bestowal? If so, how are the phenomena to be explained that appear to contradict this interpretation?

(iii) *Baptism and the Spirit in the Acts*

Here we must exercise patience as we consider the evidence of the Acts on this issue. A mere recounting of the chief occasions when the

[1] I have received eye-witness accounts of baptismal services in India during which each baptism was accompanied by a hiss of disapproval from onlooking villagers and after which the baptized were cut off from former associations in their villages.

[2] There is an echo of this teaching, whether by accident or design, in Tit. 3.6; the language used of the gift of the Spirit in baptism is curiously similar to that explaining the phenomena of Pentecost in Acts 2.33; see Bornkamm, 'Die neutestamentliche Lehre von der Taufe', *Theologische Blätter*, 1938, p. 52; Thornton, *The Common Life in the Body of Christ*, 2nd ed. 1944, p. 190.

Spirit is said to have been bestowed on men is sufficient to reveal the problem.

At Pentecost the Spirit came upon the disciples with no other condition than that of prayer; they are not baptized in the name of the Lord Jesus, either prior to or after the event.

At the close of his address on the same day, Peter calls for his hearers to repent and be baptized, with a view to receiving forgiveness and the Spirit. The impression is given that the gift of the Spirit will be given in or immediately upon baptism (2.38).

The Samaritans are evangelized by Philip and baptized by him, without receiving the Spirit. The Apostles Peter and John are sent by the Jerusalem Church; they pray for the Samaritans, lay hands on them, and the Spirit is bestowed (ch. 8).

The reverse order is seen in the Cornelius episode. He and his people hear the word and the Spirit falls upon them all; Peter concludes that this is a divine sign that they should be baptized and commands them so to be. (Observe that Peter explicitly likens this event to the experience at Pentecost, 10.47.)

Apollos is introduced as an Alexandrian Jew, mighty in the Scriptures and instructed in the way of the Lord; 'fervent in (the) spirit', he preached accurately 'the story of Jesus' (τὰ περὶ τοῦ ᾿Ιησοῦ), but he knew only the baptism of John. Priscilla and Aquila give him further instruction and he is commended by the brethren to the Church at Corinth, where he powerfully preaches the word (18.24 ff). No mention is made of any further baptism administered to Apollos. In the immediately succeeding paragraph, however, we read of twelve 'disciples', who had received the baptism of John but did not possess the Spirit; Paul imparts Christian instruction to them, baptizes them in the name of the Lord Jesus, lays hands on them, and they receive the Spirit (19.1 ff).

To account for these divergencies of practice and harmonize the theology (or theologies) presumed by them gives fair room for the exercise of ingenuity, and it cannot be said that it has been wanting in the explanations provided. Some of the difficulties are attributable to the meagreness of the descriptions; the needful information for their satisfactory solution has not been provided. For example, it is impossible for us to know with certainty whether all the disciples on whom the Spirit came at Pentecost had been baptized by John; some of them surely were, many of them may have been, but it is hazardous to build a theory on the conviction that all of them *must* have received John's baptism. Was Apollos a Christian before Priscilla and Aquila met him? Did Luke mean that he was full of zeal 'in the Holy Spirit'? Did he receive Christian baptism? We can suggest answers to these questions, but not with certainty. Much energy has been expended on trying to recover traditions which Luke has utilized in writing his narratives and thereby some plausible solutions of the puzzles have been propounded;[1] but the subjective element in these reconstructions makes them at best tentative and leaves one with a feeling of disquiet.

A well known ordering of the evidence is provided by Johannes Weiss and by Jackson and Lake. By ranging the narratives of Pentecost along with the Cornelius incident (chs. 2 and 10), and that of the Samaritan community with those of Apollos and the Ephesian disciples (chs. 8, 18, 19), they produce a well defined evolution of baptismal theology: first, the Spirit is believed to be given solely on the basis of faith in Jesus as Messiah (Peter's demand for baptism in 2.38 and the statements that he baptized converts at Pentecost and the members of Cornelius' household are to be viewed as editorial additions); secondly, the Spirit is mediated by baptism, as is seen in the additions just mentioned and in Paul's question to the Ephesian disciples, 'Did you receive the Holy Spirit when you believed?' (19.2); thirdly, the Spirit is mediated not through baptism but by the laying on of hands of Apostolic men (ch. 8).[2]

This is a neat solution, but it is produced at a price, viz. the denial of Luke's narrative at all points where the theory demands excision. If that is no refutation of the solution, neither is it a commendation of it; resort ought not to be made to such an expedient if a simpler explanation can be found. Moreover in one cardinal respect the denial is to be challenged, viz., the insistence that the practice of baptism is not primitive in the Church; this has already been considered by us and found to be improbable. But before we consider the other alleged stages of the development it would seem wise briefly to review afresh the evidence.

We have already considered the position of the original disciples on whom the Spirit came at Pentecost. There would seem to be good reason for regarding their experience as unique. The turn of the ages had occurred in the death and resurrection of the Messiah. The full significance of what they had witnessed could not have been grasped at this point by the disciples, but they knew that the exaltation of the

[1] See especially the commentary on Acts by Haenchen in the series founded by H. A. W. Meyer, *Die Apostelgeschichte*, 11th ed. 1957.
[2] Johannes Weiss, op. cit., pp. 622 ff; Jackson and Lake, op. cit., vol. 1, pp. 337 ff.

Messiah meant the beginning of the eschatological era and that the days of the outpouring of the Spirit were at hand, according to the promise through the prophets and the word of their own Lord. It was upon this expectant company that the Spirit descended; as disciples already made over to the Lord, witnesses of his resurrection, His commissioned ambassadors to the world and now possessors of His Spirit, there was no call for them to be baptized; for everything that baptism signified in its divine and human aspects had been realized in them.

That Peter's hearers on the day of Pentecost were in a different situation from this needs no demonstration. To judge of his address they had no understanding of the gospel, whatever facts they may have possessed concerning the life and death of Jesus. They had to come to terms with God, repent from their sin and turn to His Messiah. Hence the appeal: 'Repent and be baptized every one of you in the name of Jesus Christ for the forgiveness of your sins, and you will receive the gift of the Holy Spirit' (2.38). Precisely what connection is here envisaged between baptism and the gift of the Spirit? Leenhardt considers that a certain separateness between the two events is assumed. 'The promise should normally be fulfilled, and one may legitimately believe that it will be; however Peter does not appear to think that it will necessarily follow immediately on the baptism of water. God will intervene according to the promise, but the baptismal rite does not bind Him, it does not constrain Him to fulfil His promise *hic et nunc*'.[1]

As with the related question of the connection between baptism and forgiveness, this distinction between baptism and the fulfilment of the promised gift of the Spirit is hardly to be received. Naturally, God does not bind the impartation of the Spirit to the rite of baptism, any more than He binds His other gifts to it or to any other rite; but such a negative observation has nothing to do with the declaration of Acts 2.38. As S. I. Buse has pointed out, the form of statement in this passage, 'Repent and be baptized . . . and you will receive the gift of the Holy Spirit', is similar to that in Acts 16.31, 'Believe on the Lord Jesus, and you will be saved'; the kind of interpretation advocated by Leenhardt and his followers has no room in the latter passage.[2]

[1] Op. cit., p. 37. Marcus Barth enthusiastically supports this view. He insists that no appeal can be made to Acts 2.38 for support of the belief that water baptism and Spirit baptism are identical: 'The human action of getting baptized and the divine gift of the Holy Spirit are too clearly distinguished'; on the analogy of Acts 22.16, baptism should be regarded as a prayer for the Spirit, which God will answer in His time, op. cit., pp. 141 ff. A similar position is adopted by J. Schneider, op. cit., pp. 32 f.   [2] *Christian Baptism*, ed. A. Gilmore, p. 117.

Whatever the relationship between baptism and the gift of the Spirit elsewhere in Acts, there appears to be no doubt as to the intention of Acts 2.38; the penitent believer baptized in the name of Jesus Christ may expect to receive at once the Holy Spirit, even as he is assured of the immediate forgiveness of his sins.

That the situation of Cornelius and his company is related to, yet different from, the Pentecost narrative is apparent. In reporting the event to some very dubious compatriots in Jerusalem, Peter explicitly likens the experience of Cornelius and friends to their own at the original sending of the Spirit (11.17). Despite not having companied with the Lord in Galilee, nor having seen Him in the resurrection, nor having owned Him as Lord, these Gentiles received the Spirit with no other mediation than the hearing of the Word (10.44). In this they differed from the Apostles, as also from his hearers in the Temple at Pentecost, for the latter had first to be baptized before receiving the Spirit. Marcus Barth sees proof here that God is free in His gifts, that He reaches even the heathen without sacrament, and that water baptism is neither a substitute for Spirit baptism, nor its symbol, nor its vehicle, nor sacramental means for conveying it.[1] On the other hand Schlier interprets the descent of the Spirit on Cornelius and his friends as a gift of charismatic spirit; by this means God reveals that He has chosen them and that they are therefore worthy to receive baptism, which will bestow on them the Spirit who will make them members of the Church and impart salvation to them![2] Neither of these views is likely to be correct. A clue as to the way we are intended to interpret the event may be seen in the astonishment of the Judaistic Christians at the manifestation of the Spirit in these Gentiles (10.45 f) and the indication in Peter's speech that he, too, felt helpless before such a sovereign act of God (11.17). His question, 'Who was I to be able to hinder God?' shows that Peter interpreted the divine action as revealing God's acceptance of Cornelius and his company and the divine pleasure that they be baptized and so enter the Church of the Messiah. In that case the gift of the Spirit without baptism must be viewed as exceptional, due to a divine intervention in a highly significant situation, teaching that Gentiles may be received into the Church by baptism even when they have not removed their uncleanness through circumcision and sacrifice (11.18).[3]

It will be recalled that Jackson and Lake bracketed the narratives

---

[1] Op. cit., pp. 158 f.   [2] T.L.Z., 1947, p. 327.
[3] Such is the common interpretation of the narrative of ch. 10, see Lampe, op. cit., p. 75; Büchsel, op. cit., p. 257, n. 2; Heitmüller, Im Namen Jesu, p. 302; Bultmann, N.T. Theology, vol. 1, p. 139.

of Apollos and the Ephesian disciples (18.24 ff, 19.1 ff) with that of the Samaritan community (ch. 8) as representing a basically similar viewpoint and experience. This is not to be accepted without examination, nor indeed should we too hastily take it for granted that the cases of Apollos and the Ephesian disciples are identical.

What status are we to accord to these men whom Priscilla and Aquila and Paul met in Ephesus? Since the latter are described as 'disciples' ($\mu\alpha\theta\eta\tau\alpha\iota$) and in all the other thirty instances of the word occurring in Acts it means Christian disciples, it is often urged that they were Christians. Marsh affirmed this interpretation and concluded on this basis that 'the baptism of John', which they and Apollos were said to have received (18.25, 19.3), must denote the rite *originated* by John and practised during the lifetime of Jesus (Jn. 3.22 ff). Having received the earlier form of the Christian rite, they were ignorant of the supplementary Spirit baptism which Jesus had promised. The statement that Paul rebaptized these disciples is therefore to be doubted; Luke failed to appreciate the significance of the story handed on to him in the tradition.[1] Eduard Schweizer, on the contrary, considers that although Luke's terminology shows that he regarded Apollos and the Ephesian group as Christians, historically the former was a Jewish evangelist and the latter were disciples of John; Luke's interpretation is due to his inability to find a place in his theological scheme for a Jewish missionary working in the 'Spirit' and a group that remained loyal to John the Baptist.[2]

There is however, nothing improbable in the existence of groups of people baptized by followers of John the Baptist and standing at varying degrees of distance from (or nearness to) the Christian Church. There must have been many baptized by John himself, who had listened to the preaching of Jesus and His disciples, who had received the gospel with more or less intensity of conviction and faith and regarded themselves as His followers, yet who had no part in Pentecost or its developments. They would have been chiefly in Galilee, but also in Judea. The number of such people must have increased greatly as disciples of John baptized more converts, and the mission

---

[1] Op. cit., pp. 156 f.

[2] *T.W.N.T.*, vol. VI, article $\pi\nu\epsilon\hat{\upsilon}\mu\alpha$, p. 411. Haenchen pursues a similar path; he follows Loisy's conjecture that originally this narrative concerned a Baptist community in Syria (where such groups were more common) and that Luke transferred it to Ephesus to glorify Paul's ministry there and to exalt Christian baptism over against Johannine baptism. Luke's 'interest' may be freely admitted, but whether he dealt with his sources in such a manner to serve his ends is another matter. The exposition given below seems to me to deal more satisfactorily with the evidence.

of the Apostles and their associates advanced; the variety of faith will have extended almost indefinitely, as the distance from John (and Jesus) lengthened. For which reason there is no need to identify the situations of Apollos on the one hand and the Twelve Ephesians on the other, even though they were located in the same city. Of Apollos it is said that (*a*) he was powerful in the Scriptures, (*b*) he was instructed in the way of the Lord, (*c*) he declared and taught accurately the story of Jesus. If the picture of this man had not been conjoined with that of the Ephesian disciples, no one would have doubted that he was a Christian evangelist. Two further items however complicate the picture: (*d*) he was 'ardent in the spirit', (*e*) he knew only the baptism of John. On the basis of ch. 2 one would expect that, not having received Christian baptism, he did not possess the Spirit. But is it plausible to interpret $\zeta\epsilon\omega\nu$ $\tau\hat{\omega}$ $\pi\nu\epsilon\upsilon\mu\alpha\tau\iota$ as 'having a fiery temperament'? Such a use of $\tau\grave{o}$ $\pi\nu\epsilon\hat{\upsilon}\mu\alpha$ (the spirit) is very unusual, though not without parallel.[1] Preisker urged that the context strongly favours rendering $\tau\hat{\omega}$ $\pi\nu\epsilon\upsilon\mu\alpha\tau\iota$ here as 'in the Holy Spirit', for the phrase stands between a clause describing Apollos as instructed in the Gospel and another which states that he preached it: 'In that case we have before us a one time disciple of John who has gone over to the disciples of Jesus and now works with great success as an apostle of Jesus (cf. 1 Cor. 1.12, 3.4 ff). That which makes him above suspicion, and even of equal worth with all other Christian messengers, despite his not having received baptism in the name of Jesus, is the decisive fact that $\pi\nu\epsilon\hat{\upsilon}\mu\alpha$, i.e. Spirit, has come upon him'.[2] If such be true, and it seems to me to be more satisfactory than any alternative construction, it is likely that Priscilla and Aquila felt that they had no need to do more than perfect Apollos' knowledge of Christian teaching and that a further baptism was needless. Apollos, like Cornelius, had received the Spirit without Christian baptism, but under wholly different circumstances; he is to be compared rather with the hundred and twenty disciples of Jesus on Pentecost morning, though he was not a witness of the resurrection. He is representative of an unknown number of disciples of John who passed quietly unto the sovereignty of the Messiah Jesus and who were graciously visited by the Spirit without any further ecclesiastical intervention.

The Ephesian disciples were on a different footing. Acts 19.4 implies that they were not truly believers in 'the Coming One' who was

---

[1] In Acts 17.16 it is said of Paul $\pi\alpha\rho\omega\xi\acute{\upsilon}\nu\epsilon\tau o$ $\tau\grave{o}$ $\pi\nu\epsilon\hat{\upsilon}\mu\alpha$ $\alpha\mathring{\upsilon}\tau o\hat{\upsilon}$, 'his spirit was roused to anger'.

[2] 'Apollos und die Johannesjünger in Act 18.24–19.6', *Z.N.W.*, 1931, p. 301.

Jesus; Paul therefore instructs them in the Gospel. In reply to his earlier question 'Did you receive Holy Spirit when you believed?' they had stated, Ἀλλ' οὐδὲ εἰ Πνεῦμα "Ἁγιόν ἐστιν ἠκούσαμεν (v. 2). This astonishing answer is most naturally translated, 'We have not even heard that Holy Spirit exists'. But how could any Jew or Gentile instructed in Judaism, let alone disciple of John the Baptist or Christian (!), have been ignorant of the idea of a 'Holy Spirit', when it figured so distinctly in eschatological expectation and in religious thought generally? Two suggestions are possible: either these disciples are so far removed from the authentic tradition of John's teaching that they possessed but a crude notion of it — in which case they must have been Gentile converts ('God fearers'?) rather than Jews; or the language is unusually cryptic and Luke really intended to convey the thought, 'Holy Spirit is not yet given', though this is not, in fact, what is written.[1] Büchsel inclines to the former view[2] and Lake and Cadbury to the latter.[3] More important than deciding that issue is the question why Paul baptized these 'disciples', despite their having received the baptism of John.[4]

The answer is perhaps less complex than we have generally viewed it. In Paul's eyes these men were not Christians — no man who was without the Spirit of Jesus had any part in the Christ (Rom. 8.9). Probably Luke himself did not view them as Christians; his employment of the term μαθηταί, disciples, is a gesture in recognition that they were neither on a level with unbelieving Jews, nor classed with pagans. They were men who had paused on the way without completing the journey, half-Christians, occupying a zone of territory that could exist only at that period of history when the effects of John's labours overlapped with those of Jesus. It is not impossible that these men of Ephesus had known some contact with the (presumably small) Jewish-Christian community in the city (the 'breth-

---

[1] The Western text reads λαμβάνουσίν τινες instead of ἐστιν. Despite its early attestation in P. 38 and P. 41 this is obviously a paraphrase of our present text.
[2] Geist Gottes, p. 141, n. 6.
[3] Op. cit., vol. IV, p. 237.
[4] Marcus Barth's suggestion that v. 5 continues Paul's explanation to the Ephesian disciples, and is not a piece of narrative from Luke, so that Paul is made to teach that people baptized by John had in fact been baptized in the name of the Lord Jesus, is an ingenious tour de force with not a shadow of probability. It is an artificial reading of the passage; it contradicts the basic contrast between John's baptism and Christian baptism as seen in the Gospels and Acts and as demanded by the baptismal teaching of the Epistles; and it implies that in receiving John's baptism Jesus was baptized unto Himself! See Barth's exposition in his book pp. 166 ff, and the comments by S. I. Buse, Christian Baptism, pp. 120 f; J. Hering, 'Le Baptême dans le Nouveau Testament', Revue d'Histoire et de Philosophie religieuses, 1953, p. 256.

ren' of 18.27) and that therefore they had some knowledge of Jesus; if so it must have been limited and vague (cf. vv. 2–4). Men unsure of the gospel and not possessing the Spirit need Christian baptism, whatever has gone before; Paul ensured that they received it.

One important point emerges from the contrast between Apollos and the Ephesians: if we are not over-burdening the silence concerning a further baptism administered to Apollos, it would appear that the baptism of John was good enough in one case but not in another.

The exposition given above indicates why: where submission to the Messiah Jesus is accompanied by the possession of the Spirit, Johannine baptism needs no supplementing; where both are lacking, baptism in the name of Jesus must be administered. Comparing this with the Cornelius episode, it would appear that the baptism of John is viewed as an adequate preparation for Christian discipleship where it is completed in faith and by the Spirit. Apollos needs no additional baptism, but Cornelius must be baptized. But Johannine baptism without the Spirit is defective and must be followed by the baptism that bestows it.[1]

Were the phenomena concerning baptism and the Spirit in Acts confined to the incidents we have discussed, the total picture would not be unduly difficult to portray. The account of the evangelization of Samaria in no small degree complicates it. For here we meet with a baptism in the name of the Lord Jesus (8.16) administered to a people that believed the gospel preached by one of the Seven (8.12), yet which did not confer the Holy Spirit (8.15). The circumstances of the Samaritans therefore differed from those of the men of Ephesus, for the Samaritans had heard an authentic presentation of the gospel and had received *Christian* baptism; yet they were not in the happy position of Cornelius and his people, who received the Spirit immediately on hearing the gospel before baptism. The needful conditions for the reception of the Spirit had apparently been fulfilled; what lacked these people still?

Since the gift that had been withheld was bestowed through the laying on of the hands of Peter and John, it is natural to suppose that the absence of this rite had been the cause for the Samaritans not receiving the Spirit earlier. But this raises a difficulty: in only one other place in Acts is the rite of laying on of hands conjoined with baptism, Acts 19.6, and curiously that is applied to men who had also earlier received a defective baptism. Can it be that the failure to mention the laying on of hands when other baptisms are described is

[1] For the significance of the laying on of hands, see pp. 122–5.

due to its general recognition as an integral part of the baptismal initiation? We recall the well known dictum of Silva New: Belief in Jesus, baptism, remission of sins, laying on of Apostolic hands and reception of the Spirit formed a single complex of associated ideas, *any one of which might in any single narrative be either omitted or emphasized*.[1] On this interpretation the laying on of hands was an integral part of all the baptisms recorded in Acts and no reader of the book in the time of its composition would have understood otherwise. Lake and Cadbury agree and suggest that, over against John's baptism, the laying on of hands was the specifically Christian element in baptism.[2]

Despite the plausibility of this explanation and its wide acceptance, it surely involves us in an intolerable position. For the significant element in the chain of associated ideas is not that faith, baptism, forgiveness and Spirit presume laying on of hands as an integral factor, but that these come to an efficacious end by reason of Apostolic agency: it is *Apostolic* hands that bestow Holy Spirit. If laying on of hands by the administrator of baptism was regarded as part of the initiatory rite in the early church, then Philip would doubtless have laid hands on the Samaritans when he baptized them, and they would have received the Spirit! But this is excluded by Silva New's dictum. On the basis of the position assumed by her, baptism could be administered only by an Apostle, for the rite is a single whole. Yet to insist that the Apostles personally conducted every baptism in the primitive Church is an absurdity that no one, so far as I am aware, has asked us to believe.[3] Apart from the physical impossibility of the Twelve visiting so many places at once, the narrative of Acts excludes it; for in chapter 11 we read of unknown Hellenist Christians, scattered by the persecution at Stephen's death, evangelizing in Phoenicia, Cyprus and Antioch, and in the last named place 'the hand of the Lord was with them and a great multitude that believed turned to the Lord' (11.21). On Silva New's assumption the mention of the faith

[1] *Beginnings of Christianity*, vol. V, p. 134.

[2] Op. cit., vol. IV, p. 93. Bultmann gives a similar judgment, adding that this element of the rite probably accompanied the speaking of the Name, hence the bestowal of the Spirit became attached more to the naming of the Name and laying on of hands than to purification by water, *New Testament Theology*, vol. 1, pp. 134 ff.

[3] Not even Gregory Dix made the demand. In his lecture, 'The Theology of Confirmation in relation to Baptism' (London 1946), he set aside the baptism of the Eunuch by Philip as too abnormal to be viewed as a good precedent and the baptism of Paul by Ananias as too briefly described for it to be known in what circumstances it was performed, and then remarked: 'I can find no other account of a "baptism" before A.D. 200 which is not performed either in the presence of an Apostle or else of *the whole liturgical assembly of the local Church*', p. 16. I do not share Dix's concern for the Apostolic administration of baptism, but his contention that baptism is an ecclesiastical and not private ordinance is surely right.

(πιστεῦσαι) of these Antiochians includes their baptism and forgiveness, laying on of Apostolic hands and receiving of the Spirit. But no Apostle reached Antioch until Barnabas was sent from Jerusalem, by which time the Church was thriving!

It is not possible then to modify the suggestion here considered and admit that others than Apostles could administer baptism, but that in such cases laying on of hands by Apostles had to follow that the rite be fully efficacious? In my judgment the concession scarcely eases the problem, for the following reasons. (i) It involves the necessary postulate that almost from the beginning of the Church the rite of Christian initiation was in most instances divided, seeing that too many conversions in too many places took place for Apostles to be present at them all. This is to give the narrative of Acts 8 a priority over all other early Christian teaching on baptism that is scarcely to be justified, for the division of the initiatory rite at this time is hardly to be received. (ii) It demands the anachronism of imagining the Apostles travelling round Palestine conducting confirmations, and after a very few years dividing up the Mediterranean world into sees for the same purpose. Where is the evidence for such an idea? Moreover we should have to presume that this first visit to Samaria was followed by regular visitations, seeing that all subsequent baptisms by non-Apostolic persons had to receive a like completion; yet all agree that Acts 8 leaves the reader with the impression that the intervention of Peter and John was a critical affair for the regularizing of a situation, rather than administering the first confirmations in an unending series in that land. (iii) It is manifest that Ananias was no Apostle; yet he was commissioned by the Risen Lord to lay hands on Paul that he might be healed and receive the Spirit (9.17), and presumably it was he who baptized Paul in the Damascus community of believers (9.19). Certainly none of the Twelve had any hand in Paul's conversion, baptism and receiving of the Spirit, as he himself later emphatically related (Gal. 1.15 ff). (iv) The circumstances of the founding of the church in Antioch cannot be reconciled with the view we are considering, and they must have been duplicated in a number of situations unknown to us (including the founding of the church in Rome). Here is a church begun by humble Christians without Apostolic status, who had yet advanced in their evangelism beyond anything the Jerusalem Apostles had so far done. On hearing of this momentous forward move in the Christian mission, the church in Jerusalem sent to the Antiochian community an Apostolic representative, Barnabas. It is not said for what purpose Barnabas was commissioned, but there is not a hint that it was in order to lay hands on members of a congregation without the Spirit that they might receive it. On the contrary, Barnabas is reported to have seen the grace of God manifest in the church and to have rejoiced in it; the burden of his message was an appeal that they should abide still in the Lord (11.22 ff). Apart from any argument from silence, a church in which God's grace was conspicuous but from which God's Spirit was absent is hard to conceive; it is, in fact, a fiction of a bad theological imagination and a theory which demands it stands condemned.

Recognition of the difficulties involved in trying to relate the account of Acts 8 to the other baptismal narratives recorded by Luke has given rise to attempts to reconstruct the tradition or traditions utilized by him in his writing up of the story, in the conviction that he must have complicated the situation by introducing alien motifs. Attention is called to the fact that at no point in the story are Philip and Peter brought together and that it is curious that Simon Magus should seek to procure the power of the Spirit from another than the miracle-worker preacher who had so greatly impressed the Samaritan populace and himself. Accordingly it is suggested that originally but one Christian preacher featured in the story, whether Peter alone or Philip.[1] Haenchen plumps for Philip as the original hero of the narrative, for Simon would surely be more desirous of acquiring power to work miracles than to give others the gift of the Spirit; moreover the motive for the complication of the narrative is at once apparent: Peter and John are introduced into the story since the mission to the Gentiles can be fulfilled only by Apostles.[2]

It would be a relief to be able to accept such a reconstruction of the narrative, for on either view, whether it were Peter or Philip who evangelized Samaria, the embarrassment of an ineffective baptism that needed later supplementation would disappear. But tempting as it is, the suggestion cannot be received. For though Luke undoubtedly represents the Apostles as having a prime responsibility for the mission to the world, it is impossible to hold that he regarded the mission as their sole prerogative. He it is, after all, who has made it clear to us that the Hellenists took the initiative to fulfil the wider aspects of the commission of the Risen Lord recorded in Acts 1.8: 'You shall be my witnesses in Jerusalem *and in all Judea and Samaria and to the end of the earth*'. Although the first preaching of the gospel after the descent of the Spirit had a congregation representative of the wider world, the Apostolic action recorded in Acts 1–5 takes place wholly in

[1] See Lake and Cadbury, op. cit., p. 88.　　　　[2] Op. cit., pp. 265 f.

Jerusalem. The first preaching to 'all Judea and Samaria' takes place after the death of Stephen, by Christians 'scattered throughout the territories of Judea and Samaria', from whose number the Apostles are explicitly excluded (8.1), and who almost certainly were mainly the Hellenist supporters of Stephen. Philip's work in Samaria is cited as one example of this beneficial 'scattering' (8.4 ff), and the itinerant evangelism by unknown Hellenist preachers in Phoenicia, Cyprus and Antioch is given as another and parallel example, which action took place at the same time as the founding of the Samaritan church (11.19 ff). It may therefore be taken as certain that Peter was not the original preacher to Samaria in the tradition handed on to Luke; it will have been a Hellenist and there is no reason to doubt that it was Philip. The Apostles were privileged to be authentic witnesses of Jesus and the Resurrection; they were not empowered with a monopoly of obedience to the great commission.

But if they had no such monopoly they had special responsibility. The narrative of the mission in Antioch here sheds light on that concerning the Samaritan mission; for though there was apparently no question of the Gentile Church in Antioch being defective in its constitution and gifts, an Apostolic representative was sent to see that all was well; granting that such were the case, doubtless the approbation and blessing of the mother community was to be given. There is therefore nothing strange in the idea that the Jerusalem Church should have sent representatives to inspect such developments as were taking place in Samaria and Antioch. There would have been a natural desire to ensure that the new advances in the mission were duly regulated and to establish the solidarity of the new communities with the old. A parallel feature in Paul's experience may be seen, in his years-long desire to go to Rome 'to impart some spiritual gift' to the church there, that they might be 'established' (Rom. 1.11); how much more comprehensible is it that Peter and John should be sent at the epoch making juncture afforded by the Samaritan conversions for a similar purpose! Moreover if Luke thought it necessary to modify his narrative in ch. 8 for the sake of maintaining the prestige of the Twelve, why did he not do likewise in ch. 11? It would have been simple to introduce a reference to Barnabas laying hands on the disciples in Antioch. And why did he not iron out the mention of the Spirit in the report of Ananias laying hands on Paul? Ananias could have been used for Paul's recovery of sight without being instrumental in Paul's receiving the Spirit. That Luke incorporates such features shows that he had no sensitivity about this matter. It would therefore seem most in accord with the evidence he provides, to assume that he was not responsible for the tradition of Peter and John's visit to Samaria, nor for the claim that by them the Samaritans first received the Spirit; he found the tradition ready to hand and declined to adjust it to his other narratives.

It will have become evident that the problem of the Samaritan community consists not in the fact that the Apostles were sent to help them, nor even that the latter had power to impart a spiritual gift ($\tau\iota$ $\chi\acute{\alpha}\rho\iota\sigma\mu\alpha$ $\pi\nu\epsilon\upsilon\mu\alpha\tau\iota\kappa\acute{o}\nu$), but that the Samaritans needed it so urgently. Why was the baptism they received at Philip's hands so defective, if, as we have seen, Philip's ability to administer an effective baptism cannot be called into question? What caused the withholding of the Spirit in conditions under which it would be expected that the promise would be fulfilled? The answer that most readily comes to mind, and that is most commonly adopted, postulates the exercise of a divine and sovereign restraint in the bestowal of the Spirit, the uniqueness of which was due to the peculiarity of the situation; the Samaritan believers needed a divine revelation that in receiving the Christ they had become integrated into the messianic people, rooted in ancient Israel and newly created through the redemptive action of the Messiah. In the words of G. W. H. Lampe: 'Until the fact had been demonstrated that the leaders of the Church were in full accord with Philip, and that the Samaritan converts were really acknowledged and accepted by the heads of the original Apostolic body the gift of the Spirit which was received through membership of the Spirit possessed community was withheld. An unprecedented situation demanded quite exceptional methods. The imposition of hands is primarily a token of fellowship and solidarity; it is only secondarily an effective symbol of the gift of the Spirit; it becomes such a symbol solely in virtue of being a sign of incorporation into the Church of the Spirit'.[1] An objection can be raised against this interpretation: if an intervention of such proportions was required in the case of the

---

[1] Op. cit., p. 70. Lampe himself, while recognizing the plausibility of this view, hesitates to adopt it, since in his estimation it throws no light on the laying of hands on Paul by Ananias and on the experience of the Ephesian disciples. He prefers to follow up a clue offered by Dom Gregory Dix, that in Acts laying on of hands is for the ordination of prophets; this would fit Luke's stress on the duty of the Church to prosecute the world-wide mission, for which the Spirit's gifts were given, and it would fit the circumstance of Acts 8: Peter and John incorporate the Samaritans into the Apostolic Church and by the divine effecting of a Samaritan 'Pentecost' it is demonstrated that a new nucleus of the missionary Church has been established (op. cit., pp. 71 ff). Of itself this would not be an impossible variation of the above represented view; it would emphasize the nature of the fellowship into which the Samaritans are called as one of mission, which must be accepted by them in their very act of incorporation into it. But difficulties are raised when it becomes the

Samaritans, why was a like intervention not manifested in the Antiochian community, when a similarly decisive step forward in the mission was made? It could be argued that the divine restriction of grace was even more called for in the first genuinely Gentile church than in Samaria, which at least had traditions stretching back to ancient Israel. Awareness of the force of this contention excludes dogmatism in adhering to the former viewpoint, but there is one factor that could be held to distinguish Samaria from Antioch or from any other Gentile Church: its tradition of animosity towards the Jews was almost as old as its religion. The enmity was made permanent by the Jewish destruction of the Samaritan temple at Gerizim in 128 B.C., and it seems to have been mutual.[1] It is comprehensible therefore that, in the Body wherein there is neither Jew nor Greek, it should have been demonstrated by the Spirit Himself that it was specifically a Body wherein there is neither Jew nor Samaritan. The Apostolic integration of the Samaritans into the Church of the Messiah signified an effective healing of an age-long division and it was signalized with divine approval by the Spirit coming upon the estranged people, manifesting their inclusion into the Israel of God.

The major difficulty of this view is to know how to conceive of a Church consisting of believers baptized in the name of the Lord Jesus yet not possessing the Spirit sent by the Risen Lord. It seems to be a theologically impossible abstraction. To Paul the idea would have been a contradiction in terms, for the Spirit is the Mediator of the life of Christ to the Christian, as He is the soul of the Body which is the Church.[2] Luke himself was aware that Philip's ministry in Samaria was marked by the Spirit's blessing, for it was accompanied by the manifestation of 'signs and wonders' among the people (8.13). His theology was such that he would have taken it for granted that the Spirit worked in the lives of these people for their salvation (cf. 13.48). Moreover, there is much to be said for the common belief that his description of the Eunuch's going on his way 'rejoicing' ($\chi\alpha\iota\rho\omega\nu$,

major clue to all other examples of laying on of hands, such as the case of the Ephesian disciples, ch. 19, where it assumes a tenuous and artificial aspect. If we are to accept that the Spirit was in any way withheld from the Samaritans, there is more to be said for the common view, that the importance of their incorporation into the common life of the new Israel had to be grasped by them; outward integration into the community of the Messiah had to take place before the Spirit of the Messiah was given.

[1] If Jn. 4.9 relates to a Jewish conviction as to the uncleanness of Samaritans ('Jews do not use vessels together with Samaritans', so D. Daube, followed by Barrett, *St. John*, p. 194) rather than mere refraining from association with Samaritans, it yet reflects a judgment upon the Samaritans which would have been greatly resented, but which was the culmination of an attitude long held in respect to them.

[2] See e.g. Rom. 8.1 f, 8.9, 1 Cor. 12.13, Eph. 4.4.

8.39) indicates the convert's possession of the Spirit; yet Luke speaks of a similar 'rejoicing' of the Samaritans on their conversion (πολλὴ χαρά, 8.8)! Can it be, therefore, that he regarded these Christians as *not without the Spirit but without the spiritual gifts that characterized the common life of the Christian communities?* There is no doubt that Luke was particularly interested in the charismatic phenomena connected with the gift of the Spirit. Paul clearly distinguished between the charismata and the possession of the Spirit as such; all Christians possess the Spirit but not all possess the same gifts; the latter are sovereignly dispensed by the Spirit (1 Cor. 12.11) but they should be prayerfully sought by the Christian (1 Cor. 12.31, 14.1, 12). Whether Luke was sensitive to the distinction between life in the Spirit and gifts of the Spirit it is hard to say, but he has preserved for us one saying which is relevant to this discussion. In Lk. 11.13 we read, 'If you who are evil know how to give good gifts to your children, how much more will your Father in heaven give Holy Spirit to them that ask him?' It is generally agreed that this is a paraphrase of the Matthaean, 'how much more will your Father in heaven give good things to them that ask Him?' (Mt. 7.11), and that Luke interpreted the saying of the highest good that the Father gives — the Spirit. Yet since it is set in a context of teaching on prayer, thus in instruction intended for the Church even more than for them that are without, Luke will especially have had in mind the desirability of Christians praying for *the charismata of the Spirit*, though he would not have excluded the application of the saying to enquirers who should call on God for the salvation of which the Spirit is the pledge. Here we see an example of Πνεῦμα, Spirit, being used in an ambiguous manner, not dissimilar from that in Acts 8. It suggests that Luke may have been describing a Church in which the Spirit was not unknown but in which the Spirit's gifts were not yet manifest. Whether he would have viewed the lack as in part due to the Samaritans themselves cannot be known. But it is clear that the laying on of hands by Peter and John, accompanied by prayer for their lack to be made good, was at once followed by the impartation of the charismata, for such is the unexpressed assumption of Simon's desire to have the gift of imparting Holy Spirit (v. 19); an evidence of supernatural power of this order was new to him and the power of communicating it was to be coveted.

It is freely to be admitted that this interpretation can only tentatively be put forward, but it does seem to make sense of an otherwise incomprehensible situation without resorting to drastic emendation of Luke's narrative.[1] On this basis we must continue to distinguish the experience of the Samaritans from that of the Ephesian disciples: the application of laying on of hands in the case of the latter accompanied the administration of Christian baptism, with the resultant bestowal of the Holy Spirit; the former brought an increase of grace to the Church with gifts of ministry for its edification.[2]

Our review of the evidence in Acts relating to the gift of the Spirit and baptism should have made one important lesson plain: while baptism and the Spirit are set in close relation, allowance must always be made for the freedom of God in bestowing the Spirit. Bornkamm expresses this finely: 'The admitted uncertainty in the relation between baptism and the reception of the Spirit remains a sign that the Lord of the Church maintains His rule in freedom and that order in the Church must not be perverted to bind Him to itself'.[3] That goes further than the customary adage that God is not bound to his sacraments; it affirms positively that the Lord of the Church does exercise His freedom and we must ever be on the look out for its use. It is a freedom as truly in operation today as it was in the Apostolic Church.

This same evidence suggests another lesson: the really important element in baptism is not the rite but that to which it points — the work of the Spirit in the man who recognizes the claim of the Lord on him by virtue of His accomplished redemption and exaltation. Again and again we have had cause to remind ourselves that Christian baptism is baptism in the name of the Lord Jesus; in it the name of the Lord is called over the baptized, declaring him to be the Lord's, and the name is confessed and invoked by the baptized. It is this confessed relationship with the crucified, Risen Redeemer that is constitutive for Christian baptism and decisive for its significance. In this connection three recent writers on the doctrine of the Spirit in the New Testament have come to virtually the same conclusion on this matter, and it may be of value to cite their judgment. F. Büchsel sees

---

[1] It is not to be excluded that the historical facts may have been as outlined above and that Luke did not realize their precise import, assuming that the spiritual gifts so imparted denoted an initial giving of the Holy Spirit; but his hints of the Spirit's working in Samaria through the agency of Philip, before the arrival of the Apostles, seem to me to favour the interpretation here offered.

[2] The interpretation is not novel. Both J. Thomas (op. cit., pp. 382 ff) and H. Schlier (*T.L.Z.*, 1947, Sp. 328) advocated that as baptism in the name of Jesus could not be ineffective, the Samaritan believers must have received the Spirit of life and holiness but not the charismatic gifts. Thomas however seems to me to go too far in insisting that the baptism of the Spirit, in contrast to John's baptism in water, signified only the charismatic gifts, while Schlier tends to over-refinement in Luke's doctrine of the Spirit. It is surely a mistake to equate the unreflective doctrine of Spirit in Acts with the comprehensive and characteristic pneumatology of Paul.

[3] *Theologische Blätter*, 1938, p. 49.

baptism in Acts as repentance and faith coming to expression in an act that anticipates the turning and renewal of the whole course of life; by it the purely inward experience steps into the open and so comes to completion; consequently the act was the occasion for the bestowal of the Spirit. Not that the Spirit was bound to a rite; the connection was due to the turn of the ages that took place in the resurrection of Jesus, whereby baptism unto the Kingdom became baptism unto the Christ: 'It was precisely because of this union with the exalted Lord that baptism bestowed the Spirit'.[1] Von Baer went further in urging that the connection between rites of initiation (whether baptism or laying on of hands) and the Spirit was due to experience rather than to any formal schema; if a reason be sought for the experience the answer is clear: 'It is the point of the greatest religious tension, in which the soul dedicates itself to the Lord in order to submit itself wholly to His sovereignty in baptism to His name and it receives the full proof of the might of the Lord in the Holy Spirit'.[2] Such a statement needs supplementing with a reference to the Risen Redeemer and His achieved redemption if baptism is to retain its objective significance; and it is not necessary to dismiss the 'schema' that links baptism with Spirit if baptism is regarded as the 'kerygma in action'.[3] Nevertheless von Baer has expressed an essential element of baptism which is all too often minimised, and sometimes curiously despised — its nature as the climax of the soul's return to God. This is seen most starkly in Acts, where baptism is viewed more simply than in the writings of Paul. Finally we may cite Eduard Schweizer, who draws attention to the twice repeated utterance of the Lord, that John baptized with water but the disciples will be baptized with the Holy Spirit (1.5, 11.16); this shows that the supremely important matter was the outpouring of the Spirit and that baptism in water was the 'accident' of the greater gift. 'In which case', writes Schweizer, '2.38 teaches nothing other than that for Luke baptism belongs to the much more important fact of conversion'.[4] This judgment is surely true to the theology of Acts. It will cause offence to none who refuse to make conversion small, who see in it no merely human phenomenon but a turning of the sinner to God in Christ enabled by the Spirit, answered by the divine acceptance of the penitent, with all that implies of the gift of grace, hence a participation in the

---

[1] *Geist Gottes im Neuen Testament*, pp. 259 f.
[2] *Der Heilige Geist in den Lukasschriften*, 1926, p. 174.
[3] Flemington, op. cit., p. 123.
[4] Article πνεῦμα in *T.W.N.T.*, vol. VI, p. 411.

redemption of Christ through the Spirit. To such a conversion baptism 'belongs' as its embodiment, its completion and its seal.

There is therefore good reason for affirming again the description of baptism in the primitive Church, as represented in the Acts of the Apostles: it is the sacrament of the Gospel — proclaimed and received. Where the Gospel is accorded its true place in the modern Church the description can still hold good.

Note on the Laying on of Hands

The rite of laying on of hands is employed in the Old Testament in connection with:

  (i)   the offering of sacrifice (e.g. Lev. 1.3 f),
  (ii) the consecration of Levites in the service of the Temple (Num. 8.10),
  (iii) the imparting of a blessing (Gen. 48.14).

We are indebted to D. Daube for a clear differentiation of the significance of these acts.[1] The term used for the laying on of hands in the first two cases is סָמַךְ, to lean; the idea appears to be that by leaning hands on a person or animal a man 'poured' his personality into him or it, hence making him or it into a substitute. In the case of the scapegoat for example, the people as sinners were replaced by the animal, and the leaning of Moses' hands on Joshua resulted in Joshua becoming as it were a second Moses (Num. 27.18 ff, Deut. 34.9). For the conveyance of a blessing the verbs used are שִׂים or שִׁית, meaning to 'place' the hands; when Jacob placed his hands on the sons of Joseph there was no question of passing on the characteristics of his personality to them but rather of conveying some beneficial virtue. The use of hands in healing came under this same latter usage. Dr. Daube points out that there is no hint in the Gospels that Jesus laid hands on the Apostles for their ordination, for though it is conceivable that Joshua might become a second Moses, there could be no question (in the eyes of the New Testament writers) of anyone becoming a second Jesus. The blessing of the children by Jesus would have been accompanied by 'a gentle placing of the hands' — שִׂים or שִׁית, as in the healings recorded as having taken place with such action (Mk. 6.5, 7.32 f, 8.22 ff; cf. Mk. 16.16).

What kind of action is contemplated in the laying on of hands in baptism? This same writer suggests that without doubt the idea is that inherent in the term סָמַךְ — it signified the pouring of one man's

[1] See his lecture, 'The Laying on of Hands', in *The New Testament and Rabbinic Judaism*, 1956, pp. 224 ff.

personality into another. On this interpretation a complication arises, however, in the case of Ananias laying hands on Paul, for the purpose of the act is that Paul might both recover sight and receive the Spirit — which would involve both שִׂית and סָמַךְ in one act — touching *and* leaning! Dr. Daube suggests that Luke would have us understand that Ananias 'placed' his hands on Paul for healing (שִׂית) and the Holy Spirit miraculously came down from heaven as on Cornelius. It is surely more reasonable to infer that laying on of hands for baptism cannot be interpreted as coming in the category of transmission of personality (סָמַךְ); it must be an aspect of blessing (שִׂית).

Two matters of interest fall to be considered at this point, namely the extent to which laying on of hands was considered as integral to baptism and the significance of the rite. There is considerable diversity of opinion about both issues. In view of the scanty evidence at our disposal that is not to be wondered at.

It is impossible to dogmatize as to the time at which laying on of hands was conjoined with baptism. Luke records the use of the rite in connection with baptism only in Acts 19.1 ff, although its employment by Peter and John could be viewed as a completion of the baptism of the Samaritans; the laying of hands by Ananias on Paul *preceded* his baptism. In the light of the exposition given above of the narratives recorded in Acts 8 and 19, I can scarcely view with favour the commonly received notion that the experiences of the Samaritan and Ephesian disciples provided a norm for primitive Christian initiation; on the contrary, both are highly exceptional events. On the other hand, it is not to be assumed that the Samaritans were the only people on whom Peter and John laid hands that they might receive the blessing of the Spirit and it is similarly conceivable that Paul sometimes used the rite in administering baptism. The difficulty of postulating that from the beginning of the Church the rite was invariably conjoined with baptism is the absence of mention of its use in all other records of baptism in Acts, and the complete silence of Paul concerning it in his letters. That it was the normal accompaniment of baptism in the circle from which the Letter to the Hebrews emanated is certain (Heb. 6.1 f); that it was current in the whole Church from Pentecost onwards is unlikely; how long the process of adoption of the rite took is beyond knowledge.

More important to determine is the significance of the act. Here it is profoundly to be wished that some writers, enthusiastic in the cause of confirmation, would distinguish between exegesis of the New Testament and the exposition of ancient liturgies, for the two are not to be equated. To read, for example, the judgment of Gregory Dix, that the primitive Christians asserted 'with a disconcerting vehemence and frequency' that baptism of the Spirit was 'generally necessary to salvation' and that baptism in water was 'generally necessary to confirmation'[1] is to lose confidence in the ability of the writer to estimate New Testament evidence without prejudice. While the statement of R. Dix, 'In baptism we die to sin, in confirmation we rise again to righteousness; in baptism we sever our allegiance to the world, in confirmation we are admitted to the Church',[2] gives rise to a sense of futility in theological discussion, for the New Testament documents become meaningless when so alien an interpretation can be wrung from them. I confess to a similar disquiet in reading L. S. Thornton's *Confirmation, Its Place in the Baptismal Mystery*, where the view of baptism as producing the new birth and laying on of hands the gift of the Spirit is supported by tendentious expositions, as e.g. that the baptism of Jesus ended the preliminary period of His life and the descent of the Spirit upon Him began the ministry which culminated in the cross and resurrection (p. 121), or that Christian baptism is the counterpart in the individual's life to the Church's new birth at Easter and the laying on of hands the corresponding feature to the Church's experience of Pentecost (pp. 176 ff). While arguments of this kind are seriously maintained by scholars there is little hope of progress in ecumenical understanding, for minds of another cast can find no true meeting place in such discussions.

Where laying on of hands was integrated in the baptismal rite there can be no doubt that it underscored the reality of the gift of the Spirit in baptism. But the operative term is 'integrated': it was added to baptism, not in order to convey a *donum superadditum* that could not be associated with baptism as such, but to strengthen this element inherent in baptism itself. In that case the appeal currently made by many Anglicans to view the rites of Christian initiation as a single process must be taken with utmost rigour and the attempt to attribute forgiveness to one element, resurrection to another and the bestowal of the Spirit to yet another be abandoned. As Alan Richardson expresses it: 'In the New Testament the whole baptismal action is a unity which cannot be analysed into its component parts, and it is in the whole action that the Spirit is bestowed'.[3] For this reason, if the frequently advocated interpretation of laying on of hands be favoured,

---

[1] *The Theology of Confirmation in relation to Baptism*, p. 17.
[2] *Theology*, 1945, p. 252.
[3] *An Introduction to the Theology of the New Testament*, 1958, p. 355.

that it signifies the 'ordination of the laity', then the *total* baptismal event must be viewed as having that significance and not the concluding part only.[1] But in my judgment the grounds for attributing this idea to the New Testament communities are slender.

To Baptists this may appear to be a remote discussion, but historically it has not always been so. The laying on of hands in immediate connection with baptism was widely practised among Baptists in the seventeenth century, both in Britain and in the American colonies. It aroused no little controversy, but some of the protagonists were vehement in their adherence to it. An assembly of 'Messengers, Elders and Brethren' of General Baptist Churches, meeting in London 1656, stated: 'It is jointly agreed by this Assembly that mixed communion in breaking of bread with persons *denying* laying on of hands is not lawful' (!). The Standard Confession of 1660 was more positive and more explicit as to its significance: 'It is the duty of all such who are believers baptized to draw nigh unto God in submission to that principle of Christ's doctrine, to wit, Prayer and Laying on of Hands, that they may receive the promise of the Holy Spirit'. The practice gradually died out among the Baptist communities, although the desirability of liberty of judgment on the issue was urged among General Baptists as late as 1791. The practice has been retained to this day among Baptists in Denmark and Sweden, and it is being revived among other Continental Baptist groups. As an aid to the recovery of the full significance of baptism, it is to be desired that Baptists should give earnest consideration as to whether they should not once more incorporate the rite in their administration of baptismal initiation into Christ and the Church.[2]

[1] As Jerome implied in his well known saying *Sacerdotium laici, id est baptisma*; see A. M. Ramsey, 'The Doctrine of Confirmation', *Theology*, 1945, p. 198.

[2] On the relation of Baptists to the practice of laying on of hands, see the article by E. A. Payne, 'Baptists and the Laying on of Hands', *The Baptist Quarterly*, 1953–4, pp. 203 ff, to which I am indebted for much of the above information. It is an indication of the current tendency of Baptist thought in England that the service book, *Orders and Prayers for Church Worship* by E. A. Payne and S. F. Winward, 1960, contains directions for 'The Laying on of hands with prayer upon those who have been baptized', and recommends the observance of the rite either as part of the baptismal service or 'as soon afterwards as is convenient', p. 135.

CHAPTER 4

THE DEVELOPMENT OF CHRISTIAN BAPTISM IN THE APOSTOLIC WRITINGS

(i) *Baptism in the Pauline Literature*

IN considering the special contribution of the Apostle Paul to the doctrine of baptism one may either dismiss first the sayings of lesser importance and reserve the cardinal passages until last, or adopt the reverse procedure and plunge at once into a discussion of statements containing Paul's most characteristic teaching. The latter policy commends itself, since it is preferable to interpret obscure passages in the light of the clear than to proceed vice versa. Moreover it is easily possible to get started on the wrong foot with Paul's baptismal teaching. For example, an approach that starts from 1 Cor. 1.14 ff could well assume that Paul accords a minimum significance to baptism, yet to begin with 1 Cor. 15.29 invites an opposite emphasis, while 1 Cor. 10.1 ff has encouraged the view that typology is the vital clue to Paul's teaching on baptism. Accordingly we shall consider at once the most extensive exposition of baptism Paul has given, in Rom. 6.1 ff, and then move on to the related teaching in Gal. 3.26 f and Col. 2.11 f; by this means we may hope to gain a balanced estimate of the contribution of the other passages to the total picture thus outlined.

1. ROMANS 6.1 ff

In speaking of the relation of Paul's thought to that of his age, Albert Schweitzer wrote, 'One of the greatest problems of Paul's teaching is that it is something unique in Early Christianity; and yet it is not felt to be essentially different from it.'[1] That assertion holds good in respect to Paul's teaching on baptism generally and even to that contained in Rom. 6.1 ff. The Apostle's question, 'Are you ignorant that all we who were baptized into Christ Jesus were baptized into his death?' (v. 3) seems to imply that the content of the exposition that follows should be known to the Roman Christians.[2] If the

---

[1] 'Mysticism of Paul the Apostle', *E.T.*, 1931, p. 37.
[2] H. Lietzmann maintained that ἢ ἀγνοεῖτε or ἢ οὐκ οἴδατε always hints of something already agreed on. He cites Rom. 7.1., 11.2, 1 Cor. 3.16, 5.6, 6.2 f, 16, 19, 9.13, 15.24. The contention holds good for most of these but it cannot be pressed in all cases (see especially 1 Cor. 3.16, 6.16, 9.13); see *An die Römer*, 3rd ed. 1928, p. 67.

contention could be sustained that the idea of baptism as dying and rising with Christ was adopted by Hellenist Christians from the Greek Mystery Religions, there would be no reason why the Christians of Rome should not be acquainted with this teaching.[1] The relation between Paul's teaching and the Mysteries, however, is a highly debateable matter and can hardly be taken for granted at this point. It was long ago observed that the structure of vv. 3–4, 'We are baptized to his *death, buried* with him . . ., that as Christ was *raised* we should walk . . .' is reminiscent of the terms of the primitive kerygma cited by Paul in 1 Cor. 15.3 f, 'Christ *died* for our sins . . . was *buried* . . . has been *raised* . . .'. It would not be surprising if the custom had become established of applying the traditional language of the kerygma in baptism, when belief in it was confessed and its promise appropriated.[2] Michel indeed considers that Paul actually quotes a baptismal liturgy or hymn in Rom. 6.1 ff.[3] The difficulty of adopting this view without qualification lies in the absence from the other New Testament writers of this interpretation of baptism as a dying and rising with Christ and the fact that later writers who do mention it depend on Paul.[4] The 'Do you not know' of Rom. 6.3 could presume the currency of teaching analogous to that of Paul, without its possessing the precise features of Rom. 6. It was pointed out in our discussions on Acts, that a baptism in the name of the crucified and exalted Messiah for the forgiveness of sins and receiving of the Holy Spirit had at least the essential ingredients of Pauline theology. In view of the presence in the kerygmatic fragment, 1 Cor. 15.3, of the clause, 'Christ died for our sins', it is clear that the cleansing and forgiveness of sins associated with baptism must at an early date have been attributed to the power of Christ's death believed and confessed

[1] This view is, in fact, maintained by not a few exegetes and theologians. See e.g. Lietzmann, op. cit., pp. 67 f; Leipoldt, *Die Urchristliche Taufe im Lichte der Religionsgeschichte*, 1928, pp. 62 f; J. Weiss, op. cit., pp. 463 ff, 520 f; Bultmann, *N.T. Theology*, I, pp. 140 f; Dibelius, 'Paul', *E.T.*, London 1953, p. 93; Bornkamm, *Das Ende des Gesetzes*, 1952, p. 37, n. 5.

[2] This view was commonly expressed early in the present century. It may be found in von Dobschutz, 'Sakrament und Symbol im Urchristentum', *Theologische Studien und Kritiken*, 1905, p. 27; C. Clemen, *Primitive Christianity and its non-Jewish Sources*, E.T., 1912, p. 222; Rendtorff, op. cit., p. 48; A. Seeberg, *Die Taufe im Neuen Testament*, 1905, pp. 13 f.

[3] *Der Brief an die Römer*, pp. 128 ff. Michel considers that the 'we' style, in contrast to Rom. 5.12–21, betrays the language of a confession; whereas it is only rhetorical in vv. 1–2, its use in vv. 4–6, 8 is formal. The expression 'raised through the glory of the Father' is not Pauline and sounds as though it came from a confession. Similarly the key term σύμφυτοι 'united with', is not found elsewhere in Paul.

[4] This would apply to 2 Tim. 2.11 ff if the Pastorals are denied to Paul; the passage appears to cite a baptismal hymn which must be therefore older than the Epistle but which presumably comes from a Pauline circle. 1 Peter offers some slight parallels, but the Epistle is not without Pauline influences generally.

in baptism. An interpretation of baptism that regarded it as involving appropriation by the crucified and Risen Lord, forgiveness through His death and the gift of the Spirit could justly be regarded by Paul as one with his, even though none other than he stated its implications in the manner of Rom. 6.1 ff. It was Paul's task to deepen the understanding of the association with Christ in baptism, the manner of cleansing and the nature of the new life. In achieving this end his doctrine was both old and new.[1]

'Are you ignorant that all we who were baptized to Christ Jesus (εἰς Χριστὸν Ἰησοῦν) were baptized to his death (εἰς τὸν θάνατον αὐτοῦ)?' (Rom. 6.3). What is meant by baptism to Christ Jesus? Frequently εἰς after the verb βαπτίζειν denotes the goal desired and realized through baptism.[2] It would be possible to view baptism to Christ Jesus therefore as baptism in order to be *in* Christ, and so as 'baptism *into* Christ'. This interpretation is strengthened by the related passage, Gal. 3.26 f: 'You are all sons of God, through faith in Christ Jesus (ἐν Χριστῷ Ἰησοῦ). For all you who were baptized to Christ (εἰς Χριστόν) put on Christ. . . . You are all one man in (ἐν) Christ Jesus'. E. Best comments on this passage, 'The implied suggestion is that those who are "in Christ" had come "into Him" by baptism, and that therefore εἰς must carry the social and local meaning of ἐν'.[3] A difficulty is encountered by this view in that Paul declares the Israelites to have been baptized 'to Moses' (εἰς τὸν Μωσῆν, 1 Cor. 10.2), which can scarcely be said to mean 'into Moses'. Best thinks it possible to adhere to the same meaning even here, by viewing Moses as a representative of Christ: as the spiritual meat and drink partaken of by the Israelites was Christ, so the baptism was a true baptism into Christ.[4] Leenhardt, more reasonably, considers that as Moses was the instrument for carrying out the redemptive design of God, to be united with Moses was the condition for participating in the divine plan.[5] This last suggestion is more plausible, but in that case it lies near to hand to view the Israelite baptism to Moses (εἰς

---

[1] R. Schnackenburg adopts a position similar to that expounded here, and suggests that Paul *insinuates* his own interpretation into that which his readers held. (*Das Heilsgeschehen bei der Taufe nach dem Apostel Paulus*, 1950, p. 129). For reasons indicated above, the view espoused by Flemington and Cullmann, that the early connection between baptism, death and resurrection was due to the teaching of Jesus Himself concerning His own baptism (Mk. 10.38, Lk. 12.50), is to be rejected as unproven. See pp. 73–7.

[2] See Mt. 3.11, εἰς μετάνοιαν; Acts 2.38, εἰς ἄφεσιν ἁμαρτιῶν; 1 Cor. 12.13, εἰς ἓν σῶμα.

[3] *One Body in Christ*, 1955, p. 69.

[4] Op. cit., p. 72.

[5] *Épitre aux Romains*, 1957, p. 89.

τὸν Μωσῆν) as analogous to baptism *in the name of* Moses (εἰς τὸ ὄνομα Μωσῆς); the Israelites were baptized with respect to Moses, for his sake, for his allegiance.

Such a significance would suit both Rom. 6.3, and Gal. 3.27, bearing in mind that if εἰς = εἰς τὸ ὄνομα the phrase would have all the flexibility of the common לְשֵׁם. In the former passage it would fit the appeal 'Do you not know?', for this could well be the language commonly used of baptism by the Christians in Rome (as elsewhere), and represent a simplifying abbreviation of the somewhat cumbersome 'baptize in the name of Christ Jesus' (εἰς τὸ ὄνομα Χριστοῦ Ἰησοῦ), and it would enable us to see how Paul employed the traditional language of baptism to draw from it consequences in accordance with his own profounder understanding of redemption. Similar considerations apply to Gal. 3.27. We should not regard baptism to Christ (εἰς Χριστόν) as being identical with putting on Christ; rather the former act has the latter state as its effect. Paul could have well said 'Baptism to Christ *means* dying and rising with Him as it *means* putting on Christ, since he that is baptized to Christ participates in His death and resurrection even as he is united to Him'. But this is a use of *means* to denote implication, as when we render Phil. 1.21 as 'For me living means Christ and dying means gain'. Oepke is quite right in affirming that spiritual unity with the crucified and risen Christ in baptism is undeniable but that such an intention does not lie in the phrase βαπτίζειν εἰς.[1]

We may now be prepared for the possibility that baptism 'to his death' (εἰς τὸν θάνατον αὐτοῦ) of v. 3 is less complex — I nearly said less 'advanced' — than we usually take it to be. It would, of course, make good sense if we interpreted the phrase as defining precisely the implication of baptism to Christ Jesus: to be baptized to Christ Jesus is to be baptized *into* his death, to be plunged into it as it were, to participate in it in some fashion. Such is the usual under-

---

[1] Article βάπτω, *T.W.N.T.*, I. p. 537. Both Fuchs (*Die Freiheit des Glaubens*, 1949, p. 28) and Gaugler (*Der Römerbrief*, I Teil, 1945, ad loc) make a double mistake in rendering βαπτίζειν εἰς Χριστόν as 'plunge into Christ' (in Christus hineintauchen) and in defining it as meaning 'plunge into his death'. Such a rendering of βαπτίζειν εἰς is generally viewed as no longer tenable; βαπτίζειν is a technical term for baptizing *in water*, even where εἰς is used along with it, as 1 Cor. 10.2 makes clear: καὶ πάντες εἰς τὸν Μωσῆν ἐβαπτίζαντο ἐν τῇ νεφέλῃ καὶ ἐν τῇ θαλάσσῃ. And we have already seen that it is a mistake to identify the implications of baptism with its nature. The interpretation of βαπτίζειν εἰς in Rom. 6.3, Gal. 3.27 as = βαπτίζειν εἰς τὸ ὄνομα is assented to by J. Weiss, op. cit., p. 636; H. W. Bartsch, op. cit., p. 90; M. Barth, op. cit., p. 225; Schlier, *Den Brief an die Galater*, 1951, p. 125; R. Schnackenburg, in an article giving second thoughts after his book, 'Todes- und Lebensgemeinschaft mit Christus, Neue Studien zu Röm 6.1–11', *Münchener Theologische Zeitschrift*, 1955, pp. 41 f.

standing of the passage. Yet if 'we were baptized to Christ Jesus' takes up popular language, it may be more natural to interpret 'we were baptized to his death' as also possessing a vaguer meaning, i.e. we were baptized 'with reference to his death'. Its implications are then drawn out in the immediately succeeding lines.

To listen to the varied interpretations of this 'exposition' (in vv. 4 ff) is to be confronted with a veritable Babel of voices, most of which appear to be ignored or uncomprehended by the champions of the several views. The fierceness with which differing opinions are held indicates the desirability of patience in an effort to understand what the various Confessions are trying to say.

First let it be said that the consistent anti-sacramentalists need to listen. For them generally baptism is a symbolic attestation of a death and resurrection that have earlier been experienced, and the value of the action is chiefly confession and the joy of obeying the Lord's command to be baptized. This view has been espoused, though with a corrective in soteriology, by Marcus Barth; he maintains that as the burial of Jesus was an attestation of the finality, irrevocability and recognition of His death, so the burial of the believer in his baptism is a later confirmation of the finality, irrevocability and recognition of his own death in the death of Jesus on the cross.[1] This writer however has overlooked the significance of the fact, not unperceived by him, that Paul did not write, 'We were buried through baptism into death', but 'We were buried *with him* through baptism . . .'. Paul's first thought in this passage (and he has others!) is not that the believer in his baptism is laid in his own grave, but that through that action he is set alongside Christ Jesus in *His*; in baptism he is reckoned as occupying that grave as he was not before, just as an effective relationship with the Lord on the cross is assumed which did not exist before. Further the very real connection between baptism and the believer's relationship to the redemptive acts of Christ is seen in the consistent use of the aorist tenses throughout the passage Rom. 6.1–11: 'We died to sin' (2); 'All we who became baptized to Christ Jesus became baptized to His death' (3); 'We suffered a burial with Him, through baptism, unto death' (4); 'Our old man became crucified with Him' (6); 'We died with Christ and believe we shall live with Him' (8). Still more pertinently, a comparison of v. 5 with v. 8 makes it plain that Paul has baptism in mind in what he says about death to sin and death to sin in what he says about baptism: 'If we have become united with the form of His death, we shall also be united with the form of His

[1] *Die Taufe ein Sakrament?* pp. 268–82.

resurrection', so runs v. 5, taking up the language of v. 4 about burial with Christ in baptism and rising to live a new life thereafter; v. 8 takes up the same theme without mentioning baptism: 'If we died with Christ we believe that we shall also live with Him'. It may further be observed that there is no question of Paul speaking symbolically in v. 5 and literally in v. 8; he appears to maintain an even realism throughout the passage.

If then a connection between baptism and Christ's death and resurrection be admitted, how is it envisaged by Paul? The answers put forward to this question may be classified broadly into three. The most frequently represented is that *in baptism the believer suffers a death and resurrection like Christ's*; he experiences a death to sin and resurrection to righteousness at the time of his baptism. It is a viewpoint characteristic of British scholarship. Sanday and Headlam, for example, wrote in reference to baptism 'When we took the decisive step and became Christians we may be said to have died to sin'.[1] James Denney affirmed, 'If the baptism, which is a similitude of Christ's death, has had a reality answering to its obvious import, so that we have really died in it as Christ died, then we shall have a corresponding experience of resurrection'.[2] W. F. Flemington described baptism as 'a re-enactment for the believer of what once happened to our Lord'.[3] But the interpretation is not unrepresented among Continental exegetes. Schlier e.g. commented: 'The same thing has happened to Christ and to us; *as* it happened to Him, *so* it has happened to us. When? As we became baptized to Christ'.[4] The adherents of the view that Paul fashioned his baptismal theology from materials supplied by the Hellenistic Mystery Religions naturally subscribe to this interpretation also.[5]

Against this interpretation vigorous protest has been made, chiefly by Continental theologians. It is affirmed that *the death and resurrection of the baptized is the death and resurrection of Christ on the cross and at the first Easter* and there can be no talk of any other, apart from the final resurrection at the end to which baptism points. Thus Bornkamm said, 'It is of decisive importance that Paul never described baptism in the sense of a relationship or analogy between Christ and the baptized. He does not say, As Christ died on the cross, so we died in baptism. . . . He describes the event that takes place in it as dying

---

[1] *The Epistle to the Romans* (I.C.C.), 5th ed. 1902, p. 154.
[2] *The Expositor's Greek Testament*, 4th ed. 1912, p. 633.
[3] Op. cit., p. 59.   [4] *T.L.Z.*, 1947, p. 324.
[5] See e.g. Heitmüller, *Im Namen Jesu*, pp. 319 f; Lietzmann, *An die Römer*, p. 65 f; Leipoldt, op. cit., pp. 62 f.

with and a being raised with Christ (Col. 2.12). The death that the baptized and Christ die is only one, i.e. the death of Christ Himself'.[1] So also Leenhardt maintains that the believer is not invited to die to himself but to believe that he has died with Christ and to seize this reality as an accomplished fact.[2] E. Fuchs urges, 'There is no other death for us than the death of Jesus. If we were baptized in his name, then we are there, where He died, and buried when He was buried', and he suggests that to speak of our dying in baptism is to involve another death of Christ and so to crucify Him again.[3]

A third view looks with suspicion on both these interpretations and stresses the ethical nature of baptism as *a 'dying' to sinful passions and conduct by the renunciation of self and a 'rising' to a new life for the glory of God* by the grace of the Spirit of Christ. G. Kittel stated with reference to Romans 6, 'The concern of this exposition is not the gaining and retention of grace, but that we should not follow the sinful will'.[4] F. M. Rendtorff similarly wrote, 'The entire argumentation of Romans 6 culminates in the eminently ethical thought that baptism has no less a purpose than that we should enter upon a new moral way of life — ἵνα περιπατήσωμεν'.[5]

It is my conviction that each of these three views has essential truth and that none is complete in isolation from the rest. If we take into account Paul's theology generally — indeed, the text and the context provide enough evidence — it can be shown that his interpretation of baptism in relation to the redemptive event of Christ has a threefold reference: first, it relates the baptized to the death and resurrection of Christ, involving him in the actual dying and rising of Christ Himself; secondly, it involves a corresponding event in the life of the baptized believer, whereby an end is put to his old God-estranged life and a new one begins in Christ and His Kingdom and His Spirit; thirdly, it demands a corresponding 'crucifixion' of the flesh and a new life in the power of the Spirit that accords with the grace received, which 'dying' and 'rising' begins in the baptismal event.

It is our task to consider these three aspects of baptism as they are reflected in Romans 6.1–11.

(i) 'We were buried with him through baptism to death' (v. 4); so Paul deduces (οὖν) from the preceding statement that Christian bap-

---

[1] 'Die neutestamentliche Lehre von der Taufe', *Theologische Blätter*, 1938, vol. XVII, Sp. 235.
[2] Op. cit., p. 63.   [3] Op. cit., pp. 29, 37.
[4] 'Die Wirkungen der christlichen Wassertaufe nach dem Neuen Testament', *Theologische Studien und Kritiken*, vol. 87, 1914, p. 46.
[5] *Die Taufe im Urchristentum*, p. 36.

tism is to Christ's death (εἰς τὸν θάνατον αὐτοῦ, v. 3). There is some ambiguity here through uncertainty whether the last phrase in the quoted sentence belongs to the verb or to the immediately preceding noun. On the latter view we should understand the sentence as meaning, 'We were buried with him through this baptism-to-death'. That could mean that baptism is a baptism *for* death; but if the phrase 'to his death' of v. 3 has a lighter significance, conformably with 'to Christ Jesus', we cannot press its meaning here. If the phrase is related to the verb, however, it will certainly possess a more intensive sense: 'Through baptism we were buried with Him *into that death of His*'.[1] On such a construction, participation in the death of Christ will be in mind. If we cannot be confident as to what Paul did intend by the phrase, we can nevertheless be reasonably assured as to the purpose of the sentence as a whole. As pointed out above, 'We were buried with Him' indicates that the action of baptism primarily means, not that the baptistry becomes our grave, but that we are laid in the grave of Christ. To be buried along with Christ in a Jerusalem grave *c.* A.D. 30 means unequivocally that the death we died is the death *He* died on Golgotha.

Despite the frequent denials of exegetes, it is surely reasonable to believe that the reason for Paul's stating that the baptized is *buried* as dead, rather than that he *died* (as in v. 6), is the nature of baptism as immersion. The symbolism of immersion as representing burial is striking, and if baptism is at all to be compared with prophetic symbolism, the parallelism of act and event symbolized is not unimportant. Admittedly such a statement as that of C. H. Dodd, 'Immersion is a sort of burial . . . emergence a sort of resurrection',[2] can be made only because the kerygma gives this significance to baptism; its whole meaning is derived from Christ and His redemption — it is the kerygma *in action*, and if the action suitably bodies forth the content of the kerygma, so much the clearer is its speech. But we repeat, the 'with Him' of baptism is due to the gospel, not to the mimesis. It is 'to *His* death': Christ and His dying, Christ and His rising give the rite all its meaning. As one of the earliest of British Baptists put it, to be baptized is to be 'dipped for dead in the water'.[3]

---

[1] Sanday & Headlam favoured this rendering but felt too overpowered by the weight of conflicting authority to recommend it as against the former interpretation, op. cit., p. 157.

[2] *The Epistle of Paul to the Romans*, 1932, p. 87.

[3] Leonard Busher, in a work on religious liberty written in 1614 and entitled 'Religions Peace'. The statement is important since it was penned twenty years before any proved practice of baptism by immersion took place among Baptists. See W. T. Whitley, *The Baptist Quarterly*, vol. XI, 1942/1945, p. 175.

This thought comes to yet clearer expression in the succeeding sentences: 'We have become united with the form of His death . . . Our old man was crucified with Him . . . We died with Christ'. In so speaking of our death as crucifixion, Paul has abandoned the strict symbolism of the baptismal rite and made it clear beyond a doubt that our 'old man' died on the cross on Calvary.[1] Verse 5 explains how this is brought about: 'We have become σύμφυτοι τῷ ὁμοιώματι τοῦ θανάτου αὐτοῦ'. The translation of this statement in the Revised Standard Version: 'We have been united *with Him* in a death *like His*' is misleading. On the one hand it demands the insertion after σύμφυτοι ('united') of the term αὐτῷ ('with him'), and on the other it presumes that ὁμοίωμα denotes something that is similar to, yet not identical with, what is compared; both assumptions are dubious in this context. It is now generally agreed that if we can translate the sentence without the insertion of αὐτῷ we should do so.[2] There is also good reason for interpreting ὁμοίωμα in the sense of 'form' rather than 'likeness'. While the term can mean image or likeness, it is used in Deut. 4.12 of the appearance of God ('The Lord spoke to you out of the midst of the fire; you heard the sound of words but saw no *form*; there was only a voice'). Bornkamm therefore urges that ὁμοίωμα brings to expression the nature of that which is imaged in itself and writes 'ὁμοίωμα τοῦ θανάτου αὐτοῦ denotes the form of the Crucified. We have grown with it or with Him as the Crucified. Correspondingly we shall have the same relation with the form of His resurrection or with Him as the Resurrected'.[3] This use of σύμφυτοι, united *with*, should be compared with other verbs compounded with σύν in this passage: συνετάφημεν (we were buried with), v. 4, συνεσταυρώθη (we were crucified with), v. 6, ἀπεθάνομεν σὺν Χριστῷ . . . καὶ συζήσομεν αὐτῷ (we died with Christ and we shall live with him), v. 8. It will be seen that all these verbs denote the unity between the baptized believer and the person of Christ Himself in His redemptive action and do not envisage the possibility of a

[1] The 'old man' connotes the man who belongs to the age prior to the Messiah's coming and the new age of the Kingdom and whose life is dominated by the characteristics of the old aeon.

[2] R. Schnackenburg in his exhaustive study of Romans 6 contended for the kind of rendering reproduced in the R.S.V., chiefly because 'being planted together with an image' (ὁμοίωμα) is a harsh expression and σύμφυτος better suits an organic connection. In his later essay, however, this view is withdrawn. Schnackenburg notes the demonstration of O. Kuss that σύμφυτος permits various connections and that of M. M. Bourke, that σύμφυτος need not contain any allusion to the realm of botany but can be simply translated by 'united with'. He further changed his mind on the significance of ὁμοίωμα in the same direction as we here advocate. See his book, pp. 42 ff and the article in the *Münchener Theol. Zeitschrift*, 1955, pp. 35 ff.

[3] *Das Ende des Gesetzes*, 1952, pp. 41 ff.

middle term between. For this reason it is illegitimate to regard ὁμοιώματι as a dative of instrument and interpret it as a synonym for baptism: 'We have become united with Him *by the likeness of His death*', taking baptism as an image of the death of Christ; rather it would seem that Paul speaks of our being involved directly with Christ in His death and resurrection through baptism.[1]

Now on what basis of thought is Paul operating by which he is enabled to say, not simply, as in Rom. 5.8, 'Christ died for us', but yet more strikingly, 'We died with Christ'? There is little doubt that the paragraph that falls between the joyous assurance of justification and reconciliation in Rom. 5.1–11 and the exposition of baptism in Rom. 6.1–11 yields the clue: The Christ who provides a means of expiation by His blood (Rom. 3.3, 25) is the Second Man, the last Adam, the Man from Heaven (1 Cor. 15.45 ff); in Him humanity has been renewed and delivered and in union with Him the renewal and deliverance become effective.

In our approach to the thought of Rom. 5.12–21 it is necessary to bear in mind that it is not an unrelated phenomenon in Biblical thought, nor is it an odd illustration culled from Rabbinical lore for the occasion, with no real significance for Paul's theology which could be discarded without loss. We have already observed, in connection with our Lord's interpretation of Old Testament messianic teaching, that all the messianic figures in the Old Testament are representative, and none more clearly so than the two of greatest importance to Him — the Servant of the Lord and the Son of Man. From the description in 1 Cor. 15 of the Last Adam as a 'life-giving Spirit', in contrast with the first man Adam as a living soul, v. 45, and as the 'Man from heaven' in contrast to the 'man of earth', v. 47, it is clear that Paul identifies the Christ with the Son of

[1] The identification of ὁμοίωμα with baptism has been made by Schlier and given a characteristic slant by him: 'Instead of saying, "(we have become united with) his death", the Apostle says, "with the likeness of his death", because this concerns the death of Christ present in baptism, thus with the death of Christ present in a sacramental fashion and not with the death of Christ on the cross of Golgotha as such, with the death of the cross as it took place historically on Golgotha', *T.L.Z.*, 1947, p. 324. Not alone do the considerations adduced above militate against this view; a further, and, in my judgment, insuperable difficulty in the way of interpreting ὁμοίωμα in v. 5 as synonymous with baptism is provided by the immediately following clause, where it is necessary to understand a second occurrence of ὁμοιώματι: 'we shall also share *the likeness of His resurrection*'. But if ὁμοίωμα in the first clause refers to baptism ('the likeness of His death') it will have to refer to baptism in the second clause, which is surely incredible. The 'likeness of His resurrection' is the sharing in the resurrection life which the Christ has won for us in Easter. The future ἐσόμεθα would seem to point to the bestowal upon us of resurrection life at the parousia, though Schnackenburg may be right in suggesting that Paul's thought hovers between a logical and temporal future here: the baptized knows the powers of the age to come in life in Christ now (v. 4) and is to know them in fullness at the end. See *Münchener Theologische Zeitschrift*, 1955, p. 37.

Man who performs the eschatological function of raising the dead. But the Son of Man is not alone an eschatological figure; he is also linked with the creation. Cullmann, following on a suggestion of J. Héring, has pointed out that the description in Phil. 2.6 of the pre-existent Christ as 'in the form of God' (ἐν μορφῇ θεοῦ) may well reflect the language of Gen. 1.27, where man is described as made in the 'image' of God. Indeed, the synonyms of Gen. 1.26 'image' and 'likeness' of God (דְּמוּת and צֶלֶם) can both be rendered by μορφή and εἰκών; in 2 Cor. 4.4 (as in Col. 1.15) Christ is spoken of as the εἰκών ('image') of God. In 1 Cor. 15.49 Paul states that as we bore the εἰκών of the earthly man, we shall bear also the εἰκνών of the heavenly Man, again hinting of the idea of the image of God in man and the Son of Man. It would seem plausible therefore that Paul cited the hymn of Phil. 2.6 ff with the thought of Christ as the aboriginal 'image' of the Father Who, in His incarnate life, and in contrast to the 'first Adam', did not efface the image by sin.[1] It hints further that Christ is the image of God in an ultimate sense and Adam in a derived sense, seeing that 'all things were created in Him . . . through Him and unto Him' (Col. 1.16 ff).

When therefore we read that Adam is the 'type' of the 'Coming One' (Rom. 5.14), in the sense that his action involved the destiny of many, we must not regard Adam as the pattern into which the Christ has to fit, but rather see in him the promise of One transcendingly greater than he, whose greater works befit the grandeur of His person.

It is necessary to underscore this feature, since the nature of Christ's relation to the race is sometimes unduly restricted by insisting on interpreting it in strict accord with Adam's relation to the race. Nygren, for example, in wishing to prove that there is 'not even a trace of mysticism' in Paul's doctrine of participation in Christ's redemption, points out that there is no 'Adam-mysticism' in the Apostle's writings: 'That participation is not mediated by any mystical experience of oneness. It rests on the fact that our race stands in organic unity with Adam, the head of the race'. So also, 'God has made Christ the head of a new humanity; and into that new organic relationship he has brought us through baptism'.[2] Undoubtedly God has made Christ the head of a new humanity; but the 'organic relationship' with Christ into which the Christian enters as truly transcends the 'organic relationship' he sustains with Adam as the Kingdom of God transcends the natural kingdoms of this world and as the *Koinonia* of the Body of Christ transcends the *koinonia* of the world. 'In Adam' is not the same as 'in Christ', although the two phrases may be compared. E. Best has pointed out that there is a difference between solidarity and corporate personality. In the former concept what affects one affects all; Achan sinned and the whole nation lost the battle (Joshua 7). In the idea of corporate personality there is the same solidarity but

[1] See Cullmann, *Die Christologie des Neuen Testaments*, 1957, pp. 180 ff.
[2] *Commentary on Romans*, E.T., 1952, p. 237.

the 'solid' unit expresses the personality of one person. Adam is seen to be in unique solidarity with the race as the head who affects all but who is not affected by them; yet we cannot go so far as to say that all in the race express the personality of Adam; each individual may sin and die because of Adam but the whole race is not made into a personality which sins and dies. In the case of the Second Adam, however, we see One who may be viewed as an inclusive personality; when He died those who are included in Him died with Him; when He rose, they rose with Him.[1]

There is, indeed, ground for believing that Paul interpreted the relationship of solidarity between Christ and mankind in two ways. In Rom. 5.12-21 he is concerned with the universality of Christ's unity with the race and the universal scope of His redemptive action. A statement like Rom. 5.19 however makes one pause: 'As by one man's disobedience the many were constituted sinners, so by one man's obedience the many will be constituted righteous'. If the verb κατασταθήσονται ('constituted') is not simply a logical future,[2] but has also an eschatological reference to the last Day, that saying implies a strict universalism: the whole race will be acquitted in the judgment before God. In view of Paul's characterization of the judgment and its issues in Rom. 2.6 ff, that is an impossible interpretation. The 'many' who are to be justified in the judgment are those who, in the language of v. 17, 'receive the abundance of the grace and gift of righteousness' which come through Jesus Christ. If the antitheses of Rom. 5.15 ff are not to make nonsense of the teaching on justification by faith that has immediately preceded them, we must presume a double solidarity of Christ with man: in virtue of his incarnation, death and resurrection for all, Christ is 'solid' with the totality of the human race; in virtue of grace and faith Christ is 'solid' with the Church in such a fashion that the incarnation, death and resurrection attain their purposed end in man.

A similar issue faces us in the passage 2 Cor. 5.14 f, where the complicated theology of Rom. 3-6 is embodied in a mere sentence or so. 'We judge this, that one man died for all, therefore all died. And he died for all, that those who live might live no longer for themselves but for him who for their sake died and was raised.' The first statement, 'One died for all', presents Christ's death as a substitute for all men. 'All died' looks at it from the point of view of those for whom it happened, only it is spoken of as a representative death; that is, not that they escaped because Christ died, but that their death is implied in His. 'Those who live' represent a lesser number who have risen from the death they died in Christ; while the whole race rose with Christ their Representative, for them it has had peculiar efficacy, so that they are singled out as having risen, while others have not done so in comparable fashion (cf. also v. 17). If there are two levels of 'participation' in the resurrection of Christ, pre-

[1] See *One Body in Christ*, 1955, pp. 41, 56, 207. [2] Sanday and Headlam ad. loc.

sumably there are two levels of 'participation' in the death of Christ. All died, but they that are Christ's have entered into His death. All rose, but they that are Christ's have entered into the life of the resurrection. The race has been redeemed, but Christ's people have entered into its power as the world has not.[1] The difference is bound up with the fact that Christ's people have entered into a *Koinonia* with Him such as the world does not know. They are 'in Christ' and the world is not. They have become part of that inclusive personality who died and rose and therefore they died and rose with Him. The distinction between the two groups was earlier stated in terms of grace and faith; Rom. 6.1 ff expresses it in terms of baptism. The believer is baptized to the Christ who died and rose for him; hence the death on Golgotha becomes his death (the believer's) because it was *His* death (the Christ's).

Baptism, and the Christian faith it embodies, is rooted in the 'Christ event', with all that implies, and nothing of man's doing and no theological explanation must ever be allowed to detract from the uniqueness, splendour and power of that event.

(ii) To be united with Christ in his redemptive acts, and therefore to enter into His death and resurrection, cannot but have catastrophic consequences for the believer. His old life is set under the judgment of the cross and a new man begins to live. No less language than death and resurrection can suffice to describe the nature of the transition from the old creation to the new. That the experience is bound up with such an overt act as baptism serves to make it the more objective, the more definitive, the more tangible. As C. H. Dodd expressed it: 'Here in the sacrament is something actually done — a step taken which can never be retracted. Before it a man was not a member of the Church, the people of God; now he is a member. If he should thereafter be unfaithful, that would not simply be a return to his former condition. Something has happened, something overt, definable, with a setting in time and space, attested by witnesses. And behind that lies a similarly definite event in the inner life. He has grown into Christ. He is now in Christ'.[2] This aspect of baptism as an event in the life of the believer, corresponding to the Christ event of long ago, is underscored in Paul's attribution of the character of resurrection to it. There is a tendency among present Continental scholars to deny this element in baptism and regard it as solely promise or anticipation of the resurrection in the last day, in view of the future tenses in v. 5 ('If we have become united with the form of

---

[1] Cf. the comparable, but not identical, viewpoint of 1 Tim. 4.10: God is 'the Saviour of all men, especially of those who believe'.
[2] *The Epistle of Paul to the Romans*, p. 87.

His death, we shall also be united with the form of His resurrection')
and v. 8 ('If we died with Christ, we believe that we shall also live
with Him').[1] But the future aspect of these statements must not blind
us to the drift of this passage, that the Christian cannot countenance
living again in sin in view of his having died to it and risen to a new
life. The absence of a specific counterpart to 'we were buried with him
through baptism' by an outright 'we were raised with him' is due
solely to the parenetic purpose of this baptismal instruction. The
Apostle desires to stress the ethical consequences that should flow
from baptism; but there can be no doubting that the clause, 'that as
Christ was raised from the dead . . . so we also should walk in newness
of life', presumes that the Christian, as his Lord, *was* raised 'through
the glory of the Father'.[2] This thought is expressed more strongly in
vv. 10–11: 'The death He died, He died to sin, once, but the life He
lives, He lives to God. So you also consider yourselves dead to sin *and
alive to God in Christ Jesus*'. In this context the italicised clause presumes the unexpressed premiss, 'since in baptism you were raised
from death to life through your participation in the resurrection of
Christ'. It happens that we are fortunate enough to possess an authentic commentary by Paul on his own words in the Epistle to the
Colossians. Despite the later date of this letter, the closeness of
similarity between the language of Rom. 6.4 and Col. 2.12 is too great
to permit our postulating a difference of meaning in the two statements: '(You were) buried with Him in baptism, in which you were
also raised with Him through faith in the working of the God who
raised Him from the dead'. Here the resurrection of the baptized in
baptism is explicitly stated. The burden of proof must rest on any
who suggest that it represents a modification in Paul's thought. But in
truth, it is no exaggeration to say that this idea is basic to Paul's whole
view of the Christian experience of salvation. E. Sommerlath pointed
out how striking it was that the allusion to baptism in Paul's writings
is so often found in contexts in which the Apostle speaks of the new
condition of life as something accomplished and not comparable with
the previous condition.[3] He cites in support of this statement Rom.
6.2 ff, 1 Cor. 6.11, Col. 2.10 ff. Perhaps we may add 2 Cor. 5.16 f, in
the recollection that this paragraph presents in brief compass the

[1] See e.g. Lietzmann, *An die Römer*, pp. 65 ff; Fuchs, *Die Freiheit des Glaubens*,
p. 30; M. Barth, op. cit., p. 235; Bornkamm, *Das Ende des Gesetzes*, p. 38.
[2] So P. Seidensticker, *Lebendiges Opfer (Röm. 12.1), ein Beitrag zur Theologie des
Apostels Paulus*, 1954, pp. 245 f. He maintains that although the ἐσόμεθα of Rom.
6.5 is strictly a logical future, Paul implies that a fact lies at its basis whose temporal
origin is firmly anchored in baptism and whose end lies in the eternal future.
[3] *Der Ursprung des neuen Lebens nach Paulus*, 2nd ed. 1927, p. 102.

theology of Rom. 3–6: 'From now on (i.e. now that we have risen, v. 15) we regard no one from a human point of view. . . . Therefore if any one is in Christ he is a new creation; the old order has passed away, see the new has come into being!' The believer, risen with Christ and living in Christ, has become a new creature and lives in the new creation. Such a description does not refer basically to an improved moral performance in the life of the Christian but to a new existence in the eschatological order introduced in the resurrection of Christ and mediated by His Spirit. The transference into this order is as cataclysmic as the event which brought it into being: resurrection with Christ in baptism.[1]

Since baptism signifies a participation in the resurrection of Christ, in such wise that it witnesses a rising to new life in Christ, it is but natural to presume that the participation in the death of Christ is of a like order, i.e. it involves a dying with Him to the old existence. Admittedly the positive thought of entrance on to the new life is more easily conceived of as a resurrection than the forsaking of the old as a death, but if the former be considered as essentially an entry on to a new condition of life in the Kingdom in the koinonia of Christ, the severance of the believer from existence in the old aeon under the powers of this world is not unnaturally spoken of as a death. And so Paul seems to have done in Rom. 6.1 ff. It is not impossible, indeed I would think it likely, that the first reference to dying to sin in the passage is to the baptismal event, considered as something that happened within the life of the believer: 'We that died to sin, how shall we live in it still?' (v. 2). Observe the force of ἔτι — still: the people in view had lived once 'in sin', but now they do so no longer, for they died to it when they were baptized. It is converts who are in mind,[2] men of whom Paul writes in the next paragraph 'Thanks be to God that (though) you once were slaves of sin, you became obedient from the heart to the standard of teaching to which you were committed' (v. 7). Their life under the power of sin terminated when they turned to Christ. They died in their baptism because in it they shared in Christ's dying. Admittedly Paul does not say in so many words,

[1] So Sommerlath with emphasis. 'The share in the life of the exalted Lord is not understood by him (Paul) as a goal to be realized by us through moral effort, but is something that stands at the beginning of the Christian life as an event of grace (Gnadenwiderfahrnis)', op. cit., p. 108.

[2] 'Ἐπιμένειν τῇ ἁμαρτίᾳ is the life of the unconverted', Windisch, Taufe und Sünde, 1908, p. 167. Similarly Feine: 'It appears to the Apostle impossible that a Christian who has died to sin can deliberately resolve again to lead a sinful life. The 'being dead' accordingly must be understood as an occurrence in the life of the Christian. A fact has entered his life which the Apostle can describe as the experience of death', Theologie des Neuen Testaments, 8th ed. 1953, p. 295.

'The baptized convert, through participation in Christ's dying on the cross of Golgotha in baptism, thereby suffers in his own life a death to sin'; but Schnackenburg is surely right in considering that the parallel formulated of the resurrection in v. 4, 'as Christ . . . so also we', applies to our entire relation to the redemptive event. It is his conviction that Paul is concerned in this chapter to portray the believer's unity with Christ in his redemptive action *and* its subsequent effect in life and that he has not succeeded in expressing the two things in a single short sentence; instead the Apostle unfolds the *together with Christ* and the *as Christ, so also we* alongside each other and after each other.[1]

As in the positive aspect of resurrection with Christ in baptism, so in this of dying with Christ, we find illustrations of the same viewpoint elsewhere in Paul. There is a curiously similar ambiguity to that of Rom. 6.1 ff in Gal. 2.19 f: 'I through the law died to the law, that I might live to God. I have been crucified with Christ. . . .' It is uncertain whether Paul wishes to convey the notion in the first sentence that through his experience of the law (cf. Rom. 7.14 ff) he 'died' to it, renounced it to live to God by faith in Christ; or whether he means that through the death of Christ under the law, he died to the law by his participation in that redemptive death. The preceding context would favour the former view, the immediately succeeding statement favours the latter. Perhaps the latter should be given preference, in view of the clear statement of Rom. 7.4, 'You died to the law through the body of Christ, that you might belong to another, to Him that was raised from the dead'. If so, we have again a statement whose significance draws its strength from the fact of the believer's participation in the event at Calvary. So Paul continues, 'I have been crucified with Christ; *and it is no longer I that live, but Christ who lives in me*'. That is, the unregenerate man, the old Adam, the man of the old existence that Paul was, has *died*. A new man has come into being, for Paul now lives in the koinonia of the Risen Christ: 'the life I now live in the flesh, I live by faith in the Son of God'. The 'together with Christ' and the 'as Christ, so also we' of Rom. 6.1 ff are again in evidence. The relation of the two modes of participation has not been discussed, for it evidently did not occur to Paul that he should do so. The reality, not the theology of it, was his concern here. And once more the Colossian Epistle comes to aid especially the section 2.20–3.11: 'If

---

[1] *Heilsgeschehen bei der Taufe*, p. 156. O. Michel expresses himself similarly: 'The once for all historical event of the past works on in baptism, but it remains the foreordained archetype of the baptism of the individual (ὥσπερ — οὕτω)'. Commentary on Rom. 6.4.

with Christ you died to the elemental spirits of the universe,[1] why do you live as if you still belonged to the world? . . . Set your mind on things that are above, not on things that are on earth, for you died, and your life has been hidden with Christ in God. . . . Put to death what is earthly in you. . . . In these you once walked, when you lived in them, but now put them all away . . . seeing that you stripped off the old nature with its practices and put on the new nature. . . '. Language could not more clearly express the conviction of a transition from an old existence to a new, a death and resurrection, and there can be as little doubt that the passage from the old to the new existence is thought of as having taken place in baptism. In this case, however, the relation of the Christian to the redemptive event is taken for granted; it is the fruits of that participation with which Paul is concerned here, but his mode of expression serves to illuminate the passages in which the participation in the Christ event comes to the fore.

To be baptized then, according to Paul, is to undergo a drastic experience. The overworked term 'existential' is not amiss in application to his exposition of baptism given in Rom. 6.[2] It could hardly be otherwise if baptism be supremely the occasion when God draws near in Christ to a man drawing near to Him in faith. The believer comes to God through the Christ of the cross and resurrection and God meets him in the Christ of the cross and resurrection. In this momentous beginning of the I and Thou communion in Christ, the baptized learns that to be reconciled through the blood of the cross is to be conformed to it (Phil. 3.10). And in the first place this is an act of God, even as it is the act of grace. The Lutherans are quite right in calling attention to the fact that the characteristic voice in Rom. 6.1 ff is the passive: we were baptized, we were buried, we have become planted with the likeness of Christ's death, we were crucified with Christ — these are all acts of grace and power so surely as our resurrection with Christ is an act of grace and power, deeds which we can simulate but never produce by our own efforts. We that are Baptists have largely ignored this aspect of Pauline teaching; even when we

---

[1] Or, 'to the elementary knowledge of the world'.

[2] As Barth saw. He appropriates for Paul's teaching on baptism the phrase of Troeltsch, 'The theology of the absolute moment' and adds, 'Yes! That is it; provided that "absolute" be thought of as "existential", the knowledge of the most positive and most exclusive existentiality of divine grace'. His idea of the 'existentiality' of baptism is illustrated in an immediately succeeding citation from Luther, to the effect that in baptism grace *throttles a man to death!* See *The Teaching of the Church regarding Baptism*, p. 194. For a different portrayal of the existential claim of the cross in word and sacrament, see Bultmann, *N.T. Theology*, p. 303.

have heard it we have hesitated to accept it, partly no doubt because of the one-sided emphasis it has often received but partly also because we have not known how to deal with it. But misapplication of truth must never be permitted to make us insensitive to it, and this is one in which we may glory with the rest of the church — and with a cheerful conscience! For we do not forget that it is the believer who is the recipient of so great mercy and grace of God.

(iii) Precisely because it is believers who are baptized, at their own request, we have to move a further stage, as did Paul. The penitent sinner who knows that his Representative has died for him, that by the judgment and mercy of God he died in Him on Golgotha, who by faith accepts God's judgment on his sin and in Christ finds life from the dead, *in that very act of turning to God* renounces his sinful life, condemns it to the grave of baptism and by grace begins the life of discipleship to the praise of God. Whatever else lies buried deep in the theology of Rom. 6.1 ff, this lies on the surface. For it cannot be too firmly emphasized that Paul's concern in this passage was not to give a theological excursus on the nature of Christian baptism but to oppose the heretical appeal, 'Let us carry on in sin that grace may abound!' (Rom. 6.1). He could have countered with a purely theoretical consideration: 'Under no circumstances! Such conduct would frustrate the intention of grace'. Instead he appealed to an event in the past on which it would be unthinkable to go back: 'We died to sin once; how can we live in it still?' (Rom. 6.2). The exposition that follows has the purpose of bringing out the implications of that statement, by expounding the meaning of Christ's death and resurrection for the believer, his participation in those saving events and the radical change involved in the baptismal transference from existence under the powers of darkness to life in the Kingdom of God's own Son (Col. 1.13). God had wrought in merciful judgment and quickening power at that time; and the believer had both assented wholeheartedly to that judgment and committed himself to the new existence in Christ. This concept lies at the heart of the central utterance of Rom. 6.1–11, i.e. in v. 4; when the parenthetical material of the sentence is omitted we are left with the unambiguous statement: 'We were buried with him through baptism . . . *that we might walk in newness of life*'. Bornkamm maintains that the ἵνα introduces the divine determination and demand under which we now stand.[1] Without minimizing the reality of the divine purpose in baptism it could equally be insisted that the ἵνα ('in order that') introduces the pur-

[1] Op. cit., p. 38.

pose of the convert as he submits to baptism, for the baptismal act is his ultimate response to the grace of God manifest in redemption and experienced in the divine call through the Gospel; he renounces the 'oldness' of his earlier life and commits himself to the 'newness of life' opened up for him through the resurrection life of Christ. This accords perfectly with the definition of baptism given in 1 Pt. 3.21, συνειδήσεως ἀγαθῆς ἐπερώτημα εἰς θεόν, rendered by Bo Reicke as 'an undertaking to a loyal attitude of mind to God'.[1] The confessional element in baptism certainly includes a declaration of trust in Him that saves, but it also embraces the confessed intention of yielding obedience to the Lord Christ, in conduct as well as worship.

The characteristic nature of the initiation into the Christian life, as described in Rom. 6.1 ff, provides the ethical pattern for both the beginning and continuance of that life. The Christian life is rooted in participation in the event of Golgotha and the Empty Tomb through union with the Christ; that union involves a death to the old existence and resurrection to the new; it further demands that he that is so joined to the Christ accept the death sentence on his old way of life and seek grace whereby the new existence may be realized in his conduct. Death and resurrection must appear in his life. Like Paul he must henceforth ever be 'bearing in the body the death of Jesus, that the life of Jesus may also be manifested in the body' (2 Cor. 4.10). For this process baptism provides the pattern and the grace. For, be it noted, it is not alone a duty that is laid on the baptized but a new possibility of life that is opened up through the koinonia of the Risen Christ. Both the duty and the grace begin in the baptismal event. In the passage to which we have already turned for illustration of Rom. 6, namely Col. 3.1 ff, we read an appeal for the resurrection life to be actualized and pursued in the lives of the readers: '*If you have been raised* with Christ, *seek the things that are above*, where Christ is, seated at the right hand of God . . . for you died, and your life is hid with Christ in God'. There ensues a call to follow the pattern of crucifixion in conduct: 'Put to death what is earthly in you: immorality, impurity, passion, evil desire. . .'. This pattern of death and resurrection began in baptism: 'You stripped off the old nature with its practices and put on the new nature, which is being renewed in knowledge after the image of its creator'. The language has changed but the presuppositions are the same as in Rom. 6.1 ff.

Still more striking is the saying in Gal. 5.24: 'They that belong to

[1] *The Disobedient Spirits and Christian Baptism*, 1946, p. 185.

Christ crucified the flesh with its passions and desires'. The aorist tense indicates that Paul has in mind a single point of time when this event took place, and the sayings we have just considered lead us to believe that baptism provides the most suitable context. But the crucifixion of the flesh is here, remarkably enough, attributed to the Christian, not to God. This fact was perceived by Althaus in his commentary on Galatians when he wrote, 'The event in baptism is not naturalistic but entirely personal. What the baptismal act wrought in them (the baptized) they themselves confessed and made their own act. . . . Hence it comes about that that which is denoted in Rom. 6.2 ff as a happening, which a man suffers in baptism, is here spoken of as his personal act; he has crucified the old man with his passions and desires, has renounced him — a fundamental, once for all decision, which then admittedly becomes the perpetual task for the whole life of the Christian'.[1] We are grateful for this exposition of Paul's meaning, but at one point we need to exercise care: 'What the baptismal act wrought in them, they themselves confessed and made their own act' said Althaus. That may be true theoretically, but it is of vital importance to note that in experience the separation cannot be made. For a man is not baptized twice, once that God may deal with him and again that he may offer his response to the divine act; it is one baptism wherein God's *act* is *owned* by the believer — a unitary event wherein glory is given to God by fulfilling the purpose of His grace in the very act of its reception. For this reason the extraordinary deduction made by Cullmann from Rom. 6.11 ('Reckon yourselves to be dead indeed to sin, but alive to God through Jesus Christ our Lord') is wholly removed from the truth: 'This awareness of what happens in baptism', he wrote, 'together with the understanding and faith presupposed by it, is not part of the first act of the baptismal event but only of the subsequent and second act, even in the case of adult baptism'.[2] On the contrary, understanding, repentance, submission to judgment, the open heart to grace, renunciation to death, decision for life are all integral to baptism in the view of Paul. In his theology of baptism the divine action and human responsiveness are inseparable and enable baptism to be what it is.

Finally, it may not be amiss to observe that it is this aspect of baptism which is most readily linked with the teaching of Jesus. It will be recalled that the Great Commission of Mt. 28.19 associates baptism with the making of *disciples*. Now it can hardly be forgotten that on

[1] 'Die Kleineren Briefe des Apostels Paulus', *N.T.D.*, vol. 8, 5th ed. 1949, p. 48.
[2] *Baptism in the New Testament*, p. 49.

the one occasion recorded by Mark, when Jesus invited people to join the disciple band, He issued His call to discipleship in terms of shouldering a cross: 'If any man would come after Me, let him renounce himself and take up his cross and follow Me. For whoever would save his life will lose it; and whoever loses his life for My sake and the Gospel's will save it' (Mk. 8.34 f). In its setting in the gospel this is a call to follow Jesus to Jerusalem and to be prepared there to suffer and die with Him. The early Christians had cause to remember these terms of discipleship as they suffered reproach for the Name, and none more so than Paul himself (cf. Phil. 1.29 f, 3.10). It would not be surprising if Paul took account of this teaching in his own interpretation of Christian initiation. Naturally, the disciple after Easter is in a very different position from the disciple before Good Friday; he knows that however desolating his death (or life!) may be, the sting of it has been robbed by the Lord who died and rose for him. From now on the eschatological glory sheds its light over the whole of life and penetrates even the gloom of death. There can be no question of conflict between the participation in the redemptive event and following in the path that wends by Golgotha, for the latter is possible in virtue of the grace of the former. The concluding word of Rom. 6.1–11 hints of this: 'Reckon yourselves dead to sin and living to God in Christ Jesus'. The imperative λογίζεσθε ('reckon') denotes an act of faith in the efficacy of the saving act of Christ and the believer's part in it; it further includes the demand to conduct oneself as one that died and has risen from the realm of death. What Paul appealed that others should do he applied to himself:

> I have been crucified with Christ;
> it is no longer I who live, but Christ who lives in me;
> and the life I now live in the flesh I live by faith —
> faith in the Son of God who loved me and gave Himself for me (Gal. 2.20).

2. GALATIANS 3.26–27

The drift of the passage is clear. It forms the climax of the chapter in which Paul labours to refute the claim of the Judaisers that men become 'sons of Abraham' only through conforming to the law; on the contrary, urges Paul, Abraham's heirs are the 'men of faith'. And the time of faith is present! In the period when law held sway, men were held in custody, as a child is subject to the domination of his pedagogue; now that the time of faith has come through the preaching of the good news, all who exercise faith attain to sonship through

Christ, with whom we were united in baptism and in whom we are Abraham's seed and heirs of the promise. The Galatians in failing to understand this situation were denying themselves their 'majority'; Paul is concerned to recall them to the reality of their full age.[1]

So much is clear, but there are several points of detail requiring attention, chief of which is the relation of the two sentences. To assert, 'You are God's sons through faith in Christ Jesus, *for* you that were baptized to Christ put on Christ', indicates that in some manner the fact of the second statement grounds the first. But the nature of the relation postulated is vigorously debated.

First, we remind ourselves of the likelihood that the clause 'you were baptized $\epsilon i s$ $X \rho \iota \sigma \tau \acute{o} \nu$' means here, 'You were baptized *to* Christ'; the $\epsilon i s$ $X \rho \iota \sigma \tau \acute{o} \nu$ ('to Christ') is to be understood as an abbreviation of the common $\epsilon i s$ $\tau \grave{o}$ $\check{o} \nu o \mu a$ $\tau o \hat{v}$ $X \rho \iota \sigma \tau o \hat{v}$ ('in the name of Christ') and therefore has the meaning of baptism with reference to Christ, for dedication to and appropriation by Christ.[2] If the phrase had by this time become stereotyped, its associations would nevertheless have been firmly fixed in the Churches.

Secondly, the concept implied in $X \rho \iota \sigma \tau \grave{o} \nu$ $\epsilon \nu \delta \acute{v} \epsilon \sigma \theta a \iota$ ('to put on Christ') can hardly be represented by such renderings as 'to think oneself into the role of another and act accordingly, to behave and represent oneself as another' (Zahn)[3] or 'to become as Christ, to have his standing' (Burton).[4] The use of the metaphor to denote the assumption of a new character is undoubtedly frequent in Paul (e.g. Rom. 13.14, 1 Thess. 5.8, Col. 3.9 f, Eph. 4.22 ff) but ethical conditions are not in view in this passage. Nor is it certain that Burton rightly employs the Pauline citations to equate *taking on the character* of a person with *assuming his status*. There is more force in his observation, 'These passages show that the idiom conveyed no suggestion of putting on a mask, but referred to *an act in which one entered into actual relations*'.[5] That would accord with the fact that the immediate antecedent of v. 27 is the phrase $\epsilon \nu$ $X \rho \iota \sigma \tau \hat{\omega}$ $' I \eta \sigma o \hat{v}$ (in Christ Jesus); by faith the Christian shares the sonship of the Christ in whom he lives; he is in Christ because he has put on Christ. This latter idea is evidently a pictorial representation of that union with

---

[1] This last point is made by P. Bonnard, *L'Epitre de Saint Paul aux Galates*, 1953, p. 77.
[2] See pp. 90–2.
[3] *An die Galater*, 2nd ed. 1907, p. 186, n. 60.
[4] *The Epistle to the Galatians, I.C.C.*, 1921, pp. 203 ff.
[5] Op. cit., p. 204.

Christ indicated by the phrase 'in Christ Jesus' and its counterpart 'Christ in me' (Gal. 2.20).[1]

The Christian 'put on' Christ in baptism — the sequence of thought is too close knit to permit of another interpretation: 'All you who were baptized to Christ did put on Christ'. A case can be made out for deriving this belief from the mystery religions.[2] While this is not to be ruled out as impossible, it must be admitted that the figure of changing clothes to represent an inward and spiritual change was so common to the Hebrew-Christian tradition as to make a direct borrowing from such a source unlikely.[3] To link the symbol with baptism was the more natural, in that the ending of an old existence and beginning of a new one in Christ was bodied forth in this event, and Christ was the content of that new existence as well as its inspiration. Moreover baptism by immersion involved the necessity of literally stripping off and putting on clothes. In this connection it would be interesting to establish two items of information: (a) when baptism among Christians began to be practised in nudity, and (b) when the custom of presenting the newly baptized with a white robe began. The former was characteristic of proselyte baptism among Jews, for whom it was essential that *every* part of the body should be touched by water; that it came to be so practised among Christians is indicated in the comparison by Cyril of Jerusalem of the nakedness of the baptized with the nakedness of Christ on the cross, and Chrysostom's likening it with the nakedness of Adam in the Garden of Eden.[4] Similarly both Cyril of Jerusalem and Theodore of Mopsuestia mention the 'white garments' worn by the baptized; E. C. Ratcliff, in

---

[1] To 'clothe oneself with Christ' is the same as 'to be in Christ'. Ragnar Bring, *Galaterbrevet (Tolkning av Nya Testamentet,* VIII) 1958, p. 194. So also Büchsel, who regards the phrase as a periphrasis for fellowship with Christ, which is the self-giving (Hingabe) of Christ to the Christian, so that the Christian has Christ, and the self-giving of the Christian to Christ, so that Christ has the Christian, op. cit., p. 290.

[2] Leipoldt instances that the believer in Isis, at the end of the consecration, puts on the robe of Osiris; he thereby *becomes* Osiris and receives the worship of the community. The same robe is put on him on the death bed; it assures for him immortality. Op. cit., p. 60.

[3] The idea of clothing oneself with attributes is very common in the Old Testament and is used of God and man. See e.g. Job 8.22, 9.14, Ps. 93.1, 104.1 f, 132.9, 16, 18, Prov. 31.25, Is. 51–9, 52.1, but above all Is. 61.10 and Zech. 3.3 ff as precedents for the New Testament employment of the symbol for the new life of righteousness and salvation. W. L. Knox, while affirming that the practice of the mysteries had accustomed the world to the figure of a change of garments for a change of spiritual status, considers that the whole use of metaphors of clothing was so familiar in the conventional language of Judaism that it could be adapted without any thought of its origin, *St. Paul and the Church of the Gentiles,* 1939, p. 138.

[4] See H. H. Rowley, 'Jewish Proselyte Baptism', *Hebrew Union College Annual,* 1940, pp. 322 ff.

discussing this element of the baptismal liturgies, thinks it probable that Gal. 3.27 hints of its primitive origin.[1] In the nature of the case we can scarcely hope to reach certainty on these matters, but they indicate the manner in which they received embodiment. The important feature is that the baptized stripped off an old life and put on a new one. The typically Pauline presentation of the conception is seen in Col. 3.9 ff: the old man is stripped off and the new man is put on, 'which is renewed in knowledge after the image of its creator. . . . Here there cannot be Greek or Jew . . . but Christ is all and in all'. The putting on the new man represents not a determination to turn over a new leaf and be a better man but the beginning of a new existence 'renewed after the image of God', *which image is Christ*, who is 'all, and in all'. In union with the Christ who is the Second Man, the Last Adam, the Image of God, the renewal and deliverance of humanity achieved in Him become realized in the individual believer.[2]

It should not go unnoticed that the ending of an old existence (putting off the old man) and the beginning of a new one in Christ is the same reality as that represented under the image of dying and rising with Christ, in so far as the latter refers to an identification on our part with Christ in His dying and rising. This is particularly clear in the passage just quoted from Colossians, where we find an instructive series of figures representing a single idea: '*Put to death* what is earthly in you. . . . In these you once walked . . . but now *put them all away*. . . . You *put off the old man*. . . '. These statements follow the appeal, 'If with Christ you died . . . why do you live as if you still belonged to the world?' (2.20), which in turn depends on the assertion, 'You were buried with Him in baptism' (2.12), itself introduced by a reference to the death ('circumcision') of Christ for man (2.11). The renunciation of the old life is a slaying of the earthly because the baptized who has died in Christ assented to the divine condemnation of sin in the flesh (Rom. 8.3) in his baptism, even as he perpetually renews that assent and renunciation in his subsequent life. Now it is true that the aspect of relatedness with Christ with which Paul is concerned in Gal. 3.26 f is the participation in sonship that belongs to Christ by inalienable right. Yet we recall that he has just spoken of Christ's becoming a curse for us, that in Him the blessing of Abraham might come upon us (3.14). Paul's polemical interest at this point causes him to concentrate on the positive aspect of 'putting on'

[1] 'The Relation of Confirmation to Baptism in the Early Roman and Byzantine Liturgies', *Theology*, 1946, p. 263.
[2] So Cullmann, who compares Rom. 8.29, 1 Cor. 15.49, 2 Cor. 3.18 as containing related ideas, *Die Christologie des Neuen Testaments*, p. 181.

Christ, yet it is extraordinary that his statement of the baptismal putting on Christ is immediately followed by a reference to the abolition
of differences of Jew and Greek, slave and free, since all are one in
Christ, just as occurs in Col. 3.11. The train of thought is basically the
same; the thought of death and resurrection with Christ will have
been in the background, though it is not mentioned in Gal. 3.27.[1]

Assuming that the baptized entered upon the *Koinonia* of Christ in
baptism, in what sense is it explicative of the preceding statement,
'You are all sons of God, through faith, in Christ Jesus'? The importance of the issue warrants our careful consideration of it. Johannes
Schneider argues thus: 'Through this faith Christians are children of
God. The reason that they are believing children of God in Christ lies
in baptism'.[2] The basis of this mode of reasoning is given in a note,
wherein Schneider suggests that Paul distinguishes between faith
εἰς Χριστόν ('to Christ') and faith ἐν Χριστῷ ('in Christ'); the
former is faith that receives the good news and is directed to Christ at
the beginning of the Christian life; the latter is 'faith in fellowship
with Christ, faith that is maintained in life in Christ'.[3] Such a distinction is hardly to be received. It is much more likely that we are to
regard 'in Christ Jesus' as independent of the preceding 'through faith'
and render it, 'You are all sons of God in Christ Jesus through faith'.[4]

The 'through faith' evidently requires to be taken seriously. It is
not good enough to say, with Schlier, that it simply takes up the
earlier 'now that faith has come' of v. 25, and is virtually equivalent
to the 'preaching of faith' spoken of in Rom. 10.8. The principle of
v. 25 is viewed as seized and acted upon in v. 26: Christians have
heard the good news of the new age that has come with the Christ,

---

[1] This idea would be greatly strengthened if the contention of Fritz Neugebauer
could be accepted, that in such phrases as ἐν σαρκί, ἐν νόμῳ, ἐν πνεύματι, the
ἐν is adverbial, indicating the powers by which man is determined in his living;
hence ἐν Χριστῷ means 'determined by Christ', i.e. determined by the redemptive
actions of Christ. Neugebauer argues that for Paul the history of the Body of Christ
is concentrated in the cross and resurrection, as Rom. 7.4 shows, and that the Body
of Christ should not be spoken of apart from that dual event: if the community
is named the Body of Christ, that is because the same thing has happened to it as
with the Body of Christ — it has died and risen with Him. The unity of the Christian with Christ therefore is to be understood not in the sense of a spacial relationship but in being integrated into the history that began with Christ. See 'Das
paulinische "in Christo" ', *New Testament Studies*, 1958, pp. 128 ff.

[2] *Die Taufe im Neuen Testament*, 1952, p. 49.

[3] Ibid., n. 83. The interpretation is by no means new: Mundle cites Haussleiter,
Deissmann, Schmitz and Kietzig as maintaining the same view, *Der Glaubensbegriff des Paulism*, 1932, p. 75.

[4] So Burton, *Galatians*, pp. 202 f, Schlier, *Der Brief an die Galater*, p. 127. An
important instance where ἐν Χριστῷ 'Ιησοῦ follows διὰ τῆς πίστεως but refers to an
earlier element in the sentence is seen in Rom. 3.25: ὃν προέθετο ὁ θεὸς ἱλαστήριον
διὰ τῆς πίστεως ἐν τῷ αὐτοῦ αἵματι. In this latter instance there is little doubt as to
the reference of ἐν τῷ αὐτοῦ αἵματι to ἱλαστήριον.

they have believed the news and entered the new age. As Bonnard commented, 'It is not their faith that raised the Galatians to the dignity of sons. They have received this dignity in submitting themselves to the Gospel of Christ; faith is the act by which I recognize that God makes me His son in Jesus Christ'.[1]

But if faith is to be taken seriously, so is baptism. In this passage the exegetes frequently either exalt baptism at the expense of faith or faith at the expense of baptism. To Bonnard e.g. the statement about baptism in v. 27 simply illustrates the proposition of v. 26.[2] In the view of Clemen the baptism referred to in v. 27 confesses the faith spoken of in v. 26.[3] For H. A. A. Kennedy faith is *recharged* with spiritual energy and therefore achieves great things in baptism.[4] Schlier on the other hand considers that faith merely *leads* to the event in which the believer is really taken up, claimed and borne by the new basis of life in Christ Jesus;[5] this would logically mean that God works in baptism independently of faith. Rendtorff however appears to be justified in maintaining that the one sentence qualifies the other. He asserts 'The experience of baptism is the experience of faith'.[6] It would be equally permissible to affirm, 'The grace that is for faith is experienced in baptism'. Baptism is the baptism of faith and grace, so that in it faith receives what graces gives. Above all grace gives Christ, for Christ is the fullness of grace; faith therefore receives Christ in baptism. If Paul were pressed to define the relationship of the two statements in vv. 26–27, I cannot see how he could preserve the force of both sentences apart from affirming that baptism is the moment of faith in which the adoption is realized — in the dual sense of effected by God and grasped by man — which is the same as saying that in baptism faith receives the Christ in whom the adoption is effected. The significance of baptism is the objective facts to which it witnesses, the historic event of redemption and the present gift that it makes possible, embraced through faith in that God who acted and yet acts. Through such an alliance of faith and baptism, Christianity is prevented from evaporating into an ethereal subjectivism on the one hand and from hardening into a fossilized objectivism on the other. The two aspects of Apostolic Christianity are preserved in faith-baptism.[7]

---

[1] Op. cit., p. 77.   [2] Ibid., n. 1.
[3] *Primitive Christianity and its non-Jewish Sources*, p. 216.
[4] *St. Paul and the Mystery Religions*, 1913, p. 250.
[5] Op. cit., p. 128.   [6] Op. cit., p. 36.
[7] I am happy to note that a fellow-Baptist has expressed an essentially similar judgment concerning Gal. 3.26 f, viz. Kjell Kyrø-Rasmussen, *Dåben — et sakramente*, in the Scandinavian trilogy, *Dåpet, Dåben, Dåpen*, 1957, p. 41. See further Mundle, op. cit., p. 84.

3. COLOSSIANS 2.11 f

The extraordinary manner in which baptism is introduced in this passage is due to its forming part of a polemic against a 'philosophy' fashioned 'in accordance with human traditions and the elemental spirits of the universe, and not according to Christ' (2.8). The Christians of Colosse are reminded that it is in Christ that they find fullness of life, not in inferior mediators, for the fullness of God dwells in Him (vv. 9–10). They stand in no need of submission to Jewish ordinances (cf. vv. 16 ff, 20 ff), least of all to circumcision, since in Christ they have undergone a more radical circumcision than that to which their detractors would persuade them: they have been baptized into the circumcision of Christ on the cross (vv. 11–12). The violent intermingling of figures is imposed by the necessity of controversy, as is indicated by the return to the question of circumcision and Jewish ordinances in the immediately ensuing passage (vv. 13 ff). In face of such a heresy as was troubling the Christians of Colosse, it was above all necessary to demonstrate the sufficiency of Christ and His redemptive action.[1]

From this point of view Col. 2.11 ff provides a significant exposition of the theology we believed to lie at the back of Romans 6. For although v. 12 speaks of baptismal participation in the death of Christ, the preceding statement lays unmistakable emphasis on the suffering of death by Christ Himself. 'In Him you were circumcised . . . in the stripping off the body of flesh, in the circumcision of Christ'. Here is a circumcision which entailed the stripping off not of a small portion of flesh but the whole body — a gruesome figure for death. It would accord best with the language used if the two phrases 'in the stripping away of the body of death' and 'in the circumcision of Christ' were construed alike, i.e. by regarding the genitive as objective: the body of flesh was stripped off when Christ was circumcised. It will be recalled that the structure of Rom. 6.3–4 was thought to be dependent on the primary elements of the primitive kerygma: 'Christ died . . . was buried, and has been raised' (1 Cor. 15.3 f). These elements are even more clearly discernible in our passage on this interpretation, despite the change in terminology from language concerning circumcision to that of baptism: Christ's body was stripped off in his death, He was buried, He was raised; in Him the Colossian

---

[1] 'Doctrinally the false teaching was tacitly refuted by an exhibition of the true place and work of the Son', A. S. Peake, 'The Epistle of Paul to the Colossians', *Expositor's Greek Testament*, 1912, p. 487.

Christians stripped off their body of flesh, were buried with Him in baptism and were raised with Him therein. The emphasis lies on Christ's act and the participation of the Christian in that event *in Him* (ἐν ᾧ, v. 11). This is a further reason for preferring to interpret 'in the circumcision of Christ' as denoting his death and not as a synonym for baptism; the sentence in v. 11 provides a consistent application of the symbolism of circumcision, and not until the clause 'buried with him in baptism' is reached does the baptismal language really begin.[1]

The transition to the baptismal language of v. 12 is striking, though it is made a trifle ambiguous through uncertainty as to the reference of the ἐν ᾧ (= 'in which' or 'in whom') of the second clause. In v. 11 the antecedent of ἐν ᾧ is clearly Christ and it has been suggested that an excellent parallelism would result if the relative were similarly interpreted in v. 12: 'in *Him* you were also circumcised . . . since you were buried with Him in baptism; in *Him* you were also raised with Him'.[2] Several considerations militate against this interpretation. First, 'you were raised with him' is more naturally regarded as set in

---

[1] A whole line of exegetes has preferred to interpret the phrase ἡ περιτομὴ τοῦ Χριστοῦ as the 'circumcision which belongs to Christ', in tacit contrast to the circumcision which belongs to Moses and the patriarchs, and thus a periphrasis for baptism: so Lightfoot, *St. Paul's Epistle to the Colossians and Philemon*, 181 ff; Abbott, *The Epistle to the Ephesians and to the Colossians* (I.C.C.), p. 251; Jeremias, *Hat die Urkirche die Kindertaufe geübt?*, p. 40; O. Cullmann, *Baptism in the New Testament*, p. 59; J. Schneider, op. cit., p. 48; J. Crehan, op. cit., p. 41; Meyer, article περιτέμνω, *N.T.*, vol. VI, p. 82. Admittedly the phrase could be so interpreted and the significance of the saying remain unchanged, as appears in the exposition of C. Masson, *L'Épitre de Saint Paul aux Colossiens*, 1950, pp. 125 f. One could go even further in this direction and regard the prior phrase, ἐν τῇ ἀπεκδύσει τοῦ σώματος τῆς σαρκός as baptismal language, since it approximates to the unequivocal baptismal reference in 3.9, to the 'stripping off the old man with his deeds'; and the initial clause could be transferred language, as it were, speaking of baptism under the figure of circumcision. Such a procedure, however, approaches to a *reductio ad absurdum* of the view in question and rather strengthens the likelihood that Paul deliberately keeps to the circumcision symbolism throughout the verse. The fulfilment of circumcision in the Christian is his participation in the death and resurrection of Christ; this is reached by way of baptism, as the immediately ensuing clause shows, but it is the ultimate reality with which Paul begins rather than the means. In varying ways this viewpoint is adopted by Peake, op. cit., p. 525, A. Schlatter, *Erläuterungen zum Neuen Testament*, 7 Teil, p. 277; F. M. Rendtorff, op. cit., p. 44; H. A. A. Kennedy, op. cit., p. 244; G. Bornkamm, 'Taufe und neues Leben bei Paulus', *Theologische Blätter*, 1939, Sp. 238; E. Lohmeyer, *Die Briefe an die Kolosser und an Philemon*, p. 109; C. F. D. Moule, *Epistle to Colossians and Philemon*, 1957, p. 96; the reference to the cross is maintained, though with different applications in mind, by P. C. Marcel, *The Biblical Doctrine of Infant Baptism*, p. 157; *The Church of Scotland Interim Report of the Special Commission on Baptism*, part 1, 1955, p. 39.

[2] This view has been persistently maintained throughout the present century. It was held by von Dobschütz, 'Sakrament und Symbol im Urchristentum', *Theologische Studien und Kritiken*, 1905, p. 4, who cites Haupt in support of it; H. Rendtorff, 'Der Brief an die Kolosser' (*Das Neue Testament Deutsch*, vol. 8), p. 115; Schnackenburg, op. cit., p. 63; Lohmeyer, op. cit., p. 111; Masson, op. cit., p. 126, n. 4.

parallelism with 'you were buried with him'; the 'with him' binds the two verbs together; and 'you were circumcised', v. 11, takes place '*in* him' not '*with* him'. A true parallelism would have given, 'In him you were circumcised . . . in him you were also raised' (ἠγέρθητε instead of συνηγέρθητε). Secondly, the addition of 'with' to 'you were raised' (σὺν to ἠγέρθητε) causes the awkward expression: '*In* Him you were raised *with* Him', the difficulty of which is perceived if we fill out the Greek text as in the preceding clause: ἐν ᾧ καὶ συνηγέρθητε αὐτῷ. Now this could, of course, point to a profound truth: We were raised with Christ because we were in Christ at His resurrection; but the same applies to burial with Christ, so that the first clause of v. 12 should have read, 'In him we were buried with him', but that is not the case (if the first 'in him' of v. 11 is intended to cover 'buried with him', it requires a very observant reader to perceive it). Thirdly, in divorcing 'you were raised with him' from the preceding clause, the verb is loosed from any connection with baptism: 'In Him you were circumcised . . . being buried with Him *in baptism*. In Him also you were raised *through faith in the working of God*'! I doubt whether Paul intended to be so understood. Finally, it should be observed that 'in whom also you were circumcised', v. 11, does not require any further parallel statement, since it follows up in excellent progression 'in whom all the fulness of the Godhead dwells', v. 9 and, 'In him you have been brought to completion', v. 10. On all counts therefore it seems to be the simplest and most natural interpretation of v. 12 to refer the relative pronoun to its immediate antecedent, namely 'in baptism' (ἐν τῷ βαπτίσματι): 'Buried with Him in baptism, in which you were also raised with Him through faith in the working of God'.[1] That brings the saying into line with the antithetic clauses of Rom. 6.3-4, 5, 8, 11 in their relating of baptism to participation in both the dying and the rising with Christ.

It also brings the saying into close relation with Gal. 3.26 f, for as there, so here, faith is integrated into the baptismal event. *In baptism* the baptized is raised *through faith*. The divine and human aspects of the experience of salvation are accorded full recognition. Not that faith effects its own resurrection; faith rejoices in the grace revealed in Christ and directs itself wholly to the God whose almighty power raised Christ from the dead and raises helpless sinners. Marsh, after citing Moffat's translation of this passage[2] commented, 'The tre-

[1] So Peake, op. cit., p. 525; Abbott, op. cit., p. 251; Oepke, *T.W.N.T.*, I, p. 543; Lundberg, *La Typologie baptismale dans l'ancienne Église*, 1942, p. 213.
[2] 'You were buried with Him in your baptism and thereby raised with Him as you believed in the power of the God who raised Him from the dead'.

mendous change which these words describe points to an experience whose efficacy can be explained only in one of two ways: it was either intensely magical or it was intensely spiritual'.[1] The present writer has no doubt as to the alternative adequate to the Pauline teaching. This but sets in clear relief what was earlier remarked about the representation of baptism in Romans 6.1 ff: it is an existential participation in the death and resurrection of Christ.[2]

An important fact emerges from this discussion. If it be true, as we earlier suggested, that Col. 2.11 f is Paul's authentic commentary on Rom. 6.1 ff,[3] it achieves what a good commentary should do, namely brings to clear expression basic principles. On the comparison of the two passages it may be seen that Col. 2.11 f makes plain the following elements of the theology presupposed in Rom. 6: (i) The unity of the believer with Christ in *His* suffering of death on the cross. 'You were circumcised . . . by the stripping off the body of flesh in Christ's circumcision' is brutally candid. All that circumcision stands for, and more, has been fulfilled in the baptized believer through his union (ἐν ᾧ) with Christ in His passion. The primary significance of baptism is its relating the believer to the once for all reconciliation that took place on Golgotha. (ii) The unity of the believer with Christ in His *rising* from death, which signifies not alone a union with Christ in His rising at the first Easter but participation as an experienced factor in the life of the Christian now. We saw that this conviction underlies the ethical application of Rom. 6.4, 11: 'We were buried with Him through baptism . . . that we might walk in newness of life. . . . Reckon yourselves then as dead indeed to sin but living to God in Christ Jesus', for this presumes present experience of the resurrection life in Christ; but the lack of clarity on this point left sufficient room for doubt for some to deny it in Rom. 6. In the present passage there is no possibility of misunderstanding: the resurrection is a power in the life of the Christian now. Not that this means, in the heretical terms of 2 Tim. 2.18, that the resurrection is 'past already'. It is a present factor that anticipates a glorious consummation: 'When Christ who is our Life appears, then you also will appear with Him

---

[1] Op. cit., p. 203.

[2] Bornkamm explicitly stated in respect to Col. 2.11 f: 'The passage gives to baptism a peculiarly formulated relation to the death of Christ: in baptism that which happened on a cosmic scale in the death of Christ is fulfilled existentially. The disarming of the powers that occurred on the cross, the stripping them of their might, is appropriated by the believer in the stripping off his "body of flesh" ', 'Die neutestamentliche Lehre der Taufe', *Theologische Blätter*, 1938, Sp. 51.

[3] It is so characterized by Oepke, 'Urchristentum und Kindertaufe', *Z.N.W.*, 1930, p. 104.

in glory' (Col. 3.3). (iii) The existential nature of participation in
Christ's death and resurrection. This follows from the former point,
but it is sufficiently important to mention it separately. He that participates in the death and resurrection of Christ on Golgotha in baptism
thereby ends an old existence and begins a new one. The later exposition of the Epistle refers to this again and again, nowhere more clearly
than in 3.2: 'Set your minds on things that are above, not on things
that are on earth. For you died, and your life is hid with Christ in
God'. Here the ethical consequences that flow from the end of the old
life are stressed, but the context makes it plain that the transition from
the old life to the new was God-wrought (3.1). (iv) The vital part in
baptism played by faith. This we assumed in Rom. 6.1 ff in view of
the ethical implications of baptism that figure so largely in that
chapter. The only explicit mention of faith in the Romans passage
however is v. 8: 'If we died with Christ, we believe that we shall also
live with Him',[1] but the faith here mentioned is exercised in the
present and not explicitly recalled as a factor in the baptismal event.
The deduction drawn from wider implications becomes an overt and
impressive factor of baptism in Col. 2.12; so important a function is
ascribed to faith here, it is difficult to see how the experience described
can be held to be present without the exercise of faith on the part of
the baptized.

The reason for this clearer exposition in the Colossian passage is
perhaps not far to seek: it lies in the different purposes that the
Apostle had in view when he wrote the two letters. In Rom. 6.1 ff the
ethical element in baptism controls the exposition, for Paul is concerned to refute an antinomian deduction from the supremacy of
grace; his emphasis may be discerned in the conclusion of the exposition: 'Reckon yourselves dead to sin but living to God in Christ
Jesus' (v. 11). In Col. 2.6 ff Paul has to counter a false theology that
lowers the significance of Christ and advocates submission to Jewish
ordinances; he therefore alludes to the significance of baptism in a
more directly theological manner and so illuminates more clearly the
nature of the sacrament itself.[2]

It would be unfitting to leave the consideration of this passage without raising the question as to the relation of circumcision and baptism
implied in Paul's statement. Not a few interpret it as implying a very

---

[1] Its significance, however, is emphasized by Schlatter, *Der Glaube im Neuen
Testament*, 1905, p. 277, n. 1; Flemington, op. cit., pp. 80 f; Bultmann, op. cit.,
p. 318. C. F. D. Moule further pointed out to me that the λογίζεσθε of Rom. 6.11
virtually means πιστεύετε.

[2] For this observation I am indebted to Schnackenburg, op. cit., p. 67.

close connection, especially those who see in the phrase 'the circumcision of Christ' a periphrasis for baptism, 'the circumcision which
Christ gave'; it is considered that since He gave it to replace the
circumcision of Moses, it is to be interpreted on the analogy of the
earlier rite. Jeremias renders the phrase loosely as 'Christian circumcision'; he suggests that Paul hit on it in view of the kind of charge
against him referred to in Acts 21.21: it was true that he had taught
that the circumcision of children is needless, but that was legitimate,
since in the Church that rite has been replaced by baptism; hence
Col. 2.11 f supplies the first trace of the baptism of children born
Christian.[1] From a different point of view Giovanni Miegge concludes
from Col. 2.11 f that to Paul the antithesis between the old and new
circumcision is less important by far than their spiritual identity; for
in this text the significance of circumcision is not the external rite but
the 'stripping off the body of flesh'; this is the real circumcision and
this is precisely the significance of baptism; circumcision accordingly
should be viewed as the promise of which baptism is 'the truth and
the fulfilment itself'.[2]

This treatment of a Pauline text is to be regretted, for it gives the
impression of an undue desire to make hasty leaps to reach a desired
ecclesiastical position. For the belief that circumcision has been replaced in the Church by baptism by no means automatically involves
the corollary that the two rites have identical significance or identical
administration. Col. 2.11 f certainly gives no justification for the
latter presumption, nor does it point in the direction of the former.

It does not seem unjust to demand that no argument be based on
the use of the phrase 'the circumcision of Christ'. The probability
that it relates to the circumcision undergone by Christ in His death,
not that which He has given (=baptism), has already been noticed.
The argument adduced by Jeremias is therefore based on too uncertain a foundation to be given any weight. Nor is Miegge justified in
characterizing the true significance of circumcision as 'a stripping off
the body of flesh'; that phrase first and foremost relates to the stripping off the body of Christ in His death (in contrast to the stripping
off the flesh from a single member of the body) and in the second place
it refers to the death of the 'old man' through identification of the
believer with Christ in His dying. It therefore may be described as a
'spiritual circumcision' ($\pi\epsilon\rho\iota\tau\omega\mu\grave{\eta}$ $\grave{\alpha}\chi\epsilon\iota\rho\sigma\pi\omicron\acute{\iota}\eta\tau\omicron\varsigma$, Col. 2.11), since
it was wrought by God, not man, and it had the effect of cleansing a

[1] *Hat die Urkirche die Kindertaufe geübt?*, pp. 40 f.
[2] *Il Battesimo dei Fanciulli nella storia, nella teoria, nella prassi*, 1943, p. 23.

man from sin and recreating him in Christ. In this way the prophetic call for a circumcision of the heart is fulfilled (Jer. 4.4, Deut. 10.6, 30.6). It is nevertheless a mistake to affirm that such is the *meaning* of the rite of circumcision, as it is of baptism, and that therefore the two rites have the same spiritual significance. This is to confound things that differ. The prophetic call for heart circumcision is a pictorial application of the rite, not an exposition of its meaning. When Paul in Rom. 2.28 f defines 'true circumcision' as 'not external in the flesh' but 'in the Spirit, not the written letter', he is clearly maintaining the same tradition. This kind of circumcision is not *legal* circumcision, for the uncircumcized and the unbaptized may approximate to it (Rom. 2.26 f). It is written in the same vein as Phil. 3.3: 'We are the true circumcision, who worship God in Spirit and glory in Christ Jesus and put no confidence in the flesh'; the true circumcision are here defined not as the baptized but as those who yield that true worship and humble faith for which the prophets appealed. Hence Paul can say, 'Neither is circumcision anything, nor uncircumcision, but a new creation' (Gal. 6.15). Instead of characterizing the baptism that introduces to this new creation as the fulfilment of the rite of circumcision, it is better to say that it leads to the fulfilment of the prophetic hope of a spiritual circumcision. And this it does in virtue of its association with the Christ who brought the new creation into being through His death and resurrection.

In the exegesis of Col. 2.11 f it is not easy to determine whether Paul began with the idea of the greater circumcision accomplished in Christ, without any thought of baptism, or whether baptism was in his mind in the very language he used of the circumcision of Christ; and if the former be true, it has to be decided whether the passage of thought to baptism is external, even artificial, or whether it was due to a natural association of ideas, reflecting a basic element in Paul's theology. If baptism was in Paul's mind in the formulation of v. 11, then the conception of baptism as the new circumcision was very deeply ingrained in his thinking. I have suggested in the earlier exposition that it is easier to assume that the language of v. 11, describing the death of Christ as a circumcision, is adopted by Paul in view of the controversy with the Colossian heretics and that the reference to baptism is secondary. Granting that, however, I am bound to admit that the way the thought flows from circumcision to baptism hints that the association was an already formed one in the Apostle's mind and was not accidental. If the basic kerygmatic succession forms the background of this passage — Christ's death, burial and resurrection

— Paul could scarcely have passed from 'circumcised in Christ's death' to 'buried with Him in baptism' without closely relating the two ideas; moreover to be buried with Christ in baptism is to participate in that death denoted by the verb, 'You were circumcised' ($\pi\epsilon\rho\iota\epsilon\tau\mu\dot{\eta}\theta\eta\tau\epsilon$). Undoubtedly the description of Christ's death as a circumcision is figurative, in the prophetic succession; but it is used to demonstrate that no further circumcision is required by the Colossian Christians, a deduction which the prophets did not draw. The uncircumcised Colossians have been circumcised in a radical fashion in Christ through baptism, and need no other. If then the argument may be represented as: You have been circumcised in Christ's death; this you effectively entered into through baptism; therefore you need no circumcision administered by man: it would seem that in the Christian Church baptism has replaced circumcision through its mediation of the spiritual circumcision demanded by the prophets.

If this be a just assessment of Paul's teaching, two observations may be in place. First, it must be frankly recognized that the Church of Jerusalem, as the majority of Jewish Christians, did not agree with it. Jeremias has endeavoured to draw one lesson from Acts 21.21; a deduction less open to objection would be that the allegation, current among the 'thousands all zealous for the law' in the Jerusalem church, that Paul taught Jews of the Dispersion to forsake Moses and not to circumcize their children, was viewed by James as unbelievable. He advises Paul to adopt a course of action whereby 'all will know that there is nothing in what they have been told about you, but that you yourself live in observance of the law' (Acts 23.24). Doubtless the reason for Paul's submission to James' advice was to refute the idea that he advocated that all Christian Jews should 'forsake Moses'. But in the eyes of the Church of Jerusalem the practice of circumcision was included in the adherence to Moses. Since baptism was administered in Jerusalem as in all other Christian communities, the two rites were clearly maintained side by side in Palestinian churches and there was no possibility for baptism being regarded by them as in any sense a replacement of circumcision. Had the Roman war not intervened, there is no telling how long this dual practice would have continued. Secondly, it should be apparent that where Paul's teaching was current, the conditions of the administration of baptism could not be governed by those relating to the administration of circumcision. The 'circumcision of the heart, in the Spirit and not letter of law' is for 'the Jew who is one inwardly' (Rom. 2.28 f). The circumcision of the old covenant was administered, without exception so far as native

Jews were concerned, to the Jew who was one outwardly. We have to do here with a different conception of the People of God and therefore of the rite that characterizes its members. More than one exegete has pointed out that the most likely point of contact between circumcision as a rite and baptism is their joint character of being rites of initiation; circumcision was the mode of (male) entry into the Israel of the old covenant, baptism the mode of entry into the Israel of the new covenant.[1] The nature of the two rites was determined by the factors which caused their adoption for this purpose and the nature of the societies into which they admitted. Clearly this is not a matter which can be dealt with adequately at this point and its further discussion must be left till later.

4. COLOSSIANS 1.13 f, 2.15

It is possible that the doctrine of baptism to be gained from Col. 2.11 f is represented under a different form in the two passages here cited; but so much uncertainty attaches to the interpretation of the latter statement, the application to baptism can be set forth only in a tentative fashion.

In Col. 1.13 it is said that the Father 'rescued us from the power of darkness and transferred us into the kingdom of His beloved Son'. The tense in both cases is aorist; a deliverance from the satanic powers that rule the world was experienced by 'us' and simultaneously was accompanied by an entrance into the Kingdom of Christ. That this deliverance is to be understood in a baptismal context is made the more probable in that the Apostle at once adds, 'in whom we have redemption, the forgiveness of sins' (v. 14). Deliverance from the old aeon, entry into the new, redemption and forgiveness are experienced in Christ ($\dot{\epsilon}\nu$ $\ddot{\psi}$, v. 14), for He ended the old age and brought in the new when He accomplished redemption and made forgiveness available for man. It is the same theology that we have perceived in Rom. 6.1 ff and Col. 2.11 f: Christ has wrought an act of deliverance, into which the believer has been drawn and the power of which the believer has experienced through participation in Christ in baptism ($\dot{\epsilon}\nu$ $\ddot{\psi}$, v. 14!). But the portrayal of the deliverance is different in Col. 1.13 from that in the former passages: the terms used are characteristic of the eschatological process. The verb 'rescue' ($\dot{\rho}\acute{\nu}o\mu\alpha\iota$) is consistently used in the New Testament in eschatological contexts; see especially Mt. 6.13, 1 Thess. 1.10, 2 Tim. 4.18, 2 Pt. 2.9; in Rom.

[1] So substantially Preisker, 'Die Vicariatstaufe 1 Cor. 15.29', Z.N.W., 1924, p. 301; Dibelius, op. cit., pp. 30 f; Lampe, *The Seal of the Spirit*, pp. 5, 56, 83, 85.

11.26 Christ is called the Deliverer or Rescuer (ὁ ῥυόμενος), for He turns away ungodliness from Jacob in the end of the times. In our passage redemption is depicted as a rescue from the evil powers that hold sway in the world and a being planted in the Kingdom of the end that Christ has paradoxically even now established.

It is here that we find a possible connection with Col. 2.14 f. The bond that testified against us was nailed to the cross, like the *titlos* that described the crime of an executed man, but in this case triumphantly so — it was a cancelled bond! (v. 14). The Apostle proceeds, 'stripping off the powers and authorities he made a public spectacle of them and led them in the train of his triumph'. If the participle ἀπεκδυσάμενος is interpreted as in 3.9 and in the same sense as ἀπέκδυσις in 2.11, it will be most natural to understand Christ as the subject and to translate it 'stripping off Himself'. If it be asked, 'Stripping Himself of what?' the answers are various. The Latin Fathers thought of the flesh as the object, and that is not impossible, since the 'flesh' is the means by which the evil powers can exercise their tyranny over man.[1] The Greek Fathers regarded the 'principalities and powers' as the object and Lightfoot accepted their suggestion.[2] It is possible to combine both interpretations as when E. F. Scott interprets: 'In His death He threw off this contaminated nature which He had assumed for our sakes, thus breaking free from His enemies'.[3] These differences of interpretation are comparatively insignificant for they have in common one important element: they agree that Christ stripped the powers of darkness from Himself *in His death*. In so doing He rescued humanity from the powers (Col. 1.13) and in baptism we participate in His victory.[4]

This interpretation has the merit of retaining the same meaning for the key term ἀπεκδύεσθαι in Col. 1 and 2. But it is open to two objections. The subject of v. 13 is explicitly said to be God and there is no indication of a change of subject in vv. 14–15. In that case the meaning of ἀπεκδυσάμενος will be 'despoiling' or 'disarming'. The second objection is bound up with this assumption: the despoiling of the powers is not in the submission of Christ to the death they caused

---

[1] So J. A. T. Robinson, op. cit., p. 41: 'The dying Jesus, like a king, divests Himself of that flesh, the tool and medium of their power, and thereby exposes them to ridicule for their Pyrrhic victory'.

[2] 'The powers of evil, which had clung like a Nessus robe about His humanity, were torn off and cast aside for ever', *Colossians and Philemon*, p. 188.

[3] *The Epistle of Paul to the Colossians, to Philemon and to the Ephesians*, p. 48. Scott actually prefers the tradition represented in the A.V.

[4] So Lightfoot, op. cit., pp. 188 f; Bornkamm, *Theologische Blätter*, 1938, Sp. 51; Heitmüller, *Im Namen Jesu*, pp. 322 f.

(1 Cor. 2.6) but in God's exaltation of Him through resurrection. This is an attractive explanation, and is perhaps preferable to the former.[1] If accepted the statement may still be regarded as conveying an idea related to Col. 1.13, since the despoiling of the principalities and powers through Christ's victorious exaltation involves redemption for the race and the 'opening of the kingdom of heaven for all believers'. The baptismal participation in this victory will then be in the believer's sharing in Christ's resurrection rather than in dying with Him. Indeed, on the supposition of a continuity of subject from v. 12, the representation of the Colossian Christians as formerly 'dead in trespasses and the uncircumcision of your flesh' is probably being maintained; God through the resurrection of Christ has given them life from the dead. If the Colossians were thought of as dead already, the idea of dying with Christ in baptism has no place here. But the impartation of life to the dead will presumably be conceived of as taking place in conversion-baptism, in view of the immediately foregoing context (2.11–12).

It will be appreciated that the baptismal inferences from these passages are hardly clear and one would hesitate to advance them were it not for the unambiguous teaching on baptism elsewhere in the Colossian Epistle, which does not seem unrelated to 1.13 f and 2.15. If the baptismal reference be granted, their value will lie in the eschatological significance accorded to the sacrament. Baptism witnesses a deliverance from the old aeon, an entry into the Kingdom of God's beloved Son, resurrection from the dead, and participation in the victory over all evil powers.

5. I CORINTHIANS 6.11

'Do you not know that the unrighteous will not inherit the Kingdom of God?' asks Paul of the Corinthians (v. 9). To judge from his description of the 'unrighteous', the reminder, 'And such were some of you', indicates that some members of the Church of Corinth had a decidedly seamy past. 'But you had yourselves washed from those sins, you became sanctified, you were justified, in the name of the Lord Jesus and in the Spirit of our God'. The question may be raised, 'Is this a baptismal saying? Or is the Apostle relating an experience of deliverance independent of any rite of initiation?' There is an under-

---

[1] It is adopted by Lohmeyer, op. cit., p. 120 and Dibelius, op. cit., pp. 32 f. Lightfoot's objection that ἀπεκδυσάμενος could not be used in this sense in the middle is not accepted by Blass-Debrunner, who regard it as an example of a tendency in N.T. Greek to substitute the middle for active voice in certain verbs; *Grammatik des neutestamentlichen Griechisch*, 10th ed. 1959, p. 198.

standable reluctance in some quarters to recognize a baptismal context for this statement, especially as it conjoins with the cleansing spoken of justification and sanctification. But the voice of scholarship is unanimous in affirming the association with baptism. The following considerations point to the correctness of that judgment.

(i) The coincidence of language between 'you had yourselves washed . . . in the name of the Lord Jesus' and that used by Ananias to Paul, 'Get baptized and wash away your sins, calling on his name' (Acts 22.16) is so close as to make it difficult to dissociate the 'washing' of 1 Cor. 6.11 from the baptismal cleansing.[1]

(ii) The aorist points to an occasion when the washing, sanctification and justification took place. It may not be an undue pressing of distinctions to observe the change from the imperfect $\hat{\eta}\tau\epsilon$ to the succession of aorists: 'You used to be men of that kind; but there came a time when you got yourselves washed, sanctified, justified'.[2]

(iii) 'In the name of the Lord Jesus Christ' reflects the use of the Name in the baptismal formula.

(iv) 'In the Spirit of our God' associates the Spirit along with the Risen Lord as Agent of the deliverance wrought in the Corinthians. That the experience of the Spirit is linked with baptism in the Name of the Lord Jesus needs no further demonstration after our discussion of the evidence on this matter in the Book of Acts.

(v) The great baptismal utterances of Paul that we have considered show that for him there is no opposition between sacramental act and spiritual experience of grace; on the contrary, the former implies the latter. Rom. 6.1 ff, Gal. 2.26 f, Col. 2.11 f testify to the same momentous transition to the new existence that is expressed in different language in 1 Cor. 6.11.

Accordingly, the majority of exegetes concur in interpreting this statement in the context of baptism; in which case it would seem right to accord due weight to the middle voice of $\mathring{a}\pi\epsilon\lambda o\acute{v}\sigma a\sigma\theta\epsilon$ and to render it in some such fashion as above, 'You had yourself washed from (your sins)',[3] and to recognize that the verb implies voluntary action on the part of the baptized.[4] Anderson Scott is alone in believing that baptism is referred to only in this verb and that Paul describes the stages of Christian experience in reverse order: 'Ye were baptized, and behind that lay your consecration by the Spirit; ye were

---

[1] So H. T. Andrews, 'The Place of the Sacraments in the Teaching of St. Paul', *The Expositor*, 1916, p. 359.
[2] So Schnackenburg, op. cit., p. 2. [3] So Bauer, *Wörterbuch zum N.T.*, p. 174.
[4] 'Their seeking baptism was their own act, and they entered the water as voluntary agents, just as St. Paul did'. Robertson and Plummer, op. cit., p. 119.

consecrated, and behind that lay your justification, which took place the moment you "called on the name of the Lord" and were saved'.[1] This interpretation is to be rejected. The 'consecration' by the Spirit and 'justification' by the Lord Jesus occurred at the same time — it is a once for all consecration that Paul has in mind, not a process — and they took place when the Corinthians received their 'cleansing'. The three aorists are to be regarded as denoting coincidental action and all three are qualified by 'in the name of the Lord Jesus and by the Spirit of our God'.

This fact has suggested to various exegetes that Paul uses the three terms loosely here and they are not to be interpreted with theological precision: one indivisible experience of redemption is in mind, viewed under three different categories.[2] While this is so, it is hardly permissible to deny that Paul in this passage intends $\epsilon\delta\iota\kappa\alpha\iota\omega\theta\eta\tau\epsilon$ to convey the notion, 'you were justified', on the ground that in his teaching elsewhere justification is granted on the basis of faith. Perhaps we should rather gather that Paul's theological terms are more flexible than we sometimes allow and that faith and baptism are more closely interrelated than the Church has permitted them to be.

'You had yourselves washed from your sins'. It is tempting to restrict this to denote simply a 'sacramental purification' from sins.[3] If by such a phrase a merely ritual purification is intended, a kind of new covenant levitical pronouncement of being clean, the idea is unacceptable. The speaker is Paul the missionary, addressing converts among whom were numbered former adulterers, homosexuals, thieves, drunkards, gluttons, cursers (vv. 9 f). For them this 'sacramental purification' had meant a real release from their iniquity, forgiveness of their guilt and grace to forsake their evil ways. Their baptism had occasioned a revolution in their life. Just as we saw that the reality of dying and rising with Christ in baptism was reproduced in the image of stripping off the old man and putting on the new in Gal. 3.26 f and Col. 3.9, so we find it under yet another figure in this passage: in 'you had yourselves washed' is represented a dissolution of the bond with the sinful past, the end of existence under the sway of the powers of darkness; the positive aspect of resurrection life with Christ has its counterpart in the sanctification and justification in the name of Christ and in the Holy Spirit.[4]

[1] *Christianity according to St. Paul*, 1927, p. 120.

[2] So Heitmüller, op. cit., p. 321; Robertson and Plummer, op. cit., p. 120; Bultmann, op. cit., p. 136.   [3] Johannes Weiss, op. cit., p. 632.

[4] Lietzmann has the bones of the argument when he comments: 'The basic thought is clear: "since baptism the time of sin in the flesh lies behind you" ', op. cit., p. 26.

'You were sanctified' is a passive, not a middle verb, hence the accent falls on the divine act of consecration, rather than on the human act of dedication. Naturally the divine act of appropriation in the name of the Lord Jesus does not exclude the element of surrender to the sovereignty of the exalted Kurios as the baptized calls on the name of the Lord. But the addition of 'in the Spirit of our God' underscores yet further the divine operation signified in 'you were sanctified': in Christ and by the Spirit the believer is 'transferred into the kingdom of His beloved Son' (Col. 1.13), he is set apart to become a member of the consecrated people, ἅγιος a 'saint'.

'You were justified' (ἐδικαιώθητε) possibly harks back to the 'unjust' (ἄδικοι) who will not inherit the kingdom of God (v. 9); for 'such were some of you' reminds the Corinthians that some of them had been 'unjust'; in the name of the Lord Jesus and in the Spirit of God they have become 'just' (δίκαιοι). The disinclination of certain exegetes to allow 'you were justified' its normal force has already been noted — Bultmann thinks that Paul is here presenting the 'general-Christian view of baptism'.[1] Perhaps he is; but could Paul ever speak of justification in a manner unrelated to its characteristic significance as he was wont to preach it? It is hard to think so. The accent on justification in Rom. 4 is different from that in Phil. 3.9, but any presentation of Paul's doctrine that excludes the proper force of either passage is too narrow and is therefore false to Paul. Possibly the same must be said of 1 Cor. 6.11. In this passage the emphasis is on the dynamic aspect of justification — 'in the Spirit of our God' — whereby men that had been 'unjust' to a shocking degree could now be described as 'washed, consecrated, justified'. It would indicate that the baptized have something more than a changed status; men that had been dead now live, they are new creatures in a new creation, for they had been baptized in the name of the Lord Jesus and He was made by God *their righteousness*! (1 Cor. 1.30).

Marsh suggested that in this passage Paul is using 'a trick of style in which compression is used for the sake of brevity'.[2] It is a curious way of putting it, but it is not doubtful that Paul takes much for granted in expressing himself in this manner. Notably he takes his whole doctrine of baptism for granted in this brief allusion to its power. The significance of 'in the name of the Lord Jesus Christ' is presumed as known without further explanation: the Name of Jesus Christ is called on by the baptismal candidate in appeal for washing, consecration, righteousness, and the Name of Jesus Christ is called

[1] Op. cit., p. 136.   [2] Op. cit., p. 177, n. 1.

over him by the baptizer, signifying that Jesus Christ who died and rose for the baptizand cleanses, consecrates and justifies him. It may be that in this context we are to see in the twice repeated employment of the preposition ἐν an instance of its instrumental meaning: the baptized is cleansed, consecrated and justified *by* the Name of the Lord Christ and *by* the Spirit of our God; not, of course, by the magic effect of pronouncing a name, but by the prayer of the baptized as he calls on the Name of the Lord and by the action of the Lord who is invoked, operating through the Spirit who is His Agent.[1] Once more no mention of faith is found in this passage, yet it is presumed in the middle voice of ἀπελούσασθε ('you had yourselves washed') and in the inseparability of justification and faith in the Pauline theology. The implications of this recognition have scarcely been faced in traditional theology. For the inference cannot be avoided that the reality signified by justification and sanctification is apprehended *in baptism by faith*. Justification is known in Christ, as a believer, who knows that in the crucified and risen Redeemer alone grace is to be found, calls on the Name of the Lord in baptism and the Redeemer, in the calling of His name over the baptized, appropriates him to Himself.[2]

At the risk of repetition it must be explicitly mentioned that the ethical implication of baptism is once more to the fore in a baptismal context. Not alone are the Corinthians said to have experienced deliverance from the unrighteousness that excludes from the kingdom into the new existence that inherits it; the statement itself is an exhortation to live as men that are washed, consecrated and justified. The Corinthian believers stand between their experience of redemption and the consummation, when the inheritance will be fully entered upon; but that will be a day wherein the fire shall try every man's work, of what sort it is (1 Cor. 3.12); their duty is to live by the grace opened up to them at their baptism in expectation of the 'redemption of the body' (Eph. 1.13 f).[3]

Finally it is to be observed that our passage contains an approach to a Trinitarian formulation of baptism; it sets alongside the baptismal formula 'in the name of the Lord Jesus' the added phrase 'in the

---

[1] See the discussion of Heitmüller, op. cit., pp. 74 f; Windisch, op. cit., p. 130; Lietzmann, op. cit., p. 26; Schneider, op. cit., p. 43.

[2] This was emphasized by Mundle: '1 Cor. 6.11 enables us to define the significance of baptism in the context of the Pauline "faith that justifies", that is, that the believer in Christ receives justification in baptism', op. cit., p. 86. To similar effect A. Richardson, *Introduction to the Theology of the N.T.*, p. 238.

[3] The point is well made by H. D. Wendland, 'Die Briefe an die Korinther', *N.T.D.*, p. 36.

Spirit', qualified by the terms 'of our God'. This is insufficient evidence for the existence in Paul's time of a baptism in the name of the Father, Son and Holy Spirit, but it provides a hint of the way in which the Trinitarian formula arose, namely by the enumeration of respects in which baptism in the name of the Lord Jesus involved the operation of the Father and the Holy Spirit. While *the Spirit of our God* is associated with Christ in the effective working in baptism, Col. 2.12 speaks of being raised in baptism through faith in the operation of *God* who raised Christ from the dead. Sooner or later it was inevitable that the realization that baptism was essentially a Trinitarian operation should express itself in a Trinitarian formulation: and such we find in Mt. 28.19.

6. I CORINTHIANS 12.13

For the first time we meet here an explicit declaration that baptism leads into the Church: 'By one Spirit we were all baptized to one body.' English translation and exposition tends to render the ἐν ἑνὶ Πνεύματι 'by one Spirit', while the Continental tradition seems to favour '*in* one Spirit'. On the analogy of 1 Cor. 6.11 the former view would be preferred, and the immediately preceding references to the Spirit's agency in the Church might well seem to leave no room for argument: 'To one man utterance of wisdom is given through the Spirit (διὰ τοῦ Πνεύματος), and to another the utterance of knowledge, according to (κατὰ) the same Spirit, to another gifts of healing by (ἐν) the one Spirit' (1 Cor. 12.8 f). Yet baptism ἐν one Spirit inevitably recalls baptism ἐν ὕδατι, 'in water' and in 1 Cor. 10.2 we have the statement, 'all were baptized to Moses, in the cloud and in the sea' (ἐν τῇ νεφέλῃ καὶ ἐν τῇ θαλάσσῃ) suggesting that when Paul uses ἐν with the verb to baptize he has in view the element in which baptism takes place. Basically the meaning is not greatly affected, since on the one interpretation the Spirit is viewed as the Agent of baptism to membership in the Body and on the other He is the element in which one is baptized so as to be in the Body. But the point is of interest since it sharpens the question, ever and again raised by enquirers and scholars alike, whether Paul is really speaking of the normal rite of baptism or whether he uses baptism as a figure for the divine outpouring of the Spirit on the believer. Is there by chance an implicit contrast between the two 'baptisms', comparable to that in the preaching of John the Baptist, who offset his own baptism in water with the baptism in Spirit that the Messiah was to bestow?

It may assist in deciding the issue to consider the grounds on which it is held that Paul does speak here of a 'baptism of the Spirit' distinguished from the Church's rite of baptism. Griffith Thomas, opposing the plea of H. T. Andrews that the statement relates to baptism, demanded: 'How is it possible for the application of water to accomplish the spiritual act of incorporating us into the Body of Christ? How can that which is physical effect that which is spiritual?'[1] In the light of our pilgrimage thus far through the Pauline country, the question appears naive from a responsible theologian. The interrelating of gospel, faith, confession, grace, baptism appears never to have come within the horizon of this writer, nor the idea of baptism as a meeting of God and a penitent sinner on the basis of the Christ event; our exposition of Rom. 6.1 ff, Gal. 3.26 f, Col. 2.11 f etc., would presumably have been unacceptable to him. Something similar must unfortunately be said of E. Best's comment on this passage, which scarcely reflects the wealth of insight that he has given us in his book: 'The baptism of 1 Cor. 12.13 . . . is not water baptism but baptism in the Spirit. Water baptism is the sign and seal of this latter baptism — just as in Rom. 6.1–4 water baptism does not effect our death and resurrection with Christ, which took place upon the cross, but is the sign and seal of it to us. And for Paul the reception of the Spirit by the believer is connected with faith'.[2] There is no need for us to consider again the relationship between baptism and the redemptive deed of Christ, as set forth in Rom. 6.1 ff; it must be left to the reader to judge whether this summary of Paul's teaching is more just than that set forth earlier in this book. We have learned from some Pauline passages not to set faith and baptism in opposition to each other but to appreciate their inseparability in the penitent's experience of grace. This applies to the relationship of the believer with the Spirit equally as to his relationship with Christ. Finally, we may notice the view of Clemen, that baptism does not effect entry into the Church but accompanies the act of full admission to the Church.[3] Full admission by whom? By officers of the Church? Then baptism is a purely human and external rite — a view impossible to reconcile with the baptism 'in the name of Christ Jesus' that we have elsewhere considered. Is it an admission into the Church by God? Then baptism embodies the response of the convert to the call of God in the midst of his people and is the occasion when God Himself receives him as his own; the

---

[1] 'The Place of the Sacraments in the Teaching of St. Paul', *The Expositor*, 1917, p. 379.
[2] *One Body in Christ*, p. 73.   [3] Op. cit., p. 219.

difference of concept from that generally received is not great, but I fancy that Clemen did not wish to go so far. Yet can any baptismal utterance go 'further' than that which is implied in Rom. 6.1 ff? An adequate appreciation of that passage will make it apparent that the relationship between the Spirit and baptism in 1 Cor. 12.13 is no more than would be expected.

More specifically, the contention that the baptism 'in or by one Spirit', 1 Cor. 12.13, is Christian baptism in water (ἐν ὕδατι), seems demanded by the following considerations:

(i) On our reading of 1 Cor. 6.11, baptism is characterized by Paul as 'in the name of the Lord Jesus and in the Spirit of our God', a closely related conception to that in the present passage. It will be recalled that one of the operations of Christ by His Spirit in baptism is the 'consecration' of the believer, i.e. the constituting him of a member of the consecrated people.

(ii) The Book of Acts represents that the primitive Church saw the fulfilment of John's prediction of the messianic baptism 'in Spirit' (ἐν Πνεύματι) first in the outpouring of Pentecost and then in its administration of baptism to those responsive to the gospel. This saying reflects the same conviction.

(iii) Gal. 3.27 ff links baptism to Christ with baptism to the Church: 'All you that were baptized to Christ put on Christ. There is neither Jew nor Greek, slave nor free, male nor female, for you are all one in Christ Jesus'. This silent transition from Christ to the Body is reproduced in 1 Cor. 12.13, where the statement, 'So also is Christ' is followed by 'In one Spirit you were all baptized to one Body'.

(iv) The similarity between Gal. 3.27 f and 1 Cor. 12.12–13 is reproduced in Paul's emphasis that baptism to Christ and his Church entails an obliteration of social distinctions. If in Gal. 3 this happy result follows on Christian baptism and in 1 Cor. 12.13 it follows on baptism in the Spirit, the inference is not unreasonable that the two baptisms are one.

The reason for their unity is not far to seek: Christian baptism is 'in the name of the Lord Jesus', to the crucified and exalted Redeemer, who has sent to His Church the Spirit promised from the Father; and the Spirit He sends is his Agent, communicating the benefits of His redemption. Not surprisingly then the baptism 'to Christ' (εἰς Χριστόν), which Paul described as a 'putting on' Christ, setting a man 'in Christ' (ἐν Χριστῷ, Gal. 3.27 f), is also said to be a baptism ἐν Πνεύματι — by the Spirit, in the Spirit, bestowing the Spirit; for it is only by the Spirit that a man can be in the *Koinonia* of

Christ (Rom. 8.9): 'Any one who does not have the Spirit of Christ does not belong to Him'.

There is nothing automatic about this association of baptism and the Spirit, any more than there is between baptism to Christ, and life in Christ. It is incomprehensible how Johannes Weiss could deduce from the closing words of the verse ('we were all imbued with the one Spirit') the idea: 'The miracle is worked through the Spirit who is effectively present in baptism and fills the water with His powers. . . The believer is washed around and wholly penetrated by the powers of the Spirit operative in the water'.[1] On the contrary, the relation of the believer with the Spirit is to be construed in strict analogy with his relation to the Risen Christ, as Rom. 8.9–11, 14 f, 16 f, 26 f show. The imagery used in connection with the Spirit's mission should not blind us to this fact. The term 'we were given water' ($\dot{\epsilon}\pi o\tau i\sigma\theta\eta\mu\epsilon\nu$), employed in this verse, is connected with the idea of the outpouring of the Spirit in the last times, as described in the prophets (Is. 32.15, Joel 3.1 ff etc.). Apart from its other appearances in the LXX it is used in this manner in Is. 29.10: 'The Lord has poured out upon you ($\pi\epsilon\pi\dot{o}\tau\iota\kappa\epsilon\nu$ $\dot{\upsilon}\mu\hat{a}s$) a spirit of deep sleep . . .'. It is likely that it contains a similar signification in our passage: We were baptized in one Spirit to one body . . . we received the flood tide of the Spirit in the same event. Or, to keep more closely to the metaphors: We were *immersed* in one Spirit . . . and were *saturated* in His outpouring.[2]

The controlling idea of this statement, however, is not a personal, in the sense of private, receiving of the Spirit but the social concept of incorporation of the baptized through the Spirit into the Body of Christ. In this connection the following observations may be offered: (i) The believer is baptized 'to one Body'; not so as to *form* the Body but to *participate* in it, to be added to it. The Body exists before the believer is baptized; through grace he is incorporated into it by the Spirit. (ii) The believer is baptized 'to one Body' because he is baptized 'to Christ', *not vice versa*. This is abundantly clear from Gal. 3.27, where the succession baptized to Christ ($\epsilon i s$ $X\rho\iota\sigma\tau\dot{o}\nu$), putting on Christ, being in Christ ($\dot{\epsilon}\nu$ $X\rho\iota\sigma\tau\hat{\omega}$), shows clearly where the

[1] Op. cit., p. 134.
[2] See the excellent exposition of this verse in Schnackenburg, op. cit., pp. 79 f, and to the same effect Lampe, op. cit., p. 56, Flemington, op. cit., p. 56, Robertson and Plummer, op. cit., p. 272. The view maintained by Luther and Calvin, that $\dot{\epsilon}\pi o\tau i\sigma\theta\eta\mu\epsilon\nu$ refers to drinking the cup in the Lord's Supper is still represented by Leipoldt, op. cit., p. 61, Schlatter, op. cit., p. 346, Wendland, op. cit., p. 74, and Lietzmann hesitantly, op. cit., p. 63; it is scarcely feasible however, since there is no encouragement for the view that in the Supper we *drink* the Spirit, and the aorist tense points to a single occasion of receiving the Spirit, not to a habitual reception.

emphasis is conceived to lie. Doubtless it is impossible to contemplate being baptized to Christ without being baptized to the Body, but the Body must be defined in terms of Christ, not vice versa. If we appeal to the concept of corporate personality, it is Christ who is the 'inclusive personality' and who informs the members with His character, He does not receive His nature from them. The Church is subject to Christ in all things, including its very life. (iii) The twice repeated 'all' ($\pi\acute{a}\nu\tau\epsilon\varsigma$) of v. 13 is noteworthy: to be baptized into the one Body is possible only because it is a baptism in the Spirit. It is not said to be a preliminary gift of Spirit requiring later supplementation. He was 'poured in overflowing measure' upon us all. On the one hand this indicates that the Spirit is given to all and is not reserved for a privileged elite in the Church; on the other hand it clearly rules out any interpretation of baptism which requires it to be complemented by a later rite for the impartation of the Spirit.[1] (iv) Baptism into the one Body by the one Spirit overcomes the deepest religious and social divisions of mankind: in the Body there is no room for maintaining the distinctions between Jew and Gentile, and slaves and free; in Christ they are 'one man' (Gal. 3.28), and the one Spirit divides his gifts to all. The unity of the Body thus does not consist in uniformity of character and function, on the contrary Paul is about to explain how the very idea of a body presumes the necessity of members with different functions; but these differentiated functions are possible because the Body is a unity, informed by one life and inspired by one Spirit. As with the Supper, baptism obliterates the disunities of man and harmonizes them in the unity of Christ's Body in the one Spirit.

7. 2 CORINTHIANS 1.22, EPHESIANS 1.30, 4.30

'He who confirms us with you to Christ . . . is God'. Paul's ground of steadfastness in Christ is none other than the omnipotent God Himself. In this the Apostle exults; he heaps up figures to underscore its reality and to illustrate its meaning: God *anointed* us, *set his seal* upon us, gave us the Spirit as *the first instalment* of our inheritance in the Kingdom. Our concern in quoting the saying is less to explicate the images employed than to determine whether it has reference to baptism. In so doing it is impossible for us to dismiss from the mind that in the church from the second century on the term 'seal' was used

---

[1] The claim made by Goudge, that $\dot{\epsilon}\pi o\tau\acute{\iota}\sigma\theta\eta\mu\epsilon\nu$ relates to a special gift of the Spirit by the laying on of hands, apart from the baptism in one Spirit to the one Body, is without foundation in Paul's teaching and draws distinctions between the beginning and end of the verse which exist only in the minds predetermined by ecclesiastical tradition.

as a synonym for baptism. Yet there is a resistance from a variety of quarters to reading this meaning into the Pauline statements; in this the Roman Catholic R. Schnackenburg,[1] the Reformed scholar M. Bouttier[2] and the Baptist P. W. Evans[3] find themselves in agreement, while Gregory Dix denies that it refers to baptism even in the second century.[4] The motives of these writers naturally vary: Schnackenburg is laudably anxious not to let second century ideas control exegesis; Bouttier considers we have here a typical case of the Church's externalizing of the Christian religion — what originally denoted an inward outpouring of the Spirit independent of baptism became applied to the outward rite of baptism; Evans in like vein points out that the 'promise of the Spirit' in the Old Testament is connected with moral and spiritual dispositions rather than with the performance of any rite. There is truth in these contentions, but the latter two remind us of arguments we have already met that proceed from a failure to perceive the spiritual conception of baptism in the Apostolic writings. The position of Dix is different: he is concerned to retain the 'seal' for confirmation; on the ground that the 'sealing' in the rite of Hippolytus takes place in the chrismation immediately after the baptism, he contends that the same significance must be attached to the 'seal' in the New Testament and sub-Apostolic writings prior to Hippolytus.[5] Dix steadfastly discountenances the idea that there may have been a development in the thought and practice of the Church in this matter. Yet it is difficult to deny that Hermas applied the term 'seal' to baptism in view of Similitude 9. xvi. 3 f: 'Before a man has borne the name of (the Son of) God he is dead; but when he has received the seal he layeth aside his deadness and resumeth life. The seal then is the water; so they go down into the water dead and they come up alive. Thus to them also this seal was preached, and they availed themselves of it that they might enter into the kingdom of God'. When we consider the New Testament evidence that goes before Hermas there would seem justification for the statement of J. E. L. Oulton: 'I submit that the use of the term "seal" as applied to Holy Baptism underwent a change towards the end of the second century and in the early years of the third, and that its application as in "Hippolytus" and as a rule Clement of Alexandria to the laying on of hands or

[1] *Das Heilsgeschehen in der Taufe*, pp. 84 f.
[2] Article 'Seal', in *Vocabulary of the Bible*, ed. J. J. von Allmen, E.T., 1958, p. 391.
[3] 'Sealing a Term for Baptism', *Baptist Quarterly*, vol. XVI, 1955–6, pp. 173 ff.
[4] 'The "Seal" in the Second Century', *Theology*, 1948, pp. 7 ff.
[5] This position is assumed by Dix in all his writings; see e.g. *The Shape of the Liturgy*, p. 260, *Confirmation and Baptism*, p. 14

chrism or sign of the cross, as distinct from the immersion in water, is not the earliest use, according to which it meant the baptism in water or the baptismal rite as a whole'.[1] But we are in measure anticipating what must yet be considered.

The reasons for associating the seal of the Spirit with baptism may be recounted as follows:

(i) The use of the aorist tense in the three verbs, anointed, sealed, gave, in 2 Cor. 1.22 best accords with a definite point of time in the past (the same applies to the verb 'you were sealed' in Eph. 1.13, 4.30). Moreover the three verbs develop the idea contained in the clause, 'He who confirms us with you to Christ is God'. This shows that the interpretation of P. W. Evans (based on the exposition of Plummer) is untenable, namely, that the statement applies only to the Apostle and his fellow workers, whom God anointed *for their ministry* and to whom He gave an inward seal and pledge of the Spirit's appointment and equipment.[2] On the contrary, the Apostle is associating himself with the recipients of his letter: God is continuing His work of maintaining him and his colleagues along with the Christians at Corinth in the steadfastness which He secured when He anointed them, sealed them and gave them the earnest of the Spirit. This surely took place at the outset of their Christian life.

(ii) One of the basic ideas of sealing is the declaration that that which is sealed, whether object or person, is the property of him whose seal is affixed to it (or him). In popular usage this is the significance of assigning an object or person '*in the name*' of another; we have seen how closely related though on a far deeper level, is the significance of baptism in the name of the Lord Jesus. The reason for citing just now the Shepherd of Hermas was not alone its illustrating the use of 'seal' for the rite of baptism but its connection with the 'name' in baptism: 'These that had fallen asleep received the *seal of the Son of God* and entered into the kingdom of God. For before a man has borne the *name of (the Son of) God* he is dead; but when he has received the *seal*, he layeth aside his deadness and resumeth life. The seal then is the water . . .'. The impression gained from this statement is that the seal, properly speaking, is the name stamped on the baptized in his baptism, and that the term has become extended to cover the baptismal act that bestows the seal. Heitmüller believed that this was part at

---

[1] 'Second Century Teaching on Holy Baptism', *Theology*, 1947, p. 88. The most that Dix's reply to Oulton can do is to move the date of the change to some years earlier in the second century than that suggested by Oulton. The fact of the change seems to me indisputable.

[2] Op. cit., p. 173.

least of the real significance of the uttering the name of Jesus over the baptized and that it reveals the origin of the conception of baptism as a seal: by the setting of the name of Jesus on the baptized it stamped him as His property — put His brand or trade mark upon him! — and set him under His protection.[1] Here it is necessary to use caution and not claim too much; if baptism in the name of the Lord Jesus has first and foremost a Semitic origin (baptism לְשֵׁם, in the name of the Messiah) this idea could not be more than a secondary adaptation of the primary signification 'with respect to, for the sake of, etc.'. It is, however, a plausible conjecture that this made the application of the term seal to baptism natural and easily comprehensible in the early churches.

(iii) The 'seal' in 2 Cor. 1.22 etc. is not baptism, nor the name of Jesus, but the Holy Spirit. God gave us the anointing, seal and earnest *of the Spirit*. The seal is not the 'name' in this passage; rather the Spirit *is* the anointing and the seal, as He is the 'first instalment' of the inheritance. The same applies to Eph. 1.13 and 4.30. When was the first instalment of the inheritance given? According to Eph. 1.13: 'when you heard the word of the truth . . . and believed', i.e. when you were converted (cf. Rom. 13.11, for a similar use of the aorist of πιστεύω = 'begin to exercise faith'). In the light of 1 Cor. 6.11, 12.13, and the conjunction of faith and baptism in Gal. 3.26 f etc., we cannot doubt that this inward sealing of the Spirit is conceived as taking place in baptism in the name of Jesus, when the Name was invoked and called over the baptized, when he gave himself to the Lord and received Him as Lord, when he became one with the Lord in death and resurrection by Him who is called 'the Lord the Spirit' (2 Cor. 3.17).

Thus the 'seal of the Spirit' is neither baptism in water, nor a baptism of the Spirit divorced from the rite of baptism; it is *the 'baptism of the Spirit' in association with the laying of the Name of Jesus on a believer in the rite of baptism.*

This has some interesting consequences. The association of the 'seal' with the Name in baptism, and the parallel teaching in 1 Cor. 6.11, 12.13, renders untenable the plea of Dix that the seal is given in confirmation. The seal is given when a man is washed, sanctified, justified in the Name of the Lord Jesus and in the Spirit of our God, even as he is baptized to the one Body in the one Spirit. The sundering apart in the Hippolytan rite of this indivisible unity is a modification of Apostolic theology and almost certainly of Apostolic practice.

[1] *Im Namen Jesu*, p. 334. Heitmüller devoted an article to this theme in *Neutestamentliche Studien für G. Heinrici*, 1914, pp. 40 ff, which Bultmann thought decisive, *New Testament Theology*, I, p. 138.

This use of the term 'seal' for the gift of the Spirit in baptism is to be contrasted with the Jewish employment of the term for the rite of circumcision. It is repeatedly asserted that Paul adopted the term seal for baptism from the Jewish habit of referring to circumcision as a seal, and Rom. 4.11 is appealed to as proof: Abraham 'received the sign of circumcision, a seal of the righteousness of the faith he possessed as an uncircumcized man'. Unfortunately it is uncertain whether the Jews contemporary with the Apostle were accustomed to designating circumcision by this term;[1] Paul could have used the term seal (σφράγις) here in a spontaneous extension of Gen. 17.11, 'It shall be a sign of the covenant between me and you' — compare his totally unrelated use of the term in 1 Cor. 9.2. If it be granted that seal was so used by the Jews, it will have called attention to the aspect of circumcision as an *outward* sign of the Jewish covenant — 'the seal of Abraham on your flesh'.[2] The seal of the Spirit however, is an inward possession which none but God can see, apart from its effect in character, behaviour and the charismata. If the Apostle ever related the two 'seals' it would have been by way of contrast, corresponding with the difference between the circumcision of the heart which the prophets demanded and the outward circumcision which did not and could not bestow this inward transformation.[3]

Having considered the probability that the 'seal of the Spirit' is a synonym for the possession of the Spirit secured in baptism, it may be of value to enquire what connotation this symbolism had for the early Church. That it signified above all the idea of ownership by the one whose seal is stamped has already been noticed; to be sealed with the Spirit is to be 'branded as Christ's'.[4] But the really characteristic application of the figure is eschatological, that of applying the brand mark of Christ in view of the tribulation and Kingdom of the End. The background of this conception is to be sought in the vision of Ezekiel ch. 9: Six executioners advance on Jerusalem with weapons of slaughter and with them a man with a writing case at his side; the latter is bidden to set a mark on the foreheads of the men who sighed over the abominations committed in the city and the executioners are

[1] Lietzmann thought it unlikely that the Jews did refer to circumcision at so early a date, since the testimonies to the employment of seal for the rite were comparatively late. He knew of no Jewish citation earlier than the fourth century A.D. (Talm. jerus. Berachoth 9.3 Shemoth Rabba 19), *An die Römer*, pp. 53 f. Strack-Billerbeck however cite a parable containing such an allusion from Ex. Rabba. 19 (81c), attributed to R. Schimeon b. Calaphta, *c.* A.D. 190. See excursus, 'Das Beschneidungsgebot', *Kommentar zum Neuen Testament*, vol. 4, first part, pp. 32 f.

[2] The phrase is from R. Schimeon; see the full citation in Strack-Billerbeck, ibid.

[3] So Lampe, op. cit., pp. 5 f.

[4] J. G. Davies, *The Spirit, the Church and the Sacraments*, 1954, p. 150.

commanded to slay all in the city, men, women and children alike, 'but touch no one upon whom is the mark'. The passage was influential in Jewish apocalyptic writing. Compare e.g. the account of the Seventy Shepherds in Enoch 89.59 ff who destroy a certain number of the sheep while another (Michael?) is told to mark everything that the shepherds do to the sheep and to record their destructions. Still more pertinently, Rev. 7.1 ff describes how the angels of the winds of destruction are bidden not to hurt the earth 'until we seal the servants of our God in their foreheads', whereupon 12,000 of every tribe of Israel are sealed against the terrors of the wrath to come. The ensuing vision of the triumphant host whom no man could number indicates that the sealing was effective: God's people attain to the Kingdom![1] It is this latter positive note of assurance that the seal of the Spirit portrays. Nowhere in the New Testament is the possession of the Spirit taken as a charm to ward off tribulation; nor is He characteristically thought of as the protector in time of danger, though precisely that is the thought of the seal in Rev. 7.1 ff. The Holy Spirit is typically conceived of as the 'first instalment' of the Kingdom; since He is to be 'poured out' on all flesh at the end and is the means of resurrection to the Kingdom, to possess Him now is to have the most essential blessing of the Kingdom. The believer therefore who has the Spirit is 'sealed' as Christ's in the Kingdom that now is and for the Kingdom that is to be. Protection may well be an element in the figure of sealing, but to the Apostle Paul the certainty of possession will be yet more characteristic of its significance. Such is the implication of the collocation in 2 Cor. 1.22: God anointed us, sealed us and gave the first instalment of the Spirit; as also in Eph. 1.13 f, 'You were sealed with the Spirit of promise, who is the first instalment of our inheritance until we acquire possession of it'; and more briefly in Eph. 4.30, 'In Him you were sealed for the day of redemption'.[2]

[1] It is to be observed that Ezek. 9.4 ff and Rev. 7.1 ff (cf. Rev. 9.4 and 14.1 ff) provide a means of interpreting the *idea* of the seal; it is not here claimed that the seal in the Book of Revelation denotes baptism, although it has been traditionally so interpreted and is apparently still so regarded in modern Roman Catholic exposition. Rev. 7.1 ff is taken by the Seer of Revelation, with little adaptation, from Jewish originals, wherein the sealing of 12,000 from every tribe of the children of Israel represented an apocalyptic sealing of *Jews*; the idea is precisely that of Ezek. 9, with as little idea of baptism as that passage has (cf. the similar application of the idea in Ps. Sol. 15.6, 'The mark of God is upon the righteous that they may be saved', i.e. from the flame of fire and the wrath, from famine, sword and pestilence).

[2] This eschatological reference of the seal makes it the more difficult to attribute a non-Jewish original to the idea of the seal. It was inevitable that other ideas should become attached to it, as the Christian Church moved into areas with a heathen culture, but they must be reckoned as secondary. Failure to reckon with this feature marks all Heitmüller's discussions of baptism. The same must be said of Leipoldt's consideration of the seal, op. cit., p. 67.

The concept of the believer being *anointed* ($\chi\rho i\sigma\alpha s$) by the Spirit in baptism is parallel to that of receiving the seal of the Spirit. There is evidently a play of words in 2 Cor. 1.22: God confirms us to *the Anointed* and *anointed* us. The Christ was 'anointed with the Holy Spirit and with power' (Acts 10.38), a reference to the baptism in which He began his service of God and man which should end in reigning in the glory of the Kingdom. The Christian is 'anointed' with the Spirit in baptism that, having died and risen with Christ, he might be equipped to enter upon the like service as his Lord and at the last to reign with Him in the consummated Kingdom. For Paul this service is interpreted in the widest sense — in the varied ministries of the Body of Christ, in exercise of spiritual gifts, in the life of love and above all in entering into the sacrifice of Christ (1 Cor. 12–14, Col. 1.24–25). I doubt that Paul would press this parallel of Christ and the Christian as alike 'christed' in baptism, for the 'anointing' in Jordan had its counterpart in the 'anointing' in the resurrection at the right hand of God when the messiahship became fully effective (Rom. 1.3–4, Phil. 2.6 ff) and our 'anointing' is related more closely to the latter than to the former; suffice it to say that in baptism we are given the Spirit of Christ (Rom. 8.9) to engage in the ministry of the Body of Christ, with the ultimate end of participation in the eschatological glory of Christ. For God who anointed us and sealed us for that glory gave us its first instalment — the anointing and sealing Spirit.[1]

8. 1 CORINTHIANS 1.11–17

In this famous protest of Paul's against the divisiveness of the Church in Corinth the succession of questions in v. 13 is significant for us: 'Has Christ been divided out (to a privileged few)? Surely Paul was not crucified for you? Or were you baptized in the name of Paul?' The association imparting Christ as a gift, crucifixion and baptism, is in harmony with what we have already learned of Paul's teaching in the cardinal baptismal passages. Particular interest attaches however, to the last question. It follows on the statement of v. 12: 'Every one of you is saying, "I belong to Paul", "But I belong to Apollos", "And I belong to Cephas", "But I belong to Christ" '. Tactfully Paul turns to those who claimed to be his own party and asks: 'Were you baptized in the name of Paul ($\epsilon is \tau \dot{o} \ \ddot{o}\nu o\mu\alpha \ \Pi\alpha \acute{u}\lambda ov$)?' Heitmüller deduces from this employment of the phrase 'in the name' that Paul

---

[1] Observe that once more we have a Trinitarian implication of baptism: *God* confirms us to *Christ* by the anointing and sealing of the *Spirit* who is the earnest of the consummation.

interpreted it in the same way as the pagan world did generally; it signified the making over of someone so as to belong to another. He paraphrases Paul's question thus: 'Were you baptized under my name, so that you now stand under my name; were you appropriated as mine through baptism, so that you now have a right to say, I am of Paul, I belong to Paul?'[1] That this approximates to the meaning of the phrase is undeniable, but it requires a modification which is not unimportant in view of the Christian use of baptism. The series 'I am of Paul, I am of Apollos, I am of Cephas, I am of Christ' does not really mean, 'I belong to Paul as his property, as his slave; and I to Apollos and I to Cephas', for none of the Corinthians would have made themselves over to their Christian leaders in so complete a sense. In these cases the language indicates a belonging in the sense of *discipleship*: 'I follow Paul; I Apollos; I Cephas'. One could reproduce the sense by 'I am Paul's man, I Apollos' etc.', so long as it was realized that this was intended in a reduced sense. A baptism in the name of Paul accordingly is baptism with the purpose of becoming Paul's disciple. The notion of belongingness is deepened in the application to Christ, because the disciple more fully commits himself to the Lord. The idea therefore is not so remote from the Hebraic idea of baptism לְשֵׁם (in the name of) Christ as Heitmüller represented, for baptism 'for the sake of Christ' takes its colour from the Person of Christ, as the once crucified but now exalted Kurios: it is to enter into the relationship of disciple, as one crucified with Him and risen with Him, henceforth to live under His unrestricted sovereignty. This is sufficiently closely related to the Hellenistic idea for the Corinthians to be able to grasp it without difficulty, but it is not to be set without qualification in that Hellenistic milieu, for it has been decisively affected by the nature of the redemptive event it celebrates.[2]

Objection could be taken to this interpretation in view of the immediately ensuing context: 'I am grateful that I baptized none of you except Crispus and Gaius. . . . For Christ did not send me to baptize but to preach the gospel'. If this is not a minimizing of the significance of baptism, it seems perilously close to it. Nevertheless, it is generally recognized that so to read this utterance is to abuse it and to misunderstand Paul's sacramental teaching. It may be affirmed with

[1] Op. cit., p. 115. The same view is reproduced in varying terms by Johannes Weiss, '1 Korinther' (*Die Schriften des Neuen Testaments*), p. 77; Lindblom, 'Första Korinterbrevet' (*Handbok till Nya Testamentet*), p. 92; Lietzmann, op. cit., pp. 7 f; Moffatt, '1 Corinthians' (*Moffatt New Testament Commentary*), p. 11.

[2] In principle this view is implied by C. G. Findlay, '1 Corinthians' (*Expositor's Greek Testament*, vol. 2), p. 765; Robertson and Plummer, op. cit., p. 13; more explicitly by K. K. Rasmussen, op. cit., p. 42.

confidence that the man who formulated the baptismal theology reflected in Rom. 6.1 ff, Gal. 3.26 f, Col. 2.11 f did not think lightly of baptism and would not have wished to give the impression that he did. If vv. 14 and 17 are interpreted in the light of the whole paragraph they do not yield a contrary meaning without injustice.

The immediate intention of Paul is to express relief that he had baptized few in Corinth 'lest any should say that you were baptized in my name' (v. 15). It is common to invoke here the phenomenon in the mystery cults, that a novice called the priest who initiated him into the mysteries his 'Father', so attesting in Corinth the likelihood of a close relationship between one baptized and his baptizer.[1] Yet this parallel is actually a depreciation of the strength of meaning in the clause, 'lest any should say that you were baptized to my name (εἰς τὸ ἐμὸν ὄνομα)'; for on the analogy of vv. 12–13 this would express the horrifying idea that any might claim to have been baptized *so as to become the disciple of Paul*, thus setting the Apostle in the place of the *Kurios*. It is doubtful if Paul's abstention from baptizing converts sprang from a foresight that this could happen; rather his evident relief at the fewness of those he baptized in Corinth indicates that he saw in this fact a fortunate overruling of Providence.

Most scholars regard v. 17 as implying a conviction on Paul's part that his appointed task was to preach the gospel and that the administration of baptism belonged to the office or charisma of others.[2] The force of the conjunction in v. 17 would indicate that the interpretation is justified: 'I am grateful to God that I baptized none of you except . . . lest any should say that you were baptized in my name. (I did baptize also the house of Stephanas . . . I do not know whether I baptized anyone else) *For* Christ did not send me to baptize but to preach the gospel'.

It would fully accord with Paul's missionary strategy that he should encourage others to minister rather than let the life of the community revolve about himself.[3] He might well have wished to give room for his fellow missionaries to play their part; or he could

---

[1] Lietzmann cites the remarkable parallel in later Church history: marriage between a baptized person and a sponsor was forbidden, indicating that baptism formed a mystic relationship between the two. Op. cit., p. 8.

[2] So J. Weiss, op. cit., p. 77; Leipoldt, op. cit., p. 60; Lindblom, op. cit., p. 94; Mundle, op. cit., p. 125; Marsh, op. cit., p. 131; Wotherspoon, *Religious Values in the Sacraments*, 1928, p. 185; Lampe, op. cit., p. 54; Leenhardt, op. cit., p. 62; Crehan, op. cit., p. 74; Héring, *La Première Épitre de Saint Paul aux Corinthiens*, 1949, p. 19; Flemington, op. cit., p. 54.

[3] It is preferable to think in such positive terms than to insist, with Mundle, that in Paul's view the person of the baptizer is irrelevant (op. cit., p. 125). That may have been the case but it is not a necessary deduction from 1 Cor. 1.17.

have adopted the practice of leaving baptism to the leaders of the local community, since they had to perpetuate the work when he passed on to other fields'[1] It was Odeberg's belief that Paul was concerned to demonstrate that no one, not even he, the founder of the community at Corinth, had all the functions or offices in Christ's church; such a feature was consistent with the argument against partisan loyalty to a single teacher, as though *he* could give everything that pertained to the Church.[2]

Admitting all that has been said, it yet remains true that 1 Cor. 1.17 gives the impression that Paul subordinates the administration of baptism to the proclamation of the gospel. That however is consistent with the nature of baptism itself. For the latter follows the proclamation of Christ and draws its meaning from the gospel. This we saw to be implicit in the Great Commission. 'Make disciples of all the nations, baptizing them . . .' presumes the priority of preaching the gospel and the necessity of faith. It is ordained by the Lord that faith's response is made in baptism; this in turn presumes that the God-willed baptismal response should be included in the declaration of the gospel. Nevertheless the gospel to which response is given is the good news of the Christ event, the 'message' ($\dot{\alpha}\kappa o \acute{\eta}$) that is heard and that awakens faith (Rom. 10.17). From this point of view it could be said that Paul's insistence that he was sent to preach, rather than to baptize, reflected his consciousness of the essential priority of his work if there were to be any baptisms at all![3] If so, it must again be stressed that this is a matter of order. The comment of Lietzmann on this passage, that in comparison with the awakening of faith through the gospel baptism is of purely secondary importance, a non-essential no less than the wisdom of this world, is untrue to Paul. Baptism is secondary to the proclamation, in that it depends upon it and embodies it; but as it is the God-ordained mode of faith's appropriation of the gospel and of God's appropriation of the believer, it can never be said to be of *second rate* importance. It is therefore a caricature of Paul's teaching to place baptism on a level with 'the wisdom of words' as Lietzmann does; Paul goes on to show how God by the gospel had brought to nought this world's wisdom, but he does not remotely suggest that the gospel makes baptism foolish. On the contrary, baptism is the complement of the gospel. The former is empty only where the latter is despised (cf. 1 Cor. 10.1 ff).

---

[1] Schlatter adopted the second alternative, *Paulus der Bote Jesu*, 2nd ed. 1956, p. 76.
[2] 'Pauli Brev till Korintierna' (*Tolkning av Nya Testamentet*, vol. 7) 1944, p. 55.
[3] So Schlatter, op. cit., p. 76.

It may be concluded that, bearing in mind Paul's other utterances about baptism, v. 17 is to be interpreted in the light of the Semitic manner of laying stress on an issue: Christ sent Paul to preach the gospel *rather than* to baptize.[1] But this is no depreciation of the value of baptism. As Flemington remarked, 'it is just because he had so high a sense of what baptism meant that he regarded with such abhorrence its debasement by Corinthian partisanship'.[2]

9. 1 CORINTHIANS 10.1 ff

The chief requirement for understanding this greatly misused passage is to recognize that v. 1 has a context and that v. 6a is an unfinished sentence. The statement in v. 6, 'These things happened as τύποι — types, symbols, examples — for us', has led many to suppose that Paul was setting forth Old Testament types of baptism and the Lord's Supper to provide instruction on the nature of the sacraments. Discussion has accordingly centred on vv. 1–4, the Red Sea passage as the Old Covenant type of the baptism of the New Israel, and the manna and supernatural gift of water as the type of the bread and wine of the New Israel on its way to the kingdom of glory. In my judgment this procedure misses the point of the passage. It is not intended to be a typological statement of sacramental theology but a midrashic exposition of Old Testament stories for the elucidation of Christian ethics. The omission of γάρ, 'for', in v. 1 by recent translators into English is unfortunate, since the key term for 10.1 ff falls at the end of 9.27 — ἀδόκιμος, 'disapproved, good for nothing', or, in keeping with the context, 'disqualified'. If it is too much to say that Paul had a dread lest that verdict be passed on himself, at least he laboured strenuously that the possibility be avoided; he ran to *win* the race of life, even as he pummelled his sparring partner, the body, to keep himself fighting fit. But this personal note was added only to strengthen the appeal to the Corinthians: '*You* run in such fashion that you may obtain the prize' (v. 24). It was not beyond reckoning that they could lose the race and the prize; *they* could become disapproved if they grew careless, *for such was the fate of many in the long ago*. Our fathers experienced a kind of baptism in the Red Sea and

---

[1] Crehan, op. cit., p. 74.

[2] Op. cit., p. 54. Flemington draws attention to the parallel manner in which the Corinthians debased the Lord's Supper, also through the formation of 'cliques'. 'Baptism was misunderstood because the names of Paul, Apollos and Cephas became watchwords of party strife. The Eucharist was misunderstood because the social barriers separating rich and poor were maintained even at the Lord's Supper. In each context the language used by St. Paul marks his sense of how serious was the denial of Christian koinonia'.

they knew a kind of eucharist in the desert wanderings, receiving in this manner the ministry of Christ Himself; nevertheless God was displeased with most of them, for He overthrew them in the wilderness; and these things — their experience of grace, their conduct and their judgment — happened as τύποι, examples for us. The accent in the word τύποι clearly falls on the behaviour of the Fathers and the judgments that befell them, rather than on their participation in the sacraments, as the rest of the sentence shows ('so that we should not go a-lusting after evil things as they did') and as the sequence that follows to v. 11 indicates, where it is repeated, 'Now these things happened to them τυπικῶς, by way of example'. The evils that they committed and the evils that came upon them serve as warnings: 'Do not be idolaters as some of them were. . . . Let us not indulge in immorality as some of them did. . . . Let us not put the Lord to the test as some of them did . . . nor grumble as some of them. . . . Let any one who thinks that he stands take heed lest he fall. . . . Therefore, my beloved, shun idolatry !'. The last entreaty enables Paul to pass to the point he has had in mind all along, namely a plea to avoid plunging weaker brethren back into idolatry, with their consequent loss of the inheritance through thoughtless participation in pagan sacrificial foods and meals. Such is the drift of the passage, and I take space to repeat it because it is so commonly forgotten in recent discussions on baptism. Von Dobschutz was justified in protesting long ago that to make Paul's sacramental thought here the point of departure, rather than the Old Testament narrative and its contemporary exegesis, is to transform the literary clothing of the thought into the thing that matters.[1]

Had this consideration been borne in mind, along with the evident parenetic purpose of the exposition, we should have been spared many strange examples of exegesis. When E. Best, for example, follows the interpretation of T. C. Edwards and urges that, since Moses represented Christ, the baptism of the Fathers was no mere allegory but 'a true baptism unto Christ', possessing a significance even deeper than the baptism of John,[2] he is guilty of overpressing an observation of Paul (v. 4a) made in harmony with characteristic Jewish tradition: as the Rabbinical scholars reduced all the blessings of God to his people to the one principle of the Law, and the Alexandrian tradition thought in terms of wisdom or logos, so Paul claimed that *Christ* was the 'all and in all' of salvation history; but to institute historical comparisons with the baptism of John on the basis of such a homiletical principle

[1] *Theologische Studien und Kritiken*, 1905, pp. 10 f.   [2] Op. cit., p. 72.

is to violate the homiletics.[1] The comparison instituted by Bousset between Christian baptismal water, filled with divine power, and the waters of the Red Sea heaped up by the miraculous power of God, is gratuitous and needs no further consideration.[2] But not less so is the interpretation of Origen, followed by various modern scholars, that the cloud represents the Holy Spirit and the sea the baptismal water;[3] apart from the fact that that would imply a baptism in the Spirit before the baptism in the water,[4] the representation of 'baptized in the cloud and in the sea' is surely one; the Israelites were surrounded by both elements, though literally untouched by either.[5] Lundberg finds the same conception in 1 Cor. 10.1 ff as in Rev. 15.2: the crystal sea mingled with fire is related to the Red Sea, for the conquerors have just crossed it and now find themselves beside the 'glassy sea', i.e. on the other side; so too the passage through the Red Sea in 1 Cor. 10 implies the idea of baptism as a crossing of the sea of death in order to attain the promised land.[6] Such an interpretation savours of *eisegesis* that has little in common with the passage under review or the Jewish tradition on which it is based. A different kind of refinement is observable in Miegge's view that we have here a collective baptism of a whole generation of Israelites, including adults, infants and the not yet born, good and bad, believing and scarcely believing, yet in reality a Christian baptism followed by a true eucharist.[7] The 1955 Scottish Interim Report on Baptism in similar vein points out that Paul emphasizes that *all* were baptized, men, women and children, therefore if Paul had not intended children to be baptized he would have been obliged to correct the Old Testament example and explicitly exclude children from Christian baptism.[8] In view of the nature of the passage, the demand and the inference are alike unreasonable. Certainly *all* were 'baptized', and *all received the eucharist* — men, women, children, infants, good and bad, believing and scarce believing! On this argument it must be maintained that Paul specifically intended that infants, children, good and bad adults, believing and indifferent in faith should partake of the eucharist, for had he thought otherwise he

---

[1] So von Dobschutz, op. cit., p. 11; Schlatter, *Paulus der Bote Jesu*, p. 290.

[2] *Die Schriften des Neuen Testaments*, '1 Korinther', p. 114.

[3] To Origen the expression *baptizati sunt in nube et mari* was identical with *baptizati sunt in Spiritu Sancto et acqua*, Homilies on Numbers, XXII, cited by Lundberg with approval, op. cit., p. 141; see also Goudge, op. cit., p. 83; Odeberg, op. cit., p. 178.

[4] As Thornton perceived, to his consternation! *Confirmation, its Place in the Baptismal Mystery*, p. 37, n. 1.

[5] For the Rabbinic exegesis of the Red Sea passage, attaining at times the peak of fantasy, see Strack-Billerbeck, op. cit., vol. III, pp. 405 f.

[6] Op. cit., pp. 144 f.   [7] Op. cit., p. 10.   [8] Op. cit., p. 28.

should have corrected the Old Testament example. But such a mode of argumentation would be exegesis run riot. The twice repeated πάντες — all ate, all drank — is stressed to underscore the extent of the judgment: 'With most of them God was not pleased, for they were overthrown in the wilderness' (v. 5). To use a passage like this in justification of infant baptism is near to making the Word of God of no effect by our tradition. So also Cullman's deduction, 'That prototype of baptism the crossing of the Red Sea is mentioned by Paul only to show that in the first act God is active and in the second many must respond',[1] introduces an alien element into Paul's train of thought; the Apostle is not concerned with the relation of faith to baptism and the priority of divine intervention over human response, but he is very intent on underscoring the necessity for baptized Christians to live as befits their baptismal profession.[2]

The one sure inference concerning baptism that can be drawn from this passage is the inability of baptism to save from judgment and bestow the blessings of the Kingdom where it is not followed by obedience. The scope of the paragraph is very limited. We cannot even insist on its teaching the necessity of receiving baptism in faith, for faith is not once mentioned in it and it does not come into view. It has a single lesson of outstanding importance; in face of it none can impute to Paul with justice an unethical or automatic view of baptism. The whole point of his words is to illustrate the uselessness of baptism without morals, that is to say, the worthlessness and even danger of a superstitious evaluation of sacraments. Baptism must have ethical and spiritual consequences or it is of no avail. For the *positive* effects of a baptism with ethical and spiritual consequences, and what sort of a baptism it is which has such results, we must turn to other passages in Paul's letters. What they are and what they teach have been the subject matter of this chapter.[3]

To go beyond this is difficult, if only because it is obvious that Paul frames his language about the baptism and the eucharist of the Fathers at the Exodus and in the desert from their Christian counterparts. The pattern of baptism here is not the Red Sea passage but baptism in the name of the Lord Jesus, which is made a category into which the Exodus is set and by which it is interpreted. If the Jews at this time did view the Red Sea crossing as a baptism,[4] Paul has it put in Christ-

[1] Op. cit., p. 49.
[2] So Kümmel, 'Das Urchristentum', *Theologische Rundschau*, 1950, pp. 40 f.
[3] The conclusion here reached is supported by von Dobschütz, op. cit., p. 12; Leipoldt, op. cit., p. 65; Marsh, op. cit., p. 132; Oepke, *T.W.N.T.*, vol. 1, p. 540; Flemington, op. cit., p. 55; Héring, op. cit., p. 77; Schnackenburg, op. cit., p. 88.
[4] See p. 31, n.1.

ian terms, as is evident from the key phrase, 'they were baptized *to Moses*' (εἰς τὸν Μωσῆν). Baptism 'to Moses' is modelled on baptism 'to Christ' (εἰς Χριστόν); the latter is the clue to understanding the former, not vice versa.[1] It is possible, of course, that the mention of the Red Sea as a counterpart to Christian baptism brought with it associations of redemption that traditionally attached to the Exodus in Jewish and early Christian thought; if so, it is to be acknowledged that Paul has made little or no use of them here. The most plausible lesson that I have noted from this association of Christian baptism with the Exodus is based on the dual recognition that in both instances the people of God experience deliverance, yet the real counterpart to the Exodus is *the Christ event* of cross and resurrection; it could be maintained therefore that we have hinted here yet again *the unity of baptism and the redemptive action of Christ* that we perceived to lie at the root of Rom. 6.1 ff etc.[2] It must be confessed, however, that the nature of the exposition in 1 Cor. 10.1 ff forbids pressing even this conclusion. We have no alternative but to affirm once more that the purpose of this passage is parenetic, and that Paul has so severely subordinated the baptismal motif to ethical instruction as to make the former of uncertain value in constructing his theology of baptism.

10. 1 CORINTHIANS 15.29

'Of the baptism for the dead, the variety of interpretations is so great that he who would collect, I shall not say those different opinions but a catalogue of the different opinions, would have to write a dissertation'. So wrote Bengel, with pardonable exaggeration, over two centuries ago.[3] What kind of a publication would be required at this stage of history to collate the interpretations of the saying and pass a judgment on them may be left to the reader's imagination. It is no intention of mine to incorporate a minor thesis at this point, yet it may not be without value to glance at the chief modes of understanding Paul's words and it may help us to reach a decision as to the right one.

Bengel himself repudiated the notion that Paul had in mind a vicarious baptism for dead people. He followed the lead of the Greek

---

[1] So Goudge, op. cit., p. 83, Schlatter, op. cit., p. 288, Héring, op. cit., p. 78, Best, op. cit., p. 72. This has caused Moffatt to write, '*As Christians* have been baptized into Christ, *so our fathers* were baptized into loyalty to Moses, their divinely appointed leader and mediator', *1 Corinthians*, p. 129. Johannes Nörgaard expressed the same idea independently: 'As the new Israel is baptized to Christ and grace in Him, so was the old Israel baptized to Moses and to the Law', *Den kristne Daab*, p. 16.

[2] This has been pointed out with varying emphasis by Bartsch, op. cit., p. 92 and Schnackenburg, op. cit., p. 88.

[3] *Gnomon of the New Testament*, E.T., vol. 3, 1895, p. 329.

tradition in viewing 'the dead' as ordinary converts who get baptized 'with death before their eyes', knowing their mortality and therefore that they are to be added to the mass of the dead shortly.[1] In the judgment of most, the artificiality of this view is too apparent to require comment.

Several British scholars have sought to tread a parallel path and yet keep closer to the text. Robertson and Plummer favoured the idea of people being baptized 'out of affection or respect for the dead', i.e. moved by the recollection of the earnest desire that the deceased had expressed for their conversion.[2] G. G. Findlay put forward a similar interpretation, but explained 'on behalf of the dead' as indicating hope of reunion with the beloved dead, as when a dying mother wins her son by the appeal, 'Meet me in heaven!'.[3] The view has secured a topical interest, since it has been set forth recently by a pupil of Jeremias and adopted by him. Agreeing with the foregoing expositors that 'the dead' are the Christian dead, as in the context (vv. 18, 23), Maria Raeder sought to put this idea on a firmer basis by construing the preposition ὑπέρ (generally rendered 'on behalf of') as denoting purpose: the baptism is undergone with the intention of reunion with the Christian deceased at the resurrection.[4] Jeremias urged that this was the only possible meaning of the preposition in this context; in his judgment ὑπέρ cannot here denote substitution, it has a final meaning as in v. 3, 2 Cor. 1.6, Rom. 15.8.[5] Despite Jeremias' careful presentation of the argument, most scholars will find it difficult to believe that Paul really meant by the phrase ὑπὲρ τῶν νεκρῶν 'with a view to becoming united with the dead in the resurrection'; it demands the insertion of too much that has been left unexpressed. In two of the three passages Jeremias cites for a final meaning of ὑπέρ the idea 'in the interests of' is undoubtedly present; in 2 Cor. 1.6 ὑπὲρ τῆς ὑμῶν παρακλήσεως καὶ σωτηρίας can be rendered equally well by 'with a view to your encouragement and salvation' or 'in the interests of your encouragement and salvation';[6] so also in Rom. 15.8, διάκονον περιτομῆς ὑπὲρ ἀληθείας θεοῦ means 'a minister of the circumcised with a view to showing the truthfulness of God', or 'a minister . . . in

---

[1] A variety of ways of stating this interpretation, from the Greek Fathers to the Reformers, is presented by Alford, though he himself dissented from it. G. W. H. Lampe in his own manner assents to it, op. cit., p. 94.

[2] Op. cit., pp. 359 f.

[3] *Expositor's Greek Testament*, vol. 2, pp. 930 f.

[4] 'Vikariatstaufe in 1 Cor. 15.29?', *Z.N.W.*, 1955, 259 f.

[5] 'Flesh and Blood cannot inherit the Kingdom of God', *New Testament Studies*, 1956, pp. 155-6.

[6] See Blass-Debrunner, par. 231; Moule, *An Idiom Book of N.T. Greek*, 1953, p. 65.

the interests of the truthfulness of God'. The use of ὑπέρ in 1 Cor. 15.3 (ὑπὲρ τῶν ἁμαρτιῶν ἡμῶν, 'for our sins') is not on a footing with either of these, and is exceptional for Paul's usage. In only one other place does Paul speak of Christ dying ὑπέρ our sins, viz. in Gal. 1.4 (presuming that ὑπέρ is the correct reading there and not περί); in every other case where Paul connects ὑπέρ with the death of Christ a personal reference follows the preposition — e.g. ὑπὲρ ἀσεβῶν (for the ungodly, Rom. 5.6), ὑπὲρ ἡμῶν (for us, Rom. 5.8), ὑπὲρ ἡμῶν πάντων (for us all, Rom. 8.32), ὑπὲρ ἐμοῦ (for me, Gal. 2.20), ὑπὲρ ὑμῶν (for you, 1 Cor. 11.24), ὑπὲρ αὐτῆς (for the Church, Eph. 5.25) etc. It may not be accidental that the two exceptions above mentioned (1 Cor. 15.3, Gal. 1.4) are found in kerygmatic passages where Paul cites traditional language rather than his own; the evidence would suggest strongly that in both cases ὑπέρ is used loosely for περί ('concerning') or even with a suggestion of διά ('on account of').[1] A final sense cannot be given to ὑπέρ in 1 Cor. 15.3 without reading into the statement an interpolation drawn from elsewhere to make the sense required, i.e. 'Christ died with a view to *the expiation* of our sins'. Thus all the evidence is against interpreting ὑπέρ in v. 29 in another than normal fashion; ὑπὲρ τῶν νεκρῶν must be rendered, 'in the interests of the dead', hence baptism for them must be primarily for the purpose of affecting their status and condition.

There seems to be no avoiding the verdict of Oepke: 'All interpretations that try to eliminate the vicarious baptism for the dead lead astray'.[2] The majority of present day interpreters agree with this, but the manner in which such a baptism could serve the interests of the dead and what significance it had for Paul's baptismal theology are widely disputed.

For years there has been maintained virtually a three cornered fight in which the contestants have championed the following views: (i) baptism for the dead springs from a magical estimate of sacraments and Paul's approval of it reflects his own unspiritual sacramentalism;

---

[1] It is worth noting the loose way in which the sufferings of the Servant are connected with sins in Is. 53, which at an early date began to affect the Christian tradition: αὐτὸς ἐτραυματίσθη διὰ τὰς ἁμαρτίας ἡμῶν (v. 5); κύριος παρέδωκεν αὐτὸν ταῖς ἁμαρτίαις ἡμῶν (v. 6); ἀπὸ τῶν ἀνομιῶν τοῦ λαοῦ μου ἤχθη εἰς θάνατον (v. 8); δῶτε περὶ ἁμαρτίας (v. 10); διὰ τὰς ἀνομίας αὐτῶν παρέδοθη (v. 12). In the kerygmatic quotation of 1 Pt. 3.18 we read Χριστὸς ἅπαξ περὶ ἁμαρτιῶν ἐπάθη, δίκαιος ὑπὲρ ἀδίκων which preserves the kind of distinction one would like to have seen generally observed but which is too much to expect in the popular parlance of the Koine Greek. In the Letter to the Hebrews sacrifice ὑπὲρ ἁμαρτιῶν is frequently mentioned (5.1, 7.27, 9. 7, 10.12) but significantly the ὑπὲρ ἁμαρτιῶν of 10.12 is paralleled by περὶ ἁμαρτία in 10.18, showing how the author used in such contexts the preposition ὑπέρ.
[2] Op. cit., p. 540.

(ii) baptism for the dead is not to be deprecated and Paul had no grounds for disapproving of it; (iii) baptism for the dead was an alien custom adopted by the Corinthians and Paul's citation of it during the course of an argument on another subject yields no evidence as to his opinion of it.

The first is naturally supported by those who find an extreme sacramentarianism in Paul. Indeed the saying is taken as conclusive proof of their general understanding of Paul's sacramental theology: 'A stronger proof for the sacramental estimate of baptism could scarcely be imagined', wrote Heitmüller, using 'sacramental' virtually for 'magical-sacramental'.[1] Bultmann is more forthright. He cites 1 Cor. 15.29 in support of his affirmation, 'In earliest Christianity the sacrament was by no means a symbol, but a miracle working rite', and he added, 'When people have themselves baptized for the dead, as they did in Corinth — i.e. when their intention is to have the super-natural powers that the sacrament bestows made effective for the dead — then no distinction is made between the sacrament and the magical act'. The reason for Paul's lack of criticism of the custom is simple: 'the mode of thought behind it is precisely his own, too, as it was for earliest Christian thought in general'.[2]

Attempts made by the second group of scholars to turn the edge of this criticism cannot be said to be successful. Not that there has been a lack of suggestions! On the contrary they pour over the investigator with bewildering variety, and it must suffice to instance a few ex-amples. Preisker invoked the eschatological mood of the early Church to account for the practice of vicarious baptism for the dead. He recalled the common apocalyptic tenet that the end of the age could not come till the number of the elect was made up (4 Ezr. 4.35, Bar. 30.2); Acts shows that in the earliest times not a few converts entered the Church without baptism; when baptism became the invariable rule, the eschatological principle was changed into a conviction that the end awaited the enrolment of the due number of the *baptized*; hence, to hasten the end, baptisms were undergone for the Christian dead who had not received baptism in the earliest period of the Church.[3] Is it needful to give detailed consideration to this suggestion? It is ingenious but it depends on a number of assumptions for which there is no firm evidence. The sober Schlatter had a different eschato-

---

[1] Op. cit., p. 325.

[2] *N.T. Theology*, I, pp. 135 f. The like view is represented in Bousset, *Die Schriften des Neuen Testaments, 1 Korinther*, p. 153; Schweitzer, *Mysticism of Paul the Apostle*, p. 285; Fuchs, *Das Urchristliche Sakramentsverständnis*, 1958, pp. 12 f.

[3] 'Die Vicariatstaufe 1 Cor. 15.29 — ein eschatologischer nicht sakramental Brauch', *Z.N.W.*, Band 23, 1924, pp. 299 f.

logical principle to call upon: he suggested that the baptisms in view were blood-baptisms of the martyrs (cf. Mk. 10.38, Lk. 12.50); these could be said to be ὑπὲρ τῶν νεκρῶν because on the one hand such 'baptized' martyrs increased the number of the dead who stand in God's peace and on the other hand *they remained in Christ's service*; on the analogy of 1 Pt. 3.19 f they had ministry to perform in the beyond! The future 'What shall they do?' of v. 29 links on with the immediately succeeding 'Why are we also in danger?' of v. 30, for Paul 'dies daily' in his service for Christ — he is nerved by the resurrection to suffer to the uttermost even as the martyr is strengthened for his baptism in blood.[1] Again it must be said that the exegete has made a great assumption without evidence and produced an exposition less likely than the common interpretation.

Most defensive apologists for 1 Cor. 15.29 insist on confining the 'dead' (νεκροί) to a special group in order to make the explanations acceptable: Schnackenburg e.g. believes that the dead must be catechumens or people who died in confession of the faith;[2] Odeberg suggests that on the occasion of a household baptism, the deceased members of the family would be accorded a vicarious baptism to make the family complete;[3] N. Levison considers that Hebrew Christians are in view, who acted in the conviction that their departed relatives would have been obedient to the Messiah had they known of Him.[4]

All such limitations are guesses made without any justification from the text itself. Moreover it seems to be assumed that difficulties disappear when the deceased person, who benefits from a vicarious baptism, is a catechumen or is somehow related to a Christian or to a Church. But is the assumption justified? When all the allowances enumerated are made, it still remains that a sacramental action is performed on behalf of a subject without his consent and without his being able to enter into that which is being done on his behalf. The sacrament is performed in total independence of the subject, with none of the confession of faith, response to proffered grace, yielding of

---

[1] *Erläuterungen, Die Korintherbriefe*, vol. VI, pp. 198 f; *Paulus der Bote Jesu*, pp. 420 ff.

[2] Op. cit., pp. 96 ff.

[3] Op. cit., p. 290.

[4] 'The Proselyte in Biblical and Early Post-Biblican Times', S.J.T., 1957, p. 54. Levison makes the observation: 'In Jewish law vicarious baptism for the dead is approved when the body of the dead person cannot be found for burial. I know of one such case in which the Dayyam Zilberman of Safad, Palestine, ordained that the son of the dead person who was devoured by wild beasts should be baptized for the father'. This evidence, however, has to be set alongside the considerable amount of information concerning consecrations and ablutions for and of the dead available from the study of comparative religion as it affects the first century Mediterranean world.

obedience, renunciation of sin, taking up the cross which are integral to the Pauline act of baptism. To postulate that such action does, in fact, take place in the experience of the deceased in the world beyond is to assert the unknowable and savours of *Schwärmerei* — fanaticism. Yet this baptism, performed as objectively as a sacrifice for the dead, must presumably have the like signification as baptism of the living: it entails union with Christ, death and resurrection with Christ, the gift of the Holy Spirit, the forgiveness of sins, entry into the Body of Christ, participation in the sonship of Christ, becoming a new creation in Christ and entering on a new existence for Him and in His power. It is credible that some Christians in Corinth could have held such beliefs without question; it is less easy to believe that they would have been entertained by the Apostle whose baptismal utterances are permeated with the spiritual and ethical religion that we have observed in the foregoing pages. I freely allow that the exegesis of the Pauline baptismal sayings given in this book may be mistaken; but if it corresponds with any proximity to actuality, then the view of baptism presumed in the custom we have been considering represents a different order of sacramental theory. In my judgment we have to admit with Bultmann that baptism for the dead represents an unethical, sub-Christian sacramentalism, but against him we must affirm that it is a falling away from the baptismal theology implied in Paul's expositions of the subject. If Paul did hold these two sacramental views at the same time he was capable of maintaining extraordinary inconcinnities together; it is more satisfactory to infer that, since I Cor. 15.29 is solitary in Paul's letters in its representation of this kind of sacramentarianism, it reflects not the Apostle's beliefs but those of the Corinthians whom he was addressing.

For this reason I must concur with those who see in the practice of vicarious baptism for the dead a modification of Christian baptism, or an importation alongside it, that had taken root in the Corinthian Church, not of Paul's planting nor of his willing. It was intended to procure for the deceased the benefits believed to be attached to ordinary Christian baptism. Contrary to what is frequently expressed, it will not have had a special eschatological reference to participation in the coming kingdom of God; Paul calls to mind the existence of this practice among those who were *denying* the resurrection from the dead; deniers of resurrection will not have their hearts set on the Kingdom of the end, the judgment and the new creation, for they operate with a wholly different world view. Paul's adducing of the custom here can best be interpreted as a drawing attention to a contradiction in the belief and practice of the Church in Corinth: 'If it be affirmed among you that the dead do not rise, what do those of your number who get baptized for dead people expect to gain from it?' The appeal would be doubly forceful if the members in Corinth who approved of this practice were foremost in propounding the anti-eschatological doctrine opposed by Paul in 1 Cor. 15; such is not impossible, seeing that both attitudes probably sprang from antagonism to the Hebraic tradition in favour of the Hellenistic. Naturally this conjecture cannot be pressed. But Paul's procedure does seem to be fairly characterized in the well known judgment of von Dobschutz: 'Paul smites the Corinthian deniers of the resurrection with their own weapons without stopping first to estimate their value'.[1] There is no need to take exception to this view, on the ground that Paul could not have appealed to a practice that was contrary to his own convictions. An ad hominem argument can be used to demonstrate inconsistencies in people's views, without involving the speaker in agreement with any of them. Our Lord brought into his parabolic teaching some startling elements for consideration, as in His comparison of prayer for justice with a widow plaguing the life out of an unpitying judge; or His setting the unscrupulous behaviour of a dishonest administrator before the disciples as worthy of contemplation; or His representing a man as reprobate who did *not* put out his money to usury — an evil way of acquiring money in Jewish eyes! Paul similarly drew illustrations from areas of life of which it is by no means certain he would approve, e.g. his likening himself to a boxer (1 Cor. 9.27), his frequent drawing on the whole range of military metaphors and of slavery. In identifying Christ with the rock that followed the Israelites in the desert, did he really intend to express his own belief in the legend concerning the rock that moved from place to place? (1 Cor. 10.4). In Phil. 2.17 he speaks of himself as poured out as a libation on an altar; in 2.30 of Epaphroditus gambling with his life; in 4.11 he uses the Stoic watchword αὐτάρκης, 'self sufficient', to denote his attitude to life; in 4.12 he employs a term typical of mystery religion initiation, μεμύημαι, 'I have been initiated', but in no case can be held to be bound to the associations of these terms. Schnackenburg remarked, 'It is characteristic of him that he employs every usable means of proof — citations from the Scripture and rabbinic interpretations, logical and emotional appeal, traditional material and ad hoc inter-

[1] Op. cit., p. 36. With this judgment agreement is expressed by Feine, *Real-encyclopädie für Theologie und Kirche*, vol. 19, p. 401; Rendtorff, op. cit., p. 34; Lindblom, op. cit., p. 170; Leipoldt, op. cit., p. 65; Oepke, op. cit., p. 650; Wendland, op. cit., p. 99; Leenhardt, op. cit., p. 60; Flemington, op. cit., p. 55.

pretations, when he wants to support an important thesis and convince his readers'.[1] The present case is admittedly an extreme example but it is not different in kind from some of those we have quoted.

It scarcely falls within the purview of this work to determine the origin of the custom of baptism for the dead. While it is true that no precise example of its occurrence in the mystery religions and the like can be adduced, sufficient material of a related order has been found to indicate with reasonable probability that it belongs to the milieu of Hellenistic religion contemporary with the primitive Christian Church.[2] It is even more certain that the heart of Paul's doctrine of baptism cannot be explained by means of that same milieu of Hellenistic religion; his teaching is rooted in the Judaeo-Christian tradition of religion and above all in the person and the deeds of Jesus the Messiah; the affinities it has with Greek religion have been determined by the nature of the Person and his Action in whom and by which the God of the *universe* was revealed. Paul's teaching therefore is not to be determined by the implications of 1 Cor. 15.29; it has been formed by far more catastrophic factors and remains essentially unrelated to the practice of baptism for the dead.

II. 1 CORINTHIANS 7.14

It may be questioned whether this statement, 'so greatly tortured in connection with the baptismal debate',[3] should figure in an exposition of New Testament teaching on baptism.[4] Of late, however, it has featured prominently in the conversations on baptism and at this stage it cannot be ignored without reproach. The reference to the 'holiness' of the children of Christian parents has given rise to the belief that the baptism of the children concerned has either taken place or is logically demanded in the future, or some other relation to infant baptism is considered to be implied. It behoves us therefore to look afresh at the saying and endeavour to understand its implications.

Paul's immediate intention is one of encouragement. To a married

---

[1] Op. cit., p. 97.

[2] Plato knew of mendicant priests who 'came to the rich man's door with a story of a power they possess by the gift of heaven to atone for an offence that he *or his ancestors* have committed with incantations and sacrifice, agreeably accompanied by feasting'. (*Republic*, ii, 364, Cornford's translation). Lietzmann notes that the vicarious celebrations of the Dionysiac orgies for uninitiated deceased persons are parallel to the practice we are considering (*An die Korinther*, p. 82). The rites from Egypt described by Leipoldt are even more pertinent, op. cit., pp. 50 ff.

[3] Kümmel, *Theologische Rundschau*, 1950, p. 41.

[4] W. F. Flemington evidently considered that it has no place in the discussion; in his work, *The New Testament Doctrine of Baptism*, he does not even cite the saying.

man or woman who has been converted, but whose partner has not submitted to the gospel, he gives the advice not to separate if the other is willing to maintain the marriage; their union is not defiled by the continued unbelief of the one partner, nor is the believer besmirched by the unbeliever; on the contrary the non-Christian spouse is 'sanctified' by the Christian. This is demonstrated from a prior datum. Defilement of the Christian by the unbelieving partner would mean that the children of the union were unclean, but the contrary is true: *the children are holy* (ἅγιοι)! Therefore the unbelieving partner is holy (ἡγίασται)! Hence the marriage should not be broken. It may even happen that the non-Christian spouse may become converted (v. 16).[1].

The argument is remarkable in more ways than one. In contrast to the emphatic recognition in 1 Cor. 5–6 of the power of evil to corrupt the good in the Church, here the power of sanctity over sin in the marriage relationship is stressed. And over against the pessimistic view of children in the Augustinian system, the 'holiness' of the children is regarded as axiomatic, even where only one parent is Christian. We may take it, with Schlatter,[2] that the reference to '*your* children' hints that what is said would include the children where both parents were Christian as well as where one only was Christian. It is nevertheless fortunate for us that Paul has set the maxim, 'Your children are not unclean but holy', in the context where but one parent is Christian, for in so doing he has provided some signposts for our guidance which we might not have perceived otherwise.

Above all it is to be recognized that the holiness of the child is commensurate with that of the unbelieving parent; a valid explanation of the former must account also for the latter. 'The unbelieving husband has become consecrated (ἡγίασται) in the wife . . . as may be understood from the fact that your children are consecrated' (ἅγιοι).[3] It is impermissible to draw a distinction between two conceptions of holiness here, on the ground that the parent is said to be only ἡγίασται whereas the child is ἅγιος.[4] The root meaning of ἅγιος is defined by Bauer in his lexicon as 'God consecrated', i.e. ἡγιασμένος! Indeed, ἡγιασμένοι is a synonym for ἅγιοι in Paul, as may be instanced in

[1] Jeremias has pointed out that in both profane and Biblical Greek τίς οἶδεν εἰ and πόθεν οἶδας εἰ = 'perhaps', *Die Kindertaufe in den ersten vier Jahrhunderten*, p. 52, n. 1.

[2] *Paulus der Bote Jesu*, p. 224.

[3] The New English Bible draws out the connection thus: 'The heathen husband now *belongs to God* through his Christian wife . . . otherwise your children would not *belong to God*, whereas in fact they do'.

[4] Such is maintained by A. Richardson, op. cit., p. 359.

this very Epistle: 'Paul . . . to the church of God in Corinth, consecrated (ἡγιασμένοις) in Christ, called to be (members of the) consecrated people (ἁγίοις). . . .' (1.2). In the preceding chapter to this one, Paul has described the members of the Corinthian church as washed, consecrated (ἡγιάσθητε) and justified (6.11). Part of the problem of the statement we are considering is how Paul could apply so exalted a description as 'sanctified' or 'consecrated' to one whom he explicitly characterizes as ἄπιστος, an unbeliever. Whatever is signified by this consecration of the unbelieving parent, it is directly deducible from the consecration of the children: 'Since otherwise your children were unclean, but now they are holy'.

Recognition of this fact puts some of the time honoured explanations of these words out of court. For example, it is evident that the children have not derived their holiness from baptism;[1] for no argument from the state of the baptized could be applied to the obviously unbaptized. Nor is it likely that the children's holiness is due to their inclusion along with the parent in the Covenant of God with his People,[2] for this would mean that the unconverted spouse also is brought into the Covenant at the conversion of the other. Nor does it improve the situation to make the holiness derive from a participation in the parent's baptismal incorporation into the holy People of God,[3] or, more specifically, through their baptismal incorporation into the Body of Christ.[4] Schweitzer admittedly finds no difficulty in this thought. He writes, 'Because the married pair belong corporeally to one another, the unbelieving partner becomes, without his or her co-operation, attached to Christ and susceptible of receiving the powers of death and resurrection which go forth from Christ and prepare the recipient for the "being-with-Christ" in the messianic kingdom.'[5] To him this is clear proof that Paul's doctrine of the union of believers with Christ is a physical bodily union; but that in face of 1 Cor. 6.17![6] This construction of Paul's thought could be held only if it was believed that his sacramental ideas were in unmitigated opposition to his

---

[1] As is tentatively put forward in the 1955 *Scottish Interim Report on Baptism*; 'The general evidence suggests that by calling them "holy" the New Testament implies that they are baptized into Christ, initiated into the holy people of God (1 Cor. 6.1 f, 11, Heb. 2.10 f, 1 Pt. 1.2, 14 f, 22 . . .)', p. 27.

[2] Marcel, *The Biblical Doctrine of Infant Baptism*, 1953, pp. 119 f; Miegge, op. cit., pp. 26 f.

[3] *Scottish Report*, 1955, p. 27; N. P. Williams, *Ideas of the Fall and Original Sin*, p. 220, n. 2.

[4] Schweitzer, op. cit., pp. 127 f; Cullmann, op. cit., pp. 43 f; Bousset, op. cit., p. 100; Best, op. cit., p. 77; T. Preiss, *Verbum Caro*, I, N.3, p. 118.

[5] Ibid.

[6] 'He who is united with the Lord becomes one spirit with Him.'

teaching on faith, justification, life in the Spirit and the like. This we have not found in our investigations of the Apostle's baptismal utterances. For which reason I cannot but regard Lietzmann's view other than as a curiosity, that the child is sanctified by birth from a Christian parent in similar fashion as the unbelieving partner is sanctified through sexual intercourse.[1] It is one thing for Paul to point out that intercourse with a harlot is like a defiled marriage relationship (1 Cor. 6.16) and stands in violent contrast with relationship with the Lord (1 Cor. 6.15, 17); it is a debasement of Paul's thought to make him teach that an unbeliever by intercourse with a saint gains the saint's relationship with the Lord.[2] Nevertheless Lietzmann has at least seen the implications of the common idea that the believer's child is sanctified by the mere fact of *birth* from a believer, and has not shunned to state them. It is not so much birth as *belonging* that matters; the same idea would attach to adopted children in a family, even as it would have applied to a married couple that exercised strict continence (a condition of which Paul would have approved, had a pair been capable of it, 1 Cor. 7.5), and we have yet to consider the position of children born before the conversion of the Christian parent. The necessity of relating the 'holiness' of the child to that of the unbelieving parent likewise makes an appeal to the covenant idea improbable,[3] since the male at least would be required to take on himself the sign of the covenant in order to be incorporated within it.

It would seem to me necessary for the understanding of this saying to postulate the coalescence of two ideas in Paul's thought here, one fundamentally Jewish the other fundamentally Christian; the former has made the idea possible, the latter has given it power. The Jewish element has come from the ritual conception of holiness so characteristic of the Old Testament. It is illustrated for us in Rom. 11.16, which appears to be the one other passage in Paul in which the idea is given expression: 'If the dough ($\phi\acute{\nu}\rho\alpha\mu\alpha$) offered as first fruits ($\dot{\alpha}\pi\alpha\rho\chi\acute{\eta}$) is holy, so is the whole lump; and if the root is holy, so are the branches'. The first clause echoes Num. 15.20: 'Of the first of your meal (LXX $\dot{\alpha}\pi\alpha\rho\chi\grave{\eta}$ $\phi\nu\rho\acute{\alpha}\mu\alpha\tau\sigma$) you shall present a cake of your offering'; by such an offering of the first fruits of the dough the whole mass is consecrated, sanctified. Paul applies the thought to the nation Israel; through the divine consecration of Abraham and the patriarchs,

[1] Op. cit., p. 31.
[2] Observe that in 1 Cor. 6.15 Paul does not suggest that the Christian's co-habitation with a harlot would sanctify her; he speaks in terms of defilement only. The passage moves in a different universe of discourse from 1 Cor. 7.14.
[3] Contrary to Best, ibid.

the totality of Israel for ever remains holy. Similarly the holiness, consecration, separateness unto God of the root of Israel in the fathers imparts to the entire tree, including its branches (individual Israelites), the character of holiness, separateness, belongingness to God. This remains true even though Israel persists in a state of unbelief (Rom. 11.20 ff). They are still the offspring of Abraham! In an analogous fashion Paul infers that the unbelieving partner of a married Christian and the children of the marriage are 'consecrated' to God as a whole in virtue of the consecration to Him of the believing partner and parent; a part sanctifies the whole. This is plainly a reflection of Jewish ritual conceptions and is not characteristic of the thought of Paul nor of the New Testament as a whole and it must not be pressed.[1] It is to be distinguished from the conception of sanctification in Christ, as we see it in 1 Cor. 1.2, 30; 6.11; it is no more to be equated with the latter than is the 'sanctification' of unbelieving Jews to be equated with the sanctity of the Body of Christ.

This however does not wholly explain Paul's language. Büchsel has drawn attention to the analogy between the two expressions, 'in the wife', 'in the brother', and the well known Pauline formula 'in Christ', suggesting that in each case it is *personal relationship* that is in view.[2] In that case the sanctification of the unbeliever takes place in the fellowship of living with the believer, in the totality of life's exchange that occurs in the marriage relationship. The same would apply to the relationship of Christian parent and child. This element in the situation has been recognized by various critics and commentators.[3] I hesitated considerably before being persuaded that it was present in the passage, chiefly through a desire to be cautious about accepting the more attractive of two hypotheses, but I was won over by v. 16: 'Perhaps, good woman, you will save your husband! Perhaps, my man, you will save your wife!' If the believing partner is enabled to 'save' the unbelieving, that will be solely in virtue of the presence of *the grace of God, working through the Christian in the daily sharing of married life.* In that case the activity of grace cannot be excluded from Paul's thought of v. 14 and the 'consecration' referred to is not entirely external ('dinglich' as the Germans say). There is a recognition that in circumstances like these sanctity has a power that cannot

---

[1] So, urge Oepke, 'Urchristentum und Kindertaufe', *Ź.N.W.*, 1930, p. 85; Marsh, op. cit. p. 179; Kümmel, op. cit., p. 41.

[2] *Geist Gottes im Neuen Testament*, p. 293, n. 3.

[3] Notably Windisch, 'Zum Problem der Kindertaufe im Urchristentum', *Z.N.W.*, Band 28, 1929, p. 121; T. S. Evans in *The Speaker's Commentary on 1 Corinthians*, cited Robertson and Plummer, op. cit., p. 142, n.; Schneider, op. cit., p. 56; Schlatter, *Paulus der Bote Jesu*, pp. 222 f; Wendland, op. cit., p. 42.

be quenched by opposition and that grace is available to strengthen the Christian in the battle for God in the home. One is reminded of the advice to Christian wives in 1 Pt. 3.1 f: '. . . that some, though they do not obey the word, may be won without a word by the behaviour of their wives, when they see your reverent and chaste behaviour'. A similar consideration will of course be operative in what is said of the children's relationship to the Christian parent: the children are under the sanctifying influence of their Christian father or mother, with all the power for good that that involves. This, then, is the specifically Christian element in the saying, stemming from the general principle that where sin abounds grace superabounds; but it must be emphasized that it is not the only, nor even the basic element; the Jewish conception is primary, modified by the Christian.

If it be asked 'What has all this to do with baptism?' the answer must be given, 'Very little, apart from negative inferences that may be drawn'. The decisive conceptions of the saying have no relation to baptism. Indeed, many investigators have gone further and concluded that Paul's words indicate that the idea of infant baptism could not have emerged at this date.[1] Jeremias however, has strongly objected to this interpretation. He agrees that 1 Cor. 7.14 implies that the baptism of children of *Christian* parents had not arisen up to this time, as also that the language used of the holiness of a non-Christian partner and of the children of Christian and non-Christian parents reflects that of late Jewish ritual; but he suggests that the sentiment, 'Your children are not unclean but holy', has its analogy in the laws concerning the proselyte. Late Judaism distinguished between children who were not begotten and born 'in holiness' and children who were begotten and born 'in holiness' (i.e. after the parents became Jews). *The former were baptized with the parents*, the latter were not. Therefore, concludes Jeremias, since the use of the terms 'unclean' and 'holy' in relation to children in 1 Cor. 7.14 has this background, it is in the highest degree likely that *the Christian Church followed the practice of the Jews and baptized the children born before the conversion of the parents but not those born afterwards*.[2]

---

[1] This conviction has been widespread for many years even among scholars of communions practising infant baptism. See e.g. Feine, *Realencyclopädie für Theologie und Kirche*, XIX, p. 403; H. R. Mackintosh, 'Thoughts on Infant Baptism', *The Expositor*, 1917, p. 195; N. P. Williams, *Ideas of the Fall*, p. 220, n. 2; Bousset, op. cit., p. 100; Lindblom, *Handbok till Nya Testamentet*, IV, 1, p. 123; Windisch, op. cit., p. 121; Wendland, op. cit., p. 42; Leenhardt, op. cit., p. 67; *The Biblical Doctrine of Baptism* (*Study Document of the Church of Scotland*), p. 53.

[2] See *Hat die Urkirche die Taufe geübt?*, p. 40; *Die Kindertaufe in den ersten vier Jahrhunderten*, pp. 54–56.

This conclusion, however, seems to me to be in the highest degree unlikely and that for the following reasons:

(i) An analogy with terminology used in relation to the reception of the proselyte does not permit the inference that modes of procedure in proselyte baptism are also adopted. That the inference is excluded here seems to me apparent from the application of this terminology to the non-Christian parent; on the basis of the laws of proselyte baptism, such a person ought to be pronounced unclean, not 'in holiness'.

(ii) It is admitted by Jeremias that the statement of v. 14c can have its required force only if the 'holy' children are unbaptized. But on his view this is more difficult to maintain than he realized. It is likely that only three years had elapsed since the conclusion of Paul's ministry (lasting eighteen months) at Corinth; since only the unbaptized children, born after the parents' conversion, are in view, the statement is restricted to the youngest children, most of whom would be under three years of age! The *majority* of the children of the Christian men and women to whom Paul is addressing himself are thus excluded from his statement! Is this really credible? If no distinction between the children is intended, then since most of them were born before the conversion of their parents they were either baptized, in which case the argument falls to the ground, or they were unclean! In fact, there is not the slightest hint that Paul limits the reference in the expression 'your children' to those born subsequent to the conversion of the parents, in which case the argument of Jeremias is invalid.

(iii) It is assumed in the argument we are considering that the children born before the conversion of these Christians married to non-Christians are baptized and in the Church. Yet experience testifies to the fact that not infrequently children of a marriage where only one partner is converted are not allowed by the non-Christian partner to be baptized and join the Church. This would operate with particular force in a society in which the male dominated over the woman and it was the woman who was converted, for the opposition of the non-Christian was sometimes severe (cf. 1 Pt. 3.6b, Mk. 13.12). On the argument postulated, the unconverted partner is sanctified by the believer but the unbaptized children are unclean! Apart from the fantasy of this, we observe that Paul states the children are all clean. Conceivably easy going Corinth knew no difficulties and *every* child of the parents in view was in the Church; if so (and in my judgment that demands much credence from us) it ought to be recognized that the statement of 1 Cor. 7.14c almost certainly could not apply to any other church founded by Paul, for in them opposition was the order of the day, and some children at least would be prevented from coming into the Church.

All things considered, it seems to me that Jeremias has pressed his claim beyond the warrant of the evidence and a non liquet must be set against his judgment that 1 Cor. 7.14 implies the baptism of children born before the conversion of a Christian parent. As little is it legitimate for Cullmann to affirm that there is a direct line from the idea of the holiness of children here asserted to infant baptism, but 'none to a baptism based on a later decision of those sons or daughters who were born in a Christian home'.[1] On the contrary, Paul's statement concerning the unbelieving partner sanctified by the Christian spouse presumes a hope that he or she may yet exercise that repentance and faith that will be expressed in baptism (v. 16); Paul could not conceive of such a person entering the Church and enjoying the benefits of salvation on any other terms. The parallel nature of the 'holy' children makes it natural to assume that they will tread a similar path and gain that consecration in Christ, cleansing and justification that is bestowed on him who comes to baptism in faith (1 Cor. 6.11). Admittedly that cannot be proved, but the presumptive tendency of the saying is contrary to Cullmann's assertion.

It is to be concluded that Flemington's silence about this statement of Paul's was not unjustified: it yields no positive evidence concerning the Apostolic doctrine of baptism and it would be best omitted from the discussion concerning that doctrine.

12. EPHESIANS 4.5

The first thought that leaps to the mind when reading Eph. 4. 4–6, from the point of view of our interest in the doctrine of baptism, is the dignity and importance accorded to baptism in virtue of its inclusion in this enumeration of the great 'unities' of our Faith.[2] I am sure that this is right, but care must be taken in the way this impression is supported. For example, it is doubtful that we should draw conclusions as to the greater importance of baptism than the Lord's Supper or Apostolate or ministry on the ground of their lack of mention in this list.[3] Are we to draw negative conclusions also about the unimpor-

---

[1] Op. cit., p. 44.

[2] Flemington reflected this sentiment in asserting, 'When we take full account of each member of this significant sequence, there will seem perhaps no other passage in the whole New Testament that speaks more eloquently of all that baptism meant to a first century Christian', op. cit., p. 64.

[3] Such comparison is made by H. T. Andrews, in his essay incorporated in Forsyth's book, *The Church and the Sacraments*, 1917, p. 149, and by Flemington, ibid.

tance of love to this writer on the same basis? Rather than commit ourselves to such inferences, it is better to assume that the list is not intended to be exhaustive; it has probably been determined from a point of view that has made it natural to select these items and enumerate them in this order. What that viewpoint is can only be guessed. Dibelius is perhaps on the right lines in suggesting that the passage cites a confessional formula or formulae; if so, it is not impossible that the confession itself had to do with baptism and that the selection of items from it is due to the writer's interest in the Church and the Spirit who animates it and enables its ministry and growth.[1] The one *Body* and one *Spirit* are first mentioned because of the appeal just uttered to maintain the unity of the Spirit in the bond of peace (v. 3). The relationship of the one Body and one Spirit with baptism, however, needs no further demonstration after our consideration of Paul's baptismal utterances. The one *Hope* is to be interpreted in a concrete fashion, referring to the eschatological hope of the Kingdom, to the inheritance of which we have been called. The hope has been fittingly conjoined with the Spirit, since He is the seal of the believer, given in baptism in view of the last Day (1.13 f, 4.30). 'One *Lord*, one *Faith*, one *Baptism*' are interconnected, but the emphasis is probably to be placed on the first article mentioned: 'One *Lord*, the object of Faith's confession in Baptism'. And of course the *one God and Father of all* is equally a proper object of the baptismal confession.

If there is any truth in the idea that this passage is related to a baptismal confession, it would form the closest parallel in the New Testament to the Trinitarian baptismal command in the Great Commission as it is now delivered to us in Mt. 28.19.

The one faith of v. 5, similarly to the one hope of v. 4, is best interpreted objectively, as the faith avowed and acknowledged, rather than as faith in its subjective aspect as trust.[2] Its conjunction with baptism is significant as intimating yet again the connection between faith and baptism, observed frequently in Acts and Paul. Baptism is the supreme occasion of the confession of faith as it is faith's embodiment, subjectively and objectively. This we shall see illustrated in the saying immediately to be considered.

13. EPHESIANS 5.25–27

The purpose of the sacrificial death of Christ is stated in this

---

[1] See his commentary, *An die Kolosser, Epheser und Philemon*, p. 79, and Masson, *Épitre de St. Paul aux Éphésiens*, 1953, p. 187.

[2] So Abbott, op. cit., p. 109. Masson cites Michel's definition of μία πίστις as 'the Church's declaration of faith, the living confession of the Church, the professed tradition of the Church in the present', op. cit., p. 186.

passage to be the consecration, cleansing and perfection of the Church. The means whereby the consecration and cleansing take place are defined in the phrase 'with the washing of the water with (the) word'. (τῷ λουτρῷ τοῦ ὕδατος ἐν ῥήματι). There is some uncertainty as to whether the language has been determined by the custom, obtaining among both Jews and Greeks, of a bride taking a ceremonial bath as part of the marriage preparations.[1] If such a 'washing' is in mind, there can be little doubt that the readers are expected to recognize its counterpart for the Bride of Christ in baptism; indeed, the twofold addition of 'the water' and 'the word' makes the baptismal reference in the term 'washing' (τῷ λουτρῷ) even more clear than the conjectured reference to the bridal bath.

The question has been raised, however, whether the baptism here spoken of may refer to the action of Christ signified by the preceding statement 'He gave himself up for her' (v. 25), rather than to the rite of baptism applied to individuals; i.e. whether the 'washing' and consecration of the Church is viewed as having taken place when Christ gave His life for the Church.[2] This interpretation has been modified by some so as to include the idea of the Church's baptism at Pentecost; it is suggested that since the once-for-all baptism of Christ in blood on the cross and the once-for-all baptism of the Church in Spirit at Pentecost are correlative, the baptism of Christ may be spoken of as the baptism of the Church.[3] If this is intended as an exposition of Eph. 5.25 ff, rather than a theological construction taking its point of departure from the passage, it is hardly to be received. The text does not imply that the consecration and cleansing of the Church took place once-for-all in the death of Christ on the cross and gift of the Spirit at Pentecost, despite the aorist participle καθαρίσας, 'cleansing'; the statement beginning 'that he might consecrate her' denotes the purpose of the death of Christ, and the participle καθαρίσας represents the mode or means whereby the sanctification is carried out; under no circumstances is the participle to be interpreted as denoting an action taking place prior to that of the main verb 'consecrate' (ἁγιάσῃ). Indeed, the two clauses of vv. 25 and 26 introduced by ἵνα ('in order that') are closely related: Christ's death has a twofold

---

[1] Armitage Robinson thinks there is no need to invoke the parallel, *St. Paul's Epistle to the Ephesians*, 2nd ed. 1904, p. 207. Abbot accepts without question the belief that such a rite is in view, op. cit., p. 169, and so apparently Masson, op. cit., p. 212.

[2] Such is the interpretation of Théo Preiss, *Verbum Caro*, I, No. 3, p. 115 and J. A. T. Robinson, 'The One Baptism as a Category of New Testament Soteriology', *S.J.T.*, vol. 6, 1953, p. 268.

[3] *Church of Scotland Interim Report*, 1955, pp. 31 f.

end in view, the sanctification and cleansing of the Church and its ultimate glorification and perfection. If there is a sense in which *both* ends were achieved in the death on the cross, it is clear that the writer did not intend that meaning, but had in view the present condition of the Church and its future eschatological splendour. Moreover the twofold qualification of τῷ λουτρῷ, 'with the washing', must be given its full force. Whereas we are asked to accept the idea that the 'washing' denoted by τῷ λουτρῷ was not of water but in the blood of Christ and in the Holy Spirit, the writer emphatically declares that it is τοῦ ὕδατος — 'of the water'! Why this unnecessary and misleading qualification if in fact the washing is in blood and Spirit? And how is the further qualification of the 'washing' indicated by ἐν ῥήματι ('with the word') to be understood on this view? Whatever the precise significance of the phrase, all agree that it has reference to the word in which Christ and His action are embodied — the proclamation of Christ, or the confession of Christ by the believer, or the calling of the name of Christ over a believer seeking cleansing and the Spirit. This 'washing with the word' therefore looks back on the death of Christ as an accomplishment of the past and appeals to it as a means of cleansing in the present; the 'washing' cannot be viewed as accomplished in the death which is proclaimed as its condition. Still more grave however is the difficulty presented in the application of 'with the word' to the baptismal confession or the proclamation of the name over the baptized. In the case of an individual baptism the matter is clear and of deepest significance; but how is this related to the once-for-all baptism of the Church? It is conceivable perhaps that the Church is baptized as it makes its corporate confession of Christ, but this cannot apply to a baptism on the cross, for the 'Church' was then full of unbelief. And the idea of the Name being proclaimed over the Church by its ministers is intolerable, while the proclamation of the Name over the Church by a divine Agency is fantasy. Nor should appeal be made to the idea that the baptism of Eph. 5.25 ff is both that of the Church and that of the individual and that thus features of baptism are cited which are not strictly applicable to the Church; there is no evidence that the writer has such a double meaning in mind. It would seem that we are compelled by the language employed in this passage to interpret it of baptism as ordinarily received by the believer. Its application to the Church is due to the exigencies of the context; the Church as the Bride of Christ is a cleansed Body because it has baptism, but there is no thought in this passage of a once-for-all baptism in the past, or even of a baptism that is corporate rather than individual. That baptism has a corporate aspect and that there is a sense in which we may speak of the baptism of the Church at Pentecost is not to be denied; but these elements of baptismal theology are more obviously to the fore in 1 Cor. 12.13 and Gal. 3.26 ff than in the present passage, despite the paradoxical fact that the subject of baptism is here said to be the Church and not the individual. We have here an instance of those summary statements that are not infrequent in the Epistles whereby all cases of a kind are reduced under a single aorist. The Church is consecrated as its members are cleansed in baptism with the word, on the basis of the efficacious death of Christ.[1]

The discussion of this saying thus far has thrown into prominence two important elements of baptismal teaching inherent in this passage. First, baptism is seen to be rooted in the redemptive death of Christ and has in prospect the glory of the consummated Kingdom. This is demanded by the explicit mention of the death of Christ in v. 25 and the explicit mention of the hope of glory in v. 27, as well as by the language used of the baptismal act in v. 26, for 'sanctify and cleanse' is the terminology of sacrificial ritual.[2] Yet this very terminology becomes infused with new and weightier significance by its application to the action of Christ, even as the ritual idea of 'presentation' in παραστήσῃ is imbued with transcendental meaning through its eschatological reference. The effect of the whole statement in vv. 25–27 is to throw into relief the spiritual and moral transformation that the Church undergoes through the death of Christ, its reception of baptism with the word and the experience of transfiguring grace and glory that yet awaits her. We have therefore here a further example of the Apostolic transposition into another key of the basic reality declared in Rom. 6.1–11; or perhaps we should say that the theme of death and resurrection with Christ is set forth in a fresh variation, even as Gal. 3.27 employs a different one, and Col. 2.11 yet another.[3]

The second element is perhaps of even greater significance, since

---

[1] Such appears to be the preponderate view of commentators and exegetes generally. Lindblom has suggested that the aorist καθαρίσας is analogous to the so called 'complexive' aorist (see Blass-Debrunner, section 322). His citation, among other passages, of Mt. 28.19 as read in B, D, is particularly instructive: μαθητεύσατε πάντα τὰ ἔθνη, βαπτίσαντες αὐτοὺς . . ., for neither the imperative nor the participle in this case has the common aoristic force; see *Jesu Missions- och Dopbefallning*, pp. 270 ff.

[2] See Abbott, op. cit., p. 168; Armitage Robinson, op. cit., p. 205.

[3] So Dibelius, op. cit., p. 94. It should perhaps be observed that another contact with this same concept of death and resurrection is to be seen in Eph. 2.5 f, which has a close affinity with Col. 2.13. The 'quickening' to new life (συνζωοποιεῖν) of the sinner in Eph. 2.5 f and Col. 2.13 is probably to be interpreted of the rising with Christ in baptism, as in Col. 2.12, see Schnackenburg, op. cit., pp. 70–72.

it is peculiar to this statement in the Pauline corpus: the cleansing in baptism takes place ἐν ῥήματι, 'with the word'. There has been much discussion as to the precise meaning of this phrase. Whereas expositors of the last century tended to favour interpreting ῥῆμα as the gospel,[1] modern commentators incline to the view of Chrysostom, that it relates to the formula of baptism used by the baptizer, 'in the Name of the Father, Son and Holy Spirit',[2] or possibly to the confession made by the baptized in his baptism.[3] In view of the indefiniteness of ἐν ῥήματι, there is much to be said for declining to limit its reference in this context and to regard it as 'the word' in its broadest connotation — the Word of redemption and life that baptism itself enshrines, the Word summed up in the primitive confession, 'Jesus is Lord', acknowledged by the baptizand, and the Word that by divine authority apprehends the believer as the name of the Lord is proclaimed over him in his baptism.[4] If this be a reasonable postulate, its importance for our understanding of the primitive Christian teaching of baptism cannot be overstated; the baptism that sanctifies and cleanses is that in which the Word is heard, confessed and submitted to by the baptized. A baptism without the Word is a defective baptism, even as the Word is not truly heard, confessed and obeyed without baptism. The two are a unity in the will of God, forming a counterpart to the unity we have seen elsewhere in the conjunction of faith and baptism in the teaching of Paul. But though God has joined the two together, it can hardly be doubted that the emphasis in the extended phrase 'with the washing of water, with the word' falls on its conclusion, as 1 Pt. 3.21 more than hints and Jn. 17.17, 15.3 would imply. The power of baptism is the Word of God.[5]

14. 1 TIMOTHY 6.12-13

The pertinence of this saying to our study lies in its reflection of the importance attached in the Church to the confession made and vow

---

[1] Meyer, *Ephesians*, E.T., 1880, p. 295; Alford, vol. iii, 1897, p. 137; Kennedy, op. cit., p. 252.

[2] Abbott, op. cit., p. 169; A. Robinson, op. cit., p. 125, 205 f; Dibelius, op. cit., pp. 94 f with hesitation; Schlier, *T.L.Z.*, 1947, p. 325.

[3] E. F. Scott, *Colossians, Philemon, Ephesians*, p. 239; F. M. Rendtorff, op. cit., p. 48; Anderson Scott, op. cit., p. 119; Flemington, op. cit., p. 65.

[4] So Masson, op. cit., p. 212, n. 5, citing in agreement S. Hanson, cf. Schlatter, *Erläuterungen*, vol. 7, p. 236. A closely parallel ambiguity in the use of the term ῥῆμα occurs in Rom. 10.8 ff, for in v. 8 the ῥῆμα is defined as 'the word of faith which we preach', i.e. the gospel, but in v. 9 it is concentrated in the formula κύριος Ἰησοῦς whom God raised from the dead. The parallel is the more striking if, as is commonly believed, κύριος Ἰησοῦς is the primitive baptismal confession.

[5] So E. F. Scott, op. cit., pp. 239 f; Dibelius, ibid.; Johannes Schneider, op. cit., p. 62.

undertaken by the believer at his baptism. While a few exegetes contest this reference of the passage, preferring to relate the confession before many witnesses to ordination,[1] or to trial before a court,[2] the setting by the author of 'You made the good confession' in parallelism with 'the eternal life to which you were called' shows fairly conclusively that the confession was made by Timothy at the beginning of his Christian life, when he responded to the call of God made through the gospel. Consequently there is fairly general agreement that the context of the 'glorious confession' made by Timothy is that of his baptism.[3]

The making the baptismal confession 'before many witnesses' calls attention to the publicity of baptism, which ensures a fulfilment of the demand of Jesus that would-be-disciples of His must not fear to confess Him before men (Mt. 10.32). Michel points out two further aspects of the baptismal confession: its binding obligation, since the confession involves a vow of obedience that must not be broken; and its finality, for confession of the Son of Man before men will be acknowledged by the Son of Man's confession of the disciple before God in judgment (Mk. 8.38).[4] Both these aspects appear in our passage. The eschatological element is alluded to in the appeal to Timothy to lay hold of the life eternal to which he was called. The binding nature of the obligation undertaken in the baptismal confession is presumed in the call to fight the good fight of faith begun at that time, and in the demand ($\pi\alpha\rho\alpha\gamma\epsilon\lambda\lambda\omega$), to which the impressive declaration of v. 13 forms the introduction, that Timothy 'keep the commandment spotless, without reproach, until the appearing of our Lord Jesus Christ'. While the 'commandment' could admittedly be a general summing up of the exhortation given to Timothy in the Epistle,[5] it would suit the context best if it referred to the charge laid on Timothy in his baptism, for the once-for-all confession of

---

[1] Jeremias, *Die Briefe an Timotheus und Titus*, 5th ed. 1949, p. 37; E. K. Simpson, *The Pastoral Epistles*, 1954, p. 88.

[2] Cullmann, *The earliest Christian Confessions*, E.T., 1949, p. 26, in dependence on Baldensperger, *Révue d'Histoire et de Philosophie Religieuses*, 1922, pp. 1 ff, 95 ff.

[3] So N. J. D. White, 'The First and Second Epistles to Timothy' (*Expositor's Testament*), p. 145; Lietzmann, 'Symbolstudien', *Z.N.W.*, Band 22, 1923, pp. 269 ff; Lock, *The Pastoral Epistles* (I.C.C.), 1924, p. 71; E. F. Scott, *The Pastoral Epistles*, 1936, p. 77; R. Falconer, *The Pastoral Epistles*, 1937, p. 157; B. S. Easton, *The Pastoral Epistles*, 1948, p. 166; A. Richardson, *N.T. Theology*, p. 337; O. Michel, art. $\dot{o}\mu o\lambda o\gamma\dot{\epsilon}\omega$, *T.W.N.T.*, vol. V, p. 211; Dibelius, *Die Pastoralbriefe*, 3rd ed. revised by H. Conzelmann, 1955, p. 67. It is of interest that Cyril of Jerusalem, when recalling the baptismal ceremonies to the newly baptized, spoke of their professing faith in the Trinity as $\dot{\omega}\mu o\lambda o\gamma\dot{\eta}\sigma\alpha\tau\epsilon$ $\tau\dot{\eta}\nu$ $\sigma\omega\tau\dot{\eta}\rho\iota o\nu$ $\dot{o}\mu o\lambda o\gamma\dot{\iota}\alpha\nu$ (Cat. xx.4).

[4] *T.W.N.T.*, vol. V, p. 211.

[5] Dibelius thought of it as similar in scope to the $\pi\alpha\rho\alpha\theta\dot{\eta}\kappa\eta$ delivered to Timothy, op. cit., p. 68.

obedience to the divine Lord made in baptism can fittingly be appealed to at any subsequent time.[1]

The terms of introducing the appeal to 'keep the commandment' in
v. 13 are reminiscent of credal statement and therefore may well
reflect the baptismal confession itself. Timothy is charged before

> 'God who gives life to all things
> And Christ Jesus who testified before Pontius Pilate
> the glorious confession'.[2]

Such a reference to God the Creator and Christ Jesus the Witness
reminds us of the bipartite confessions elsewhere in the New Testament, e.g. 1 Cor. 8.6 and 2 Tim. 4.1, the latter being of particular
importance to us since it characterizes Jesus as Messianic Judge and
King. That hints of the reason why the reference to Jesus making confession before Pilate is included at this point. The confession of God
the Creator is natural in a baptismal creed and is typical of the later
creeds,[3] but the appearance of Christ before Pilate is generally recorded in relation to His suffering of death. We must presume that the
earliest forms of the creed retained a reference to the confession made
by Jesus in His trial as well as to His death under Pilate's sentence.
And the reference is significant, for Timothy was reminded that the
confession he made before witnesses at his baptism was the same as
that made by Jesus before Pilate at His trial. As Jesus answered
Pilate's question, 'Are you the King of the Jews?' with the affirmation,
'You say it' (Mk. 15.3), so Timothy had confessed at his baptism,
'Jesus is Lord'.[4] Having made such a confession, following so great an
example, Timothy must carry out its obligation as befits one who has
yielded his submission to the King of Kings. We may surmise that
such a use of the baptismal confession was not infrequently made by
early Christian preachers.[5]

[1] So Lock, who recalls 2 Clem. 8, τηρήσατε τὴν σάρκα ἁγνὴν καὶ τὴν σφραγῖδα
ἄσπιλον, which is clearly a call to live up to one's baptismal profession.

[2] Dibelius suggested that the second occurrence of τὴν καλὴν ὁμολογίαν in
this credal snatch may be an addition of the author, harking back to Timothy's
making τὴν καλὴν ὁμολογίαν and so rendering the parallel more explicit. Op. cit., p. 68.

[3] For early examples Lock cites Justin, Apol. i.61, ἐπ' ὀνόματος τοῦ πατρὸς τῶν
ὅλων; Ireneus, c. Haer. 1.10, τὸν πεποιηκότα τὸν οὐρανὸν καὶ τὴν γῆν καὶ πάντα τὰ ἐν
αὐτοῖς; Tertullian, de Praescr. 36, unum Deum novit, creatorem universitatis.

[4] It is evident that the answer of Jesus to Pilate, Thou sayest (συ λέγεις) was
interpreted in the primitive Church as affirmative and not evasive. In this respect
the tradition embodied in Jn. 18.33 ff is instructive, for therein Jesus makes known
to Pilate the true nature of his royalty and Pilate confesses his Kingship both to
Jesus Himself (18.37) and to the Jews (18.37) and to the chief priests (19.19–22).

[5] It would in no wise conflict with the interpretation here given if Cullmann's
belief were adopted, that vv. 12 ff were spoken with the prospect of persecution and
trial in mind; the greater force would be then attached to the exhortation to be
faithful to the baptismal confession and vow. See Cullmann's The Earliest Christian Confessions, E.T., 1949, pp. 25 ff.

15. 2 TIMOTHY 2.11–12

It is now generally recognized that the couplet of v. 11 is cited from an early Christian hymn, but there is dissent as to the extent of the quotation in the text of 2 Timothy. Easton considers that the 'faithful saying' extends only to v. 12a, on the ground that the two couplets have a rhythm and an assonance absent from the lines that follow.[1] Moffatt, followed by Lock and the translators of the R.S.V., takes the poem as far as v. 13a, regarding the last line as a comment of the writer of the Epistle. More generally the three verses 11–13 are viewed as wholly reproduced from the poem, for they cohere well, are pertinent to the context, and provide a striking exposition of 'the salvation which in Christ Jesus is with eternal glory' (v. 10), thus:

> If we died with Him, we shall also live with Him;
> If we endure, we shall also reign with Him;
> If we deny Him, He also will deny us;
> If we are faithless, He remains faithful,
> For He cannot deny Himself.[2]

More important than determining the precise limits of the poem is the question of its reference. Schnackenburg admits that v. 11 strongly reminds us of Rom. 6.8 but he considers that the continuation of the hymn forbids a sacramental interpretation of the 'dying with Christ' in this context; it reflects the Pauline Christ-mysticism and confirms the general exhortation of the poem to persevere in tribulation and suffering.[3] Similarly, the implicit exhortation to endurance and warning against denial of Christ in v. 12 has encouraged the view that the whole poem is a 'Hymn to Martyrdom'.[4] Jeremias agrees with this, though regarding v. 11 as a quotation of Rom. 6.8 and originally referring to baptism; its employment here extends its application to martyrdom, thereby yielding the deeply significant teaching that to die *for* Christ in such circumstances is to die *with* Christ.[5] Although

---

[1] Op. cit., p. 42.

[2] So Köhler, *Die Schriften des Neuen Testaments*, 2nd ed. 1908, II, p. 425; Bernard, *The Pastoral Epistles*, 1899, p. 120; Jeremias, op. cit., p. 44 who considers that the poem is 'completely unGreek' and must have emanated from a Jewish-Christian writer — possibly Paul, in view of its dependence on Rom. 6.8; E. F. Scott, op. cit., p. 106; Dibelius-Conzelmann, op. cit., pp. 80 ff; D. Guthrie, *The Pastoral Epistles*, 1957, pp. 144 f; *The British and Foreign Bible Society's second edition of the Greek New Testament*, 1959. Since these verses are a citation from an earlier composition, the possibility must be reckoned with that their echo in Polycarp's *Epistle to the Philippians*, 5, is due to a reminiscence of the original hymn and not to the use of 2 Timothy.

[3] Op. cit., p. 76.   [4] Köhler, op. cit., pp. 425 f; Bernard, op. cit., p. 121.

[5] Op. cit., p. 44. Lock also regards v. 11 as applying both to baptism and to martyrdom, citing in support Chrysostom's comment: θάνατον, τόν τε διὰ λουτροῦ καὶ τὸν διὰ τῶν παθημάτων, op. cit., p. 96.

this interpretation is attractive it is unlikely to be correct; the aorist tense of v. 11, 'we died with him' (συναπεθάνομεν), shows unmistakably that the death with Christ is not a possibility of the future but an event of the past finished and done with, as in Rom. 6.8, 2 Cor. 5.14, Gal. 2.19. It may have consequences for the present and nerve to suffering for Christ in the future (v. 12) but there is no question of the dying with Christ in v. 11 having a dual relation to past and future; it is the death with Christ in baptism, according to the teaching of Rom. 6.1 ff, that is solely in view.[1]

The probability that the hymn before us has a baptismal setting makes the conjunction of the further clauses after v. 11 of significance for our interpretation of baptism. 'If we endure, we shall also reign with Him': endurance of suffering for Christ is a natural outcome of dying with Christ in baptism. This confirms our interpretation of Rom. 6.1 ff, that dying with Christ signifies not alone a being drawn into the event of the cross with Christ on Golgotha but a renunciation of the self, a 'slaying' of the flesh (Gal. 5.24, Col. 3.5) in the very act of baptism. The eschatological prospect of baptism is also emphasized. The συζήσομεν ('we shall live with him') of v. 11 may possibly, as in Rom. 6.5, hover between a present and a future resurrection with Christ.[2] In v. 12 however the eschatological future alone is in mind and the prospect is held out, not alone of rising with Christ for the Kingdom, but of *reigning* with Him in the Kingdom. This is the consequence of dying with Christ in baptism and living out the baptismal life of endurance in faith and obedience; it is a following through of the messianic pattern by the messianic people (Lk. 24.26), for a dying with Christ that is followed by a life lived for self is a manifest contradiction, but a life in accordance with the messianic pattern of lowliness, concern 'for the things of others' and obedience unto death, brings a participation in the messianic glory (Phil. 2.3–12; 3.10–11). Accordingly the second couplet of v. 12 warns of the consequence of denying Christ or defection from Him, in manifest dependence on Mt. 10.33; but the couplet of v. 13, with its triumphant addition of a third line, indicates the source of the Christian's perseverance; Christ abides faithful evermore, pitiful to his followers in their frailty, their unchanging ground of assurance and hope of final glory.

---

[1] So Schlatter, *Erläuterungen*, VIII, pp. 210 f; N. J. D. White, op. cit., p. 163; Scott, op. cit., p. 105; Easton, op. cit., p. 52; Guthrie, op. cit., p. 145.

[2] Observe that in the Pastorals 'salvation', the subject of v. 10, which the poem is intended to illustrate, is both past (2 Tim. 1.9, Tit. 3.5) and future (1 Tim. 4.16, 2 Tim. 3.15, 4.18).

To be baptized to Christ is thus to die and live in grace and rise to glory.[1]

16. TITUS 3.5-7

We have in this passage the last of the 'faithful sayings' of the Pastoral Epistles (v. 8, see 1 Tim. 1.15, 3.1, 4.9, 2 Tim. 2.11). The rhythmic structure is not so immediately obvious as in 2 Tim. 2.11-13, but it is probable that here also we have an early Christian hymn.[2] In this case the issue once more requiring to be determined is whether or not it is a baptismal hymn. In particular, is baptism in view in v. 5? Of the commentators who have written on these Epistles, I can find but one who denies it. E. K. Simpson writes 'That baptism has a symbolic reference to cleansing we do not deny; but a spiritual economy cannot be tied to a material agency as an indispensable channel of grace. How can a sign engross the virtue of the thing signified?'[3] This is a now familiar sentiment. He that has accompanied us through this review of Paul's teaching on baptism will know that for the Apostle and his contemporaries baptism cannot be reduced to a bare sign, any more than the cross of Christ can be described as a 'mere symbol'; the sacrament is the meeting of God and man in grace and faith, a spiritual transaction that cannot but have spiritual consequences for one engaged in it. The language and thought of the

---

[1] It is possible to interpret v. 13 as a grim assurance of the inflexibility of Christ in the judgment and the impossibility of His doing other than condemn the defaulters. But the strong asseveration of the faithfulness of the Lord in v. 13, as well as the analogy of passages in which a like assurance is given (cf. especially Rom. 3.5, 11.29 ff, 1 Jn. 3.20), favour the positive interpretation of a reference to covenant faithfulness. Conzelmann cites a good parallel from the Manual of Discipline, XI, 11, translated by Kühn and which may be rendered thus:

'And if I totter, the mercies of God are my help for ever;
And if I stumble through a sin of the flesh,
My right stands eternally on the righteousness of God', op. cit., p. 82.

[2] As in 2 Tim. 2.11 ff the limits of the citation are uncertain. Dibelius goes back as far as v. 3, since the comparison between the old life and the new begins at that point, op. cit., p. 24; Moffatt, followed by Scott, begins at v. 4. Lock seems to have hovered on the matter, for he first provides a poetic paraphrase of vv. 4-6, op. cit., p. 151, but later suggests that the Saying is contained in 5-7, or possibly only in v. 5, vv. 6-7 being added by way of comment (p. 155). Easton restricts the poem to vv. 5b-7 (p. 102). Jeremias includes vv. 5-7 as a whole and sets forth the lines as follows:

Not through deeds and righteousness which we performed,
But in virtue of his own mercy,
He saved us through the washing of regeneration
And renewal by the Holy Spirit,
Which he poured out upon us lavishly
Through Jesus Christ our Saviour,
That justified by his grace
Heirs we might become in hope of life eternal (op. cit., p. 61).

[3] The Pastoral Epistles, p. 115.

hymn are such as we have encountered and are to meet in baptismal passages of other Epistles: λουτρόν, denoting the 'washing' of baptism, occurs in Eph. 5.26; baptism in the Spirit in 1 Cor. 12.13 and the Acts (frequently); justification in Christ and the Spirit, in 1 Cor. 6.11; and the conjunction of salvation with baptism in 1 Pt. 3.21. (The connection of regeneration with 'water and Spirit' in Jn. 3.5 we have yet to examine.) All things considered, it requires a real hardiness of spirit to refuse the weight of this evidence; it is the 'wealth' (πλουσίως) of the gift poured out on the baptized that causes hesitation to recognize the connection — a curious attitude for the Christian to adopt to God's 'kindness and love for man'! We should compare with the quotation from Simpson the reflections on this saying of another conservatively minded New Testament scholar, Adolf Schlatter: 'He (Paul) can declare the word of Jesus, not in part but completely, without the sacraments being once mentioned. But if they do appear he links with them the entire riches of the grace of Christ, because in them he sees the will of Jesus not merely partially but wholly stamped and effective. In baptism he possessed union with the Lord, who gives us a new life through His Spirit'.[1] This sentiment is in agreement with our findings thus far and with the tenor of this passage.

'He saved us through the washing of regeneration
And renewal of the Holy Spirit.'

What force is to be ascribed to these genitives and how are they to be related? A long tradition, stretching back to Theodoret, interprets the clause as a virtual chiasmus: He saved us 'by a regeneration effected through the water and the renewal effected through the Holy Spirit'. By this means a distinction is drawn between the crisis of the new birth bestowed by baptism and the continual renewing of life by the Spirit — a view not inimical to the practice of confirmation.[2] This interpretation is nevertheless to be rejected, despite its apparent support by the parallelism of the two lines. It is fairly certain that 'regeneration' (παλινγενεσία) and 'renewal' (ἀνακαίνωσις) represent the same reality, although their derivations differ. The former is an eschatological term for the new creation of God at the end of the times (Mt. 28.19) and applied to the individual represents his recreation (cf. 2 Cor. 5.17); the latter denotes a new beginning of life, a

[1] Schlatter, Die Briefe an die Thessalonicher, Philipper, Timotheus und Titus (Erläuterungen VIII), p. 262.
[2] It is favoured by Alford, op. cit., pp. 424–5 and White, op. cit., p. 198. Lock is drawn to it, though he also expresses his conviction that παλινγενεσίας and ἀνακαινώσεως alike depend on λουτροῦ, op. cit., pp. 154 f.

making over again rather than a renewal of former powers.[1] Since the two terms are used synonymously, we should view the καί as resumptive — 'through the washing of regeneration, *even* the renewal of the Holy Spirit'.[2] Thus the Holy Spirit is the Agent of the action denoted by both words: the regeneration and renewal are alike wrought by the Spirit. It is misleading to imply that regeneration is effected by the washing but renewal by the Holy Spirit; the Spirit is the Author of both. λουτροῦ παλιγγενεσίας καὶ ἀνακαινώσεως Πνεύματος Ἁγίου must therefore be rendered in such a way as to show that the Holy Spirit is the Agent in each case, as e.g. 'the washing characterized by the regeneration and renewal wrought by the Holy Spirit', or even, following the Scandinavian translations, 'the washing for the regeneration and renewal that the Holy Spirit effects'.[3]

The immediately succeeding clause hints as to how the hymn writer conceives this to happen: 'He poured out (the Spirit) upon us richly through Jesus Christ our Saviour'. The verb ἐκχέω ('pour out') occurs infrequently in the New Testament. It is used in Mt. 9.17 of the gushing of wine from burst wineskins, in Jn. 2.15 of the money poured on the ground from overturned tables of the changers, and in Rom. 3.15 of blood shed (an O.T. citation). Leaving out of account the Book of Revelation, its only other occurrences have to do with the Pentecost narrative: it appears in Acts 2.17–18, quoting the prophecy concerning the outpouring of the Spirit in the last days (Joel. 3.1 f) and in Acts 2.33, Peter's explanation of its fulfilment in the Pentecostal phenomena: 'He (Jesus) having been exalted by the right hand of God and having received the promise of the Holy Spirit from the Father, poured out this that you see and hear'. There is no likelihood that Tit. 3.6 cites Acts 2.33, but it is very probable that the association of Joel 3.1 f with Pentecost and the conviction that the Spirit was sent by the exalted Jesus had become fixed elements in Christian teaching. The total effect of vv. 5–6 is to represent baptism as the counterpart in the individual's experience of the sending of the Spirit at Pentecost. Baptism is the occasion when the Spirit works creatively in the believer, as He made out of the community of the disciples the Body of Christ and will produce at the end a new creation for the everlasting Kingdom.[4]

---

[1] So Dibelius, op. cit., p. 111; Easton, op. cit., p. 100; Behm, article καινός, *T.W.N.T.*, vol. III, p. 455.　　[2] Jeremias, op. cit., p. 61.

[3] 'Ett bad till ny födelse och förnyelse i helig ande' (Swedish); 'Badet til gjenfødelse og fornyelse ved den Hellige Ånd' (Norwegian); 'Badet til genfødelse ved Helligånden' (Danish).

[4] So Lock, op. cit., p. 155 and especially Bornkamm: 'Baptism is the work of our deliverance through Christ the Saviour, the bath of regeneration and renewing in

The question has been raised concerning the origin of this conception and its relation to the Pauline teaching on baptism. On the one hand it is maintained that the conception of regeneration and renewal in baptism has been taken over from the Mystery Religions,[1] and on the other that it comes close to a magical estimate of the rite, indicating that the move from Paul's theology to that of the later Catholic Church was by this time well on its way.[2] The matter is not simple to resolve, for the origins of these concepts are complex and it is not easy to determine at which stage in the development the Pastoral Epistles stand. In my judgment, however, critical writers tend to over-simplify the situation and, in their anxiety to differentiate between Paul and the writer of these Letters, to exaggerate the distance between the Apostle and this writer. For example, Dibelius produces evidence from the Mysteries for the use of παλινγενεσία to denote rebirth, points out that ἀνακαίνωσις ('renewal') is synonymous with it in this passage, showing that its meaning is the same as that in the Mysteries, and concludes that the concept has been taken from them.[3] The term παλινγενεσία certainly originated among the Greeks in connection with Stoic ideas of the renewal of the world and was adopted by the adherents of the Mystery Religions. But it was also employed in Diaspora Judaism, as by the unmystical Josephus, and early became a common word among educated people generally.[4] Its use in Mt. 19.28 is significant, for in this case there is no contact with Hellenism; the term was employed by the translator of the Aramaic source to render the simple idea of the new world or new age, in accordance with traditional Jewish eschatology.[5] The significance of παλινγενεσία could be extended to represent the experience in this age of the life of the age to come, an easy transition for one who believed that Jesus by His resurrection had brought that age into being and by His Spirit had released its powers into this. Such is the source of 2 Cor. 5.17 and it seems to me gratuitous to invoke the Mystery Religions to explain it. It is no far cry from 2 Cor. 5.17 to Tit. 3.5. Its

the Holy Spirit, that is the appropriation of the regeneration and renewing through the Spirit, and so the corresponding event for faith that was given to the entire Church in the event of Pentecost', 'Die neutestamentliche Lehre von der Taufe', *Theologische Blätter*, 1938, p. 52. See also Thornton, *The Common Life in the Body of Christ*, p. 190; J. G. Davies, *Spirit, Church and Sacraments*, p. 104.

[1] Dibelius, op. cit., p. 111; Bultmann, *N.T. Theology*, I, p. 142.
[2] So Oepke with restraint, *T.W.N.T.*, I, p. 541; Easton, op. cit., pp. 100 ff; and Scott, op. cit., pp. 175 ff with emphasis.
[3] Ibid.
[4] Cicero even used it of returning from exile, Att. 6.6. See Büchsel's discussion of the word, article παλινγενεσία, *T.W.N.T.*, I, pp. 685 ff.
[5] Dalman, *The Words of Jesus*, E.T., 1909, p. 177.

language is consistent with the Pauline tradition and, as Windisch pointed out, is characteristic of Jewish-Christian eschatology.[1] That its thought is related to that of the Mystery Religions need no more signify dependence on those Religions than the kinship of Paul's exposition in Rom. 6.1 ff to that of the Mysteries prove that his view is derived from them.[2]

As to the relationship of Tit. 3.5 to Paul's doctrine, one must protest at the representation of it in Scott and, to a lesser extent, at that in Easton. It is inexcusable for the former to say that for Paul baptism is 'only setting the seal on the essential act of faith', but in Tit. 3.5 baptism is efficacious by itself; and that for Paul baptism represents dying with Christ, but for the Pastorals baptism is little more than a purifying rite.[3] Neither of these contentions is worthy of the discussion. Easton has, however, lighted on a more serious matter: whereas justification appears in v. 7, its inseparable Pauline correlative, faith, does not once occur in vv. 4–7; the appearance is given that justification is the fruit of baptism worked in the soul by the entrance of the Holy Spirit, whereas for Paul this is rather the beginning of sanctification.[4] This seems to me to rest on a misunderstanding. Easton perhaps overlooked that if faith is not mentioned in Tit. 3.5 ff, neither does it occur in most of the Pauline baptismal sayings, e.g. Rom. 6.1–11 (v. 8 is a doubtful exception), 1 Cor. 6.11, 12.13, 2 Cor. 1.21 f, Eph. 5.25–27, Col. 1.13 f, 2.15. It has been our contention, however, that Gal. 3.26 f and Col. 2.11 f, to say nothing of the implications of the 'word' for baptism in Rom. 10.9 f and Eph. 5.25 f and the theological content of Rom. 6.1 ff, demand the recognition that faith is integral to baptism in Paul's teaching. In the Pastorals we have noted the confessional context of baptism in 1 Tim. 6.12 f and the binding of baptism with endurance in faith in 2 Tim. 2.11 ff; in these two sayings faith is clearly important for baptism; its omission from Tit. 3.5 ff is therefore as little significant as it is from the Pauline texts quoted above. In particular we must not fail to observe that the view of justification, as interpreted by Easton, is remarkably close to that in 1 Cor. 6.11, where it is hardly distinguishable from consecration and

---

[1] He cites the appearance of grace, the deliverance wrought by God, the outpouring of the Spirit through the exalted Christ, and the inheritance of eternal life; *Taufe und Sünde*, 1908, p. 247. Büchsel came to a similar conclusion: 'The idea is fundamentally eschatological, but it therefore includes a moral renewal', op. cit., p. 688.

[2] See the discussion on regeneration and the Mystery Religions by W. L. Knox, *Some Hellenistic Elements in Primitive Christianity*, 1944, pp. 190 ff.

[3] Op. cit., pp. 176 f.

[4] Op. cit., p. 103.

cleansing 'in the name of our Lord Jesus Christ and in the Spirit of our God'. It could even be maintained that the reference to justification by grace in Tit. 3.7 is more characteristic of Paul than that in I Cor. 6.11! But such comparisons are odious. In our passage the Pentecostal experience in baptism is renewed for faith (v. 5), as justification by grace is for faith (v. 6) and the promise of life eternal is for faith (v. 7). We do injustice to the unknown composer of this 'faithful saying' if we insist on setting the lowest possible interpretation on his theology.

With all this the *possibility* must nevertheless be admitted that the author of the hymn may not have been so fully aware as we are of the eschatological background of the concepts with which he worked, and still more that his language could be misunderstood by Christians from a purely Hellenistic background and be interpreted by them in accordance with the traditions with which they had been familiar. The writer has certainly used current coinage in setting forth the Christian understanding of baptism; that it is a debased coinage is not to be admitted. His exposition is set forth in such a fashion as could be appreciated by Christians of the Hebraic and Hellenistic traditions — and differently interpreted. If he had his feet planted in both traditions it would not be surprising.

As in the 'faithful saying' of 2 Tim. 2.11 ff, this hymn is rich in baptismal significance and we do well to call its elements briefly to mind.

The believer experiences 'salvation' in baptism (ἔσωσεν, v. 5) because a saving event has happened: 'the kindness and love for man of God our Saviour appeared' (v. 4). By this short statement the Incarnation in its totality is described — as in Jn. 3.16 and Gal. 4.4 f; it is God our *Saviour* who saved us through the λουτρόν. We perceive here the same rooting of baptism in the redemptive action of God in Christ that appears in the great baptismal utterances, Rom. 6.1 ff, Col. 2.11 f, Eph. 5.25 ff.

God saved us 'not by reason of works . . . but in accordance with His mercy' (v. 5). A two fold contrast is here drawn between deeds that earn and faith that receives, and the power of God that mercifully achieves what man cannot do for himself. This, we observe, is related to baptism (ἔσωσεν ἡμᾶς, 'he saved us'); the emphasis on the powerful operation by the Spirit in the 'washing' underscores this very fact that God does for us what we are powerless to perform — He makes us anew and gives us new life.

God saved us 'through the washing wherein the Holy Spirit

wrought regeneration and renewal'. No statement of the New Testament, not even Jn. 3.5, more unambiguously represents the power of baptism to lie in the operation of the Holy Spirit. Schlatter was justified in commenting on these words: 'That God has given baptism to the Church and effects through it her deliverance is not based on the water but on that which is bound up with this bath as God's work in man. He produces thereby a new man, not through water, but through the Holy Spirit'.[1]

God saved us that 'having been justified . . . we might become . . .'. It would be possible to loose δικαιωθέντες ('having been justified') from ἔσωσεν ('he saved us') and to think of justification as independent of the washing,[2] but the impression is undoubtedly given that it took place at the time indicated by 'he saved us through the washing' (ἔσωσεν ἡμᾶς διὰ λουτροῦ). This is precisely what we found in the conjunction of aorists in 1 Cor. 6.11 — 'you became washed, consecrated, justified'. Further indications of a related point of view may be observed in a comparison of the two texts. It will be recalled that the setting of 'you were justified' in 1 Cor. 6.11 led to the conclusion that a dynamic rather than a purely forensic conception of justification was therein implied. A similar judgment applies here, as is evident when we compare the phrase 'justified by his grace' with the appearance of the same phrase in Rom. 3.24, 'justified freely by his grace', for the latter is strictly related to God's provision of a means of forgiveness apart from the Law, but in our context the emphasis falls on renewal of life in the Spirit. We earlier compared two related passages Rom. 8.1 ff, Phil. 3.9, for they too go beyond a purely forensic view of justification; in these latter passages, however, justification is 'in Christ', whereas in 1 Cor. 6.11 the cleansing, consecration and justification take place 'in the name of our Lord Jesus Christ and in the Spirit of our God'. Is it without significance that in Tit. 3.5 ff justification is entwined with the renewal of *the Holy Spirit whom God poured out richly through Jesus Christ our Saviour*, i.e. by the Spirit bestowed through the mediation of the Christ in whose name baptism was performed? However that may be, there is excellent reason for affirming that the relation of baptism to justification in 1 Cor. 6.11 and

---

[1] Op. cit., p. 261.

[2] Wohlenberg urges that δικαιωθέντες denotes a time antecedent to ἔσωσεν . . . διὰ λουτροῦ, since Paul would consider that it is the justified believer who comes to baptism, 'Die Pastoralbriefe' (*Kommentar zum N.T.*, ed. T. Zahn, 1911, p. 259). This however is to make grammar subserve a theological notion that can by no means be extracted from the present text and that is difficult to reconcile with Paul's baptismal teaching generally.

Tit. 3.5 ff is fundamentally the same: the grace that baptizes is the grace that justifies, inseparably one and experienced as one.

God saved us through baptism . . . 'that we might become heirs of life eternal'. The theme of the faithful saying in 2 Tim. 2.11 ff is echoed and the eschatological goal of baptism once more declared. Baptism was given with a view to obtaining the Kingdom of heaven. The heirs who have received the Spirit have already been given the first instalment of the promised blessing; the 'hope' of life eternal is therefore sure and certain.

With so broad a view of the grace of God bestowed upon us in baptism it is not to be wondered at that the writer of the Letter, after concluding the citation, adds, 'These things I want you to emphasize, so that those who have professed faith in God may devote themselves to good works'. A true understanding of what God has done for us in baptism should stimulate us to a right concern for our fellows. Only so is gratitude worthily expressed.[1]

(ii) *Baptism in the Johannine Literature*

1. *The Sacramentalism of the Fourth Gospel*

It is characteristic of the Fourth Gospel that it provides no account of the baptism of Jesus nor command to baptize, no account of the Last Supper nor charge to perpetuate the eucharist, yet it is universally acknowledged to contain sacramental teaching of deepest significance. The manner in which eucharistic teaching is expounded in the discourse on the bread of life after the feeding miracle, instead of being set in the context of the Last Supper, indicates the preference of the Evangelist for indirect teaching. By the same method instruction on the significance of baptism is included in the conversation with Nicodemus in ch. 3. Of late it has become a subject of lively debate whether the Evangelist has had a more sustained interest in baptism than the Nicodemus discourse would indicate and whether intimations of baptismal teaching are scattered throughout the Gospel for the discerning eye to catch. That such is the case is the conviction of Oscar Cullmann and he has contended for it in considerable detail in his work, 'Early Christian Worship'.[2]

From early times in the Church writers have seen references to baptism in the healing of the man born blind (ch. 9) the washing of

---

[1] Observe that again a Trinitarian view of baptism is implied in the central statement of this passage: '*God our Saviour* saved us through the washing unto new life by *the Holy Spirit*, whom He poured out upon us through *Jesus Christ our Saviour*'.

[2] *E.T.*, 1953, first issued as *Urchristentum und Gottesdienst*, 1950 and in French with a more suitable title, *Les Sacraments de l'Évangile Johannique*, 1951.

the disciples' feet (ch. 13) and the flowing of water and blood from the Saviour's side on the cross (ch. 19). Cullmann has revived certain elements of patristic interpretation of the Gospel in support of the view that from first to last the Evangelist was concerned to relate the narratives of the ministry to the two sacraments, especially to baptism. This is believed to be due to the Evangelist's desire to demonstrate the connection between the earthly life of Jesus and the Church's experience of the Risen Lord. The presence of Christ among his people is actualized in the service of worship, and early Christian worship was especially characterized by the Lord's Supper and baptism. Cullmann's examination of the Fourth Gospel leads him to believe that sacramental allusions partake of the very warp and woof of the Gospel and in his demonstration it happens that baptism looms even larger than the eucharist. Since his discussion has occasioned the necessity of considering a wider range of evidence from the Gospel than it would have been otherwise necessary, we shall pay special attention to his treatment of this evidence before proceeding to the exposition of Jn. 3.1 ff. At the outset I must acknowledge that, although several notable reviewers have expressed the opinion that Cullmann has completely established his case, in my judgment the exegesis demanded by the view is so often questionable as to put in grave doubt the major premiss.

An unfortunate beginning is made by Cullmann in his endeavour to prove that the relation of John the Baptist to Jesus is portrayed by the Evangelist in the interests of demonstrating the true relationship between John's baptism and Christian baptism, i.e. to show the superiority of the latter to the former. This is considered to be indicated by the setting of the witness of John to Jesus: it is given when *Priests* and *Levites* come to question the Baptist (1.19): 'In the composition of the delegation, the context of public worship of the passage is immediately evident. The delegation is composed of men who specialize in questions of liturgical propriety'.[1] This inference strikes me as highly improbable. It is nevertheless typical of the manner in which Cullmann finds connections between the Gospel history and the Christian sacraments; with such a method the links can most certainly be found, and that in abundance.

John declared to the Priests and Levites that he was not the Christ: 'He confessed and denied not, and he confessed, "I am not the Christ" ' (1.20). 'It is already a question of baptism', comments Cullmann, 'and more specifically it is a question of a rejection of a con-

[1] Op. cit., p. 60.

tinuance of the baptism of John after Christ has introduced baptism by the Spirit'.[1] Surely it is a question of the status and mission of John as compared with that of Jesus the Messiah, not of the baptism administered by the one and that administered in the name of the Other. Admittedly John is asked by his questioners why he baptizes, if he is not the Messiah, nor Elijah nor the Prophet, and replies, 'I baptize with water; in the midst of you stands one whom you do not know' (1.26). The implication of his statement, however, is not that the significance of all baptism is in Jesus, as Cullmann maintains, but the contention of v. 31, which is the real continuation and exposition of v. 26: '*That He should be manifested to Israel, therefore have I come baptizing in water*'; John's baptism is for the revelation of the Messiah.[2]

The brief allusion to the baptism of Jesus in 1.32 ff is seen by Cullmann as having a double reference: on the one hand it closely follows the proclamation by John of Jesus as the Lamb of God (1.29) and on the other hand it comes after the account of the Jewish delegation to the Baptist (1.19–28). Since the theme of the latter narrative is believed by Cullmann to be the rejection of John's baptism, the juxtaposition of the narrative with the story of Jesus' baptism is considered to point to the same lesson: the activity, or baptism, of John the Baptist is confronted with the baptism of Jesus, i.e. Christian baptism, and found superfluous. Further the description of Jesus' baptism coming immediately after his description as the Lamb of God is seen to illustrate the close connection of Christian baptism with the death of Christ: by this proclamation Jesus is revealed as the Servant, whose baptism foreshadows a general baptism for the sins of the world, manifests the nature of Christian baptism as baptism into His death and proves yet again the superfluity of John's baptism.[3] Again the argument appears to me to overreach itself. We have already considered the improbability of the exegesis that interprets the baptism of Jesus as a consecration for death; this setting of it affords no improvement of the case. The deduction from the supposed link between the baptism of Jesus and the interview of the Priests and Levites with John has nothing in its favour.

In the passage that gives the final witness of John to Jesus (3.22–36), the Evangelist's chief concern is once more expounded as a defining

[1] Op. cit., p. 62.

[2] So Gardiner-Smith, *St. John and the Synoptic Gospels*, 1938, pp. 4 f; Barrett, *The Gospel according to St. John*, p. 148; Bultmann, *Das Evangelium des Johannes*, p. 62 f.

[3] Op. cit., pp. 63 ff.

of the new baptism in Spirit over against the baptism of John, and the evidence is of an extraordinary nature. Cullmann draws attention to the description of Jesus in v. 31 as 'He that comes from above' (ἄνωθεν), in contrast to the man of the earth, i.e. John the Baptist. He suggests that the term ἄνωθεν ('above') links the whole paragraph with the Nicodemus discourse (2.1–21). There ἄνωθεν occurs in the statement that a man must be born 'from above' if he would see the Kingdom of God (v. 3), which is explained in v. 5 as a birth 'of water and of the Spirit'. The question of Nicodemus, 'How can these things be?' receives its answer in v. 13: 'Because the Son of Man who descended has ascended', i.e. He has brought redemption. The language and thought of vv. 5 and 13 are brought together in v. 31, on which Cullmann comments: 'He (the Evangelist) is concerned to show that John's baptism cannot be that baptism "from above" which is here discussed, for it was not John who ascended into heaven after he descended out of heaven, but Jesus'. Hence, by setting alongside each other in this manner the originators of the two baptisms, the baptisms themselves are placed in proper relationship.[1] Anyone acquainted with the content of Jn. 3 will surely agree that this is an astonishing argument. Verse 13 is not the direct answer to the question, 'How can these things be?' The words indicate that these things are true on the authority of Him who alone has descended from heaven and therefore witnessed the heavenly realities ('testifies to what He has seen', vv. 11, 32 f). The answer to the 'How' is implied in v. 14 f — the work of the Spirit in baptism is in virtue of the redemptive power of Christ's death and resurrection responded to in faith.

I cannot resist the conclusion that Cullmann has failed to establish his case for a consistent baptismal interest in Jn. 1–3. That the Evangelist was interested in John's baptism and its relation to Christian baptism none would wish to deny, but it is not a predominating theme of the early chapters of this Gospel. The investigation illustrates the frame of mind in which Cullmann has approached the Gospel evidence generally and suggests the desirability of exercising care in relation to passages commonly thought to be sacramental. Not all these passages stand on the same footing, but we must beware of doing injustice to the thought of John by making exaggerated claims for his sacramental interests.

This is illustrated as we turn to Jn. 4.14 and 7.37 ff. 'Everyone who drinks of this water will thirst again; but whoever drinks of the water that I shall give him will never thirst; the water that I shall give him

[1] Op. cit., pp. 77, 79–80.

will become in him a spring of water welling up to eternal life'. This saying is considered to reflect the giving of the Spirit in baptism, for Jn. 3.5 teaches that the Spirit is bestowed in baptism, and Jn. 7.37 ff is 'certainly a baptismal passage'.[1] On the contrary there is no suggestion that Jn. 7.37 is a baptismal passage. Both sayings illustrate how the Evangelist (as other New Testament writers) can speak of the bestowal of life in the Spirit without mentioning baptism. Cullmann admits that the fact that the Evangelist speaks of *drinking* water makes it difficult to relate the two passages to baptism; he recalls however that in many Gnostic baptist sects the baptismal water was drunk (!). Has Cullmann perchance overlooked that the Christ bids *all* to come and drink of the water that He gives? (see especially Jn. 7.37 f). Or does he seriously maintain that John would have all men drink the water of their baptism? Or that to drink water is a periphrasis for baptism? To interpret these sayings in such a manner is surely to fall into the like error of early Christian writers, who read baptism into every mention of water in the Old Testament. Jn. 4.14 and 7.37 ff have no sacramental significance.

The two healing miracles of Jn. 5 and 9 are of another order and could conceivably have in view baptism, especially by illustrating the nature of the change that occurs when a man receives Christ and is baptized. Nevertheless we must beware of the error above mentioned that assumes that every appearance of water must relate to baptism.

The healing of the man by the pool of Bethesda is thought by Cullmann to set forth baptism as a miracle; for both healing and forgiveness of sins are granted at the pool and Christian archaeology shows us that Christian baptisms early took place in this pool.[2] On the other hand one can hardly fail to observe that the Lord did not command the sick man to plunge into the water; He sent him away from the pool, healed and forgiven by the power of His word. No clear baptismal motives occur in the following discourse. The miracle appears to be regarded as an illustration of Christ's power to raise the dead and to exercise judgment because He is Lord and Son of Man. These conceptions would be consonant with baptism, if its presence were plainly indicated in the text; but in the absence of such indications the connection with baptism can at best be admitted as possible but unproven.

The miracle of the man born blind can more plausibly be linked with baptism. The connection is maintained chiefly on the ground that the blind man receives *sight* after *washing* his eyes in a pool that bears

[1] Op. cit., p. 82.   [2] Op. cit., pp. 81, 83.

a significant name, *Sent*. Apart from the washing, the association of 'enlightenment' with baptism appears to have been made at least as early as the Epistle to the Hebrews (6.4). Moreover, Cullmann urges, 'We are actually called upon to ask what it means when a pool of water is brought into connexion with Christ the "Sent". To ask the question is to answer it'.[1] The answer, however, is not so plain. It is well known that the name Siloah properly belonged to the spring that fed the pool. The counterpart to this is not another pool (for baptism) but Jesus Himself. Godet therefore remarked that for the reader of the Gospel, 'Go to Siloam' really signifies, 'Come to Me!'[2] It may further be noted that the man was commanded to wash clay from his eyes, not to bathe himself in the pool. The baptismal reference in this narrative, therefore, is to be judged as uncertain; it is by no means self-evident.[3]

More than in any other narrative of the Gospel, apart from ch. 3, expositors have been inclined to relate the account of the foot washing in ch. 13 to baptism. Cullmann goes further and accepts the interpretation earlier put forward by Loisy and Bauer that v. 10 teaches the necessity of receiving both sacraments. In reply to the request of Peter to have his hands and head as well as his feet washed, Jesus answers: 'He that has been completely washed has no need for a further washing [except for his feet] but is completely clean'. Two deductions are thought to be involved here: on the one hand the complete efficacy of baptism is taught, in denial of tendencies to desire frequent baptisms, manifest in the Hemerobaptists who baptized every day; on the other hand the necessity for cleansing sins committed after baptism is admitted, and this is met in the frequent celebration of the eucharist in fellowship with Christ and the brethren. In this conclusion the disputed phrase, 'except his feet' plays a great part; the argument is considered to have such cogency as to demonstrate the authenticity of the phrase, as against those early textual authorities that omit it.[4]

[1] Op. cit., p. 104.

[2] 'Commentary on St. John's Gospel', *E.T.*, 1899, vol. 2, p. 366. It remains an open question whether Barrett is right in concluding from the fact that Jesus himself is ὁ ἀπεσταλμένος: 'He gives light to the blind, just as He is himself a spring of living water', op. cit., p. 297. Unlike Jn. 4.14, 7.37 ff no reference is made in this passage to drinking the waters of Siloam, although in fact the drawing of water from Siloam in the ceremony of the Feast of Tabernacles provides the background for the saying in 7.37 ff.

[3] So Strathmann emphatically, *Das Evangelium nach Johannes* (*Das Neue Testament Deutsch*), 1955, p. 158. The idea advanced by Cullmann, that since the Good Shepherd is a favourite baptism symbol in early Christianity, the discourse of Jn. 10 is related to ch. 9 as the eucharistic discourse of Jn. 6 to the feeding miracle, is impossible; Jn. 6 is full of eucharistic symbolism and is difficult to interpret without the aid of the eucharist, but Jn. 10 is remote from baptism.

[4] Cullmann, op. cit., pp. 108 f.

The interpretation appears to me precarious. There is no hint that repeated *baptisms* are in view nor any suggestion that the *eucharist* is symbolized under the form of washing the feet. To understand the phrase 'except [to wash] the feet' as relating to a different mode of cleansing is to do defiance to the whole story. Verse 10, after all, represents an explanation of the action of Jesus in washing the feet of the disciples. It is unreasonable to relate the words of that explanation, 'He that has been washed has no need of a further washing', to the foot washing just done, but relate the explicit mention of washing feet ('*save for the feet*'), to *an action of a wholly different kind* not so much as hinted at in the narrative, an action which itself requires further explanation, since it is not obvious in the statement, an action so unrelated to that performed by Jesus as the celebration of the eucharist. If the disputed phrase in v. 10, 'except (to wash) the feet' is allowed, it must certainly relate to the action of Jesus just completed: the 'bath' referred to in the words 'he that is bathed' (ὁ λελουμένος) must then be viewed as having taken place at an earlier point of time — the nature of the occasion or mode of cleansing is not stated. Contrary to Cullmann, the interpretation thus demanded is so muddling and unsuitable to the action it is supposed to explain, it strongly favours the view that the phrase 'except the feet' (εἰ μὴ τοὺς πόδας) is a later interpolation, due to a scribe who misunderstood the narrative.[1] Whoever inserted the phrase 'except for the feet' did not realize that v. 10a indicates that in washing the disciples' feet Jesus had given them, as it were, a complete bath. The action had this significance because, as Hoskyns tersely put it, 'the washing of the disciples' feet rests upon and interprets the death of the Lord'. The love of God for man is supremely seen in the humiliation of the Son of God unto death, and this is the meaning of the action which, according to v. 7, the disciples could not grasp at that time but which they would understand later.[2]

That this accords with the primary intention of the Evangelist seems to me to be reasonably certain. The real difficulty is to determine whether the writer wished to convey a secondary lesson concerning some other washing. Hoskyns believed not, for the Evangelist was here concentrating attention on the efficacy of the death of Jesus.

---

[1] It is omitted by ℵ c z gat vg^w Tertullian, Origen. The addition in P. 66 (μόνον) and still more that in D (οὐ χρείαν ἔχει τὴν κεφαλὴν νίψασθαι εἰ μὴ τοὺς πόδας μόνον) shows that the original expansion was considered inadequate by some scribes, who could not resist the temptation to embark on clarification.

[2] See the excellent discussion of the meaning of this incident in E. C. Hoskyns, *Fourth Gospel*, pp. 435 ff.

With this Strachan agrees,[1] and apparently R. H. Lightfoot.[2] C. H. Dodd has had other thoughts; in his major work on the Fourth Gospel he considered that λούεσθαι ('wash') here reminds of the λουτρὸν παλινγενεσίας ('washing of regeneration') in Titus 3.5,[3] but in his review of Cullmann's Early Christian Worship he makes the interesting suggestion that contact may here be made with the use in the Pentateuch of λούεσθαι for the ceremonial bath which forms part of the ritual of consecration to the priesthood and νίπτειν ('rinse') of ad hoc ablution before officiating.[4] On this basis the washing of the disciples' feet could be viewed as a consecration to their ministry of reconciliation.[5] By an application one stage further removed, it would be possible to include in the action the idea of baptism as a consecration to ministry, but the connection would be tenuous.

Most interpreters prefer to see in the narrative a simple reference to the adequacy of baptism, noting on the one hand the strong language of v. 8, 'If I do not wash you you have no part with me', and on the other assurance of v. 10, 'He that has been washed . . . is completely clean'. If this were acceptable it would have a nuance in keeping with the Pauline interpretation of baptism: the cleansing of baptism is in virtue of its relation to the death of Christ. It might even be said that the believer is cleansed from sin in baptism by Christ because he was cleansed from sin by Christ's dying for him; that is, baptism is an application to the believer of the atonement wrought by the Christ for him. This is the foundation doctrine of Romans 6 in yet another guise. Why hesitate, then, to accept that John intended to convey this teaching in Jn. 13.1 ff? My chief ground of hesitation is that this is not a secondary interpretation of the narrative but a tertiary. We tend to forget that the primary lesson drawn from the foot washing, and the only one explicitly mentioned by John, is its example of humility and love towards one another (13.12 ff). A secondary lesson is intimated in v. 7, for 'thou shalt know these things afterwards' presumably relates to the completer understanding that the disciples are to gain after the death and resurrection of Christ and not simply to the explanation recorded in vv. 12 ff (cf. 2.22, 12.16, 14.25 f, 20.9). This secondary meaning we have considered to be the nature of the foot washing as a prophetic symbol, setting forth the

---

[1] The Fourth Gospel, p. 267. [2] St. John's Gospel, p. 273.
[3] Op. cit., p. 401. [4] Journal of Ecclesiastical History, 1952, p. 219.
[5] W. L. Knox made a related suggestion that the proverbial necessity of not embarking on tasks with 'unwashed feet' (ἀνίπτοις ποσίν, Lucian, Pseudolog. 4.165) is in view: the Evangelist provides a solemn ritual introduction to the revelation of Jesus that follows in chs. 14–16, Some Hellenistic Elements in Primitive Christianity, 1944, p. 76, n. 1.

humiliation of the Son of God unto death for the forgiveness of sinners. It is the perfect illustration of Mk. 10.45, denoting the last act of service of the Son of Man for the provision of a ransom for many. If now we go a stage further and see in the foot washing an illustration of baptism, we have to do so as a lesson deduced from a secondary lesson. We have observed the possibility that the foot washing could denote baptism as a consecration to the ministry of reconciliation; that would make it a secondary lesson of the secondary lesson. How much further are we supposed to go? And did John write with the express intention that we should so interpret his words? Some commentators no doubt cheerfully answer in the affirmative. For my part I can but record my misgivings at such a procedure. A reference to baptism in the narrative of Jn. 13 is not impossible, but in my judgment probability is against it.

Finally, in this review of possible references to baptism in the Fourth Gospel, we must note Jn. 19.34 — the piercing of the side of Jesus, with the consequent flowing of blood and water from His body. Cullmann sees in the incident the concentration of all the Evangelist's connexions of the life of Jesus with the sacraments. It shows that Christ gives to His Church in the two sacraments the atonement accomplished in his death. It is also to be understood chronologically: 'Scarcely is the historical Jesus dead . . . when He shows in what form He will from now on be present upon earth, in the sacraments, in baptism and Lord's Supper'.[1] Only on this understanding of the incident can we explain the emphatic statement of v. 35 of the truth of the witness borne to it: 'He that has seen has borne testimony and his testimony is true'. This interpretation is a highly respectable one and Cullmann can claim great support for it.[2] For my part the considerations adduced in connection with the narrative of Jn. 13 weigh

---

[1] Op. cit., p. 115.

[2] But he has over-stated the unanimity of opinion for it. Though supported among the Fathers by Chrysostom, Cyril of Alexandria and Augustine, there was a great variety of views; the interpretation in terms of two baptisms, one in blood and one in water, was favoured by Tertullian, Rufinus, Ambrose, Cyril of Jerusalem, Euthymius Zigabenus; an intimation of deliverance through blood and washing through water was seen in it by Marcarius Magnus, Apollinarius and John of Damascus; Theophylact believed it taught the necessity of the mixed chalice, Origen that it signified Christ's divinity, Novatian Christ's humanity, Leo that it proved both the manhood and the deity of Christ (see the appendix on the interpretation of Jn. 19.34 in Westcott's Commentary). Among modern commentators Westcott, Macgregor, Hoskyns, Temple, R. H. Lightfoot, Barrett, Heitmüller, Schlatter, Bauer, Bultmann agree that the two sacraments are in view in the Johannine record. But besides the 'single' exception mentioned by Cullmann, viz. Büchsel, who rejected the view, Burkitt did likewise (in the Gospel History and its Transmission, p. 233, n. 1) and in their commentaries Godet, Bernard, C. J. Wright, Strachan, J. A. Findlay, C. H. Dodd (The Fourth Gospel, pp. 428 f) and Strathmann.

here also. Under no circumstances can it be admitted that the sacramental interest was John's primary one in this passage. Cullmann and others are mistaken in relating the emphatic protestation of the truth of the record in v. 35 to the sacramental view. The Evangelist makes his solemn asseveration, 'He that has seen has borne testimony . . . *that you too might believe!*' The piercing of the side of Jesus is an evidential fact and possesses a significance that the enquirer after Christ should know. '*For* these things happened that the Scripture might be fulfilled, A bone of him shall not be broken. And again another Scripture says, They will look on him they pierced'. The Evangelist described the spear thrust and its effects, according to his own admission, primarily to show how certain Scriptures were fulfilled, above all those that relate to the Passover Lamb, for Jesus in His dying fulfilled that type of redemption (cf. Ex. 12.46, Num. 9.12). The interest in the blood and water is subordinate to the major motif of Jesus as God's Passover Lamb. Nevertheless blood and water are mentioned. For what purpose? 1 Jn. 5.6 suggests what was the chief intention of the writer: the efflux of blood and water from the body of Jesus reveals his true humanity and disposes of the contentions of the Docetists, who denied that the Christ had a body of flesh and blood and died.[1] This may be a less exciting conclusion to draw from John's words than the founding of the two sacraments, but the existence of Christianity depends on its truth; in a time when the doctrine of a real Incarnation was being challenged it was basic to demonstrate it, hence the urgency of the anti-Docetic interest in both the Gospel and First Epistle of John. Without assurance concerning the flesh and blood of the Son of God it is senseless to talk about sacraments.

Granting this to be the major concern of the Evangelist, is it feasible that a lesser one is also in view as in ch. 13? Yes, it is possible, but we must recognize that less assurance attaches to it than in Jn. 13, for in the latter passage a broad hint is given that a further lesson lies beneath the surface, but here the stress is on the relation of Christ's death to the Scriptures. Nevertheless it is not to be ruled out that John may have had in mind the blood of the Son of Man which is 'real drink' (Jn. 6.55); on this analogy the water will signify the 'living water' which is the life of the Spirit, given to those who believe on the Christ and 'drink' (Jn. 7.37 f).[2] This is more suitable than to relate the passage to the two sacraments; partly because of the congruence of drinking blood and drinking water (instead of drinking one and being

---

[1] See Burkitt, *The Gospel History and its Transmission*, p. 233, n. 1.
[2] So C. H. Dodd, *The Fourth Gospel*, p. 428.

baptized in the other); partly because this Gospel lays so much stress on drinking the living water which Christ gives; and especially because 7.37 ff sees the prophetic anticipation of living waters flowing from the Temple fulfilled in Christ *after His death* — 'Out of that man's body rivers of living water shall flow. But this he said concerning the Spirit, which they that believe on Him were to receive; for the Spirit was not yet (given), because Jesus was not yet glorified'. If, therefore, we are to read a secondary significance in the blood and water that flowed from the side of Jesus, this interpretation is congruous with the teaching of the Gospel in a manner in which the idea of the founding therein of the two sacraments is not. Even so, I do not think it can be pressed and I would prefer to recognize it as a possible but uncertain interpretation.

2. JOHN 3.3-5

It is important for the understanding of the famous v. 5 to consider its simpler form in v. 3, where the issues are more sharply presented. Nicodemus is told that a man cannot inherit[1] the Kingdom of God unless he be 'born from above' ($\gamma\epsilon\nu\nu\eta\theta\hat{\eta}$ $\check{\alpha}\nu\omega\theta\epsilon\nu$). A more shattering short sentence addressed to one characterized as 'the Teacher of Israel' (v. 10) can hardly be imagined. Nicodemus has spent his life in the service of God and in hope of the Kingdom. He is told that if he would attain the Kingdom he must have a wholly new beginning — not merely a fresh start but a fresh *origin*, a new birth. And the birth is not of a kind that can be produced by human effort; it must be $\check{\alpha}\nu\omega\theta\epsilon\nu$, from above, from heaven, therefore from God.[2] By this statement the whole life and work of Nicodemus are set in question. It is as though the message of Jesus to the nation, 'Repent for the Kingdom of heaven has drawn near', (Mk. 1.15) were reformulated for him in the most drastic manner possible, in the strain of Jesus' reply to the question as to who could be saved: 'With men it is impossible! But not with God' (Mk. 10.26 f). What Nicodemus can gain alone from God he must seek in penitence and humility from God.

As Peter and his fellow disciples were astonished, and even indignant, at the teaching of Jesus on the impossibility of being saved apart from a divine intervention, so Nicodemus asks an incredulous ques-

---

[1] That the expressions 'see the Kingdom of God' and 'enter the Kingdom of God' are identical is clear from v. 36, where the believer is said to *have* eternal life (the life of the Kingdom) but the unbeliever will not *see* life. Cf. also Lk. 2.26, Acts 2.27.

[2] It is generally recognized that $\check{\alpha}\nu\omega\theta\epsilon\nu$ includes the lesser meaning 'again', (cf. Gal. 4.9) but in this context has primarily the significance of 'from above', as in v. 31, and yet more particularly 'from God', as in 19.11. The concept of $\gamma\epsilon\nu\nu\eta\theta\hat{\eta}\nu\alpha\iota$ $\dot{\epsilon}\kappa$ $\theta\epsilon o\hat{\upsilon}$ is basic to the First Epistle of John, see 2.29, 3.9, 4.7, 4.18, 5.1.

tion, implying the response 'Nonsense! A man can't enter his mother's womb, can he? For this the Evangelist has been taken to task, since Rabbinic writings contain not a few references to the idea of a man becoming a 'new creature', and the comparison of a proselyte to a new born child is well known; v. 4 is therefore regarded as an indication that we here deal with a fictitious dramatic setting of the Johannine teaching on regeneration. It should be observed, however, that when the Rabbis spoke of a man becoming a new creature, they were not really concerned with *moral* renewal. A man became physically a new creature when God healed him; and he became a new creature in a sense of living in a different environment when his tribulations and dangers were removed, or when his sins were forgiven, bringing thereby renewal in health and in circumstances and a changed relationship with God. Moral renewal, however, was particularly associated with the resurrection in the last day.[1] Moreover if the examples of Rabbinic quotations, even of this physical or external kind of renewal, be examined in the collection provided by Strack-Billerbeck, it will be found that almost without exception they are late.[2] It looks as though we must reckon seriously with the possibility that the application of the concept of regeneration to the spiritual life of the individual was uncommon both in Judaism and in the world of Hellenistic syncretism before the advent of Christianity.[3] It cannot be doubted that the Fourth Evangelist had frequently debated with Jews concerning the theme of the Nicodemus discourse; if the reactions he experienced were so different from v. 4, how could he have represented so great a Rabbi to be so ignorant? And if his experience accorded with that answer, ought we not regard that fact as an important datum concerning Jewish opinion at this time, in view of the indications in his Gospel that he was well acquainted with the theological ideas of contemporary Rabbinic Judaism?[4] If the teaching on regeneration represented in this chapter were a commonplace among educated Jews of the Evangelist's day, he would not have permitted even a dramatic setting to be so manifestly false.

The answer to the question, 'How is this thing possible?' is con-

[1] See Strack-Billerbeck, op. cit., vol. ii, pp. 420 ff.

[2] Chiefly third and fourth centuries A.D. Some sayings concerning the proselytes fall in the second century, but even these in the estimate of Strack-Billerbeck, relate to the consequences of the forgiveness of sins. The use of παλινγενεσία in Josephus in connection with the renewal of the nation after the Exile (Ant. ii.66) is scarcely pertinent.

[3] For Judaism, see Dodd, *The Fourth Gospel*, 303 f; for Hellenism, W. L. Knox, *Some Hellenistic Elements in Primitive Christianity*, 1944, pp. 91 ff.

[4] See Schlatter's commentary, *Der Evangelist Johannes*, and Dodd's *Fourth Gospel*, part 1, ch. 4.

veyed by the significant replacement of ἄνωθεν in the otherwise
repetitive assertion of v. 5: 'Unless a man be born *of water and of the
Spirit* . . .'. The conjunction of birth, Spirit and Kingdom is significant; it hints of the eschatological background presumed in the idea
of being born from above. The Spirit is poured out in the last days,
enabling God's people to walk in his statutes (Ezk. 36.26 ff) and even
to experience resurrection from the dead (Ezk. 37.9 ff).[1] The language
presumes that the Spirit is even now at work in the righteous or is
about to be given for the attainment of such ends. The miracle
demanded in v. 3 accordingly either has become or is shortly to be a
possibility. But what is intended by the mention of 'water' in such a
connection? The former passage cited from Ezekiel conjoins with the
gift of the Spirit the sprinkling of clean water for the 'cleansing of
uncleannesses' (36.25), so the idea of a ritual use of water in connection with the gift of the Spirit would not be without precedent. But at
a time when the employment of water for cleansing in view of the last
day had taken the specific form of baptism, it is difficult to take
seriously any other reference than baptism in the words ἐξ ὕδατος.[2]
As in Jn. 6.51 ff the exposition on eating the flesh of the Son of Man
and drinking His blood cannot fail to bring to mind the Lord's Supper,
so the reference to new birth by water and Spirit inevitably directs

---

[1] 'In the future God will punish the wicked and destroy them out of the world,
but he will make the righteous as a new creature and put Spirit in them', Tanch B.
12 (19a); Strack-Billerbeck, op. cit., p. 421.

[2] The popular idea, that the water represents human birth, whether the semen of
man or waters in the womb, in contrast to the divine birth given by the Spirit, is
excluded by the fact that the *whole* expression ἐξ ὕδατος καὶ Πνεύματος defines
the manner in which a man is born ἄνωθεν and Jn. 1.13 declares that the birth from
God has nothing to do with human begetting. Calvin considered that water and
Spirit mean the same thing, 'for it is a frequent and common way of speaking in
Scripture, when the Spirit is mentioned, to add the word *Water* or *Fire*, expressing
his power', in support of which Mt. 3.11, Lk. 3.16 are quoted. But in the latter two
passages it is unlikely that 'fire' is a symbol for the Holy Spirit; it represents a quite
different notion of judgment. Calvin's exegesis was forced on him because he could
not endure the idea that baptism was necessary to salvation ('Commentary on St.
John's Gospel', vol. I, *E.T.*, 1846, p. 110); but that deduction from the words does
not necessarily follow and they must be allowed their proper force without prejudice.
Odeberg's interpretation, that the water represents the celestial or spiritual waters,
spoken of in Jewish and pagan Gnosticism as seed of the divine begetting, is a
curious combination of these two views; while Odeberg thereby eliminated reference
to baptism, Strachan (op. cit., p. 135) and Flemington (op. cit., p. 86) favour combining this thought of the divine seed with Christian baptism; Bultmann however is
probably right in thinking that the early Christian parallels to the use of 'water and
Spirit' for baptism are much closer than the Gnostic evidence and render the latter
of doubtful worth (op. cit., p. 98, n. 2). The refusal to accept the authenticity of
ἐξ ὕδατος is the last resort of an attitude that will not permit the text to stand on its
own merits and speak for itself; Bultmann, following in the steps of Wendt, Wellhausen, Merx, von Dobschutz and Kirsopp Lake, believes the words to have been
inserted by the same ecclesiastical redactor who interpolated 6.51b–58 (ibid.). This
is nevertheless an arbitrary supposition, without evidence in the external tradition,

attention to Christian baptism. But just as the exposition of participating in the flesh and blood of Christ in ch. 6 has a history, so has
the birth of water and Spirit in ch. 3 and it is necessary to understand
that history to grasp the significance of the passage.

Contrary to the often expressed opinion that the Fourth Evangelist
has no historical sense in his dialogues and addresses, there are clear
indications that he is sensible to the situations in which his teaching is
set, and he provides signposts for the right perspective in which to
view it. The future tense of 6.27, 6.51, for example, shows that the
eating of the flesh and drinking the blood of the Son of Man strictly
belong to the time future to those addressed in the synagogue at
Capernaum, though the presence of the Christ made a participation
in the 'living bread' possible in a preliminary fashion even then.
Similarly with regard to the life of the Spirit, 7.39 is a crucial saying
and is to be compared with the consistent portrayal of the sending of
the Spirit in the Last Supper discourses as a *promise*, even for the
disciples who had in measure experienced the Spirit's ministry but
not his indwelling presence (14.17). It may be taken as certain, then,
that the baptism in which birth by the Spirit is known is regarded by
the Evangelist as a phenomenon future to the time of Nicodemus.
But there was a baptism open to Nicodemus which gave, if not
promise, at least hope of birth by the Spirit and entrance into the
Kingdom of God: the baptism of John, despised by the Pharisaic
colleagues of Nicodemus (Lk. 7.30) and presumably insufficiently
valued by Nicodemus for him to humble himself and submit to it.
But still more pertinently, a baptism was being administered at this
time yet more closely related to the promise of the Spirit and of the
Kingdom: the baptism of Jesus Himself! It is extraordinary how it
has been universally overlooked that Jesus, who authorized his
disciples to baptize and whose baptisms at this time are said to have
exceeded those of John (3.26, 4.1), might have laid on a Pharisee the
necessity of submitting to baptism in the light of the imminence of
redemption and sending of the Spirit. Or, if more cautious speech is
desired, it is strange how neglected the idea is that the Johannine Jesus
conjoined baptism with new life and the Kingdom of God, in view of

and is due to an inability to appreciate the compatibility of sacraments with spiritual religion. W. L. Knox's verdict on the matter is worth pondering: 'If the words
ἐξ ὕδατος are part of the original text . . . no Christian reader could have understood them except as an allusion to baptism; if they are a later insertion, we still have
to explain the interpretation of conversion as a "new birth" instead of a death and
resurrection, as they are to St. Paul; and the separation of conversion and baptism
would have been meaningless to a Christian of the first century', *Some Hellenistic
Elements in Primitive Christianity*, p. 91.

the references made in this chapter to the baptismal ministry exercised by his disciples and the greater value that the Evangelist would have attached to this baptism than that assigned to the baptism of John.

If Nicodemus would be born anew, he must be baptized on repentance and faith in the word of the Kingdom preached by its herald, John the Baptist, and its representative, the Son of Man. That is the first thing. A second follows: he must know the life of the Spirit, for entrance to the Kingdom is ministered by the Spirit. In the proclamation of John these two things were separated as a prophecy and a hope of fulfilment, since the baptizer in water was one and the baptizer in Spirit another. On the lips of Jesus they come closer, as a promise 'in sure and certain hope' of fulfilment, for the baptism is from Him who shall baptize with Spirit. This baptism of the Spirit is not to be postponed until the end of all things; it awaits the 'lifting up' of the Son of Man on the cross, and thence to the presence of the Father, after which the Spirit is given and life in Christ becomes a reality (Jn. 3.14 f, 7.39). Then the baptism commanded by Him will be a baptism in Spirit — a being born of water and Spirit.[1]

That Jesus brought together what were separated in John's baptism as act of obedience and object of hope gives one pause as to the precise meaning of birth 'of water and Spirit' ($\dot{\epsilon}\xi$ $\ddot{\upsilon}\delta\alpha\tau\sigma\varsigma$ $\kappa\alpha\dot{\iota}$ $\Pi\nu\epsilon\acute{\upsilon}\mu\alpha\tau\sigma\varsigma$) in v. 5. The unity of the two elements is shown by the use of the single preposition $\dot{\epsilon}\kappa$: '*by* water and Spirit'. But is the water an agency of the new birth in the same fashion as, or in a manner comparable to, the Spirit? Some would reply in the affirmative, but that is surely mistaken. The explanatory discourse that follows v. 5 does not mention again birth 'of water and Spirit' but emphasizes the agency of the Spirit as the divine begetter: 'that which is born of the Spirit is spirit' (v. 6); 'The Spirit breathes where He wills . . . so is everyone born of the Spirit' (v. 8). Moreover we observed that the objective basis of the gift of Spirit and the efficacy of baptism is the exaltation of the Son of Man on the cross and in heaven, the subjective counterpart to which in v. 15 is *faith*. The Evangelist in the prologue writes of the begotten of God who received the Logos *in faith*.[2] In

---

[1] The conviction that the primary reference of $\dot{\epsilon}\xi$ $\ddot{\upsilon}\delta\alpha\tau\sigma\varsigma$ is to John's baptism is at least as early as Bengel, *Gnomen*, vol. II, p. 275; see further Cremer, op. cit., p. 42; Schlatter, *Evan. Johannes*, p. 89; Westcott, op. cit., p. 50; Temple, *Readings in St. John's Gospel*, 2nd ed. 1945, p. 45; Hoskyns, op. cit., p. 214; Barrett, op. cit., p. 174; Lightfoot, op. cit., p. 131.

[2] 'It is by "receiving the Logos" that man gains the right ($\dot{\epsilon}\xi\sigma\upsilon\sigma\acute{\iota}\alpha$) to be God's child. This effectively dissociates the idea of rebirth, in the Johannine sense of the term, from all mythological notions of divine generation such as were current in wide circles of Hellenistic society, and it must be taken to overrule the whole discussion of the theme in the present passage', Dodd, op. cit., p. 305.

face of such statements it is impossible to attribute to the water as such an efficacy for rebirth of the same order as the work of the Spirit. As baptism in Tit. 3.5 is 'the washing for the regeneration and renewal that the Spirit effects', so in Jn. 3.5 it is the occasion when the Spirit gives to faith the regeneration that qualifies for the Kingdom.[1]

In conclusion it is to be observed that the major elements of the Apostolic teaching on baptism have appeared during our discussion of Jn. 3.5 ff. Christian baptism is seen to be rooted in the Christ event, with especial emphasis on the exaltation of the Christ in death and to the throne of God, whence He sends his Spirit to his people. If Jn. 3.5 has any relation to the baptism administered on the authorization of Jesus, it will be unique as bringing the baptism that anticipates the gift of the Spirit into connection with the baptism in which the Spirit is given — a characteristic which has affinity with the teaching on the bread of life in ch. 6, and which reflects the Evangelist's consciousness of the unity yet distinction between the ministry of the incarnate Son and that of the exalted Lord at God's right hand.

The emphasis on the miracle of God wrought by the Spirit in baptism is underscored by the teaching of a new life bestowed by the Spirit in that context, the equivalent of a divine begetting. The sovereignty of the Spirit and the mystery of His work are manifest in operations other than baptism (v. 8), but the stress in this passage is on the priority of His action in baptism: He effects the life unattainable by man's efforts. But though this life is such as man cannot produce, it is not without his assent: the new life from the Spirit in baptism (v. 5) is indistinguishable from the eternal life in Christ granted on the basis of redemption to the man of faith (v. 15); and the right to be sons of God is given to those who believe on the name of the incarnate Word of God (1.12), sons who are begotten not of flesh and blood but of God alone (1.13). This conjunction of sayings concerning sonship to God and the life of the Spirit demonstrates that the redemption of Christ, faith and baptism are as inseparably intertwined in John as in Paul. To diminish the significance of faith in

---

[1] The statement of Hoskyns cannot be too carefully heeded: 'The embracing of water and spirit in one single phrase . . . and the linking together of two births by an adverb whose derivative meaning *a second time* can never become wholly dormant, are theologically possible only when the vast distinction between natural birth and birth from God and between cleansing by water and creative purification by the Spirit is clearly recognized and acknowledged', op. cit., pp. 214 f. See further Wheeler Robinson, 'Believer's Baptism and the Holy Spirit', *Baptist Quarterly*, 1938–9, p. 393; Creed, 'Sacraments in the Fourth Gospel', *The Modern Churchman*, 1926–7, p. 369; Büchsel, *Das Evangelium nach Johannes* (N.T.D.), p. 52; Schneider, op. cit., p. 58; Strachan, op. cit., pp. 134 f; Michaelis, *Die Sakramente im Johannes-evangelium*, 1946, p. 13; Rasmussen, op. cit., p. 46.

baptism because of the lack of their explicit integration in Jn. 3.3–5 is as unjust to John's thought as it is to Paul's when that is attributed to Rom. 6, as becomes apparent when we consider the weight of emphasis laid on faith throughout this Gospel.[1]

The eschatological associations of baptism in this discourse are striking. The new life of the Spirit, bestowed in baptism, is the *sine qua non* for possessing the Kingdom. Presumably the consummated Kingdom of the end is in view, as in the Synoptic sayings generally that speak of entry into the Kingdom of God,[2] and as the eschatological passages 5.19–29, 14.1–3 etc. suggest; the Fourth Evangelist, like the other New Testament writers, anticipates the judgment, resurrection and final glory of the new creation. But the idea of possessing the new life of the Spirit now, without which indeed there is no hope of participating in the future kingdom, implies a present experience of the blessings of the age to come. The same implication is involved in the concept of present possession of eternal life in Christ through his redemption (v. 15); the exposition that follows vv. 14–15 (vv. 16–21) moves on the basic assumption that both the judgment and deliverance of the end are being manifested among men in the present time. And this deliverance, this blessing of the Spirit and resurrection life are bestowed in baptism! Baptism thus gives hope of resurrection unto the Kingdom by bringing the life of the Kingdom into this one. It is a sacrament of realized eschatology for the inheritance of the consummated glory.

Finally, a baptism which witnesses a new existence in the Spirit, life eternal in Christ on the basis of his redemption and assurance of the future glory is manifestly closely related to a baptism which signifies death and resurrection with Christ and possession of the Spirit as seal of participation in the final Kingdom. Schweitzer is surely wrong in his radical divorce of the Pauline doctrine of the new creation from the Johannine doctrine of the new birth.[3] The emphasis, background and presentation of the doctrine are different in the two writers, but the basic content is one. Resurrection, New Creation, New Birth through the Christ event mediated by the Spirit in baptism by faith is fundamentally one experience, one doctrine, one baptism.[4]

---

[1] Precisely the central significance accorded to faith in the Fourth Gospel distinguishes the sacramentalism of the Evangelist from that of the later Church writers who echo his language; see Schneider, op. cit., p. 58.

[2] Mk. 9.43–47, 10.15, 23 ff, Mt. 5.20, 7.21, 19.23, 23.13, 25.46. For the classic exposition of these sayings, see the article by Windisch, 'Die Sprüche vom Eingehen in das Reich Gottes', *Z.N.W.*, 1928, pp. 165 ff; also W. G. Kümmel, *Verheissung und Erfüllung*, 2nd ed. 1953, p. 46.

[3] *Mysticism of Paul the Apostle*, p. 15.   [4] So W. L. Knox, op. cit., p. 62.

3. I JOHN 2.20, 27

'You have an anointing from the Holy One and you know all things'.[1] The possession by the readers of this letter of a *chrism* (from χρίω, to anoint, whence Χριστός, anointed) enables them to discern and combat the false teaching of the antichrists among whom they dwell. From the aorist ἐλάβετε in v. 27 — 'the chrism which you *received* from him' — it would seem that this gift was bestowed on a particular occasion. In the light of the parallel statement in 2 Cor. 1.21, 'He that confirms us with you to Christ is God, who anointed (χρίσας) us and sealed us and put the earnest of the Spirit in our hearts', and of the analogy of our Lord's anointing with Spirit at his baptism (Acts 10.38), it is all but universally agreed that the occasion for the impartation of the chrism was baptism and that the chrism was the Holy Spirit. Through the chrism the readers know the 'truth', that is, the truth concerning the person of Christ (vv. 21 ff); it dwells in them, teaches them concerning all things and is no lie: we are reminded of the teaching in the upper room discourses concerning the Paraclete (cf. Jn. 15.26 f, 16.12 f) and what is written elsewhere in this letter concerning the witness of the Spirit (note especially 5.7, 'The Spirit is the witness, because the Spirit is the truth'; in 4.6 the influences at work in the Church of the Apostles and those in the heretical groups are described as 'the spirit of truth and the spirit of error'). On the interpretation here mentioned, this saying reflects in a casual manner the doctrine we have seen in so many other passages of the New Testament, that the Spirit is imparted to the believer at baptism, but it applies it in this context to the witness that the indwelling Spirit bears to the Christ, particularly with respect to his incarnation and redemption.[2] If it is adopted it will surely be admitted that the language is not explicit enough to support the opinion that it reflects the custom of anointing with oil, attested by Tertullian and Hippolytus, to symbolize the imparting of the Spirit.[3] Such an act would admittedly have set forth in excellent manner the idea that the

---

[1] Most scholars prefer to read πάντες with ℵ B, 'you all have knowledge', rather than the neuter πάντα, which is not so well attested. But the parallel statement of v. 27, τὸ αὐτοῦ χρίσμα διδάσκει ὑμᾶς περὶ πάντων, favours the latter reading; it is preferred by T. W. Manson, on the ground that οἶδα is not used absolutely in the Fourth Gospel and Johannine Epistles; see his article, 'Entry into Membership of the Early Church', *J.T.S.*, 1947, p. 28, n. 1.

[2] Such is basically the interpretation represented by Westcott, *The Epistle of St. John*, 4th ed. 1902, p. 73; A. E. Brooke, *The Johannine Epistles*, 1912, p. 221; A. Schlatter, *Erläuterungen*, vol. x, pp. 45, 51; F. Hauck, *Die Kirchenbriefe, Das Neue Testament Deutsch*, 5th ed. 1949, p. 130; H. Windisch, *Die Katholischen Briefe*, 3rd ed. edited by H. Preisker, 1951, pp. 117, 119; G. W. H. Lampe, op. cit., p. 61.

[3] Contra Gregory Dix, *Confirmation or the Laying on of Hands?* pp. 10 f.

believer baptized to Christ was thereby made a χριστός in Christ; but whereas Acts attests the occasional use of the laying on of hands at baptism, no mention of this custom is to be found in its pages and no clear evidence of it occurs elsewhere in the New Testament. In the present passage, v. 27 makes the interpretation of the chrism as a literal anointing with oil hardly feasible: 'The chrism which you received abides in you and . . . teaches you concerning all things'; such language is not consistent with the idea of the chrism being an outward anointing and there is no indication that the chrism represents both the anointing and the Spirit conveyed by the anointing. It is more likely that the passage, along with 2 Cor. 1.21, gave rise to the idea of embodying the chrism by an anointing with literal oil, although the term naturally originated in practices applied in other circumstances.[1]

It is possible, however, that a quite different conception of the chrism is in mind of the writer of this letter. The subject of the passage is the Truth of Christ, denied by the antichrists but known to the readers in virtue of the chrism. From this point of view the coincidence of language in vv. 27 and 24 is noteworthy. In the former we read:

'*The chrism which you received from him* abides in you',

in the latter:

'Let *what you heard from the beginning* abide in you'.

In v. 27:

'As his *chrism* teaches you about all things and is no lie,
just as it has taught you, *abide* in him';

in v. 24:

'If *what you heard from the beginning* abides in you,
then you will *abide* in the Son and in the Father'.

The strong affirmation in v. 27 of the truth of the chrism, which 'teaches you concerning all things and is true and is no lie', in a similar manner repeats the thought of v. 21 concerning the truth of the 'message': 'I did not write to you because you do not know the truth but because you know it and know that no lie is of the truth'. The natural conclusion to draw from these parallel statements, and which would have been generally admitted had it not been for the

[1] Such is the belief of Westcott, op. cit., p. 73; Heitmüller, op. cit., p. 30; Dodd, *The Johannine Epistles*, 1946, p. 59; Lampe, op. cit., p. 81. T. W. Manson leaves it an open question, op. cit., p. 29.

strong influence of the tradition embodied in the Hippolytan rite, is that the chrism is *the truth of the Gospel*. If the aorist ἐλάβετε ('you received') of v. 27 is to be interpreted as pointing to its adoption in baptism, it will relate, as in Eph. 5.26, to the Word embodied in baptism and the confession of Jesus Christ as Lord (with possibly other elaborations at this time), and perhaps to the loyal submission to the Lord whose name is proclaimed in baptism.[1] Such an appeal to the chrism received and confessed in baptism would be pertinent to this context; whereas the heretical teaching involved a denial of the very basis of the Gospel, the baptismal confession set it forth as the revelation of God in Christ, who was true man, who truly died on the cross and was truly raised, in whom our humanity was renewed and in union with whom we participate in the renewal.

Dodd aptly cites Ignatius to the Ephesians, 17.1 f, for a striking parallel to the thought of this passage: 'Be not anointed with the ill-odour of the doctrine of the Prince of this world, lest he take you captive from the life that is set before you. Why do we not all become wise, receiving the knowledge of God which is Jesus Christ?' The anointing with the odoriferous doctrine of Satan is the counterpart of the Johannine description of the doctrine of the heretics as the lie of the antichrists; the knowledge of God which is Jesus Christ is evidently the fragrant anointing corresponding to the chrism of 1 Jn. 2.20, 27. This use of the symbol seems to have emanated from Gnostic circles. Hippolytus cites the Naassenes as maintaining, 'We alone of all men are Christians, who complete the mystery at the third portal and are anointed there with speechless chrism', where the chrism is an initiation into a mystery.[2] If this be the origin of the employment of *chrism* for receiving right doctrine, we have a parallel to the polemical use made by the writer elsewhere in his letter of Gnostic conceptions for the purpose of claiming the orthodox Christian faith as the true Gnosis. It need not surprise us that some variation in the employment of baptismal symbols should appear in the writings of different Apostolic men. The Johannine teaching on recreation through Christ, as compared with Paul's relation of it to dying and rising with Christ, is such a variation.

---

[1] So C. H. Dodd: 'It seems natural to conclude that the "chrism", which confers the knowledge of God, and is also a prophylactic against the poison of false teaching, is the Word of God, that is, the Gospel, or the revelation of God in Christ, as communicated in the rule of faith to catechumens and confessed in baptism', op. cit., p. 63. Windisch in his commentary on the Catholic Epistles mentions that Reitzenstein advocated a similar view in *Die Hellenistischen Mysterienreligionen*, 3rd ed., pp. 393 ff.

[2] Dodd, op. cit., p. 61.

While some uncertainty therefore remains in the interpretation of the chrism in 1 Jn. 2.20, 27, we conclude that it is plausible to view it as derived from the contemporary background of Hellenistic religion, and that it represents the Gospel as the true chrism into which the Christian is initiated at baptism, to which appeal can be made against the spurious Christianity advocated by Gnostic deniers of the Christ come in the flesh.

4. 1 JOHN 5.5–8

'The faith that conquers the world' has been the theme of the writer's reflections in the immediately preceding context, and he has summed it up in the brief confession, 'Jesus is the Son of God' (v. 5). Over against the insidious modifications of the Church's faith that would threaten its destruction, John makes explicit once more its essentials and the nature of the witness borne to it. In so doing he brings to a climax the polemic contained in the letter against the 'false prophets' who have gone out into the world (4.1), the 'many anti-christs' who have proceeded from the bosom of the Church itself (2.18 ff), and 'those who would deceive you' (2.26). There can be little doubt that the manner in which the divine witness to Christ is presented in this passage has been dictated by the form of heresy prevalent in the area to which the letter was sent. The statement, 'This is he who came *through* water and blood', is a strange mode of describing the ministry and redemption of the incarnate Son of God. It is possible that the false teachers themselves coined the expression, 'He came *through water*', and that John made the needful correction by the addition, '*and blood*'. For the idea of the Lord coming 'through water' would well suit the conception that the divine Christ descended on the man Jesus at his baptism. Entering without birth, He could as easily depart without death; there was no involvement in humanity by this Spirit. That such teaching was current about this time we know from the summary of the preaching of Cerinthus given by Irenaeus: 'After the baptism there descended upon him in the form of a dove the Christ from the Ruler who is supreme over all things. He then announced the unknown Father and wrought miracles. In the end the Christ departed again from Jesus and while Jesus suffered and rose again Christ remained impassible, continuing to exist as a spiritual being'.[1] As Findlay remarked, on this view of Cerinthus, the Christ who came through water went away from blood rather than came through blood. To the heretics the death of Jesus could signify

[1] *Adv. Haer.*, I, xxvi, 1.

only abandonment by God, not revelation of God; the cross was not redemption but the suffering of defeat at the hands of the powers of darkness. However much of right was gathered into this system by its advocates, John was correct in perceiving that it struck a fatal blow at the faith that was rooted in the revelation of God in Christ; it was not even half the gospel, it was no gospel at all. Without the death of the Son of God there was neither a life of the Son of God, nor life for those who have believed in Him. John therefore proclaims again the historic basis of the gospel by taking up the Gnostic slogan and amplifying it by one significant particular. 'This is he who came through water *and* blood'.

If this be the correct background on which to set the statement, it has decisive consequences for our understanding of its meaning. The term ὁ ἐλθών, 'He who came', can hardly be held to echo the messianic title, ὁ ἐρχόμενος, 'He who comes', as Westcott believed; but Westcott was right in insisting that the sense of the phrase points to a past historic fact, and that consequently 'through water and blood' must also have an historic meaning and refer to 'definite events characteristic of the manner in which the Lord fulfilled his office upon earth'.[1] As we have seen, 'through water' relates to the baptism of Jesus, his first messianic act, wherein He demonstrated and established his solidarity with sinners; 'through blood' refers to the death on the cross, the consummation of that solidarity with sinners maintained through his ministry and which issued in suffering as the Representative of all. But the nature of this polemic makes it difficult to see any justification for the common view that the writer alludes to the two sacraments of the Christian Church. The reality of the incarnate life of Jesus is being defended. John insists that Jesus Christ did not appear as a meteorite from heaven to Jordan, to disappear into heaven again without any true contact with flesh and blood; Jesus Christ was baptized as flesh and blood and died as flesh and blood: 'Again I repeat', says John, 'he came not alone "with the water" of Jordan but "with the blood" of the cross'. To interpret the second statement as 'He came *bringing* the water and *bringing* the blood' of Christian baptism and the Christian eucharist, as Windisch-Preisker maintain on the basis of the replacement of δι᾽ ὕδατος καὶ αἵματος by ἐν ὕδατι καὶ ἐν τῷ αἵματι is remote from the writer's mind.[2] The second statement repeats the first with emphasis and with the same meaning.

[1] Op. cit., p. 181

[2] Op. cit., p. 132. The change of prepositions is stylistic; compare the closely parallel replacement of διά by ἐν in Heb. 9.12, διὰ τοῦ ἰδίου αἵματος εἰσῆλθεν and Heb. 9.25, εἰσέρχεται εἰς τὰ ἅγια κατ᾽ ἐνιαυτὸν ἐν αἵματι ἀλλοτρίῳ.

Westcott considered that the second clause, 'not with the water only, but with the water and the blood', echoes Jn. 19.34, the flowing of blood and water from the side of the crucified Lord: 'While He hung upon the cross, dead in regard to mortal life, but still living, He came again "by water and blood" '.[1] It seems to me, however, that we are dealing with a different kind of statement in our passage from that in Jn. 19.34. The latter calls attention to an event viewed as significant beyond anything a casual observer could have understood at the time, by which the death of Jesus is seen to fulfil prophecy and type and so to actualize God's redemptive purpose in history; 1 Jn. 5.6, on the contrary, pleads for a recognition of something that only he cannot see who will not see — that the same Jesus Christ who was baptized in Jordan really died on the cross, a Messiah who shared our life in fact and not in appearance. Of this there is nothing mysterious. John wants less spiritualizing here and more acknowledgment of flesh and blood. In this connection we may recall that the secondary motif in Jn. 19.34 has nothing to do with baptism and the eucharist but establishes that Jesus was true man, and that He truly died on the cross; and that is precisely the contention of 1 Jn. 5.6. It would seem to me that this passage gains in force if its purpose in relation to the heretics is given full recognition and its historic testimony to Jesus the Christ be allowed to stand alone.

'And the Spirit is the one who bears testimony, because the Spirit is the truth'. To what does the Spirit bear testimony? In this context it must relate to the fact that Jesus Christ came through water and blood, i.e. that in his baptism and in his death Jesus was seen to be the Christ and the Christ was seen to be Jesus. Brooke considers that the present tense excludes the necessity of any definite historical reference being in mind, as the Voice at the Baptism or the Voice from heaven shortly before the Passion (Jn. 12.28).[2] It is perhaps better to recognize that the present tense indicates that the witness of the Spirit is not *confined* to any one occasion; but the continuity of the Spirit's testimony does not exclude the possibility that certain occasions of his witness are outstanding. In the latter category the descent of the Spirit at the baptism of Jesus would come, especially in the light of the statement of John the Baptist in Jn. 1.31 ff, indicating that the purpose of his baptism was for the revelation of the Messiah through the Spirit to Israel: 'That he might be revealed to Israel, therefore came I baptizing with water . . . I saw the Spirit coming down like a dove out of heaven and it remained on him. And I did not know him; but he that

[1] Op. cit., p. 182.   [2] Op. cit., p. 136.

sent me to baptize with water said to me, "He on whom you see the Spirit coming down and remaining on him is the one who baptizes in Holy Spirit". And I saw it and bear testimony that he is the son of God'. It will be observed that the Spirit's descent on Jesus marks him out as the one who should later baptize with Spirit. It is an integral element of the theology of the Fourth Evangelist that the sending of the Spirit awaits the glorification of the Son of God through death and exaltation to heaven; conversely the giving of the Spirit through the Risen Lord may be viewed as a testimony to his presence at the right hand of the Father, since God alone can give the Spirit of promise. It is as Risen Son of God, whom the Father has sent into the world, that Jesus gives the Spirit on Easter Day (Jn. 20.21 f); we must presume that He bestows the Spirit because of a prior 'giving' or commission from the Father (Jn. 15.26). Yet it is manifest from John's language in 1 Jn. 5.6 that the testimony borne by the Spirit is viewed as continuing after Easter. The Paraclete passages inevitably spring to mind, above all Jn. 15.26: 'When the Paraclete comes, whom I will send to you from the Father, the Spirit of truth who proceeds from the Father, he will bear testimony concerning me'; compare also Jn. 14.26, 16.8 ff. That the Spirit bears witness to the coming of Jesus 'through water and blood' gains in pertinence when it is remembered that the heretics believed that *the Spirit would have nothing to do with the Jesus of the cross* and that the Spirit's present work was to give a higher gnosis than that taught by the leaders of the Church. John declares, on the contrary, that the Spirit's supreme task is to bear witness to the incarnate Lord who was Jesus Christ and to the reality of his redemption; this He has borne in the ministry and in the resurrection and this He bears still in the communities of the faithful and in their fellowship with Him.

The writer now brings together into a single statement what he has written but casts it into a slightly different form: 'Three there are who bear testimony, the Spirit and the water and the blood; and the three subserve one end'. It is immediately noticeable that the water and the blood are spoken of as witnesses, not merely events through which Jesus passed, and that their testimony is set in the present time: Jesus *came* through water and blood, but the water and blood *bear* witness now. Is a difference of viewpoint involved in this presentation of the water and blood as witnesses along with the Spirit? C. H. Dodd has suggested that there is, and that the clue is to be found in the analogy afforded by the witness of the Spirit. The Spirit was a factor in the historical life of Jesus, bearing witness to Him in his redemptive acts, and is a continuing experience of the Church; this witness is not so much the 'interior witness' of the Spirit as the outward expression of that inner witness in the corporate life of the Church, particularly in the prophetic utterance by which the Church proclaimed the truth of the gospel. So also, 'the baptism and the crucifixion are authenticated facts in history, and as such bear witness to the reality of the incarnate life of the Son of God; but further, the Church possesses a counterpart to the baptism of Christ, in the sacrament of baptism, and a counterpart to his sacrificial death, in the sacrament of the eucharist. Both sacraments attest and confirm to believers the abiding effect of the life and death of Christ. It seems likely that our author is thinking of these two sacraments as providing a continuing witness to the truth of Christ's incarnation and redemptive death. . . . Thus the Apostolic faith is authenticated against all false teaching by a threefold testimony: the living voice of prophecy and the two evangelical sacraments; and "the three of them are in accord" '.[1]

This is an attractive interpretation and it has never been better expounded than in the above citation. I am almost persuaded by it, but not quite. There are certain difficulties in the way of its acceptance which are not generally given due consideration. For example: (i) Brooke pointed out that αἷμα ('blood') by itself is never found in the New Testament as a designation of the eucharist.[2] The frequent adducing of Jn. 3 and 6 as parallel representations of indirect teaching on the sacraments is inadequate, for 'birth from above, of water and of Spirit' as needful for entering the Kingdom leaves no doubt that a baptism of some kind is in view, and the post-resurrection perspective of the Evangelist and his readers makes its ultimate reference to Christian baptism unambiguous; similarly in the eucharistic discourse the statement about eating the *flesh* and drinking the *blood* of the Son of Man brings both elements of the Christian sacrament into view and invites reference to it. But the mere fact of witness given by 'blood' is not an unambiguous reference to the eucharist; were there no reference in our passage to 'water' alongside it, no one could justly have considered that the Supper was in mind; but whether 'water' here denotes Christian baptism as distinct from the baptism of Jesus in Jordan is a point at issue. (ii) W. F. Flemington is impressed with Brooke's objection and suggests that the water could refer to the Christian's baptism but the blood to the blood baptism of Jesus on the

[1] Op. cit., pp. 129 ff. A similar viewpoint is expressed by Westcott, op. cit., p. 182; Findlay, op. cit., pp. 384 f; Windisch, op. cit., p. 133; E. K. Lee, 'The Sacraments and the Fourth Gospel', *Theology*, 1954, p. 415.
[2] Op. cit., p. 132.

cross.[1] Yet it is difficult to relate the one element, water, to the baptism of Jesus *and* our baptism, and the other, blood, to something experienced by Jesus alone, the 'baptism' on the cross. Moreover, we noted the improbability of Jn. 19.34 having any relation to Christian baptism; for if we are to relate the water flowing from the Saviour's side to the individual believer, it will more plausibly be linked with the gift of living water which Christ gives to the thirsty. Dodd is so impressed with this argument that he dissociates our saying altogether from Jn. 19.34.[2] (iii) Above all, v. 9 indicates that the perspective of v. 8 has not actually changed. After speaking of the threefold testimony of the Spirit, water and blood John writes, 'If we receive the testimony of men, the testimony of God is greater; because this is the testimony of God that he has borne concerning his son'. The witness of the Spirit, water and blood is apparently in the last analysis the witness which God *bore*: the weight is on the facts of the life of Jesus — that He was baptized and died by the will of God and was attested by the Spirit sent from the Father. The repetition of the three witnesses in v. 8, after the initial statement of v. 6, is most plausibly to be accounted for by the desire to bring together three witnesses to bear testimony to the incarnate life of the divine redemption of Jesus Christ, in accordance with the Deuteronomic law, 'Only on the evidence of two witnesses, or of three witnesses, shall a charge be sustained', Deut. 19.15. That this diverse witness is in reality from God naturally makes it the more impressive. A similar procedure may be observed in Jn. 5.19–47, where the witness borne to Jesus by John the Baptist (v. 33), his miracles (v. 36) and the Scriptures (v. 39) is in reality the testimony of God Himself (v. 32). Such testimony could conceivably be seen in the sacraments of baptism and the eucharist, especially the former; but since believers only were permitted to be present at the latter the scope of the testimony is restricted in a fashion that was probably not intended by the writer.

These objections to the common interpretation are not conclusive, but they appear to me to take away confidence from it. In view of the fact that all are agreed that the primary emphasis of the Johannine passage is on the witness borne to Jesus by his baptism, his cross and his Spirit, it would seem safer to concentrate attention on them and regard as only tentative the idea that the Christian sacraments are present to view as secondary witnesses. The importance of the passage is its significance for the doctrine of the Incarnation: the Christ of God was true man, baptized according to the Will of God, crucified

[1] Op. cit., p. 89.   [2] Op. cit., pp. 129 f.

according to the Will of God, attested by the divine Spirit sent from the Father. If the sacraments do come into reckoning it is that they might support this same truth ('the three are directed to the same end'): they bear witness to the fact that Jesus is the incarnate Son of God and Redeemer. In that case the passage is unique in relating the sacraments solely to the glory of the giver and not at all to their recipients. In view of our constant concern with their effect on us, that is not an unhealthy corrective.[1]

(iii) *Baptism in Hebrews and 1 Peter*

1. HEBREWS 6.1–6

The writer of this letter has reproached his readers for their lack of maturity in Christian understanding: whereas they should have been in a position to instruct others, they required to learn again the very alphabet of the revelation of God (5.12). He desired his friends to leave behind this childhood stage of religious development and carry them with him to maturity of spirit and judgment; surely it was not necessary for him to lay again the foundation of Christian faith, as though they were but enquirers after the Gospel or mere catechumens not yet initiated into the Church! (6.1–2). It would appear that in this passage 'the first principles of God's word' (5.12), 'the elementary doctrines of the Christ' (6.1a) and the 'foundation' of the Christian confession (6.1b) are synonymous expressions, whose content is indicated in the three pairs of doctrines enumerated in 6.1b–2: (i) repentance from dead works and faith toward God; (ii) ablutions and the laying on of hands; (iii) the resurrection of the dead and eternal judgment. Otto Michel takes up the suggestion of Delitzsch, that the first two items have in mind the unbeliever and set forth the negative and positive conditions required for beginning the Christian life, and the last four, separated by the introductory term, 'instruction about . . .', have in mind the catechumen.[2] In view however of the conjunction of the demand for baptism with the appeal for repentance and faith in the early Christian proclamation (see e.g. Acts 16.31–33, 18.8), it is better not to make such a separation but to regard all six items as elements of the primitive ὁμολογία ('confession') (10.23). It is likely

---

[1] The interpretation of 1 Jn. 5.6 ff by T. W. Manson, who holds that 'the Spirit, the water and the blood' represent (possibly) the chrism, the laver and the chalice, bearing testimony to a primitive initiation rite *in that order*, viz. reception of the Spirit through the laying on of hands and anointing, baptism and first communion, does not commend itself in the light of the above discussion. It is highly tenuous and is supported by doubtful interpretations of Pauline evidence. See 'Entry into Membership of the Early Church', *J.T.S.*, 1947, p. 29.

[2] *Der Brief an die Hebräer*, *Meyer-Kommentar*, 8th ed. 1949, p. 145.

that vv. 4b–5 select further items from this catechesis, and that they have particular reference to the nature of the Christian initiation hinted at in the 'ablutions and laying on of hands' of v. 2.[1]

The conjunction of 'washings' (βαπτισμοί) and 'laying on of hands' in a list of foundational elements of faith affords a plain hint as to how both are to be understood: they are set in the context of the beginning of the Christian life. While therefore the term βαπτισμοί can have a quite general connotation, and has such in 9.10 (as in Mk. 7.4, 8), it is tolerably clear that 'baptisms' in a more technical sense are chiefly in view. And since the plural 'baptisms' is so unusual in the New Testament, we may safely set aside the view that repeated immersions are thereby intended.[2] The employment of βαπτισμός instead of the usual βάπτισμα confirms what in any case most naturally occurs to the reader, that the writer implies a *contrast* between Christian baptism and other religious 'washings'. The term is wide enough to include the ritual washings of the Old Testament and every kind of baptism of initiates known in the writer's time, including the baptism of John, the baptisms practised in the Jordan Valley and by the Dead Sea, Jewish proselyte baptism, and whatever ritual washings existed among the various Mystery Religions. Instruction as to the distinctive nature of the Christian rite will have been especially appropriate among the people to whom the Pentateuchal ordinances were known, but in any case ceremonial washings were common enough in the ancient world for such instructions to have been deemed advisable among converts generally.

In like fashion, although the laying on of hands was a long established custom in Israel[3] and was carried over into the early Church with a variety of significations,[4] it can hardly be doubted that in association with βαπτισμοί ('washings') it relates to the laying on of hands in Christian baptism. As such the passage is an important datum. Whereas the evidence of Acts is too inconclusive to permit the inference that the rite formed an integral element in baptism from the beginning of the Christian Church and in all areas of its operation, it is evident that its inclusion in this list of cardinal elements of Christian

[1] See further Westcott, *The Epistle to the Hebrews*, 1889, p. 143; E. C. Wickham *The Epistle to the Hebrews*, 1910, p. 39; J. Moffatt, *A Critical and Exegetical Commentary on the Epistle to the Hebrews* (I.C.C.), 1924, p. 73; T. H. Robinson, *The Epistle to the Hebrews*, 1933, p. 75; O. Michel, op. cit., pp. 144–147.
[2] Contra Windisch, *Der Hebräerbrief*, 1913, p. 48. Tertullian thought of the threefold immersion in the name of the Trinity, *Adv. Prax.*, 26.
[3] Cf. Lev. 16.21 for its use in connection with sacrifices and Num. 27.18 ff for ordination.
[4] As a mode of blessing, see e.g. Mk. 10.16; for healing, Mk. 6.5 etc.; for ordination, Acts 6.6, 1 Tim. 4.14.

faith shows that in the communities in which the writer and his readers moved the laying on of hands was at this time an unquestionable feature of Christian baptism. Nor need we doubt the reason for this integration of laying on of hands with baptism: the association of such an action with the communication of divine blessing, in prayer, healing, ordination, and above all the gift of the Spirit, would naturally tend to its inclusion in a rite that embodied the transition of a convert from a life in sin to a life for God, from life in the old age to life in the new, from life in estrangement from God to life *in the Spirit*. The variations in the experience of the Spirit, attested in Acts, would strengthen the desire that the convert should receive the gift of the Spirit at the beginning of his Christian life. Experience of the Spirit's work and desire for his fullness, as well as conviction of his absence and yearning for his reception, would all combine to make it natural for the practice of laying on of hands to be united with baptism and at length to make the union unexceptional.

After declining to lay again the foundation of Christian faith, the writer issues a warning on the frightful nature of the apostasy into which his readers are in danger of falling. The tarrying in the elementary stage of religion has involved them in a looking back and a possibility of retreating, which could mean only irrevocable ruin. To underscore the gravity of the situation the writer recalls for them the significance of the transition that a convert experiences in baptism. Such a man (i) receives a once-for-all enlightenment, (ii) tastes the heavenly gift, (iii) becomes a partaker of the Holy Spirit, (iv) tastes the goodness of the word of God and (v) knows the powers of the age to come. Reflection on this description of God's gracious action in the believer suggests that we are not to analyze the separate items too closely but that we should recognize in them an attempt to characterize the manifold grace of God vouchsafed to the believer.[1] Interest has not unnaturally centred in the phrase τοὺς ἅπαξ φωτισθέντας, 'the once-for-all enlightened' since the verb φωτίζω ('illumine'), with its noun φωτισμός ('illumination') became technical from the time of Justin (Apology i.61, 65) for the 'illumination' of Christian baptism. Interestingly, the Syriac versions paraphrase the verb in this passage in

---

[1] Westcott's division of the five elements into illumination by divine action (i–iii) and experience of the 'beauty' of revelation and powers of the new order (iv–v) illustrates the difficulty of such dissection; for the reception of enlightenment is scarcely to be distinguished from tasting the goodness of the word of God, and to become a partaker of the Holy Spirit is to taste the powers of the age to come. See Westcott, op. cit., pp. 147 f and for a different view Wickham, op. cit., p. 40, and Moffatt, op. cit., p. 78.

order to make this meaning explicit: the Peshitta renders it, 'who have once descended to baptism', the Harclean Syriac, 'who have once been baptized'. That the writer to the Hebrews does in fact have baptism in mind is not to be contested: the occurrence of his characteristic term ἅπαξ ('once for all') alongside the aorist verbs throughout the statement φωτισθέντας ('having been enlightened'), γευσαμένους ('having tasted'), μετόχους γενηθέντας ('having become sharers') shows that the most critical moment of a man's spiritual life is being portrayed, wherein he tasted 'the heavenly gift' — the salvation of Christ by the Spirit — received the Holy Spirit, discovered how good is God's word that promises forgiveness and life in the Gospel, and experienced in the present the powers of the age to come. We recognize in these descriptions ideas already encountered in Acts, Paul and the Johannine writings. The 'powers of the age to come' alone could summarize for us the chief elements of Paulinism, viz. deliverance from the guilt and power of sin and thraldom of the evil powers (Rom. 6.1 ff, 1 Cor. 6.11, Col. 1.13, Eph. 5.25 f), resurrection in Christ (Rom. 6.1 ff, Col. 2.12) and participation in the new creation in Christ (2 Cor. 5.16); the further contact with Tit. 3.5 ff and Jn. 3.5 needs no demonstration. That by no means justifies the Syriac translators, however, in rendering the participle τοὺς φωτισθέντας as 'the baptized', any more than they would have been justified in translating 'those that tasted the powers of the age to come' by the same verb. Illumination is associated with baptism, as is the bestowal of the Holy Spirit, but we have no right to regard the verb as a synonym for βαπτίζω ('baptize'), either here or in Heb. 10.32. The situation is similar to the development of the expression 'sealed with the Spirit' to represent the inward operation of the Holy Spirit in baptism; in the New Testament it is never used synonymously with the verb βαπτίζω, but quite soon after the Apostolic age its cognate noun σφραγίς ('seal') became an established term for baptism.

The idea of illumination through reception of the truth of the Gospel is not unfamiliar to the New Testament — we may recall 2 Tim. 1.10, 2 Cor. 4.4–6, and even the prologue to the Fourth Gospel. The employment of the verb in Eph. 1.18 is worth noticing ('the eyes of your heart being enlightened' — πεφωτισμένους), since there is no ground for considering that baptism is in view in the passage; it forms a variant for the preceding clause, 'that the God of our Lord Jesus Christ . . . may give you a spirit of wisdom and of revelation in the knowledge of him', and its object is indicated in that which follows, namely the nature of the Christian hope, the glorious inheritance in the saints and the greatness of the power of the resurrection. Contemporary Judaism was not unfamiliar with the metaphor, as is seen in 2 Esd. 14.22 ff: 'If I have found favour before thee, send the Holy Spirit into me and I shall write all that hath been done in the world since the beginning, even the things that were written in thy law, that men may be able to find the path and that they which would live in the latter days may live. And he answered me and said . . . I shall light a lamp of understanding in thine heart, which shall not be put out until the things be ended which thou shalt write. And when thou hast done, some things shalt thou publish openly, and some things thou shalt deliver in secret to the wise . . .'. The two passages illustrate how contemporary religious writers can use images in a manner related to religions of a very different order, for the Jewish apocalyptist and the Christian Apostle (or disciple) have come remarkably close in their language to that of adherents of the Mystery Religions, who sought 'illumination' through the vision of God in their consecration rites. There is nevertheless one significant difference between the apocalyptic passage and the conception of illumination in the Mystery Religions, a difference perceptibly lessened in Eph. 1.18 ff and almost eliminated in Heb. 6.4 f: for the Jewish seer, knowledge of the truth is chiefly in mind; for the initiate, the goal is transformation into the divine nature which is Light; so also in Heb. 6.4 f the illumination is inseparably associated with receiving the heavenly gift, the good word of God, the powers of the age to come and the life of the Spirit. The possibility must be allowed, therefore, that the writer to the Hebrews has taken into his vocabulary a term associated in some quarters with the mystic's transfiguring vision of God, but which had also occupied a firm place in the Jewish and Christian traditions, and that he claimed it as expressing the Christian experience of divine grace known in baptism.[1]

The importance of baptism to the writer of this letter is not left in doubt. Its significance to him is crucial. At the beginning of this passage baptism is aligned with repentance and faith on the one hand and

---

[1] So Heitmüller, *Taufe und Abendmahl*, pp. 36 f; Clemen, op. cit., p. 345; Michel, op. cit., p. 147, n. 2; Bultmann, *N.T. Theology*, I, p. 143. Some writers have seen in the reference to tasting the heavenly gift an allusion to the Christian eucharist; see Michel, op. cit., p. 148, Héring, op. cit., p. 59. The 1956 *Interim Report of the Church of Scotland on Baptism* suggests that both the eucharist and 'the baptismal milk and honey' are in view in the text, p. 55. The interpretation is doubtful; the aorists indicate a single experience of the saving grace of God. Enlightenment, partaking of the Holy Spirit, tasting the heavenly gift of life in Christ, and the goodness of God's word and the powers of the age to come all describe the one great experience of saving grace. There is no ground for introducing the milk and honey at this juncture of the Church's history.

the resurrection from the dead and eternal judgment on the other (vv. 1–3). The concepts associated with it in vv. 4–5 are such as we commonly denote by the term 'realized eschatology': the powers of the age to come have entered this age and the Christian knows the reality of the new creation already. If alongside these associations of baptism with the Kingdom now and the Kingdom to come we set the fact that the writer is conscious of living in the last times (10.37), we may understand in part at least the gravity with which he views apostasy: such individuals step away from the company of the Son of God, so abandoning the ranks of the heirs of the Kingdom, and take their stand with the crucifiers of the Lord to face the wrath that is *ready to be revealed*![1] In such a situation nothing more remains to be done. The lesson is plain and must ever be emphasized: 'Since God has made you in these last times an heir of the Kingdom which cannot be shaken, *improve your baptism and be sure of the inheritance!*'

2. HEBREWS 10.22–23

The once-for-all sacrifice for sins by which Christ 'perfected for ever those who are sanctified' has been the theme of the writer's exposition in this chapter. He rejoices that through that offering the new covenant has been initiated and its promise become reality: 'Their sins and their misdeeds I will no more remember' (v. 17). In language of which every syllable is reminiscent of the Old Testament cultus, he encourages his fellow Christians to exercise their high-priestly privileges. Under the old covenant the High Priest had the awful prerogative of entering the Most Holy Sanctuary on the Day of Atonement, to make atonement for the tabernacle, for himself, the priests and the people (Lev. 16.11 ff, 33); under the new covenant every believer may exercise the right to enter the true sanctuary, of which the old was but a shadow (8.2, 9.11, 24), since their great High Priest, Jesus, in the offering of Himself had rent asunder the curtain that shut it off from mankind and consecrated them to join Him there. In having direct access to God in that Most Holy Place, the Christian is privileged beyond anything vouchsafed to the High Priest of the old order.

It is the exercise of this privilege that the writer has in view when he bids us 'draw near', i.e. to God in the Most Holy Sanctuary:

> 'with our hearts sprinkled from an evil conscience
> and our bodies washed with pure water'.

[1] Heb. 10.26–27.

R

The language is determined in part by the ritual of the Day of Atonement. In the instructions concerning that event the High Priest must 'bathe his body in water' (Lev. 16.4) and enter the Most Holy Sanctuary with the blood of a bull slain as a sin offering; the blood of the sacrifice, however, has to be sprinkled on and before the mercy seat, not on himself (v. 14, vv. 15 ff). In this particular the parallel fails, as the writer must have known, for the cleansing of the shrine on the Day of Atonement is referred to by him elsewhere (9.23). Accordingly he will also have had in view the consecration of the High Priest, instructions for which are given in detail in Exodus 29 and a description of which is reproduced in the account of the consecration of Aaron and his sons in Lev. 8. 'You shall bring Aaron and his sons to the door of the tent of meeting and wash them with water. . . . You shall kill the ram and take part of its blood and put it upon the tip of the right ear of Aaron and upon the tips of the right ears of his sons, and upon the thumbs of their right hands, and upon the great toes of their right feet, and throw the rest of the blood against the altar round about. Then you shall take part of the blood that is on the altar, and of the anointing oil, and sprinkle it upon Aaron and his garments, and upon his sons and his sons' garments with him; and he and his garments shall be holy, and his sons and his sons' garments with him' (vv. 4, 20 f). If the fusion of ideas from these two passages is self conscious, it would seem that the writer to the Hebrews has in mind the consecration of the Christian for priestly ministry within the Most Holy Sanctuary of heaven — a figure for the closest fellowship with God that can be conveyed by means of symbolism of this order.

We must now enquire as to what reality in Christian faith and experience the writer alludes in the terms, 'our hearts sprinkled clean . . . and our bodies washed with pure water'. It is evident that the imagery is that of sprinkling a person with *blood* and washing him with water, although in the former case it is the heart that is cleansed and in the latter the body. The inference lies to hand that a contrast is being made between an internal and external cleansing, the one through the sacrifice of Christ, the other through the water of baptism, the one on the basis of repentance and faith, the other through sacramental efficacy, and so many exegetes have interpreted the passage.[1]

---

[1] Nairne for example writes, 'In accordance with this double aspect, outer and inner, of "the faith" we have a double description in v. 22 of the concomitants of access — cleansed heart and baptized body'. *Epistle of Priesthood*, p. 381. Windisch cites Philo as making a comparable distinction in speaking of people 'cleansed in

Despite the plausibility of this view, there is surely something wrong with it. This becomes the more apparent when we recognize that the water that washes the body is described as 'pure' or 'clean', not because the Holy Spirit is thought to be in it, but simply in deference to cultic usage, as in Ezk. 36.25 ('I will sprinkle clean water upon you and you shall be clean from all your uncleannesses') and Test. Levi 8.4 f ('The first man anointed me with holy oil. . . . The second washed me with pure water'). Is it conceivable that the writer who characterized Christian initiation in the glowing terms of 6.1–5 could represent baptism as a mere washing of the body? Such an interpretation proceeds from a misunderstanding of both the ritual imagery employed by the writer and the simple parallelism in which he has expressed his thoughts. In the Old Testament ritual the blood of sacrifice was sprinkled upon the body but in the New Testament fulfilment the blood cleanses the whole personality, just as the water washes the whole man. The two lines express one indivisible reality:

> 'sprinkled in the heart from an evil conscience,
> washed in the body with pure water'.

The parallelism is not antithetic, it is purely rhetorical. We may recall the continuation of Ezk. 36.25: 'I will sprinkle clean water upon you. . . . A new heart I will give you and a new spirit I will put within you; and I will take out of your flesh the heart of stone and give you a heart of flesh. And I will put my spirit within you . . .'. The writer to the Hebrews will not have meant less in his statement. The term 'heart' has been employed because of the appeal to which the clauses with which we are concerned are subordinate:

> 'Let us draw near with *a true heart* . . .
> having a *heart* sprinkled from an evil conscience . . .'.

We draw near to God like the High Priest of ancient times, but with

their bodies and souls, the former with washings, the latter with streams of laws and right education', σώματα καὶ ψυχὰς καθηράμενοι, τὰ μὲν λουτροῖς, τὰ δὲ νόμων καὶ παιδείας ὀρθῆς ῥεύμασι, de plant. 162. Schneider takes it that the water is 'pure' because the Spirit of God is active in it; the sprinkling with the blood of Christ, which reaches our heart, and the bath of baptism, through which God cleanses our body, work together to the sanctification of our whole being: 'The blood of Christ and baptism are the basis of the new existence of man', op. cit. p. 65. In the judgment of Strathmann the relation between the inner and outer event posed a problem for the author of the Epistle: the possibility of receiving the one without the other evidently had not entered his head, but neither did the writer think of baptism in a 'mystical' fashion, as did Paul: to him it was a purely cultic action, after the nature of the Old Testament cleansings through water, *der Brief an die Hebräer*, p. 129.

the infinitely better cleansing afforded by the sacrifice of Christ, the power of which is known in baptism.[1]

Once more, therefore, we meet with an expression of the conviction, basic to the writers of the New Testament, that the cleansing power of baptism is the death of Christ, to which we are related in the sacrament. In Paul's teaching we participate in the death of the cross in baptism by union with Him who died thereon, so that we died with Him *there* and by grace ended an old existence in baptism and began a new one in the power of his resurrection. The writer to the Hebrews expresses the same reality in terms of the Levitical sacrificial ritual: the once-for-all sacrifice of Christ has once-for-all *sanctified* us who have drawn near in repentance and faith to find the cleansing through his sacrifice that none other can impart (10.2 ff). In this sanctification the laws of God are set within the heart and a new kind of life begins (vv. 15 f). The meeting place of the sanctifying power of Christ's death and the individual is the baptism wherein the believer turns to God in faith for cleansing through Christ.

It should not go unmentioned that the immediately succeeding exhortation, 'Let us hold fast the confession of our hope without wavering' (v. 23), is almost certainly an appeal to maintain the confession made in baptism. The term ὁμολογία came to be especially employed for the baptismal confession. In view of the eschatological associations of baptism in ch. 6 it is noteworthy that the confession is concentrated in the term *hope*. That is characteristic of this writer, for whom faith and hope are bound in one and hope rests on the double guarantee of the promise of the God who cannot lie and his oath (6.17 f). Hence the apt comment of Theophylact: 'We confessed, when we made the covenants of faith, to believe in the resurrection of the dead and in the life eternal'.[2] To be baptized to Christ is to be baptized into life and unto life. For 'Christ, having been offered once to bear the sins of many, will appear a second time . . . to save those who are eagerly waiting for him' (9.28), and, 'We are not the men to shrink back and be lost, but to have faith and win our souls' (10.39).

---

[1] This is well expressed by Moffatt: 'The distinctive feature which marked off the Christian βαπτισμός from all similar ablutions (6.2, 9.10) was that it meant something *more* than a cleansing of the body; it was part and parcel of an inward cleansing of the καρδία, effected by τὸ αἷμα τῆς διαθήκης. Hence this as the vital element is put first, though the body had also its place and part in the cleansing experience. The καρδία and the σῶμα are a full, plastic expression for the entire personality, as an ancient conceived it', op. cit., pp. 144 f. See also Wickham, op. cit., p. 85; Michel, op. cit., p. 231; Bultmann, op. cit., p. 183; Flemington, op. cit., p. 98; I. Buse, *Christian Baptism* (ed. by Gilmore), p. 183.

[2] Cited by Westcott, op. cit., p. 323.

3. THE FIRST LETTER OF PETER: A BAPTISMAL TREATISE?

The place occupied by baptism in the thought and composition of this Letter has long been a matter of debate and in recent time it has become a focal point of interest. The discussion was initiated by R. Perdelwitz in 1911, in a monograph entitled, 'Die Mysterien-religionen und das Problem des 1. Petrusbriefes'. As the title indicates, the major interest of this author was to relate the baptismal teaching of the Letter to conceptions of initiation found in the Mystery Religions, but his investigations as to the composition of the Letter were independent of his views on that subject. Perdelwitz was struck by the difference of attitude towards suffering and persecution in 4.12 ff from that in the section of the Letter that preceded it: whereas in 4.12 ff the fiery trial was in process, in the earlier part everything is hypothetical (note especially the εἰ καὶ πάσχοιτε of 3.13 and εἰ θέλοι τὸ θέλημα τοῦ θεοῦ of 3.17). He then urged that 4.12 ff does not suitably follow on the section headed up by the doxology and Amen of 4.11; the progress of thought, excellently continued to this point, is suddenly broken off, to be followed by yet another treatment of suffering, with exhortations in part repetitive of what has gone before. He therefore ventured the view that the present writing was composed of two independent and self-contained documents. The shorter one, consisting of 1.1–2, 4.12–5.14, is a hortatory discourse to strengthen Churches enduring suffering, as well as to rebuke them for their shortcomings. The former, 1.3–4.11, is wholly concerned with 'edification'; its preaching style had already been observed (by Zahn and Gunkel); the idea suggested itself that this part of the Letter might be based on a homily. If so, for what purpose and occasion? In 1.3, 1.23 men 'born anew' are addressed, (in 2.1 they are *newly* born, ἀρτιγέννητα — very recently indeed!). Tremendous joy has just come to them (1.8). They have reached the goal of which prophets spoke and which men of old longed to attain (1.10 f). Called out of darkness to God, they are now his people (1.9 f) and salvation has now come to them in baptism (3.21). 'This "now" runs like a red thread through all the utterances of the writer'. It is therefore proposed that 1.3–4.11 is the record of an address delivered on the occasion of a baptism to the newly baptized. Read from this point of view the train of thought is seen to be thoroughly compact and many items become illuminated.

The second section of the Letter is believed to have been written to the same community when it was under pressure of persecution. At a later date the two documents, long kept separately in the archives of the Church were brought together, and the longer one was placed first.

This thesis received a fresh treatment from W. Bornemann.[1] He repudiated any idea that 1 Peter was composite; apart from the address, 1.1-2, and conclusion 5.12-14, the whole letter is too compact to permit interpolation hypotheses. On the other hand in the Letter proper, i.e. 1.3-5.11, there is no allusion to the personality and circumstances of the writer, except the brief mention in 5.1 that he is an elder and witness of the sufferings of Christ. There is no mention of any mutual relationships between him and the addressees, no hint that he knows them personally, not a word as to his right to exhort or console the readers, no declaration of the authority on which he addresses them, no trace of what impels him to intervene in this manner. If we ignore 1.1-2 and 5.12-14 we must admit that this is not a letter at all but a *discourse*. Bornemann therefore advanced the thesis that originally this entire writing was a baptismal sermon, in loose association with Psalm 34, and that it was preached by the aged Silvanus in a city of Asia Minor about A.D. 90.[2]

The baptismal context of the 'sermon' is strongly suggested (in Bornemann's view) by the credal references in it and even the credal like structure of the whole. Of passages in the New Testament that may be regarded as foreshadowings of the Apostolic Symbol, 1 Pt. 3.18-4.5 is foremost. Not that it is formal, but it gives a free reproduction of elements concerning the person and work of Christ that came to be embodied in the second member of the Apostles' Creed and they are here reproduced with a baptismal reference. The call to sanctify Christ as *Kurios* in 3.15 suits this same context. If 3.18-4.5 reproduces a second member of the creed, are the other two members in view elsewhere? Bornemann finds that 1.13-3.12 is dominated by the first member and 4.1-19, 5.10 by the third member. Moreover the introductory section 1.3-12, is triadic in form, speaking first of the Father who begets us anew, then of Christ who mediates salvation to faith, and finally of the Spirit who gave prophetic intimation of salvation and now realizes it. That the baptism has just taken place is seen in a comparison of 3.21, 'baptism, which *now saves you*', with Tit. 3.5,

---

[1] 'Der erste Petrusbrief — eine Taufrede des Silvanus?' *Z.N.W.*, Band. 19, 1919-20, pp. 143. He made no reference to Perdelwitz, but it is scarcely possible that he knew nothing of his work; he must have taken over the idea of his predecessor and developed it according to his own predilections. The like happened to Streeter. He did not read the book by Perdelwitz and clearly knew nothing of Bornemann's article; but his attention was drawn by A. E. J. Rawlinson to a sentence in Gunkel's commentary on 1 Peter, wherein the view of Perdelwitz was alluded to but dismissed. Streeter took up the idea and made it a point of departure for his own theory of the origin of 1 Peter. See *The Primitive Church*, 1929, pp. 122 ff.

[2] The same date lighted on by Streeter, op. cit., p. 128.

'He *saved us* through the washing of regeneration'; the present instead of aorist is strengthened by the 'now', and the 'you' instead of 'us' suggests that the addressees are distinguished from other Christians through their experience of salvation at this present time. The exhortations to the presbyters (5.1 ff) are especially appropriate when new members of the church are being received, especially if they had responsibility to look after them in their early period of membership. The sermon was written down, presumably at the request of visiting brethren, that they might take it back to their own communities in Pontus, Galatia, Cappadocia etc. It became ascribed to Peter because 2.25, and 5.2 f seemed like an echo of Jn. 21.17, and the whole content, especially the concluding 5.10, was seen as a fulfilment of Lk. 22.32.

Bornemann's belief that the Letter must be considered a unity was questioned in some quarters but the support provided for the basic idea that 1 Peter embodies a baptismal address was welcomed.[1] H. Preisker, however, favoured Bornemann's view, but he modified it with the suggestion that the Letter represents not an address but an entire baptismal *service* in which many participants contributed to the whole.[2] Preisker urged that there was nothing extraordinary in a service being preserved in writing; Paul demanded as little improvisation as possible in a service of worship, 1 Cor. 14.26, 30. Preparations made at home and spontaneous inspiration in the service would complement each other. On so important an occasion as a baptismal service those intending to take part would write down their contributions.

In England Preisker's presentation of the case for a baptismal origin of 1 Peter was enthusiastically adopted by F. L. Cross, who systematized the baptismal references and gave the whole a precise setting. He recalled that Easter was pre-eminently the season for baptism in

---

[1] The limitation of the address to the point reached in the doxology of 4.11 was accepted by Windisch, *Die Katholischen Briefe*, H.N.T., 2nd ed. 1930 and 3rd ed. 1951; Hauck, *Die Kirchenbriefe*, N.T.D., 5th ed. 1949; Beare, *The Epistle of Peter*, 1947; and Cranfield, *The First Epistle of Peter*, 1950.

[2] This entailed a careful analysis of the text to reveal its component parts and an estimate of the different styles revealed in it. The result was as follows: (1) a prayer psalm in 1.3–12; (2) an address of instruction with echoes of confessional and liturgical formulae, 1.13–21. The baptism at this point takes place, as may be deduced from the language used in verses 22, having purified your souls; 23, having been born anew; 2.2, as new-born infants; 2.3, you tasted. Hence follow (3) the dedication of the baptized, 1.22–25; (4) a festal hymn in three verses from a Spirit inspired Christian, 2.1–10; (5) an exhortation from another preacher, 2.11–3.12; (6) an eschatological discourse from an apocalyptist seer, 3.13–4.7a; (7) a prayer and doxology, concluding the baptismal service proper, 4.7b–11. A closing service for the entire church now takes place, consisting of (8) an eschatological revelation, 4.12–19, (9) an exhortation to the presbyters, younger church members and the whole company, (10) a doxology uttered by a presbyter, 5.11. See Preisker's appendix to his edition (the 3rd) of Windisch's commentary, 1951, pp. 156 ff.

the early Church. It happens that there are more appearances in this Letter of the verb πάσχειν, to suffer, than there are in the rest of the New Testament. This is perhaps due to the idea, attested by Melito of Sardis and Hippolytus, that the term for passover, τὸ πάσχα, has been derived from the great event that took place in it, the πάσχειν or suffering of Jesus: Christians who suffer (πάσχειν) do so in mystical union with the Lord who suffered at τὸ πάσχα, and they enter upon this in their baptism at Easter, the Christian's passover. The eucharistic reference in 2.2 suggests that the Letter reproduces the bishop's preparations for *a baptismal eucharist taking place on the night of the Paschal Vigil*. As such it is both a homily and a liturgy combined. On this basis a simple analysis is given: (1) 1.3–12, opening prayer; (2) 1.13–21, charge to the candidates; (3) 1.22–25, welcome of the newly baptized into the Church (the baptism having taken place after v. 21); (4) 2.1–10, the fundamentals of the sacramental life; (5) 2.11–4.11, the duties of Christian discipleship. Cross recognizes the possibility that 4.12 ff was directed to the whole congregation, but he has less confidence in this suggestion than in the belief that 1.3–4.11 reproduces the paschal baptismal eucharist.[1]

It is not easy to assess the probabilities of this view concerning the 'baptismal' origin of 1 Peter; different elements in the argument appeal with varying degrees of plausibility to different people. For my part I confess that the liturgical argument, set forth by Preisker and Cross, seems to me unlikely. It presses sayings to yield doubtful implications. In particular it demands much credence to accept that between 1.21 and 1.22 f a baptism has taken place. The 'red thread' of the 'now' in these chapters has an attractive appearance, but we cannot be sure that it binds the seam of a baptismal robe donned by a still damp candidate (e.g. in 1.6 the 'now' contrasts this time with the age to come, in 1.8 it contrasts believers in this time with those who saw the Lord, in 1.12 it contrasts this age with the dispensation of the prophets). It may be natural for a member of a Church that uses written liturgies in all worship services to assume that prayers, exhortations, prophecies and liturgies were written out beforehand by participants in the worship of the primitive Church, but to any acquainted with services in which the charismatic element is given room, it appears very dubious. Can any imagine what a sermon in tongues would look like when written down? The interpretation could not be prepared — it had to await the 'tongue'! Why should it be thought that the other elements of 1 Cor. 14.26 were normally written

[1] *1 Peter, A Paschal Liturgy*, 1954.

out? In the very different atmosphere of the twentieth century, I myself, a Free Churchman, have not yet written a prayer in extenso, though I have naturally used on occasions prayers of the ancient Church and still more frequently the Psalms of the Old Testament. Sermons I have never written out, except for examinations and the Press! I am sure that is not exceptional for large numbers of Free Church ministers. That is not to imply that services are conducted without preparation, or that they do not tend to become stereotyped. Every service is drawn up in detail, prayers have their themes selected, and sermons are given prolonged preparation: but the result does not remotely resemble 1 Peter! Any who have been present at the Breaking of Bread in a Brethren assembly will know that such preparation far exceeds what is common among them, who consciously take 1 Cor. 12-14 as their model for worship. Undoubtedly Hippolytus represents a considerable remove from such an ethos, but this raises the real point of issue with Preisker and Cross: they presume that 1 Peter is to be interpreted in the light of Hippolytus rather than of Paul; in my judgment that is a basic error, as erroneous as to assume that the baptismal theology of Hippolytus is the same as that of Paul.

Even from within the liturgical tradition, C. F. D. Moule finds this interpretation difficult. 'I do not find it easy', he writes, 'to conceive how a liturgy-homily, shorn of its "rubrics" . . . could have been hastily dressed up as a letter and sent off (without a word of explanation) to Christians who had not witnessed its original setting'.[1] With that judgment few will be inclined to disagree. Yet Moule in his anxiety not to over-estimate the baptismal associations of the Letter, has seemed to me perhaps to under-estimate their significance. He urges that many other parts of the New Testament are concerned with baptism (e.g. Rom. 6, Col. 2, Heb. 6), but 'in itself it proves no more than that the early Church writers continually had the "pattern" of baptism in mind, and often cast the Gospel into that dramatic form'.[2] One is nevertheless constrained to ask: *Does any other writing of the New Testament contain so much baptismal material in comparable proportions to that of 1 Pt. 1.3-4. 11?* I doubt it. The Letter to the Romans contains much more than 6.1-11; Colossians 2 has the baptismal theme only in vv. 11-15 (though ch. 3 is certainly dominated by baptismal ethics) and Hebrews is much longer than ch. 6. It would be absurd to put forward the thesis that these Letters were written as

[1] 'The nature and purpose of 1 Peter', N.T.S. vol. 3, 1956, p. 4. For more detailed criticism of the theory of Preisker and Cross I would refer the reader to this searching article of Moule's.
[2] Op. cit., p. 4.

baptismal treatises, but it is not absurd to suggest the same of 1 Pt. 1.3–4.11, even though it be a mistaken thesis. Whatever be the truth of its origin, 1 Pt. 1.3–4.11 is unique among New Testament writings in its fullness of baptismal allusions, as a glance through its contents serves to show.[1]

Accordingly, in the present stage of investigations, it would seem justifiable to put forward a modest claim. While proof is not forthcoming, the evidence suggests that 1 Pt. 1.3–4.11 reflects the pattern of baptismal instruction followed by the writer of the Letter, and may reproduce an address given by him to newly baptized converts; its incorporation is perhaps due to the writer having in view young Christians recently won in a forward movement of the Church in the areas to which it is addressed.[2] No one who has been under the necessity of writing pastoral letters, or even of contributing to church magazines, will be surprised at a missionary having recourse to a sermon he has preached when writing an Epistle of this length. Paul himself illustrates the same process on occasion.[3]

[1] In view of the baptismal association of 3.18–22 and 4.1 and the conversion theme of 4.3–5, the whole section 3.18–4.6 ought to be regarded as unitary in its baptismal relation. The same applies to 1.22–2.10; granted that exaggerated claims have been made on behalf of 1.22, it remains that it does allude to the baptismal turning, that 1.23 follows with a reference to regeneration, that 2.1–3 is particularly apt for lately baptized converts (note the baptismal term ἀποθέμενος with which it begins), and 2.4 ff ('Come to him that living stone . . .') is especially suitable as an appeal to converts to be firmly rooted in their new faith and to fulfil their vocation in the Church they have joined. The thrill and joy of a new found life in Christ, referred to by Perdelwitz, is especially discernible in ch. 1: 'Without having seen him you love him . . . you believe in him and rejoice with unutterable and exalted joy, receiving as the outcome of your believing the salvation of your souls' (1.8 f); recent entry on to this faith, love, joy, salvation (with future joyous prospect) is a natural inference from these words, for otherwise they are a very idealized picture of the average Christian attitude. With this agree the underscoring of the consciousness of being heirs to the ages (10–12), the appeal for a changed life in the light of Christ's coming (13–16) and of the priceless redemption of the Lamb of God, (18–22) — all which leads straight into 1.22 ff and is integral to baptismal instruction and theology. The chief remaining section 2.11–3.17 is representative of the ethics that Selwyn has sought to derive from the primitive baptismal catechesis, the outworking of the new life of the baptized in his every-day existence; see Selwyn's essay, 'On the Interrelation of 1 Peter and other New Testament Epistles', in his commentary, *The First Epistle of St. Peter*, 1949, pp. 363 ff.

[2] Following a hint of Windisch, who however considers it unhistorical, op. cit., p. 51. Jeremias has gone a long way towards expressing himself as in the text above, *Die Kindertaufe in den ersten 4 Jahrhunderten*, p. 36. For an excellent discussion on the whole problem see Buse in the symposium *Christian Baptism*, ed. Gilmore, pp. 171 ff.

[3] It would be illuminating to know how much preaching material has been worked up into Romans; chs. 2–3 reflect Paul's approach to Jews, ch. 6 his baptismal instruction, chs. 12–14 his ethical instruction, while chs. 9–11 could well be a synagogue sermon virtually unchanged; see Dodd, *The Epistle to the Romans*, pp. 148 ff. With a product of the standard of Romans as the result of such a mode of composition, none need complain at the method. If the same procedure was adopted in the case of 1 Peter we have a double testimony as to its effectiveness!

If then baptismal instruction be the key to 1 Pt. 1.3–4.11, the chief value of such knowledge will be the understanding gained of associations that clustered about the doctrine in first century Christian teaching. These have become manifest in our discussion of the Letter and they revolve about two focal points. First, the joy of actualized redemption into which the believer enters at baptism and hope of coming glory to which he is baptized in prospect. This theme dominates the opening chapter; its tension of 'now' and 'not yet' is summarized in the opening sentence: 'born anew to a living hope!' The new life is thus lived *by* the grace of the Lamb that was slain and *for* the grace of the revelation of Christ — i.e. in faith and hope (1.13–21). The second point concerns the nature of the life that knows redemption by the Lamb and expects the judgment and resurrection. It is on this aspect that the emphasis chiefly falls in the homily: on holiness (1.13–21) and brotherly love (1.22–25); on the need for growth and realization of one's calling to be a member of the new People of God (2.1–10); on specific applications regarding behaviour towards them that are without (2.12), towards rulers (2.13–17), masters (2.18–20), husbands (3.1–6), wives (3.7), fellow Christians (3.8–12) and persecutors (3.13–17). The contact with the Pauline theology of baptism comes to the fore in these hortatory sections. For the command to gentle submission by servants to masters is underscored by the recollection of the life and death of the Servant of the Lord, into whose patient endurance of suffering for righteousness the believer has been baptized (2.21: 'to this you have been called'). The same association of thought has prompted an appeal to the whole body of the baptized to 'reverence Christ as Lord' when their allegiance to Him is challenged, but with meekness and a pure conscience when abused: 'For it is better to suffer for doing right . . . than for doing wrong. *For* Christ also died for sins. . . . Since therefore Christ suffered in the flesh, arm yourselves with the same principle, for whoever has suffered in the flesh has ceased from sin, so as to live for the rest of the time in the flesh no longer by human passions but by the will of God' (3.14–4.2). The relevance of this to baptism would have been evident, even if the writer had not made the point explicitly in 3.21. As it is, we see in new terms the Pauline appeal to put to death the fleshly life, namely as a call to the *imitatio Christi*, a suffering as He did but withal in fellowship with Him as the resurrected and exalted Lord (3.21 f, 4.1 f). The baptismal creed, the 'pattern of teaching to which you were committed' (Rom. 6.17), has become the pattern of living and dying — of death in life and of life in death. Thus in simpler terms than Romans 6 we see the ethical power of baptism in the name of the Christ; for baptism to the Christ of the cross is to be lived out in a suffering for Christ on whatever cross may be provided, yet ever in the light of the resurrection and parousia. Hence there is no repining: the end is the glory of God in Christ and a doxology (4.11)!

4. I PETER 3.20–21

It is essential to pay particular attention to this crux of New Testament exegesis, to glean what it has to teach on the subject of baptism. The confessional nature of the setting, vv. 18–22, has already been mentioned. It is reasonably clear that confessional elements have been incorporated into the passage, but there is doubt as to their extent and firmness of connection. Not a few consider that the entire passage is taken from a Christological hymn.[1] It is difficult to resist the impression, however, that the reference to Noah and baptism has been inserted by the writer into the context, true though it be that the 'interpolation' was of importance to him. Cullmann[2] and Bultmann[3] consider that the quotation from the confession or hymn extends to vv. 18, 19, 22, while Cross prefers to confine it to vv. 18, 22.[4] It may be prudent to recognize that we have in vv. 18 and 22 a framework of confessional elements or formulae into which the intervening verses have been inserted by natural association and assume nothing as to the original connection of these verses.[5] For our purpose the mention of the 'spirits in prison' has significance through their implication in the Flood and their becoming recipients of the ministry of Christ after his death. Despite the very learned dissertations in which the contrary is maintained, I am convinced that no exegesis of v. 19 is sound that divorces it from 4.6; the primary reference of both statements is the same, and the primary lesson in the writer's mind is to exemplify the universal reach of Christ's redeeming work and the divine willingness that all should know it. The preaching of Christ between his cross and his Easter is intended to prove that the wickedest generation of history is not beyond the bounds of his pity and the scope of his redemption, hence there is hope for *this* generation, that has sinned even more

[1] Windisch includes vv. 20 f in the citation, considering the whole to be a baptismal hymn, op. cit., p. 70, citing for support Feine, *D. Apostolische Glaubensbekenntnis*, pp. 55 f; similarly Lundberg, *La Typologie baptismale dans l'ancienne Église*, p. 101 in dependence on Kroll, *Gott und Hölle*, 1932.

[2] *The Earliest Christian Confessions*, p. 20.

[3] 'Bekenntnis und Liedfragmente im 1 Petrus', *Coniectanea Neotestamentica*, XI, 1947, 1 ff.

[4] Op. cit., p. 32.

[5] So Jeremias, *Z.N.W.*, 1949, pp. 194 ff, cited by Preisker in the appendix to Windisch's commentary, p. 154.

greatly than the Flood generation in refusing the proclamation of a greater Messenger of God and that faces the *last* judgment (4.7).

When God brought the judgment of the Flood upon the earth, an ark was built 'in which (εἰς ἣν) . . . eight souls were brought to safety through water (διεσώθησαν δι᾽ ὕδατος)'. The saying has been unduly complicated by commentators. The preposition διά ('through') is most easily interpreted not in an instrumental sense,[1] since the eight persons were saved by the ark from the waters, nor in a double sense, '*through* the water and *by* the water',[2] but in a local sense: the eight persons were 'brought to safety *through* the water'. The author of the Wisdom of Solomon has used similar language when generalizing about the rescue from sea that Noah experienced:

> It is thy will that the works of thy wisdom should not be idle;
> Therefore also do men intrust their lives to a little piece of wood,
> And passing through the waves by a raft are *safely brought through*.[3]

Josephus employs the same term, declaring 'The ark was strong, so that from no side was it worsted by the violence of the water and Noah and his household *were safely brought through*', διασώζεται (Ant. I, iii.2). The import of v. 20 is therefore clear: Noah and his family were saved in the Flood that overwhelmed their contemporaries.

What relation is conceived by the writer to obtain between this event and Christian baptism? It is indicated in the statement: ὃ καὶ ὑμᾶς ἀντίτυπον νῦν σώζει βάπτισμα. The majority of Continental scholars appear to favour referring the relative pronoun ὅ to its immediate antecedent, ὕδατι, the water, and to render the clause: 'which (water), in a counterpart, now saves you also in the form of baptism'.[4] This is the simplest rendering proposed, but it involves regarding the water as the means of salvation, which is contrary to what v. 20 says of the salvation of Noah and is difficult to harmonize with the immediately following words, '*not* the removal of dirt from the flesh but . . .'.[5]

---

[1] As Lundberg, op. cit., p. 112.

[2] As Gunkel, op. cit., p. 562; J. H. A. Hart, *Expositor's Greek Testament*, V. p. 69; Selwyn, op. cit., pp. 202 ff; Cranfield, op. cit., pp. 86 f.

[3] Wisd. 14.5: διελθόντες κλύδωνα σχεδίᾳ διεσώθησαν. A reference immediately follows to Noah's family 'taking refuge on a raft' in the flood, 'Thy hand taking the helm.'

[4] So Windisch: '. . . das in einem Gegenbild auch euch jetzt rettet als Taufe', op. cit., p. 72.

[5] Selwyn's variation of this is yet more doubtful: 'And water now saves you too, who are the antitype of Noah and his company, namely the water of baptism', op. cit., p. 203. It is antecedently more probable that ἀντίτυπον agrees with βάπτισμα than with ὑμᾶς and that one saving act of God should be viewed as the type of another saving act of God, rather than one group be viewed as the type of another. In 1 Cor. 10.6–11, which Selwyn cites in support of his view, it is clearly the *events* of the Exodus that are the τύποι, which events include the judgments of God as well as the sinful acts of the people.

Reicke therefore proposes to regard βάπτισμα as an apposition to the previous sentence drawn into the relative clause and to view ἀντίτυπον as an adjectival attribute to βάπτισμα, so translating, 'which antitypical baptism now saves you'.[1] I cannot help thinking that it is the unusual term 'antitypical' that makes such a rendering appear acceptable. If we interpret the statement by means of Heb. 9.24, as Reicke would have us do, we must understand it as meaning 'which *copy-* or *shadow-* or *provisional*-baptism now saves you', an idea which the writer to the Hebrews would view as heresy (Heb. 6.2)! It is most unlikely that the writer of this Letter wishes us to understand that Noah's family passing through the waters of the Flood and the Christian passing through the waters of baptism are included within the term 'antitype'. That would imply that there is a higher baptism that both Noah's rescue and Christian baptism alike foreshadow — an idea foreign to this context.

Reluctantly I am compelled to believe with Hort,[2] who is followed in this by Beare,[3] that the neuter nominative relative pronoun ὅ has been corrupted from a primitive ᾧ, and thus that the reading of the later tradition of cursives, which reproduces ᾧ, is a correct reversal of the corruption. It is well known that there was frequent confusion between omicron and omega in our texts, due no doubt to the tendency in the Koine Greek of the first century A.D. to assimilate the vowels o, ω and the diphthong ου in pronunciation.[4] On this reading it will be natural to regard the antecedent of ᾧ as the whole clause that precedes it and so to refer it to the salvation of Noah, translating, 'the counterpart to which now saves you also, I mean baptism'.[5] Is not this the idea which the writer meant to express when he set Noah's salvation in conjunction with Christian baptism? Noah's deliverance through water was a prefiguring of Christian baptism. It is not the prefiguring baptism that saves us, nor the water used in Christian baptism. It is *baptism in the sense to be defined in the next clause that saves* and that answers to the salvation of Noah.

This baptism is said to be 'not the removal of dirt from the flesh but the συνειδήσεως ἀγαθῆς ἐπερώτημα εἰς θεόν'. The negation presumably puts out of court false ideas and forms of baptism, with particular reference to the ceremonial cleansings of Judaism that relate to outward and physical purification, and perhaps also to pagan

---

[1] Op. cit., p. 145.
[2] *Notes on Select Readings*, p. 102.
[3] Op. cit., p. 148.
[4] See Moulton-Howard, *Grammar of New Testament Greek*, vol. II, 1929, p. 44.
[5] So Beare, ibid.

consecrations that produce automatic effects. The positive affirmation is less simple. The most popularly received interpretation has proceeded on the assumption that ἐπερώτημα reflects the basic meaning of ἐπερωτάω, to ask or to question, meaning in this context: 'the *prayer* to God for a good conscience'.[1] I cannot agree with Reicke that the idea of baptism as a prayer is 'quite unthinkable' in a definition of its nature, for the conception of baptism as a vehicle of surrender in faith and obedience to God is inseparable from the thought of prayer in the act of baptism, and the definition so understood would suit the context. Nevertheless there is evidence for an official use of ἐπερώτημα in the sense of oracular declaration, and in more popular usage as the equivalent of the Latin *stipulatio*, the clause in an agreement containing a formal question and consent (ὁμολογία) of two parties making a contract.[2] It seems better to follow this clue and interpret the definition of baptism in our passage as 'the pledge to God proceeding from a good conscience',[3] (taking συνειδήσεως as a subjective genitive) or, 'the pledge to God to maintain a good conscience'[4] (taking the genitive as objective). On either view the 'pledge' is given in response to a demand: the baptismal candidate answers affirmatively to God's request for faith and obedience. It is possible that a formal question from the baptizer and answer from the baptized are reflected in this definition. Selwyn observes that the idea of baptism as a seal of contract between a convert and God is not far removed from that which led to the application of the term *sacramentum*, military oath, to baptism and the eucharist.[5]

But we have not completed the statement. 'Baptism now saves you, not as a removal of dirt . . . but as a pledge to God . . . *through the resurrection of Jesus Christ*'. According to this declaration, the power of baptism is the resurrection of Christ. The first thought in the

[1] So Gunkel, op. cit., p. 563; Hart, op. cit., p. 69; Windisch, op. cit., p. 73; Hauch, op. cit., p. 71; Moffatt, *The General Epistles*, p. 143; Flemington, op. cit., p. 99; Schneider, op. cit., p. 64; Bultmann, *N.T. Theology*, I, p. 136; Greeven, in Kittel's *T.W.N.T.*, vol. II, p. 686; Lundberg, op. cit., p. 115.

[2] See the note on ἐπερώτημα by G. C. Richards, *J.T.S.*, vol. XXXII, 1931, p. 77.

[3] So G. C. Richards, ibid; Selwyn, op. cit., p. 205; Crehan, op. cit., p. 11; Cross, op. cit., p. 32.

[4] Given as an alternative by Beare, op. cit., p. 149. This is the interpretation favoured by Reicke, who however believes that συνείδησις in the New Testament usually denotes a practical direction of the will and attitude, rather than the inner voice of conscience, and translates the phrase, 'an undertaking before God to a loyal attitude of mind', op. cit., pp. 185 ff.

[5] Op. cit., p. 205. It has been observed more than once that this conception of baptism may lie behind the statement of Pliny to Trajan, that Christians, 'bound themselves by an oath (*sacramentum*) not to commit theft or robbery or adultery, not to break their word and not to deny having received a deposit when demanded' — a practical demonstration of the clear conscience pledged at baptism.

writer's mind will be the impartation of new life to the believer (as perhaps in some fashion it might be said that Noah emerged into a new world after the Flood), as indicated in 1.3: 'the Father regenerated us to a living hope by the resurrection of Jesus Christ from the dead'. This is not the identical doctrine of Rom. 6.3 ff but it is close to it. In baptism the Lord who rose from his redemptive death acts for the believer's deliverance from sin and death to new life and righteousness (hence the 'clear conscience'). But the Lord who rose ascended into heaven — Lord of angels, rulers and powers. No power therefore can assail the Christian baptized to his name.[1] The victory of Christ is complete and assures us of our part in the final redemption when we, too, shall know resurrection from God.

The chief lesson of this passage is its emphatic denial that the external elements of baptism constitute either its essence or its power.[2] The cleansing in baptism is gained not through the application of water to the flesh but through the pledge of faith and obedience therein given to God, upon which the resurrection of Jesus Christ becomes a saving power to the individual concerned. Observe carefully: it is not said that the giving to God of an answer saves; the Risen Lord does that, 'baptism saves . . . through the resurrection of Jesus Christ'. But the response is at the heart of the baptism wherein the Lord makes the resurrection effective. Surely we are not interpreting amiss in believing that once more we have the representation of baptism as the supreme occasion when God, through the Mediator Christ, deals with a man who comes to Him through Christ on the basis of his redemptive acts. It is a meeting of God and man in the Christ of the cross and resurrection; it is faith assenting to God's grace and receiving that grace embodied in Christ. This is more important than Noah and the Flood and the disobedient spirits, but all together combine to magnify the greatness of the grace revealed in the suffering and exalted Lord who meets us in the Christian $\beta \acute{a} \pi \tau \iota \sigma \mu a$.

---

[1] So Reicke: 'The spiritual Powers of this world are behind the aberration of the heathen. But the Christian cannot suffer any real harm from them, for by means of baptism into Christ, the Lord of the Spirits, he has been set free in principle from any dependence on the pagan world. In consideration of this fact the believers should, without fear, allow the light of the Gospel to shine out on their pagan environment, however unwilling it may be', op. cit., pp. 200 f.

[2] 'Any magical sacramental conception of baptism is hereby repulsed', Preisker, op. cit., p. 155. See further Gunkel, op. cit., p. 563; Crehan, op. cit., p. 12; Flemington, op. cit., pp. 100 f; Reicke, op. cit., pp. 187 f.

CHAPTER 5

THE DOCTRINE OF CHRISTIAN
BAPTISM IN THE NEW TESTAMENT

(i) *Baptism and Grace*

IN the light of the foregoing exposition of the New Testament representations of baptism, the idea that baptism is a purely symbolic rite must be pronounced not alone unsatisfactory but out of harmony with the New Testament itself. Admittedly, such a judgment runs counter to the popular tradition of the Denomination to which the writer belongs, as it does to some of the significant contributions to the study of baptism that have appeared from theologians of other Churches in recent years. But the New Testament belongs to us all and we all stand judged by it. Few, if any, are concerned to oppose the contention that baptism is 'a beautiful symbol'.[1] The Apostolic writers make free use of the symbolism of the baptismal action;[2] but they go further and view the act as a symbol with power, that is, a sacrament. 'Whoever says sacrament says grace', wrote H. J. Wotherspoon, 'for grace is the differentia of the sacrament, by which it is more than a symbol'.[3] The extent and nature of the grace which the New Testament writers declare to be present in baptism is astonishing for any who come to the study freshly with an open mind. Adolf Schlatter, who was no traditionalist sacramentarian, stated, 'There is no gift or power which the Apostolic documents do not ascribe to baptism'.[4] He meant, of course, that there is no gift or power available to man in consequence of the redemption of Christ that is not available to him in baptism. Though many will expostulate at the statement, there is little doubt that Schlatter is right. On the basis of the exposition offered above, and without any attempt to give exhaustive references, the 'grace' available to man in baptism is said

---

[1] R. E. Neighbour defined baptism as 'a beautiful and expressive symbol of certain basal facts in the redemptive mission of the Lord Jesus Christ, together with certain correlated and dependent ideas', 'The Moral Significance of Baptism', *Review and Expositor*, vol. 6, Louisville, 1911, p. 420.

[2] Especially immersion, Rom. 6.3 f, and the stripping off and putting on clothes, Gal. 3.27, Col. 3.9 f.

[3] *Religious Values in the Sacrament*, 1928, p. 60.

[4] *Die Theologie des Neuen Testaments*, II, *Die Lehre der Apostel*, 1910, p. 495.

by the New Testament writers to include the following elements: forgiveness of sin, Acts 2.38 and cleansing from sins, Acts 22.16, 1 Cor. 6.11; union with Christ, Gal. 3.27, and particularly union with Him in his death and resurrection, Rom. 6.3 ff, Col. 2.11 f, with all that implies of release from sin's power, as well as guilt, and the sharing of the risen life of the Redeemer, Rom. 6.1–11; participation in Christ's sonship, Gal. 3.26 f; consecration to God, 1 Cor. 6.11, hence membership in the Church, the Body of Christ, 1 Cor. 12.13, Gal. 3.27–29; possession of the Spirit, Acts 2.38, 1 Cor. 6.11, 12.13, and therefore the new life in the Spirit, i.e. regeneration, Tit. 3.5, Jn. 3.5; grace to live according to the will of God, Rom. 6.1 ff, Col. 3.1 ff; deliverance from the evil powers that rule this world, Col. 1.13; the inheritance of the Kingdom of God, Jn. 3.5, and the pledge of the resurrection of the body, Eph. 1.13 f, 4.30.

How are we to explain this attribution of the fullness of saving grace to the performance of an outward act like baptism? One answer would take us back to our earliest chapter: such a theology of sacraments is a throw back to primitive religion. Bultmann evidently so understands the position. Explaining the New Testament view he writes: 'The concept "sacrament" rests upon the assumption that under certain conditions supranatural powers can be bound to natural objects of the world and to spoken words as their vehicles and mediators. If the conditions are fulfilled (if, for instance, the prescribed formula is correctly spoken and the material is thereby "consecrated" — i.e. laden with supranatural power), and if the act is consummated according to the prescribed rite, then the supranatural powers go into effect, and the act, which apart from these conditions would be only a purely worldly, natural one like a bath or a meal, is itself a supranatural ceremony which works a miracle'.[1] This reduces the baptism of the New Testament to the level of magic: by the correct recitation of the formula the water is laden with supranatural power, the pronouncement of the name brings the god on the scene and the miracle is performed. From such a standpoint Windisch spoke of Paul's teaching of baptism as due to his 'standing under the *ban* of mystical, messianic and mystery modes of thought'.[2] Such an interpretation of the Apostolic writings seems to me in no small measure due to a habit of interpreting the utterances of the New Testament writers on the lowest plane possible: sacramentalism *can* be magical, therefore it is to be presumed that the sacramentalism of the primitive Church *was*

[1] *New Testament Theology*, I, p. 135.
[2] *Taufe und Sünde*, 1908, p. 172.

magical.[1] Now while it is undeniable that the Church in all generations of its history, including the first, has been prone to lapse into lower forms of sacramentalism,[2] we have not perceived that lapse in the Apostolic teaching itself. Paul in 1 Cor. 10.1 ff gave a clear warning against a magical-sacramental view of the sacraments, and 1 Pt. 3.21 yields an emphatic denial that the external elements of baptism constitute either its essence or its power: 'Baptism saves . . . *through the resurrection of Jesus Christ*'. Does not this very saying point in the direction to which we should look for the solution of our problem? Baptism saves, not because water washes dirt from the body, but as the occasion when a man is met by the Risen Christ. Johannes Schneider pointed out that nowhere in the New Testament is any decisive significance imputed to water, in the sense of its possessing magical sacramental power. In every place except Heb. 10.22 it is unambiguously stressed that it is the Name of Christ, the resurrection of Christ, the Holy Spirit or the Word of God or of Christ that brings the new creation into being: '*They* are the divine powers of salvation and grace that in baptism bring to pass the decisive work within the baptized'.[3] We may add that even in Heb. 10.22 the baptized in his baptism is related to the redemptive act of Christ, and so experiences the cleansing power of the blood of the cross. It is no new thought, but it cannot be too often before our eyes, that the grace offered in baptism, as in the eucharist, is no impersonal influence, injected through material substances, but *the gracious action of God Himself*.[4] This, as we pointed out, is the great lesson of the passive mood of Rom. 6, which perhaps comes to even more pointed expression in

---

[1] For an example of this kind of exegesis, see the lengthy excursus on Rom. 6 in Lietzmann's commentary on the Epistle, *An die Römer*, pp. 65 ff. Windisch considered that Paul taught in that chapter a real annihilation of the sinful organism, ibid.

[2] 1 Cor. 15.29 is probably to be classed as a very early instance of this. For an example of the way in which a cultured man can accommodate himself to sacramentarianism, consider the following statement of J. H. Newman: 'To feel yourself surrounded by all holy arms and defences, with the Sacraments week by week, with the priests' benedictions, with crucifixes and rosaries which have been blessed, with holy water, with places or with acts to which Indulgences have been attached, and "the whole Armour of God" — what can one desire more than this?' Cited by A. Fawkes, *The Modern Churchman*, vol. XV, 1925–6, p. 448.

[3] Op. cit., pp. 78 f.

[4] Grace 'is always God Himself, who in the sacrament gives Himself to us. Grace is God's will in Christ, the very life of God Himself — it is the Holy Ghost working in us', A. Rinkel, Archbishop of Utrecht, 'Christianity, Church and Sacrament', *Theology*, vol. L, 1947, p. 458. 'χάρις cannot be detached from Jesus Christ and therefore for Paul it is not an energizing principle nor an infused quality but the loving kindness of a personal God in action', J. G. Davies; *Spirit, Church and Sacraments*, p. 86. 'What Pentecost means, grace is. . . . It is known to us only as a presence, as the operation in us of a presence, and as the result of that operation',

[continued overleaf]

Col. 2.12: 'You were *buried* with him in baptism, in which also you were *raised* with him through faith in *the working of God who raised Him from the dead*'. As truly as Christ was the object of the working of God's almighty power in the resurrection, so is the believer the object of that same working of God in baptism. The sacrament is the occasion of God's personal dealing with a man in such fashion that he henceforth lives a new existence in the power and in the fellowship of God. The death and resurrection of Christ are not alone the acts of God for man's redemption, they are the pattern of the acts of God in man's experience of redeeming grace.

To speak thus is not to claim to understand all. We can no more give a complete account of our participation in the resurrection of Christ through baptism than we can give a complete account of our anticipated participation in the resurrection of Christ in the Last Day. The perplexity is occasioned not simply by the nature of baptism, as though our embarrassment made a mystery of an unreasonable inconcinnity; the position would not be relieved if we substituted the term 'grace' for 'baptism' in the above sentence. The difficulty — perhaps I should say profundity — in which we are involved is that of attempting to describe the dealings of God with man in baptism or at any other time. Our consolation is drawn from the realization that in baptism we are concerned less with water than with the Living God. We recall in this connection the common sense comment of Bernard Manning: 'God's way with men in Word and Sacrament, as in other things, is sure; but it is past finding out. *Why not say as much?*'[1]

Where the flame of God burns so brightly, yet incomprehensibly, it behoves us to draw near in worship and be grateful (Heb. 12.28).

(ii) *Baptism and Faith*

Christian faith, as distinct from religious faith in general, has to do with the Gospel: 'Faith springs from hearing the message, and the message comes through the proclamation of the Christ', writes Paul (Rom. 10.17). In an earlier passage (v. 9) he sums up that proclamation as the Lordship of Jesus and his resurrection: 'If you confess "with your lips" that Jesus is Lord and believe "in your heart" that

---

Wotherspoon, op. cit., pp. 67 f. 'Baptism is no human manipulation, no secret procedure through which something difficult of attainment is won. The blessings of salvation thereby mediated are given by God', Schnackenburg, op. cit., p. 102. 'Believers' Baptism is primarily God's act. . . . Here Christ gives Himself in all his fullness to those whom He has chosen and called', R. C. Walton, *The Gathered Community*, 1946, p. 164. These citations come from the Old Catholic, Anglican, Reformed, Roman Catholic and Baptist traditions.

[1] *Essays in Orthodox Dissent*, 2nd ed. 1953, p. 76.

God raised him from the dead you will be saved'.[1] Here faith *believes* something about Jesus, it receives the message of his death and resurrection; but 'believe' is paralleled by the term '*confess*', which involves both a statement of belief and a dependence on Jesus confessed as 'Lord'.[2] Paul's thought has a yet more characteristic stamp in Rom. 1.16 f, the 'text' of his exposition to the Romans: The Gospel is 'the power of God for salvation to everyone who believes . . . for in it the righteousness of God is revealed *through faith for faith*' ($\dot{\epsilon}\kappa$ $\pi\iota\sigma\tau\epsilon\omega\varsigma$ $\epsilon\iota\varsigma$ $\pi\iota\sigma\tau\iota\nu$). The concluding phrase of this statement emphasizes faith as the sole mode of appropriation of the Gospel: the revelation of God's righteousness is 'a matter of faith from start to finish'.[3] Such passages are instructive as showing alike the priority of the divine redemptive action and its proclamation over the believing of man, and the nature of faith as man's appropriate answer to God's saving deed. It is perhaps especially this relation of faith to the proclamation of the Gospel that prompted Paul frequently to replace faith by obedience, so indicating that for him obedience is integral to the Christian conception of faith.[4] The Gospel lays a demand on man, to which an obedient response should be given. It calls for a man to cease from himself, to own allegiance to Christ and repose trust in Him. This conception of faith is set forth with particular clarity in the Fourth Gospel, a book written for the avowed purpose of awaking faith in Christ (20.31); it has a whole succession of promises of grace for 'everyone who believes', and it declares that the first 'work' a man must do is to 'believe in him whom He has sent' (6. 29). Such a 'work', of course, is to cease from 'works' and to depend on the Christ from whom alone comes life; that was a 'work' the Jews declined to perform.

All this makes it clear that in the New Testament faith is no mere intellectual acceptance of a set of religious propositions. It has the

---

[1] The language has been accommodated to Deut. 30.12 f but doubtless reflects a primitive formulation of faith, providing clear testimony as to where the emphasis of the earliest Christian preaching lay.

[2] $K\acute{\nu}\rho\iota o\varsigma$ would embrace within itself a whole complex of ideas through its association in the Old Testament with the covenant theology attaching to the name Yahweh and its association in the Hellenistic world with the cult deities and especially the cult of the Emperor. See Dodd, *Romans*, pp. 167 f; Cullmann, *The Christology of the New Testament*, E.T., 1959, p. 195 ff.

[3] Dodd, *Epistle to the Romans*, p. 14. So also Denny, 'In the revelation of God's righteousness everything is of faith from first to last', *E.G.T.*, II, p. 591, and Jülicher, who translates the phrase, 'faith the first word and faith the last', *S.N.T.*, 2nd ed., II, p. 225.

[4] See especially Rom. 10.16, 2 Thess. 1.8, and compare Rom. 1.8 with 16.19. Bultmann renders $\dot{\upsilon}\pi\alpha\kappa o\grave{\eta}$ $\pi\iota\sigma\tau\epsilon\omega\varsigma$ in Rom. 1.5 as 'the obedience which is faith', *N.T. Theology*, I, p. 314.

Lord Christ as its object and calls forth a response of the whole man to Him. To confess Christ is to acknowledge the truth of the Gospel about Him, to turn from the world and self to the God revealed in Him for mercy and deliverance, and in grateful acknowledgement of the divine love, to make of obedience the total surrender of the self. Mind, heart and will are involved in the faith that turns to the Lord, even as the Lord redeems the whole man in his 'spirit and soul and body' (1 Thess. 5.24).

When considering the relation of this faith to baptism, it is impossible to avoid the cognate issue of the relation of faith to grace. Manifestly, the solution of the latter problem (for problem it is) affects the attitude taken to the former; but conversely, belief and practice arising out of the attitude assumed towards faith and baptism have determined much that has been written on faith and grace, and it is notoriously difficult to view the matter without one's confessional spectacles (I admit it of myself, even as I see it in others). The major issue is whether the gift of grace, and therefore of the salvation of God, is in any sense dependent on faith, or whether the reverse is not rather true. There is a strong tendency for the latter position to be adopted and for it to be insisted on that faith is not to be viewed as a condition of grace and salvation. Two reasons are urged in support: (i) to lay down any condition for receiving grace and salvation is to revert to the legalism Paul contested and to deny the Gospel;[1] (ii) faith is beyond the ability of unaided man to produce, it is the gift of God, hence it is misleading to speak of it as a condition of salvation.[2]

Some profound misunderstandings are involved here. If appeal is

---

[1] 'Assert that God's grace can only come to such men as earn it by preceding merit of faith or works, and you have denied all that makes Christianity a religion; you have reduced it to the level of a moral code, though the noblest of codes, no doubt', Kenneth Kirk, 'Magic and Sacraments', *Theology*, vol. XI, 1925, p. 329. 'Our salvation ultimately depends upon something other than our faithfulness within the covenant relationship; that would be a salvation by works, and who then would be saved?' *The Biblical Doctrine of Baptism, A Study Document issued by the Special Commission on Baptism of the Church of Scotland*, 1958, p. 57. It should not go unobserved that these citations so overstate the position that few would wish to assert what is being denied!

[2] 'The over-emphasis on faith, making it a condition of baptism, springs from a Pelagian view of human nature, which imagines that unregenerate man can choose whether to sin or not', J. Heron, 'The Theology of Baptism', *S.J.T.*, vol. 8, 1955, p. 44. Similarly Cremer: 'We have freedom to refuse grace, not the freedom to enter on it. Our unbelief is our free deed which we do in the freest decision', *'Taufe, Wiedergeburt und Kindertaufe, in Kraft des Heiligen Geistes'*, 1917, 3rd ed., pp. 85 f. If it be asked, How then is freedom to believe gained? the answer is given: through regeneration in baptism. 'Regeneration is to believe. . . . To be born of the Spirit is to believe, nothing else. Grace was not imparted to me through my faith but it became my life's salvation, constancy and power through my baptism', op. cit., pp. 98 ff, 104.

to be made to Paul it must be recognized that he fought against making salvation depend on any condition *except* faith, and this Gospel of salvation by grace through faith he opposed to the gospel of works. That he did insist on the necessity of faith is self-evident. When e.g. Paul declared that God set forth Jesus as a means of expiation διὰ πίστεως ἐν τῷ αὐτοῦ αἵματι ('through faith, by his blood', Rom. 3.25) he clearly meant to say that God forgives men *through Christ* and *through faith*. Nobody on the basis of such a juxtaposition equates the significance of faith with that of Christ's redemptive deed, as though in our believing we are partners with Christ in the joint production of our salvation. He is the Redeemer and we the redeemed, He the Giver and we the receivers; by his action He has brought into being a new creation, and faith's part is to affirm its dependence on the Creator-Redeemer who alone can give entrance into his renewed Creation. The nature of Christ's giving and of faith's receiving are of two different orders, to be contrasted, rather than compared. But the necessity for faith's response is nonetheless indisputable. This is underscored by Paul's employing the same expression διὰ πίστεως, used in Rom. 3.25, in Rom. 3.29: 'God is one, and He will justify the circumcized on the ground of faith (ἐκ πίστεως) and the uncircumcized through faith' (διὰ πίστεως — the difference of prepositions is stylistic). To deny the necessity of faith in the light of such statements is to make Paul's words meaningless and to nullify his preaching. Paradoxically enough, this is done in the name of his Gospel! A Lutheran writer found it possible to affirm: 'It is indisputable Reformation teaching that neither the Church nor the individual can add any contribution to the saving deed of God, neither in preaching, nor in hearing, nor in the sacraments. The attempt to teach and to act in any other way, somehow again to introduce man and his activity or the activity of the Church, is the basic temptation which keeps breaking out from the legalistic understanding of the Gospel and of the unevangelical use of the law'.[1] The danger of an assertion of this kind is its ambiguity. If the writer wished to affirm that neither the Church nor the individual can add anything to the once-for-all redemptive act of God in Christ, no one will dissent from it; but if he intended to convey the notion that the redemptive act of God in Christ needs neither proclamation by the Church, nor the hearing of faith by the individual for its end to be achieved among men, it is nonsense. Where the Church does not proclaim the Gospel, and where men do

---

[1] H. Höhler, 'Die theologische Hintergründe des Taufgesprächs', *Evangelische Theologie*, 1948–9, pp. 473 f.

not receive it with the hearing of faith, men live and die in their sins, strangers to the grace Christ has brought for them. Where the Gospel is made known and received, the redeeming grace of the new age is known and received; where it is made known and refused, the judgment of the Last Day is anticipated; and man is responsible for this difference of effect of the Gospel. To describe such a view as 'legalism' is to betray a failure to grasp Paul's teaching and to misapply his terms in a manner of which he would have strongly disapproved.[1]

This position is in no way weakened by a recognition of Paul's doctrine of grace. The priority of God's action over the faith of the Christian extends not alone to his redemptive acts in history but to the divine dealings with the individual. Admittedly it is difficult to point to a clear statement in Paul's letters to the effect that faith is the gift of grace, but his emphasis on the electing grace of God is sufficient evidence to show that he considered grace to be active in faith.[2] Yet the Apostle of grace is also the minister of reconciliation, who sums up his message as, 'We entreat you on behalf of Christ, be reconciled to God' (2 Cor. 5.20). Such an entreaty presumes an ability to respond to it. It is apparent that we stand before the old problem of how to relate the freedom of God in his bestowal of grace with the responsibility of man to repent and yield the 'obedience of faith' to the Gospel. At this stage of history we ought to know better than to attempt a solution of the problem by the denial of either reality; to adopt such an expedient is rapidly to find ourselves in trouble. When Cremer, for example, permitted himself to write, 'God justifies the heathen through the

---

[1] It should be carefully observed that Paul opposed works to faith (Rom. 3.27 ff, Gal. chs. 2–4) and works to grace (Rom. 4.3 f, 11.5 f, Eph. 2.8 f) but never faith to grace; and he never bracketed faith with works as in any respect alike. Mundle protested against the tendency among his fellow Lutherans to do precisely this thing: 'To understand this faith itself as a "work" which could be co-ordinated with the works of the law would have been impossible to the Apostle. Whoever draws such consequences from the Pauline doctrine of grace moves far off from the thought of the Apostle. Even if such reflections cannot be forbidden to the systematic theologian, it must nevertheless be emphasized from the exegetical standpoint that to do it is to introduce into the Pauline utterances an essentially alien point of view and it is to leave out of account the historical connection of the Pauline doctrine of justifying faith', op. cit., p. 102.

[2] So above all Rom. 8.29, 9.6–29. I take it, with most exegetes, that the καὶ τοῦτο of Eph. 2.8 relates to salvation as the gift of God, not to faith through which the gift is given (so Ellicott, *Ephesians*, 3rd ed. 1864, p. 41; Abbott, op. cit., p. 5; Armitage Robinson, op. cit., pp. 156 f; Salmond, 'Ephesians', *E.G.T.*, p. 289; Masson, *Ephésiens*, p. 161; Dibelius-Greeven, op. cit., pp. 66 ff). Lohmeyer considers that Phil. 1.29 implies that faith was granted as a gift to the Philippians, even as their privilege to suffer, *Philipper.*, p. 78, and he may be right, though the allusion is uncertain. Bultmann, in his article πίστις, *T.W.N.T.*, vol. VI, p. 221, contrasts Paul's view with that of Augustine and declares that the former does not teach that faith is the gift of the Spirit, but in his *Theology of the N.T.*, vol. I, p. 329 he cites Phil. 1.29 in proof that Paul regards faith as a gift from Christ.

means of faith in that He through the gift of justification . . . works faith in the heart',[1] he neatly reversed Paul's doctrine of justification by faith to become faith by justification. The result is a perversion of the Gospel! Bishop Nygren put the view much more attractively when he wrote, 'It is not man's faith that gives the Gospel its power; quite the contrary, it is the power of the Gospel that makes it possible for one to believe'.[2] Naturally, it is the Gospel that calls forth faith and its power is the power of Christ proclaimed in the Gospel; but the Gospel is almost always refused to some, when it is preached, and accepted by others; in such circumstances men are divided according as they have or have not faith, and faith becomes, as Asmussen puts it, a 'separating wall' between the hearers.[3] The human element in faith cannot be eliminated nor man's responsibility for his decision denied. It seems that we are compelled to recognize a polarity here, such as Schlatter expressed: 'In faith two characteristics are inherent: *it is worked by God and willed by man*'.[4] We are called on to recognize 'the mystery of free grace and the mystery of free faith'.[5] Beyond this we cannot penetrate.[6]

The relation of faith to baptism is illuminated for us by this recognition of the relation of faith to the Gospel and to grace. For baptism is the embodiment of the Gospel. The objective givenness of baptism lies in its being a representation of the redemptive act of God in Christ, whereby life from the dead became possible for men, and the means of participation in that act and life through participation in the Christ. God Himself must grant this participation, even as He gave the Christ on the cross and raised Him from death. Yet the very term 'participation' (κοινωνία) is meaningless without the assenting will

[1] Op. cit., p. 119. [2] *Romans*, p. 71.
[3] *Der Römerbrief*, 1952, p. 19.
[4] *Der Glaube*, p. 267. His remark in *Theologie d. N.T.*, II, p. 336 is worth noting: 'The statement, that faith is the gift of God, has nothing to do with the idea that it could be in us without our perception and willing. As assurance requires one who knows, so faith must have one who trusts'.
[5] K. Barth, 'The Real Church', *S.J.T.*, vol. 3, 1950, p. 341.
[6] A similar conclusion is forced on us if the relation of faith and grace be considered in terms of faith and the Spirit. That Paul viewed faith in Christ as a gift from the Spirit could be inferred from 1 Cor. 12.3, 2 Cor. 4.13; yet in Gal. 3.2, 14 he unambiguously states that the Spirit is given to faith. Here too, Schlatter would make the double affirmation without attempting to resolve the difficulty: The Spirit is given through faith and faith is gained through the Spirit; the relation is that of a personal fellowship, perfected in the harmonious working together of both, op. cit., p. 366. I have cited Schlatter's great work on faith, for I doubt if any comparable work on the subject exists. But for similar expressions of this same viewpoint, see Denny, *The Christian Doctrine of Reconciliation*, 1918, p. 169; Bartlet, art. 'Regeneration', *H.D.B.*, vol. IV, p. 218; Anderson Scott, *Christianity according to St. Paul*, p. 102; Sommerlath, op. cit., p. 147; Lampe, op. cit., p. 54; Richardson, op. cit., p. 30; J. G. Davies, *Spirit, Church and Sacraments*, pp. 81 f.

of the human κοινωνός. We recall that the statement of the Gospel in Rom. 10.9 embodies the baptismal confession, 'Jesus is Lord'. From the human side baptism is a confession of that faith in Jesus as Lord, a joyful committal of self to Him unto the sharing of his death and resurrection, and an appropriation by faith of the boundless grace the Lord has brought through his redemption. In baptism the Gospel proclamation and the hearing of faith become united in one indissoluble act, at one and the same time an act of grace and faith, an act of God and man.[1] There is, indeed, much to be said for the contention, independently advocated by theologians of varied schools, that in the New Testament faith and baptism are viewed as inseparables whenever the subject of Christian initiation is under discussion, so that if one is referred to, the other is presupposed, even if not mentioned.[2] Care must be taken not to press this beyond warrant, but it is undoubtedly true that in the New Testament it is everywhere assumed that faith proceeds to baptism and that baptism is for faith.[3] This has repercussions on our understanding of both. For example, what was said in the preceding section of this chapter on the grace associated with baptism in the New Testament finds its completion here; for *in the New Testament precisely the same gifts of grace are associated with faith as with baptism*. Forgiveness, cleansing and justification are the effect of baptism in Acts 2.38, 22.16, 1 Cor. 6.11; in 1 Jn. 1.9 forgiveness and cleansing attend the believing confession of sin, while the doctrine of justification by faith in Rom. 3–4 scarcely needs citation. Union with Christ comes through baptism in Gal. 3.27 and is ac-

---

[1] Bultmann sees in Rom. 10.9 evidence that the appropriation in baptism is of the same order as the appropriation of the preached word. 'If, as can scarcely be doubted, Rom. 10.9 is a reference to the confession made at baptism . . . then baptism on the part of him who is being baptized is an act of faith confessing itself. And as acceptance of the word in faith is the acknowledgement of the Lord who is speaking in it, so baptism also brings a man under the domination of the Lord', *N.T. Theology*, I, p. 312.

[2] The saying of James Denney has now become famous, 'Baptism and faith are but the outside and the inside of the same thing', *The Death of Christ*, p. 185. Mundle endeavoured to demonstrate this position in great detail, being convinced that in the Pauline writings πιστεῦσαι includes both faith and baptism, op. cit., pp. 79–124. See also the writers of the Scandinavian trilogy on baptism (*Dopet, Dåben, Dåpen*): 'Everywhere in the New Testament faith and baptism belong together. . . . We find no baptism without faith and no faith without baptism', K. K. Rasmussen, pp. 34 f. 'Where baptism is spoken of faith is presumed, and where faith is spoken of baptism is included in the thought', N. J. Engelsen, p. 58.

[3] I have not seen this more strongly stated than by the Roman Catholic writer Schnackenburg, who affirmed, 'Baptism without faith in Christ is *unimaginable* for the thinking of the primitive Church', citing Mk. 16.16, Acts 16.31, Jn. 1.13. He viewed the relation between faith and baptism as complementary, since they belong together yet have their own significance, op. cit., p. 120. We even find him rebuking a Baptist theologian, J. Schneider, for separating conversion and baptism and virtually denying their inner connection! (op. cit., p. 59, n. 199).

corded to faith in Eph. 3.17. Identification with Christ in his death and resurrection is rooted in baptism in Rom. 6.3 ff, Col. 2.11 f; faith alone is in view in Gal. 2.20, and in Col. 2.12 faith is the means whereby new life is gained in baptism. Participation in Christ's sonship is bound up with baptism in Gal. 3.26 f, since it becomes possible through union with Christ; but in v. 26 faith is explicitly mentioned as the means whereby sonship is possible, and in Jn. 1.12 faith alone is in view. Membership in the Church, the Body of Christ, is through baptism in 1 Cor. 12.13, Gal. 3.27 ff; while it is quite certain that in the New Testament Church membership would have been normally dated from baptism (the Acts shows that exceptions were for a time possible), faith is so strongly the hall mark of the Church that it can be called 'the household of faith' (Gal. 6.10), and union with Christ is, as we have seen, through faith. The Spirit is given through baptism according to Acts 2.38, 1 Cor. 12.13, but to faith in Gal. 3.2, 14. The new life of the Spirit is given in baptism according to Tit. 3.5, Jn. 3.5, but to faith in Jn. 1.12–13. The inheritance of the kingdom is for the baptized in Jn. 3.5 but for faith in Mk. 10.15, Jn. 3.14–18, 5.24, 20.31. One New Testament writer makes the summary statement, 'Baptism saves you' (1 Pt. 3.21); another makes the yet more characteristic assertion, 'By grace you have been saved through faith' (Eph. 2.8); the former asseveration had to be qualified by the writer, but the latter stands luminously self-evident!

This identity of the grace given by God to faith and to baptism has a corollary which appears to me to be inescapable: *God's gracious giving to faith belongs to the context of baptism, even as God's gracious giving in baptism is to faith.* Faith has no merit to claim such gifts and baptism has no power to produce them; all is of God, who brings man to faith and to baptism, and in his sovereignty has been pleased so to order his giving. Faith therefore ought not to be represented as self-sufficient; Christ comes to it in the Gospel, in the sacraments, in the Church, and it needs them all. Nor should baptism be regarded as self-operative. It is wrong to represent the function of faith as merely that of asking for baptism in which God works irrespective of man's attitude, or of understanding what God does in baptism, or of evidencing an intention of making the appropriate response after baptism. Baptism is rather the divinely appointed rendezvous of grace for faith. It is, as Ernst Fuchs has put it, the *goal* of faith,[1] or, according

---

[1] 'God's act demands that it remains faithfully attested. Therefore Paul makes the concept of faith with its goal in baptism (den auf die Taufe zielenden Begriff des Glaubens) the central conception of his theology', *Das urchristliche Sakramentsverständnis*, 1958, p. 31.

to N. P. Williams, 'the indispensable external expression and crowning moment of the act of faith'.[1]

Admittedly both these definitions view baptism from the human point of view, but we are not at liberty to overlook this aspect or to make it of small consequence, any more than we are to make light of the hearing of faith in relation to the Gospel. Faith is needful *before* baptism, that Christ and his Gospel may truly be confessed in it; *in* baptism, to receive what God bestows; and *after* baptism, in order to abide in the grace so freely given and to work out by that grace what God has wrought within (Phil. 2.12 f).

It goes without saying that this theology of faith and baptism, which is found throughout the New Testament, has been constructed by the Apostolic writers on the presupposition that baptism is administered to converts. This is commonly recognized now,[2] though not by all. Cremer has many successors. His statement, 'Faith must be the *effect* of our baptism, if the latter has effected anything at all',[3] is manifestly constructed on the basis of infant baptism as the norm of baptismal practice; whatever may be said of it in the modern institutional church, it is anachronistic in the consideration of New Testament teaching. In the New Testament faith *comes* to baptism; the idea of baptism creating faith is not on the horizon. For the Apostle of justification by faith, who also associated justification with the Name of the Lord invoked in baptism and the Spirit of our God received in baptism (1 Cor. 6.11), it is clear that faith was as integral to the reception of baptism as it was to the reception of justification.[4] That faith is strengthened in baptism is to be expected, since God is present in baptism, so surely as He enables faith. Our duty is to make sure that we neither deny the reality of man's part in faith and baptism nor underestimate the wonder of grace in both. In this respect the authors of the earliest Interim Report of the Church of Scotland's Special

---

[1] *The Fall and Original Sin*, p. 31.

[2] There is no need to multiply names, but one may mention Schnackenburg among the Roman Catholics, op. cit., pp. 116–120; Lindblom, op. cit., p. 217; Schlatter, *Theologie des Neuen Testaments*, II, p. 499, Althaus, *An die Römer*, p. 52, Bultmann, op. cit., p. 135, among the Lutherans; Gore, *The Reconstruction of Belief*, London, 1926, pp. 749 f, Quick, *The Christian Sacraments*, pp. 168 ff, and the Report, *Baptism and Confirmation Today*, London 1955, among Anglican statements; Leenhardt, op. cit., p. 69, D. M. Baillie, *The Theology of the Sacraments*, London 1957, pp. 74 f, of Reformed scholars; P. T. Forsyth, *Church and Sacraments*, London 1917, p. 168, Dodd, *Romans*, pp. 86 f among Congregationalists; Flemington, op. cit., p. 135, J. R. Nelson, *The Realm of Redemption*, London 1951, p. 129 among Methodists.

[3] Op. cit., pp. 105 f, 115.

[4] So W. G. Kümmel explicitly, 'Das Urchristentum', *Theologische Rundschau*, 1950, p. 36.

Commission on Baptism have words worth heeding: 'As in the doctrine of Christ the divine and the human natures must neither be confounded nor be separated, so in the doctrine of the Sacraments the act of God and the act of man must neither be confounded nor be separated. We cannot penetrate the mystery of Christ and understand fully how God and Man are one in Him. That is a Mystery more to be adored than expressed. Nor can we penetrate into the Mysteries of Baptism and Holy Communion, to give precise expression of the relation between the act of God and the act of man in them. As the Church found it necessary to repudiate errors that separated the divine and the human natures in Christ or confounded them, so we must repudiate errors that seek to confound the divine and the human aspects of the Sacraments and those which seek to separate them'.[1]

(iii) *Baptism and the Spirit*

In view of what has been written above on baptism and grace it may seem superfluous to add a special treatment of baptism and the Spirit. Yet much controversy has centred upon this aspect of the meaning of baptism and it is well to clarify our attitude towards it.

G. Kittel voiced the feelings of not a few theologians concerning views currently held on baptism when he wrote: 'The chief mistake appears to me to lie in the fact that there is not a sharp enough distinction drawn between water-baptism and Spirit-baptism'.[2] In his view the New Testament never affirms that water baptism bestows the baptism of the Spirit or calls forth any spiritual change; it is solely a witness to an inner change that has already taken place.[3] This, of course, is the position that has been adopted by many Free Churchmen, but as an exegetical judgment it is hardly to be received. On the contrary, in the Acts and Epistles baptism is the supreme moment of the impartation of the Spirit and of the work of the Spirit in the believer. Ernst Fuchs wrote, 'If the Spirit is received in baptism, that is because his operations are received with baptism'.[4] I would be inclined to affirm that the operations of the Spirit are known because the Spirit is received, but the difference is of small consequence; what is incontestable from the New Testament point of view is the impossibility of dividing *Christ* and his gifts of grace from *the Spirit* whom

---

[1] Op. cit., p. 53.
[2] 'Die Wirkungen der christlichen Wassertaufe nach dem N.T.', *Theologische Studien und Kritiken*, vol. 87, 1914, p. 25.
[3] Op. cit., p. 53.
[4] *Das urchristliche Sakramentsverständnis*, p. 29.

He has given to his Church. We earlier saw that the Apostolic writers attribute to baptism and to faith forgiveness and cleansing, union with Christ in his death and resurrection, and consequently the becoming a new creation in Christ, participation in the sonship of Christ, membership in the Body of Christ, regeneration, deliverance from the evil powers and the entry upon the life of the Kingdom of God. I have omitted from this list the gift of the Spirit, evidenced from Acts 2.38, 1 Cor. 6.11, 12.13, though these Scriptures seem to most exegetes to bear an incontrovertible testimony. Yet in a sense we do not need this testimony, for the New Testament writers could never have postulated such things of a Christian apart from the presence and the operation of the Holy Spirit in the believer. To imagine that one could be in Christ, in the Body, in the Kingdom, participating in the life of the new age and therefore a new creature, born anew and renewed by the Spirit, yet not possess the Spirit of Christ, the Spirit of the Body, the Spirit of the Kingdom and the life of the new age is to be guilty of serious misunderstanding of the Apostolic teaching. Where Christ is, there is his Spirit. A man is either in Christ or not in Christ; the New Testament does not allow of a compromise position. Similarly a man either has the Spirit or has not the Spirit; the Pauline theology allows of no compromise in this respect also. 'If a man does not possess the Spirit of Christ he does not belong to Him' (Rom. 8.9). Hence baptism in the name of Christ, which is a 'putting on' Christ and a setting of a man in Christ, cannot be other than a baptism in the Spirit. So primitive Christianity believed. 'You were washed, you were sanctified, you were justified *in the name of the Lord Jesus Christ and in the Spirit of our God*' (1 Cor. 6.11). 'In *one Spirit* we were all baptized into *one Body* . . . and were all saturated in his outpouring' (1 Cor. 12.13). There can be little doubt that this doctrine would never have been seriously challenged in the Church, as has been the case, had there not existed a strong desire to maintain a particular doctrine of Confirmation, the inspiration of which lies in later liturgical developments rather than in the New Testament writings.[1]

Free Churchmen, and especially Baptists, have had different scruples from these. Their stress on the necessity of faith and con-

[1] See the review of Thornton's book, *Confirmation, its Place in the Baptismal Mystery*, by L. S. Sladden in *Theology*, vol. LVIII, 1955, pp. 69 f. Archbishop Ramsey, in an earlier article, cited Dr. William Bright as urging that when it is believed that a man may be in Christ but not in the Spirit, and in the Body but without the Spirit who is its formative principle, then 'a separation will be established between the work of the Son and the work of the Spirit, to the great disturbance of theological unity', 'The Doctrine of Confirmation', *Theology*, vol. XLVIII, 1945, p. 197. This last contention seems to me to be indubitable and of grave consequence.

version for entry into the Church has led them to emphasize the interior work of grace rather than any external rite of initiation; since Baptists insist on profession of faith prior to baptism, they have tended to conceive of the function of baptism solely as witness to a faith already embraced and an experience of the Spirit already known. 'That Baptism of itself confers the Holy Spirit we do not hold', wrote H. Clarkson. 'The New Testament affords us no warrant for any such assumption. But we do know by experience of the grace of the Lord Jesus mediated to them by the Spirit'.[1] Now I have neither warrant nor desire for doubting that such has been the common experience among Baptists; but neither have I warrant for doubting that the New Testament witnesses to a different experience, in which the reception of the Spirit was not divorced from the confession of Christ in baptism. The primitive Church knew not simply 'a *fresh* experience of grace' in baptism but *the* experience of grace by the Spirit: union with Christ, death and resurrection, new creation, the life of the age to come by the Spirit of the age to come. And this teaching is by no means necessarily inimical to Baptists. In a little volume, which every Baptist minister in Britain has at some time read, Wheeler Robinson wrote, 'When we speak of believers' baptism we mean that baptism in the Spirit of God of which water baptism is the expression. . . . *Baptism, in its New Testament context, is always a baptism of the Spirit*'.[2] It was the writer's conviction that this teaching, far from being alien to Baptist tradition, could be held with a good conscience *alone* by Baptists![3]

Because of this association of baptism with the work of the Spirit, baptism in the New Testament is the true context for regeneration — if I may be permitted to use the term 'true' in its Johannine sense of 'real, authentic' ($\dot{\alpha}\lambda\eta\theta\iota\nu\acute{o}s$). Those who belong to the Catholic, Lutheran and Anglican traditions accept this as a matter of course, but members of other communions find it a stumbling block. Whether or not members of the former Churches realize it, 'baptismal regeneration' is an abomination of desolation to a multitude of believers. Yet there can be little doubt that bad exegesis and fires of

[1] 'The Holy Spirit and the Sacraments', *Baptist Quarterly*, vol. XIV, 1951–2, p. 269. Cf. D. S. Russell: Baptism 'is an experience in which the Holy Spirit, who was given to us at our conversion, deepens still further the experience of God's grace'; 'Ministry and Sacraments', *Baptist Quarterly*, vol. XVII, 1957–8, p. 72.

[2] *Baptist Principles*, 3rd ed. 1938, pp. 27, 77.

[3] Preface to the third edition: 'Those who follow the practice of the New Testament of administering baptism to believers only, ought also to follow it by more closely associating it with the baptism of the Holy Spirit; they are the only people who can do this without risk of "sacramentarianism", since they alone require those moral and spiritual conditions in the recipient of baptism which rule out a materialistic mediation', p. 1.

controversy have greatly beclouded the issue. The New Testament evidence demands care and candour on the part of us all in this matter. Any reader who has read the preceding section on faith and grace will realize that the present writer believes the *ex opere operato* view of baptism to be not alone absent from the New Testament but alien to it. 'Baptismal regeneration' is understood in attachment to that interpretation of baptism. The New Testament writers, however, think of baptism in terms of grace and faith — always grace, always faith. To Paul baptism witnesses a rising from the dead (Rom. 6.1 ff, Col. 2.12), the reception of the Spirit (1 Cor. 12.13), life in Christ (Gal. 3.27), which involves the believer in participation in the new creation (2 Cor. 5.17); the believer puts on the 'new man' (Col. 3.9 ff), which is the new nature bestowed through union with the Second Adam, thus again signifying the life of the new creation.[1] What is all this but 'regeneration' under different images? It is the reality without the word. The reality and the word come together in Tit. 3.5 ff, wherein baptism is spoken of as 'the washing characterized by the regeneration and renewal wrought by the Holy Spirit', the counterpart in the individual's experience of the constitution of the Church at Pentecost to be the Body of Christ, and an anticipation of his participation in the Kingdom of Glory at the last day. As we pointed out, this passage is even more unambiguous than the more famous Jn. 3.5, which speaks of the necessity to be born 'by water and Spirit' if a man would enter the Kingdom of God. But both passages make it plain that regeneration is not by the *agency* of water. In Tit. 3.5 baptism is 'the washing for *the regeneration and renewal that the Spirit effects*'. In Jn. 3.6 it is emphasized: 'That which is *born of the Spirit* is spirit', and again in v. 8: 'The Spirit breathes where He wills . . . so is everyone *born of the Spirit*'. Baptism is thus represented as the occasion when *the Spirit* brings to new life him that believes in the Son of Man lifted up on the cross to heaven (Jn. 3.14 f). As we earlier contended that the New Testament does not permit us to divide the Christ and the Spirit in baptism, so here we must ungrudgingly recognize that the New Testament does not permit us to divide between the new life of Christ and the new life of the Spirit in baptism. The name by which we term that life is of little consequence, but the reality is of eternal consequence. We do despite to the God of grace by making it sound small. That we shall not be tempted to do if we bear steadily in view that the difficulties and the misunderstandings that have surrounded this doctrine

---

[1] For the connection between baptism and the new creation, see J. G. Davies, *Spirit, Church and Sacraments*, pp. 101 f.

through the change of context in which the Churches have set baptism do not arise in the New Testament; they should not be permitted to affect our interpretation of its evidence.

(iv) *Baptism and the Church*

Baptism to Christ is baptism to the Church; it cannot be otherwise, for the Church is σῶμα Χριστοῦ, the Body of Christ. One gains the impression from Paul's writings that this thought must have been much more fundamental to him than it is to us, for his mind passes from the one conception to the other with a spontaneity that suggests it was part of the warp and woof of his thinking. In Gal. 3.27 f, for example, we read: 'All you who were baptized to Christ put on Christ. There is neither Jew nor Greek, there is neither slave nor free, there is neither male nor female, for you are all one (man) in Christ Jesus'. The expression 'one (man)' is significant: it is εἷς, masculine, not ἕν, neuter, which would denote the simple idea of a unity; the 'one man' evidently represents Christ Himself, in the sense of σῶμα Χριστοῦ. The pith of the statement then is simply 'You were baptized to Christ. . . . You are Christ's Body'.[1] Precisely the same mode of thinking is presumed under different images in Col. 3.9 ff: 'You put off the old man with its practices and put on the new man, which is being renewed in knowledge after the image of its creator. Here there cannot be Greek and Jew . . . but Christ is all and in all'. The 'new man' put on in baptism is a shorthand expression for the renewal that takes place through 'putting on' Christ, the Image of God, the Second Adam, the Head of the new creation; in Him social distinctions are abolished, for Christ is *all* and *in all*. Once more the central idea is, 'You "put on" Christ in baptism . . . you became one Body'. The thought is presented without trappings in 1 Cor. 12.13: 'As the body is one and has many members. . . so also is the Christ. For in one Spirit we were all baptized into one Body'. The statement is unusual by its declaration that the Christ, not the Church, is the Body and that baptism is into the Body, not simply to Christ; yet it is wholly in accord with the two sayings we have considered, Gal. 3.27 f, Col. 3.9 ff. The passage makes another elementary yet important fact plain: the Church is *there*, before we are baptized, and we are incorporated into it. The authors of the first Interim Report of the Church of Scotland's Commission on Baptism (1955) rightly lay stress on this, although unfortunately they support it with some questionable exegesis (e.g. the employment of Eph. 5.25–27 for the idea of a once-for-all baptism

[1] So Schlier, *Der Brief an die Galater*, p. 130.

T

of the Church is dubious). Their chief contentions are that through the baptism of the Spirit the Church was incorporated into Christ and given to share in his baptism of blood on the cross, in his baptism in the Jordan, and in his incarnational baptism (=birth) by the Spirit. 'This corporate baptism of the Church stands behind every baptism of every individual and is prior to every administration of the sacrament of baptism. . . . When an individual is baptized within this Church he too is baptized into Christ who was born of the Spirit, who died and who rose again'.[1] Setting aside the manifest over-working of baptismal terminology, the quoted sentence represents an important insight into the context of baptism. The Church existed prior to Pentecost, but the gift of the Spirit was an epochal event for it, of such magnitude as to justify the application of 'new creation' to it. The death and resurrection of Jesus became effective in the lives of the believers and the life and powers of the age to come became available to them when the Spirit came upon them. The followers of the Lord became the Body of Christ in a new dimension as they became the *Koinonia* of the Spirit. Henceforth baptism in the name of the Lord Jesus meant baptism into his Body in the fullest sense, so that baptism itself assumed a transformed meaning. But one fact must be clearly grasped. True though it be that the Church calls men into the *Koinonia* of Christ and the Spirit; true though it be that the Church through its representatives baptizes the converts made, and thus that baptism is properly a Church act: the power of baptism does not derive from the Church. Baptism is what it is through the operation of Christ by His Spirit. He works through his servants, but *He* gives the grace, *He* incorporates into the Body, *He* makes a believer to become a new creation. The only control over baptism that the Church or its representatives has is to grant it or withhold it, but its spiritual significance first and last is from the Lord. This needs to be said because a widespread tendency exists to weaken this insistence. The opinion is frequently voiced that the prime meaning of baptism is that it introduces the convert into the Church and *therefore* into Christ. In considering the meaning of Gal. 3.26 ff we recalled the view, advocated by prominent theologians, that 'in Christ' is an ecclesiological formula: the convert is in the Church and consequently is in Christ. Mozley relates this to baptism and affirms that entry into the Church through baptism gives promise of entry into the Kingdom and *so* brings about the regeneration of the believer and bestows the forgiveness of sins.[2] The sentiment is echoed by the secretary of the Scottish

[1] Op. cit., p. 32.   [2] *The Gospel Sacraments*, pp. 62-7, 71-4.

Commission when he writes, 'It is as incorporation into the Church, the *Koinonia* of the Spirit, that the New Testament speaks of baptism as "regeneration" '.[1] If this reflects the meaning of the Commission's statement it must be repudiated; but it appears to be either a restatement of it or a corollary of it, and in neither aspect does it appear acceptable. When we read Paul's words, 'As the body is one and has many members . . . so also is the Christ', we should remember that in the Hebrew-Greek tradition which he represents the term 'body' is the nearest equivalent for what we mean by person. The body expresses the person, and the person (the Hebrew would not object to 'personality' here) is in every limb and member. The accent in the concept 'Body of Christ' should fall on *Christ* when we so think of the Church. The modern theologian likes to think of the Christ as a corporate personality, and that is a helpful manner of representing the Pauline idea, but we are not thereby justified in thinking only of the adjective 'corporate'; the notion includes the very important idea that Christ's personality is expressed in all the members. The unity of the Body of Christ is not simply sociality but a *Koinonia* in the Spirit after the pattern of the *Koinonia* of the Blessed Trinity (Jn. 17.21 ff). The difficulty for us is to avoid the danger of extremes — of pressing the symbolism of the Body so that one practically deifies the Church, and of thinking exclusively of the members so that one forgets that the Body is Christ. In the symbolism of the Body in 1 Corinthians the Body is Christ and the limbs are the believers; no differentiation is made between the Head and the rest of the Body; the unity is such that Christ cannot be separated from his members nor the members be thought of as members without including them in Him. Yet the members are the Body only because Christ has made them so. The emphasis must fall on Him, as is done explicitly in the modification of the symbol that differentiates Christ as the Head and the Church as the rest of the Body (Ephesians-Colossians). Against all tendencies to a misplaced stress on the Church it must be insisted that baptism takes place in the name of the Lord Jesus, not in the name of the Church. The believer is ingrafted into the Body because he is united with the Christ in his saving work by the Spirit; the reverse is never contemplated in the New Testament. Not even the richness of the symbol of the Body must be permitted to minimize the fact that there is a Redeemer and there are the redeemed, there is a Lord and there are his servants, there is a King and there are his subjects, there is a Judge and there are those to be judged — and judgment begins at the

[1] *S.J.T.*, vol. 8, 1955, p. 49.

house of God! In every symbol representing the relationship of Christ and his people, including that of the Body, Christ dominates the scene. Our theological expositions of the relationship must never blur that priority.

The really important fact, then, of which we have to take account is the indivisibility of the two aspects of baptism: it is baptism to Christ and into the Body. It is at once intensely personal and completely corporate, involving the believer in relationship simultaneously with the Head and with all the members of the Body. 'The special feature of baptism', wrote the Lutheran missionary H. W. Gensichen, 'is that it testifies that there is no saving relation to Christ without the fellowship of the brethren being at the same time grounded with it and in it'.[1] We are called to recognize therefore that a purely private relationship to Christ cannot exist, nor a bestowal of the Spirit given to be enjoyed on our own, as it were, in isolation from the Christian fellowship. *Koinonia* is a key term of the Christian life, connoting fellowship in the Holy Spirit with Christ and with his saints and it takes its rise in baptism to Christ and the Body.

While the Churches have for long paid lip service to this twofold relationship of baptism, so deeply rooted in New Testament thought, it cannot be said that they have recognized it in practice. Most of the churches of the Reformation have been to some extent subject to a false individualism in their administration of baptism. One sees this in the widespread tendency to make baptism an affair of the family rather than of the Church (the fact that it takes place in a church building does not make it a Church act!); a baptism in which the Church is not interested is a curious development of baptism into the Church! Many Free Churchmen have lost all sense of baptism as entry into *membership* of the Church and would be surprized at the suggestion that it should be so regarded. Even Baptists in Britain not infrequently baptize young people on profession of faith without raising the question of Church membership (though that is a fall from Baptist theology rather than an expre: sion of it). The Churches need to be delivered from careless practice, for theoretically they know better than what they do.

But that raises a question. Baptism is to Christ and the Church; but to which Church? The Church visible or invisible? This is one of the questions that have been thrust forward through the exigencies of Church history, particularly through the rise of State Churches, wherein baptism tends to become a token, accepted without question,

---

[1] *Das Taufproblem in der Mission*, p. 35.

of one's membership in a 'Christian' society, a kind of ecclesiastical imprimature of citizenship in a professedly Christian nation. Whatever difficulties were entailed in the administration of baptism in the primitive Church, this was not one of them. Admittedly there were true and false brethren in the Churches, but the communities were composed of ostensible believers in Christ, set in an unbelieving world, and measures existed for the discipline of such as needed it. In such circumstances baptism was a genuine demarcation of the Church from the world which none would consider passing through without strong conviction. Such a consciousness is reflected in the earliest part of the Acts. The summary of Peter's appeal in Acts 2.40, 'Save yourselves from this crooked generation', is followed by the statement, 'They that received his word were baptized and on that day about three thousand souls were added', v. 41. By their baptism the converts thus separated themselves from their unbelieving compatriots and numbered themselves among the followers of the Messiah Jesus; so doing they secured for themselves 'salvation', i.e. the inheritance of the Kingdom, of which the gift of the Spirit was the pledge. It is noteworthy that Luke's statement that three thousand souls were 'added' must be completed in thought by the words 'to the Church', and presumes the existence of the Church already. This is not likely to mean that they were added to the Church that had been born at that moment, but rather that they were joined to the Church constituted by the group of believers in Jesus, who had just received the promise of the Spirit.[1] The Church was not born at Pentecost but it did receive the promised baptism of the Spirit from the ascended Lord (Acts 1.5, 2.33), and the converts of that Day showed by the nature of the fellowship they experienced (2.42–47) that they, too, had been added to the Church by baptism and had received the like gift of Spirit. In this situation the question of the visible and invisible Church could not be expected to rise; the Church consisted of believers in Christ who possessed his Spirit and no further reflection was needful. Nor would distinctions have been obvious when the concept of the Church as the Body of Christ was formulated, for baptism was viewed as entrance into the Church in the fullest sense; so that to be baptized to Christ in Corinth was to become a member of the Church at Corinth and a member of the Body of Christ.

There is a sense in which the Church could be considered to be invisible, inasmuch as the Risen Lord is invisible, and the Spirit who

[1] So G. Westin, *I Urkristen Tid*, p. 8; T. Bergsten, *Dopet och Församlingen*, in the trilogy *Dopet, Dåben, Dåpen*, p. 4.

mediates the *Koinonia* of the Body is invisible, and Christ by the Spirit is the constitutive factor of the Church — He *is* the Body. But the Church is on earth as in heaven, the Lord by his Spirit is among his people on earth, and they, the members of the Body, are very visible; baptism as a visible act is a fitting mode of representing the action of Christ by his Spirit in constituting the Body of Christ on earth. In fact, baptism is extraordinarily well fitted to be a means of incorporating a believer into the Church in both aspects of its nature. When a representative of the Church baptizes a believer, he acts in the name of Christ and in the name of the Church. It is of the essence of the act that in it the exalted Lord appropriates to Himself the one who is baptized in his name and that He incorporates him into the Body; for baptism is a spiritual transaction, signifying baptism in Spirit and into the salvation history of the Christ. Yet baptism takes place in water, a visible act among a visible community of Christ's people; by it a man that was formerly not a member of the people of God is identified with the Lord and his people, and in an open, visible, public fashion he is admitted to the Church. There can be no question of the doctrine of baptism having been formulated by the New Testament writers with a view to its suiting the concept of the Church as both the Body and the Bride of the Risen Christ in the Spirit and the empirical community of his professed followers on earth, for those writers were not interested in such a distinction, but there is no doubt that the twofold aspect of baptism as an external, visible rite, yet having an essentially spiritual (one is tempted to write transcendental) significance, admirably fits it for being the means of entry into the Church in both senses. In the will of God the outward act of baptism, witnessing the outward entry into the Church, should coincide with the baptism of the Spirit and incorporation of the believer into the Body of Christ. How to give expression to that ideal in the empirical Churches of today is perhaps the greatest problem of the Church of Christ.

(v) *Baptism and Ethics*

Our consideration of the New Testament evidence has frequently led us to the recognition that baptism in the Apostolic Church is a moral-religious act. Against those on the one hand who can see in baptism only an external rite, it is to be affirmed that it is a deeply spiritual event, decisive in its consequences even where it is not experienced by the baptized in a catastrophic manner; against those on the other, who would eliminate all significance of the human element from baptism, it is to be affirmed that the repentance and faith of the baptized are integral to New Testament baptism, involving a response of the whole man to the grace of God therein made known. The responsive element of baptism is underscored by the confessional context in which it appears to have been set from the beginning: the candidate confessed Jesus as Lord and faith in the Gospel (Rom. 10.9). In the earliest years the confession must have been very simple and instruction confined to the elements of the Gospel. Of every baptism recorded in the Acts of the Apostles, the circumstances are such as to exclude the possibility that a long period of catechetical instruction preceded them; the baptisms were administered as soon as faith was professed. Not that the primitive Christian communities considered instruction unnecessary, but the teaching was given *after* baptism, just as the baptized converts of Pentecost 'continued in the instruction of the Apostles, in the fellowship, in the breaking of bread and in the prayers' (Acts 2.42).[1] That Christian instruction properly belongs to baptized Christians is a thought that could well be heeded by the modern Churches. Yet it is clear that at an early date the baptismal confession of the *kerygma* was supplemented by an acceptance of certain basic ethical obligations. This appears to have been in Paul's mind in his statement, following on the baptismal exposition of Rom. 6.11: 'Thanks be to God that you who once were slaves of sin became obedient from the heart to the standard of teaching to which you were committed' (Rom. 6.17); both the context and the tense of the verbs (aorist) support the view that baptism was the occasion of receiving the teaching. A similar twofold pattern of doctrine and ethical teaching received at baptism may be reflected in 1 Tim. 6.12 ff: 'Fight the good fight of faith, take hold of the eternal life to which you were called when you made the good *confession* in the presence of many witnesses. . . . I charge you to keep the *commandment* unstained and free from reproach until the appearing of our Lord Jesus Christ'. The first four chapters of 1 Peter, with their admixture of *kerygma* and ethical instruction, suit perfectly the kind of context presumed for the administration of baptism, and we recall the possibility that those chapters may embody a baptismal address.

If the characterization of baptism as a 'religious-moral' act be accepted, it would yet be misleading to give the impression that the 'religious' aspect of baptism was the divine impartation of grace, and the ethical aspect consisted of the candidate's acceptance of moral

---

[1] See the article on this theme by William Robinson, 'A Historical Survey of the Church's Treatment of New Converts, with reference to Pre- and Post-Baptismal Instruction', *J.T.S.*, vol. XLII, 1941, pp. 42 ff.

obligations laid upon him at that time. The basic significance of baptism is participation in the death and resurrection of Christ, with the tremendous consequences that involves of a new life in the Holy Spirit orientated towards the all holy God. The death of the baptized is a death *to sin*, and the life is a life *in* God, a life *after* God, a life *for* God. The divine and human elements in baptism are alike directed to the ending of an existence that is hostile towards God and the beginning of a new one in which the defaced image of God should be renewed in his redeemed creature. This is true of every aspect of the believer's participation in the death and resurrection of Christ. It will be recalled that in Romans 6 participation meant in the first instance an inclusion in Christ's death and resurrection through union with Him, our Representative; it was a becoming 'united with the form of his death' and, in an anticipatory way, with the form of his resurrection: he that is so united with the Son of God in his obedient death unto sin and resurrection in triumph over all powers of sin and death has as little to do with sin and evil powers as the Christ with whom he is joined; the event that marks such participation is both wholly 'religious' and wholly 'ethical' — if ethical be a term we can apply to the holy life of the Risen Son of God in the communion of the Father and the Holy Spirit! Further, this participation in Christ's death and resurrection involved an 'existential' dying to sin and rising to live in the *Koinonia* of the Christ by the Holy Spirit; 'as Christ . . . so also we' is the keynote of this aspect of baptism, in which the baptized suffers a death to his own sin and rises to be a new creation in Christ Jesus, receiving through the Holy Spirit a new existence in the eschatological order that the Redeemer brought into being. This new life from God the Holy Spirit must of necessity be Godward in its nature, partaking of the holiness of his own Being. And finally, participation in Christ's redemptive act meant a renunciation by the baptized of his sinful life, a condemning it to the grave of baptism and a dedication of self into the obedience of Christ. The depth of earnestness with which Paul viewed the renunciation of sin in baptism is reflected in the manner in which he attributed to the Christian an *imitatio Christi* even to the laying down of life — a condemning to death the old life of the old order: 'They that are Christ's crucified the flesh with its passions and desires' (Gal. 5.24); 'You stripped off the old nature with its practices and put on the new nature, which is being renewed in knowledge after the image of its Creator' (Col. 3.9 f). From whatever angle we view it, baptism signifies the end of the life that cannot please God and the beginning of a life in Him and for his glory. In baptism we *put on* Christ; the baptismal life *is* Christ; in so far as it is truly lived it will be Christ-like.[1]

The decisive consideration concerning the new mode of life set before the Christian is that God has already wrought in him the renewal demanded of him. God himself has broken the fetters that formerly chained the believer in the world of sin; He has brought him into the sphere of the divine righteousness and there with given him his Spirit. At the heart of the Pauline baptismal theology lies the conviction that baptism witnesses not alone to a *cleansing* from guilt of sin, but to a *release* from the power of sin. The old existence has been ended by the might of the Redeemer; henceforth the baptized lives by the power of divine grace, in communion with the Risen Lord, and in the possession of the Holy Spirit. If he had ever said with Paul, 'O wretched man that I am! Who will deliver me from this body of death?' he now answers with him, 'God alone, through Jesus Christ our Lord! Thanks be to God! The law of the Spirit of life in Christ Jesus has set me free from the law of sin and death!' (Rom. 7.24 f; 8.2). As Windisch put it, 'Now that he is determined by a newly created way of life, "ought" has become subordinated to "can" '.[2] This is so because the baptized man knows himself to be under grace.

The baptismal ethic is of a unique order. It is the outworking of an achieved redemption, into the power of which he has been drawn. Henceforth the form of that redemption becomes the pattern of the life of the redeemed — and the form, of course, includes the participation of the believer in that redemption in baptism. Bornkamm pointed out a remarkable feature of the Pauline parenesis, obvious as soon as it is mentioned, but foundational for the Christian life, that the exhortations in his Epistles simply repeat what has happened in baptism: 'The content of the appeal is nothing other than dying with Christ, though now carrying it through life; nothing other than living in Christ, living out just *this* life; nothing other than the putting on of the Lord Jesus Christ'.[3] This becomes particularly clear in Col. 3,

---

[1] Schnackenburg raised the question whether the effect of baptism was purely ontic or purely ethical and concluded that it was false to select one alternative, since both aspects were indissolubly joined together in Paul's thought: 'The divine life that is bestowed carries in itself, without thereby affecting the freedom of man, the tendency and inclination to transform the walk of the Christian according to God and his Will', op. cit., p. 160. Bornkamm expressed a similar conviction: 'In that the Christ draws his own into his death and his life, He draws them also into this movement, separating them from sin and giving their life the perpetual direction away from sin to God; the new behaviour accordingly is at once set in association with the new being', *Das Ende des Gesetzes*, p. 45.

[2] *Taufe und Sünde*, p. 172.

[3] Op. cit., p. 47.

where appeal is made for a renewal of the baptismal allegiance to God in Christ: '*You died*, and your life is hid with Christ in God . . . *Put to death* therefore what is earthly in you . . . (vv. 3 and 5). '*Take off* all these things, anger, wrath, malice, slander, foul talk . . . seeing that *you stripped off* the old nature with its practices' (vv. 8–9). '*You did put on* the new nature, which is being renewed in knowledge after the image of its Creator . . . *Put on* then, as God's chosen ones . . . compassion, kindness, lowliness, meekness, and patience, forebearing one another . . . as the Lord has forgiven you, so you also must forgive' (vv. 12–13). The same rationale lies behind the exposition of baptism in Rom. 6. It owes its appearance at this point in the Letter to the Apostle's desire to refute an antinomian response to redemption through grace, 'Let us continue in sin that grace may abound!' Such an attitude is deemed to be an impossible one for Christians to adopt: they had died to sin in baptism, how then could they possibly live in it again? On the contrary; 'We were buried with him by baptism into death . . . that we might walk in newness of life' (Rom. 6. 3 f). Formerly slaves of sin, they had become obedient to the 'standard of teaching' delivered to them at baptism, and thereby become 'slaves of righteousness' — their direction of life had been changed, they were under new ownership and owed no allegiance to their former way of existence. Henceforth their attitude must be: 'Consider yourselves dead to sin and alive to God in Christ Jesus' (v. 11); 'Offer yourselves to God, as men who have been brought from death to life, and your members to God as instruments of righteousness' (v. 13). They are to renew now and perpetually the surrender made in their baptism of body, soul and spirit (the verb in v. 11 is in the present tense, 'Continually consider yourselves dead to sin and alive to God . . .', in v. 13 the aorist, 'Make an offering of yourselves to God . . .'). This was the pattern of life that Paul had adopted for himself: 'I have been crucified with Christ, and it is no longer I who live, but Christ who lives in me; and the life that I now live in the flesh I live by faith in the Son of God' (Gal. 2.20). '. . . always bearing in the body the death of Jesus, that the life of Jesus may also be manifested in the body' (2 Cor. 4.10).

The baptismal pattern of doctrine and conduct appears to be at the root of most of 1 Peter (we have noticed this especially in 1 Pt. 1.3–4.11, but the latter part also contains reminiscences of many baptismal motifs). The joy of redemption entered upon and the wealth of the inheritance anticipated in baptism forms the theme of the opening paragraph of the Letter; it gives place to an outline of the new quality of life to which baptism introduces, determined on the one hand by the redemption through which the new life was made possible and on the other by the goal set before the convert in baptism (viz. the judgment and Kingdom). While the investigation of the baptismal associations of 1 Peter was of particular importance for us, it will be recalled that lists of duties closely parallel to those given in 1 Peter appear elsewhere in the New Testament, notably in Eph. 5–6, Col. 3–4, Jas. 1–4 and more briefly in Rom. 12, Heb. 12. These lists have been investigated by Archbishop Carrington,[1] E. G. Selwyn,[2] and W. D. Davies.[3] The interrelation that exists between these lists makes it reasonably certain that the likenesses are due to the writers of these Letters drawing upon an earlier common tradition, rather than to their borrowing from each other. The key terms in the lists include ἀπόθεσθαι ('put off'), ἐνδύσασθαι ('put on'), ὑποτάσσεσθαι ('submit to'), γρηγορεῖτε ('watch'), στῆτε ('stand'), ἀντίστητε ('resist'), νήψατε ('be sober'); the plausibility that the tradition they embody reflects the primitive baptismal catechesis will immediately be recognized. The last four terms relate especially to the necessity for endurance of persecution from those who would deter the converts from continuing in their faith, and for spiritual alertness in the light of the coming of Christ, the judgment and the Kingdom. The command to submission — of wives to husbands, of servants to masters, of citizens to rulers — presumes a basic code of social duties, needful both for conscience sake, as Paul put it (Rom. 13.5), and for the sake of the good name of the Church (1 Pt. 3.16 f, 4.14 ff). It is generally recognized that this item of the catechesis came from Jewish catechetical instruction; in the view of W. D. Davies[4] and D. Daube,[5] it is possible, and even likely, that the catechetical tradition itself both in concept and content was strongly influenced by the Jewish tradition. If the latter point be conceded, it must be noticed that the tradition has been suffused throughout with the specifically Christian baptismal motifs. The appeal to servants, for example, that they be submissive to their masters, including the overbearing and cruel, is supported by citing the example of the sufferings of Christ, with language deliberately reminiscent of Is. 53 (1 Pt. 2.18 ff). The call for submission to

---

[1] A convenient summary of his views appeared in an article, 'The Baptismal Pattern in the New Testament', *Theology*, vol. XXIX, 1934, pp. 162 ff. They are more fully worked out in his book, *The Primitive Christian Catechism*, 1940.

[2] 'Essay on the Inter-relation of 1 Peter and other N.T. Epistles' in his commentary, *The First Epistle of St. Peter*, 1946, pp. 363 ff.

[3] *Paul and Rabbinic Judaism*, pp. 121 ff.

[4] Op. cit., p. 121.

[5] 'A Baptismal Catechism', in *The New Testament and Rabbinic Judaism*, pp. 106 ff.

authorities is likewise set in the light of the supreme necessity to fear no man but to reverence Christ as Lord and to keep before the mind his example of suffering injustice for the sake of others (3.9–22). The latter appeal concludes, 'Since Christ suffered in the flesh, arm your-selves with the same thought, for whoever has suffered in the flesh has ceased from sin, so as to live for the rest of the time in the flesh no longer by human passions but by the will of God' (4.1 f). Paul's teaching on the necessity to put to death the flesh life is thus here presented in terms of a call to follow in the footsteps of the suffering Redeemer. Baptism to Christ entails a willingness to suffer as He did, but in the light of the fact that the Risen Lord Himself is the power of Christian baptism and of Christian living (3.21); the end of both is the glory of the parousia (1.3 ff, 13). A similar diffusion of specifically Christian baptismal motives appears throughout the parenetic teach-ing of Ephesians-Colossians; relationships among Christians are set in the light of the baptismal putting off the 'old nature with its deeds' and the putting on of the new nature (Col. 3.8 ff, Eph. 4.22 ff); but whereas the statement of this is more Christological in Colossians than in Ephesians (note especially Col. 3.1 ff), the call to wives to submit to their husbands is given in Colossians with the cryptic com-ment 'as it is fit in the Lord' (Col. 3.18), while in Ephesians it is set in the light of the Church's relation to Christ (Eph. 5.21 ff).

In his baptism, thus, the Christian's participation in the redemption of Christ becomes the means of deliverance, the pattern of living, the fount of renewal, and the anticipation of glory. 'Baptism is the appro-priation of the new life, and the new life is the appropriation of bap-tism' said Bornkamm.[1] If this be so we have to do with something more than ethic; this is grace for grace. And only the antinomians do not know that grace means divine *action!*

(vi) *Baptism and Hope*

The baptism of John was essentially an eschatological rite. It was administered in anticipation of the judgment and Kingdom of the Messiah, assuring the repentant of the forgiveness of sins, and so of escape from the Wrath of the Last Day, and sealing them as members of the covenant people to whom inheritance in the Kingdom would be given. The messianic work of judging the world and refining the people for the Kingdom was itself described as a baptism (Mk. 1.8).

In that context the baptism of Jesus took place. The phenomena accompanying it were such as to indicate that the divine intervention,

[1] Op. cit., p. 50.

proclaimed by John, was beginning its course in Jesus' baptism: the heavens were torn apart, the Spirit descended as a dove upon Him and the Voice of the Father declared his messianic status (Mk. 1.10 f). Since both the Messiah and the Spirit belong to the age to come, it is to be inferred that the submission of Jesus to the baptism of John was made of the Father an eschatological act, inaugurating the eschatological deliverance that should issue in the Kingdom. True, the Voice made known the Son as the Servant, designated to fulfil the role of the Servant of the Lord; but whatever unknown ways of suffering and humiliation were ahead, the vision of the opened heaven left no doubt as to their end: it would be the downfall of the evil powers, the gift of the new creation, the glory of the eternal Kingdom and the resurrection from the dead. The baptism of Jesus thus confirmed the authority of John's ministry as summed up in his baptism and added an unexpected actuality to the connection between that baptism and the coming of the Kingdom of God.

Yet the fulfilment of the baptism of Jesus, and therefore of the baptism administered by John, was beyond the ability of John to imagine. The baptism of fire was endured by the Messiah Himself! (Lk. 12.49). And the baptism of the Spirit refined the people of the Kingdom through the cleansing blood of the messianic sacrifice and the power of his resurrection. A fresh baptism was inaugurated, wherein the hope of the Kingdom was set in a new perspective. For this baptism first looked *back* to the accomplished redemption of the cross and resurrection, wherein the Kingdom of God came in a way commensurate with the ministry of the Servant — in weakness and might, in forgiveness and recreative grace; therein hope found a new foothold, in a redeeming act of God that was committed to a consummation. Christian baptism of necessity signifies more than hope, for Christian faith rests in a cry, 'It is finished!' (Jn. 19.30). Yet Christian baptism of necessity includes hope; for the Kingdom and the Christ are veiled from sight, and sin and death are in the world and will not be eradicated till the Christ steps forth and utters his almighty word. The Church occupies a time that no prophet understood — a 'time between the times', as it has been described. 'It is a period in which we may say that the Kingdom has come (since it came with the coming of Christ) and yet has still to come because the final consummation is not yet. Christ is present with us, yet not in a way in which He was present in the days of his flesh, and again not in the way in which we shall enjoy his immediate presence in the final consummation. In this interim period He is present with us through the Holy Spirit in the

Church. And in this interim period the Church is always looking back and looking forward. *That is why the Church needs sacraments.* And in both baptism and the Lord's Supper the Church looks both back to the death and resurrection of Christ, which have to be reproduced in us, and forward to the full enjoyment of the Kingdom. . . .'[1]

Naturally in baptism (as in the Supper) we do more than simply *look* back; we *participate* in the event whereby the Kingdom came! That means that the forward look in baptism is much more than a wistful longing for a place in the Kingdom that is to be; we have been united with the Christ who brought the Kingdom in his death and resurrection and shall complete it in his parousia, and we have received the Spirit who mediates the powers of the Kingdom and is the binding link between the two appearings. The forward look of baptism therefore, by reason of its participation in the event that inaugurated the Kingdom, is an anticipation with joyous confidence of the event that shall consummate it. It is a 'strong encouragement' for those who have fled for refuge to 'seize the hope set before us' (Heb. 6.18).

Baptism is thus an entry into the eschatological order of the new creation. For the primitive Church this was the consequence of the exaltation of Jesus as Messianic Lord; He had by his death and resurrection conquered the evil powers and sent the Holy Spirit of promise. There is little doubt that the manifestations of the Spirit, together with the knowledge that the Messiah had risen from the dead, convinced the early Christians that the last times had dawned and that the blessings attaching to those times were theirs. Apart from the stress laid on the Spirit's manifestations in the Acts, no passage more eloquently speaks of the earliest Christians' consciousness of receiving the blessings of the Kingdom than Heb. 6.4–5: believers in their baptism received the 'enlightenment' of the Spirit, tasted the heavenly gift of Christ's salvation by the Spirit, received the Spirit Himself, discovered the power of God's word that promises forgiveness and life in the Gospel, and experienced the powers of the age to come. These 'powers' would include deliverance from sin and the evil powers, as well as the more positive gift of the life of the coming age. All the blessings of God's new world are bound up with the possession of the Holy Spirit. What Schweitzer wrote of Paul's doctrine of the Spirit was not confined to Paul alone, but was common possession of his contemporaries: 'His conviction that with the resurrection of Jesus the supernatural world-period has begun, makes itself felt in his

[1] D. M. Baillie, *The Theology of the Sacraments*, pp. 69 f.

thinking in all directions, and determines also his conception of the Spirit. Paul inevitably comes to see in the manifestation of the Spirit an efflorescence of the messianic glory within the natural world'.[1] Anyone, however, who had a consciousness of possessing the life of the age to come anticipated with keenest expectation the coming in fullness of that age. The possession of the Spirit brought with it a forward look. So commonly is this attested in the New Testament, it is hardly needful to point to the passages that speak of it, but we recall especially the intense expectation of the End in the early chapters of the Acts; the eschatological context of 'baptisms and the laying on of hands' in Heb. 6.1 f; the description of the baptismal confession in Heb. 10.23 as 'the confession of our hope'; the joyous assurance of the opening doxology of 1 Peter ('By his great mercy we were born anew to a living hope through the resurrection of Jesus Christ from the dead, to an inheritance . . . kept in heaven for you, who by God's power are guarded through faith for a salvation ready to be revealed in the last time', 1.3–5); and the essentially identical though un-apocalyptic expression of confidence in Jn. 3.5, that the baptized in water and Spirit will receive the Kingdom of God.

This eschatological connotation of baptism in the Spirit was deepened by the Christological reference of baptism in Paul's teaching. Since baptism to Christ is baptism to his death and resurrection, the most critical experiences that human beings can know after birth, namely death and resurrection, have already happened to the baptized! They have happened because they happened to Christ; the baptized died and rose in *his* death and resurrection. They have happened because the union of the baptized with Christ ended their old God-estranged life, as they assented to the divine judgment on sin, and received life in Christ in the power of the Holy Spirit. Henceforth they share in the existence of the new creation, brought into being in the resurrection of Christ. Such is the basic teaching of Paul presumed in Rom. 6.4 ff and Col. 3.1 ff. But of course he could not stay at that point. He had to press on to its logical conclusion in the future: 'If we died with Christ, we believe that we shall also live with Him' (Rom. 6.8). 'You died and your life is hid with Christ in God. When Christ, who is our life, shall appear, then you also will appear with him in glory' (Col. 3.3 f). Dying and rising with Christ in baptism points to the day of the resurrection. He who believes that Christ has raised him to the life of the eternal Kingdom, giving him to participate in the fruits of his own Easter, must go on to anticipate that Christ will

[1] *The Mysticism of Paul*, p. 166.

raise him from death to the glory of the consummated Kingdom at the parousia. 'The day of baptism presses forward and calls for the day of the Lord', wrote Schnackenburg. 'The sacramental dying and rising with Christ imperatively demands the (bodily) resurrection with Christ at his parousia'.[1] The 'demand' of course is that of logic, not of right. It is the kind of logic contained in the early hymn, cited in 2 Tim. 2.11 ff:

> If we died with Him, we shall also live with Him;
> If we endure, we shall also reign with Him. . . .
> If we are faithless, He remains faithful,
>   For He cannot deny Himself.

Our union with Christ is the assurance that we shall rise with Him in the last day — and not alone live with Him but share the privilege of serving with Him: 'we shall also *reign* with Him!' The promise is guaranteed by the faithfulness of the Redeemer, who stands as the embodiment of the messianic law that glory is entered through suffering (Lk. 24.26, 46); they who tread the path of the cross with Him will tread the way of resurrection with Him.

There is an inner connection between dying and rising with Christ in baptism and rising from death in the last day, a 'logic' which is deeper than that of mere reasonableness and which is rooted in the nature of the *Koinonia* which Christ instituted with us through his redemption. For as the Spirit is the 'first instalment' of the Kingdom and bestows its powers in this age, so resurrection in Christ is the 'first instalment' of the resurrection unto the consummated Kingdom and it is perpetually renewed by the transforming grace of the Risen Lord. Such at least appears to have been the conviction of Paul; and it finds frequent illustration in 2 Corinthians. 'Though our outer man is wasting away, our inner man is being renewed every day', in preparation for 'the eternal weight of glory beyond all comparison' (4.16 f). With this 2 Cor. 3.18 should be compared: 'We all, with unveiled face, reflecting the glory of the Lord, are being changed into his likeness from one degree of glory to another, for this comes from the Lord who is the Spirit'; while the words could include reference to moral renewal, the context demands that the primary significance relates to the eschatological order of the Spirit (as against the fading splendour of the old order), of which the prime characteristic is glory and in which glory the believer participates by the Spirit. The idea is directly connected with baptism in the next chapter. The coincidence

---

[1] Op. cit., p. 199.

of baptismal terminology concerning the 'putting off' the body at death and 'putting on' the new embodiment at resurrection may be purely accidental, but the assurance that we shall receive the new embodiment is rooted in the fact of our having received the Spirit in baptism: 'He who has prepared us for this very thing is God, who has given us the Spirit as the first instalment' (v. 5). On this R. F. Hettlinger comments: 'It is a fresh, but logical deduction from the fact that the Christian already experiences the earnest of the final resurrection in this life; those who have been baptized into Christ have already put on the new Body, that of Christ . . . and can never again be naked'.[1] By this the impression must not be given that resurrection is by growth; the resurrection at the Last Day is a creative act of God, but it is not a creation *ex nihilo*; its relation to the new life in Christ may be compared with that of the consummated Kingdom to the hidden existence of the Kingdom between Easter and the parousia. On any view the Last Day is a bursting forth of glory and not the last stage in organic evolution. The idea is further illustrated in the imagery of the Spirit as the seal of God, put upon the believer in baptism. By that seal the believer is secured as Christ's 'for the day of redemption' (Eph. 4.30). That it is no merely external mark on the believer is obvious. The Spirit is 'the first instalment of our inheritance' (Eph. 1.13 f), above all because He is the means of resurrection to the Kingdom: 'If the Spirit of Him who raised Jesus from the dead dwells in you, He who raised Christ Jesus from the dead will quicken your mortal bodies also by his Spirit that dwells in you' (Rom. 8.11). There is thus a kind of inner necessity of resurrection in the Last Day for those who have been raised in Christ by the Spirit in baptism; for they are joined to the Lord of Easter on his way to the parousia and have received the Spirit of life from Him who is to raise the dead at the last.

Here is an element in the significance of baptism that deserves recovery, for whereas it was once basic to the outlook of the ordinary Christian it can hardly be said to be typical of the faith of our contemporaries: *the beginning of God's dealing with us, which is the true beginning of Christian experience, bears within itself the assurance of our immortality*. As the grace of God in the Gospel gives an unfaltering promise to the believer, so the grace of God in baptism gives sure and certain hope to the believer concerning his final destiny. Dying with Christ the believer has been justified before the bar of God; rising with Christ he has entered the new creation; possessing the Spirit he

[1] '2 Corinthians 5.1–10', *S.J.T.*, vol. 10, 1957, p. 185.

has the first fruits of the Kingdom of God; a member of Christ, he shares his sonship and his inheritance. This is the indicative language of the Gospel, as C. F. D. Moule has called it — idealistic language, absolute language, the language of realized eschatology.[1] Admittedly baptism is *not* the last judgment, any more than it is the final resurrection and the parousia of Christ. The absolute language of faith has nothing to do with the presumptuous antinomianism that imagines that because we are under grace and are heirs of the Kingdom of God, we may be careless of morals. 1 Cor. 10.1 ff has said the needful word against the gross view of the sacraments that sees in them charms against the judgment of God: 'Let him that thinks he stands take heed lest he falls' (1 Cor. 10.12). Wherever there is hope there is warning, for resurrection in the Last Day is inseparable from judgment in the Last Day; the ethical appeal of the entire New Testament gains no little actuality by reason of this duality of the Christian outlook on the future. Nevertheless it remains that baptism declares that we were 'born anew to a living hope through the resurrection of Jesus Christ from the dead' (1 Pt. 1.3). *Baptism means hope!* The earliest Christians were acutely conscious of the eschatological reference of baptism, hence it was possible for it to be perverted at an early date into a practice of baptism for the dead (1 Cor. 15.29). But its power to nerve and inspire is strikingly illustrated in the record of Thecla who, when exposed to wild beasts in the amphitheatre, threw herself into a pond containing 'ferocious seals', uttering the cry, 'In the name of Jesus Christ I baptize myself for the Last Day!'[2] Modern Christians would be strengthened by a fresh grasp of this aspect of the meaning of Christian baptism. For men still look for ground to hope and there is no secure basis for it but in Christ. When we know Him to be 'our life' (Col. 3.4) we need no other.

(vii) *The Necessity of Baptism*

In this chapter we have been concerned to gain a synoptic view of the New Testament teaching on baptism and to grasp its relations to certain basic aspects of Christian thought. Had an early Christian

[1] 'The Judgment Theme in the Sacraments', in Dodd's Festschrift, *The Background of the New Testament and its Eschatology*, ed. W. D. Davies and D. Daube, 1956, p. 468.

[2] The ethos of the saying remains, whatever the judgment as to the historicity of the account. H. W. Gensichen gives some interesting illustrations of the strength of the eschatological significance of baptism among the 'Dschagga' Christians of modern times. The custom of taking a new name at baptism is frequent among them, and of such names Gensichen cites some typical examples: 'Wait for the Life', 'Wait for the Joy', 'I shall not die'. An East African woman is reported to have died with the words, 'I now go to Him whom I saw in baptism', op. cit., p. 64.

teacher handed on in writing a systematic treatment of this subject, which alas none ever did, it is conceivable that he could have included in his discussion all six aspects we have considered, viz. baptism and grace, faith, the Spirit, the Church, the good life, and hope. But I cannot think it would have entered his head to round it off with a section entitled, 'The necessity of baptism'. Who would have wished to raise the question? It would have sounded as strange to a first generation Christian as many other queries characteristic of our time such as, 'Is it necessary for a Christian to join the Church? Is it necessary to pray? Is corporate worship necessary? Is preaching necessary? Is the Lord's Supper necessary? Is the Bible necessary?' Such matters are self-evident, for they belong to the very structure of the Christian life. On the other hand, some necessities are more stringent than others. A Christian suffering from ill health may be desultory in attendance at the worship of his Church and even prevented from going to it. The habits of individual Christians with regard to prayer differ enormously, as does the place which different Churches give to the preaching of the Word and to the Lord's Supper. Yet not even a sick Christian can cease to believe and still remain a Christian. A Church which *prohibited* the reading and proclamation of the Word of God would cease to be a Church. Where in the scale of necessity does baptism stand? At an early point in the progress of the Christian mission a group of Jewish Christians asserted to Gentile believers, 'Unless you become circumcized according to the custom of Moses, you cannot be saved' (Acts 15.2). The issue was fiercely debated and although, according to Acts, the assertion was denied by the assembled Church of Jerusalem, it is clear from Paul's letters that some Jewish Christian teachers never accepted the majority decision, for they continued to infiltrate the Gentile churches with their teaching. Would a debate have arisen if one had asserted, 'Unless you become *baptized* according to the custom of the Church, you cannot be saved'? The answer is not immediately apparent, for the two statements are less similar than their form suggests, since they raise different issues. The principle at stake in the circumcision question was even more portentous than that which would have arisen for a Jew, had he been told, 'Unless you receive proselyte baptism you will not enter the Kingdom'. For Paul, circumcision stood for Judaism and baptism stood for the Gospel; for a Gentile to be circumcized entailed a committal to obedience to the Law of Moses in its entirety (Gal. 5.3), and after baptism to Christ that would mean a virtual cancellation of the believer's professed dependence on Christ (Gal. 5.2);

baptism, however, meant committal to obedience to Christ. The assertion, 'Unless you become baptized you cannot be saved', would have sounded to a first generation Christian like saying 'Unless you believe and are Christ's you cannot be a Christian', and no controversy could have arisen on that basis. It is only because in the development of the Church the whole complex of baptism — faith — confession — Spirit — Church — life — sanctification has been torn asunder that the question has been forced upon us as to the relationship between baptism as an act and that which it represents, and whether the reality can be gained apart from the act with which it is associated in the New Testament. If the issue had been raised in those terms the theologians of the primitive Church would certainly have had something to say, above all the Jew whose reflection drove him to the revolutionary assertion, 'Neither circumcision counts for anything nor uncircumcision, but a new creation' (Gal. 6.15). Indeed, the first generation Church as a whole had cause enough to ponder, had any wished to gather the data.

That the rite of baptism is represented in the New Testament as necessary for salvation is believed by many exegetes. Their reasons may be summarized as follows:

(i) In all parts of the New Testament baptism is presupposed as normative for the acceptance of the Christian faith and entrance into the Church. Its place in the Gospels is naturally different from that in the Acts and Epistles, but even so there is sufficient evidence to show that the former were written in Churches for which baptism was the rule of initiation. Some have contended that baptism was not practised in the earliest years of the Church's existence, but the reasons for this view are dubious, and no one contests that by the time of Paul's activity baptism had established itself generally in the Church. Schlier urged that the very fact that baptism was everywhere presupposed and practised without question suggests that it was viewed as 'a means for salvation and necessary for salvation'.[1]

(ii) The significance attributed to baptism by the Apostolic writers shows that they viewed it as a means of grace. We recall again Schlatter's dictum: 'There is no gift or power which the Apostolic documents do not ascribe to baptism'. Does not that imply that this means of grace is needful for such 'gifts and powers'? Joachim Beckmann, in a book devoted to this theme, affirmed a positive answer: 'God's saving will in Christ comes to men in the means of grace and *only* through them. They are the means or instruments which the

[1] 'Zur kirchlichen Lehre von der Taufe', *T.L.Z.*, 1947, Sp. 326.

exalted Lord as the eternal Mediator uses to procure for us personally and in the present, the grace of God, the forgiveness of sins, the Holy Spirit, the life from God, in order that we may become participators in salvation. Without these means there could be no appropriation of grace, no share in redemption . . . this is the only way by which men can receive the salvation that God has appointed for them'.[1] Apart from the cumulative argument from Apostolic sayings concerning the efficacy of baptism, there is one passage in the New Testament that comes close to the form of, 'Except you are circumcized . . . you cannot be saved', namely Jn. 3.5: 'Except a man be born of water and the Spirit, he cannot enter the Kingdom of God'. On this Schlier remarks, 'How Jn. 3.5 should not serve as a proof for the necessity of baptism for salvation is beyond understanding. Yet its content, positively expressed, is this: Only he who is born of water and Spirit, thus of baptism, can enter the Kingdom of God. . . . If Jn. 3.5 does not express the necessity of water in the sense of necessitas medii, then it also does not stress the necessity of the means, or better the Mediator, who is the Spirit'.[2]

(iii) Faith admittedly is required for the appropriation of salvation but it is questioned whether saving faith can exist without baptism. Cremer denies that it can.[3] Alan Richardson denies its adequacy, for without baptism faith is like a disembodied soul. 'To regard sincere faith as adequate to salvation apart from baptismal incorporation into Christ's Body is sheer "Christian Science" by the standards of New Testament theology; by ignoring the reality of the Body it makes salvation a subjective affair, a disembodied soul-salvation of individuals who have "enjoyed" a certain "experience" . . . . Believing while dispensing with the act of obedience, with the act of baptism, is a kind of docetism, and is thus not belief in the New Testament sense at all. . . . The actual historical baptism of the individual Christian is important precisely in the sense in which the actual historical death of Christ is important. Both are ἐφάπαξ, unrepeatable'.[4]

(iv) Since saving faith cannot exist without baptism, faith without

---

[1] *Die Heilsnotwendigkeit der Taufe, Schriftenreihe der Bekennenden Kirche*, Heft 8, 1951, p. 12. When a multiplicity of sacraments is accepted, the necessity of baptism is the more imperative, since it is the first without which the others cannot be gained. Hence Darwell Stone cites with approval from the Constitutions of Richard Poore, Bishop of Sarum: baptism is 'the gate of all the sacraments and the first plank after shipwreck without which there is no salvation', *Holy Baptism*, 1905, p. 258.

[2] Op. cit., Sp. 327.

[3] Op. cit., pp. 105 f.

[4] *Introduction to the Theology of the New Testament*, p. 348. In brief compass Schneider expresses virtually the same view, op. cit., p. 35.

baptism is obviously unprofitable. 'One receives nothing from his baptism without faith', said Cremer, 'and *one receives nothing from his faith without baptism*'.[1] Mundle contends that, though faith and baptism are inseparable in the New Testament, baptism is the event wherein God acts, hence it is indispensable: 'Through it, and through it alone, does the Christian enter into fellowship with Christ; here that fellowship is grounded, independently of the subjectivity of our faith-knowledge and religious experience'.[2] As a result of this view the missionary Gensichen draws the logical conclusion: Missions must be conducted in order that the heathen may receive baptism whereby they may be regenerated into the Kingdom of God.[3]

I confess to a distaste in entering into controversy on this matter, for I have no wish to detract from the New Testament emphasis on baptism. Yet I cannot but feel that the writers quoted have over-stated their case to a dangerous degree. Oepke warned us long ago that whoever would rightly evaluate the New Testament teaching on baptism and salvation must steadily keep before him the fact that criticism of any purely external, materialistic estimate of religious objects and actions is constitutive for the Bible from the days of the prophets.[4] The writers quoted do not support a materialistic view of baptism, but they stress the material of the sacraments to an extent hardly compatible with awareness of the necessity for prophetic criticism of the 'cult'; in so doing they seem to me to have parted company with the prophets and to have 'progressed' a long way off from Jesus. To gain a balanced view we must recall some further factors in the total picture of the New Testament view of baptism.

(i) The so-called Great Commission of Mt. 28, 18–20, is a call to Mission. Is it really a sober evaluation of that Commission to view it, with Gensichen, as a command to preach the Gospel in order to baptize, that through baptism the nations may receive salvation? I am persuaded that no unprejudiced exegete would so expound the words. Indeed, no commentator to my knowledge has ever advocated that they should be so understood. But is it not a serious thing to advance a view of baptism that involves a distortion of the dominical institution of baptism? The emphasis of the Commission lies on the proclamation of the Word of the cross and resurrection. I appreciate Alan

---

[1] Op. cit., pp. 96 f.
[2] Op. cit., p. 178.
[3] 'We Lutherans must therefore engage in missions in order to bring holy baptism to the heathen, for he that is not born anew of water and Spirit cannot come into the Kingdom of God', op. cit., p. 67.
[4] *T.W.N.T.*, vol. 1, p. 538.

Richardson's point in saying that baptism, like the cross, is ἐφάπαξ, 'once-for-all', but to affirm it to be important 'precisely in the sense in which the actual historical death of Christ is important' is to come close to an equation that ought never to be made and to overlook the margin of ambiguity that exists in the New Testament with regard to baptism.

(ii) The Acts of the Apostles shows that this margin of ambiguity must be taken seriously. As the Gospel has to take the Gospels seriously, and neglects them at its peril, so the Church has to take the Acts seriously along with the Epistles in its attempt to understand itself. The complex phenomena of the Spirit in relation to baptism in Acts compel a dual recognition: first that baptism is closely linked with the reception of the Spirit, howsoever it may be received; secondly that allowance must be made for the freedom of God in bestowing the Spirit, since *God exercises that freedom*. The Day of Pentecost itself provides a supreme example of this freedom. We cannot now know, and it is useless for us to pretend to know, how many of the hundred and twenty had received the baptism of John, how many had received baptism from the hands of followers of Jesus, and how many had received no baptism at all; but we do know that the Spirit came upon all without distinction! Nor can any say how many of the three thousand baptized on that day had received proselyte baptism, how many had received John's baptism, how many had received the baptism of Jesus, and how many had received no baptism; but no differentiation was made by the Apostles, for *all* were baptized in the name of the Lord Jesus. A differentiation, however, between recipients of John's baptism seems to have been made in the case of Apollos and the Ephesian disciples; for whereas they all had received the baptism of John, presumption is strong that Apollos was not baptized in the name of Jesus but the Ephesian disciples were; the reason for the difference, we suggested, lay in the fact that Apollos had received the Spirit of Jesus and the other disciples had not. Why had Apollos received the Spirit? Because he was a believer in Jesus. And he ministered in the name of Jesus powerfully (Acts 18.27). Objection may be taken to citing examples from a time of transition of the Church, yet it must be stressed that these narratives almost certainly would have been duplicated many times over in the Palestinian Church and beyond, when the effects of the labours of John and of Jesus, and of their respective followers, continued to overlap and the news of the Gospel spread through all kinds of channels other than those directly connected with the Apostles. We have no authority for believing that they alone sought and received the Spirit who heard the Word in the 'orthodox' manner. This is in no way to minimize the teaching of the Epistles as to the significance of baptism, but one point is made abundantly clear by the evidence of Acts, namely that *life is more complicated than formulations of doctrine* and the Lord is able to look after the exigencies of life outside the range of the formulas. This is a lesson of incalculable importance for the modern Church, for the Church has become engulfed in a complication of life of such proportions as to make the divergencies of belief and practice in the New Testament Church of small account. For years the Churches have been confused in their thought and practice of baptism; but in the mercy of God the Church is still the Church and not another Body! God is *still* able to take care of the exigencies beyond the formulas! The Apostolic doctrine of baptism remains for our instruction and as our ideal (we deceive ourselves if we think we reproduce it in our Churches), but manifestly it is wrong to put a construction on it that can neither take account of the realities existing in the first generation of the Church nor come to terms with those existing in ours.

(iii) Does Jn. 3.5 mean that, in the view of the Fourth Evangelist, baptism is 'necessary' for salvation? Schlier's interpretation will be recalled: If the water is not necessary as a means, neither is the Spirit; the one is as needful as the other as the means for bestowing regeneration and entrance into the Kingdom. Beckmann speaks similarly: 'The word of God works its will on the baptized through the water, and with the water, and not without the water, which it makes its seal and instrument, for through the word of God the water of baptism is "a water of life rich in grace" '.[1] Such words involuntarily call to my mind the sacred pool of the early Semite; apart from the transcendentalism of the word of God, the concept and language would be easily understood by the primitive. But it does *not* reflect the theology of the Fourth Evangelist. John has unquestionably conjoined water and Spirit for the gift of the new birth, but it is a grave misrepresentation of his teaching to say that water and Spirit are conjoint means for bestowing the gift. John knows that there is a history to baptism in the Church: John the Baptist baptized, the disciples of Jesus baptized, the Church baptizes. He knows that John's baptism did not convey the Spirit, nor the baptism of the disciples of Jesus — the testimony of 7.39 is incontestable. Nicodemus then could have a baptism in water at once, but not a baptism in Spirit; *that* awaited the lifting up of the Son of Man on his cross to heaven and the sending of the Paraclete

[1] Op. cit., p. 22.

from the Father. This shows clearly enough that for the Evangelist there is no life in water, not even when the Word of God in the flesh commanded its use. By the time the Gospel was composed, baptism in water and baptism in Spirit had come together, and the Evangelist was addressing his readers. Yet he himself immediately makes it plain that 'water and Spirit' are not *instruments* for regeneration; the Spirit alone is the Lifegiver. In the sentence following v. 5 we read: 'That which is born of the flesh is flesh, and that which is born of the *Spirit* is spirit'. He did not write and could not write, '. . . and that which is born of *water and Spirit* is . . .'! How can it be affirmed that the word of God does not work 'without the water', when the Evangelist declares that the Spirit in his operations is as free and mysterious as the air in its movement? And how can one dogmatize about the process whereby man is born anew when the Evangelist adds that the operation of the Spirit for the regeneration of man is equally unfathomable? ('So is everyone born of the Spirit', v. 8.) Schlier's grave mistake in interpreting Jn. 3.5 is to fasten on the phrase 'of water and Spirit' and to disregard the context in which the saying is set. The regeneration of man 'of water and Spirit' is possible because of the Incarnation of the Logos, his redemptive death, his exaltation to heaven, the sending of the Spirit and faith in the Word (Jn. 1.12 f, 3.14–18). The one authentic commentary on Jn. 3.5 is Tit. 3.5: 'He saved us according to his mercy, through the washing for *the regeneration and renewal which the Spirit effects*'. Whether the Spirit effects that regeneration and renewal apart from the 'washing', neither Tit. 3.5 ff nor Jn. 3.5 ff consider. What they do declare is that God has given this conjunction, and it is to be received with gratitude. And Jn. 3.8 warns against denying the freedom of the Spirit. The denial is in any case useless — the Spirit breathes where He wills!

(iv) The relation of faith to baptism has already occupied our attention in this chapter. The view of Richardson, that faith without baptism is 'Christian Science' or 'docetism', is an unhappy exaggeration. The classic description of faith in the Pauline Epistles is to be found in Rom. 4, revolving about the typical faith of Abraham. It is part of Paul's polemic in that chapter that this pattern-faith of Abraham's was wholly independent of an external rite — in this case it was circumcision that was regarded as obligatory for faith. To regard as 'Christian Science' the faith that against all hope believes in God's word in steadfast hope, that despises death-in-life because God can give life even to bodies as good as dead, that gives glory to God by believing in the apparently impossible promise of God, is itself a judgment more characteristic of Christian Science than Pauline theology. And how can faith be characterized as 'docetic', when it is directed to the flesh and blood of the Son of Man, crucified and risen for us men and for our salvation? Similarly, when another scholar affirms, 'One receives nothing from faith without baptism',[1] I am tempted to wonder what he did with the life and teaching of Jesus, and in what section of the New Testament Apocrypha he placed the Epistle to the Galatians. His statement should be compared with the following utterance of Wotherspoon: 'The sacraments are central to the life of grace — they are its shrine and core; but they are contained, embraced and supported by faith in that which they "signify, seal and apply". Their place can be spiritually supplied, as in the case of the "baptism of blood", or a quest for baptism which is frustrated by intervening death, or of the spiritual communion of such as die beyond the reach of ministry: but nothing save the gift of faith can supply the lack of faith. *He who has faith, but cannot obtain a sacrament, has Christ: he who has a sacrament but has not faith has nothing*'.[2] Against every tendency of New Testament theologians to minimize the Pauline doctrine of faith it must be insisted that in his teaching faith in God manifested in Christ is *prior* to baptism, and faith receives the gift of God *in* baptism, and faith in God is the constitutive principle of the Christian life *after* baptism. There is not a line in Paul's writings that justifies a reversal of this emphasis in the relationship between the two.

These considerations incline me to the view that it is desirable to avoid the term 'necessary' when considering the meaning of baptism, since the word has given rise to so much misunderstanding. Most Christians would be prepared to accord to baptism a *necessitas praecepti*, or *necessitas non absoluta sed ordinata*. But is it not better to recognize positively that God has graciously given us sacraments for our good and that it is our part to receive them gratefully? It is not customary for us to argue whether it was 'necessary', or in what sense, that Christ should have become incarnate of the Virgin Mary, that He should have been born a Jew, that He should have died on a cross and risen from the dead, that He should have united humanity to Himself in the one Body by the Spirit, that He should bestow on us the Kingdom prepared for us from the foundation of the world; in these events we perceive the unspeakable grace, love, wisdom and power of God, and we adore Him for it. And I see in baptism a gift of grace, at which I wonder the more as I ponder it the more. The sacramental principle

[1] Cremer, op. cit., p. 97.   [2] Op. cit., pp. 119 f.

is rooted in life as God has created it. 'Through the visible as a school we rise up to the appreciation of the invisible', said F. W. Robertson.[1] Hence Quick contended that, if you consider the needs and capacities of the race, the need for a sacramental system in a spiritual religion becomes clear: 'We may say that, although individuals can be, and most undoubtedly are, saved without baptism, yet the world as a whole, so far as experience seems to show, could not'.[2] I would prefer to say that experience shows that the world 'needs baptism', rather than to draw so definite a negative conclusion; but the sentiment otherwise is sound. It is almost poignantly expressed by N. Levison, a converted Jew: 'At this distance of time it is possible for some to argue that baptism is not necessary to becoming a Christian. That may all be very well for the good people of the Society of Friends and others not as good, but for the Hebrew Christian it is a very important matter, for he is cast out from his own people when he confesses his faith in Christ, and thus he needs to have assurance that he is incorporated into the New Israel, for that is in part what Christianity means to him. His reception by baptism into the Church, the Body of Christ, gives him a sense of continuity with the past, and the new relationship to God through the New Covenant realized and ratified in the New Covenant made in his broken body and shed blood'.[3]

It behoves us accordingly to make much of baptism. It is given as the trysting place of the sinner with his Saviour; he who has met Him there will not despise it. But in the last resort it is only a *place*: the Lord Himself is its glory, as He is its grace. Let the glory then be given to whom it belongs!

[1] *Life and Letters of F. W. Robertson*, Phillips Brooks, vol. ii, p. 67.
[2] *The Christian Sacraments*, p. 178.
[3] 'The Proselyte in Biblical and Early Post-Biblical Times', *S.J.T.*, vol 10, 1957, pp. 52 f.

CHAPTER 6

THE RISE AND SIGNIFICANCE OF INFANT BAPTISM

1. THE ORIGIN OF INFANT BAPTISM

(a) INFANT BAPTISM A NEW TESTAMENT INSTITUTION?

'THE Church has received a tradition from the Apostles to give baptism even to little children.' So wrote Origen,[1] and thereby provided our earliest witness to the belief that the Apostles themselves commanded the baptism of infants. How much further back, beyond Origen, that conviction went is a matter of dispute;[2] but we need not doubt that wherever Christians baptized little children they would have assumed that they were continuing Apostolic practice. The widespread hesitations about infant baptism current in the fourth century were set aside, chiefly through the commanding authority of Augustine, and from that time the major part of the Church has given unquestioned adherence to belief in the Apostolic institution of infant baptism. Even today the majority of the baptized in Europe have never heard any other opinion concerning the origin of the rite, and of those who do know that some dissent from it, most assume that such people must be sectaries outside the orthodox Church of Christ.[3] That, however, illustrates the cleavage that can exist between Biblical scholarship and ecclesiastical belief and behaviour, for the rise of the critical study of the Bible has transformed the scene to such an extent that the upholders of the traditional view

---

[1] Comm. in Rom. 519, Patrologia Graeca (Migne) 14, 1047.

[2] Jeremias takes it that Origen could not have asserted the Apostolic origin of infant baptism unless he himself had been baptized as an infant; and since, according to the testimony of Eusebius, Origen's forebears had been Christians, he considers that both the father and grandfather of Origen will have been baptized in infancy, which takes us back into the first half of the second century; see *Die Kindertaufe in den ersten vier Jahrhunderten*, pp. 76 f. A. Argyle, however, has urged that Origen shows no acquaintance with the practice of infant baptism in his period of writing at Alexandria, and he cites Bigg, Harnack and N. P. Williams for the view that Origen became acquainted with infant baptism in the latter period of his life, when living in Caesarea; see *Christian Baptism*, ed. Gilmore, pp. 204 f.

[3] That does not apply to Britain, but the statement is unfortunately true of most Continental countries. Quite recently a prominent German theologian of the Faith and Order Movement addressed a question to me on the assumption that Baptists deny the doctrine of the Trinity!

are now compelled to struggle hard in their endeavour to recall the Churches to the old paths. In the realm of Biblical scholarship the issue of the Apostolic origin of infant baptism is no longer a question of confessional loyalty, any more than the exposition of the Apostolic doctrine of baptism is bound by denominational ties; the formerly unquestioned tradition of the Church is now set in jeopardy from all quarters.[1]

In a review of Continental work on baptism, Reider Bjornard suggested that the present era in baptismal discussions should be seen as beginning with Heitmüller's work, Im Namen Jesu, published in 1903.[2] Significantly that book was written in the conviction that baptism in the primitive Church was of believers only.[3] The same position was adopted in a very different work by F. M. Rendtorff, issued two years later,[4] by Feine in 1907,[5] and by Windisch in 1908.[6] The last named showed himself strengthened in his conviction twenty-one years later, in his well known article written against Oepke.[7] It would be possible to produce an impressive list of scholars who concurred with these men in their judgment, but it should be observed that they were less responsible for the reversal of the traditional belief among New Testament scholars than symptomatic of the change that was taking place everywhere. While these scholars were Lutherans, the strongest statements repudiating the traditional view have come from Reformed scholars. Leenhardt, for example, in his valuable treatment of the New Testament teaching on baptism, wrote, 'It is generally agreed by defenders of infant baptism that the New Testament does not offer us explicit teachings capable of settling the problem of infant baptism. . . . It is the evidence of the facts which lead to this established position; *only the fanatics will contest it!*' He goes on to ask 'Why will people constantly take up arguments which have already been shown a hundred times to be untenable?'[8] This is indeed a startling reversal of the cry, '*Schwärmerer* — Fanatics!' addressed to the Anabaptists by both Lutherans and Reformed. Barth's strictures

---

[1] It is, I trust, clear that I am speaking of the *origin* of infant baptism, not its *legitimacy*, which is quite another issue.

[2] 'Important Works on Baptism from Continental Protestants', in *Foundations*, vol. III, Rochester, New York, 1960, p. 41.

[3] This was further stated by Heitmüller in his more popular volume, Taufe und Abendmahl, 1911, in which, unlike some recent expositors, he saw a proof for his viewpoint in 1 Cor. 7.14, see pp. 15, 19.

[4] *Die Taufe im Urchristentum im Lichte der neueren Forschungen*, 1905.

[5] Art. 'Taufe I, Schriftlehre', *R.T.K.*, 3rd ed. vol. 19, pp. 396 ff.

[6] *Taufe und Sünde im ältesten Christentum bis auf Origenes*, 1908.

[7] 'Zum Problem der Kindertaufe', *Z.N.W.*, vol. xxviii, 1929.

[8] *Le Baptême chrétien*, pp. 66 f.

on the commonly received exposition of baptism in the New Testament are better known and are no less severe: 'From the standpoint of a doctrine of baptism, infant baptism can hardly be preserved without exegetical and practical artifices and sophisms — the proof to the contrary has yet to be supplied! One wants to preserve it only if one is resolved to do so on grounds which lie outside the Biblical passages on baptism and outside the thing in itself'.[1] Here Barth goes beyond our immediate concern, which is to show how scholars have reacted from the accepted belief that infant baptism stems from the Apostles; Leenhardt agreed with Barth's judgment against seeking infant baptism in the New Testament but not against the institution itself.

As an indication of the strength of New Testament opinion on this issue it will be difficult to find anything more significant than the carefully prepared statement of the theological faculty of the university of Tübingen to the 'Landeskirche' of Württemberg. The churches had asked guidance of their theologians concerning the attitude they should adopt towards those of their number in ecclesiastical office who, by reason of their repudiation of infant baptism and acceptance of believers' baptism, were advocating the 'rebaptism' of such as asked for it. The Tübingen Faculty in their reply strongly opposed this practice; while believing it desirable to administer adult baptism along with infant baptism, they went so far as to counsel that clerics who taught, administered, or even regarded as possible 'rebaptism' (i.e. the baptism of adult believers who had been baptized in infancy) ought not to remain in office, and that members who had submitted to it and refused to admit that they had thereby been guilty of heresy should no longer be regarded as members of the Evangelical Church. Despite this, in my judgment, extreme and harsh advice, and their energetic defence of infant baptism, the Tübingen theologians freely admitted: 'A compelling, direct proof from Scripture for the possibility of infant baptism cannot be brought'. The Faculty however were not thereby unduly dismayed: 'The decisive issue is whether infant baptism can be identified with that which baptism essentially is in the light of the New Testament kerygma'.[2] I agree that that is the decisive issue: but that scholars with such strong views on the validity of infant baptism could not find compelling evidence in the New Testament for the practice is highly significant for the nature of

---

[1] Op. cit., p. 49.

[2] 'Gutachten der Evangelisch-Theologischen Fakultät der Universität Tübingen über Fragen der Taufordnung', in *Für Arbeit und Besinnung*, 5. Jahrgang, Nr. 21, 1951, p. 419. The statement was first published in *Zeitschrift für Theologie und Kirche*, August 1950.

the 'proofs' that are still being offered us today and which we must shortly consider.

In Britain the scene has varied widely, owing to the rich variety in the life and organization of the Churches. For Congregationalists[1] and Methodists[2] it has not been difficult to adjust to the new viewpoint. The Presbyterians have been more reluctant to abandon belief in the Apostolic institution of infant baptism; H. R. Mackintosh was one of the few in their ranks who counselled the frank admission that the New Testament provides no evidence for infant Baptism,[3] and T. W. Manson has been even more emphatic in stating the conviction.[4] It is the Anglican theologians, however, who have been most exercised in heart and conscience over this matter. Unlike some of the writers we have quoted, the burden of many of their foremost scholars is not the silence of the New Testament as to infant baptism, which they admit, but still more its eloquent testimony to the fact that the theology of baptism in the Apostolic writings is consistently stated with respect to the baptism of believers. The strong statements of such outstanding Churchmen as N. P. Williams,[5]

[1] H. T. Andrews, e.g. wrote 'There is no shred of real proof that baptism was ever administered to infants in the Apostolic age', 'The Place of the Sacraments in the Teaching of St. Paul', incorporated in Forsyth's *Lectures on the Church and the Sacraments*, p. 150. Forsyth himself agreed with this position: 'The point of origin for infant baptism is obscure . . . it is not in the New Testament', op. cit., p. 198. See also Micklem, *Christian Worship*, p. 248; Dodd, *Epistle to the Romans*, pp. 86 f.

[2] J. R. Nelson affirmed: 'That the New Testament says nothing explicitly about the baptizing of little children is incontestable. . . . In current discussion therefore greater weight must be placed for the defence of the practice upon theological, rather than scriptural grounds', *The Realm of Redemption*, pp. 129 f. It is striking that the only statement as to the significance of baptism in the document, *The Nature of the Christian Church according to the Teaching of the Methodists*, 1937, declares: 'Baptism is for St. Paul a symbol that *believers* have entered into communion with Christ in His death and resurrection', p. 19. Snaith is unusually forthright: 'In these days, for the majority of people, both Christian and non-Christian, the whole matter of baptism is hedged about with confusion and error. In the first days of the Christian Church things were different and the significance of the rite was clear. It was baptism of believers and it was baptism by immersion', *The Methodist Recorder*, June 17, 1948.

[3] See his article 'Thoughts on Infant Baptism', *The Expositor*, 8th Series, vol. XIII, London, p. 195, in which he brushes aside the familiar attempts to find infant baptism in the Lord's blessing of the children, in household baptisms and in 1 Cor. 7.14.

[4] 'As a matter of history, of what in fact went on in the Early Church, the antipaedobaptist case is a very strong one. The argument from silence on the matter of infant baptism is almost complete; and even Oscar Cullmann's powerful argumentation does not seem to me to do more than establish that there *may* have been infant baptisms in New Testament times'. The authority for infant baptism, to Manson, is the faith that the Church learns by experience what Christ means her to do, 'Baptism in the Church', *S.J.T.*, vol. 2, 1949, p. 403.

[5] 'The New Testament references to Initiation assume that its recipients are adults, and that the dispositions required in them are those of conscious and deliberate renunciation of sin and idols, and of personal faith in the allegiance to Christ,' *Ideas of the Fall and Original Sin*, p. 550.

O. C. Quick,[1] the present Archbishop of Canterbury,[2] and Dom Gregory Dix,[3] are impressive and deserve to be pondered by their fellow Anglicans. Even more notable is the persistent acknowledgement of this circumstance in all the Reports of the Anglican Joint Committees on Baptism, Confirmation and Holy Communion. We take as typical the following: 'It is assumed in all the New Testament language about the rites that the convert receives them with a lively faith and a renunciation of the old world'.[4] 'It is clear that the doctrine of baptism in the New Testament is stated in relation to the baptism of adults, as was also the case (with two or three exceptions) in the writers of the first three centuries. In every recorded case of baptism in the New Testament, the Gospel has been heard and accepted, and the condition of faith (and presumably of repentance) has been consciously fulfilled prior to the reception of the Sacrament'.[5] 'In the New Testament Adult Baptism is the norm, and it is only in the light of this fact that the doctrine and practice of Baptism can be understood.'[6] In consequence of this reiterated recognition made by successive reports through the years, the revised orders of service for Baptism and Confirmation, drawn up by the Liturgical Commission to the Archbishops of Canterbury and York in 1958, attempted to put into practice the principle that adult baptism is the norm for Christian initiation: in the service book the baptism and confirmation of adults is treated as the archetypal service and is printed first.[7]

[1] Quick's whole baptismal discussion centres upon the difficulties raised by the fact that the Church has seen fit to change from adult baptism as a normal mode of initiation to that of infant baptism; see *The Christian Sacraments*, pp. 168–80.

[2] 'The Apostolic practice was the admission of adults to the Church and their anointing with the Holy Spirit in the closely linked rites of baptism and confirmation, through faith. The Church must be loyal to this Apostolic fact in its totality, including the important words 'through faith', A. M. Ramsey, 'The Doctrine of Confirmation', *Theology*, vol. XLVIII, 1945, p. 201.

[3] 'From the earliest days repentance and the acceptance of the belief of the church was the condition sine qua non of baptism into the Body of Christ', *The Shape of the Liturgy*, p. 485. Similarly in his lecture, *The Theology of Confirmation*, 'Christian Initiation in the New Testament is described and conceived of solely in terms of a *conscious* adherence and response to the Gospel of God, that is, solely in terms of an *adult* Initiation' (Dix's italics), p. 31. Dix is almost contemptuous in speaking of those who read back modern ideas of baptism and confirmation into the Apostolic age: 'When Bucer and Melanchthon declared that confirmation in the primitive Church was a catechising of children on reaching maturity for the public ratification of their faith, followed by a solemn blessing, they were talking historical nonsense. But they reached this astounding fantasy quite simply and innocently by reading back into antiquity the mediaeval "set up" of universal infant baptism, followed in childhood by the parish priest's instructions . . . leading up to confirmation by the bishop at the end of youth as a solemn ceremony with no very precise meaning', p. 28.

[4] *Theology of Christian Initiation*, 1948, p. 9.

[5] *Baptism and Confirmation Today*, 1955, p. 34.

[6] *Baptism and Confirmation*, 1959, p. x.

[7] *Baptism and Confirmation*, 1959, pp. x, 2 ff.

That a State Church with the peculiar history and dignity of the Church of England should be so advised by its theological and liturgical experts, and that it would be prepared to experiment in its liturgical practice in order to conform to these fresh insights into the New Testament pattern of initiation is a most significant sign of the times, setting an example of courageous thought and action to other Churches, and providing the most striking illustration of that change of opinion we have been considering concerning the nature of the New Testament teaching on baptism.

In view of this widespread change of viewpoint, which I have not in the least attempted to document fully, for I have ignored the contribution of the commentaries to this debate, it is astonishing that Alan Richardson could write in 1957: 'In the light of recent New Testament scholarship *there can be no reasonable doubt* that the practice of baptizing in infancy the children of Christian parents goes back to the days of the Apostles themselves'.[1] It is understandable that this eminent Anglican writer might wish to adhere to earlier views now being revived in certain quarters, but to affirm it in these terms in face of the immense weight of responsible opinion to the contrary is quite *unreasonable!* The exaggeration has a cause, which will be known to every reader of this book. The last decade has witnessed a marked swing of popular opinion back to the traditional ways of thinking of infant baptism and it has been due, not to a sudden change of mind on the part of New Testament scholarship generally, but to two scholars above all, Joachim Jeremias and Oscar Cullmann. They have deeply influenced the production of the Interim Reports of the Special Commission of the Church of Scotland on Baptism, and in turn the members of the Commission have written numerous articles in support of their views, which have deservedly evoked considerable interest and discussion. But we must keep our heads at this juncture and not generalize so rashly as Richardson has done. Both Cullmann and Jeremias are sharply opposed by many Continental scholars, and whereas the theological and historical learning of the Scottish Commission has put the whole Church in their debt, their exegetical work has been inferior and out of harmony with the scientific exegesis of New Testament scholarship generally.[2] Accordingly, it will be our

[1] Op. cit., p. 358, my italics.
[2] It would interest me to know whether there is an occupant of a chair of New Testament studies in any reputable university, in Scotland or out of it, who would endorse the exegesis of sayings relating to Children in the Gospels and Children in the Epistles given in the *Scottish Report* of May 1955, pp. 22–9. Some of that exegesis appears to me to be so improbable, I cannot understand how a responsible body of mid-twentieth century theologians could permit it to be published in their name.

x   [continued overleaf

task to give careful consideration to the grounds offered by these scholars, and those in agreement with them, for the revived conviction that the practice of infant baptism was observed from the first in the Christian Church, and we shall then proceed to consider the significance attached to the rite in contemporary thinking.

(i) Household Baptism and the Solidarity of the Family

Several instances of the conversion of a whole 'house' to the Christian Faith are provided in Acts. The first to be mentioned is that of Cornelius: the angelic message to him, in Peter's account, runs, 'He will declare to you a message by which you will be saved, you and all your house' (Acts 11.14). Of Lydia at Philippi it is recorded, 'She was baptized with her household' (16.15); of the Jailor, 'He was baptized at once, with all who belonged to him' (16.33); of Crispus, the synagogue ruler, that he 'believed in the Lord together with all his household, and many of the Corinthians hearing Paul believed and were baptized' (18.8). Paul, in reviewing his limited baptismal activity in Corinth, wrote, 'I baptized also the house of Stephanas' (1 Cor. 1.16). In the Pastoral Epistles we read of the 'house of Onesiphorus' (2 Tim. 1.16, 4.19), which presumably had a similar history to those mentioned above. This phenomenon of the conversion of a 'house' may have been more frequent than we have commonly allowed. Michel has urged that its importance for the building up of the Church has not been given due recognition, for the family was the natural unit of the Christian community.[1] Certainly it would be an obvious procedure for the Apostle to seek to integrate entire families into the infant communities; by this means the Churches would rapidly find stability and their life and organization assume a natural pattern.

From this general consideration and from the narratives in the Acts two related problems fall to be considered: Were very young children in a family baptized on the entrance of a 'house' into the Church? What was the role of the head of the house in the conversion of those who belonged to him? The questions have been endlessly debated, and the following points are urged in elucidation of them.

(a) It is a priori unlikely that there were no infants in the households converted to Christianity; if such were present they were surely

The temper of the Reports as a whole can be judged by the assertion in the 1959 Report (p. 32) that believer's Baptism is 'essentially a modern phenomenon, first found in 1140 A.D.'! (The reference is to the heretical Paulicians of Armenia, see the 1956 Draft Interim Report with supporting material, p. 91.)

[1] Article οἶκος in T.W.N.T., vol. 5, p. 133.

baptized, as on the analogy of Jewish circumcision and reception into the Hellenistic cults.[1]

(b) The accounts in Acts make this a priori likelihood certain, for Luke continually stresses that the *entire* household was baptized. We read of the conversion, baptism or salvation of 'all your household' (11.14), 'all that belonged to him' (16.33), 'his *whole* house' (18.8). No members of the family therefore could have been excepted from these baptisms.[2]

(c) The term οἶκος, 'house', in Judaism had acquired virtually a technical meaning in religious contexts. Its use in the Old Testament indicates not alone that very young children were included along with the rest of the house but that they were *especially* in mind when it was employed. For examples of this use in the Old Testament see Gen. 17.12 f, 23.27; Ex. 12.27, 30; 1 Sam. 1.21 ff. For parallel examples in the New Testament see 1 Cor. 1.16, Acts 16.15, 33 f.[3]

(d) Even if, by some extraordinary coincidence, there were no children in the households mentioned in the New Testament, the principle of baptism on the ground of another's faith is more strongly exemplified by the baptism of the slaves of the household, since they will have been added to the Church by baptism on the ground of their master's faith. Such a principle must naturally be allowed an extension to the children of the house when such existed.[4]

(e) The role of the head of the house in ancient society had an importance beyond that which pertains in modern society and its application in this particular must be given due recognition. All important questions were decided by the head of the house and his decisions were binding on all. In religious matters the household was a unity, so that if the head of the house decided on a change of allegiance from one religion to another the rest of the members unquestioningly followed suit. That this applied to the conversions in the primitive Church is illustrated in the account of the Philippian Jailor: he asks what he should do to be saved, and the reply is given,

[1] 'Who can believe that in so many families there was not a single infant, and that Jews, who were accustomed to circumcize their infants, and the Gentiles, to purify their infants by lustrations, did not also present them for baptism?', Bengel, *Gnomon*, E.T., vol. II, p. 657.

[2] Jeremias, *Hat die Urkirche . . .*, p. 23, *Die Kindertaufe in den ersten vier Jahrhunderten*, p. 24.

[3] E. Stauffer first presented this argument in an article, 'Zur Kindertaufe in der Urkirche', *Deutsches Pfarrerblatt* 49 (1949), pp. 152 ff. This has not been available to me, but the viewpoint is outlined in his *New Testament Theology*, E.T., pp. 161 f, 298, n. 540.

[4] C. Anderson Scott, art. 'Baptism', Hastings I Vol. *Dictionary of the Bible*, 1909, p. 84.

'Believe on the Lord Jesus Christ, and you will be saved, and your house'; whereupon he was baptized, 'he and all his immediately', and 'he rejoiced with his whole house as he believed on God' (Acts 16.31–33). The implication is surely unmistakable: The Jailor is informed that if *he* believes, *he and his whole house* will be saved; the record states that he did believe and *he and his whole house* were baptized; and they *all* rejoiced because *he* believed in God![1]

(*f*) Baptism in the primitive Church was an eschatological sacrament; it signified being taken out of a world facing the impending Last Judgment and incorporation into the company of the redeemed — an eschatological sealing in the last hour before the catastrophe. In such circumstances a division of families coming over to the company of the saved, purely on the ground of age, is 'utterly improbable'.[2]

On these grounds it is maintained that the practice of baptizing whole households into the Christian Church makes infant baptism in the first generation Churches, 'as good as certain'.[3] It was in this connection, encouraged, no doubt, by the anthropological conceptions involved in this view of family solidarity, that the first Interim Report of the Church of Scotland's Commission on Baptism made its declaration, since frequently quoted, that the idea of believer's baptism only is 'entirely modern, bound up with the Renaissance idea of human individualism and autonomy, and representing a radical divergence from the Biblical teaching about the nature of man'.[4]

It cannot be overlooked, however, that a very considerable number of exegetes are unhappy about the whole train of thought we have reviewed. It is needful to take into account considerations of another kind before coming to a decision about it.

(*a*) The insistence of Jeremias that statements concerning 'all' the household must necessarily relate to all its members without exception would appear to be reasonable. But has he noticed to what the statements in Acts about these 'whole' households refer? Acts 11.14 repeats the word to Cornelius: 'He will declare to you a message by which you will be saved, you and *all* your household'. Peter continues,

---

[1] Compare Jeremias, *Die Kindertaufe . . .*, pp. 26 ff and especially Cullmann: 'Where solidarity in baptism on the basis of the New Testament connection between the family and the body of Christ is presupposed, there can be no question of preceding instruction or of a faith present at the moment of baptism on the part of the member of the family. This is certain, quite independently of the insoluble question whether there were infants in these "houses" or not', op. cit., p. 53.

[2] Jeremias, *Die Kindertaufe*, p. 28.

[3] Oepke, article παῖς, *T.W.N.T.*, vol. V, pp. 648 f. See further Marcel, op. cit., p. 195; Flemington, op. cit., p. 131; Richardson, op. cit., pp. 358 f.

[4] Op. cit., p. 20.

'As I began to speak, the Holy Spirit fell on them just as on us at the beginning. . . . Who was I that I could withstand God?' Hence he commanded them to be baptized. Let us then refer back to 10.44 ff: 'The Holy Spirit fell on *all* who heard the word. And the believers from the circumcision were amazed . . . For they heard them speaking in tongues and extolling God . . . And he commanded them to be baptized in the name of Jesus Christ'. On Jeremias' principle no doubt is to be entertained concerning the meaning of this passage: *all* the house of Cornelius heard the word, *all* received the Spirit, *all* spoke with tongues, *all* were baptized; the infants present also heard the word, received the Spirit, spoke with tongues and so were baptized. To this *no* exception is permissible!

In the episode of the Jailor it is written, 'They spoke the word of the Lord to him and to all that were in his house . . . and he was baptized at once, with all his family' (16.33). *Every* person in the house, then, heard the word of the Lord: the infants were brought out of their beds at this early hour of the morning and listened to the instruction before being baptized; and they rejoiced with the servants at their father's faith in God as they joined in the meal with Paul and Silas (v. 34). Such is the plain meaning of the narrative on Jeremias' principle.

Of Crispus it is stated: 'Crispus the ruler of the synagogue believed in the Lord together with all his household; and many of the Corinthians hearing Paul believed and were baptized' (18.8). Here a notable advance is made. Every member of the household believed in the Lord, including the infants. The Acts of the Apostles teaches that infants have faith. Luther is vindicated by none other than St. Luke!

In so writing I would cite Paul's words, 'I have been a fool! You compelled me to it!' (2 Cor. 12.11). But has not this nonsense an important lesson? Luke, in writing these narratives, does not have in view infant members of the families. His language cannot be pressed to extend to them. He has in mind ordinary believers and uses language applicable only to them. Abuse of it leads to the degradation of the Scripture.

(*b*) The case is not dissimilar with respect to Stauffer's 'οἶκος-formula'. He maintains that the term does not alone include little children but it especially relates to them. Apart from the objection raised by Schneider, that it is by no means clear that Luke the Hellenist understood so technical a Hebraic use of the Greek term,[1] we

[1] Op. cit., p. 37.

have seen that the relevant passages in Acts do not permit the claim that they refer *especially* to children; so to treat them is to make nonsense of them. Unfortunately for Stauffer the one instance of the οἶκος-formula he is able to cite from Paul, as proof for its continuance in Apostolic circles, is 1 Cor. 1.16: 'I baptized also the household of Stephanas'. But the phrase occurs again in the last chapter of the same Letter:[1] 'Now brethren, you know the household of Stephanas were the first converts in Achaia, *they have devoted themselves to the ministry of the saints*; I urge you to be *subject to such and to every fellow worker and labourer*' (16.15 f). Corinth had some gifted members, but these precocious leaders of the flock must have commanded the utmost admiration![2] Perhaps it is better to admit that this οἶκος-formula was unknown to the New Testament writers and to allow the myth to be buried, unlamented.

(c) That the New Testament is acquainted with the idea of solidarity is not to be denied: the very titles Messiah, Son of Man, Servant of the Lord, Second Adam have corporate overtones; the idea of representation is basic to the New Testament soteriology; and the Body of Christ and like symbols imply a solidarity that extends to our fellow Christians as well as to Christ. But it would be false to the New Testament presentation of the Christian Faith to deny on this account the personal element in Christianity. There is a tension between these two factors that must be maintained, and the view we are considering comes perilously close to losing the element which provides the tension. Too often reference is made to the 'Biblical doctrine of man', as though it were on a level throughout. It is notorious, however, that such is not the case. The story of Achan could not have been written in the Acts of the Apostles, nor could anything else in the Old Testament on the same level. Significantly the first example Jeremias reproduces to illustrate Old Testament solidarity is the annihilation of Nob by Doeg the Edomite: 'You shall die, Ahimelech, you and all your father's house', said Saul, on the mistaken assumption that Ahimelech was a traitor; and not alone eighty five priests died, but their city was put to the sword, 'both men and women, children and sucklings, oxen, asses and sheep' (1 Sam. 22.19). And this is cited to help us grasp the nature of family solidarity in the New Testament! In fact, it is not pertinent to contemporary Judaism, let alone the

---

[1] In 1 Cor. 16.15 Paul speaks of the οἰκία Στεφανᾶ instead of the οἶκος Στεφανᾶ, but in such a context the meaning cannot be different.

[2] Schlatter should have saved Stauffer and Jeremias from this slip; he had already seen that the household of Stephanas must have been of mature persons, *Paulus der Bote Jesu*, p. 76.

Christian Church. There is a growing belief among Old Testament scholars that the exaggerated view of family solidarity, which these Old Testament narratives exemplify, was less a corollary of the national religion than a failure to rise to its height. Eichrodt has pointed out that in the Book of the Covenant, which he believes to go back at least to the time of entry into the promised land, collective retribution as a principle of punishment has been eliminated; the Code seeks to maintain a balance between the needful protection afforded by the Law to the community and the claim made on the Law by the individual. 'As the "Thou shalt" of the categorical command is directed at the individual Israelite, whether male or female, full citizen or sojourner in Israel, so the punishment of the Law is executed only on the guilty person, his kin not even being incriminated in those cases where the ancient Eastern conception of justice (as is borne out by Babylonian and Assyrian laws) unhesitatingly includes them, for example in cases of indirect talion.'[1] Moreover, it has to be recalled that this 'Thou shalt' is the word, not of a human legislator, but of the Lord of the Covenant who had brought the nation out of slavery into the freedom of the promised land, so that grace and gratitude are at the heart of this relation, ideally at least. It is apparent that an apostasy from the Lord of the Covenant to the religion of Israel's neighbours entailed a reversion to primitive views of the relation of man to God and to the social entity. That such persisted through the centuries may be seen in the struggle maintained by Jeremiah and Ezekiel with a solidarity which could not distinguish between the responsibility of parent and child and recognize personal accountability: 'In those days they shall no longer say, "The fathers have eaten sour grapes, and the children's teeth are set on edge". But everyone shall die for his own sin; each man who eats sour grapes, his teeth shall be set on edge' (Jer. 31.29 f). Since Jeremiah's contemporaries continued to use the proverb, in spite of his teaching, Ezekiel delivered a whole sermon, pressing home a like conclusion to that of Jeremiah (Ezk. 18). It is not infrequently maintained that Ezekiel over-pressed the lesson, but the fierceness of his teaching illustrates how necessary he felt the struggle to be in order to emancipate his people from an idea of solidarity which was incompatible with personal religion. Neither Jeremiah nor Ezekiel wished to loose the pious individual from the nation; they both anticipated a new covenant of God with 'the *house* of Israel and the *house* of Judah', but it belonged to a time when every

---

[1] *Man in the Old Testament*, E.T., 1951, p. 10.

man would know the Lord. Personal religion was to be the hall mark of the new age.[1]

When the Herald and Bringer of the New Age came, He uttered an even more drastic statement of the necessity for personal obedience to the word of God, though that obedience should tear asunder for the hearer his closest ties on earth. 'If any one comes to me and does not hate his own father and mother and wife and children and brothers and sisters, yes, and even his own life, he cannot be my disciple' (Lk. 14.26). The statement is hyperbolical, but its meaning is deadly plain to any Christian who has known the circumstance depicted by the Lord. It is easy for us, who live in the semi-Christian society in which the Church is tolerated along with all other institutions, to forget that Jesus did not anticipate such a situation of ease for his Church. His Church was the eschatological community of the Last Days wherein the ultimate powers of the universe should come to decision. Here we should call to mind Jeremias' plea that since baptism is an eschatological sacrament and the Church was living in the last days, baptism would not be envisaged as dividing a family. On the contrary, the Lord's teaching contemplates the opposite possibility for his disciples, and the Epistles reflect occasions wherein it had come to pass. Facing the issues of his ministry, Jesus asked, 'Do you think that I came to give peace on earth? No, I tell you, but rather division; for henceforth in one house there will be five divided, three against two and two against three; they will be divided, father against son and son against father, mother against daughter and daughter against mother, mother in law against her daughter in law and daughter in law against her mother in law' (Lk. 12.51–3). This admittedly is a reversal of the natural order of God's ordination for the family, but it indicates the catastrophic effect of the message of Christ in the apocalyptic times initiated by his bearing the divine judgment (Lk. 12.49 f).

[1] I think that the authors of the Ecumenical Biblical Study, *The Biblical Doctrine of Man in Society*, G. E. Wright, London 1954, have exaggerated the situation when they explain the 'individualism' of Jeremiah and Ezekiel purely by their sense of loneliness through being apparently torn by God from their social mooring (p. 27). If it be true that earlier critics failed rightly to estimate the reality of personal religion in the early centuries of Israel's experience, there is no need to underestimate the greatness of the prophetic contribution to this vital aspect of religion. Such is freely recognized by Eichrodt: 'This new way of describing the individual's right attitude to his God not only expresses that bowing before the overwhelming majesty of the holy God, which was proclaimed by the prophets with unheard of passion; but the strongest possible emphasis falls upon the spiritual initiative of the individual, which is no purely passive abandonment but demands a conscious grasp of the newly offered reality of life. . . . The man to whom God's demand comes is recognized as a person, an I, who cannot be represented or replaced by any other. Even his belonging to the nation cannot provide him with a cover behind which he might retreat from the divine demand', op. cit., pp. 21 f.

Clearly, a confrontation of the Gospel, in which the head of the family decides for the rest and they submit to his decision, is far from the mind of Jesus. His word initiates a division more radical than anything the world has known. The very basis of society is shaken. It is the time that precedes the Coming of God to bring his final deliverance (Mic. 7.7 ff). And this is to happen 'henceforth' — that is, from the time of speaking to the parousia! For the first disciples that could but signify a characterization of the period of the Church.

Did the primitive Church experience anything commensurate with this expectation? Assuredly it did. The early dissemination of the Eschatological Discourse (Mk. 13) reflects that the Church already knew something of this situation and was bracing itself for the last trials (cf. Mk. 13.9 ff). Yet more certainly, how has it escaped the notice of the enthusiasts who find proof for their view of family solidarity in 1 Cor. 7.14 that the problem there faced by Paul was the situation wherein a husband had been converted *without* his wife and a wife *without* her husband? The fact that the Corinthians were constrained to write to Paul about the matter shows that the problem was not ephemeral: the unconverted husbands and the unconverted wives were not relenting. Apart from the rightness of sharing life with a pagan (which was the basic consideration) there can be no doubt that these circumstances brought difficulties and tensions, which may well be in the mind of the author of 1 Pt. 3.1–6. To say the least, it is plain that the early Church had experience of other kinds of conversions than those of whole households and to exaggerate the normality of the latter is to forget the situation out of which the Gospels came.

Above all, we should return to the text of Acts and look again at the narrative of the Philippian Jailor. Here it should be admitted in candour that the statement, 'Believe on the Lord Jesus, and you will be saved, you and your household' (16.31) has been abused. It is not intended to teach that the faith of the householder suffices for his wife, children and slaves. Alford rightly commented: 'καὶ ὁ οἶκός σου does not mean that *his* faith would save his household, but that *the same way was open to them as to him*: "Believe, and thou shalt be saved; and the same of thy household" '.[1] That is why the word of the Lord was spoken to 'all who were in his house' (v. 32), namely that all might hear and all might believe along with him. The process is the same as that which happened to Crispus and his family: 'Crispus

---

[1] Alford's *Greek Testament*, vol. II, 7th ed. 1899, p. 184. The same interpretation is given in R. J. Knowling, *Expositor's Greek Testament*, vol. II, p. 346 and in Haenchen, *Die Apostelgeschichte*, p. 203.

believed on the Lord *with his whole house*'; he did not believe *for* them, but they shared his faith *with* him. Such is the common pattern in Acts: the Gospel calls for faith, and both come to expression in baptism. The baptized hear and believe.[1]

Finally it should be observed that the contention that households became the nuclei of churches, carries limitations with regard to the families in the churches. Michel is not alone in urging that the household was constitutive for the church. Dom Gregory Dix did the same, having a special interest in the pattern of the eucharist that thereby emerged. In his view the eucharist was essentially a family affair — therefore *private and exclusively for believers!*[2] Possibly children in arms were regularly brought to the eucharist, but they did not participate in the feast. Schlatter also emphasized the significance of the family for the Church. He urged that a man was called in the Gospel, not as an abstract man, but in his concrete relationships as a husband and father. Yet he added, 'The personal and free manner of Christian piety in repentance and faith is not thereby diminished, and Jesus' saying that justifies renunciation of the family and the tearing of all natural relations, remains in force. It is not the will of the husband that can make his wife believing, nor the command of the father his children Christians. Only God's grace that moves a man inwardly can cause these natural relationships to be fruitful also for the religious goal of man. Christianity acts, however, in faith that He who created the natural fellowship also fills it with his grace'.[3]

That statement would be approved by any Baptist. To characterize it as Renaissance individualism is light heartedly anachronistic: it springs from the Gospels and Acts.

(ii) *Jesus and the Children*

In the minds of not a few the ultimate authority for the baptism of infants is found in the Gospel narrative wherein Jesus welcomed children brought to Him, rebuked those who would hinder them, and gave the children his blessing (Mk. 10.13–16, Mt. 19.13–15, cf. Mt. 18.3 ff, Lk. 18.15–17). This conclusion as to the significance of the event has been reached by two distinct modes of argument: the one concerns the nature of the event itself, the other the manner in which it was used by the primitive Church. The former viewpoint is represented by H. Vogel: 'Ultimately we dare to bring infants to baptism,

---

[1] So Windisch, *Z.N.W.*, 1929, p. 123; R. Knopf, *Die Schriften des Neuen Testaments*, II, p. 604; W. G. Kümmel, *Theologische Rundschau*, 1950, p. 40.
[2] *The Shape of the Liturgy*, pp. 16 ff.
[3] *Theologie des N.T.*, vol. II, pp. 467 f.

not because of an ancient tradition — which does in fact reach back into New Testament times — but because of the mystery of the promise under which He, the Lord of baptism, places infants by blessing them and indeed granting to them the Kingdom of God'.[1] Observe that it is not here claimed that all children are in the Kingdom of God; the decisive factor is the action of Jesus. He gives the inheritance of the Kingdom to those brought to Him.[2] If children brought to Jesus receive the Kingdom, which is the sum of the blessings bestowed on the believer sealed in baptism, how, it is asked, can one deny them the baptism itself?[3] H. J. Evander even suggested that the laying on of hands by Jesus was virtually a baptism, 'a consecration, an initiation to become Christians — it might be said, baptism without water'.[4]

As an alternative to the foregoing view (though sometimes in combination with it) it has been proposed that the narrative of the Blessing of the Children was included in the Gospels in order to answer the query, already raised in the first generation Church, as to whether baptism ought to be administered to very young children. The narrative was meant to supply the answer: 'Bring them to Jesus, as they did in the days of his flesh, and let them be baptized'. This viewpoint, earlier advanced by Wohlenberg,[5] is especially associated with Jeremias and Cullmann. Both agree that the narrative in itself

[1] 'The First Sacrament — Baptism', *S.J.T.*, vol. 7, 1954, pp. 56 f. Similar statements are made by Wotherspoon, op. cit., p. 166; Thornton, *Confirmation*, p. 150; N. Johansson, 'Making Christians by Sacraments', *S.J.T.*, vol. 5, 1952, p. 132.

[2] So explicitly the Church of Scotland study document: 'This saying states that the Kingdom of God, the sphere into which we are incorporated in Baptism, belongs in a special way to such children as are brought to Jesus. This belonging does not depend on some special spiritual qualities in the children, but on the fact that, being brought to Christ as children, they can begin anew their lives with Him', *Biblical Doctrine of Baptism*, p. 48.

[3] So Calvin. His exposition of Mt. 19.13 ff is instructive as exemplifying the Church's traditional approach to the incident: 'He declares that he wishes to receive children; and at length, taking them in his arms, he not only embraces but blesses them by the laying on of hands; from which we infer that his grace is extended even to those who are of that age. And no wonder; for since the whole race of Adam is shut up under the sentence of death, all from the least even to the greatest must perish, except those who are rescued by the only Redeemer. To exclude from the grace of redemption those who are of that age would be cruel; and therefore it is not without reason that we employ this passage as a shield against the Anabaptists. . . . And for what did He pray for them, but that they might be received into the number of the children of God? Hence it follows that they were renewed by the Spirit to the hope of salvation. In short, by embracing them He testified that they were reckoned by Christ among his flock. And if they were partakers of the spiritual gifts, which are represented by Baptism, it is unreasonable that they should be deprived of the outward sign'. *Commentary on a Harmony of the Evangelists*, vol. II, Edinburgh 1945, pp. 390 f. This exposition is approved by Marcel, op. cit., pp. 122, 193; Schlier, *T.L.Z.*, 1947, Sp. 335; *Interim Report of Church of Scotland*, 1957, p. 40.

[4] Op. cit., p. 177.

[5] 'Das Evangelium des Markus', in the *Zahn-Kommentar*, 1910, p. 272.

has nothing to do with baptism — it is 'pre-sacramental', as Jeremias puts it. But in his view the purpose of its inclusion in the Gospel is hinted at by its present position, set between the conversation about divorce (Mk. 10.1–12) and the story of the Rich Young Ruler (Mk. 10.17–31); the three sections form a little catechism, instructing disciples as to the attitude they should adopt towards marriage, children and possessions. The second catechetical item, by implication, lays upon Christian parents the task and responsibility of bringing their children to Jesus, and that not in a general way but for the purpose of their receiving baptism. Jeremias finds confirmation of this in the manner in which the episode has been treated by the Evangelists. He considers that Mk. 10.15 and Jn. 3.5 are variant forms of Mt. 18.3, which last is the original form of the saying. The Fourth Evangelist has interpreted it as implying the necessity for baptism, and not alone he but Justin and the Apostolic Constitutions have treated it likewise.[1] Luke's modifications are also believed to be peculiarly significant. Luke replaces the term παιδία ('children'), by βρέφη ('babies'), thereby hinting, not simply of the baptism of children, but of the baptism of infants. The omission of Mark's v. 16 (the embracing of the children and laying hands on their heads), the inclusion of the article *the* infants, and the apparent adaptation of the introductory sentence so as to address it to *parents* rather than to disciples, are all to be explained from the liturgical use of Luke's account in baptismal services. The ambiguity of the phrase, 'as a child', in Mk. 10.15, Lk. 18.17, is thought to be due to the same cause: whereas Mt. 18.3 shows that it originally meant 'becoming as a child', in Mark and Luke it can mean, 'he that does not receive the Kingdom of God as a child (i.e. in childhood) will not enter it', so suiting better the application to infant baptism.

Cullmann's mode of linking the narrative with the liturgical language of baptism is better known. In his view it would appear from Acts 8.36, 10.47, 11.17 that the term κωλύειν ('hinder') had acquired a certain liturgical character in primitive baptism. We are to gather that in the first century, when a convert was brought for baptism, enquiry was made whether any 'hindrance' existed, that is, whether the candidate had fulfilled the conditions demanded. 'In every case, and whatever the conditions imposed, when conviction was reached that the candidate had fulfilled them, the declaration nihil obstat was

[1] *Die Kindertaufe*, pp. 63 ff. Jeremias thinks the versions in Justin, 'Except you be born again, you will not enter the Kingdom of heaven', and Apost. Const., 'Except a man be baptized of water and Spirit he will not enter the Kingdom of Heaven' are independent renderings of the Synoptic saying.

certainly made before baptism took place — οὐδὲν κωλύει (there is no hindrance) or ἔξεστιν (it is permitted, Acts 8.37)'. The saying in Mk. 10.14 uses the same term: 'Allow the children to come to me, μὴ κωλύετε αὐτά — do not hinder them'. By this means says Cullmann, the Evangelist reproduced the narrative in such a manner as to provide an answer to the question of the propriety of infant baptism. Though not being directly related to baptism, the story 'was fixed in such a way that a baptismal formula on the first century gleams through it'.[1]

For convenience, let us consider first the proposal concerning the use of the narrative by the Evangelists. It should be observed that Jeremias depends much for his view on the non-Marcan versions of the incident and sayings; our primary source, Mark, does not so easily lend itself to the hypothesis of liturgical use. There is reason to believe that the secondary features in the secondary sources are less significant than is suggested. For example, much is made of Luke's replacement of παιδία ('children') by βρέφη ('infants'). Here, it is urged, is clear proof that Luke has *infant* baptism in mind. Let it be realized, however, what this interpretation postulates: In Luke's narrative no mention is made of children of maturer years, only infants in arms were brought to Jesus ('They brought to him even the infants'); in that case the saying that follows 'Whoever does not *receive* the Kingdom of God as a child does shall not enter it', has no relevance to the passage, for an infant's unconscious passivity is no example for the reception of the Kingdom by a grown person.[2] Nevertheless it is almost certain that Luke had no intention of so nullifying the word of Jesus; his replacement of Mark's παιδία by βρέφη in v. 15 is either a thoughtless slipping into a favourite but rare word of his, or, as Lagrange suggests, he considered βρέφη to be synonymous with παιδία in meaning.[3] That he had no wish to change the scene is

---

[1] Cullmann, op. cit., pp. 72–8.

[2] Creed is in agreement here: 'βρέφη is less appropriate, as some conscious capacity in the children seems needed to give point to the saying concerning receiving the Kingdom of God as a little child', *Gospel Acc. to St. Luke*, p. 225; so also Luce, *St. Luke* (C.G.T.) 1933, p. 283. The suggestion that Luke and Mark wished their readers to understand the saying, 'Unless a man receives the Kingdom of God *as an infant*, he will not enter it', as implying the necessity of receiving baptism *in infancy*, is typical of the kind of defence of infant baptism from the Bible that leaves one weakly despairing. It is unworthy of its advocates.

[3] Lagrange considered that βρέφη was, in fact, used by Luke in the sense of παιδία, since the children in question were able to *approach*, *come to* Jesus; the added touch, '*even* the children', implies that it was not alone sick people who were brought to Jesus in order to be touched, *Évangile selon S. Luc*, p. 479. The term occurs in the LXX only in the Apocrypha — once in Sir. 19.11, and once in each book of Maccabees. Luke uses it four times in the infancy narratives and also in Acts 7.19. Elsewhere in the N.T. it appears in 2 Tim. 3.15 (of Timothy's knowing the Scriptures ἀπὸ βρέφους) and in 1 Pt. 2.2.

apparent in his reverting to Mark's παιδία in the next sentence: 'Allow the *children* to *come* to me', which could easily have been rendered, 'Allow the *infants* to be *brought* to me', had he been of a mind to make the change.

Luke's omission of Mk. 10.16 (the laying on of hands on the children) is hardly due to abbreviation for liturgical purposes; one would have thought that a liturgical use of the narrative would rather have prompted him to retain it, in view of his interest in laying on of hands at baptism. The omission has probably no profounder reason than that Luke had already replaced Mark's ἰδών ('on seeing them') by προσεκαλέσατο αὐτά ('he called them to him'), thereby implying the coming of the children to Jesus.[1]

Nor is the attempt any happier to show Mt. 18.3 as the original of Mk. 10.15 and Jn. 3.5, and to view thereby the two first sayings as baptismal declarations. It is generally agreed that the Matthaean saying is a rewriting of the Marcan rather than vice versa.[2] If the Fourth Evangelist has used Mk. 10.15 as the basis for Jn. 3.5, he has transferred it to so different a situation that one ought not to draw conclusions as to his understanding of the original context; if otherwise we should have to take note about John's teaching on faith in relation to sonship! But I do not believe that the Fourth Evangelist has used this quarry for his teaching on regeneration.[3]

Cullmann's theory of the liturgical use of κωλύειν ('hinder') in the administration of baptism has more plausibility, but two observations should be made: first, on all counts its employment in a technical sense in the primitive Church is highly conjectural;[4] secondly, its employment in non-baptismal contexts is so frequent as to make it hazardous to draw any inferences concerning narratives not plainly

---

[1] So Holtzmann, *Die Synoptiker*, p. 397.

[2] See Bultmann, *Geschichte der synoptischen Tradition*, p. 32; Percy, *Die Botschaft Jesu*, p. 36; Kümmel, *Promise and Fulfilment*, p. 126, n. 77.

[3] See the exposition of Jn. 3.5 on pp. 226–32.

[4] Of the four passages cited by Cullmann, the questions in Acts 8.36, 11.17 appear to me not in the least liturgical, nor is it readily apparent that liturgical fragments are being employed in them. As Markus Barth has shown, the latter passage involves one in grave difficulties if it is taken as a divine *request* for Cornelius to be baptized (op. cit., p. 157). I find it difficult to believe that the change from the Matthaean διεκώλυεν to ἐκώλυσεν in the Gospel of the Ebionites was motivated by a desire to approximate to the customary baptismal formula. A. Argyle has provided a striking number of parallel occurrences in Greek writers and in the LXX of the New Testament phrases in which κωλύει occurs, thereby weakening Cullmann's case very considerably; see his article, 'O. Cullmann's Theory concerning κωλύειν', *E.T.*, vol. LXVII, 1955, p. 17. My chief ground for not dismissing the theory altogether is the fact that later occurrences of the term in connection with baptism have been found in Christian literature, reflecting possible earlier usage, see Jeremias, *Die Kindertaufe*, pp. 66 f.

baptismal.[1] The theory is fraught with such uncertainty, it cannot be justly claimed to make good the contention that this narrative supplies the chief New Testament evidence for infant baptism.[2] If we are concerned to understand the Evangelists' interpretation of the meeting of Jesus with the children there are some hints much closer to hand than this.

All would surely agree that Mark has two transparently clear motives in recounting the narrative: one is his desire to illustrate the attitude of Jesus to children, and so implicitly that which his followers ought to adopt concerning the religious life of the child; the other relates to the lesson that children have to teach adults in their approach to God. It is reasonable to presume that Mark viewed these two concerns as a harmonious unity. From this point of view it is of secondary importance to decide whether v. 15 is in its original context or whether Mark has added it from his store of isolated sayings of Jesus. The chief necessity is to grasp that, in Mark's view, v. 15 *explains* the statement in v. 14 that children are heirs of the Kingdom;[3] that the Kingdom to be received 'as a child' is the eschatological reign of God that is to come; and that the 'reception' inculcated relates to the good news concerning its impending fulfilment.[4]

In this context therefore, it is most natural to interpret v. 15 as affirming the necessity of receiving the good news of the Kingdom of God *as a child receives it*. And v. 14 provides a supreme illustration of children receiving the good news: they come to the Saviour with a love and trust answering to his love. The idea, accordingly, that children are adduced as models of that passivity which adults should show towards God[5] is inadmissible. In relation to the Good News it

[1] Would Cullmann be prepared to maintain that the command in Mk. 9.39, 'Do not *hinder* him', said of the exorcist not belonging to the company of the disciples, indicates that such a one should be baptized and received into the Church? The relationship between such individuals and the orthodox Church must have occasioned no little perplexity in the early period! The charge to the scribes, 'You *hindered* those who were entering' (Lk. 11.52), could equally well apply to hindering applicants to baptism in the Church. The Jews *hindered* Paul from speaking the word to the Gentiles (1 Thess. 2.16): did Paul mean to imply that they registered objection to the validity of their baptism? The Corinthians are bidden not to *hinder* speaking with tongues — at baptism? Ingenuity would be severely taxed to consider the potential baptismal allusions in the other New Testament occurrences.

[2] Cf. C. T. Craig: 'It may be correct that the Greek word here translated "hinder" had acquired a technical use in the early Church in relation to baptism. Yet it is not very conclusive evidence that Jesus meant as the opposite of "hindering" children the "baptizing" of them', *The One Church*, 1952, p. 68.

[3] So Bultmann, ibid., Percy, op. cit., p. 35, and apparently Lohmeyer, *Ev. des Markus*, pp. 204–6.

[4] So Loisy, *Les Évangiles Synoptiques*, vol. II, p. 205; Lohmeyer, op. cit., p. 204; Kümmel, ibid.

[5] Oepke, *Z.N.W.*, 1930, p. 98.

is their receptivity that is in view,[1] and in relation to Christ their trust and their love towards those who show them love.[2] Perhaps we should not distinguish too sharply between the Gospel and Christ, since the good news of the Kingdom is inseparably bound up with the person and action of the Christ. Both the Catholic Lagrange and the Lutheran Lohmeyer stress this point in relation to our passage. 'To receive the Kingdom is to receive the Christ, the Gospel, grace. In a word the reign of God is an invitation, a call. Children respond at once to a call from people they know and they run and throw themselves into their arms. Those who will have responded will enter into the Kingdom.'[3] Lohmeyer considers this to be the vital point of v. 14. Rabbis were sometimes asked to give children their blessing and pray for them,[4] and Jesus would have been so approached. But the answer of Jesus sets Him on a different plane from this. The children should be permitted to come to Him, for to come in faith to Him is to become an heir of the Kingdom. He is not simply a famous Rabbi, but the Lord and Bringer of the Kingdom. To have a part in Him as Messiah is to have a part in the Kingdom.[5]

One cannot consider these things without being conscious of the tremendous weight of tradition, and still more of popular Christian sentiment, that attaches to the conventional understanding of this passage, but if it were possible to banish from our minds the invariable association of this incident with infants in arms brought to the font (or, in Baptist circles, to a dedication ceremony), how should we construe the Lord's words: 'Let the children come to me . . . Whoever does not receive the Kingdom as a child does will not enter it'? How, but to think of children coming to Jesus — or even, more naturally, of them running to Him and clinging to Him, so affording a picture of the ideal human response to the Lord's call in the Gospel? To Lohmeyer the saying recalls the great invitation of Mt. 25.28–30, 'Come unto Me . . . Learn of Me': for the primitive Church that would mean that the exalted Lord calls the children, not to draw near on one occasion, but to begin a continuing relationship with Him.[6]

The rest of the saying, 'For of such is the Kingdom of heaven', is

---

[1] So Bultmann, *Jesus and the Word*, London 1935, p. 206; Otto, *Kingdom of God and Son of Man*, London 1938, p. 120; Guardini, *The Lord*, London 1956, pp. 267–9; Percy, op. cit., pp. 32 f.

[2] So Swete, *St. Mark*, p. 221; Lindblom, op. cit., p. 232; Lagrange, *St. Marc*, p. 262.

[3] Lagrange, op. cit., p. 263.

[4] See the examples in Strack-Billerbeck, op. cit., vol. 1, pp. 807 f, vol. 2, p. 138.

[5] See Lohmeyer's exposition in his *Ev. des Markus*, pp. 203 ff.

[6] Op. cit., p. 205.

peculiarly difficult to define with certainty. The interpretation, as old as Origen, that τοιούτων ('of such') means, 'such people as the children', has fallen out of favour, though it has been advocated by weighty names.[1] Whereas it would admirably suit v. 15, the difficulty of this interpretation lies in the conjunction γάρ, 'for': 'Let the children come to me *because* the kingdom belongs to people who are like them'. That would seem to imply that Jesus wants the children to come to Him because it is fitting to have those about Him who *resemble* the heirs of the Kingdom; which is not very plausible! Not a few exegetes incline to interpreting τοιούτων as meaning, 'the children and those who are like them',[2] though the grounds for the suggestion are not always clear. There is, however, no doubt that the term τοιοῦτος is frequently used in the New Testament without implying the idea of comparison. Blass-Debrunner point out that now and again the term is weakened to an indefinite determination for οὗτος ('this'), and they cite as examples 1 Cor. 5.5; 2 Cor. 2.6, 7; 12.2, 3, 5.[3] The same usage is evident in Acts 22.22, 2 Cor. 3.4. More striking, perhaps, is the fact that many normal occasions of the use of τοιοῦτος are intended to denote a *class*, of which the one mentioned in the context is an example; see e.g. Jn. 4.23, Rom. 1.32, 16.18, 1 Cor. 7.15, 28, Gal. 5.21, Heb. 7.6. It will be observed that in all these cases it is impossible to make the primary reference of τοιούτοι a comparison with *other* individuals. When e.g. the Jews cried, 'Away with such a man', (Acts 22.22), they did not refer to another person like Paul; and the saying, 'We have such a High Priest', (Heb. 7.26) makes the exalted Christ the only priest of his class.[4] Accordingly it would seem most plausible to relate the τοιούτων of our saying to the children themselves: they should be permitted to come to Jesus because the Kingdom of God belongs to precisely such as them.

In what sense does the Kingdom of God 'belong' to them? Not, assuredly, in the signification that the children are already 'in' it. The popular Christian idea that children are born into the Kingdom of God has no contact with the teaching of Jesus on the Kingdom. The saying shares the same form as the Beatitudes in Mt. 5.3, 10, αὐτῶν

---

[1] See Plummer, *Gospel of Matthew*, p. 262; Dalman, *Words of Jesus*, p. 128; J. Weiss, *Die Schriften d. N.T.*, I, p. 168; J. Schmid, *Das Ev. nach Markus*, 1950, p. 151; R. E. O. White, *Christian Baptism*, ed. Gilmore, p. 105.
[2] Loisy, op. cit., p. 204; McNeile, *St. Matthew*, p. 277; Schlatter, *Ev. Matthäus*, pp. 575 f; Lagrange, *S. Marc*, pp. 262 f; Gould, *St. Mark* (I.C.C.), p. 188.
[3] *Grammatik des neutestamentlichen Griechisch*, 10th ed. 1959, par. 304. Percy cites E. Mayser, *Grammatik der griechischen Papyri aus der Ptolermäerzeit*, II, 2, 1934, pp. 82 ff for examples in the papyri and inscriptions for this usage, op. cit., p. 31.
[4] I owe this observation to J. Murray, *Christian Baptism*, 1952, p. 64.

ἐστιν ἡ βασιλεία τῶν οὐρανων, 'theirs is the Kingdom of heaven';
i.e. they will inherit the Kingdom of heaven at the end of the times.
The children are thus said to be the destined heirs of the future
Kingdom. Consonant with this, the following saying states that those
who do not receive the good news of the Kingdom like a child *will* not
enter it; sayings concerning entering the Kingdom generally relate to
the eschatological kingdom of the End.[1] This gives precision and
depth to the saying concerning the children: they are to be allowed
access to Jesus, for the Kingdom of heaven will be given to just such at
the Judgment and glory of the parousia. On what grounds is the Kingdom of heaven to be given to them? In virtue of their coming to Jesus
(v. 14) and receiving the word of the Kingdom (v. 15).

It is possible that some will recoil in annoyance at this interpretation as pedantic and precious, but it is surely closer to the text than the
vague generalities about the Kingdom of God belonging to children
because of their supposed sinlessness, or by virtue of their membership by birth in the people of the covenant, or because they are
covered by the redemptive work of Christ, or through their belonging
to the last generation of history that is to see the Kingdom, or the view
which reduces the Kingdom of God in the teaching of Jesus to the
idea of a beneficent divine Providence. There is nothing strange in the
idea of children listening to Jesus, receiving in simplicity his 'call'
(=invitation) to the Kingdom, and loving Him with all their hearts.
This is not a question of foisting on children an 'adult experience', or
pretending that they are what they are not. It remains true today that
there is nothing that moves a parent to gratitude to God so much as to
see his children opening their hearts to the word of God and responding in simplicity of heart and mind to the love of God. And that is
what Jesus in the narrative before us wished to encourage. Whether
any infants were in the company of those brought to Him on this
occasion, it is naturally impossible to affirm or deny.[2] As in the household baptisms we have considered, the passage is not concerned with

---

[1] For the classic treatment of this theme see Windisch, 'Die Sprüche vom Eingehen in das Reich Gottes', *Z.N.W.*, 1928, pp. 163 ff. Exegetes are now realizing
that the same applies to Mk. 10.14 f; see e.g. Wellhausen, *Ev. Marci*, p. 79; Wernle,
Die Reichsgotteshoffnung in den ältesten Christlichen Dokumenten, 1903, p. 31;
Lindblom, op. cit., p. 146; Lohmeyer, op. cit., pp. 203 f; Kümmel, op. cit., p. 118,
n. 77; Jeremias, *Die Kindertaufe*, p. 62.

[2] It is sometimes suggested that the παιδία who came to Jesus must have been
infants since Jesus 'took them in his arms', ἐναγκαλισάμενος, v. 16; so Wohlenberg, op. cit., p. 270. This is by no means a sure deduction from the statement. The
term occurs elsewhere in the New Testament only in Mk. 9.36, where we read
that Jesus 'took a child and set him in the midst of them, and taking him in his arms
he said . . .'. The child in this case was clearly no infant. Many translators prefer to

them; it has in view the young who come to the Lord and receive his word; to such the Kingdom, the resurrection and the life will be given — and to all who share their faith and love.

(iii) *Proselyte Baptism and the Church*

From time to time the question is raised whether infants and very young children in the family of a proselyte to Judaism were baptized with older members of the family. Johannes Schneider doubted our right to answer affirmatively, in view of the lack of early attestation to the practice.[1] It is, indeed, curious how late the evidence is on the matter. In the literature of the Tannaitic period there is frequent mention of female proselytes under the age of 'three years and one day', who were reckoned to be on the same level as Israelite girls; presumably they were baptized, but it happens that their baptism is nowhere mentioned.[2] The earliest explicit reference to the baptism of a very young child falls just before A.D. 300. R. Huna (died A.D. 297) counselled that a child whose father had died and whose mother wished him to become a proselyte should receive the bath 'according to the judgment of the court': 'What is our justification for this? Because it is for his advantage, and an advantage can be applied to a man without his knowledge of it'.[3] Such a statement presumes that the child was too young to answer for himself. Even more significant is a citation made by a pupil of this Rabbi in the funeral oration over his master, quoting one R. Hithqijja, who in turn spoke in the name of R. Abba for the practice of baptizing a foundling child that was rescued, even in Israel; the baptism was evidently applied for fear the child was of heathen parentage.[4] Such a judgment is highly illuminating, since it does not come under the category of family solidarity; if children in these circumstances were baptized, it may be assumed with confidence that infant children of proselytes were also baptized in this era. Despite the very late date of this evidence, it is likely to reflect practice of an earlier time, since there are no obvious factors which would indicate a development of practice among the Jews in this respect.

To Jeremias this is of first importance, since it appears to dispose of

render the verb by some such phrase as, 'putting his arms round', so Moffatt; Lagrange (*embrassant*); *Bible de Jérusalem* (*ayant embrassé*); J. Weiss, Schlatter, the *Zürcher Bibel* (*umarmte*); Luther (*herzte*); the Dutch translation (*omarmde*), etc. In Prov. 6.10 it is used of a lazy man who enfolds himself in sleep. The noun ἐναγκάλισμα means a consort (!).

[1] *Die Taufe im Neuen Testament*, 1952, p. 21, n. 5.
[2] See Oepke, art. παῖς, *T.W.N.T.*, vol. V, p. 646; Jeremias, *Die Kindertaufe*, p. 45.
[3] Keth 11a, cited in Strack-Billerbeck, I, p. 112.
[4] Jeremias, *Die Kindertaufe*, p. 46.

an objection raised by Windisch as to the possibility of infant baptism being practised in the primitive Church: baptism in the New Testament presupposes knowledge of good and evil, confession of faith and acceptance of obligation; but, urges Jeremias, similar considerations apply to Jewish proselyte baptism, for it was bound up with mission preaching, conversion and ethical obligation, yet it was freely applied to infants; the same modification of principle could have existed in the primitive Christian communities.[1] In Jeremias' view, 1 Cor. 7.14 demonstrates that the Jewish precedent was, in fact, followed, for Paul in that passage cites the terminology of Jewish proselyte baptism, indicating that in his churches, as with proselytes to Judaism, children were baptized with their parents on the conversion of the latter, but those born after the conversion of the mother were not baptized.[2] With this Oscar Cullmann agrees,[3] as also G. Miegge; but the latter moves a stage further and argues on the same basis that parents would also have brought their young children to John the Baptist to be baptized along with themselves; admittedly such children could not and did not need to repent, but they could receive the messianic seal of the Kingdom and we may confidently presume that they were baptized for it.[4] In like manner J. C. S. Nias cites Walls, in his well known History of Infant Baptism, for the view that the Risen Lord in the Great Commission willed that this element in the practice of proselyte baptism should be continued in his Church: 'For when a commission is given in such short words, and there is no express direction what they shall do with the infants of those who become proselytes, the natural and obvious interpretation is that they must do in that matter as they and the church in which they lived always used to do'. With this sentiment Nias is in full agreement.[5]

At this point it is necessary for us to recall that in our examination of the relationship between proselyte baptism and Christian baptism we found no clear trace of influence from the Jewish rite on the interpretation of baptism in the New Testament. The weight of theological significance of the passage of the proselyte to life in the Jewish fold did not fall on his receiving the bath but on his circumcision, and we observed what a profound transformation the ideas of death and resurrection and new birth gained through their relation to baptism in

[1] Hat die Urkirche . . ., p. 28.
[2] Op. cit., pp. 37–40.
[3] Op. cit., pp. 43 f.
[4] Il Battesimo dei Fanciulli, pp. 10, 14 f.
[5] See his article, 'William Wall's History of Infant Baptism', Theology, vol. LXIX, 1946, p. 139.

the name of the Christ of the Cross and Resurrection. So great a difference between the interpretation of Jewish proselyte baptism and Christian baptism does not predispose to assume an identification of procedure in the administration of the two baptisms.

Further, when considering the import of 1 Cor. 7.14, we concluded that a careful exegesis of the saying actually forbids this equation of administration in proselyte baptism and Christian baptism. That there is contact between the terminology of the saying and that of proselyte baptism is undoubted; the statement, 'Else were your children unclean, but now they are holy', reminds of the distinction drawn between children begotten and born 'in holiness' and children not begotten and born 'in holiness'. But two considerations militate against pressing this analogy to identity of procedure. The category of holiness is applied in 1 Cor. 7.14 to the non-Christian parent in a manner which, so far as I am aware, was not done in proselyte baptism, for on the basis of the laws of the proselyte a non-Christian husband of a Christian wife ought to be pronounced unclean, not consecrated; if Paul was conscious of using the language of proselyte baptism with respect to the children, he must have known that he was departing from it in speaking of the unbelieving parent; to say the least, that would indicate that he did not feel himself bound to the concepts associated with proselyte baptism. But more important, the argument of 1 Cor. 7.14 proceeds on the assumption that the 'holy' children in Corinth had not been baptized, for they were in a position comparable to that of the unbaptized parent — otherwise Paul could not have argued from the status of the children to the status of the unbelieving parent; but we saw that the Church at Corinth was too young at the time of the writing of the Letter for that to have been the case, if the procedure of proselyte baptism was applied to their children.[1] Since the majority of the children in the Church at Corinth must have been born *before* the conversion of their parents, and they had therefore been baptized with them according to the argument under review, the application of their status to that of the unbaptized parent is unwarranted and Paul's argument falls to the ground. But if, as most recognize, there is no limitation of reference in the expression 'your children', and Paul's argument is presumed sound, the procedure of proselyte baptism did not obtain at Corinth, for the children

[1] Reckoning on a ministry of one and a half years at Corinth and three years since his departure, no child of the converts born after their conversion could have been four years of age, most would have been younger. That is, only a very small proportion of the children of the Corinthians could have been reckoned as born 'in holiness'.

at Corinth had not been baptized. I am accordingly compelled to the conviction that, far from demonstrating that the children of Christians in the primitive Church were baptized as in proselyte baptism, 1 Cor. 7.14 fairly conclusively proves that the Churches of the Pauline foundation diverged from the Jewish tradition and baptized *none* of their children. From this conclusion I can see no way of escape.

Whether or not infants were brought by their parents to the baptism of John is beyond our ability to prove or disprove. It is impermissible, however, to insist that John must have followed the precedent of proselyte baptism in this respect, presuming that he knew it. We ought not to dismiss from the mind the fact that John's nearest neighbours, the Covenanters of Qumran, did not admit children to the lustrations. From the Two-column fragment we learn that children began to receive instruction in the teaching of the group when they became ten years of age, and they continued in it until they reached the age of twenty, at which time they became eligible for examination with a view to entering the community.[1] It is as unnecessary to suggest that John followed in the steps of the Covenanters in his administration of baptism as that he adhered to the procedure of proselyte baptism when baptizing Jews, but it is worth reminding ourselves that there were other views in Judaism concerning the rightness of baptizing young children besides those which came to prevail in proselyte baptism. It is further necessary to recall the results of our comparison between John's baptism and proselyte baptism, for we found considerable differences between them: the strong eschatological element in John's baptism, referring both to judgment and hope, is absent from proselyte baptism, while the relation of proselyte baptism to the Temple worship and to sacrifice in particular has no analogy in John's baptism. In both these respects John is nearer to Qumran than to the proselytization of Jerusalem. But if the two rites, John's baptism and proselyte baptism, have so little in common, in their associations and significance, why should it be assumed as axiomatic that their conditions of administration were identical?

The differences between proselyte baptism and John's baptism, however, were not so marked as those between the former and Christian baptism. It is, in fact, common knowledge that the administration of baptism to proselyte families had contacts with Christian baptism at best within severely defined limits. The baptism of infant proselytes had a provisional character that is in strong contrast to all repre-

---

[1] For the text, see Gaster, *The Scriptures of the Dead Sea Sect*, pp. 285 f, and compare the Zadokite Document xv, op. cit., p. 92.

sentations of baptism in the New Testament. Children who had been baptized with their proselyte parents had the right to exercise their own discretion as to their relationship to the Jewish faith and nation when they attained their majority, and they were at liberty to renounce their proselyte status without blame if they so desired. It is stated by Strack-Billerbeck, 'If an offspring of a proselyte baptized in infancy later resolved to turn his back again on Judaism, he was not treated like a renegade Jew but *was looked on as one who had lived all his life as a non-Israelite*'.[1] On such a basis it is clear that the baptism of infant proselytes was provisional in a way that the baptism of a person of mature years was not. One cannot but contrast the strong sentiments expressed by many writers on Christian baptism concerning the gravity of the situation of those who renounce in adult life the baptism that had been imparted to them as infants.[2] Of yet weightier significance is the consideration that proselyte baptism was solely a rite of conversion and was not applied to children born after the initiation of the parents into Judaism. H. H. Rowley has frequently stressed this point, and I think convincingly. For if the primitive Church had been decisively influenced by the regulations governing proselyte baptism, Christian baptism would have been administered only to converts with their families and *never* to the offspring of members of the Church. On this Rowley says: 'It is not here affirmed or denied that the Church followed Jewish practice in this matter, but merely affirmed that if it did, its practice was wholly different from what is meant by Infant Baptism today, and it is wholly fallacious argument to pretend that the one is a copying from the other. Not seldom, indeed, modern defenders of infant baptism hold that it should be administered only to the children of Christian parents — that is, to precisely those corresponding to the children who did not receive the Jewish baptismal rite'.[3]

Allowing for all positive relationships between the Jewish and Christian rites, is it not plain that the New Testament presents us with a different understanding of baptism from that met with in

[1] Op. cit., vol. I, p. 110; see citations from the Rabbinical literature on pp. 111 f.

[2] 'It is infinitely worse for those who are baptized than for those who are not, if they fall from the participation in Christ's death and resurrection bestowed upon them at their reception into the Church, that is, if faith, the response which ought unconditionally to follow, does not occur. It is in this connection that the New Testament words are to be understood, which speak of a sin which is not forgiven, for which no repentance is possible, as well as the kindred passages which talk of final exclusion from the community', Cullmann, op. cit., p. 36.

[3] 'The Origin and Meaning of Baptism', *Baptist Quarterly*, vol. XI, 1945, pp. 310 f. See also his article, 'Jewish Proselyte Baptism', *Hebrew Union College Annual*, 1940, p. 321, and *The Unity of the Bible*, 1953, pp. 154 f.

proselyte baptism? And does not this sense of a new thing coming into the world lie at the heart of the Great Commission of the Risen Lord? The theological setting of the scene in Mt. 28.16–20 — the Easter adumbration of the parousia, with the exultant consciousness of the new order that has broken into the world and the presence of the Risen Kurios to make it known — is far from the attitude that thinks in terms of a perpetuating Jewish proselytism. Christian baptism was a newer, more radically different sacrament from its predecessor than Wall or any of his school ever dreamed. On any view, a divergence from the application of proselyte baptism to children took place in the Christian Church. Bartsch put the question whether we are not driven to postulate that precisely the abstention of applying baptism to infants provides a decisive illustration of the difference between Christian baptism in the primitive Church and the rites of Greeks and of the Jews.[1] In view of the depth of meaning attaching to baptism in the New Testament, in the setting of the unique salvation-history of the Christ, he is surely right.

(iv) *The Covenant, Circumcision and Baptism*

The apologetic thus far considered for infant baptism as a New Testament institution is represented among most branches of the Christian Church. A group of the Reformed tradition[2] takes a somewhat exclusive way of its own in finding the sole basis of infant baptism in the one covenant which God has made with man and which continues throughout all time. None in our generation has so strenuously advocated this view as Pierre Marcel, whose exuberance in expounding it, however, tends by its very extravagance to detract from its strength.[3] He explicitly states that it is not enough to find the foundation of baptism in Christ; one must go higher still and see it in the eternal decree of God revealed in the Covenant. 'No a priori argument, no reason, no motive, however valuable it may at first appear to be, no supposed demonstration can, according to the Scriptures invalidate this vital point and cause the foundation of baptism to be anything other than the covenant of grace, or cause baptism to signify and seal anything else in the first place than our adoption and recep-

---

[1] *Evangelische Theologie*, 1948–9, p. 77.

[2] It appears to be in rapid progress of securing the allegiance of the Evangelical Anglicans, one of whom translated Marcel's articles and issued them in book form.

[3] I feel bound to say that no work which I have read in connection with this study has appeared to me so unsatisfactory as his book *The Biblical Doctrine of Infant Baptism*, 1953. The exegesis and deductions drawn from it frequently have seemed to me unworthy of the seriousness of the discussion.

tion into the covenant'.[1] Consequently no store is set on attempts to justify infant baptism such as those we have earlier considered: 'That the opponents of infant baptism should be led to reject all these supposed foundations of baptism does not surprise us in the least, and in this connection we can but approve their perspicacity, for we are in full agreement with them. . . . With the rejection of the covenant of grace every possible foundation of infant baptism disappears'.[2]

If it be asked what interpretation of the covenant of grace makes such confidence possible, the answer appears in a series of postulates which are all interconnected and which presume a single basic attitude to the relation of the Old Testament faith to the New. Chief among them are the following:

(i) Throughout history there has been and is but *one covenant of grace*, essentially the same in all its dispensations. That the New Testament speaks of a 'new' covenant must not mislead us; this chiefly relates to the change in forms of administration, as in Heb. 8–10, or to the contrast with Judaistic misconceptions which perverted the Mosaic covenant into a covenant of works, as in Paul.

(ii) There always has been and is now but *one Gospel*, that is the announcement of the plan of salvation through Christ, with its offer of salvation to all who believe. Paul said that the Gospel was preached to Abraham (Gal. 3.8), and Jesus stated that Abraham rejoiced to see his day (Jn. 8.56); hence, 'The Hebrew believers are described as those who hoped in Christ before his coming, because they received the Gospel (Gal. 3.8, Eph. 1.12)'.[3]

(iii) The *condition of receiving salvation* has always been the same — faith in the promises of God. Abraham is the prototype of New Testament believers, 'the father of us all,' both Jews and Gentiles, who share a like faith with him (Gen. 15.6, Rom. 4.9–25, Gal. 3).

(iv) Throughout history the *Church* has been and remains but one. The nation of Israel was the Church, and the Christian Church is the same Church, for it comes under the same covenant of grace. (See especially Rom. 11.16 ff.)

(v) The *sacraments* of the two dispensations have essentially the same significance. 'Since the sacraments were seals . . . by which the promises of God were sealed, and since no promise of God has been

---

[1] Op. cit., pp. 151, 154.

[2] Op. cit., p. 199. It is not that Marcel rejects such conceptions as vicarious faith and the common interpretation of the bringing of children to Jesus, of proselyte baptism and the like. But to him these issues are secondary and are to be viewed as consequences of baptism, or rather of the covenant of which baptism is the sacrament, hence they cannot form its basis.

[3] Marcel, op. cit., p. 77.

made to man except in and through Jesus Christ (2 Cor. 1.20), all the sacraments exhibit Christ to us and teach and remind us of the promises of God. All that we have today in our sacraments the Jews had formerly in theirs, namely Jesus Christ and his spiritual riches.'[1]

The argument thus heads up into the last affirmation, wherein the virtual equivalence of circumcision and baptism is maintained. It is urged that even in the Old Testament the true meaning of circumcision is set forth as the circumcision of the heart (Deut. 10.16, Jer. 4.4); since Abraham received circumcision as 'a seal of the righteousness of faith' (Rom. 4.11), circumcision must have been viewed as a sign of the cleansing away of sins in the same way as baptism is in the new dispensation; and Jesus himself is described by Paul as a 'minister of the circumcision' conclusively proving the spiritual significance of the rite.[2] It is therefore laid down: 'Circumcision was the sign and seal of the remission of sins, of justification, of change of heart, of sanctification, of the objective work of the grace of God. It conveyed the promise of eternal life; it was the sacrament of admission into the covenant of grace. Its basis was the promise of God's mercy, its content Jesus Christ. According to the New Testament all this applies equally to baptism. . . . Their usage and efficacy are identical, as are also the conditions of admission'.[3]

While Marcel is extreme in his statement of views, he faithfully reflects the tradition in which he stands. So that while Cullmann, in his exposition of the relation of circumcision to baptism, moderates his claims, his position is essentially identical with that of Marcel. He makes two major assertions: first, that baptism is, in Paul's thought, the fulfilment and thus repeal of circumcision (explicitly so in Col. 2.11, implicitly in Rom. 3.25 ff, 4.1 ff, Gal. 3.26 ff, Eph. 2.11 ff); secondly that the two sacraments correspond to each other as sacraments of reception into the covenant (observe that circumcision is called a seal in Rom. 4.11, as baptism is in Eph. 1.13 etc.; that the Jews attributed new life to the circumcision of proselytes; and they spoke of the circumcized as 'holy'). 'If circumcision is repealed only because there is now baptism into Christ's death and resurrection as reception into the new covenant of Christ's Body, and if consequently

---

[1] Marcel, op. cit., p. 90.

[2] 'If, in spite of the texts, it is insisted that the true circumcision . . . is a carnal institution, then Christ was the minister of a carnal institution. If, however, it is impossible to attribute to Christ a carnal ministry, then it follows that the true circumcision is spiritual', Marcel, op. cit., pp. 87 f.

[3] Op. cit., p. 155 f.

baptism is no radically new gift of grace, the suggestion is confirmed that the meaning of the "seal" at one decisive point cannot be different from that at another.'[1] It is but natural therefore, to apply baptism to the infant children of believers, as circumcision was applied to the infant sons of the members of the old covenant. Peter's declaration on the Day of Pentecost is seen as confirmation of this view: 'The promise is to you and to your children and to all that are afar off, everyone whom the Lord our God calls to him' (Acts 2.39): the principle of incorporating children along with their parents into the covenant continues from the old order into the new.[2] Accordingly Knox the Reformer declared that it is not only 'right and natural' that we should baptize children of Christians but that we *must* do so if we are to obey the command of God: 'He has promised that He will be a God to us and the God of our children unto the thousandth generation . . . instructing us thereby that our children belong to Him by covenant and therefore ought not to be defrauded of those holy signs and badges whereby his children are known from infidels and pagans'.[3]

One of the difficulties in coming to grips with this view is the presence in it of elements of truth, to which all would accord fullest recognition, alongside a distortion of the Biblical evidence that makes the interpretation unacceptable. The major mistake of the writers of this school is their one-sided stressing of the elements of unity in the Covenant, Gospel and Church of both dispensations, and their ignoring of the equally clear elements of discontinuity, elements which, in fact, often take the attention of the New Testament writers more than the elements of unity because they are so overwhelming. For example, it is unjust to the consciousness of the New Testament Church to tone down the 'newness' of the new covenant to a truer understanding of the covenant of grace perverted by Pharisees to appear as a covenant of works, or to a new administration of that covenant. Admittedly, under some aspects the new covenant *is* a new 'administration' — for that is not a bad translation of διαθήκη, covenant![4] The new covenant is the divine 'dispensation' of redemption and the Kingdom. But Paul

---

[1] Op. cit., pp. 56 ff, 69.

[2] Of this text John Murray said, 'It is the certification of the Holy Spirit to us that this method of the administration of the covenant of grace is not suspended', *Christian Baptism*, p. 71. A like interpretation of the saying is given by Grossmann, *Ein Ja zur Kindertaufe*, 1944, pp. 17 f; Jeremias, *Hat die Urkirche . . .*, p. 27, *Die Kindertaufe . . .*, p. 48; *Church of Scotland Interim Report*, 1955, p. 21.

[3] *Church of Scotland Interim Report*, 1958, p. 13.

[4] See Behm in the article διαθήκη, *T.W.N.T.*, vol. II, pp. 132–7 and Bauer's *Wörterbuch*.

contrasts the old and new covenants as a dispensation (διακονία) of death and a dispensation of life, a dispensation of condemnation and one of forgiveness and righteousness, a transient administration and an eternal one, a dispensation of fading glory and one of surpassing glory (see 2 Cor. 3.5 ff). This is not a contrast between a misunderstanding or perversion of the divine order and a revelation of truth, but of two providential orders of history, each serving its own purpose, as Paul's doctrine of Law makes plain. Even more striking, the new covenant of which our Lord spoke (Mk. 14.24) was nothing other than the gift of the Kingdom of God through the redemption He was about to accomplish: it granted promise of inheritance in the coming glory (Lk. 22.29 f) and brought into this time all those blessings characteristically associated with the new age of the divine sovereignty — forgiveness, a personal relationship with the Father, resurrection, Holy Spirit, emancipation from the world, the flesh and the devil, life in the new creation, the *Koinonia* of the Body of Christ and so on, of which Paul never tires of glorying. It is not otherwise with the Gospel of the Kingdom: that Gospel is undoubtedly rooted deep in the Old Testament, where it is seen as the undying hope of the prophets; but there is a vast difference between possessing a *promise* and possessing its *fulfilment*, and those two terms not unfairly describe the distinction between the old and new dispensations, despite the forward look of the New Testament community. And because the new covenant was made in the blood of the Christ, who was raised from the dead and sent the promised Spirit, the people of God became a new phenomenon — the *Body of Christ*, a mystery hidden since the world began but now a reality to amaze angels (Eph. 3.4 ff, 9 f). The Church is one, but the difference between the two 'administrations' is cataclysmic, for they are separated by a gulf and an unscalable height, the death of the Christ and the glory of his Easter, with the age of the Spirit ensuing. Allowing for all elements of continuity between the old and the new covenant, old and new revelation, old and new people, to put them under a common denominator is to identify the unidentifiable — life and death, flesh and Spirit, old creation and new creation, life of this age and the life of the age to come. This attempt to reduce to uniformity the old and new covenants and their respective sacraments belongs to an unrealistic mode of exegesis that fails to distinguish between shadow and substance, that fails to understand New Testament eschatology and that fails to take into account the significance of the resurrection of Christ and the coming of the Holy Spirit. In a word, it cannot come to terms with precisely those insights into the teaching of the New Testament which are so marked a feature of our age.

Apart from modern insights, it is difficult to see how this view is reconcilable with the teaching of Paul on the covenant in Galatians 3. Paul is concerned to demonstrate who are the true 'sons of Abraham' and by what means they receive the promise of the covenant. Abraham's sons are they who share Abraham's faith (v. 7). This is seen in the dual fact that Abraham believed God and it was accounted to him for righteousness (v. 6) and that the Gospel was made known to him beforehand — 'In thee shall all the nations be blessed' (v. 8), i.e. the nations were to be justified as he was through a faith like his (v. 9). Above all, the covenant promise was made to 'Abraham *and his seed*' and *that seed is Christ* (v. 16, the Christ is here not an isolated individual but includes His people in Himself). The Lord has wrought a redemption, that in Himself the blessing of Abraham might come upon the Gentiles (vv. 12–14). Apart from his coming the purpose of the covenant could not be fulfilled even in the Jews, for the Law's effect was to multiply transgressions (vv. 19 f); justification and life could come to all only when the Christ had redeemed men from the curse of the Law (20 f). Now, however, the age of faith has come: in Christ Jesus we are sons of God, Abraham's seed, heirs of the covenant promise (vv. 25–9). Nothing could demonstrate more clearly the continuity and discontinuity of the two dispensations. The *covenant* with Abraham remains in force, unaffected by the giving of the Law, and it reaches fulfilment in Christ; but under the Law none could receive the inheritance; that required the redemption of Christ. The *Gospel* preached to Abraham gave hope of a promise being one day realized; now the Christ has come the promise has been actualized. The *people* of the covenant are no longer the Jews but the Body of Christ, wherein all distinctions disappear. And how do men enter the covenant and become heirs of the promise? The answer is unequivocal: in baptism by faith. 'It is men of faith who are the sons of Abraham' (v. 7); 'Those who are men of faith are blessed with Abraham who had faith' (v. 9); 'That in Christ Jesus the blessing of Abraham might come upon the Gentiles, that we might receive the promise of the Spirit through faith' (v. 14); 'The scripture consigned all things to sin, that what was promised to faith in Jesus Christ might be given to those who believe' (v. 22); 'Before faith came we were confined under the law, kept under restraint until faith should be revealed; so that the law was our custodian until Christ came, that we might be justified by faith' (vv. 23 f);

'For in Christ Jesus you are all sons of God through faith, for as many of you as were baptized into Christ did put on Christ' (vv. 26 f). Could words be plainer? Not a line of this remotely suggests that the covenant in Christ operates on a hereditary basis. The promise is explicitly for those baptized in Christ in faith. Had Paul shared the so-called covenant theology he could never have written Galatians 3 in this manner; that is evident by the fact that the chapter represents one world of thought and Marcel's volume another, as is evident on reading them.

What then is the relation between circumcision and baptism? No unequivocal answer to this question is given in the New Testament. It is clear that attitudes to it must have differed in the primitive Church. In the Palestinian Church the two rites must have been regarded as having quite separate functions, for Jewish Christians continued to circumcize their children, as part of their loyal observation of the Law, and they also baptized converts. The Council of Jerusalem had to consider the question whether both circumcision and baptism should be administered to Gentile converts; the Pharisaic Christians wanted to make both compulsory, as Jews did when Gentiles became proselytes to their faith. That the whole Church of Jerusalem, and not merely the ex-Pharisees, were unanimous in retaining circumcision among themselves is seen in the report passed on by James to Paul: many thousands of Jews had joined the Church and had heard that Paul was teaching Jews of the Dispersion not to circumcize their children and observe 'the customs'; this was an offence to them, and James counselled Paul to purify himself along with certain others; 'Thus all will know that there is nothing in what they have been told about you, but that you yourself live in observance of the law' (Acts 21.20 ff). In an environment wherein circumcision was so firmly rooted, there was no possibility for baptism to be regarded as its fulfilment, or for the two rites to be viewed as possessing the same meaning. Nor was there any possibility of these Christians regarding circumcision as denoting the 'circumcision of the heart', for in that case what need was there of baptism? If the circumcision they had received meant to them 'the sign and seal of the remission of sins, of justification, of change of heart, of sanctification, of the objective work of the grace of God', conveying 'the promise of eternal life' and its content was Jesus Christ,[1] baptism in the name of Jesus Christ was superfluous, or possessed a considerably reduced significance, for the circumcized had already received everything that baptism

[1] Marcel, op. cit., p. 155.

meant.[1] This is important, for in the Jerusalem Church we see a group of Christians who perpetuated the Jewish understanding of circumcision, but their view had nothing in common with the interpretation offered by the Reformed theologians. To equate the circumcision of the old covenant with the baptism of the new covenant evidently does two things: it exalts circumcision to a height of significance it never had in Israel, not even when the Christ was known and believed in, and it diminishes the uniqueness and power of the New Testament rite that is rooted in the cross and resurrection of Jesus Christ.

By this time it should be clear that 'the circumcision of the heart' is something other than the rite of circumcision. The latter was administered to every male child in Israel as a sign of his membership in the covenant people and had no relation to moral renewal; the prophetic call for heart circumcision is an application of the rite in symbol, not an exposition of the rite itself. In Deut. 30.6 it is said, 'The Lord your God will circumcize your heart and the heart of your offspring, so that you will love the Lord your God with all your heart and with all your soul, that you may live'. This is nothing less than a promise of salvation to be wrought by God Himself. The promise is fulfilled in Jesus Christ. This is the true approach to make to the disputed saying in Col. 2.11. We saw earlier that the view advocated by many scholars, that the phrase ἡ περιτομὴ τοῦ Χριστοῦ means 'Christian circumcision', i.e. baptism, is almost certainly mistaken; it denotes the death of Christ. The employment of circumcision as a figure for the redemptive death of Christ and our part in it is due to the exigencies of controversy with the Colossian heretics; whereas they were being persuaded to receive Jewish circumcision, Paul argues: 'You have already been circumcized in Christ's death and you entered effectively into it through your baptism; therefore you need no circumcision administered by human hands'. Baptism, then, did away with the need of circumcision because it signified the union of the believer with Christ, and in union with Him the old nature was sloughed off. A lesser circumcision has been replaced by a greater; the spiritual circumcision promised under the old covenant has become a reality under the new through baptism.[2] If circumcision is needless, on the ground that through participation in the redemption of Christ in baptism the circumcision of the heart has become a reality, then circumcision is a far lesser thing than that which has supplanted it.

[1] Marcel himself says of the two rites, 'Their usage and efficacy are identical', op. cit., p. 156.
[2] 'For Paul the circumcision of the heart is identical with the redemption through Christ', Meyer, art. περιτέμνω, T.W.N.T., vol. VI, p. 82.

As Ernst Fuchs said, 'Over against circumcision baptism brings brilliantly to expression the new factor of the divine saving event, namely *its eschatological power*'.[1] Baptism differs from circumcision as the new aeon differs from the old; the two rites belong to different worlds.[2]

In view of this utter newness of baptism compared with circumcision, there is no a priori case for postulating an identity of administration of the two rites. No appeal to the contrary can legitimately be made to Acts 2.39. I am inclined to agree with Jeremias that the most natural interpretation of Peter's statement, 'The promise is to you and to your children', is that it denotes that the promise belongs to the hearers and their own children, even as the citation from Joel at the beginning of Peter's speech declares, 'Your *sons* and your *daughters* shall prophesy' (v. 17).[3] Probably Luke at least would have extended the reference to 'your children' to include later descendants, as Acts 13.32 would encourage us to believe: 'We bring you the good news that what God promised to the fathers, this he has fulfilled to us their children by raising Jesus'.[4] But that does not warrant the conclusion that the new covenant embraces children to a thousand generations and commands their baptism in infancy. If 'your children' in v. 39 are the same as 'your sons and your daughters' who shall prophesy in v. 17, the indication is that they are such as can repent and be baptized for the remission of sins and the reception of the Holy Ghost, according to v. 38.[5] Indeed the promise is explicitly said to apply 'to you, and to your children, and to all that are far off, *every one whom the Lord our God calls to him*'. That presumes a call to which a response is made, for the prophecy of Joel is still being quoted: following immediately on the sentence cited in v. 21 the prophecy continues, 'for

---

[1] *Das urchristliche Sakramentsverständnis*, p. 35.

[2] It is not to be denied that when circumcision was applied to the proselyte it received a more critical significance than was usual in Israel, for it signified to the former his passage from paganism to the people of God, hence a transition from one kind of life to another under the blessing of the God of Israel. By virtue of this circumstance the ideas of new birth and an emergence from death to life became attached to the circumcision of the proselyte, but this was clearly an extension of meaning over that of the rite when applied to a Jewish child. If the primitive Church was influenced by this teaching in forming its own doctrine of baptism, it transformed it by its relation to the actual death and resurrection of Christ, *in whom* we die and rise again and are transferred to the new aeon and are born of his Spirit — a related set of concepts which the circumcision of the proselyte could not have possessed.

[3] *Kindertaufe*, p. 48.

[4] I. Buse would wish to confine the meaning of Acts 2.39 to the descendants rather than children of the hearers in the light of this saying, *Christian Baptism*, p. 124.

[5] As Windisch urged against Oepke, *Z.N.W.*, vol. XXVIII, 1929, p. 123.

in Mount Zion and in Jerusalem there shall be those who escape as the Lord has said, and *among the survivors shall be those whom the Lord calls*' (Joel 2.32).[1] Probably, however, the language ought not to be pressed to make it yield precise information as to the age when children can repent and be baptized. Such a question is outside the range of the interest of the saying; it is better to let its message carry due weight without being maltreated by the proponents and opponents of infant baptism.

That the lack of a rite of initiation for children of Christian parents sets them in an inferior position to that of the children under the old covenant is plausible, providing one dismisses teaching of the New Testament to the contrary. Paul makes it clear that the divine election cuts right across the distinctions of circumcision and uncircumcision: not all of Israel are Israel (Rom. 9.7), though all Israel be circumcized. It is significant that the first child of Abraham to receive circumcision, Ishmael, was not reckoned among the heirs of the promise, according to Paul (Rom. 9.7, Gal. 4.30). Contrariwise, in Paul's view, the child of Christian parents sustains a special relation to God and his people; such is the implication of 1 Cor. 7.14, where the unbaptized children are described as 'holy'. Such children are brought up in the environment of faith and prayer, at home and in the Church, and are under the constant instruction of the Word of God. They are the most privileged children of all time, under the shadow of the wings of God and his Christ, being prepared in the midst of his people for his Kingdom of grace and glory. Recognizing to the full the blessings of such a situation, it is a mistake not to recognize its limitations. Birth in a Christian home is a priceless privilege, but it is not a guarantee of inheritance in the Kingdom of God.[2] In the inscrutable providence of God, neither all the members of Christian families repent and believe the Gospel, to be incorporated into Christ and the Church, nor, mercifully, are all the members of unbelieving families doomed to irreparable loss. For election also cuts across the distinctions created by the Churches' institutions. The problem of the child dying before reaching the age of responsibility has no relevance to our subject; only an evil doctrine of God and man sets them among the lost or in limbo, and fortunately the Lord is not bound by our ignorance and mistakes. God is good, his Word is good, and his grace is ever about us and our children; our chief responsibility is to see that

[1] See Lake and Cadbury, *The Beginnings of Christianity*, vol. IV, London 1933, p. 27.
[2] See the observation on this made by Paolo Bosio, a Waldensian, in his book *Ritorno al Battesimo*, 1942, p. 41.

we, and they, hear the Word and live. For as Paul said, 'Neither is circumcision anything, nor uncircumcision, but a new creation' (Gal. 6.15).

(v) *The Objectivity of Baptism and the Function of Faith*

That salvation is of God is an axiom of Biblical religion. The Gospel declares what God has done in Christ for the redemption of the world. The sacraments are embodiments of that Gospel, deriving significance from their relation to the acts of God in Christ. Of this there is no question among the Churches, for it lies deep in their traditions, however poorly it may be expressed in practice. This very givenness of the Gospel, this relatedness of the sacraments to acts of God done without our knowledge or consent, seems in the judgment of not a few to point to the desirability of infant baptism for the sake of the truth of God. It is a view characteristic above all of the Lutheran tradition of exegesis.

Typical of the approach is the position maintained by Oepke, in his debate with Windisch. He stressed that Paul's teaching on baptism starts from the basic fact that the divine righteousness is an objective fact, a *justitia extra nos posita*; the Apostle's doctrine of baptism is thus of a transcendent order; had the dependence of Rom. 6 on Rom. 5.12–21 been observed, we would have been saved from the psychological misrepresentations of the former and recognized that justification in Christ takes place through transference from the realm of sin and death of the first Adam into the realm of life of the second; and this transference is effected solely through the act of God in baptism, not through the conversion or decision of the individual.[1] We recall Schlier's view of the relation of faith to baptism: faith looks to and prepares for the moment in which its confession is given and from which the Christian life is reckoned, viz. *the self-effective baptism*: 'In this saving act faith has only the significance of disposing man for baptism; it has no influence on the effectiveness of baptism'.[2] So also the Tübingen theologians stressed that the decisive character of baptism is given by the fact that in it the baptized is set in relation to Jesus Christ in an irrevocable manner; every objection to the validity of infant baptism is a denial that salvation comes exclusively from God's grace in Jesus Christ.[3]

Not surprisingly it is maintained by theologians in this tradition

---

[1] *Z.N.T.*, vol. XXIX, 1930, pp. 104–10.
[2] *T.L.Z.*, 1947, Sp. 332–3.
[3] Op. cit., pp. 419–20.

that baptism is independent of all disposition of man, hence it is *always* effective.[1] As baptism has such a decisive effect, independent of human conditions, baptism ought not to be denied to any; there is no reason to refuse it, for it is God who works in the sacrament, not man. If this view is especially associated with certain Anglicans, it is espoused in other traditions. J. K. S. Reid, a Presbyterian, gave it as his conviction, 'There is something so precious offered in Holy Baptism, that it should in no wise be withheld, except under the most compelling circumstances'.[2] A Swedish Lutheran advocated that baptism should be administered, even where it is viewed by the parents as a mere naming ceremony, for the promise of the Spirit is there, if the baptized will later take it.[3] An Anglican writer urged that to refuse a child baptism because of the parents' lack of Church status savoured of visiting the sins of the father upon the children![4] On such a view faith is an irrelevancy in the administration of baptism to infants. And not alone irrelevant: H. Höhler affirmed that to insist on the presence of faith in the baptized is to deny grace and pervert the Gospel, as the Anabaptists did; their refusal of infant baptism was due to their denial of justification by faith, seeking instead the conditions of baptism in the spiritual qualities of men.[5] To restrict baptism to believers is to abandon the rock of the Word of God and dissolve the Gospel into a vapourous subjectivity.[6]

[1] 'Baptism is God's work; through baptism He chooses a man and incorporates him into his Church. . . . Therefore Luther considered that all the baptized — according to the yardstick of love — are to be called saints', R. Josefson, 'Kirche und Taufe', an article in *Ein Buch von der Kirche*, ed. by G. Aulen, A. Fridrichsen, A. Nygren, etc., 1950, p. 367. The same point is made by N. Johannson, *S.J.T.*, vol. 5, 1952, p. 134: 'All baptized persons must be regarded and treated as fellow-Christians'.

[2] 'Notes on the Administration of Holy Baptism', *S.J.T.*, vol. 3, p. 166.

[3] B. Rodhe, *Att döpa barn*, 1953, p. 41.

[4] D. B. McGregor, *Theology*, 1940, p. 111.

[5] 'Who was it who looked on infant baptism as frivolous and ineffective? And did it not spring from a misinterpretation of the Gospel? Have not the Reformers looked on this confusion as so grave that they demanded the death penalty for it? The Baptists did not agree with the confession of the Church. Because they could not let *simul justus et peccator* stand, they could not assent to infant baptism, which attests this understanding of the Gospel in a particular manner', *Evangelische Theologie*, 1949, p. 477. One gains the impression that this writer regrets that the penalty for denying infant baptism was removed.

[6] Giovanni Miegge cites with approval the statement of Luther: 'If today a man gets rebaptized because he thinks that when an infant he had not believed well, tomorrow, when the devil comes, and he looks at his heart, he will say, "Look you, now I feel I truly believe, but yesterday I did not really believe well; then I will get baptized a third time. . . ." It often happens that he who believes he believes does not in fact believe, and that he who believes he does not believe, but rather despairs, believes fully', op. cit., p. 58. To Baptists this kind of argument is an example of the manner in which a great man of God can lose touch with actuality in his zeal to defend infant baptism. It has not the remotest contact with Baptist life.

There is no little irony in the fact that a group of Christians who resist the doctrine of justification *without* faith should be accused of both denying the doctrine of justification by faith and of worshipping the idol 'faith' — and this in the name of New Testament Christianity! Paul is said to have testified both to Jews and to Greeks 'of repentance to God and of faith in our Lord Jesus Christ' (Acts 20.21); he characterized the Gospel as 'the word of faith, which we preach' (Rom. 10.8); his missionary aim was to bring Gentiles to 'the obedience of faith' (Rom. 1.5): was he, too, an idolater? Mark summarizes the message of Jesus as, 'The Kingdom of God is at hand; Repent and believe . . .' (Mk. 1.15), and another Evangelist records stern words of condemnation on cities of Galilee for their lack of repentance and faith (Mt. 11.20 ff). In the Fourth Gospel life eternal is for faith and wrath of God for unbelief (Jn. 3.16, 18, 36). 'You will die in your sins unless you believe . . .', said the Christ to the Jews (Jn. 8.24). According to these words life and death, heaven and hell hang upon faith and unbelief. 'Woe to me if I preach not the Gospel!' said Paul (1 Cor. 9.16). And woe to us if we hide these issues of faith and unbelief from men — including the baptized.

This is not the place to defend the denomination to which the writer belongs from the misunderstandings of theologians of other traditions. In the confusion of Luther's time there is perhaps some excuse for his failure to understand the Anabaptists, but there is less reason for the ignorance of his successors. Anyone who knows the modern Baptist Churches realizes that the shapers of their thought chiefly identified themselves with the theology of Calvin — indeed, the British Baptists nearly throttled themselves with hyper-Calvinism more than once, and some Strict-Baptists are successfully doing so today. Anxiety over their faith is far from their hall mark: the doctrine of assurance and of the perseverance of the saints is far more characteristic of them, even of the stream deriving from General Baptists. Any reader of Spurgeon's sermons will know that he often inveighed against the religion of Law and proclaimed justification by faith as though he still lived in the Reformation. The average Baptist minister today would indignantly repudiate the suggestion that he did not believe in justification by faith, but he would admittedly not understand a presentation of that doctrine which interpreted it as justification by a faith bestowed in baptism; *that* he would suspect as justification by a work and priestly interposition in subtle disguise. Just as he holds together the sovereignty of God in election and the responsible freedom of man toward the Gospel, so he views faith as both gift of God and response of man and declines to deny either reality. The issues come together in baptism: if it is the kerygma in action, proclaiming divine redemption and offering its fruit to man, it is to be received as the kerygma must ever be received — in faith. Justification by faith can be viewed as fitly expressed in infant baptism only when a view of faith is held that is foreign to Jesus and his Apostles.[1]

The belief that baptism conveys its grace irrespective of the presence or absence of faith, however, is acceptable to none of the Protestant traditions. The New Testament link between baptism and faith is too strong for it to be broken completely. Even when it is urged that faith receives, not makes, a sacrament, place is somehow found for faith. Hence the stress on the objectivity of grace in baptism is qualified by an emphasis on the faith of the *infant* receiving baptism, or on the faith of the *sponsors*, or on the faith of the *Church* present at the baptism.

Contrary to the extraordinary notion that infant baptism corresponds best to justification by faith, Luther postulated the presence of faith in an infant, *in order to bring his doctrine of infant baptism into line with justification by faith*.[2] He found proof of the reality of infant faith in the account of the leaping of the child John the Baptist in the womb of his mother, when she greeted Mary in her pregnancy: as John became a 'believer' and holy when Christ came and spoke through his mother's mouth, so a child becomes a believer when Christ speaks to him through the mouth of the baptizer, for his word can never be in vain.[3] I can understand Luther in his day applying exegesis of this kind to infant baptism, but I find it difficult to comprehend how men of our time can take it seriously.

---

[1] It is well known that Luther distinguished two sorts of faith — one self-manufactured, by which a man could give assent to Christian doctrine, and the other which was the gift of God; the former was the faith of the Sophists (=the Schoolmen), Jews and Turks! T. L. Lindsay pointed out that in so approaching faith Luther had his own experience in mind: 'When Luther, oppressed with a sense of sin, entered the convent, he was burdened by the ideas of traditional religion, that the penitent must prepare himself in some way so as to render himself fit to experience that sense of the grace of God which gives the certainty of pardon. It was not until he had thoroughly freed himself from that weight that he experienced the sense of pardon he sought', *History of the Reformation*, vol. I, 2nd ed. 1907, pp. 444 f. One can sympathize with Luther's concern to free others from a like burden, but it is a major mistake to confuse the approach to grace via ecclesiastical institutions, sacraments, good works, etc. with the divine demand for repentance and faith in Christ. It is also wrong to oppose faith as the response of man to faith as the gift of God as irreconcilable opposites; in the New Testament faith is neither exclusively the one nor the other but both at once. That many Lutherans are today ready to admit.

[2] Kattenbusch, art. 'Taufe, II, Kirchenlehre', *Realencyklopädie f. Theologie u. Kirche*, vol. 19, p. 418.

[3] Kattenbusch, ibid.

Even Calvin seemed to be uneasy in propounding the theory: suggesting that God sows the seeds of repentance and faith in the mind of the child in baptism, he nevertheless fell back on the appeal to the power of God to do the incomprehensible and on the affirmation that we must not deny God's ability to furnish infants with the knowledge of Himself in any way he pleases.[1] Yet a modern missionary apologist not long ago asserted: 'The Mission can continue with a good conscience to baptize children only if it holds fast to the famous statement in Luther's Longer Catechism: 'With respect to children we foster the opinion and hope that the baptized child believes and we pray God to give him faith, but we do not baptize him on this basis, but solely on the ground that God has commanded it'.[2] This sounds like an uneasy realization that the ground beneath the feet is insecure; but the refuge that God has commanded infant baptism is the very point at issue. When are we going to be candid enough to admit that the idea of infant faith is an arbitrary and inconceivable accommodation of the New Testament theology of baptism to a circumstance not imagined by the New Testament writers; that it is, in fact, a *deus ex machina* device?[3]

More characteristic of the traditions of the Churches is the provision of sponsors to answer for the child at baptism. The necessity of such is strongly asserted by Calvin: 'We confess that it is indispensable for (the infants baptized) to have sponsors. For nothing is more preposterous than that persons should be incorporated with Christ, of whom we have no hopes of their ever becoming his disciples. Where none of its relations present himself to pledge his faith to the Church that he will undertake the task of instructing the infant, the rite is a mockery and baptism is prostituted'.[4] Here, it should be noted, the

---

[1] A. Dakin, 'Calvin's Doctrine of Baptism', *Baptist Quarterly*, vol. IX, 1938-9 p.163.

[2] Gensichen, *Taufproblem und Mission*, p. 60.

[3] In face of appeals to modern psychology to reinforce the idea of divine operation in the subliminal consciousness in baptism, H. R. Mackintosh wrote: 'It certainly will not commend the Christian religion to thoughtful men with a keen ethical sense if infant baptism should come to be defended by reference to the subliminal consciousness. . . . We can only say that if the divine new creation is a process in the unconscious depths of the soul, it is unrelated to the Gospel, which is a message addressed to moral spirit and seeks to elicit a change in our willed attitude to God. Truth as it is in Jesus operates by its meaning, and for unconsciousness meaning simply does not exist. We turn salvation into a nature process, like atmospheric influences telling on the body, when we divorce it from conscious appreciation and personal trust', *Expositor*, XIII, 1917, pp. 197 f. Compare also Forsyth's judgment on subconscious faith: 'Theologically such a notion of faith is fatal to the evangelical idea. It is one of its chief depressants and demoralisers. It leads to all kinds of theosophic theories about an implanted germ affecting unconsciously the child's human nature. It transfers the religious interest to the nature from the conscience', *Church and Sacraments*, p. 2.

[4] Letter to John Knox, 1559, quoted by J. K. S. Reid, op. cit. p. 171.

position that baptism 'makes Christians' is virtually denied by setting discipleship as a future prospect for the baptized, for one cannot distinguish between a Christian and a disciple. But Calvin has twisted the usual interpretation of the function of the sponsor; traditionally the latter has a more important task at the baptism than simply to promise future instruction of the child in the faith: the sponsor provides the *response* which the baptized would make if he were able to speak for himself. As in so many matters connected with infant baptism, the Churches have silently modified the explanations of their procedure, and their substitutions do not really coincide with the practice. In the Anglican Prayer Book the sponsor is addressed by the one baptizing and makes profession of repentance, faith and promise of future obedience to the command of God in the name of the child.[1] E. C. Whitaker, however, pointed out that for a thousand years before the Reformation the important questions about renunciation and faith were addressed *to the child*, exactly as to the candidate in believer's baptism, and that they were taken over virtually without modification from the form in Hippolytus. He writes, 'A ruthlessly logical interpretation of the implications of this passage (concerning the interrogations) seems to show that it depends upon the following presuppositions: that the child is capable of, and has experienced, a present faith and a present repentance (for questions and answers are all in the present tense); and that the sole function of the godparent at this point of the rite is to supply the child's lack of articulate speech. The child is thus treated as a responsible but inarticulate person; the formulas would be suited well to the baptism of a deaf mute'.[2] It was Cranmer who changed this by making the sponsors the sureties for the *future* response of the child, so assuming the right of sponsors to make promises in the name of the child. The assumption is frequently accepted without question, yet I am under the impression that, if we lifted this issue out of the baptismal debate, most people would admit that one cannot morally pledge another to repentance,

[1] The revised form of baptism, recommended by the Liturgical Commission, modernizes the language and shortens the statements but retains the fundamental idea:

'Do you renounce the devil and all his works, the wickedness that is in the world and the sinful desires of the heart?
I do.
Do you believe in God the Father . . . and in his Son Jesus Christ . . . and in the Holy Ghost?
I do.
Will you therefore obey him in whom you have believed?
I will.'

Baptism and Confirmation, p. 28.
[2] 'The Baptismal Interrogations', *Theology*, vol. LIX, 1956, p. 104.

faith and obedience towards God; in view of the Churches' experience, it is even more evident that one cannot do it practically, for the baptized so often refuse the pledge given on their behalf.

Currently an appeal is being revived to instances of vicarious faith exercized on behalf of sick people in the miracle stories of the Gospels, in justification of the practice of sponsors acting on behalf of the baptized. Théo Preiss has called attention to the fact that though Jesus often refused to perform a miracle without the exercise of faith, the faith demanded and given was that of others than the one to be healed. Naturally it is anticipated that the person affected will himself come to faith but, said Preiss, 'The action of God in Christ urges a man to faith, to recognition, but it does not necessarily presuppose it'. Moreover the Evangelists show that healings and forgiveness of sins alike constitute a sign of the Kingdom that comes in Christ (Mt. 11.5), hence it is plain that the parallel to baptism in this respect is justifiable.[1] What is not so plain is the belief that a healing vouchsafed to a dependent on the entreaty of faith justifies us in postulating that by the vicarious faith of another an individual can be *united with Christ in his death and resurrection in baptism*. W. G. Kümmel is surely right in his criticism of Preiss in asserting, 'The New Testament knows in no form a "vicarious faith", when it has to do with the question of gaining σωτηρία, salvation'.[2] In fact, as we have seen, the liturgies of the Church suggest that it was a late idea to think in terms of the sponsors believing for the baptized child; the notion that the healing miracles could encourage salvation by the faith of a proxy would not have come within the purview of the Evangelists.

In my judgment the one plausible theological justification of the function of sponsors is that advanced by Whitaker, who observed that in the Bobbio Missal the reply to the three questions, 'Dost thou believe in God the Father . . .' in each case runs, 'Respondet *credat*' — 'May he believe!' The reply of the sponsor is a prayer that the repentance and faith, present in a person of mature years at baptism, may one day be manifested in the infant being baptized. This is as much as can be hoped for in a baptism. 'If any conditions at all are demanded in infant baptism, they can only be that the godparents will bring up the child in a Christian manner. This is in fact the only condition that we can exact. The gratuitous affirmation of the godparents' faith and repentance, though doubtless edifying, is of no significant importance: it is the faith and repentance of the infant which we may

[1] *Verbum Caro*, vol. I, no. 3, p. 119.
[2] *Theologische Rundschau*, 1950, p. 37.

seek, for which there can be no substitute, and of which we can have no certainty. The best we can do is to follow the Bobbio Missal and express our faith and hope and prayer that the child will grow into these things; in fact that he will grow into his baptism'.[1] The suggestion is a valuable one, but it raises an important question as to the relation of such a baptism to that of the New Testament. Can a baptism in which the sponsors do not exercise a decisive faith, and which has only a *prospective* faith of the baptized in view, have any decisive effect in the present, and be anything more than a prayer that one day the baptism may have power? If not, it must be recognized that the significance of such a baptism is considerably changed from that ascribed to baptism in the New Testament.

A perceptible tendency has become manifest in recent works on baptism to stress faith of the *Church*, as exercized along with that of the sponsors (parents?), and into which faith the child is baptized.[2] From the point of view of responsibility and future action the faith of the Church can be a highly significant factor and it is desirable that it should be taken with increasing seriousness. But the objections voiced above to the notion of a group believing unto the salvation of another remain, and are even increased. If the faith of the Church sufficed to have the momentous effect attributed to it, the multitudes of lapsed baptized would not be so apparent in history and in the contemporary scene.

Indeed the whole lamentable situation in which the Church finds itself today with respect to baptism is sufficient proof that the objective power of baptism, unaffected by the presence or absence of faith is a tragic mistake. The outcry against 'indiscriminate baptism' is a protest against its continued advocacy. On this matter thoughtful members of the great Churches have expressed themselves with vehemence. Bishop Gore saw indiscriminate baptism as 'the real disaster'.[3] N. P. Williams characterized it as 'senseless and cheapening'.[4] The authors of the Minority Report in *Baptism and Confirmation* spoke of it as 'closely akin to sacrilege and to be exposed to the censure of the Gospel'.[5] For Brunner it is nothing short of 'scandalous'.[6] C. B. Law summarized his view on it by the epigram: 'Christ without baptism is one of God's possibilities; baptism without Christ is one of man's futilities', and he asked, 'Who can deny that the

---

[1] Op. cit., pp. 111 f.
[2] See Flemington, op. cit., p. 144; D. Baillie, op. cit., p. 83.
[3] *The Reconstruction of Belief*, pp. 749 ff.
[4] Op. cit., p. 552.
[5] Op. cit., p. 25.
[6] *Divine Human Encounter*, p. 132.

fact that England today swarms with baptized heathen is a source of real weakness to the Church?'[1] If baptism is 'self-operative' one can but say that its effect is short lived in the lives of multitudes who receive it. It needs neither wisdom nor courage to admit that such a situation is a far cry from the picture of baptism in the New Testament. From the theological aspect, the objective view of the efficacy of baptism is vastly superior to the crude animism of earlier popular notions, but in practice it is doubtful that it makes much difference; it has become a sop to the people's conscience, resulting in a dulling of their ears to the trumpet call of repentance and faith towards God. Such a charge is not to be defended by the observation that Paul himself was accused of antinomianism (Rom. 3.1–8); that is a sop to the theologian's conscience! For the Apostle, and for his contemporaries, baptism was for *faith*. They never envisaged it being administered to any but believers. Admittedly the Church has entered upon many situations not envisaged by the Apostles and developed institutions begun by them in ways not contemplated by them. Why, in view of the evidence, should it hesitate to admit that the like phenomenon is to be seen in its development of baptism?

(b) INFANT BAPTISM AND ALIEN INFLUENCES

In the foregoing pages we have considered the popular attempts to demonstrate that infant baptism was an Apostolic institution in the primitive Church, and we have observed the difficulties inherent in these arguments. It is not only that the New Testament is silent on the practice of infant baptism, but that the thought and practice of the primitive communities, as reflected in the New Testament documents, appear to be contrary to the ideas and practices that accompany infant baptism in the later Churches. The counter question might well be posed: If the baptism of infants was not instituted by the leaders of the primitive Church, how is its rise and universal adoption among the Churches to be accounted for? A definitive answer cannot be given to the question, or it would have been supplied long ago. Yet we are not without some broad hints for the solution of the problem, and those hints suggest to me the thesis that *infant baptism originated in a capitulation to pressures exerted upon the Church both from without and from within*. That thesis we shall proceed to examine.

In 1929 Hans Windisch wrote an influential article,[2] prompted by

[1] 'The Administration of Holy Baptism — Indiscriminate or not?', *Theology*, vol. XXVI, 1933, pp. 138 f.

[2] 'Zum Problem der Kindertaufe im Urchristentum', *Z.N.W.*, vol. 28, 1929, pp. 118 ff.

a defence of infant baptism from Oepke. In it he affirmed his conviction that in the beginning of the Church baptism was a confession and a personal act of decision on the part of the baptized. The participation of children at an early age in the Greek cults (to secure for them the benefits of the sacrifices etc.), the analogy of circumcision and the baptizing of children of proselytes in Judaism, made it natural to introduce the baptism of *children*, but the theology of the Church prevented it from becoming the baptism of *infants*. When infant baptism did prevail, the personal-religious element fell away and the sacramental soteriological element of baptism which for the common people meant the sacramental-magical element, became the essential thing in the rite. 'Although the sacramental element already exists in primitive Christianity, *the infant baptism of the Catholic Church signifies a "falling away"*[1] *from primitive Christianity*'.[2] Oepke wrote a further article in reply to Windisch, in which he admitted that the 'falling away from Apostolic Christianity' could point in the right direction; but he urged that the germs of this 'falling away' already lay in Apostolic Christianity. The Apostolic idea of baptism was itself contradictory, embracing at one time a spiritual-ethical element and certain magical-sacramental conceptions: 'The sacrament in Christianity is from the beginning a hybrid phenomenon, *half spiritual symbolism and half primitive magic*'.[3] This was a surprising statement from Oepke, for in all his writings he takes baptism, whether of believers or of infants, seriously and champions its necessity. Indeed, he immediately sought to mitigate the sharpness of the statement, but it is not difficult to see the implication that it was this 'half-primitive magic' in early Christianity that made the rise of infant baptism possible.[4] Most exegetes do not believe that there was any magic inherent in Paul's doctrine of the sacraments, but it is easy to understand how his teaching could become perverted in this direction. The same process took place, of course, with respect to other elements of his teaching: e.g. his doctrine of justification by grace apart from the deeds of the Law rapidly produced among the fringe of his circle a sub-Christian antinomianism. That such perversion of baptism took place in very early days in the Pauline churches is illustrated from 1 Cor. 15.29. If the baptism for the dead refers to a practice of baptizing living persons for dead persons, then we have a

---

[1] *Abfall*, the usual term for apostasy.
[2] Op. cit., pp. 124 ff, 142.
[3] 'Urchristentum und Kindertaufe', *Z.N.W.*, vol. 29, 1930, p. 100.
[4] The apologetic that the doctrine of baptism was tinged with magic is in any case a doubtful warrant for lowering it further!

sub-Christian use of the sacrament, presumably adapted from pagan customs, introduced into a Pauline church within a few years of its founding. The attitude that could adapt the baptism of believers to baptism for dead people, that they might gain the benefits believed to attach to the rite, would find it a short step to baptize infants, that they too might receive its blessings.[1]

It is astonishing to note the candour with which observations in harmony with this view are made from time to time by exponents of infant baptism. The Swedish writer H. J. Evander, for example, freely admitted that, as he put it, 'in Paul's baptistry[2] there was as yet no font for small children'. 'But', he added, 'the field was made ready for infant baptism, partly by the sacramental-magical character which baptism gradually took under the influence of the mystery cults, partly through the analogy with circumcision on the eighth day, partly through the teaching on inherited sin . . . and finally to the conception of the Church as the exclusive institution of salvation, into which one came through baptism and from which it was desired not to exclude the infants'.[3] Not a few writers would agree with that statement. If the church at Corinth could so soon be susceptible to the influence of Greek religion (and there are other traces of it in 1 Corinthians apart from the sacraments); if the young church in Colosse could find its very foundations threatened by incipient Gnosticism with a strong Judaistic tinge; and if the whole group of Galatian churches could be invaded with a Christianity accommodated to Judaism, one can well understand that by the end of the first century these pressures from both Jewish and pagan quarters, and from the imperfect grasp of Christianity by its adherents, made it increasingly difficult for the Church to maintain its sacramental thought and practice unimpaired.

The suggestion of N. P. Williams therefore, that infant baptism was a spontaneous popular *development from below*, gradually forcing its way into official recognition, is more than likely.[4] For in addition to the factors making for change, there was a lack of competent leadership in the Church, capable of correcting and guiding the movement of the masses. G. W. H. Lampe has some pertinent observations on this matter. He characterized the period between the Apostles and Irenaeus and Tertullian as 'emphatically the Century of the Common

[1] So Leipoldt: 'Churches which practise the custom of baptism for the dead cannot refuse the baptism of infants', op. cit., p. 76.

[2] The building in which the baptisms took place.

[3] *Det Kristna Dopet*, p. 92. Evander made the interesting suggestion, in keeping with the above, that infant baptism was first practised in cases of emergency, p. 44.

[4] *Ideas of the Fall and Original Sin*, p. 221.

Man'. After the Apostles 'no single character of outstanding spiritual and intellectual power comes forward to take up their part . . . The Church was left with second class leaders at its head to face the critical period of consolidation'. The little Christian congregations, chiefly drawn from the lower middle class, were set in the confused religious milieu of the Gentile world, side by side with the guilds and other hero cults, and the devotees of the numerous mysteries; sometimes they were also in close contact with the fringe of Judaism. 'The Christians must often have brought into their obscure assemblies many of the ideas which were current in the pagan environment, in which they had been brought up, and in which they still lived and worked'. When one recalls how easily the early Christians tended to be drawn to a Judaistic religion of moralism on the one hand, and to the antinomian version of Paulinism on the other, it is easy to comprehend that there was a weakened grasp of the doctrines of justifying faith and of the believer's incorporation into Christ through faith; and this must have had a far reaching effect on the theology of baptism. Moreover, observed Lampe, *'It was in this age of confusion, while the Church was still evolving the means by which this confusion was soon to be reduced to order . . . that the liturgical tradition took shape'*.[1]

This last observation is of great significance in view of the claims that are made for the primitive character of the liturgical tradition of the Church. Gregory Dix has asserted that the Apostolic παράδοσις ('tradition') of practice, like the Apostolic παράδοσις of doctrine, antedates the writing of the New Testament documents by some two or three decades, being presupposed by them and referred to in them as authoritative.[2] With regard to its basic elements that may be true, but Dix, like so many others has glossed over the indubitable fact that in this tradition the simple structure of the New Testament baptism has become a complex system of initiation rites and *in these rites a most unexpected and extraordinary emphasis is laid on exorcism*. At the commencement of the initiation the bishop lays his hand on the baptismal candidates and exorcizes the evil spirits to flee away and never return. He breathes on the candidates and 'seals' their foreheads, ears and noses; that is, he shuts up the convert's body against the powers of evil and fortifies it against their attempts to regain the possession from which the formula of exorcism has driven them.[3] The importance attached to these acts is illustrated in the preliminary address of Cyril to catechumens anticipating baptism: 'Receive with earnestness

---

[1] Op. cit., pp. 97–102.   [2] *Theology of Confirmation*, pp. 9 f.
[3] See Lampe, op. cit., p. 135.

the Exorcisms; for whether thou art breathed upon or exorcized, the ordinance is to thee salvation. . . . For as the goldsmith, conveying the blast of fire through delicate instruments, and as it were breathing on the gold which is hid in the hollow of the forge, stimulates the flame it acts upon, and so obtains what he is seeking, so also exorcizers, infusing fear by the Holy Ghost, and setting the soul on fire in the crucible of the body, make the evil spirit flee, who is our enemy, and salvation and the hope of eternal life abide; and henceforth the soul, cleansed from its sins, hath salvation'.[1]

The process of exorcism is by no means finished at this point. After the renunciation of Satan, his service and works, the candidates are anointed with the oil of exorcism. For this purpose a prayer is offered for the oil. In the Apostolic Constitutions it is sought that God would 'sanctify the oil in the name of the Lord Jesus and impart to it spiritual grace and efficacious strength, the remission of sins and the first preparation for the confession of baptism, that so the candidate for baptism, when he is anointed, may be freed from all ungodliness and may become worthy of initiation, according to the command of the Only begotten' (VII. 2). The water itself is then blessed, and that for a twofold purpose: first that it may be freed from the demons and secondly that it may become filled with the Spirit's power. In the Roman rite prayer is made that every unclean spirit may be expelled from the water and that it may by the operation of the Holy Spirit become 'a regenerating water, a purifying stream' to those about to be baptized.[2] The extent to which the consecration of the water partook of exorcism is illustrated from the Sarum ritual: the priest recites a long prayer for the blessing of the water, and in the course of this prayer he signs the water with the cross with his right hand, casts some of it out of the font in four directions, breathes upon it three times in the form of a cross, drops wax into it from a lighted candle in the form of a cross, divides it crosswise with the candle placed in the font, removes the candle and pours holy oil and chrism in the form of a cross into the water.[3] In a ritual of this order we should have the candour to acknowledge that it is not a hair's breadth removed from incantation: it is an adulteration of the religion of Christ by pure animism.

[1] St. Cyril of Jerusalem's Lectures on the Christian Sacraments, the Protechesis, 9, ed. by F. L. Cross, 1951, p. 45.
[2] E. C. Ratcliffe mentions that in the Barberini MS. God is prayed to cause the Spirit to come upon the water for its sanctification and is asked to protect it from the activity of the demon of darkness and the wicked spirit, 'The Relation of Confirmation to Baptism in the Early Roman and Byzantine Liturgies', Theology, vol. XLIX, 1946, p. 262.
[3] See Darwell Stone, op. cit., p. 177.

This prolonged series of exorcisms undoubtedly indicates an extension of belief in demons in the Church. We read in the Apostolic Constitutions, for example, 'Every man is filled either with the holy or with the unclean spirit; and *it is not possible to avoid the one or the other unless they can receive opposite spirits*'.[1] The exorcism of demons is thus achieved only by the receiving of a holy spirit. A like view occurs in Barn. 16.7: 'Before we believed on God the abode of our heart was corrupt and weak, a temple truly built by hands, for it was full of idolatry and was a house of demons. . . . By receiving the remission of our sins and hoping on the Name we became new, created afresh from the beginning'. This comes to pass through 'the word of his faith, the calling of his promise, the wisdom of the ordinances'. It is difficult to resist the conclusion that the doctrine of baptism in the liturgical tradition has become suffused with the exorcistic idea; hence the concept of forgiveness as the gift of the sacrament has become overshadowed by the setting aside of uncleanness and defilement and being freed from the devil and his hosts, and even the idea of regeneration has been similarly affected.[2]

It is sometimes asked, Where is the voice of protest against the introduction of infant baptism, if it were a post-Apostolic innovation? I am constrained to ask, Where is the voice of protest against this blatant accommodation of the Apostolic doctrine of baptism to pagan infiltrating into the Church? I know of none. On the contrary the great thinkers of the Church seem to have been blind to the process going on in their midst and some of them, like Tertullian, contributed to the trend. On considering the evidence available to us I am constrained to believe that the long process of spiritualizing and elevating the interpretation of religious lustrations, such as we see taking place in the Old Testament and which came to its height in late Judaism and in the Apostolic Church, is set in reverse in the sub-Apostolic Church as it progressively opened its doors to contemporary paganism. It is impossible to ascribe such views to the Apostles and their associates; they must have entered the Church through converts who were unable to rise to the heights of their teaching. In this we find parallels in modern missionary endeavour. The missions to non-Christian lands show that the tendency to accommodate Christianity to heathenism is a perpetual temptation of young Churches, not alone in their beginnings but in succeeding generations. At the time of writing there is an ominous movement in Central and South Africa,

---

[1] Book VI, par. 27.
[2] See further Heitmüller's discussion of this theme, *Im Namen Jesu*, pp. 279 f.

in which Christian faith and worship are being infused with revived pagan views and forms of worship; it is making rapid strides and is seriously affecting established orthodox Churches. At the other end of the scale, Gensichen tells that missionaries from Herrnhut in the early days of the Nyasa mission found that women refused to be baptized, although their husbands readily submitted to baptism. It was eventually discovered that water used for baptism was generally believed to have been placed under a spell and that in consequence a woman who came into contact with it would be made sterile. Elsewhere baptismal water has often been looked on as potent in healing,[1] while in Papua Christian evangelists found that natives believed that blood had been mixed with the baptismal water in order to give it its cleansing power.[2] Clearly the missionaries in their preaching and baptismal instruction had no intention of conveying notions of this order, but the native hearers brought to their instruction minds imbued with traditions of many generations concerning the nature and operation of religious rites, and without any wilful intention on their part they gained an understanding harmonious with their traditions concerning the efficacy of baptism. Is this not what happened in the early Christian mission? Missionaries today go out with a firmly defined doctrinal tradition and established missionary techniques; they are able generally to correct misinterpretations of Christian teaching and support evangelism with Christian education. The earliest Christian mission was far less closely integrated and after the deaths of the Apostles and the fall of Jerusalem there was no central authority to maintain a check on the development of the thought and practice of the Churches. The miracle was that the Churches held together so well as they did in the period prior to the activity of the great teachers.

Here then are the data. The New Testament gives no evidence that infant baptism was practised in the primitive Church; its theology of baptism is lofty, with no taint of magical conceptions, and it does not allow of application to the baptism of infants. In the succeeding century the doctrine of baptism was considerably modified in the direction of a lowered and externalized sacramentalism; this theology is capable of being applied to the baptism of infants, since the emphasis falls on the efficacy of the rites and on the materials used; by the close of the period infant baptism appears to be established. The suggestion

---

[1] This idea was in circulation in early centuries, when baptismal water was sometimes viewed as the best medicine! See Heitmüller, op. cit., p. 283.
[2] *Das Taufproblem in der Mission*, p. 31.

lies to hand that the modified views made possible the application of the rite to infants, and when once the rite began to be applied in this manner, the process of externalizing the mode of its operation became accelerated.

The argument falls short of proof; but it is uncomfortably plausible.

2. THE SIGNIFICANCE OF INFANT BAPTISM

If there is any cogency in what is written in the preceding pages on the origin of infant baptism it might be considered a devastating exposure of the practice and that there is nothing further to be said in its favour. This is not a necessary deduction. It will have been observed that most of the writers cited in support of the position here laid down are or were members of Churches practising infant baptism and their citations are chiefly taken from works expounding the meaning of the rite. My main concern has been to show that this mode of administering baptism did not arise in the primitive Church and that the New Testament utterances concerning the nature and meaning of baptism have been made with believers in mind. Nevertheless I am ready to admit that the principle that the origins of an institution do not necessarily serve as a criterion for its developed condition may be applied here also. The undesirable practices and conceptions of the early centuries, following the deaths of the Apostles, could conceivably be regarded as regrettable but inevitable concomitants of developments that were to issue in something entirely good. Setting aside therefore the question of origins we now seek to discover the significance of infant baptism, using, as throughout our investigation, the New Testament doctrine of baptism as our yardstick.

But the mention of the 'yardstick' gives cause for reflection. Is it right to measure infant baptism by the pronouncements of the New Testament on the baptism of persons of maturer years? Should the application of the rite to infants be expected to bear the same significance as when the subject is a responsible and responsive convert? Here the theologians speak with a divided voice. Some deny emphatically that the baptism of infants can have the same meaning as that of converts of mature age. Flemington writes: 'It cannot be too strongly emphasized that many of the difficulties about the doctrine of baptism arise because statements of St. Paul and others in the New Testament about adult baptism as they knew it in the first century A.D. are applied, without modification, to infant baptism as most Christian communions know it today. . . . It is obvious that the most

characteristic New Testament baptismal teaching, originally formulated with specific reference to the baptism of adults, must undergo
some measure of restatement before it can be applied to a situation in
which the typical subject of baptism is an infant'.[1] The leading
Anglican authorities on baptism have consistently acknowledged this
viewpoint. Canon Quick devoted a major proportion of his treatment
of baptism to discussing the kind of restatement needful on the application of baptism to infants.[2] The Commission on Baptism and
Confirmation has uniformly adopted a similar attitude.[3] The Liturgical Commission has endeavoured to give it practical recognition by
making the baptism of adults (with confirmation) as the norm for
baptismal services, to which infant baptism is accommodated in such
measure as may be possible.[4]

Resistance to this view, however, is offered by representatives of the
Reformed and Lutheran traditions. John Murray, a Presbyterian,
stated, 'If it is proper to administer baptism to infants, then the
import of baptism must be the same for infants as for adults. It cannot
have one meaning for infants and another for adults'.[5] Cremer, a
Lutheran, expressed himself more strongly. He asked, 'Is our baptism
also, which we received as new born children, the appropriation of the
grace of God, forgiveness of all sins, a bath of regeneration? If this
question is answered with a "No", then our baptism, or the baptism
as it is now practised within Christianity, is not the baptism commanded by the Lord Christ. If it is not that, then it is no baptism at
all: no washing of sins, no burial with Christ, no resurrection with
him — it is *nothing* . . . no *less than nothing!* For then it hinders the
real baptism which the Lord Christ has commanded, and therefore it
hinders the attainment of grace and the fulfilment of redemption in
us. . . . If this baptism were in vain, then the Holy Spirit would be
given to nobody; nobody would be saved; in short there would be no
church'.[6] These are strong words, even rash words which could be
highly embarrassing if Cremer's assumption proved mistaken. They

---

[1] Op. cit., pp. 82, 130.

[2] Op. cit., pp. 168 ff.

[3] 'It is not to be thought that the baptism of infants . . . can bear the whole weight
of theological meaning which the New Testament places upon the Initiation of
adults. . . . We believe the practice (of infant baptism) to be sound and defensible,
provided that the error is avoided of equating it with the fulness of Christian
initiation', *The Theology of Christian Initiation*, pp. 12, 14. The same point was
made by Dix, *Theology of Confirmation*, p. 31; N. P. Williams, op. cit., pp. 552 f;
F. C. Tindall, *Christian Initiation*, p. 8; J. R. Nelson, op. cit., p. 129; Leenhardt,
op. cit., p. 69.

[4] *Baptism and Confirmation*, pp. x ff.

[5] Op. cit., p. 48.

[6] Op. cit., pp. 30–2, 150.

reveal an attitude that assumes that the universe itself is at stake in infant baptism. But neither high emotions nor traditional dogmatics must be permitted to becloud our judgment. We must attempt a dispassionate estimate of the significance of infant baptism in the light of the New Testament teaching on baptism.

(i) *Infant Baptism and Confession*

It is universally recognized that in the primitive Church baptism was the occasion par excellence for the confession of faith in Christ. Acts 8.36 ff (Western text), Rom. 10.9, Eph. 5.26, 1 Pt. 3.18 ff provide sufficient evidence on this point. Moreover the baptism itself was a confession, expressing before men a faith embraced in the hidden man of the heart. In a similar way it was both an occasion of calling on the name of the Lord for forgiveness (Acts 22.16), and itself a prayer in action, at once the surrender of faith to the Saviour and the surrender of obedience to Him as Lord. No attempt to deny this element of New Testament baptism is made by modern apologists for infant baptism, but it is urged that the confession of faith can be as well made after as before baptism, and that to insist on any relative order is unwarranted.[1] Yet there is at least one aspect of the believer's confession in baptism mentioned in the New Testament that cannot be postponed in this fashion. In 1 Pt. 3.21 it is said, 'Baptism ... now saves you, not as a removal of dirt from the body but as a συνειδήσεως ἀγαθῆς ἐπερώτημα εἰς θεόν through the resurrection of Jesus Christ'. We have seen that the disputed phrase can be rendered either as 'a prayer to God for a good conscience', or 'a pledge to God to maintain a good conscience'. On the first interpretation baptism is declared to be an appeal to God on the part of the baptized, which appeal is answered through the saving act of the Risen Christ; this personal dealing between the believer and his Lord makes the rite what it is. On the second view the essence of baptism is represented as being a pledge of fidelity to God, which is made possible through the saving power of the Risen Christ; it would be the nearest instance in the New Testament of the conception of baptism as a *sacramentum*, a military oath. Reicke commented on the passage, interpreted in this latter sense: 'To define the Christian act of initiation as an undertaking to be loyal towards God and men fits very well in this connec-

---

[1] 'To systematize the actions of Christ in baptism according to some rational pattern of our own, either by requiring the priority in time of faith to baptism, or by asserting the simultaneity of regeneration and sacramental administration, is to do wrong. Such systematization is an attempt to control the Holy Spirit', *Interim Report of the Scottish Commission*, 1955, p. 52.

tion. It is quite natural that baptism is defined as an undertaking in an ethical meaning'.[1] The observation 'quite natural' is true when the baptized person is a believer, able to make of his baptism a pledge of faith and obedience, but when applied to the baptism of an infant it becomes meaningless. We should be honest enough to recognize that 1 Pt. 3.21 is one example of a New Testament baptismal utterance that cannot be applied to infant baptism. The baptism of an infant is neither his prayer to God for a pure conscience nor his promise to God to maintain such. This aspect of New Testament baptism, accordingly, we must ungrudgingly confine to the baptism of believers.[2]

(ii) *Infant Baptism and Dying and Rising with Christ*

The statement, 'Baptism saves you ... through the resurrection of Jesus Christ', has contact with the theology of baptism in Rom. 6.1 ff. True, there is no mention in this sentence of participating in the death of Christ; the emphasis falls on baptism as a participation in Christ's *resurrection*. The Lord who rose from death acts in baptism for the deliverance of the believer who pledges himself to God; only so can the 'pledge' be maintained (or, on the alternative interpretation, the 'prayer' be answered). Self-evidently, the 'answer' or 'appeal' to God has no power to save, except as it directs the believer to the Risen Christ who can do so. But if the Risen Christ is viewed as the power of that baptism whose definitive element is confession or prayer to Him, the question is raised whether the writer would have envisaged the power of Christ's resurrection operative in a baptism from which the definitive element of confession or prayer to Him is absent. The answer is surely clear: had the writer known such a baptism he would not have defined baptism in the terms he has used in 1 Pt. 3.21. A similar standpoint appears to be assumed in Rom. 6.1 ff.

It will be recalled that in the latter passage, along with other related statements in the Pauline Epistles, we distinguished three aspects of Paul's doctrine of the believer's dying and rising with Christ in baptism. First he becomes 'united with the form of Christ's death', or with Him as the Crucified, to become 'united with the form of his Resurrection', or with Him as the Resurrected (Rom. 6.5). That is to say, he participates in the death and resurrection that Jesus himself suffered and experienced. Baptized to the Christ who died and rose as his Representative, the believer dies and rises in Him. Secondly, in

[1] Op. cit., p. 185.
[2] This is explicitly granted by the Swedish Lutheran Hjalmar Evander, *Det Kristna Dopet*, pp. 191 ff.

baptism the believer suffers a death like Christ's and rises as He did. The old God-estranged, God-displeasing life in the flesh is ended, and in Christ the believer is a new creature living in the new creation. Baptism is for the believer a transition from the old aeon to the new. Thirdly, the believer in baptism renounces the sinful ways in which he formerly lived, henceforth to set his affection on things above and live according to the pattern of Christ's dying and rising. 'We were buried with him through baptism . . . that we might walk in newness of life' (Rom. 6.4). 'You stripped off the old nature with its practices and put on the new, which is being renewed in knowledge after the image of its creator' (Col. 3.9 f). At this point it is important to grasp that in *each* of these aspects the grace of Christ is active in a responsive believer.

Under the first aspect the crucial matter is Christ's solidarity with men as the Second Adam. Because of his unity with the race, all men are involved in his redemptive action: 'As one man's trespass led to condemnation for all men, so one man's act of righteousness leads to acquittal and life for all men' (Rom. 5.18). Yet other utterances of Paul presuppose within the universal solidarity of Christ with mankind a narrower solidarity with those in whom his death and resurrection have unique power. For example, 'If because of one man's trespass, death reigned through that one man, much more will those who *receive* the abundance of grace and the free gift of righteousness reign in life through the one man Jesus Christ' (Rom. 5.17, see also 2 Cor. 5.14–17). In virtue of his incarnation, death and resurrection, the whole race is included in Christ's redemption; in virtue of grace and faith, Christ's incarnation, death and resurrection attain their purposed end in his people; they enter a koinonia with the Lord such as the world does not know, for they are 'in Christ' — and *they are in Christ through baptism in faith* (Gal. 3.26 f).

Under the second point of view the 'existential' aspect comes to the fore, but the primary emphasis still lies on the act of Christ, as the passives in Rom. 6 testify ('We were buried . . . became planted in the form of Christ's death . . . were crucified with Christ'): the 'crucifixion' of the 'old man' is as truly the action of grace as resurrection with Christ is deed of divine power. On the other hand, this 'passivity' is matched by 'response', even as grace is met by faith. For in Col. 2.12 we read, 'You were buried with him in baptism, in which you were also raised with him through faith in the working of the God who raised him from the dead'. A view which maintains that resurrection with Christ in baptism is independent of faith is irreconcilable with this statement. Once more we freely grant that faith itself has no power to raise the believer from the dead — it can only look to God to do that; but according to this statement, God acts in his almighty power to raise the dead in baptism in response to the faith of the baptized. A baptism wherein God raises from death apart from the active faith of the object of his action is not contemplated. A baptism of this kind would be of a different order from that which is in view here. Evidently the Apostle had never considered such a phenomenon, or he would not have framed his statement in this fashion, nor were there any in Colosse who had experienced such a baptism.

The third aspect has in view especially the ethical implication of baptism: in the act of turning to God in Christ the believer renounces his sinful life, condemns it to the grave and begins the life of discipleship. Attention is concentrated in this case on the action of the baptized: '*You* stripped off the old nature with its practices and put on the new' (Col. 3.9). 'They that are Christ's *crucified* the flesh with its passions and lusts' (Gal. 5.24). And the baptismal turning is imitated in later life: 'Consider yourselves dead to sin and alive to God in Christ Jesus' (Rom. 6.11), 'ever bearing in the body the death of Jesus, that the life of Jesus may also be manifested in the body' (2 Cor. 4.10). But the extent to which this new quality of life is rooted in the action of God in Christ is illustrated in such sayings as Rom. 6.18: '*Having been set free from sin*, you have become servants of righteousness', Col. 3.1 ff: '*If you have been raised with Christ*, seek the things that are above'. In every aspect of redemption and the Christian life, grace is foundational, and faith is crucial.

The important conclusion from this review is the unity of these aspects of death and resurrection with Christ and the unity of grace and faith in them all. Contrary to the assumption, regarded as axiomatic by the theologians of the great Churches, that baptismal incorporation in Christ takes place in the due administration of baptism to an infant, the teaching of Paul negates it. For there is no incorporation in Christ without participation in his death and resurrection and there is no death and resurrection in and with Christ apart from the response of faith. *The most characteristic teaching of Paul concerning baptism is accordingly inapplicable to infant baptism.*

(iii) *Infant Baptism and the Forgiveness of Sins*

'Repent and be baptized every one of you in the name of Jesus Christ for the forgiveness of your sins', exhorted Peter on the day of Pentecost. 'Rise and be baptized and wash away your sins, calling on his name' said Ananias to Paul (Acts 22.16). 'We acknowledge one baptism unto remission of sins', runs the Creed. In the popular mind the forgiveness of sins, or cleansing from them, is the first thought associated with baptism, and it is applied without hesitation to the baptism of infants. In the Anglican Book of Common Prayer the priest before baptism prays, 'We call upon Thee for this infant, that he, coming to Thy holy baptism, may receive remission of sins by spiritual regeneration' and, after the baptism, 'We yield Thee hearty thanks . . . that it hath pleased Thee to regenerate this infant with Thy Holy Spirit', thus presuming cleansing from sins to have taken place in the baptism.

The difficulty raised by this application of the theology of baptism to infant baptism has long been felt. The mature person is made to be aware of his sins, hence Peter's first word, '*Repent* and be baptized. . .' Expression is given to this repentance in the renunciation of the devil and all his works, the world and the flesh, therefore the typical addition of Ananias is made, '*calling on his Name*', for only by coming under the power of Christ's redemption can such a deliverance be effected. The baptized, like the Prodigal Son, is one who has 'come to himself', and in recognition of his need returns to the Lord with the cry, 'I have sinned against heaven and before you'. For such a person baptism is a true expression of penitence; the Father comes to welcome his child, assure his forgiveness and bestow restoration — the robe and the ring and the shoes; joy is proclaimed, 'for this my son was dead and is alive again, was lost and is found' (Lk. 15.17 ff). The entire symbolism of baptism is suited to a conception of this order; but how can it be predicated of infants a few days old?[1]

The classical answer of the Churches to this question has been that infants, though not culpable of sins committed after this fashion, are nevertheless embroiled in 'original sin'; infant baptism cleanses away that sin. Admittedly it has not been easy to be precise about its

[1] This was the major contention of Windisch. Of the New Testament teaching on baptism he wrote, 'This symbolic-sacramental interpretation of the actual baptismal event presupposes that the baptized already have a life behind themselves and that they have besmirched their life through their own iniquity, that they have committed many sins, consciously denied obedience to God and have served another God-opposed power. Baptism then means that the iniquity of the old life is wiped out, that the service of sin is broken, that the old man is dead and that a new life has been given to the baptized', *Z.N.W.*, 1929, p. 127. Set against this background, the renunciation of the devil and his works in infant baptism, which, as we saw, for a millennium was applied to the *present* state of the child, is unrealistic. The thoughtlessness of framers of liturgies in this connection comes to its height in the Coptic Church rite, wherein the priest prays that all the remains of the worship of idols should be cast out of the infant's heart! See F. C. Tindall, 'The Theology of Original Sin and Original Guilt', an appendix to the report *Baptism Today*, p. 43.

nature. Origen, who appears to have been the first to consider the question, in one place suggests, 'By the sacrament of baptism the pollution of our birth is taken away' (Hom. 14.4, in Luc.); but elsewhere he says that the Apostles gave baptism to infants, 'for they knew that there were inborn corruptions of sin in all people, which must be washed away by water and the Spirit' (Comm. on Romans 5.9). Yet if we are to speak of forgiveness, and not merely of cleansing away the pollution of birth (!) it is impossible to avoid the notion of the guilt of infants, and from Augustine onward that has been the standard doctrine. In the Anglican formularies for example, 'original sin . . . is the fault and corruption of the nature of every man . . . and therefore in every person born into this world it deserveth God's wrath and damnation' (Art. IX). We repeat, if *forgiveness of sins* in infant baptism is to be taken seriously, no less language than that will do, though no Anglican theologian will be found who subscribes to it. However acceptable to the age of Augustine and the next millennium it may have been, the logic of infant baptism is too cruel for modern man. For this reason lesser terms are used in reference to original sin remitted in baptism. Darwell Stone, e.g. speaks of 'the taint and distortion of original sin': 'The love of God provides that they may be unconsciously set free from that which they have unconsciously received, and that they may possess grace which may enable them from their earliest years to respond to the teaching of divine truth and the voice of conscience'.[1] Giovanni Miegge states this aspect of baptism to mean 'the proclamation and solemn attestation of the remission of that offence'; since this is an impersonal sin, contracted without knowledge through mere birth into humanity, it may be forgiven without knowledge, 'not in virtue of a personal act of repentance, but simply in virtue of the redemptive solidarity of Christ'.[2] There is some sense here: infant baptism is the *proclamation* of the forgiveness of this child through the redemptive solidarity of Christ; but does not that imply that the 'redemptive solidarity' existed all along, as it exists with every child born into the humanity for which Christ died, and that infant baptism can do no more than *proclaim* this truth? If this is what Miegge means, infant baptism is not efficacious for forgiveness; it is purely declaratory. But that is a considerable reduction of the Apostolic doctrine, which attributes to baptism much more than a declaratory effect. With regard to the problem of the relation of children to original sin, I think Miegge points in the right direction for its solution. In view of Rom. 5.12–21 there seems to be no doubt

[1] Op. cit., p. 100, cf. p. 214.　　[2] Op. cit., p. 81.

that Paul taught the entailment of the whole race in Adam's sin; but he also taught the entailment of the whole race in Christ's deed of righteousness. Naturally he had no explicit concern for infants in his brief exposition; he was concerned with men that sinned, whether in possession of or without the Law, and their relationship to the disobedience of the First Adam and the obedience of the Second Adam. The logic of his argument would appear to imply, however, that as truly as the reach of Adam's deed is universal, so is that of Christ's redemptive act. No act of the Church is required to bring infants within the scope of Christ's action, any more than an act of the group is required to bring the child under the dominance of Adam's sin. When assent is given to sin by the individual, so that in some measure he too sins 'after the likeness of Adam's transgression', then sin is both personal and culpable; only the cry of repentance and faith towards Christ can then bring the deliverance from the sin which slays (Rom. 7.11).[1] At that point Christian baptism becomes meaningful.

It is not surprising that desire is increasingly manifest by theologians to be rid of this theological burden of forgiveness of sins in infant baptism. O. C. Quick explicitly repudiated the idea of cleansing original sin and impartation of the supernatural gifts which Adam enjoyed before the fall; his solution was to view infant baptism as a symbol of the many purifications from sin and gifts of new life which go towards the achievement of salvation.[2] Flemington, in similar vein, also denied the removal of original sin through infant baptism; he views it as a pledge and promise of the divine conquest of sin in the life of the baptized.[3] These interpretations of baptism as promise and symbol will engage us shortly. More thoroughgoing is the viewpoint of N. P. Williams and those who follow him. In his judgment the item in the Creed, 'We acknowledge one baptism unto remission of sins', was drawn up at a time when baptism was predominantly that of mature persons, and it should be restricted to baptism in that context: 'The true meaning of this clause must be the meaning which it would have borne for Cyril and for the Church of Jerusalem in the middle of the fourth century. And there can be no reasonable doubt that the thought in their minds was that of baptism as administered to adults according to Apostolic and primitive usage, preceded by "repentance" and immediately followed by "confirmation" and first communion.

---

[1] A brief, clear exposition of this viewpoint is given by Nils Engelsen in his article, 'Tro og dåp', in the trilogy *Dopet, Dåben, Dåpen,* pp. 62 f.

[2] Op. cit., pp. 168–72, 173 ff.

[3] Op. cit., pp. 139 f.

When therefore we repeat this clause in the Creed as a part of the Eucharistic Liturgy, what we affirm is our belief in baptism as anciently administered to adults, for the washing away of actual sins, and as still so administered, habitually in the mission field to converts from heathenism, and rarely in Christian countries'.[1] Dr. Williams proposed, accordingly, to distinguish between the sin-remitting and strength-bestowing aspects of baptism; the baptism of adults involves both kinds of operation, but the baptism of infants only the positive operation of making its recipients members of the Church and of Christ, capable of receiving the grace given in confirmation, after which time they will gradually be enabled to overcome the 'inherited infirmity' common to us all.[2] This exposition has been of considerable influence in the Anglican Communion. It was espoused by C. B. Law,[3] and by F. C. Tindall in the report Baptism Today.[4] There seems to be a move towards it in the yet more basic document, The Theology of Christian Initiation, wherein it is affirmed that in baptism 'children are brought from a realm which is dominated by "original sin" into one wherein the grace of God in Christ abounds, where the benefits of the divine forgiveness are at work'.[5] This represents a distinct modification of the historic position that forgiveness is granted in infant baptism. If those responsible for drawing up the revised service for infant baptism have hesitated to express this in the Liturgy,[6] the foundations of the doctrine have nevertheless been ominously shaken and there must come a time when it shall tumble to the ground. Forgiveness of infants, even in baptism, is a notion exegetically unjustifiable and theologically indefensible.

(iv) Infant Baptism and Entry into the Church

It was observed in the preceding discussion that N. P. Williams, denying that infant baptism bestowed forgiveness of sins, restricted its significance to making its recipients 'members of the Church and of Christ'. In a similar manner the Anglican Report, The Theology of Christian Initiation, avoided speaking of the removal of original sin in baptism and stressed instead the function of baptism as bestowing regeneration, 'not as the infusion of something into the child, but as the

[1] Op. cit., p. 552.
[2] Ibid.
[3] 'The Administration of Holy Baptism', Theology, vol. XXVI, 1933, p. 137.
[4] P. 46.
[5] P. 22.
[6] The ancient prayer that God would sanctify the water to the mystical washing away of sin has been retained. One wonders whether its implication in this context has been fully realized. That it relates to the present and not future time is intimated in the prayer of thanks that the child is regenerated.

bringing of the child within the Church and Body of Christ, wherein the "powers of the age to come" are at work'.[1] Citations to a like effect could be made from a variety of works expounding the significance of infant baptism. If doubts are entertained about some aspects of the practice, here is one as to which none exists among the representatives of the Churches: baptism incorporates a child into the people of God, where the Spirit of God is at work. On this point no weakening is conceivable. To not a few it is the basic issue in the baptismal debate.

Behind this apparent unanimity and simplicity of view, however, lurk deep seated differences and difficulties that are not always brought to light of day. In what way does infant baptism 'bring' a child into the Church? Most Free Churchmen would concur with Forsyth's answer: 'Baptism is at least a formal introduction of the child to these influences of a loving Church and a Church of grace, which are meant to surround the growing life with a Christian atmosphere of sympathy and instruction. And it should be easier to grow up a Christian inside the Church than outside of it, as so many children are'.[2] Baptists would have no little sympathy with this viewpoint, for they commonly bring their own children to a service for the Blessing of Infants, with just such an intention.[3] If this represented the mind of the Churches in their practice of infant baptism, a rapprochement between those holding differing views on baptism would be far simpler than it has been thus far.[4] But in fact, the classic Catholic, Lutheran and Reformed traditions have intended far more than this in their administration of infant baptism. For them infant baptism incorporates a child into the Body of Christ, so making him a member of Christ, 'a redeemed member of the order of Christ's new creation'.[5] Such a view is vigorously maintained on all hands in the current debate. To Cullmann there can be no valid reason to contest it, since the baptized, whether adult or infant, is a purely passive object of God's dealing.[6] Reformed theologians in Britain are again urging that from this basic point of view infant baptism better accords with God's

---

[1] Pp. 21 f.   [2] *The Church and the Sacraments*, p. 162.

[3] They normally explicitly include in the service thanksgiving for the life, intercession for the well-being and salvation of the child and dedication of parents and church to that end.

[4] Forsyth was a Congregationalist. It should not be overlooked that in England there are many Union churches, following the tradition of John Bunyan, composed of Baptists and Congregationalists; and there are many Evangelical Free Churches, open to membership of all Free Churches, in whose membership Baptists usually preponderate.

[5] *The Theology of Christian Initiation*, p. 22.

[6] Op. cit., pp. 32 f.

mode of incorporating men into the redeemed society than does the baptism of mature believers.[1]

. Nevertheless, despite these claims on behalf of the baptism of infants, it seems impossible for most Churches to maintain the practice without minimizing the participation in salvation and the Church, attributed to baptism in the New Testament, and therefore without minimizing baptism itself. In the Anglican tradition full membership in the Church is not accorded to infants baptized; that must await their later confirmation. Many members of the Lutheran and Reformed Churches incline to the same view. But it leaves the unconfirmed baptized in an ambiguous position with regard to the Church, and for the majority that ambiguity remains throughout life. There is even greater confusion over the doctrine of the Spirit and infant baptism. Logically the practice of confirmation sunders baptism from the gift of the Spirit, and many Anglican theologians and clergy contend for this as the correct view: baptism *prepares* for the gift of the Spirit bestowed in confirmation. That interpretation reduces the significance of baptism in a manner unknown to Apostolic theology; it sunders the Spirit from the Risen Lord, and involves the curious notion of birth by the Spirit without the possession of the Spirit. Other Anglicans of a different persuasion join ranks with the Lutherans and Reformed in reducing the concept of regeneration to an ambiguous phenomenon that, whatever it is supposed to be, is not that which the New Testament writers represent it to be; expressed bluntly, these theologians fear to apply the full blooded Apostolic doctrine to infant baptism.[2] We have the extraordinary situation therefore, that the Churches, in order to retain a non-Apostolic ap-

---

[1] In its advocacy of this position the Church of Scotland radically differs from the Church of England. In the Book of Common Order the basic pattern of baptism is that of infants. 'The Scottish Reformers did not offer a doctrine of baptism primarily applicable to adults and then seek to adapt it to infants. For them baptism by its very nature as the sacrament of our first entrance into God's Household was essentially relevant for children, but therefore equally adaptable to adults who can only enter into the Kingdom of God as little children', *Interim Report of the Scottish Commission*, 1958, p. 12.

[2] The traditional Lutheran view, in no kind of relation to the New Testament teaching on the subject, reduces regeneration to signify the gift of faith; or it is seen as the effect of justification that enables renewal of life to take place; sometimes it is extended to denote the whole work of grace in the Christian; some Swedish Lutherans apparently still maintain the view of Martensen that the seed of regeneration is sown in the baptized infant. The Reformed Tradition considers regeneration to be adoption into the family and household of God, sometimes adding to this the thought of new life from the Spirit. The Church of Scotland's commission emphasized the belief that regeneration is that which took place in Christ on our behalf, in which we are given to share in baptism — a right view which is wrongfully used as soon as it is implied that to be in Christ is *not* to become a 'new creature' (see the *Reports*, 1957, pp. 42 ff; 1958, p. 14; 1959, p. 31).

plication of baptism, find themselves compelled to diminish the Apostolic doctrine of baptism, compromise their doctrine of the Church and confuse their doctrine of the Spirit. Far from being a matter to view with equanimity, this unclear conception of the Church is the most unfortunate fruit of infant baptism. We have already noticed the view, very common among the masses in Europe and supported by theologians, that all the baptized must, in charity, be viewed as Christians and so as members of the Church. But with the best endeavour after charity, we cannot shut our eyes to the fact that there are *millions* of baptized people in Europe who have no contact at all with the Church; yet they are still claimed as members of the Church, members of the Body, members of Christ! Surely Brunner is justified in his protest, 'He who does not want to confess Christ does not belong in the Church', and in affirming that the sufferance of manifest atheists in the Church is a relinquishment of an essential mark of the Church.[1] The belief that the baptism of infants makes them members of the Church has resulted in the distinction between Church and world being blurred, to the loss of both.

A quite different approach, however, has been made to this question from the angle of the child of Christian parents, nurtured in Christian faith: what is *his* status in the Church? On this matter D. M. Baillie has spoken with eloquence and deep feeling. In his view Christians have to face the alternative whether their children are in the Church or are outsiders, whether they are children of God or children of wrath, whether they are Christian children or 'little pagans'. To him the answer is indubitable: God desires children to experience grace as children and to be Christian children: therefore they should be regarded as part of the Church, the entrance to which is marked by baptism. 'The sacrament of baptism brings the child into a new environment, the environment of the Church of Christ, which Calvin, following Cyprian, called the Mother of all who have God as their Father. . . . If "a baby must have love", it is also true that a baby must have the grace of God in order that it may grow as a truly Christian child. And it is through the faith and love of the Church and the parents, directed upon the children through physical channels and using the effective symbolism of baptism, that the grace of God reaches the scarcely conscious child'.[2]

One sympathizes with the attitude manifest in this argument, for it springs from concern for children and not for the retention of traditional forms for their own sake. Yet Baillie surely drew contrasts

[1] *Divine Human Encounter*, p. 133.   [2] *The Theology of the Sacraments*, pp. 80–7.

which do not exist. It is unreal to ask whether children are children of God or children of wrath, still less to suggest that the children of Christian parents are the former and those of non-Christian parents are the latter. In the Pauline and Johannine theology, at least, children are neither the one nor the other by virtue of birth. Young or old, men become children of God in baptism by faith (Gal. 3.26 f, Jn. 1.12) and no unbaptized infant is a 'child of wrath'.[1] If the phrase 'child of God' were to be extended, as it is sometimes, to signify one made in the image of God and existing under the love of God, it would be true of infants universally and they need no baptism to make them such.

The children of Christian parents, nurtured within the fold of the Church, are certainly not outsiders nor 'little pagans', though they may be little terrors. But neither are they, in the fullest sense of the term, 'in the Church' in the sense of members of the Body, that is, *in Christ*. Nor should we regard such a view as an insult to our children. To be baptized into the Church is to possess Christ and the Spirit (1 Cor. 12.13, Gal. 3.26 ff), to be 'washed, consecrated, justified' (1 Cor. 6.11); Paul evidently did not envisage a person 'consecrated' to be a member of the consecrated people who was not justified, cleansed from his sins, a participator in Christ and the Spirit (1 Cor. 6.11), hence dead to sin and risen to righteousness in Christ (Rom. 6.1 ff). But we have already seen that to predicate these effects of infant baptism is bad exegesis and an application of categories unsuitable to infants. To say that a child needs the grace of God like mother-love is undoubtedly true; but the point at issue is whether that grace comes in infant baptism. Dr. Baillie declared his anxiety to let children be children and not to foist an unnatural adult experience on to them, but in reality his view entails attributing such an experience to *infants*.

Admittedly, to define satisfactorily the relation of children in the nurture of the Church to the Body of Christ is not easy; but it is a mistake to permit an issue, on which the New Testament is almost silent, to becloud the doctrine of baptism, on which the New Testament speaks with clarity. 1 Cor. 7.14 may be held to afford some guidance: the children of a Christian parent are 'holy' and the non-Christian partner is 'consecrated' by virtue of belonging to the believer; such a family (in a manner undefined by the Apostle) stands

---

[1] The statement in Eph. 2.3, 'We are by nature children of wrath', employs a Greek idiom (by nature) and a Hebrew (children of wrath); it has nothing to do with the notion of divine wrath directed to a humanity born twisted.

under the wing of divine grace, whatever the relation of its individual members to the local Church may be. The conception belongs to the world of Jewish sacrificial ritual and I do not think that it can be pressed; it does indicate, however, that God looks in pity and grace on a family within the sphere of the Church, though it does not allow of the deduction that the members are ipso facto members of the Church (consider the non-Christian partner in 1 Cor. 7.14). From the human angle, the children of Christian parents are the objects of the perpetual intercession of their parents and recipients of the inestimable blessings that enrich a Christian home. Within the Church they are participators in the gracious influences of worship, the proclamation of the Word of God, and the various means of Christian education; that is to say, they are in a position peculiarly comparable to that of the catechumen. Now the catechumen was certainly not regarded as a member of the Church: he was permitted to attend part of the Church's worship but not the Supper; yet neither was he viewed as a pagan; such a person was *in the care of the Church, being discipled unto Christ.* Something similar may be said of our children in their tender years. Admittedly there is a difference between catechumens of mature years, undergoing instruction for a defined period at their own request, and young children, whose preparation for the Church commences even before birth in the prayers of the parents, and whose nurture for the glory of God begins long before they can appreciate what they receive. Nevertheless, where Christian parenthood is regarded as a vocation from God, the blessing of God is not withheld, and often the prayers are wonderfully answered in lives guided unto Him. But it must be stressed that in this circumstance the catechumenate does not begin with baptism but has baptism as its goal, and with it the full entry on to the rich inheritance of the Church's fellowship. A restoration of the catechumenate for their children would prove of inestimable blessing to the Churches and would do more than anything else yet suggested for the restoration of baptism and Church membership to their original dignity and glory.[1]

(v) *Infant Baptism as a Promise of Salvation*

There are not wanting exegetes who perceive the difficulties raised by the traditional interpretation of infant baptism and are ready to grant that it cannot signify a means of present committal to Christ, of forgiveness of sins, of death and resurrection with Christ and of

---

[1] For an instructive discussion on this theme, see G. W. Rusling, 'The Status of Children', *Baptist Quarterly*, vol. XVIII, 1960, pp. 245 ff.

ingrafting into the Body of Christ; this they acknowledge because, in the absence of responsive faith, the accent in infant baptism appears to them to be transferred from *appropriation* to *anticipation*. When a child is at the threshhold of life, it seems reasonable to view the rite as 'the sacrament of his future',[1] or, in the picturesque phrase of H. R. Mackintosh, as 'a promise clothed in sense'.[2]

This view has appealed with particular force to Leenhardt, for he sees in it a means of retaining the Biblical exposition of baptism, despite the altered perspective. He observes how frequently things are said about baptism, which in themselves are good, but which have nothing to do with the sacrament, and conversely how even a writer like Calvin does not appear to be interested in the New Testament texts that deal with baptism, but draws his material from elsewhere: *Eh bien*, says Leenhardt, 'we are in the presence of a new sacrament!'[3] In his judgment we must see baptism as the sign of what God has done in Christ for sinners and of what He does when faith seizes his action. It is the sign of the divine *will* to regenerate, rather than the sign of an accomplished regeneration. 'The effusion of the Spirit is a "promise" of which the sacrament marks the actuality and of which faith lays hold'.[4] Admittedly a baptism in these circumstances implies a 'deviation' from, or 'defect' (malfaçon) in the sacrament, but 'it is not a misinterpretation' of its essential significance.[5]

This represents a candid attempt to face the difficulties arising from the application of New Testament teaching to the baptism of an infant incapable of entering into a sacrament. It raises the dual problem, however, in what sense baptism may be regarded as a promise, and the legitimacy of relating a sacrament solely to the future. The former point is illustrated in W. F. Flemington's exposition of this approach to the doctrine. He defines the baptism of an infant as 'the divine pledge and promise for a particular human life, that all sin (whether original sin or actual sin) shall ultimately be overcome, because Christ overcame it once-for-all in the victory of the cross'.[6] How are we to interpret this statement? Can anyone know at the font that all sin will be overcome in the unfolding life of a particular infant? Flemington has already agreed with Quick's contention relating to original sin and baptism, that experience shows that sinful tendencies or spiritual defects of the baptized and unbaptized child are much the same; does not this apply here also — that baptized children often

---

[1] Forsyth, op. cit., p. 168.   [2] *The Expositor*, 1917, p. 202.
[3] Op. cit., p. 70.   [4] Op. cit., p. 71.
[5] Op. cit., p. 72.   [6] Op. cit., p. 140.

grow up without fulfilment of the 'promise' of baptism? If, however, appeal is being made by Flemington to the ultimate destiny of the race, what special need does baptism meet? For according to the Universalist, all will be saved at the last, baptized and unbaptized, while the Calvinist expects to see the triumph of God over sin in *hell* as in heaven, and he will not consent to the simple proposition that all the baptized will be in heaven and all the unbaptized in hell! Flemington, in fact, later modifies his language to suggest that baptism embodies 'the divine *purpose* for that human soul'.[1] Again one is in doubt: if the divine 'purpose' means the willingness of God to save, it is too weak, for God wills all men to be saved and come to the knowledge of the truth (1 Tim. 2.4); but who dares affirm that baptism pledges the will of God to the effectual calling of the child, thus identifying the elect with the baptized? The like question is raised by the later characterization of baptism as a 'prophecy and anticipation' of the forgiveness, new life, gift of the Spirit, sonship, etc. which the New Testament ascribes to adult baptism;[2] for baptism is not a divine declaration that the infant *shall* be forgiven, *shall* be granted the Spirit, *shall* be made an heir of God etc., on the contrary the prophecy is all too often falsified by the event.

Leenhardt is much more cautious in his presentation of the argument. In his view infant baptism is *a promise with a condition*, viz., that the response of faith will later be made by the child. 'The significance of the sacrament as a symbolic action has escaped the infant; those who take the responsibility of administering the sacrament to the child, who today is unconscious of what has been done over him, must supply his lack. They have the charge to make this child conscious of what has been done over him, so that his faith may respond with full knowledge to the act of God in Christ which baptism has sacramentally expressed'.[3] In a comparable manner Mackintosh imagined that a Christian baptized in infancy might look back and confess, 'He met me at life's threshhold and by the pledge of this sacrament declared me to have an interest in that love of his which Jesus represents, announcing that for me there was a great inheritance awaiting, which should be mine in proportion as I accepted it. He held forth to me, even then, the blessings that are in Christ, and this offer He confirmed and sealed by the appointed sign'.[4] The sentiment is very beautiful; but observe what a drastic change has been wrought

[1] Op. cit., p. 142.   [2] Op. cit., p. 143.
[3] Op. cit., pp. 71 f.   [4] Op cit., p. 202.

in the nature of baptism so administered. Baptism has been reduced from a sacrament to a sermon, from a gift to an offer, from an event of eternal consequence to an uncertain possibility. Undoubtedly there is an element of proclamation in every sacrament, but the person for whom this sermon is preached and on whom it is acted cannot understand a syllable of the speech nor a gesture of the action; it will all have to be repeated later by instruction and proclamation of the Word. The rationale of preaching a sermon that cannot be understood till other sermons with the same content are heard years later is not readily perceptible. Strictly speaking, of course, the baptized child will never hear a sermon with the same accent as his baptism contained. His baptism proclaimed, 'If this child, now placed under the sign of redemption, at some later date on attaining years of discretion responds to the Gospel in faith, he will receive forgiveness and all the blessings of salvation'. Such a Gospel is never heard in the Churches for no preacher appeals for a future repentance; the Christian message is a word for today (2 Cor. 6.2), but infant baptism is a gospel for tomorrow. In so changing the time reference, the sacrament itself has been made as uncertain as tomorrow.

This cannot be too strongly underscored. In the baptism of the New Testament we have no offer for tomorrow but gift for today — a gift taken in the very act of receiving the rite. All that Christ can be in life is received by the baptized as he opens his heart to the Redeemer, sealing his surrender of faith; forgiveness of sins is ratified; the Spirit is poured out; the dead is raised; all things become new; the cry sounds forth, 'It is done'. The offer and promise made known in the word are sealed before heaven and earth — the whole emphasis is one of assurance.

In the words of Philip Doddridge:

> Tis done! the great transaction's done,
> I am my Lord's and He is mine;
> He drew me, and I followed on,
> Charmed to confess the voice divine.

For this a baptism is substituted in which nothing is received but an uncomprehended word that must later be explained. And, most alarming of all, the explanation may never be heard or, if heard, may never be received. There is no assurance about infant baptism. In the best of circumstances it is a hope, and in multitudinous administrations it is a forlorn hope.

I am not unmindful that the person of mature years who comes to baptism may also fall away and subsequently repudiate his baptism.

But such a possibility must not confuse this issue, for the confirmed person may also repudiate his confirmation, as the ordained minister may repudiate his ordination and labour for the destruction of the Church. The important point is that *the person who asks for baptism has heard the word* and desires that his baptism become the actualization and seal of the promise. That infant baptism can never be. The baptism of the believer also has a future reference, in that it is a sealing unto the day of redemption and Kingdom of glory; it looks back to Easter and forward to the parousia, signifying a participation in the blessings of the former and a pledge of participation in the latter. The future reference in infant baptism is quite different from this: it intimates a future possible participation in both events, providing that the condition is fulfilled; but the fulfilment of the condition is at the time of administration quite unpredictable.

It is no intention of mine to minimize the wonder of the fact that God's redemptive act includes in its scope the child baptized and that the fullness of that grace is available for him as soon as he will receive it. But precisely the same applies to every child in a world under the redemption of Christ. The offer of grace is not a whit less true for the unbaptized child than for the baptized; and the unbaptized child is not a whit less under obligation to give heed to the Word of God when he hears it later than the baptized child is. Admittedly the baptized child is more likely to hear the Word of God than the unbaptized child growing up in China or the heart of Brazil, but he is not more likely to hear it than the unbaptized child in a Christian church that places its children under instruction before baptism.

Accordingly, despite Leenhardt's good intentions to preserve the identity of infant baptism with New Testament baptism, I am constrained to suggest that in face of this tremendous change, whereby baptism has become a word instead of an event, an offer instead of a gift, possessing an uncertain future reference instead of a powerful present assurance, we are still in the presence of *another* sacrament. Once more we witness how infant baptism reduces the fullness of significance of the baptism given by the Risen Lord and administered and expounded by his Apostles and makes of it a far, far poorer thing. Why should the Church continue to deprive itself of treasure committed to it?

(vi) *Infant Baptism and Prevenient Grace*

Whatever special interpretation of infant baptism be adopted by theologians, it is common at the present time to view it as a supreme example of the grace that comes to man before it enters his heart to come to God. So Nathaniel Micklem wrote: 'Baptism is pre-eminently the sacrament of the prevenient grace of God, of the historic, finished work of Christ. It declares that whilst we were yet sinners, or before ever we were born or thought of, Christ died for us'.[1] Aulen, in his systematic theology, entitles his discussion on baptism, 'The Sacrament of Prevenient Love'; he has in view not alone the love that gave itself in the redemptive event but the particularizing of that love in baptism: 'God uses this symbolical act to declare and realize his loving will. Divine love meets man in the act of baptism as "prevenient grace", or, in other words, the act of baptism testifies that God's love is always prevenient love'.[2] The preacher of the Zürich Grossmünster, H. Grossmann, sets the confessional element of baptism in this context; it is a confession not of the infant, but of the Church, precisely of this *gratia praeveniens*: 'Against all righteousness of works it is an express confession of the free grace of God in Jesus Christ that comes in advance to meet us'.[3]

In some quarters this conception merges into a view of infant baptism as a mode of operation of the divine election. In the words of Théo Preiss, it is 'the sign of our election in Christ'.[4] Not surprisingly this interpretation is favoured by scholars of the Reformed Church, though the precise relation postulated between baptism and election is far from clear. Marcel is content to speak of the covenant as 'the seed-bed at whose centre election to life eternal is realized'; i.e. God chooses his elect normally 'in the covenant', among the children of believers.[5] Some groups of the Dutch Reformed Church, desirous of preserving the connection between baptism and regeneration but not inclined to the doctrine of baptismal regeneration, administer baptism to all children of believers, on the presupposition that they are the elect in whom the Holy Spirit has (already) wrought regeneration — this being presumed until the contrary is proved in later life.[6] Preiss

---

[1] *Christian Worship*, p. 248.
[2] *The Faith of the Christian Church*, 1954, p. 380.
[3] *Ein Ja zur Kindertaufe*, 1944, p. 31.
[4] *Verbum Caro*, vol. 1, p. 117.
[5] Op. cit., pp. 105 ff.
[6] A long controversy took place on this question. In 1905 the General Synod of Utrecht stated, 'According to the confession of our churches the seed of the covenant must be held regenerated according to the promises of God, until in their growing up, out of their acting or teaching, the opposite becomes clear'. A continuous debate on this teaching of 'supposed regeneration' occurred until a severe split resulted in 1944. A competent examination of the problem is given by J. Bouritius in an unpublished thesis in the library of the Baptist Theological Seminary, Rüschlikon, Switzerland, 'The Relation between the Doctrines of Predestination and Baptism as taught in the Reformed Churches of the Netherlands', 1958.

himself anchors the election in the redemptive event of Christ.[1] Miegge prefers to speak more generally: 'It may be said that the proper object of the divine election is not so much the elect persons individually as the divine Person of the Son of God, and his Body in him at the same time — the individuals, thus, solely as members of his Body. If this conception of predestination be allowed, all the objections that people bring against paedobaptism fall to the ground'.[2]

From this point of view infant baptism is once more claimed to be a more suitable embodiment of the Gospel of grace than believers' baptism, since it is performed on subjects who can offer nothing, and without their request, yet for their eternal good.[3]

As often in our discussions, there are elements in this argument that few will wish to discount. It is impossible to take Biblical religion seriously without recognizing the importance of grace and election, however they may be defined. That baptism should be regarded as exemplifying the 'grace that precedes us' is also legitimate and natural. What is not obvious is the contention that infant baptism embodies such grace in a manner the baptism of a believer does not. Is Principal Flemington really serious in stating that the Apostolic Baptism, which he so excellently expounded, embodies less effectively than infant baptism 'the primary truth of the Christian Gospel, that the grace of God comes before everything else, and that man's only hope of salvation rests upon that Act of God in Jesus Christ, from which this sacrament draws all its meaning and efficacy'? Does grace not come before all else in the baptism of a convert? Does the baptism to Christ in his death and resurrection, described by Paul, draw its meaning elsewhere than from the cross and resurrection? Is baptism in the name of Jesus, administered to one who calls on the name of the Lord as the name of the Lord is called over him, salvation by Works? Any such imputation, even indirectly, is a slander on the baptism

---

[1] 'We are dead and risen through our election in Jesus Christ, in the year A.D. 29, by the sole event which can be decisive. . . . One cannot meditate too long on the reply of Kohlbrügge: "When was I converted? At Golgotha!" ', op. cit., p. 115.

[2] Op. cit., p. 80.

[3] 'If under the present viewpoint (i.e. baptism as an act of election) we pose the question, infant baptism or adult baptism, it seems that the decision must be absolutely given in favour of infant baptism', Evander, op. cit., p. 167. 'Infant baptism, so far from being less evangelical than believers' baptism, is in reality more so, because it even more unmistakably embodies the primary truth of the Christian gospel, namely that the grace of God comes before everything else...', Flemington, op. cit., pp. 146 f. 'The nature of baptism is such that it should be infant baptism, and it is as such that it demonstrates its inner power. No other form of baptism is so effective or so essential for the Christian life', G. Aulen, op. cit., p. 381.

practised and taught by the Apostles![1] Surely no person of sober judgment, surveying the Church from the second to the twentieth century, with its perpetual lapses into crude baptismal theology, can maintain that it has improved on Apostolic baptism. Even where infant baptism is administered with the greatest care, it must fall short of believers' baptism in its doctrine of grace; for only on an extreme view of opus operatum teaching can infant baptism be believed to have the same total significance as the baptism of a believer, and such a notion of grace is not a higher but lower estimate of its nature. It is fallacious to argue that grace is greater where the recipient is unconscious of it, incapable of recognizing it and of responding to it![2] Moreover, it could be argued that prevenient grace is seen more grandly in believers' baptism than in infant baptism, since the believer recognizes both the wonder of Christ's prior self-giving and the reality of the divine overruling in his life, leading him to the knowledge of Christ and confession of Him in baptism. That guiding providence appears the more ineffable in the kind of experience undergone by the present writer, who was not brought up in a Christian home and who still views with astonishment the leading of God that brought him under the sound of the Gospel and so to Christ and the Church. But competition is out of place here: we are all debtors to grace, wherever we have been set in the providence of God, and whoever confesses Christ recognizes with gratitude his indebtedness.

It does seem, however, a mistake to postulate a direct connection between infant baptism and election. How can it reasonably be maintained that infant baptism is 'the sign of election in Christ'? No doubt, multitudes of those baptized in infancy do show the fruits of election in their lives; but multitudes do not, since they ignore the Church throughout their lives. How can that which is common to elect and non-elect be a sign of election? It is to be admitted with alacrity that none of us can draw the line between the elect and the non-elect, for God alone is Judge; but on what grounds does one presume to superior knowledge in the case of infants and regard *them* as elect? In the light of the Church's age-long experience, it is not open to us to maintain a pious hope that all the baptized are, in fact, elect. A sign of election, liberally distributed among all who care to have it, as it is

---

[1] H. H. Rowley makes the same point in replying to the view of J. Barr (in *S.J.T.*, vol 4, 1951, p. 274) that the practice of believers' baptism may obscure the antecedence of Christ's work to faith: 'Since it can scarcely be denied that we have many instances of believers' baptism recorded in the New Testament, this implies a condemnation of Apostolic practice and of New Testament teaching that is quite astonishing', *The Unity of the Bible*, p. 166.

[2] See J. Nørgaard, *Den Kristne Daab*, 1944, pp. 102–4.

in the State Churches of Europe, is so manifestly ineffective that it ought no longer to be claimed as possessing that significance. Election cuts across all ecclesiastical administrations, for many, by their repentance and faith toward Christ, suggest that they are among the elect, although they have not received baptism in infancy. If we are to attempt to relate baptism to election, it would seem wiser to presume the elect to be those who confess Christ and to reserve the sign of election for such, rather than to anticipate the divine working by applying the sign to those who give no evidence of election.[1]

Finally, this whole view ignores, as is so often the case, the element of demand that goes with the gift in baptism. Aulen, for example, writes: 'The significance of infant baptism for the congregation lies in the fact that it shows how membership in the Christian church is based entirely on the loving will of God and consequently is entirely independent of the caprice of men'.[2] But what a manner in which to refer to the Apostolic demand for repentance and faith: 'Caprice'! Even the great H. R. Mackintosh permitted himself a similar lapse. Infant baptism, he said, stands for the the priceless truth, enshrined in the words, 'Herein is love, not that we loved God, but that He loved us' and, 'We love, because He loved us first'; 'If it stands for this' he wrote, 'then it embodies the very core of Christianity'.[3] Quite so: baptism is the recognition of this priority of God. It is the confession: 'We love, because He loved us first'! But no infant in his baptism has ever confessed a love for the God who first loved Him! It is a constant mistake in this debate to aver that Christian preaching consists of a recital of God's saving acts, and nothing more. Any preacher knows that that is false, and it is belied by the Acts of the Apostles. The Apostolic preaching, as recorded in the Acts, on every occasion consists of a declaration of the redemptive acts of God in Christ together with a call for repentance and faith.[4] At Pentecost

[1] Bouritius points out the inconsequential manner in which Reformed scholars assume that the same line which separates believers and unbelievers may also be drawn between the children of believers and the children of unbelievers, 'thereby ignoring the fact that as the result of God's election, which is and must be sovereign, there are as well potential believers among the latter as there are potential unbelievers among the former. If a line is to be drawn human activity is limited to a recognition of *the line drawn by God himself*, which we on our side can recognize by the indispensable result of election, being regeneration, faith and conversion and their visible fruits', op. cit., p. 31. The same point is made by Bosio, *Ritorno al Battesimo*, p. 31.

[2] Op. cit., p. 381.

[3] Op. cit., p. 199.

[4] As Dodd points out: 'The kerygma always closes with an appeal for repentance, the offer of forgiveness and of the Holy Spirit, and the promise of "salvation", that is, of "the life of the Age to Come", to those who enter the elect community', *The Apostolic Preaching and its Developments*, 2nd ed. 1944, p. 23.

Peter exhorts, 'Repent and be baptized', 'Save yourself from this crooked generation' (Acts 2.38, 40); on a later occasion, 'Repent and turn again, that your sins may be blotted out' (3.19 f), and again, 'God exalted Him at his right hand as Prince and Saviour, to give repentance to Israel and forgiveness of sins' (5.31); to Cornelius and his friends, 'To him all the prophets bear witness that every one who believes in him receives forgiveness of sins' (10.43). Paul's closing words in the typical sermon at Pisidian Antioch are, 'By him everyone that believes is freed. . . . Beware lest there come upon you what is said in the prophets, "Behold you scoffers, and wonder and perish" ' (13.40); to the Lycaonians, 'We bring you good tidings, that you should turn from these vain things unto the living God' (14.15); to the Athenians, 'He commands all men everywhere to repent' (17.30). Is it needful to continue the citations? Yet this elementary fact is consistently minimized in the baptismal debate; indeed, more than minimized: again and again it is represented that the baptism that eliminates this essential element of Apostolic proclamation is more 'evangelical', more faithful to the Gospel, than believers' baptism, and that those who insist on the call to repentance and faith being proclaimed and heard are preachers of work-righteousness and betrayers of the Gospel! It is an incomprehensible development of theology that has brought about such an attitude; it is due, I suspect, in part to the heat of controversy, and in measure at least to the irrational antipathy that still exists in Europe towards any movement that may be suspected of having even a remote connection with the Anabaptists.[1]

Prevenient grace is an essential element of Christian theology. But it is not the whole of Christianity. Grace also brings to fruition and perfects what it begins — but never without faith. The baptism of the New Testament embodies the whole Gospel — grace and faith, beginning and end, this life and the world to come. No lesser baptism can contain this Gospel.

(vii) *Infant Baptism a Symbolic rather than an Instrumental Rite*

One final interpretation of infant baptism should be included in our review, since it has been put forward by the most influential modern exponent of the Anglican interpretation of the sacraments. O. C. Quick urged that the formalism of the orthodox doctrine of baptism, which has proved such a stumbling block to the modern mind, is due to the attempt to regard the baptism of infants as possessing instru-

---

[1] Compare the remark of Höhler, *Evangelische Theologie*, 1949, p. 477, cited above on p. 345, n. 5, of which I hope he now repents!

mental power in the same way as the baptism of adult converts; whereas it should have been apparent that the change from adult baptism to infant baptism as the Church's normal practice ought to have been accompanied by a shift of emphasis from the instrumental to the symbolic aspect of the sacrament.[1] Quick was encouraged in his view by observing that baptism in Paul's teaching symbolizes much more than what it effects at the time, particularly when considered with respect to its outlook on the future. To the Apostle it symbolizes 'a perfect washing from sin, a perfect resurrection to new life, a perfect membership in God's family through Christ', hence the final salvation of the soul. 'Baptism therefore in symbolizing the ultimate end of salvation, symbolizes also by anticipation all those many purifications from sin and gifts of new life, of which the progress towards final salvation is made up. The end is identical with the completed achievement of the process, and both end and process are appropriately symbolized at the beginning'.[2] Baptism has also a retrospective aspect, since the goodness and power and grace of God have been with the baptized from the beginning, even if unknown and unrealized.

Is then the baptism of an infant symbolic only, with no 'instrumental' power? That an Anglican theologian could never believe! If it be true that the symbolic rather than the instrumental aspect of the sacrament has to be emphasized, Quick was constrained to add, 'At the same time we must not allow the instrumental to be wholly absorbed into the symbolic'.[3] A means of retaining the latter element is found in considering the uniqueness of the symbol. The belief that baptism is an 'extension' of the incarnation and atonement is accepted in the modified sense that it symbolizes for each individual the whole process and end of the new human life which the life of Jesus Christ brought into the world: 'Baptism itself must be regarded as one event in that process; and since it is that event which is in a special sense appointed to symbolize the whole, it is only natural to hold that it is also in its actual effect specially important and decisive'. The precise nature of this 'effect' cannot be defined, but it may be said to initiate the 'process of the Christian life'.[4]

Here, then, an attempt is made to break away from the biblicist approach to baptism, while endeavouring to preserve the values of the biblical teaching on baptism. Quick will not attribute to infant baptism the great spiritual change in the life of the baptized such as is associated with baptism in the New Testament. He would preserve the rite

---

[1] *The Christian Sacraments*, 2nd ed. 1932, p. 168.
[2] Op. cit., p. 173.   [3] Op. cit., p. 179.   [4] Op. cit., p. 174.

because of its value as symbolizing the effect of the incarnation and redemption of Jesus Christ in the life of an individual, with the further postulate that, since it has been divinely instituted to be such a symbol, its administration must have a decisive effect on the person to whom it is administered. The nature of this 'effect' remains undefined: it is more than a beginning of grace, since grace is ever at work in human life, but the Christian life may be said to date from this point.

It will be at once evident that this view is not without its difficulties, not the least of which is to know how seriously to take Dr. Quick in his concessions and how seriously to take his reservations. At first sight the former appear to be very considerable: the concept of infant baptism as a sacrament with power has apparently been abandoned in favour of baptism as a symbol of the meaning of the incarnation and atonement for an individual life. If this were the real intention of the writer, he would then be advocating in a fresh way the declarative view of baptism, held by such influential figures as F. W. Robertson,[1] F. D. Maurice,[2] The Congregationalist theologian R. W. Dale,[3] Ryder Smith, speaking for many in Methodism,[4] Karl Barth,[5] and his son Marcus Barth.[6] Yet Quick did not wish to rest in this position, for in his view the instrumental element in baptism must not be wholly lost; the symbol belongs to the processes set in motion by the incarnation and may itself be said to initiate the Christian life. But if baptism *begins* the process it typifies, must it not be regarded as the first of 'the many purifications from sin and gifts of new life' of which the process of salvation consists? More affirmatively, if baptism *initiates* a participation in the new life that Jesus Christ brought into the world through his incarnation and atonement, we must presume it to be a participation specifically in the life, death and resurrection of Christ, in his Spirit, his Kingdom, his new creation, for none can participate in Christ without being involved in this radical manner. But that brings us to a position expressly repudiated by Quick! In reality he has fallen into a double error. First, he substituted the term 'symbol' for 'sacrament', with the intention of reducing its significance; but he proceeded to fill it with a content that made it a *symbol with power*, and a symbol that has consequences of the order he ascribed to it is precisely what we mean by sacrament. Secondly, he seems to have

---

[1] *Life and Letters of F. W. Robertson*, Phillips Brooks, vol. ii, p. 60 ff.

[2] *Theological Essays*, 5th ed. 1905, p. 172.

[3] *Manual of Congregational Principles*, Book III, cap. ii, cited by J. Huxtable, 'Christian Initiation in Congregational Churches', *Theology*, vol. LV, 1952, p. 168.

[4] 'Methodism and Baptism', *Baptist Quarterly*, vol. vii, 1934–5, pp. 97 ff.

[5] *The Teaching of the Church regarding Baptism*, p. 13.

[6] 'Baptism and Evangelism', *S.J.T.*, vol. 12, 1959, p. 39.

considered that by restricting baptism to be an initiation to the Christian life he thereby diminished its power; but there is no beginning of Christian life without Christ and there is no Christ for man apart from his cross, his resurrection and his Holy Spirit; to be united with Christ can never be of small consequence and should never be represented as such. If the 'instrumental' nature of baptism is to be admitted at all, then it comes with completeness. 'He does not give the Spirit by measure' (Jn. 3.24) is a saying that applies in principle to the individual joined to Christ as to the Christ Himself in his incarnate life.

Doubtless a doctrine of infant baptism, viewed as a significant symbol, can be worked out, relating it to the accomplished redemption which avails for the baptized child and to the possibility of the child receiving the fruits of redemption through union with Christ by faith. But are the Churches willing consciously to take the step of adjusting their viewpoint and practice to such an interpretation and of accepting its consequences? In the case of the Free Churches it means the frank abandonment of sacramental initiation into the Church, replacing it with something after the order of a covenant service; in Churches that practice confirmation it involves transferring the significance of baptism to confirmation, which raises serious questions concerning the legitimacy of emptying a dominical rite of its appointed significance to give it to one which at best can be regarded only as the completion of the rite. Both these possibilities, of course, have become actualities in many quarters, but I have always been under the impression that they have been deviations from the official attitudes and traditions of the Churches concerned. Where this happens, we are presented with the spectacle of Apostolic baptism being reduced to the level of a symbol effecting an unknown and unknowable blessing, whose lack can be made good by later ecclesiastical remedies. I am reminded of the caustic remark of the Lutheran writer, Götz Harbsmeier, when he commented on the 'dabs' of water that are used in baptism, fitly corresponding to the minimum substance of the word of proclamation given at most celebrations of infant baptism, with the result that baptism becomes 'a tiny drop' of itself.[1] It seems that a small amount of water is bestowed on a small infant with a very small result. And this, it is alleged, is *baptism!* Can it be wondered at that Baptists should be strengthened in their determination to strive for the retention of the fullness of baptism, ordained of the Lord and continued in

[1] ' "Wort und Sakrament" in ihrer Bedeutung für die Erneuerung des Gottesdientes', *Evangelische Theologie*, 1953, p. 262.

the Apostolic Communities, and that they should continue to lift up their voices among the Churches to plead for a return to this baptism? It has never been the property of an exclusive group within the Church but the gift of the Risen Lord to the whole Church. It is time his people took it afresh from his ever gracious hands.

POSTSCRIPT: BAPTISMAL REFORM
AND INTER-CHURCH RELATIONSHIPS

IT IS but a short time since controversy on the sacraments was pursued in the spirit of gladiatorial combat, with results that were sometimes not dissimilar. In an era of ecumenical discussion the smart of controversy is of a different kind: the pain of inflicting wounds on Christian colleagues can be more acute than that of receiving them. This is no expression of unctuous piety. Anyone sharing the author's convictions and who has participated in ecumenical discussion knows that such fellowship at times becomes embarrassing, and that to be compelled to maintain those convictions, in opposition to one's fellow-participants in Christian conversation, is grievous. It would be far easier to be silent on points of difference, or at least to blunt them, and to welcome partial solutions of problems. Yet the Kingdom of God is not served by insincerity; until better solutions are found for the problems we have enumerated in the preceding pages, the pain of exposing them must be endured.

The most distressing difficulty of the present discussion concerns the validity of infant baptism. How can any who maintain the standpoint from which this book is written accord to infant baptism the significance of Apostolic baptism? And in such case, how should a convert not be urged to receive Apostolic baptism, even though in infancy he had received the very defective rite of infant baptism? In these circumstances scandal cannot be avoided. The Baptist considers the Paedo-Baptist unbaptized; the Paedo-Baptist theologian regards a submission to believers' baptism after the receiving of infant baptism to be an affront to the Word of God and nigh to blasphemy. Conscience thus strikes on conscience: the Paedo-Baptist bridles with indignation and the Baptist feels compelled staunchly to maintain his here-I-stand-I-can-do-no-other attitude.

The breaking of the deadlock is conceivable only if either group, or both, move from positions traditionally held. And that cannot happen without hurt, for every surrender of cherished traditions brings pain and any attempt at compromise creates opposition. Yet the issue is of crucial importance; if we try to dodge it, it will continue to haunt us and be an open sore throughout the years.

It seems to me that some difficulties are going to be solved only by walking, and that in unaccustomed paths. I am prepared to believe that problems at present apparently insoluble may receive light from further study of the Word of God in mutual fellowship. But some possibilities present themselves as open to consideration even now; they affect both the Churches that practise infant baptism and those that practise believers' baptism, and they make demands on both.

Foremost among the issues which Churches that maintain the traditional baptism have to face is the desirability of exercising discipline with respect to families whose infant children receive baptism. It is to be doubted whether any single factor has weakened the Church in its history so gravely as the practice of indiscriminate baptism; that there are theologians and clergy who defend its legitimacy even today, and multitudes more who administer it without knowing why, illustrates the abysmal depths to which the sacramental practice of the Church has sunk. No major baptismal reform is possible without this abuse being rectified, though no other step of baptismal reform would prove so far-reaching in its effects. Certainly it is difficult to conceive of any kind of rapprochement in the matter of baptism between groups holding Baptist convictions and the great Churches while a rite that is held to be the door to the Church is administered to multitudes whose only use for the Church is to adorn ceremonies of birth and death. Such a misapplication of baptism degrades the conception of membership in the Body of Christ and makes the confession of faith and promise of discipleship undertaken in baptism meaningless when it is not hypocritical. Fortunately this point of gravest vulnerability is also the point of greatest sensitivity on the part of many who wish to see a reinstatement of baptism to its rightful place in the Church; it is the place for a beginning of hope and that beginning ought to be made without delay.

Pending some such minimum baptismal reform, the exaggerated language used about the 'blasphemy' of 'rebaptism' should cease. In countries whose populace has largely received the infant baptism of the State Church but of which only a very small minority attends it, is it to be wondered at that adherents of Baptist Churches conclude that infant baptism is without effect, and that therefore a convert should receive *Christian* baptism on conversion? And in such circumstances is it the 'rebaptizers' who degrade baptism or the ministers of the State Churches? The existence of a situation in which 'rebaptism' is possible is doubtless tragic, but the source of the wrong should be pondered. Baptists, of course, have never accepted the name 'Rebaptizers'; they have never made a practice of baptizing again Christians who received baptism in another communion as *believers*, even if the baptism was by sprinkling or affusion; their protest has been directed to the application of the rite in such wise that its significance has (in their estimate) been nullified. If a concordat between Baptists and Churches administering infant baptism with discipline is conceivable, their protest where it is *undisciplined* should be understood and their conviction respected, even if believed to be mistaken.

A more positive step in rehabilitating Biblical baptism would be an increase in the number of baptisms of believers of responsible age in the ordinary services of the Churches. This should be done, not so much for the increase of interest in baptism which such services would create but, as at least one group of Paedo-Baptist theologians has perceived, because the fullness of significance which Christian baptism possesses can be conveyed only in the baptism of a believer, when the confession, pledge and prayer of faith are integrated within the rite itself, answering to the redemptive grace bodied forth in the rite.[1] In this respect the Church of England has an unrivalled opportunity for setting forth the 'wholeness' of baptism, by its 'archetypal' baptismal service for a believer of mature years and which consists of the baptism, confirmation and first communion of the initiate.[2] If the Anglican bishops would utilize some of the Anglican baptistries built for the immersion of believers and conduct services in accordance with the revised order of their Liturgical Commission, the most impressive celebration of baptism in all Christendom would thereby be provided and, incidentally, a most impressive witness given of the Church's ability to recover its sacramental riches.

Lastly, in this list of recommendations addressed to the great Churches, I would pose the question: Is a return to believers' baptism as the normal Christian baptism really inconceivable? That many members of Churches practising infant baptism are profoundly disturbed by it and would willingly accept a change is evident. There never has existed such dissatisfaction with the older views of baptism as today. Ministers and clergy of every Protestant denomination have expressed and still express their disquiet; and it is not without significance that support for criticisms made of infant baptism in this book has been drawn almost entirely from theologians of the great Churches and hardly at all from those sharing the writer's own persuasion. There is a willingness everywhere to think again concerning the Church's interpretation and practice of baptism.

[1] *Gutachten der Evangelisch-Theologischen Fakultät der Universität Tübingen über Fragen der Taufordnung*, p. 423.
[2] *Baptism and Confirmation*, p. x.

For this reason it seems to me that Barth's counsel to the Churches ought to be given fresh consideration. Unfortunately it appears to be comparatively unknown, and certainly unheeded. When Barth delivered his lecture on baptism in May 1943, he ventured an opinion on how to implement changes in the Churches' administration of baptism, but when publishing the lecture he omitted this section, desiring not to deflect attention from his main thesis.[1] In his view baptism is too eminently an affair of the Church for it to be left to isolated individuals to propagate their views and for anyone to please himself, as it were, on which side he chooses to be. Nor does he consider it right to remit the matter to the leaders of the Churches, to Church councils, synods, ecumenical conferences, or even to the result of mass voting. 'It ought not to be impossible — and this should be regarded as the theologically correct way — to strive for a better understanding of the ordinance of baptism, and at the last for an agreement concerning its restoration, in the individual congregations first, in pastoral care, instruction, preaching and open conversation. Where such agreement is attainable it would be practicable to carry it into effect in the circle of the individual congregation — with or without the approbation of the other churches! with or without the consent of the superior church courts!' Barth evidently feels that it is insufficient for baptismal reform to be a matter solely of theoretical argument; it needs to come down to earth and to confront the Church as a church fact or situation, and then it would be better estimated by everybody concerned. There is much to be said for this point of view. Baptismal reform needs the guidance of the Church's theologians, but it is a matter of worship as well as theological reflection; yet the liturgiologists alone are not adequate for the matter, since it is even more a pastoral concern, an element of the Church's mission to the world on which the pastors and clergy themselves ought to be heard. And is it not also a matter on which the congregations should bear their testimony? In this regard insufficient attention has been paid to the experience of Churches which still practise on a large scale the baptism of mature believers. Apart from the Baptists and the Churches (Disciples) of Christ, there is a rich source of experience to be examined in the foreign missionary agencies of all the Churches.[2] This hardly features in the present baptismal discussions but it ought to be

---

[1] The omitted section of the lecture was published in the journal *Evangelische Theologie*, 1949, pp. 189 f.

[2] Gensichen, *Das Taufproblem in der Mission*, Gütersloh, 1951, uses some of this material to good effect and illustrates how much more could be done in this direction.

brought to light; its relevance is increased by the fact that the Churches of the West are increasingly finding themselves in a mission situation, and every deterioration of the Church's position in society makes infant baptism more difficult to administer and to justify. It need scarcely be pointed out that experimentation in the Churches would be feasible only if greater freedom were accorded to local churches than that which now exists. Such freedom need not occasion chaos, by reason of diversity of practice; in fact, the experimentation would certainly be on a limited scale; if it increased to some extent the diversity that already exists, the end would justify the inconvenience to the few.

It must be faced that even if experiments of the kind here advocated were to be attempted, there is no likelihood of a cataclysmic change in the Churches' baptismal thought and action in the near future, however profoundly some of us may wish it were otherwise; the Churches are not yet prepared for so complete a revolution. Presupposing, however, their willingness to initiate reforms, what is to be the attitude of the Baptist Churches and those who share their outlook? Are they to stand aside and wait till the Churches fall in line before attempting to enter into positive relations with them? That cannot be, for generations may pass before such a condition is reached, and it may never arrive! The Baptists, too, must consider their ways.

First, they should not take it for granted that differing views on baptism from those held by other Churches of necessity means perpetual alienation from them. There are Churches in Europe that for centuries have practised both believers' baptism and infant baptism in the same communities, notably the Waldensians in Italy, and on a smaller scale the Reformed Church in certain Cantons of French-speaking Switzerland, and the Swedish Missionsförbundet. Notable experiments in this regard have been made among the younger Churches, such as the Church of Christ in Congo and the Church of Christ in China. In England a not inconsiderable number of churches are composed of Baptist and Congregationalist members (Union Churches); the Baptists and Congregationalists of the Bunyan country (Bedfordshire) have traditionally maintained themselves in a single union, and there are even more Evangelical Free churches scattered through the land with memberships that contain a preponderance of Baptists.

Does this, then, mean that Baptists should at last take the step they have consistently refused and recognize the validity of infant baptism, even though they deny the wisdom of this mode of

2C

administration? Long before the publication of Karl Barth's lecture on baptism Baptists were to be found who urged this view on their fellows, and their number has increased in recent years. I confess my inability to concur with them. For the reasons earlier made known, I find myself unable to recognize in infant baptism the baptism of the New Testament Church and nothing that my fellows have written has helped to mitigate this difficulty for me. Moreover I think it right to disabuse the minds of any who have been led by the utterances of some of my Baptist colleagues to imagine that a change of view on this matter is taking place in Baptist circles; there is strong resistance to any such change among British Baptists and the mere voicing of it is looked on with astonishment among Baptists in the rest of the world, who form the bulk of our people. This may well provide a disappointment to many who hoped for a more positive attitude of Baptists to infant baptism. Yet testimony has here been given to the reasons for the Baptist persistence in these convictions; to all who remain unpersuaded by the criticisms of infant baptism here advanced I address the plea that at least they will recognize our sincerity and not interpret our attitude as the product of blind obscurantism.

There is more, however, to be said on this matter. It lies in the power of Baptists to take a significant step towards the establishing of closer relations with the other Churches: in respect for the conscience of our fellow-Christians and the like charity, which we trust will be exercised towards us, could we not refrain from requesting the baptism of those baptized in infancy who wish to join our churches and administer baptism to such only where there is a strong plea for it from the applicant? This would leave room for freedom of conscience for those who believe they should be baptized, despite their having received infant baptism, but it would involve a change of policy with respect to the majority who come to us from other Denominations.

This step would be a small one for the English Baptists to take, since their policy of having 'open-membership' Churches has long since been established. In charity towards other communions, submission to believers' baptism is not required for membership in such Churches; no other form of baptism is practised in them and all who grow up within them are urged to receive baptism when making a profession of faith in Christ. This policy is open to criticism and is often misunderstood, both by Baptists in other parts of the world and by members of Churches practising infant baptism, but it has been shaped as a compromise in a complex ecclesiastical situation. Relations between the Free Churches in Britain have from the beginning been close, and Baptists have been anxious to make possible fullest participation in their life for members of sister communions who desire to come among them but believe they ought not to receive believers' baptism after their baptism as infants. That this does not involve a 'despising' of baptism, as some allege, is evident in that it is in precisely these Churches that the deepened appreciation of the significance of baptism has taken place among Baptists. An extension of this practice among Baptist Churches throughout the world would be desirable and the further step would then be feasible of abstaining, so far as possible, from administering believers' baptism to those baptized in infancy.

Alongside this preparedness, in Christian love, to mitigate demands of others, it would seem to me to be our bounden duty as Baptists to do all in our power to allow baptism in our own churches to be what God has willed it to be. A call for reform according to the Word of God has to be heeded first by those who issue it. In this connection there is room for improvement in our own administration of the rite of initiation.

First, there ought to be a greater endeavour to make baptism integral to *the Gospel*. It is taken as axiomatic amongst us that the proclamation of the Gospel consists of making the redemptive acts of God in Christ known and calling for faith in Christ as the due response; baptism is then a proper subject for exposition in the enquirers' class, along with instruction as to the nature of the Church, of worship, of Christian obligation in the Church and to the world etc. Peter's response, however, to the cry of his conscience stricken hearers on the Day of Pentecost was not, 'Repent and believe', but 'Repent and *be baptized*'! (Acts 2.38). Naturally faith was presumed in repentance, but Peter's answer told the Jews how to become Christians: faith and repentance are to be expressed in baptism, and *so* they are to come to the Lord. Baptism is here a part of the proclamation of Christ. In an Apostolic sermon it comes as its logical conclusion. An effort ought to be made to restore this note in our preaching.

Secondly, there should be a serious endeavour to make baptism integral to *conversion*. This is a corollary of the previous point. The preaching of the Gospel is directed to the conversion of men and women (at least it is if it has any contact with him whose burden for the multitude was, 'The Kingdom of God is upon you; *turn to God, and believe the Gospel*' (Mk. 1.15)). This involves, as we have seen, not simply the acceptance of an idea but a reception and submission in action. Baptism and conversion are thus inseparables; the one demands the other, for neither is complete without the other. This, although elementary, is not obvious to all and it requires to be made explicit. Yet it is not immediately apparent how to give effect to this insight. The experience of the Churches in missionary enterprise has led them to introduce an extended catechumenate, as was universal in the Church of the early centuries; there is much to be said for an extension of that practice in the Churches of the West rather than its diminution. Care is needed lest people mistake the sway of emotion for faith. Some individuals request baptism long after their conversion (in Russia the baptism of adolescents in any case is impermissible). The child growing into faith in a Christian family is in a different situation from that of the child coming from a pagan home. The relationship of these groups to the catechumenate is to be wisely differentiated, as is that of man in western civilization from the Australian aboriginal. A pastoral problem of great magnitude is involved here, but it would help if a few simple considerations were kept steadily in view. The instruction of converts, always necessary, need not wholly precede baptism; much of it can more fittingly come after baptism, and in any case the instruction ought *never* to cease at baptism. If the point earlier made were carried into effect and the nature and significance of baptism were given their rightful place in the proclamation of the Gospel, hearers would understand what baptism is and that the response of faith should find its fitting embodiment in the sacrament. Above all, whether the time between baptism and conversion be little or much, baptism should be regarded as the ultimate and unreserved ratification of the individual's turning to God and of God's gracious turning to the individual, with all that means of dedication on the one hand and of grace on the other.

Finally, there should be an endeavour to make baptism integral to *Church membership*. In Britain, at least, our baptismal practice has tended to obscure the fact that New Testament baptism is at once to Christ and the Body. The baptized are customarily welcomed into the Church, not at the baptismal service but at a later communion service, which may follow after weeks, or months, or even years in the case of young adolescents in some Churches. It is profoundly to be wished that this anomaly be rectified. This is most easily done if the service of baptism is concluded with the Lord's Supper. The newly baptized may then be welcomed into the Church and partake of their first communion at one time.

Is it not possible to consider a further action and include the laying on of hands as an integral part of the service? It would underscore the aspect of baptismal symbolism as initiation into Christ and the Church by the Spirit. Some European Baptist communities have long adhered to this method and more are accommodating to it. There is little doubt that it would enrich both our understanding and experience of baptism; it would put us into continuity with the development observable in the New Testament and with that which continued after (but without the undesirable elements that entered from other quarters); it would deepen the fellowship of the Church; and it would anchor the newly baptized members in the community.

All of us in all the Churches need to consider afresh our ways before God, with the Bible open before us and a prayer for the guidance of the Holy Spirit and a preparedness to listen to what the Spirit is saying to all the Churches. With such prayer answered — and it would be unbelief to assume that it will not be — and obedience pledged to guidance vouchsafed, the inadequate insights of frail individuals and of our very fallible traditions would surely give place to a fuller understanding of the divine will made known, and the glory of God in Christ be furthered through the Church by the Spirit.

SELECTED BIBLIOGRAPHY

No account is taken in this bibliography of articles in dictionaries and encyclopaedias, nor of commentaries on books of the Old and New Testament. Although such are prime sources for the study of baptism, they are too numerous and too well-known to require enumeration.

I. Abrahams, 'How did the Jews Baptize?', *Journal of Theological Studies*, vol. XII, 1911.

R. Aldwinkle, 'Believer's Baptism and Confirmation', *Baptist Quarterly*, vol. XVI, 1955–6.

P. Althaus, *Was ist die Taufe?*, Göttingen, 1950.

H. T. Andrews, 'The Place of the Sacraments in the Teaching of St. Paul', *The Expositor*, 8th Series, vol. XII, 1916.

A. W. Argyle, 'O. Cullmann's Theory concerning κωλύειν', *Expository Times*, vol. LXVII, 1955.

H. J. D. Astley, 'Primitive Sacramentalism', *The Modern Churchman*, vol. XVI, 1926–7.

F. J. Badcock, 'The Significance of the Baptism of Christ', *The Interpreter*, vol. 13, 1916–17.

S. Bailey, 'Baptism and the Outpouring of the Holy Spirit in the New Testament', *Theology*, vol. XLIX, 1946.

D. M. Baillie, *The Theology of the Sacraments and other papers*, London, 1957.

T. A. Bampton, 'The Sacramental Significance of Christian Baptism', *Baptist Quarterly*, vol. XI, 1942–5.

Baptism and Confirmation Today. The Schedule attached to the Final Reports of the Joint Committees on Baptism, Confirmation and Holy Communion, London, 1955.

Baptism and Confirmation, A Report submitted by the Church of England Liturgical Commission, London, 1959.

Baptism Today, Schedule attached to the Second Interim Reports of the Joint Committees on Baptism, Confirmation and Holy Communion, London, 1949.

J. Barr. 'Further Thoughts about Baptism', *Scottish Journal of Theology*, vol. 4, 1951.

K. Barth, *The Teaching of the Church regarding Baptism*, translated by E. A. Payne, London, 1948.

M. Barth, 'Baptism and Evangelism', *Scottish Journal of Theology*, vol. 12, 1959.

M. Barth, *Die Taufe ein Sakrament?*, Zollikon-Zürich, 1951.

H. W. Bartsch, 'Die Taufe im Neuen Testament', *Evangelische Theologie*, Heft 1/3, 1948–9.

J. Beckmann, 'Die Heilsnotwendigkeit der Taufe', *Schriftenreihe der Bekennenden Kirche*, Heft 8, Stuttgart, 1951.

F. Bennett, 'Indiscriminate Confirmation', *Theology*, vol. XLVIII, 1945.

J. S. Bezzant, 'Sacraments in Acts and the Pauline Epistles', *The Modern Churchman*, vol. XVI, 1926–7.

H. G. Blomfield, 'Baptism and the Catechumenate', *Theology*, vol. L, 1947.

P. Bosio, *Ritorno al Battesimo, Saggio dottrinale presentato al Corpo Pastorale Valdese*, Rome, 1942.

W. Bornemann, 'Der erste Petrusbrief—eine Taufrede des Silvanus?', *Zeitschrift für die neutestamentliche Wissenschaft*, 19ter Jahrgang, 1919/1920.

G. Bornkamm, 'Die neutestamentliche Lehre von der Taufe', *Theologische Blätter*, vol. XVII, 1938.

G. Bornkamm, 'Taufe und neues Leben bei Paulus', *Theologische Blätter*, vol. XVIII, 1939.

G. Bornkamm, *Das Ende des Gesetzes*, München, 1952.

J. Bouritius, 'The Relation between the Doctrines of Predestination and Baptism, as taught in the Reformed Churches of the Netherlands', Unpublished B.D. Thesis, Rüschlikon-Zürich, 1958.

W. H. Brownlee, 'John the Baptist in the New Light of Ancient Scrolls', *The Scrolls and the New Testament*, ed. K. Stendahl, London, 1958.

J. C. Campbell, 'Considerations on the Definition of a Sacrament', *Scottish Journal of Theology*, vol. 9, 1956.

P. Carrington, 'The Baptismal Pattern in the New Testament', *Theology*, vol. XXIX, 1934.

R. L. Child, 'The Baptist Contribution to the One Church', *Baptist Quarterly*, vol. VIII, 1936–7.

R. L. Child, 'Church of Scotland on Baptism', *Baptist Quarterly*, vol. XVI, 1955–6.

R. L. Child, 'The Ministry and the Sacraments', *Baptist Quarterly*, vol. IX, 1938–9.

N. Clark, 'An approach to the Theology of the Sacraments', *Studies in Biblical Theology*, no. 17, London, 1956.

B. G. Collins, 'The Sacrament of Baptism in the New Testament', *Expository Times*, vol. XXVII, 1915.

F. Coventry, 'Initiation not disintegrated', *Theology*, vol. LI, 1948.

C. E. B. Cranfield, 'The Baptism of our Lord—A Study of St. Mark, 1.9–11', *Scottish Journal of Theology*, vol. 8, 1955.

J. M. Creed, 'Sacraments in the Fourth Gospel', *The Modern Churchman*, vol. XVI, 1926–7.

J. H. Crehan, *Early Christian Baptism and the Creed*, London, 1950.

H. Cremer, *Taufe, Wiedergeburt und Kindertaufe in Kraft des Heiligen Geistes*, 3te Auflage, Gütersloh, 1917.

F. L. Cross, 'The Patristic Doctrines of the Sacraments', *The Modern Churchman*, vol. XVI, 1926–7.

F. L. Cross, *I Peter, A Paschal Liturgy*, London, 1954.

O. Cullmann, *Baptism in the New Testament*, London, 1950.

O. Cullmann, *Early Christian Worship*, London, 1953.

O. Cullmann, 'The Significance of the Qumran Texts for Research into the Beginnings of Christianity', *The Scrolls and the New Testament*, ed. Krister Stendahl, London, 1958.

N. A. Dahl, 'The Origin of Baptism', *Interpretationes ad Vetus Testamentum pertinentes S. Mowinckel*, Oslo, 1955.

A. Dakin, 'Calvin's Doctrine of Baptism', *Baptist Quarterly*, vol. IX, 1938–9.

J. G. Davies, 'The Disintegration of the Christian Initiation Rite', *Theology*, vol. L, 1947.

J. G. Davies, *Spirit, Church and Sacraments*, London, 1956.

G. Delling, βάπτισμα βαπτισθῆναι, *Novum Testamentum*, vol. 2, 1957.

E. C. Dewick, 'Psychology and Sacraments', *The Modern Churchman*, vol. XVI, 1926–7.

E. von Dobschutz, 'Sacrament und Symbol im Urchristentum', *Theologische Studien und Kritiken*, vol. 78, 1905.

Dopet: Dåben: Dåpen—Tre nordiske teologiska uppsatser (T. Bergsten, *Dopet och församlingen*, K. Kyro-Rasmussen, *Dåben—et sakramente*, N. J. Engelsen, *Tro og dåp*), Stockholm, 1957.

G. Dix, *The Theology of Confirmation in relation to Baptism*, London, 1946.

G. Dix, 'The "Seal" in the Second Century', *Theology*, vol. LI, 1948.

D. L. Edwards, 'Science, Sin and Sacrament', *Theology*, vol. LVII, 1954.

Hjalmar Evander, *Det kristna dopet, dess uppkomst och betydelse: Några synpunkter till ledning för diskussionen vid prästmötet i Lund den 20, 21 och 22 September 1938*, Lund, 1938.

P. W. Evans, 'The Baptismal Commission in Matt. 28.19', *Baptist Quarterly*, vol. XV, 1953–4.

P. W. Evans, 'Sealing a Term for Baptism', *Baptist Quarterly*, vol. XVI, 1955–6.

J. V. Fenton, 'Baptism and Circumcision', *Theology*, vol. LIII, 1950.

L. Finkelstein, 'The Institution of Baptism for Proselytes', *Journal of Biblical Literature*, vol. LII, 1933.

W. F. Flemington, *The New Testament Doctrine of Baptism*, London, 1948.

P. T. Forsyth, *The Church and the Sacraments*, London, 1917.

A. Fridrichsen, ' "Accomplir toute justice", *La rencontre de Jésus et du Baptiste* (Mt. 3.15)', *Congrès d'Histoire du Christianisme, Jubilé Alfred Loisy*, vol. I, Paris and Amsterdam, 1928.

E. Fuchs, 'Das Urchristliche Sakramentsverständnis', *Schriftenreihe der Kirchlich-Theologischen Sozietät in Württemberg*, Heft 8, Bad Cannstatt, 1958.

E. Fuchs, *Die Freiheit des Glaubens*, München, 1949.

R. H. Fuller, 'Baptism and Confirmation', *Theology*, vol. XLIX, 1946.

F. Gavin, *The Jewish Antecedents of the Christian Sacraments*, London, 1928.

H. W. Gensichen, *Das Taufproblem in der Mission*, Gütersloh, 1951.

P. Gardner, 'The Pagan Mysteries', *The Modern Churchman*, vol. XVI, 1926–7.

T. S. Garrett, 'Baptism in the Church of South India', *Scottish Journal of Theology*, vol. 8, 1955.

A. Gilmore, editor, *Christian Baptism, A Fresh Attempt to understand the Rite in Terms of Scripture, History and Theology*, London, 1959.

A. Gilmore, 'Some recent trends in the Theology of Baptism', *Baptist Quarterly*, vol. XV, 1953–4, vol. XVI, 1955–6.

H. Grisshammer, 'Kindertaufe oder Erwachsenentaufe?', *Evangelische Theologie*, Heft 5, 1948–9.

H. Grossmann, 'Ein Ja zur Kindertaufe', *Kirchliche Zeitfragen*, Heft 13, Zürich, 1944.

G. Harbsmeier, ' "Wort und Sakrament" in ihrer Bedeutung für die Erneuerung des Gottesdienstes', *Evangelische Theologie*, Heft 6, 1953.

W. Heitmüller, *Im Namen Jesu, Eine sprach—und religionsgeschichtliche Untersuchung zum Neuen Testament, speziell zur altchristliche Taufe. (Forschungen zur Religion und Literatur des Alten und Neuen Testaments*, herausg. von W. Bousset und H. Gunkel, I Band, 2 Heft), Göttingen, 1903.

W. Heitmüller, 'Taufe und Abendmahl in Urchristentum', *Religionsgeschichtliche Volksbücher*, herausg. von F. M. Schiele, I Reihe, 22/23, Heft, Tübingen, 1911.

J. Heron, 'The Theology of Baptism', *Scottish Journal of Theology*, vol. 8, 1955.

L. Hickin, 'Public Baptism of Infants', *Theology*, vol. LVII, 1954.

H. Höhler, 'Die theologischen Hintergründe des Taufgesprächs', *Evangelische Theologie*, Heft 10, 1948–9.

L. S. Hunter, 'The Arts in Relation to the Sacraments', *The Modern Churchman*, vol. XVI, 1926–7.

J. Huxtable, 'Christian Initiation in Congregational Churches', *Theology*, vol. LV, 1952.

F. J. F. Jackson and Kirsopp Lake, 'The Development of Thought on the Spirit, the Church, and Baptism', *The Beginnings of Christianity*, part 1, *The Acts of the Apostles*, edited by F. J. F. Jackson and K. Lake, vol. 1, Prolegomena I, London, 1942.

J. G. Jenkins, 'The Baptists and the New Testament', *Baptist Quarterly*, vol. VII, 1934–5.

J. Jeremias, *Hat die Urkirche die Kindertaufe geübt?* 2 völlig neu bearbeitete Auflage, Göttingen, 1949.

J. Jeremias, *Die Kindertaufe in den Ersten Vier Jahrhunderten*, Göttingen, 1958.

J. Jeremias, 'Der Ursprung der Johannestaufe', *Zeitschrift für die Neutestamentliche Wissenschaft*, 28ter Band, 1929.

N. Johansson, 'Making Christians by Sacraments', *Scottish Journal of Theology*, vol. 5, 1952.

R. Josefson, *Kirche und Taufe—Ein Buch von der Kirche*, herausg. von G. Aulen, A. Fridrichsen, A. Nygren, H. Linderoth, R. Bring, Berlin, 1950.

A. R. S. Kennedy, *St. Paul and the Mystery Religions*, London, 1913.

K. E. Kirk, 'Magic and Sacraments', *Theology*, vol. XI, 1925.

G. Kittel, 'Die Wirkungen der christlichen Wassertaufe nach dem Neuen Testament', *Theologische Studien und Kritiken*, 87, 1914.

K. G. Kuhn, 'Römer 6.7', *Zeitschrift für die neutestamentliche Wissenschaft*, 30 Band, 1931.

W. G. Kümmel, 'Das Urchristentum', *Theologische Rundschau*, Neue Folge, Heft 1, 1950.

W. G. Kümmel, 'Vom Ursprung der Kindertaufe', *Die Christliche Welt*, Nr. 13, 1939.

K. Lake, 'The Gift of the Spirit on the Day of Pentecost', *The Beginnings of Christianity*, part 1, *The Acts of the Apostles*, ed. by F. J. F. Jackson and K. Lake, vol. V.

K. Lake, 'The Holy Spirit', *The Beginnings of Christianity*, part 1, *The Acts of the Apostles*, vol. V.

G. W. H. Lampe, 'Baptisma in the New Testament', *Scottish Journal of Theology*, vol. 5, 1952.

G. W. H. Lampe, *The Seal of the Spirit, A Study in the Doctrine of Baptism and Confirmation in the New Testament and the Fathers*, London, 1951.

C. B. Law, 'The Administration of Holy Baptism—Indiscriminate or not?', *Theology*, vol. XXVI, 1933.

E. K. Lee, 'The Sacraments and the Fourth Gospel', *Theology*, vol. LVII, 1954.

F. J. Leenhardt, 'Le Baptême Chrétien, son origine, sa signification', *Cahiers Théologiques de l'Actualité Protestante*, No. 4, Neuchatel, 1946.

J. Leipoldt, *Die urchristliche Taufe im Lichte der Religionsgeschichte*, Leipzig, 1929.

N. Levison, 'The Proselyte in Biblical and Early Post-Biblical Times', *Scottish Journal of Theology*, vol. 10, 1957.

W. Lillie, 'Faith and Baptism', *Scottish Journal of Theology*, vol. 10, 1957.

J. Lindblom, *Jesu Missions—och Dopbefallning, Tillika en Studie över det Kristna Dopets Ursprung*, Stockholm, 1919.

E. Lohmeyer, *Das Urchristentum I, Johannes der Täufer*, Göttingen, 1932.

P. Lundberg, 'La Typologie baptismale dans l'ancienne Église', *Acta Seminarii Neotestamentici Upsaliensis*, edenda curavit A. Fridrichsen, X, Leipzig and Uppsala, 1942.

R. P. McDermott, 'Holy Baptism', *Theology*, vol. XLVI, 1943.

H. R. Mackintosh, 'Thoughts on Infant Baptism', *The Expositor*, 8th series, vol. XIII, 1917.

H. D. A. Major, 'Why we value Baptism and Confirmation', *The Modern Churchman*, vol. XV, 1925–26.

T. W. Manson, 'Baptism in the Church', *Scottish Journal of Theology*, vol. 2, 1949.

P. C. Marcel, *The Biblical Doctrine of Infant Baptism*, translated by P. E. Hughes, London, 1953.

D. W. Margoliouth, 'Baptizing with Fire', *The Expositor*, 8th series, vol. XIII, London, 1917.

H. G. Marsh, *The Origin and Significance of the New Testament Baptism*, Manchester, 1941.

H. Martin, 'Baptism and Circumcision', *Theology*, vol. LIII, 1950.

H. Martin, 'Baptism and Cleansing', *Baptist Quarterly*, vol. XVI, 1955–6.

H. Martin, 'Baptism and the Fourth Century', *Baptist Quarterly*, vol. XIII, 1949/50.

R. Mehl, 'Zur Bedeutung von Kultus und Sakrament im Vierten Evangelium', *Evangelische Theologie*, Heft 2, 1955.

P. H. Menoud, 'Le baptême des enfants dans l'Église ancienne', *Verbum Caro*, vol. 2, no. 5.

W. Michaelis, *Die Sakramente im Johannesevangelium*, Bern, 1946.

O. Michel, 'Der Abschluss des Matthäusevangeliums', *Evangelische Theologie*, Heft 1, 1950–1.

N. Micklem, *The Sacraments, Christian Worship, Studies in its History and Meaning by Members of Mansfield College*, ed. by N. Micklem, Oxford, 1936.

G. Miegge, *Il Battesimo dei Fanciulli nella storia, nella teoria, nella prassi*, Torre Pellice, Torino, 1943.

C. F. D. Moule, 'Baptism with Water and with the Holy Ghost', *Theology*, vol. XLVIII, 1945.

C. F. D. Moule, 'The Nature and Purpose of 1 Peter', *New Testament Studies*, 1956.

J. K. Mozley, *The Gospel Sacraments*, London, 1933.

W. Mundle, *Der Glaubensbegriff des Paulus, Eine Untersuchung zur Dogmengeschichte des ältesten Christentums*, Leipzig, 1932.

John Murray, *Christian Baptism*, Philadelphia, 1952.

R. E. Neighbour, 'The moral Significance of Baptism', *The Review and Expositor*, vol. VI, 1911.

F. Neugebauer, 'Das paulinische "In Christo"', *New Testament Studies*, vol. 4, 1958.

S. New, 'The Name, Baptism and the Laying on of Hands', *The Beginnings of Christianity*, Part 1, *The Acts of the Apostles*, ed. by F. J. F. Jackson and K. Lake, vol. V, 1933.

J. C. S. Nias, 'Gorham and Baptismal Regeneration', *Theology*, vol. LIII, 1950.

J. C. S. Nias, 'William Wall's "History of Infant Baptism"', *Theology*, vol. XLIX, 1946.

A. Oepke, 'Urchristentum und Kindertaufe', *Zeitschrift für die Neutestamentliche Wissenschaft*, 29ter. Band, 1930.

W. O. E. Oesterley and G. H. Box, *The Religion and Worship of the Synagogue*, London, 1911.

J. E. L. Oulton, 'Second Century Teaching on Holy Baptism', *Theology*, vol. L, 1947.

E. A. Payne, 'Baptism and Church Membership among the Baptists', *Theology*, vol. LV, 1952.

E. A. Payne, 'Baptism and the Laying on of Hands', *Baptist Quarterly*, vol. XIV, 1953/4.

R. Perdelwitz, *Die Mysterienreligionen und das Problem des I Petrusbriefes*, Giessen, 1911.

H. Preisker, 'Apollos und die Johannesjünger in Act. 18. 24–19.6', *Zeitschrift für die neutestamentliche Wissenschaft*, 30. Band, 1931.

H. Preisker, 'Die Vicariatstaufe 1 Cor. 15.29–ein eschatologischer, nicht sakramentaler Brauch', *Zeitschrift für die neutestamentliche Wissenschaft*, 23ter Band, 1924.

O. C. Quick, *The Christian Sacraments*, London, 2nd ed. 1932.

M. Raeder, 'Vikariatstaufe in 1 Cor. 15.29?' *Zeitschrift für die Neutestamentliche Wissenschaft*, 46 Band, 1955.

A. M. Ramsey, 'The Doctrine of Confirmation', *Theology*, vol. XLVIII, 1945.

E. C. Ratcliff, 'Justin Martyr and Confirmation', *Theology*, vol. LI, 1948.

E. C. Ratcliff, 'The Relation of Confirmation to Baptism in the Early Roman and Byzantine Liturgies', *Theology*, vol. XLIX, 1946.

B. Reicke, 'The Disobedient Spirits and Christian Baptism', *Acta Seminarii Neotestamentici Upsaliensis*, edenda curavit A. Fridrichsen, XIII, København, 1946.

T. K. S. Reid, 'Notes on the Administration of Holy Baptism', *Scottish Journal of Theology*, vol. 3, 1950.

F. M. Rendtorff, *Die Taufe im Urchristentum im Lichte der Neueren Forschungen*, Leipzig, 1905.

R. D. Richardson, 'The Mystics and the Sacraments', *The Modern Churchman*, vol. XVI, 1926–7.

A. Rinkel, 'Christianity, Church, Sacrament', *Theology*, vol. L, 1947.

J. E. Roberts, 'Thoughts on Infant Baptism', *The Expositor*, 8th series, vol. XIII, 1917.

A. T. Robertson, 'Paul not a Sacramentarian', *The Expositor*, 8th series, vol. XIII, 1917.

F. W. Robertson, 'Baptism, Two Sermons preached March 1950', *Sermons*, Second series, London, New edition 1869.

H. W. Robinson, *Baptist Principles*, London, 3rd ed. 1938.

H. W. Robinson, 'Believer's Baptism and the Holy Spirit', *Baptist Quarterly*, vol. IX, 1938–9.

H. W. Robinson, 'Christian Sacramental Theory and Practice', *Baptist Quarterly*, vol. X, 1940–1.

H. W. Robinson, 'Five Points of a Baptist's Faith', *Baptist Quarterly*, vol. 11, 1942–5, London.

H. W. Robinson, *The Life and Faith of the Baptists*, London, 2nd ed., 1946.

H. W. Robinson, 'The Place of Baptism in Baptist Churches Today', *Baptist Quarterly*, vol. I, 1922–3.

H. W. Robinson, 'Present Day Faiths, The Faith of the Baptists', *Expository Times*, vol. 38, 1926–7.

J. A. T. Robinson, 'The Baptismal Interrogations', *Theology*, vol. LIX, 1956.

J. A. T. Robinson, 'The One Baptism as a Category of New Testament Soteriology', *Scottish Journal of Theology*, vol. 6, 1933.

W. Robinson, 'Christian Sacramental Theory and Practice', *Theology*, vol. XXXVI, 1938.

W. Robinson, 'Historical Survey of the Church's Treatment of New Converts with reference to Pre- and Post-Baptismal Instruction', *Journal of Theological Studies*, vol. XLII, 1941.

W. Robinson, 'The Sacraments and Eschatology', *Theology*, vol. LV, 1952.

B. Rodhe, *Att Döpa Barn*, Andra Tider—Samma Tro, 9–10, Stockholm, 1953.

C. F. Rogers, 'How did the Jews Baptize?', *Journal of Theological Studies*, vol. XII, 1911.

C. F. Rogers, 'How did the Jews Baptize?', *Journal of Theological Studies*, vol. XIII, 1912.

T. G. Rogers, 'The Value of the Sacraments Today', *The Modern Churchman*, vol. XVI, 1926–7.

J. M. Ross, 'The Theology of Baptism in Baptist History', *Baptist Quarterly*, vol. XV, 1953–4.

H. H. Rowley, 'The Baptism of John and the Qumran Sect', *New Testament Essays, Studies in Memory of T. W. Manson*, edited by A. J. B. Higgins, Manchester, 1959.

H. H. Rowley, 'The Origin and Meaning of Baptism', *Baptist Quarterly*, vol. XI, 1942–5.

H. H. Rowley, *The Unity of the Bible*, London, 1953.

H. H. Rowley, *The Zadokite Fragments and the Dead Sea Scrolls*, Oxford, 1952.

G. W. Rusling, 'The Status of Children', *Baptist Quarterly*, vol. XVIII, 1960.

D. S. Russell, 'Ministry and Sacraments', *Baptist Quarterly*, vol. XVIII, 1957–8.

A. Schlatter, *Der Glaube im Neuen Testament*, Dritte Bearbeitung, Stuttgart, 1905.

H. Schlier, 'Zur kirchlichen Lehre von der Taufe', *Theologische Literaturzeitung*, 72. Jahrgang, No. 6, 1947.

R. Schnackenburg, *Das Heilsgeschehen bei der Taufe nach dem Apostel Paulus, Eine Studie zur paulinischer Theologie*, München, 1950.

R. Schnackenburg, 'Todes- und Lebensgemeinschaft mit Christus, Neue Studien zu Röm. 6. 1–11', *Münchener Theologische Zeitschrift*, 1 Heft, 1955.

J. Schneider, *Die Taufe im Neuen Testament*, Stuttgart, 1952.

Church of Scotland, *Interim Reports of the Special Commission on Baptism*, Edinburgh, 1955, 1956, 1957, 1958, 1959.

Church of Scotland, *Draft of Interim Report 1956, Containing detailed reference and supporting material not included in the Printed Report to the General Assembly*, Prepared by T. F. Torrance, Edinburgh, 1956.

Church of Scotland, *The Biblical Doctrine of Baptism, A Study document issued by the Special Commission on Baptism of the Church of Scotland*, Edinburgh, 1958.

W. A. Smellie, 'Confirmation in the Church of Scotland', *Theology*, vol. LIV, 1951.

Ryder Smith, 'Methodism and Baptism', *Baptist Quarterly*, vol. VII, 1934–5.

H. V. Soden, 'Sakrament und Ethik bei Paulus', *Marburger theologische Studien I*, Gotha, 1931.

E. Sommerlath, *Der Ursprung des neuen Lebens nach Paulus*, 2te. erweiterte Auflage, Leipzig, 1927.

Church of South India, *An Order for Holy Baptism: authorized by the Executive Committee of the Synod of the Church of South India on 7th Oct. 1954 for optional and experimental use wherever it is desired*, London, 1955.

R. V. Spivey, 'Admission to Full Membership in the Methodist Church', *Theology*, vol. LV, 1952.

J. Starr, 'The Unjewish Character of the Markan Account of John the Baptist', *Journal of Biblical Literature*, vol. LI, 1932.

Darwell Stone, *Holy Baptism*, London, 1905.

N. Sykes, 'The Reformers and the Sacraments', *The Modern Churchman*, vol. XVI, 1926–7.

F. C. Synge, 'The Holy Spirit and the Sacraments', *Scottish Journal of Theology*, vol. 6, 1953.

T. M. Taylor, ' "Abba, Father" and Baptism', *Scottish Journal of Theology*, vol. 11, 1958.

T. M. Taylor, 'The Beginnings of Jewish Proselyte Baptism', *New Testament Studies*, vol. 2, 1956.

Theological Commission appointed by the Archbishops of Canterbury and York on Baptism, Confirmation and Holy Communion, '*The Theology of Christian Initiation*', London, 1948.

Joseph Thomas, *Le Mouvement Baptiste en Palestine et Syrie*, Gembloux, 1935.

W. H. Griffith Thomas, 'The Place of the Sacraments in the Teaching of St. Paul', *The Expositor*, 8th series, vol. XIII, 1917.

L. S. Thornton, *Confirmation, Its place in the baptismal mystery*, London, 1954.

F. C. Tindall, *Christian Initiation, Anglican principles and practice*, Reprinted from *Church Quarterly Review*, London, 1951.

Canon Tollington, 'Sacraments since the Reformation', *The Modern Churchman*, vol. XVI, 1926–7.

T. F. Torrance, 'The Origins of Baptism', *Scottish Journal of Theology*, vol. 11, 1958.

T. F. Torrance, 'Proselyte Baptism', *New Testament Studies*, vol. I, 1954.

H. W. Trent, 'Ourselves and the Ordinances', *Baptist Quarterly*, vol. XVII, 1957–8.

Tübingen, 'Gutachten der Evangelisch-Theologischen Fakultät der Universität Tübingen über Fragen der Taufordnung', *Für Arbeit und Besinnung*, 5 Jahrgang, Nr. 21, 1951. (First published in *Zeitschrift für Theologie und Kirche*, August, 1950).

H. W. Turner, 'Confirmation', *Scottish Journal of Theology*, vol. 5, 1952.

A. C. Underwood, *Conversion: Christian and Non-Christian, A Comparative and Psychological study*, London, 1925.

G. Vermes, 'Baptism and Jewish Exegesis, New Light from Ancient Sources', *New Testament Studies*, vol. 4, 1958.

A. R. Vidler, 'Baptismal Disgrace', *Theology*, vol. XLI, 1940.

H. Vogel, 'The First Sacrament: Baptism', *Scottish Journal of Theology*, vol. 7, 1954.

J. Warns, *Baptism, Studies in the Original Christian Baptism*, English translation by G. H. Lang, London, 1957.

G. Westin, *I Urchristen Tid*, Stockholm.

G. Westin, *I Efterapostolisk Tid*, Stockholm.

E. C. Whitaker, 'The Baptismal Interrogations', *Theology*, vol. LIX, 1956.

E. C. Whitaker, 'A Case for Exorcism in Baptism', *Theology*, vol. LX, 1957.

E. White, 'Sacraments and the Synoptic Gospels', *The Modern Churchman*, vol. XVI, 1926–7.

R. E. O. White, *Biblical Doctrine of Initiation*, London, 1960.

W. T. Whitley, 'Baptized—Dipped for Dead', *Baptist Quarterly*, vol. 11, 1942–5.

N. P. Williams, *The Origins of the Sacraments, Essays Catholic and Critical*, edited by E. G. Selwyn, London, 1926.

W. Williams, 'Some Thoughts upon the Sacramental', *Theology*, vol. XLVII, 1944.

H. A. Wilson, 'The Misuse of the Sacraments', *The Modern Churchman*, vol. XVI, 1926–7.

H. Windisch, *Taufe und Sünde im ältesten Christentum bis auf Origenes*, Tübingen, 1908.

H. Windisch, 'Zum Problem der Kindertaufe im Urchristendum', *Zeitschift für die Neutestamentliche Wissenschaft*, 28ter Band, 1929.

World Council of Churches, 'One Lord one Baptism', *Reports by the Theological Commission on Christ and the Church*, London, 1960.

H. J. Wotherspoon, *Religious Values in the Sacraments*, Edinburgh, 1928.

W. G. Young, 'Baptism—Is Missionary Practice Inconsistent?', *Scottish Journal of Theology*, vol. 5, 1952.

S. Zeitlin, 'The Halaka in the Gospels and its Relation to the Jewish Law at the time of Jesus', *Hebrew Union College Annual*, vol. 1, 1924.

S. Zeitlin, 'A Note on Baptism for Proselytes', *Journal of Biblical Literature*, vol. LII, 1933.

S. Zeitlin, 'Studies in the Beginnings of Christianity', *Jewish Quarterly Review*, vol. XIV, 1923-4.

Additional works published since the first edition of this book:

K. Aland, *Die Säuglingstaufe im Neuen Testament und in der alten Kirche*, München, 1962 (E.T. *Did the Early Church Baptize Infants?* London, 1963. A German second ed., 1964, contains an appendix in answer to Jeremias' reply to the first edition).

J. Jeremias, *Nochmals:Die Anfänge der Kindertaufe*, München, 1962.

E.T. *The Origins of Infant Baptism*, London, 1963: a reply to Aland.

K. Barth, *Dogmatik, Part IV*, Edinburgh, 1969.

G. R. Beasley-Murray, *Baptism Today and Tomorrow*, London, 1966.

N. Cryer, *By What Rite?*, London, 1969.

G. Delling, *Die Taufe im Neuen Testament*, Berlin, 1963.

H. Frankenmölle, *Das Taufverständnis des Paulus*, Stuttgart, 1970.

D. Moody, *Baptism: Foundation for Christian Unity*, Philadelphia, 1967.

E. Schlink, *Die Lehre von der Taufe*, Kassel, 1969.

G. Wagner, *Das religionsgeschichtliche Problem von Römer* 6: 1–11, Zurich, 1962 (E.T. *Pauline Baptism and the Pagan Mysteries*, Edinburgh, 1967).

G. Wainwright, *Christian Initiation*, London, 1969.

INDEX OF SUBJECTS

INDEX OF AUTHORS

INDEX OF SCRIPTURE REFERENCES

OLD TESTAMENT